AFFIRMATIVE PRACTICE

AFFIRMATIVE PRACTICE

Understanding and Working with Lesbian, Gay, Bisexual, and Transgender Persons

SKI HUNTER AND JANE C. HICKERSON

NASW PRESS

National Association of Social Workers
Washington, DC

Gary Bailey, MSW, *President*
Elizabeth J. Clark, PhD, ACSW, MPH, *Executive Director*

Cheryl Y. Bradley, *Publisher*
Paula L. Delo, *Executive Editor*
Susan Fisher, *Editor*
Andre Barnett, *Editor*
January Layman-Wood, *Acquisitions Editor*
Christina Bromley, *Editorial Assistant*
Louise Goines, *Copy Editor*
Robin Bourjaily, *Proofreader*
Bernice Eisen, *Indexer*

Cover and interior design by Metadog Design Group, Washington, DC
Printed and bound by Port City Press, Baltimore, MD

Library of Congress Cataloging-in-Publication Data

Hunter, Ski
    Affirmative practice: understanding and working with lesbian, gay, bisexual, and transgender persons / Ski Hunter, Jane Hickerson.
        p. cm.
    Includes bibliographical references and index.
    ISBN 0-87101-352-5
    1. Social work with gays—United States. 2. Social work with lesbians—United States. 3. Social work with bisexuals—United States. I. Hickerson, Jane. II. Title.

HV1449 .H865 2002
362.8—dc21

2002021903

TABLE OF CONTENTS

ABOUT THE AUTHORS

Ski Hunter, MS, MSW, PhD, LMSW, is a professor in the School of Social Work at the University of Texas at Arlington. She teaches courses on human behavior and the social environment, adult development, personal relationships, and LGBT issues. Along with Martin Sundel, she was an editor of *Midlife Myths*, published in 1989. She was the lead author of *Lesbian, Gay, and Bisexual Youths and Adults*, published in 1998, with Coleen Shannon, Jo Knox, and James I. Martin and coauthor with James I. Martin of *Lesbian, Gay, Bisexual, and Transgender Issues in Social Work: A Comprehensive Bibliography with Annotations*, published in 2001. She was the lead author of *Women at Midlife: Life Experiences and Implications for the Helping Professions* with Sandra Sundel and Martin Sundel, published in 2002. She is currently working on a book on midlife and older gay and lesbian persons.

Jane Hickerson, MSW, PhD, LMSW-ACP, was an assistant professor in the School of Social Work at the University of Texas at Arlington. She taught courses at the undergraduate and graduate levels on diverse populations. In addition, she worked for five years in direct practice in Arlington, Texas, seeing a wide range of clients, including lesbian and gay persons. Currently, she is vice president, social services, Praesidium, Inc., in Arlington, Texas.

ACKNOWLEDGMENTS

Ski and Jane express appreciation to the NASW Press staff. Special thanks are also extended to Lou Goines, copy editor, who did a wonderful job of editing and keeping in contact. Ski extends special thanks and appreciation to all NASW staff who offered their distinctive support during the early period of this project.

Jane expresses her love and gratitude to Hal and their sons, Blake and Cole, for their unconditional support in this and all projects.

Ski expresses thanks to lesbian, gay, bisexual, transgender, and intersex persons throughout history for invaluable contributions to the world.

Ski dedicates this book to Bev, artist and sign painter, and thanks her for sharing her experiences of life and her wisdom, which includes learning from and acting from experience.

INTRODUCTION

Following the removal of "homosexuality" as a diagnostic category from the American Psychiatric Association's *Diagnostic and Statistical Manual of Mental Disorders* in 1973 (see Chapter 8), the views of human services professionals about "homosexuals" began to change. In 1975, the Delegate Assembly of the National Association of Social Workers (NASW) passed a resolution supporting the civil rights of these persons and in 1977 adopted a policy statement opposing discrimination against them. In 1979, NASW formed a National Task Force on Lesbian and Gay Issues. The task force issued a position statement recommending that social workers hold nonjudgmental attitudes toward lesbian and gay persons, offer optimal support and services, and advocate for supportive environments (Gramick, 1983). NASW created the National Committee on Lesbian and Gay Issues in 1982, and in 1993 a change in the bylaws made the committee mandatory, to provide guidance and direction to NASW on gay and lesbian issues and represent lesbian and gay members of NASW and the social work community at large (National Association of Social Workers, 1999). In 1999, the NASW Board of Directors approved an affirmative action goal of 10 percent representation of lesbian, gay, and bisexual members in the association's national leadership ("Sexual orientation goal," 1999). The *NASW Code of Ethics* (1996) also has clear expectations regarding sexual orientation—practitioners cannot discriminate against clients because of their sexual orientation. Nor, can they refuse to provide services for a person solely because of their sexual orientation.

A former editor-in-chief of NASW's journal *Social Work* urged educators, students, and practitioners to be more proactive on behalf of lesbian and gay persons on individual, organizational, and educational levels. At the individual level, we are challenged to examine the effects of a heterosexist society, put aside assumptions about lesbian and gay persons, and hear their own understandings of themselves and their lives. We must familiarize ourselves with oppression and its effects on lesbian and gay persons, couples, families, and communities, and become advocates on their behalf. At the organizational level, we must examine our educational programs, agencies, and organizations for oppressive policies or heterosexist biases. We must work to change nonaffirmative policies and educational content. At the national level, we must push our professional organizations to be proactive in supporting affirmative policies, laws, and political candidates (Hartman, 1993).

The Council on Social Work Education (CSWE), the accrediting body of social work education programs, also has a committee that focuses on lesbian and gay and also bisexual and transgender (LGBT) issues. The CSWE Commission on Sexual Orientation and Gender Expression advocates for inclusion of educational material on LGBT persons in social work programs. Not until 1991, however, did CSWE require content on sexual orientation in social work programs as part of its nondiscrimination standard.

Currently, CSWE requires that social work programs make "specific and continuous efforts to provide a learning context in which respect for all persons and understanding of diversity... are practiced" (CSWE, 2002, p. 17). This standard on "nondiscrimination and human diversity" includes sexual orientation (http::/ /www.cswe.org/). Nevertheless, some of the actions of this organization reflect incompatible ideologies (Van Soest, 1996). For example, CSWE exempts religious institutions from the nondiscrimination standard related to sexual orientation. In a debate on this action between two social work educators, R. G. Parr claimed that religious institutions have codes of conduct for faculty and students limiting sexual conduct to heterosexual marriages. Exempt programs are not required to provide affirmative knowledge about gay and lesbian persons. This situation is troubling in a profession that seeks social justice for all persons. L. E. Jones contended that the issue is not one of codes of sexual conduct but discrimination against a particular group of persons (Parr & Jones, 1996). The NASW board passed a motion regarding this exemption. It opposed "any effort which could diminish the profession's commitment to and support of nondiscrimination in educational or professional arenas as explicated in NASW's *Code of Ethics*" ("CSWE standard," 2001, p. 8).

All human services professional associations now require their members to deliver knowledgeable and unbiased services to LGBT persons and to advocate against discrimination directed at them. Although transgender is a sexual identity, transgender persons experience the same range of sexual attractions and sexual orientations as any other group. Even if heterosexual, these persons also have issues in common with LGB persons such as prejudice and discrimination. Across the United States coalitions of LGBT communities recognize common goals of sexual freedom and sex–gender expression. Transgender persons also experience other common issues such as coming out and disclosing information about their sexual identity, sexual orientation, or both.

Knowledge of LGBT populations is the educational foundation from which unbiased human services practice begins (for example, Croteau & Kusek, 1992). The purpose of this book is to add to the contemporary resources of knowledge on LGBT persons. It is noted in this book, however, that practitioners are also required to not only demonstrate intellectual competency but emotional competency (for example, no attitudes and feelings that can impair capacity to effectively and compassionately offer services to LGBT clients). Reaching emotional competency and learning unbiased or affirmative practice skills depend on field placements and agencies with supervisors who can guide students and practitioners in attaining this competency and the skills to work with LGBT clients.

CONTENTIOUS ISSUES: CAUSES, CHOICES, AND NUMBERS

Many contentious issues surround nonheterosexual sexual orientations. Among the most fiercely heated issues are what causes differences in sexual orientations, whether or not sexual orientation is a choice, and what are the proportions of LGB persons. Scholars, scientists, and the lay public debate these issues, as well as LGB persons themselves.

Causes

Typically, various proposed causes of sexual orientation fall on either side of a dichotomy: nature–biological (essentialism) or nurture–social (social constructionism). Are same-sex or bisexual sexual orientations biologically caused, permanent, and found in every culture; or are they arbitrary and socially created and maintained phenomena (for example, Bailey, 1995; E. Stein, 1990)? So far, no sufficient evidence supports either biological causes (for example,

Affirmative Practice: Understanding and Working with Lesbian, Gay, Bisexual, and Transgender Persons

Bailey & Pillard, 1991) or social–environmental causes (for example, Kitzinger, 1995). Many studies fail to find any associations between various proposed causative factors (for example, prenatal hormones, early psychosocial factors) and same sex–gender or bisexual sexual orientations.

Most likely, nonheterosexual sexual orientations result from a complex interaction of biological, psychological, and cultural factors. A discovery of either a definitive set of components or a single path to sexual orientation is unlikely (T. S. Stein, 1993). Different "causes" may operate not only across persons but also within subgroups of populations (for example, sex–gender, ages, social classes, racial and ethnic groups) (Bailey, 1996; Savin-Williams, 1998). Most likely, research will eventually identify a cluster of routes that lead to some forms of nonheterosexual sexual expression (Dynes & Donaldson, 1992).

Choices

The question of whether LGB sexual orientations are choices is central to the essentialist–constructionist debate. Essentialists assume that persons do not consciously choose their sexual orientation (Gonsiorek & Weinrich, 1991; Herdt, 1990). In distinct contrast to this view, one of the most basic tenets of social constructionism is that persons make a conscious, intentional choice of sexual orientation (for example, Vance, 1988; Weeks, 1991).

Even within LGB communities, opinions differ. Some LGB persons distinguish between sexual orientation, which they do not choose, and sexual identity, which they do choose. Many lesbians studied by Golden (1996, 1997) believed they had no control over their sexual orientation, but that they chose their sexual identification or the labels for it. Yet, these women appear to have chosen more than just their self-label. Some talked about deciding to become sexually attracted to and involved with other women. Though they had no previous same sex–gender sexual experience, they became "open" to attractions to women. Certain experiences, such as a specific film or TV program, lecture, article, or discussion with a lesbian, prompted their interest as well as more general experiences such as women's studies classes or exposure to lesbians within feminist groups. Some "chose" to be lesbians because the feminist movement legitimated this choice. Women identifying as bisexual found it easy to move into this choice once they discovered bisexuality. Sometimes these women reinterpreted close female friendships and attachments as evidence that they had always had attractions to women but had not acknowledged them as having anything to do with being lesbian or bisexual. These various experiences could support either the constructionist or essentialist views.

Although sexuality is not experienced as a choice by all women, or even by most, Golden (1997) thought it is a choice for a significant minority of women. Such does not seem to be the case, however, for gay and bisexual persons (for example, Diamond & Savin-Williams, 2000; Kitzinger, 1995). Biology may play a larger role for them (Golden, 1997; Veniegas & Conley, 2000). A question posed by Bohan and Russell (1999a) was why choice is debated at all. If LGB identities are healthy variations, why not choose them? Many persons choose these identities and experience happy and satisfying lives.

A related issue is the stability–fluidity of one's sexual identity (Savin-Williams, 1998). But, the longitudinal stability or instability of sexual orientation or identity over one's adult life is an open question because of the lack of research on this topic (Gonsiorek, Sell, & Weinrich, 1995).

Numbers Question

Pursuit of the numbers question started with the Kinsey reports in 1948 and 1953 and continues to date (for example, Laumann, Gagnon, Michael, & Michaels, 1994; Sell, Wells, & Wypij, 1995). Despite many definitional and measurement difficulties in these pursuits, Gonsiorek and colleagues (1995) concluded that the approximate prevalence of predominantly same sex–gender sexual orientation in the United States ranges from 4 percent to 17 percent. Exclusive same sex–gender sexual behavior or substantial same sex–gender attraction is probably in the middle of this range.

Estimates of the prevalence of lesbian and gay persons are simply guesses—what the actual figures are remains unknown. The exact prevalence of bisexual behavior and attraction is also unknown (Stokes, McKirnan, Doll, & Burzette, 1996) as is the prevalence of transgender persons, although one estimate is that they make up .01 percent of the U.S. population (Gainor, 1999).

UNSETTLED TERMINOLOGY

Terminology is also unsettled; it varies across geographical areas, across cultures, across time periods (American Psychological Association [APA], 1991; Donovan, 1992), as well as from inside and outside LGBT populations. In the second half of the 1860s, K. M. Benkert, writing under the noble name of his family, Károly Mária Kertbeny, invented the term homosexual for persons who felt attractions to others of the same sex–gender (Herzer, 1985). Later, others such as Krafft-Ebing (1892), Havelock Ellis (1942), and Magnus Hirschfeld (1948) adopted and popularized this term. Though other terms were in use such as "homophile"—meaning "loving the same" in Greek (Dynes, 1990)—"homosexual" was by far the most predominant term applied to persons with same sex–gender attractions for more than a century (Herdt & Boxer, 1992).

Community Terms

Before the turning point of the rebellion at the Stonewall bar in Greenwich Village in 1969 (see Chapter 1), few used the terms "lesbian" and "gay." When opportunities for collective organizing and socializing increased, the phenomenon of self-identification as lesbian or gay also began to appear (Cohler, Galatzer-Levy, Boxer, & Irvin, 2000).

Gay. Gay and lesbian persons dismissed the term "homosexual" after the 1969 Stonewall Rebellion because of the link between this term and negative stereotypes as well as its use as a pathological diagnosis. Though its origins are unknown, an alternate term—"gay"—was in widespread use by the late 1960s. The group itself chose this term "as a sign of its refusal to be named by, judged by, or controlled by the dominant majority" (Cruikshank, 1992, p. 91). Gay and lesbian persons no longer identified with sin or sickness ("homosexual") but with a social status (gay). Though not accepted by everyone, this term was the standard community term by the 1980s (Herdt & Boxer, 1992) although primarily it applied to males. Unless noted otherwise, in this book "gay" means males.

Lesbian. The term "lesbian" was not in wide use in the United States until the 19th and 20th centuries. The historical record of who introduced this term apparently no longer exists but the source for it was probably the name of the home of the poet Sappho who lived on the Greek island of Lesbos around 600 BC (Money, 1998; Nakayama & Corey, 1993). Because of the primary identification of the term gay with men, women wanted a label of their own. By the late 1980s, groups for both women and men usually included lesbian in the group identity (Cruikshank, 1992). Lesbians wanted a name to represent women's distinct and separate experiences and culture (Jeffreys, 1994; T. S. Stein, 1993). In the 1940s and 1950s, before the consistent usage of the term lesbian, women had no concept of a cohesive lesbian community (Kennedy & Davis, 1993).

Bisexual. Though not a term chosen by its community, "bisexual" seems to be an acceptable term to contemporary bisexual men and women. Current affirmative books, networks, and other resources on bisexual men and women use this term or sometimes the shorter version "bi." Another related term is "bisexualities," which reflects the wide diversity among bisexual persons (Stokes & Damon, 1995).

Intersex. "Intersex" is a clinical term applied to persons born with varying degrees of both male and female sexual reproductive organs (Feinberg, 1996). This term, which emerged in the 19th century, has largely replaced an older term, "hermaphrodite." In the 19th century, "intersex" was also applied to persons who sexually desired others of the same sex-gender (Epstein, 1990; Hekma, 1994). As with transgender persons, intersex persons may or may not be lesbian, gay, or bisexual.

Transgender. The medical establishment also imposed clinical terms on transgender persons that implied pathology such as "transvestite" and "transsexual" or "sexual dysphoria" (Denny, 1999). In 1966, *The Transsexual Phenomenon* by New York endocrinologist Harry Benjamin popularized the term "transsexual," although this term has largely been rejected by transgender persons. The use of "transgender" began in the 1990s (coming into widespread use in 1994) as a new way to think about sex–gender. This term fits almost anyone who resists gender stereotypes or who transgresses sex–gender norms through sexual orientation—gay, lesbian, and bisexual persons—and sex–gender—women who are not stereotypically "feminine" or men who are not stereotypically "masculine" (Denny, 1999).

Terms for Racial and Ethnic LGBT Persons

Racial and ethnic LGBT persons contend not only with the terms that signify sexual identity or sex–gender expression but also their racial and ethnic groups. Most of the research findings on LGBT persons in racial and ethnic groups include those who are African Americans, Asian Americans, Latinos, and Native Americans. In this book, the ethnic and racial terms generally used are those recommended by the APA *Publication Manual* (2001). These include black or African American, Latino, Asian American, and Native or Native American. Yet, racial and ethnic persons may prefer other terms based on differences in region, age, culture, and philosophies. Examples include Latina/Latino, Chicana/Chicano, Mexican American, or person of color (Martinez, 1998).

Minority cultures may or may not use the same terms as the white gay and lesbian communities. Many Latino men in same sex–gender relationships, for example, do not identify as gay but as "homosexual." No term fits the diversity of motivations, behaviors, and identities of Latino men (González & Espin, 1996), so Manalansan (1996) suggested using the phrase "men who have sex with men." Many Native American persons identify powerfully with the labels of lesbian, gay, bisexual, transgender, or queer—depending on their social–economic, regional, generational locations, or on their political attitudes (Tofoya, 1996). Other Native American persons, though, find these categories too confining. They may prefer instead one of several "sex–gender styles" that exist among Native Americans: women, men, not-men (biological women who perform some male roles), not-women (biological men who perform some female roles), lesbian, and gay. Not-men and not-women may seem bisexual because they experience sexual attractions to both men and women (Brown, 1997). In addition, the term "two spirit" is used among some Native Americans because it represents more of a spiritual–social identity or an integration of alternative sexuality, alternative sex–gender, and Native American spirituality (Tofoya, 1996, 1997).

Emerging Terms

The terms gay, lesbian, bisexual, and transgender are currently the standard terms in use, but terms used by community members rise and fall in popularity (Champagne, 1993) and vary in different social and political situations (Rust, 1996b). Along with queer politics and queer activism, the term "queer" recently reemerged as a label within some LGBT communities. Yet, it is a controversial term because of politically radical associations (for example, "Queer Nation"), past use as a taunt by heterosexuals (Jeffreys, 1994), and particularly derogatory definitions such as something unusual, abnormal, worthless, or counterfeit (Bryant & Demian, 1998). Queer is also a generic word applied to both males and females and, as argued by Jeffreys (1994), generic words typically only refer to men.

Terms also develop and change with socially available sexual identities. Today among bisexual women the most common identities not only include bisexual and queer but "lesbian-identified bisexual" and "bisexual lesbian" or "bi dyke" and "byke." Some bisexual women include the term lesbian in their current identification because of a previous lesbian identification or a political commitment to women or to the lesbian community (Rust, 1995). Some women identify as bisexual lesbians because of sexual involvements with women and identification as lesbians, but this does not exclude the possibility that they might also experience sexual desire for men. Other women identify as "transient lesbians" because although at some point they identified as lesbians and sexually involved themselves with women, they subsequently became sexually involved with men (Golden, 1996). "Gay bisexual" is a recent identification among men. Other identifications among both men and women include "bisensual" (indicating a sensuality that expresses human connecting more accurately than genital sex does), "polysexual" or "polyamorous" (indicating separation of sexuality from sex–gender and sexual dichotomies), and "polyfidelitous" (indicating fidelity to a group of three or more persons; Rust, 1996a).

The transgender movement continues to define itself beyond the existing terminology (Maurer, 1999). Many transgender persons are creating words or terms to describe their own experiences including "two spirit" (from Native American traditions), "genderblend," "androgyne," "drag king," and "drag queen" (Cole, Denny, Eyler, & Samons, 2000; Maurer, 1999).

We must be sensitive to what persons want to be called. The terms used among transgender persons and persons attracted to the same sex–gender, including terms used among racial and ethnic persons with same sex–gender attractions, vary and change. Language sensitivity also applies to intersex persons although little discussion of their preferred terms appears in the literature.

Another important perspective on terminology is the use of nonbiased terms that do not perpetuate old stereotypes (Bernstein, 1992). The Committee on Lesbian and Gay Concerns of the APA identified acceptable terminology in 1991, and some of these terms are now in the APA *Publication Manual* (2001) such as "lesbian and gay" instead of "homosexual." The terms "homosexual(s)" or "homosexuality" sometimes appear in this text but usually only in the context of historical discussions and past research. They appear with quotation marks to indicate that these terms are not currently acceptable unless, as observed earlier, persons prefer them. Quotation marks are also used with the term "transsexual" to indicate its decreased acceptance in the transgender community. The terms "preoperative," "postoperative," and "nonoperative" are also not used because they make sexual reconstruction surgery (SRS) the primary event in the lives of transgender persons, overshadowing everything else (Denny, 1997).

Additional Clarifications about Terminology

Several other terms in this book also require clarification. The terms "link" or "linkup" are sometimes used for relationship. The terms "coming out" and "disclosure" represent different processes. Coming out refers to the internal process of same sex–gender identity development in this book, whereas disclosure refers to the declaration of one's identity to others (Strommen, 1989). More recently, Savin-Williams and Diamond (1999) used "sexual questioning" instead of coming out. A concept recommended by Longres (2000), "subordinated group(s)," is used as a replacement for "minority group(s)." The terms "problem" and "problems" are often replaced with the terms "difficulty" or "difficulties" to indicate that problem-oriented terminology is less acceptable now because of more emphasis on the strengths of persons. Also the terms "therapy" and "therapist (s)" are rarely used because they signify a narrow approach to what clients may require. The terms "practitioner (s)" and "practice" are more often used.

Uses of the terms "gender" and "sex" also require clarification because sometimes these terms appear as if they are the same. In its standard usage, sex distinguishes males and females mostly by biological characteristics (Rutter & Schwartz, 2000). Biological aspects such as genitalia, chromosomes, reproductive organs, gametes, and hormones assign a person to the distinct categories of male or female. Gender is what society expects people to be, based solely on sex (Maurer, 1999), including roles, characteristics, and stereotypes (E. Stein, 1999). But, gender can be imposed (feminine–masculine) on experiences that may have no relation to the sex (male–female) of a person (Bohan & Russell, 1999b; McKenna & Kessler, 2000).

Many of the biological factors used to classify persons as male or female do not divide persons into two distinct groups (Coombs, 1998). This is seen in persons who are born with different combinations of genitals, chromosomes, and secondary sex characteristics (for example, body hair, breasts) not classifiable as male or female (E. Stein, 1999). The sex–gender assignment for others may come into question later, such as an XY (chromosomal) baby who has external female genitals but will never fully develop internal female sexual organs (Maurer, 1999). Some cultures recognize more than two sexes (for example, Blackwood, 1984).

Because our current views about what biological features distinguish males from females might be inaccurate and controversial, E. Stein (1999) used the term sex–gender to encompass the standard usage of both sex and gender. Sex–gender includes all the characteristics (for example, biological, psychological, cultural) that distinguish males–men from females–women.

In this text, we also use the term sex–gender to indicate the complex and unsettled issues surrounding sex and gender. Sometimes the terms masculine and feminine and "butch" and "femme" are used, indicating that these terms are often unclear because what differentiates a male from a female is unclear.

WHAT READERS CAN EXPECT

This book will lead the teacher, student, and practitioner through many contexts of the lives of LGBT persons, including the oppressive responses of the heterosexual world and the psychological and social development of primarily lesbian and gay persons across the life course. We also identify various practice issues related to the topics we address. The initials LGB or LGBT are often used in this book but, as noted earlier, being transgender does not imply a connection with any particular sexual orientation (Lee, 1998). These initials also do not imply that material on these all of these groups of persons is available in any equivalent way. Far more material is currently available on lesbian and gay persons.

Part 1 addresses the development of communities among LGBT persons (Chapter 1), and then discusses cultural, social, political, and legal issues and advances (Chapter 2). Finally, sexual orientation, sexual identities, and evolving identifications are examined (Chapter 3). In Part 2 of the book, we present a knowledge base on individuals, with a focus on coming out and disclosure across the life course (Chapters 4 and 5), couples (Chapter 6), and families and children (Chapter 7). In Part 3 of the book, the history of practice with LGBT persons, contrasting the former, highly oppressive "conversionist" practice with the newer affirmative practice, is reviewed (Chapter 8). The requirements of affirmative practitioners and social agencies are then addressed (Chapter 9). Some ideas for practice with individuals, couples, and families, and institutions and communities are presented in Part 4 (Chapters 10, 11, and 12). Part 5 focuses on knowledge and interventions with LGBT persons in special groups including adolescence, middle age, and old age (Chapters 13 and 14). The epilogue looks at research issues. The Appendix is a more general review of the values and principles of practice and pointers on assessment, intervention goals, and various practice approaches.

Because of space limitations, some topics in this book are not addressed as fully as others or not at all. Examples of topics not addressed include physical violence in some LGBT couples and alcoholism. Although there are discussions of HIV/AIDS in almost every chapter, they are not extensive except in the chapter on youth. Numerous materials on HIV/AIDS are available elsewhere.

The reader can also expect a positive or affirmative approach to the lives of LGBT persons. After the major modification made by the American Psychiatric Association in 1973, approaches to treatment of lesbian and gay persons changed from approaches focused solely on changing sexual orientation to those that focused on helping these clients to accept and value their sexual identities. These new approaches become known as *affirmative* (see Chapters 8 and 9).

The book is intended for use by both undergraduate and graduate students. It can serve as a required main text in courses on oppressed populations and as a supplemental text for many courses that prepare students to practice in applied human services fields (for example, social

Affirmative Practice: Understanding and Working with Lesbian, Gay, Bisexual, and Transgender Persons

work, counseling, mental health, nursing, psychology, sociology, and education). In social work, where content on LGBT persons is required, the book can be used in several of the core courses: human behavior, direct practice, and oppressed populations.

Practicing professionals, such as social workers, clinical psychologists, policy planners, and human resource providers in the human services, can also use the book. It can be used for in-service training and workshops—also, it should be of interest to LGBT populations and to the organizations and agencies, both public and private, servicing these populations.

INTRODUCTION
REFERENCES

American Psychological Association. (2001). *Publication manual of the American Psychological Association* (5th ed.). Washington, DC: Author.

American Psychological Association, Committee on Lesbian and Gay Concerns. (1991). Avoiding heterosexist bias in language. *American Psychologist, 46,* 937–974.

Bailey, J. M. (1995). Biological perspectives on sexual orientation. In A. R. D'Augelli & C. J. Patterson (Eds.), *Lesbian, gay, and bisexual identities over the lifespan: Psychological perspectives* (pp. 102–135). New York: Oxford University Press.

Bailey, J. M. (1996). Gender identity. In R. C. Savin-Williams & K. M. Cohen (Eds.), *The lives of lesbians, gays, and bisexuals: Children to adults* (pp. 71–93). Fort Worth, TX: Harcourt Brace.

Bailey, J. M., & Pillard, R. C. (1991). A genetic study of male sexual orientation. *Archives of General Psychiatry, 48,* 1089–1096.

Benjamin, H. (1966). *The transsexual phenomenon: A scientific report on transsexualism and sex conversion in the human male and female.* New York: Julian Press.

Bernstein, G. S. (1992). How to avoid heterosexual bias in language. *Behavior Therapist, 15,* 161.

Blackwood, E. (1984). Sexuality and gender in certain Native American tribes: The case of the cross-gender females. *Signs, 10,* 27–42.

Bohan, J. S., & Russell, G. M. (1999a). Afterword: The conversation continues. In J. S. Bohan & G. M. Russell (Eds.), *Conversations about psychology and sexual orientation* (pp. 183–209). New York: New York University Press.

Bohan, J. S., & Russell, G. M. (1999b). Conceptual frameworks. In J. S. Bohan & G. M. Russell (Eds.), *Conversations about psychology and sexual orientation* (pp. 11–30). New York: New York University Press.

Brown, L. B. (1997). Women and men, not-men and not-women, lesbians and gays: American Indian gender-style alternatives. *Journal of Gay & Lesbian Social Services, 6,* 5–20.

Bryant, S., & Demian. (1998). Terms of same-sex endearment. *Siecus Report, 26,* 10–13.

Champagne, J. (1993). Seven speculations on queers and class. *Journal of Homosexuality, 26,* 159–174.

Cohler, B. J., Galatzer-Levy, R. M., Boxer, A., & Irvin, F. (2000). Adolescence and youth: Realizing gay and lesbian sexual identity. In B. J. Cohler & R. M. Galatzer-Levy (Eds.), *The course of gay and lesbian lives: Social and psychoanalytic perspectives* (pp. 144–192). Chicago: University of Chicago Press.

Cole, S. S., Denny, D., Eyler, A. E., & Samons, S. L. (2000). Issues of transgender. In L. T. Szuchman & F. Muscarella (Eds.), *Psychological perspectives on human sexuality* (pp. 149–195). New York: John Wiley & Sons.

Coombs, M. (1998). Sexual dis-orientation: Transgendered people and same-sex marriage. *UCLA Women's Law Journal, 8,* 217–266.

Council on Social Work Education. (2002). *Educational policy and accreditation standards.* Alexandria, VA: Author.

Croteau, J. M., & Kusek, M. T. (1992). Gay and lesbian speaker panels: Implementation and research. *Journal of Counseling and Development, 70,* 396–401.

Cruikshank, M. (1992). *The gay and lesbian liberation movement.* New York: Routlege.

CSWE standard reviewed. (2001, May). *NASW News,* p. 8.

Denny, D. (1997). Transgender: Some historical, cross-cultural, and contemporary models and methods of coping and treatment. In B. Bullough, V. L. Bullough, & J. Elias (Eds.), *Gender blending* (pp. 33–47). Amherst, NY: Prometheus Books.

Denny, D. (1999). Transgender in the United States: A brief discussion. *Siecus Report, 28,* 8–13.

Diamond, L. M., & Savin-Williams, R. C. (2000). Explaining diversity in the development of same-sex sexuality among young women. *Journal of Social Issues, 56,* 297–313.

Donovan, J. M. (1992). Homosexual, gay, and lesbian: Defining the words and sampling the populations. In H. L. Minton (Ed.), *Gay and lesbian studies* (pp. 27–47). New York: Haworth Press.

Dynes, W. R. (1990). Homophile. In W. R. Dynes (Ed.), *Encyclopedia of homosexuality* (p. 552). New York: Garland.

Dynes, W. R., & Donaldson, S. (1992). General introduction. In W. R. Dynes & S. Donaldson (Eds.), *Homosexuality and psychology, psychiatry, and counseling* (pp. v–xx). New York: Garland.

Ellis, H. (1942). *Studies in the psychology of sex* (Vols. 1–2). New York: Random House.

Epstein, J. (1990). Either/or–neither/both: Sexual ambiguity and the ideology of gender. *Genders, 7,* 99–142.

Feinberg, L. (1996). Transgender warriors: *Making history from Joan of Arc to RuPaul.* Boston: Beacon Press.

Gainor, K. A. (1999). Including transgender issues in lesbian, gay and bisexual psychology: Implications for clinical practice and training. In B. Greene & G. L. Croom (Eds.), *Psychological perspectives on lesbian and gay lives* (Vol. 5, pp. 131–160). Thousand Oaks, CA: Sage Publications.

Golden, C. (1996). What's in a name? Sexual self-identification among women. In R. C. Savin–Williams & K. M. Cohen (Eds.), *The lives of lesbians, gays, and bisexuals: Children to adults* (pp. 229–249). Ft. Worth, TX: Harcourt Brace.

Golden, C. (1997, Winter). Do women choose their sexual identity? *Harvard Gay & Lesbian Review,* 8–20.

Gonsiorek, J. C., Sell, R. L., & Weinrich, J. D. (1995). Definition and measurement of sexual orientation. *Suicide & Life-Threatening Behavior, 25,* 40–51.

Gonsiorek, J. C., & Weinrich, J. D. (1991). The definition and scope of sexual orientation. In J. C. Gonsiorek & J. Weinrich (Eds.), *Homosexuality: Research implications for public policy* (pp. 1–12). Newbury Park, CA: Sage Publications.

González, F. J., & Espin, O. M. (1996). Latino men, Latino women, and homosexuality. In R. P. Cabaj & T. S. Stein (Eds.), *Textbook of homosexuality and mental health* (pp. 583–601). Washington, DC: American Psychiatric Press.

Gramick, J. (1983). Homophobia: A new challenge. *Social Work, 28,* 137–141.

Hartman, A. (1993). Out of the closet: Revolution and backlash. *Social Work, 38,* 245–246, 360.

Hekma, G. (1994). A female soul in a male body: Sexual inversion as gender inversion in nineteenth-century sexology. In G. Herdt (Ed.), *Third sex, third gender: Beyond sexual dimorphism in culture and history* (pp. 213–239). New York: Zone Books.

Herdt, G. H. (1990). Developmental discontinuities and sexual orientation across cultures. In D. P. McWhirter, S. A. Sanders, & J. M. Reinisch (Eds.), *Homosexuality/heterosexuality: Concepts of sexual orientation* (pp. 28–38). New York: Oxford University Press.

Herdt, G. H., & Boxer, A. (1992). Introduction: Culture, history, and life course of gay men. In G. Herdt (Ed.), *Gay culture in America: Essays from the field* (pp. 1–28). Boston: Beacon Press.

Herzer, M. (1985). Kertbeny and the nameless love. *Journal of Homosexuality, 12,* 1–26.

Hirschfeld, M. (1948). *Sexual anomalies: The origins, nature and treatment of sexual disorders.* New York: Emerson Books.

Jeffreys, S. (1994). The queer disappearance of lesbians: Sexuality in the academy. *Women's Studies International Forum, 17,* 459–472.

Kennedy, E. L., & Davis, M. D. (1993). *Boots of leather, slippers of gold: The history of a lesbian community.* New York: Routledge.

Kitzinger, C. (1995). Social constructionism: Implications for lesbian and gay psychology. In A. R. D'Augelli & C. J. Patterson (Eds.), *Lesbian, gay, and bisexual identities over the lifespan: Psychological perspectives* (pp. 136–161). New York: Oxford University Press.

Krafft-Ebing, R. (1892). *Psychopathia sexualis.* Philadelphia: F. A. Davis.

Laumann, E. D., Gagnon, J. H., Michael, R. T., & Michaels, S. (1994). *The social organization of sexuality: Sexual practices in the United States.* Chicago: University of Chicago Press.

Lee, L. J. (1998). Transgender students on our campuses. In R. L. Sanlo (Ed.), *Working with lesbian, gay, bisexual, and transgender college students: A handbook for faculty and administrators* (pp. 37–43). Westport, CT: Greenwood Press.

Longres, J. F. (2000). *Human behavior and the social environment* (3rd ed.). Itasca, IL: F. E. Peacock.

Manalansan, M. F., IV. (1996). Double minorities: Latino, black, and Asian men who have sex with men. In R. C. Savin-Williams & K. M. Cohen (Eds.), *The lives of lesbian, gay men, and bisexuals: Children to adults* (pp. 393–425). Fort Worth, TX: Harcourt Brace.

Martinez, D. G. (1998). Mujer, Latina, lesbian—Notes on the multidimensionality of economic and sociopolitical injustice. *Journal of Gay & Lesbian Social Services, 8,* 99–112.

Maurer, L. (1999). *Transgressing sex and gender: Deconstruction zone ahead?* Siecus Report, *28,* 14–21.

McKenna, W., & Kessler, S. J. (2000). *Retrospective response.* Feminism & Psychology, *10,* 66–72.

Money, J. (1998). Homosexuality: Bipotentiality, terminology, and history. In E. J. Haeberle & R. Gindorf (Eds.), *Bisexualities: The ideology and practice of sexual contact with both men and women* (pp. 118–128). New York: Continuum.

Nakayama, T., & Corey, F. C. (1993). Homosexuality. In R. Kastenbaum (Ed.), *Encyclopedia of adult development* (pp. 208–115). Phoenix: Oryx.

National Association of Social Workers. (1996). *NASW code of ethics.* Washington, DC: NASW Press.

National Association of Social Workers, National Committee on Lesbian and Gay Issues. (1999). *We're out for you* [Brochure]. Washington, DC: Author.

Parr, R. G., & Jones, L. E. (1996). Point/CounterPoint: Should CSWE allow social work programs in religious institutions an exemption from the accreditation nondiscrimination standard related to sexual orientation? *Journal of Social Work Education, 32,* 297–313.

Rust, P. C. (1995). *Bisexuality and the challenge to lesbian politics: Sex, loyalty, & revolution.* New York: New York University Press.

Rust, P. C. (1996a). Finding a sexual identity and community: Therapeutic implications and cultural assumptions in scientific models of coming out. In E. D. Rothblum & L. A. Bond (Eds.), *Preventing heterosexim and homophobia* (pp. 87–123). Thousand Oaks, CA: Sage Publications.

Rust, P. C. (1996b). Sexual identity and bisexual identities: The struggle for self-description in a changing sexual landscape. In B. Beemyn & M. Eliason (Eds.), *Queer studies: A lesbian, gay, bisexual, and transgender anthology* (pp. 64–86). New York: New York University Press.

Rutter, V., & Schwartz, P. (2000). Gender, marriage, and diverse possibilities for cross-sex and same-sex pairs. In D. H. Demo, K. R. Allen, & M. A. Fine (Eds.), *Handbook of family diversity* (pp. 59–81). New York: Oxford University Press.

Savin-Williams, R. C. (1998). *". . . and then I became gay": Young men's stories.* New York: Routledge.

Savin-Williams, R. C., & Diamond, L. M. (1999). Sexual orientation. In W. K. Silverman & T. H. Ollendick (Eds.), *Developmental issues in the clinical treatment of children* (pp. 241–258). Boston: Allyn & Bacon.

Sell, R. L., Wells, J. A., & Wypij, D. (1995). The prevalence of homosexuality in the United States, the United Kingdom and France: Results of population-based surveys. *Archives of Sexual Behavior, 24,* 234–248.

Sexual orientation goal is set. (1999, November). *NASW News*, p. 7.

Stein, E. (1990). Conclusion: The essentials of constructionism and the construction of essentialism. In E. Stein (Ed.), *Forms of desire: Sexual orientation and the social constructionist controversy* (pp. 325–354). New York: Routledge.

Stein, E. (1999). *The mismeasure of desire: The science, theory, and ethics of sexual orientation.* New York: Oxford University Press.

Stein, T. S. (1993). Overview of new developments in understanding homosexuality. *Review of Psychiatry, 12,* 9–40.

Stokes, J., & Damon, W. (1995). Counseling and psychotherapy for bisexual men. *Directions in Mental Health Counseling, 5,* 4–15.

Stokes, J. P., McKirnan, D. J., Doll, L., & Burzette, R. G. (1996). Female partners of bisexual men: What they don't know might hurt them. *Psychology of Women Quarterly, 20,* 267–284.

Strommen, E. F. (1989). "You're a what?" Family members' reactions to the disclosure of homosexuality. *Journal of Homosexuality, 18,* 37–58.

Tofoya, T. N. (1996). Native two-spirit people. In R. P. Cabaj & T. S. Stein (Eds.), *Textbook of homosexuality and mental health* (pp. 603–617). Washington, DC: American Psychiatric Press.

Tofoya, T. N. (1997). Native gay and lesbian issues: The two-spirited. In B. Greene (Ed.), *Ethnic and cultural diversity among lesbians and gay men* (pp. 1–10). Thousand Oaks, CA: Sage Publications.

Vance, C. S. (1988). Social construction theory: Problems in the history of sexuality. In A. van Kooten Niekerk & T. van der Meer (Eds.), *Homosexuality, which homosexuality?* (pp. 13–34). Amsterdam: Jhr. Mr. J.A. Schorerstichting.

Van Soest, D. (1996). The influence of competing ideologies about homosexuality on nondiscrimination policy: Implications for social work education. *Journal of Social Work Education, 32,* 53–64.

Veniegas, R. C., & Conley, T. D. (2000). Biological research on women's sexual orientations: Evaluating the scientific evidence. *Journal of Social Issues, 56,* 267–282.

Weeks, J. (1991). *Against nature: Essays on history, sexuality, and identity.* London: Rivers Oram.

PART I
HISTORY AND CONTENT

CHAPTER 1
COMMUNITY DEVELOPMENT

What have been the major trends in community development for gay and lesbian persons?

What kinds of diversity exist in the gay and lesbian community?

How have White lesbian and gay communities responded to ethnic and racial gay and lesbian persons and vice versa?

What are the trends in community development for bisexual and transgender persons?

What means do persons have to connect with LGBT communities?

DEVELOPMENT OF COMMUNITY FOR GAY AND LESBIAN PERSONS IN THE UNITED STATES

Today, many national and international organizations and a multitude of Internet lists and Web sites connect LGBT persons throughout the world. This is a dramatic change compared to the time before World War I when LGBT persons had no sense of community or culture. Except for a few small, secret friendship networks and a few clubs and bars in large cities, these persons experienced isolation from each other (Herdt, Beeler, & Rawls, 1997). In friendship networks, members protected each other by not disclosing their identities. Outside these groups, persons maintained total anonymity, including the use of fictitious names (Henry, 1941). Clubs and bars did not advertise their locations, partly to maintain the patrons' anonymity (James & Murphy, 1998). Although some women in the 1920s openly identified as lesbians, they were not a part of any lesbian subculture (Faderman, 1991).

The 1940s and 1950s: War Links and the Beginnings of National Organizations

Between the two World Wars, no community provided contacts, support, resources, role models, or language for same sex–gender attractions (Bohan, 1996). "Homosexuality" was illegal in every state (D'Augelli & Garnets, 1995; D'Emilio, 1983). Police raided lesbian and gay bars; subjected patrons to verbal, physical, and sexual mistreatment; arrested them; and provided the names of those arrested to newspapers. Lesbian and gay persons were also subjected to other harsh reprisals, such as the loss of jobs, residences, their children, and, sometimes, visitation rights with their children. Often, even their parents disowned them (D'Emilio, 1983; Martin & Lyon, 1995). Losing or being barred from jobs was particularly frequent since the police notified employers of the arrests conducted in bars. Military bases performed periodic purges of "homosexuals" followed by court marshals and dishonorable discharges (Bohan, 1996; Martin & Lyon, 1995). Because of Senator Joe McCarthy's hearings during the early 1950s, persons suspected of being communist or "homosexual" lost jobs in the federal government. Also, "homosexuals" could not work in many state and local governments, as well as in many institutions and businesses in the private sector (Bohan, 1996; Esterberg, 1996). Such repressive events provoked greater group identity among some lesbian and gay persons. But because public identity was still dangerous (D'Augelli & Garnets, 1995; D'Emilio, 1983), most of these persons were isolated and afraid of negative consequences if identified (Martin & Lyon, 1995).

Not until World War II did communities begin to emerge (D'Augelli & Garnets, 1995). In the sex–gender-segregated makeup of military units, men and women stationed overseas, interested in same sex–gender relationships, often met others with the same interests (Bérubé, 1990; D'Emilio, 1983). Upon return to the United States, many couples as well as single persons remained in the cities where they disembarked, such as New York and San Francisco (Bohan, 1996). Some of these persons organized various social and political groups (D'Emilio, 1983) under the general title "homophile rights." The Mattachine Society for gay persons that began in 1951 in Los Angeles was the first "gay rights" group in the United States; in 1955, a group for lesbians, the Daughters of Bilitis, was organized in San Francisco (Martin & Lyon, 1995; Schultz, 2001). Persons in these groups wanted acceptance; they dressed and acted in accordance with mainstream standards and avoided overt displays of their sexual identity. Given the political climate, these early group formations were courageous ones, but attempts to fit in with mainstream society did not achieve social acceptance (Bohan, 1996).

Persons in other settings in the 1950s were unconcerned with approval by mainstream society. This includes the lesbians in Buffalo, New York, described by Kennedy and Davis (1993). These women often went to bars and parties, and experienced solidarity and feelings of pride. They lived independent and nonconformist lives by crossing acceptable boundaries for women, as in avoiding marriage to men and living with women.

The 1960s and 1970s: Decades of Stonewall and Major Growth in Culture and Community

During the 1960s, sexual contact between two persons of the same sex–gender was still a criminal offense in most states (Levine, 1992). Given this situation, the dramatic events that happened on the night of June 28, 1969, seem almost impossible to imagine. A riot erupted following a routine police raid at the Stonewall Inn bar in Greenwich Village, New York. The patrons at this bar included local gay persons, "drag queens" (men who dressed in women's clothes), and "butch" lesbians (women who displayed masculine-type behavior), many of whom were racial and ethnic persons (Gainor, 2000). The police loaded three men attired as women into a police van, but released them and retreated when persons in the streets threw bottles and cans at them. Police reinforcement arrived to clear the streets, but the next night hundreds of protesters gathered to support the resistance and to battle the police, a situation that lasted several days (Bohan, 1996; Herdt & Boxer, 1993; Jost, 2000).

Although Stonewall was not the first act of resistance by lesbian and gay persons, it emerged as the key symbol of the contemporary lesbian and gay movement (Stein, 1999) and as a watershed event that evoked political activism. Bolstered by slogans painted on walls such as "Gay Pride" (Bohan, 1996), LGBT persons reframed the problem not as themselves but rather as society. This inspired a mass liberation movement to overcome the oppression of secrecy and isolation (for example, Jay & Young, 1972). The movement also drew strategies from the civil rights movement, including black militants who provided models for transforming stigma into pride and strength; the New Left and other movements that provided critiques of

American society and models of confrontational political action; and the women's liberation movement that provided political analysis of sexism and sex–gender roles (D'Emilio, 1993). Two political strategies were adapted from the decades of the 1940s and 1950s—accommodationist strategies of the homophile movement that paved the way for dialogues with heterosexuals and entry into the political arena, and confrontational strategies from the resistance culture of working-class or bar lesbians in Buffalo and in other midsize industrial cities in the United States (Kennedy & Davis, 1993).

Inspired by the Stonewall incident, the lesbian and gay culture evolved from isolated and fragmented elements to group consciousness and cohesiveness (Cruikshank, 1992). In June 1970, a march in New York to commemorate Stonewall drew about 5,000 participants (D'Emilio, 1993); the largest demonstrations before Stonewall included only a few dozen participants. Only 50 gay and lesbian organizations existed at the time of Stonewall, but more than 700 lesbian and gay groups existed by 1973. Mostly concentrated in New York and other urban areas, political activist and civil rights organizations, social clubs, community centers, businesses, social services organizations, and newspapers and magazines gained popularity. The new visibility of lesbian and gay persons, however, had a downside because of attacks fueled by conservative political and religious trends (D'Augelli & Garnets, 1995).

The 1980s, 1990s, and Beyond: HIV/AIDS, Community, Politics, and Culture

Political solidarity continued to escalate. "Gay liberation" was synonymous with a politically aware identity, but it also connoted for many a new community-oriented identity accompanied by personal, social, and sexual freedom (Bohan, 1996). This all changed in the 1980s, however, when the medical and social crises of the HIV/AIDS epidemic became the predominant focus in the lives of urban gay persons. Illness, death, loss of friends and partners, and the fear of diagnosis pervaded the lives of these persons (Paul, Hays, & Coates, 1995).

The indifference of governmental and social agencies to this crisis challenged the AIDS-affected community to develop ways to care for its own (James & Murphy, 1998). The community met this challenge with energetic voluntarism by both gay and lesbian persons, and existing programs were adapted to meet the needs of persons with the disease (Omoto & Crain, 1995; Paul et al., 1995). An array of informal social services, such as self-help and support groups, developed to supplement formal social services organizations (D'Augelli, 1989). Yet, because of the immense scope of the epidemic, the community could not meet all the needs. Therefore, considerable political organizing in the gay and lesbian community was directed at expanded funding for more services and for research focused on a cure for HIV/AIDS (Paul et al., 1995).

During the 1990s and the current decade, HIV/AIDS and the need for more resources still has consumed much of the energy in the lesbian and gay communities. But the focus has also broadened to include the lack of legal protections across many areas and the need for civil rights at all levels of government and in business, universities, and other institutions (Paul et al., 1995). Other issues coming to the forefront in these decades are the rise in lesbian and gay unions and the debates going on about lesbian and gay marriages, and the increased visibility of lesbians having children or the gay baby boom (Crespi, 2001). These issues continue to be in the forefront of gay and lesbian interests in the current decade.

DIVERSITY OF COMMUNITIES

The lesbian and gay community is essentially based on a shared sense of identity instead of on residential areas or territories (Bernard, 1973). The solidarity of an identificational community flourishes in large part through its culture or the values, common experiences, and sentiments that it produces (Gruskin, 1999). This includes art, music, literature, and jewelry; groups and organizations, including political associations, baseball teams, and choruses; and special events, including music festivals and marches. The lesbian and gay community is also a subculture of the larger American culture and thus shares many broader social values (Murray, 1992).

Just as no unified American culture or community exists, no monolithic gay and lesbian culture or community exists. "Community" can mean different things to different persons, for example, being a member of the worldwide population of lesbian and gay persons versus the population of lesbian and gay persons in the San Francisco Bay area. It can mean participation in a social network, the social "scene," or the lesbian and gay institutions operating in a certain area (Saulnier, 1997). Cultural norms and behaviors also vary because of factors including social class, ethnicity, and residential area (Appleby & Anastas, 1998). Diversity is evident in large events such as Lesbian and Gay Pride Day that is celebrated every year across the United States with parades. Although "solidarity" is present in rhetoric, considerable diversity and pluralism are evident among the parade participants (Herrell, 1992).

The diversity of lesbian and gay communities is not often evident because most of these communities may seem largely middle or upper class, young, and White. In addition, most respondents to surveys on gay and lesbian persons have higher than average incomes and educational levels. Many survey instruments are distributed at social venues requiring discretionary income or distributed at colleges and universities. Those persons who are older or poor may not be "out" (that is, openly lesbian or gay) and, therefore, are invisible (Gonsiorek, 1991).

The diverse segments of the community often experience discord (for example, D'Emilio, 1993; Franzen, 1993). The primarily European American lesbian and gay communities show the same prejudices as the larger society regarding racial- and ethnic-subordinated groups including those who are LBG or T. The lesbian and gay community also does not fully welcome bisexual or transgender persons whatever their racial and ethnic background. Many lesbians also claim that they do not feel welcomed among gay persons. The tensions among these various groups have resulted in separate communities, many of which never cross paths or communicate with each other. Some persons identify only with their particular community—radical lesbian socialists, bar crowds, or study groups, for example (Icard, 1985–1986; Rust, 1996).

GROUPS EXPERIENCING DIFFICULTIES INTEGRATING WITH MAINSTREAM GAY AND LESBIAN COMMUNITIES

Lesbian Feminists

The rebirth of the feminist movement in the 1960s encouraged many lesbians to see themselves as oppressed both as lesbians and as women and to begin to value themselves as both (Kennedy & Davis, 1993). Lesbians played only a marginal part or participated in largely secondary roles during both the pre- and post-Stonewall years. This history and the minimal involvement and lack of gay person's interest in women's issues resulted in the emergence of the lesbian feminist movement (Cruikshank, 1992; D'Emilio, 1993; Jay, 1995). This movement advanced different goals from those pursued by the male-dominated gay liberation movement. Whereas liberation for gay persons meant freedoms such as sexual expression, for lesbian feminists it meant intimacy and communities that were not patriarchal (Pearlman, 1987; Raymond, 1986). Many lesbians also wanted to focus more on women's health issues—breast cancer, for example, which was far behind in garnering the attention and resources provided for HIV/AIDS (Winnow, 1989). Lesbian feminists also experienced tensions with heterosexual feminists who thought lesbians were barriers to attaining women's rights. Some chapters of the National Organization of Women (NOW), which was founded in 1966 and currently has chapters in all 50 states and the District of Columbia, attempted to exclude lesbians from membership. Eventually, however, these prejudicial attitudes modified (Adler & Brenner, 1992; D'Emilio, 1983) and NOW began to advocate on behalf of lesbian rights issues (Jordan & Davis, 1998; Toledo, 1999; see http://www.now.org/issues/lgbi/index.html).

In the 1990s, the unequal power alignment between lesbian and gay persons in organizations began to change. Lesbians were in positions of power in lesbian and gay organizations at local, state, and national levels. Even so, many lesbian feminists continued to desire an autonomous group and political action movement that concentrated on their concerns including health, abortion, child care facilities, child custody, economic discrimination, and sexism (Cruikshank, 1992; Paul et al., 1995). Lesbians, therefore, developed more groups and projects around their particular concerns, including support groups and political activism projects, as well as social and sports groups (Wight, 1996).

Racial and Ethnic Lesbians and Gay Persons

Because there are often exceedingly negative reactions to same sex–gender sexual orientation, many racial and ethnic lesbian and gay persons separate from their families and community and connect with other lesbian and gay persons. They hope to replace family and peer support by joining the White lesbian and gay community. What often happens, however, is that they experience discrimination rather than acknowledgment or acceptance (for example, Chan, 1989; Greene, 1995). Many report that they cannot freely participate in lesbian and gay bars, social groups, political organizations, and social services agencies (for example, Mays & Cochran, 1988; Morales, 1992).

Another barrier that ethnic and racial gay and lesbian persons experience in White gay and lesbian communities includes stereotypes about them and insensitivity of the importance of their family ties—for example, some members of these communities view Asian American lesbian and gay persons as "exotic, non-American, or foreign" (Nakajima, Chan, & Lee, 1996, p. 571). Some White gay persons often view Japanese American gay persons as "feminine," passive, and easy pickups (Wooden, Kawasaki, & Mayeda, 1983). In addition, White gay and lesbian persons often display insensitivity to the significance of family to many ethnic and racial lesbian and gay persons. Conflicts occur between these groups regarding activism and public disclosures. Racial and ethnic persons may respond negatively to both because they do not want to embarrass or disgrace their families (Savin-Williams, 1996).

Conflicting Loyalties

Racial and ethnic lesbian and gay persons spend considerable effort managing conflicting allegiances among their divergent social worlds (Cazenave, 1984; Gock, 1985; Mays, 1985). They often face difficult choices concerning which of multiple communities to identify with most: their racial and ethnic community, the lesbian and gay community, or the majority White, heterosexual community. Additionally, ethnic and racial women may also want to participate in a feminist community (Kanuha, 1990; Mays & Cochran, 1988). The most troublesome dilemma regarding identification issues usually involves the racial or ethnic community as opposed to the lesbian and gay community. Whereas one community provides cultural grounding, the other provides intimacy with peers (Gock, 1985). Although intimacy with peers is desired, these persons may feel that they betray their cultural groups if their primary identification is to the lesbian and gay community (Sears, 1989).

Managing conflicting loyalties is not an easy endeavor. To be accepted by each community may require racial and ethnic lesbian and gay persons to hide or minimize significant parts of themselves. They may feel that they are not completely a part of any group. Even in their own racial and ethnic groups of lesbian and gay persons, they may feel alone and isolated (Greene, 1995).

Variations in Primary Allegiances

Primary allegiances vary among different ethnic and racial groups. For example, Asian American lesbian and gay persons are generally more firmly committed to their lesbian and gay identity than to their Asian American identity (Chan, 1989). Self-awareness as an Asian American is often low, which fosters a preference for interactions with White lesbian and gay persons instead of with Asian American lesbian and gay persons (Nakajima et al., 1996). Depending on need or stage of identity formation, however, the primary allegiance may shift (Chan, 1989). A diagnosis of HIV or a breakup of a primary relationship, for example, may motivate these persons to seek support from other Asian Americans (for example, Hom, 1992).

The primary allegiance for Latino lesbian and gay persons usually remains with their ethnic identity, their community, and most prominently their family (for example, González & Espin, 1996; Marsiglia, 1998). The family or "familism" is a core value in Latino culture that transcends the nation of origin and, to some extent, acculturation (for example, Morales, 1990, 1992) or social, economic, and political integration into mainstream society (Keefe & Padilla, 1987). Latino families often include strong ties with grandparents, aunts, uncles, and cousins (Marín & Marín, 1991). These families protect and buffer their members from the socioeconomic and political pressures of immigration, the stress of acculturation, and racism (González & Espin, 1996). For these and other reasons, the family remains of central prominence throughout the lives of Latino lesbian and gay persons. To identify more with the lesbian and gay community can be a costly move from these underpinnings of family support (Espin, 1984).

Different groups and subgroups of LGB persons also exist within each racial or ethnic culture, with varying allegiances (Conerly, 1996). For example, Carrillo and Maiorana (1989) discovered a range of participation in gay subcultures and allegiances among Latino gay persons living in San Francisco. This range included Latino men who self-identified more as Latino than as gay but did not participate in the Latino gay subculture; those who openly self-identified as gay and participated in the Latino gay subculture; and those who had marginal Latino identity and fully assimilated themselves in the White gay community. Diaz (1997) also found acculturated men to be identified with and integrated into the White gay culture—they did not highly identify with Latino culture and seldom participated in the Latino community; nonacculturated Latino men who highly identified as Latinos preferred Latino groups and establishments and to speak Spanish.

In a qualitative study with African American gay and bisexual men, Stokes and Peterson (1998) found that because they were sexually subordinated both by ethnic group and sexual orientation, this group felt pressured to choose between a gay or bisexual community, which was mostly White and frequently racist, and a black community with its heterosexism. Conerly (1996) suggested that where allegiances lay could depend on whether one was a black-identified lesbian, gay, or bisexual person or a lesbian, gay, bisexual–identified black person.

Though many lesbian and gay Native Americans identify themselves as members of LGB communities (Tofoya, 1997), others do not because of the discrimination they face. They want to find a place in their traditional communities (Wilson, 1996) and are searching for "Indian" identities and ways of life as opposed to those associated with White gay and lesbian persons or with racial and ethnic gay and lesbian persons. Turning to their native cultures in search of identity and role models, they rediscover the tribal traditions of multiple sex–genders that include women–men and men–women who experience acceptance by their tribes. Many Native American gay and lesbian persons in the cities see their contemporary roles as a continuation of the tradition of women–men and men–women in their tribal cultures. Taking the roles of these gay and lesbian predecessors entails not only sexual attraction but also special roles and responsibilities (for example, artists, providers, healers). The term "two spirit" reflects these roles. Contemporary urban two-spirited persons usually view the combination of masculine and feminine as a spiritual quality and maintain that it is innately inherent in lesbian and gay persons (Lang, 1999).

Not all Native American lesbian and gay persons view themselves as two-spirited. This concept is more prevalent in the cities and at intertribal gatherings than on reservations. Furthermore, a considerable number of lesbian and gay Native Americans still choose an identity and way of life closer to White gay and lesbian persons. They use gay and lesbian bars and other gathering places to merge into the gay and lesbian urban subcultures (Lang, 1999).

Counterdevelopments in Communities

One reaction to isolation is the establishment of specific ethnic and racial support and social groups (for example, Icard, 1985–1986). African American lesbian and gay communities in urban areas provide resources not only for social contacts but also for health and mental health needs, political needs, and economic needs. African American gay and lesbian churches are also emerging across the country. These resources, plus the successes of African American gay and lesbian writers, musicians, moviemakers, politicians, and scholars, are contributing to a new sense of community for African American lesbian and gay persons (Icard, 1996; Jefferson, 1998).

Political and social organizations for Asian American lesbian and gay persons are also developing across the country, especially in large urban cities (Chan, 1990; Nakajima et al., 1996). Southeast Asians frequently form their own organizations, believing that general Asian American organizations ignore or are unaware of their issues (Nakajima et al., 1996). The Gay

American Indians group recently organized yearly meetings to explore Indian American culture and spirituality and to help build solidarity among Indian North American lesbian and gay persons (Jacobs & Brown, 1997). Native American lesbians often work closely with men in organizations like the Gay American Indians and attend the annual two-spirit gatherings with gay Native American men, as few events focus on Native American lesbians. Some Native American lesbians, however, participate in small communities of their own (Lang, 1999). (See the Native American Gay Pride Web site: http://www.pe.net/-~whtwolf/gaypride.html) In most urban centers with a substantial Latino population, a Latino gay subculture also exists. (For a Web site that lists various sites of interest to lesbian persons who are Latino and belong to other racial and ethnic groups, see http://www .jwpublishing.com/gayscape/lat.html/)

Bisexual Persons

Like members of other subcultures, many bisexual men and women experience isolation (Esterberg, 1996, 1997; Hutchins & Kaahumanu, 1991). Neither heterosexual nor lesbian and gay communities fully accept them (Fox, 1996; Rust, 1996) and, in fact, lesbian and gay communities may exclude them from their activities and social circles (Bohan, 1996; Fox, 1996). A quarter or more of gay and lesbian persons studied by Mohr and Rochlen (1999) excluded bisexual persons as best friends (25 percent) or dates (32 percent). Some lesbians think bisexual women are too free-floating in their identifications to be reliable friends (Esterberg, 1997) and that they remain implicitly loyal to their heterosexual sexual orientation, whereas lesbians explicitly reject heterosexual relationships. Bisexual women can always assimilate into the more comfortable dominant culture or pass as heterosexual (Bohan, 1996). Lesbians may view women who do not sever ties with men as colluding with the patriarchy and with sexism (Ochs, 1996). Lesbian feminists particularly see women who align themselves with heterosexuals as "sleeping with the enemy" (Bohan, 1996) and as a health threat in spreading sexually transmitted diseases such as HIV/AIDS from the heterosexual mainstream (Golden, 1996; Ochs, 1996; Weinberg, Williams, & Pryor, 1994).

The Political Road

Hostile reactions in lesbian and gay communities can induce bisexual men and women to label themselves publicly as lesbian or gay, denigrate heterosexual persons, devalue their own heterosexual feelings, and hide the heterosexual part of their identity. Yet, this makes them feel like impostors and outsiders in both communities (Bohan, 1996; Ochs, 1996). Some bisexual men and women join groups such as Queer Nation (which started in New York City in 1990) that are more accepting of a broader range of sexual identities (Esterberg, 1996; Klein, 1993). Other bisexual persons want their own community and culture (Rust, 1995). They do not want inclusion in gay and lesbian communities because they think such participation dilutes their own culture. They view the interests of bisexual men and women as different from those of lesbian and gay persons and want a separate movement with independent organizations and communities (Esterberg, 1996; Klein, 1993).

Early bisexual groups provided a supportive framework for developing a political movement comparable to the gay and lesbian homophile groups of the 1950s. Bisexual activists began to associate with the political liberal left, feminism, and lesbian and gay communities to learn how to build a framework for their political movement. This movement advanced rapidly, over about a decade. Today, bisexual political activists are meeting each other at national and international conferences (Rust, 1995).

Alignments among Lesbian, Gay, and Bisexual Persons

Having a separate political movement is a minority view among most bisexual persons because they see inclusion in the lesbian and gay community as beneficial to them. Their community is much smaller and less politically powerful (Rust, 1995, 1996). They also feel that they have much in common with gay and lesbian persons because of the HIV/AIDS crisis and because of persecution by right-wing hate groups (Hutchins, 1996). Many bisexual persons fight hard for acceptance by lebian and gay persons because they have been part of the gay and lesbian movement all along (Rust, 1995).

A national contingent of bisexual men and women participated in the second national march on Washington for lesbian and gay rights in 1987. "Bisexual" appeared in the official name of the march in 1993, and a bisexual person spoke on the main stage of the rally (Hutchins, 1996). Not all lesbian and gay persons, though, support this inclusion. Some of them believe that bisexual men and women did none of the work in the gay liberation movement (Guidry, 1999; Rust, 1995), that they do not care enough about gay and lesbian political causes to support them, and that they may not be willing to fight heterosexism (for example, Golden, 1996; Rust, 1993).

Transgender Persons

The movement for transgender liberation is even more recent than the bisexual movement (Feinberg, 1993; Hemmings, 1996). About two years ago, organizations for transgender persons were invisible and without political focus. The thinking then was that the less known about them the better. Now, however, transgender persons are organizing for social change that includes a legitimate existence in society, the right to choose or display whatever sex–gender identity they are comfortable with (Lombardi, 1999), the need for services and support, and a desire to participate in diagnostic and treatment issues (Bolin, 1997; Lombardi, 1999). No longer do transgender persons feel shame about themselves; instead they feel pride (Denny, 1999). Once rare, there is now a trend for positive presentations of transgender persons in popular print media and in films (Denny, 2002). A new commitment has emerged to be "out"— to be honest, to share personal experiences, and to educate others about transgender persons (Allen, 1997; Boswell, 1997; Maurer, 1999). Understanding of variability in gender expression is growing, with many contributions from transgender persons themselves (Denny, 2002).

Transgender persons are learning quickly to form alliances for political change and are increasingly building bridges with LGB communities (Allen, 1997). They want to be involved with these communities, as many transgender persons are gay, lesbian, or bisexual. The National Gay and Lesbian Task Force (2000) now includes the issues and concerns of transgender persons, particularly in policy deliberations on civil rights, hate crimes, and health.

More alliances are developing between bisexual and transgender persons. The bisexual magazine *Anything that Moves* regularly includes substantive transgender content. Maybe these groups feel more in common because they share a middle ground against conventional dichotomous thinking (Maurer, 1999). Transgender persons are also building coalitions between subgroups such as male–female persons, female–male persons, and intersex persons (Bornstein, 1998). But as with most coalitions with diversse members, there are tensions because of varying goals (Lorber, 1998). Some transgender persons have little interest in these alliances and coalitions because of a stronger desire to blend into society, physically, socially, and legally. Once they assumed a new sex–gender, they wanted to downplay their past. They want to live as the men or women they have become and may not want to be part of any transgender group, way of life, or social cause (Stuart, 1991).

Intersex Persons

During the 1990s, intersex persons began to talk to each other and question the genital surgery they had as children and the resulting sex–gender assignment (Denny, 2002). Advocacy groups for intersex persons began to emerge in this decade along with research that challenged the success of sex–gender assignment shortly after birth. This intersex medicalization was not only ineffective but also harmful, including incorrect sex–gender gender assignment or sexual dysfunctioning. Now, in opposition to intersex medicalization, advocacy groups have developed new clinical guidelines to protect the rights of intersex persons—for example, surgery is not recommended unless there is immediate risk to an infant if not done (Preves, 2002).

HOW CAN LGBT PERSONS CONNECT WITH COMMUNITIES?

Lesbian and gay persons can meet each other in well-identified gay and lesbian communities in large urban areas, such as Dallas, Houston, San Francisco, San Diego, Seattle, Minneapolis, New York, Chicago, Los Angeles, Miami, Boston, Santa Fe, northern California, western Massachusetts, and some resort areas as Provincetown, Massachusetts, and Key West, Florida. Concentrations of lesbian and gay persons are also emerging in some residential areas of some large cities. Such locations exist in the Castro in San Francisco, West Hollywood in Los Angeles, New Town in Chicago, Coconut Grove in Miami, and Greenwich Village in New York. Even in smaller cities, lesbian and gay persons tend to live close to each other (D'Emilio, 1993; Nakayama & Corey, 1993; Pope, 1995).

In large urban areas, weekly lesbian and gay newspapers or magazines and Web sites advertise groups and activities open to new members. There are gay and lesbian yellow pages and lambda pages in concentrated areas of gay and lesbian persons that list numerous organizations and resources as well as places to meet. Most large cities also have Parents, Families, and Friends of Lesbians and Gays (PFLAG) groups open to anyone interested in affirmative actions on behalf of families with LGBT children. PFLAG is an international organization represented in 444 communities across the United States and in 11 other countries. Many gay and lesbian persons communicate with each other via e-mail lists, which are especially useful for those who live in small towns, small cities, and rural areas (Miller, 1990). Often, in rural areas, a small lesbian or gay bar provides the only meeting place (D'Augelli & Garnets, 1995). The same is often true in suburbs (Lynch, 1992).

Groups for bisexual men and women now exist in almost every state in the United States and in many other countries. The larger cities have special interest groups for bisexual women and men who are, for example, artists, children of alcoholics, or racial and ethnic women. In addition, expanding numbers of publications, cable television shows, college courses, and e-mail lists address bisexual topics. The regularly updated *Bisexual Resource Guide* (Ochs, 2001) provides lists of bisexual organizations throughout the world and other information such as books and films. A national bisexual political and educational organization, BiNet USA, also exists. This organization developed in 1992 out of the North American Bisexual Network that was established in 1990. An international network of various bisexual groups including support groups and political action groups is also available. An identifiable bisexual press and a forum exist for debates on bisexual political ideology (Hutchins, 1996; Rust, 1995).

Transgender persons who are out usually desire to contribute to the development of other transgender persons. This occurs through various means—being visible and providing support groups and newsletters are two examples. Online computer forums publish autobiographies that introduce newcomers to the rest of the community (Nakamura, 1997). To find another transgender person, through the media, online computer services, or support groups, is a tremendous emotional and psychological relief (Gagné & Tewksbury, 1999). The magazine *Transgender* provides news, views, and features for the transgender community and friends. Books on transgender issues are increasingly available (Maurer, 1999).

SUMMARY

- After World War II, gay and lesbian persons began to create their own communities and to become politically active in many arenas such as HIV/AIDS and civil rights.
- These community developments have not been easy nor have they been the work of groups with a consistent and unified focus. Persons with different orientations and divergent personal, ethnic, and political interests can collide, leading to the creation of separate social and activist organizations.
- Ethnic and racial LGBT persons experience the same cultural prejudice and discrimination among their LGBT White peers as they do among their ethnic and racial heterosexual peers. Different ethnic and racial groups have successfully organized their own resources, mostly in urban areas, to provide social outlets, education, support, and advocacy. The members of these groups also experience the dilemma of primary identification with their families of origin and racial or ethnic culture versus identification with their same sex–gender sexual orientation. Although the strong encouragement of families is invaluable, it does not always supplant the need for intimacy among peers with the same sex–gender sexual orientation.
- Similarly, bisexual and transgender persons experience prejudice and discrimination not only in society at large but also in gay and lesbian communities. Although many of these persons want to align themselves with gay and lesbian persons for political strength, these groups have established their own networks, publications, and organizations.
- In this time of expanding technology and media, LGBT persons have been able to interact with others in their groups via print publications, e-mail, and the Web. Yet, the most enduring connection of these groups remains proximity as they gather in urban areas and neighborhoods to build an infrastructure that offers not only individual support, but also public identity and a sense of pride. Intersex persons are also experiencing these kinds of connections.

CHAPTER 1
REFERENCES

Adler, S., & Brenner, J. (1992). Gender and space: Lesbians and gay men in the city. *International Journal of Urban and Regional Research, 16,* 24–34.

Allen, M. P. (1997). The changing face of the transgender community. In B. Bullough, V. L. Bullough, & J. Elias (Eds.), *Gender blending* (pp. 311–382). Amherst, NY: Prometheus Books.

Appleby, G. A., & Anastas, J. W. (1998). *Not just a passing phase: Social work with gay, lesbian, and bisexual people.* New York: Columbia University Press.

Bernard, J. (1973). *The sociology of community.* Glenview, IL: Scott, Foresman.

Bérubé, A. (1990). *Coming out under fire: The history of gay men and women in World War II.* New York: Free Press.

Bohan, J. S. (1996). *Psychology and sexual orientation: Coming to terms.* New York: Routledge.

Bolin, A. (1997). Transforming transvestism and transsexualism: Polarity, politics, and gender. In B. Bullough, V. L. Bullough, & J. Elias (Eds.), *Gender blending* (pp. 25–32). Amherst, NY: Prometheus Books.

Bornstein, K. (1998). *My gender workbook.* New York: Routledge.

Boswell, H. (1997). The transgender paradigm shift toward free expression. In B. Bullough, V. L. Bullough, & J. Elias (Eds.), *Gender blending* (pp. 53–57). Amherst, NY: Prometheus Books.

Carrillo, H., & Maiorana, H. (1989). *AIDS prevention among gay Latinos in San Francisco: From behavior change to social change.* Unpublished manuscript.

Cazenave, N. A. (1984). Race, socioeconomic status, and age: The social context of American masculinity. *Sex Roles, 11,* 639–656.

Chan, C. S. (1989). Issues of identity development among Asian-American lesbians and gay men. *Journal of Counseling and Development, 68,* 16–20.

Chan, C. S. (1990). Asian-Americans, gay and lesbian. In W. R. Dynes, W. Johansson, & W. A. Perry (Eds.), *Encyclopedia of homosexuality* (pp. 84–85). New York: Garland.

Conerly, G. (1996). The politics of black lesbian, gay, and bisexual identity. In B. Beemyn & M. Eliason (Ed.), *Queer studies: A lesbian, gay, bisexual, and transgender anthology* (pp. 133–145). New York: New York University.

Crespi, L. (2001). From baby boom to gayby boom: Twenty-five years of psychoanalysis in the lesbian community. In E. Gould & S. Kiersky (Eds.), *Sexualities lost and found: Lesbians, psychoanalysis, and culture* (pp. 261–275). Madison, WI: International Universities Press.

Cruikshank, M. (1992). *The gay and lesbian liberation movement.* New York: Routlege.

D'Augelli, A. R. (1989). The development of a helping community for lesbians and gay men: A case study in community psychology. *Journal of Community Psychology, 17,* 18–29.

D'Augelli, A. R., & Garnets, L. D. (1995). Lesbian, gay, and bisexual communities. In A. R. D'Augelli & C. J. Patterson (Eds.), *Lesbians, gay, and bisexual identities over the lifespan* (pp. 293–320). New York: Oxford University Press.

D'Emilio, J. (1983). *Sexual politics, sexual communities: The making of a homosexual minority in the United States, 1940–1970.* Chicago: University of Chicago Press.

D'Emilio, J. (1993). Gay politics and community in San Francisco since World War II. In L. D. Garnets & D. C. Kimmel (Eds.), *Psychological perspectives on lesbian & gay male experiences* (pp. 59–79). New York: Columbia University Press.

Denny, D. (1999). Transgender in the United States: A brief discussion. *Siecus Report, 28,* 8–13.

Denny, D. (2002). A selective bibliography of transsexualism. *Journal of Gay & Lesbian Psychotherapy, 6,* 35–66.

Diaz, R. M. (1997). Latino gay men and the psycho-cultural barriers to AIDS prevention. In M. P. Levine, P. M. Nardi, & J. H. Gagon (Eds.), *In changing time: Gay men and lesbians encounter HIV/AIDS* (pp. 221–224). Chicago: University of Chicago Press.

Espin, O. M. (1984). Cultural and historical influences on sexuality in Hispanic/Latin women: Implications for psychotherapy. In. C. Vance (Ed.), *Pleasure and danger: Exploring female sexuality* (pp. 149–163). London: Routledge and Kegan Paul.

Esterberg, K. G. (1996). Gay cultures, gay communities: The social organization of lesbians, gay men, and bisexuals. In R. C. Savin-Williams & K. M. Cohen (Eds.), *The lives of lesbian, gay men, and bisexuals: Children to adults* (pp. 377–391). Fort Worth, TX: Harcourt Brace.

Esterberg, K. G. (1997). *Lesbian and bisexual identities: Constructing communities, constructing selves.* Philadelphia: Temple University Press.

Faderman, L. (1991). *Odd girls and twilight lovers: A history of lesbian life in twentieth century America.* New York: Columbia University Press.

Feinberg, L. (1993). *Stone butch blues.* Ithaca, NY: Firebrand Books.

Fox, R. C. (1996). Bisexuality in perspective: A review of theory and research. In B. A. Firestein (Ed.), *Bisexuality: The psychology and politics of an invisible minority* (pp. 3–50). Thousand Oaks, CA: Sage Publications.

Franzen, T. (1993). Differences and identities: Feminism and the Albuquerque lesbian community. *Signs, 18,* 891–906.

Gagné, P., & Tewksbury, J. R. (1999). Knowledge and power, body and self: An analysis of knowledge systems and the transgendered self. *Sociological Quarterly, 40,* 59–83.

Gainor, K. A. (2000). Including transgender issues in lesbian, gay and bisexual psychology: Implications for clinical practice and training. In B. Greene & G. L. Croom (Eds.), *Education, research, and practice in lesbian, gay, bisexual, and transgendered psychology* (Vol. 5, pp. 131–160). Thousand Oaks, CA: Sage Publications.

Gock, T. (1985, August). *Psychotherapy with Asian/Pacific gay men: Psychological issues, treatment approach and therapeutic guidelines.* Paper presented at the meeting of the Asian American Psychological Association, Los Angeles.

Golden, C. (1996). What's in a name? Sexual self-identification among women. In R. C. Savin-Williams & K. M. Cohen (Eds.), *The lives of lesbians, gays, and bisexuals: Children to adults* (pp. 229–249). Fort Worth, TX: Harcourt Brace.

Gonsiorek, J. C. (1991). The empirical basis of the demise of the illness model of homosexuality. In J. C. Gonsiorek & J. Weinrich (Eds.), *Homsexuality: Research implications for public policy* (pp. 115–136). Thousand Oaks, CA: Sage Publications.

González, F. J., & Espin, O. M. (1996). Latino men, Latino women, and homosexuality. In R. P. Cabaj & T. S. Stein (Eds.), *Textbook of homosexuality and mental health* (pp. 583–601). Washington, DC: American Psychiatric Press.

Greene, B. (1995). Lesbian couples. In K. Jay (Ed.), *Dyke life: From growing up to growing old—A celebration of the lesbian experience* (pp. 97–106). New York: Basic Books.

Gruskin, E. P. (1999). *Treating lesbians and bisexual women: Challenges and strategies for health professionals.* Thousand Oaks, CA: Sage Publications.

Guidry, L. L. (1999). Clinical intervention with bisexuals: A contextualized understanding. *Professional Psychology: Research and Practice, 30*, 22–26.

Hemmings, C. (1996). From lesbian nation to transgender liberation: A bisexual feminist perspective. *Journal of Gay, Lesbian, and Bisexual Identity, 1*, 37–59.

Henry, G. (1941). *Sex variants: A study of homosexual patterns.* New York: Harpers.

Herdt, G. H., Beeler, J., & Rawls, T. W. (1997). Life course diversity among older lesbians and gay men: A study in Chicago. *Journal of Gay, Lesbian, and Bisexual Identity, 2*, 231–246.

Herdt, G. H., & Boxer, A. (1993). *Children of the horizons: How gay and lesbian teens are leading a way out of the closet.* Boston: Beacon Press.

Herrell, R. K. (1992). The symbolic strategies of Chicago's gay and lesbian pride parade. In G. Herdt (Ed.), *Gay culture in America: Essays from the field* (pp. 225–252). Boston: Beacon Press.

Hom, A. Y. (1992). *Family matters: A historical study of the Asian Pacific lesbian network.* Unpublished master's thesis, University of California, Los Angeles.

Hutchins, L. (1996). Bisexuality: Politics and community. In B. A. Firestein (Ed.), *Bisexuality: The psychology and politics of an invisible minority* (pp. 240–259). Thousand Oaks, CA: Sage Publications.

Hutchins, L., & Kaahumanu, L. (1991). *Bi any other name: Bisexual people speak out.* Boston: Alyson.

Icard, L. D. (1985–1986). Black gay men and conflicting social identities: Sexual orientation versus racial identity. *Journal of Social Work and Human Sexuality, 4*, 83–93.

Icard, L. D. (1996). Assessing the psychosocial well-being of African American gays: A multidimensional perspective. *Journal of Gay & Lesbian Social Services, 5*, 25–49.

Jacobs, M. A., & Brown, L. B. (1997). American Indian lesbians and gays: An exploratory story. *Journal of Gay and Lesbian Social Services, 6*, 29–41.

James, S. E., & Murphy, B. C. (1998). Gay and lesbian relationships in a changing social context. In C. J. Patterson & A. R. D'Augelli (Eds.), *Lesbian, gay, and bisexual identities in families: Psychological perspectives* (pp. 99–121). New York: Oxford University Press.

Jay, K. (1995, Winter). Lesbian New York. *Harvard Gay & Lesbian Review, 2*, 19–22.

Jay, K., & Young, A. (Eds.). (1972). *Out of the closets: Voices of gay liberation*. New York: Douglas Book.

Jefferson, T. R. (1998). Toward a black lesbian jurisprudence. *Boston College Third World Law Journal, 18*, 263–291.

Jordan, C., & Davis, B. J. (1998, Fall). NOW calls activists to come out against homophobia. *National NOW Times*, p. 16.

Jost, K. (2000). Gay-rights update. *Congressional Quarterly Researcher, 10*, 307–327.

Kanuha, V. (1990). Compounding the triple jeopardy: Battering in lesbian of color relationships. *Women and Therapy, 9*, 169–184.

Keefe, S. E., & Padilla, A. M. (1987). *Chicano ethnicity*. Albuquerque: University of New Mexico Press.

Kennedy, E. L., & Davis, M. D. (1993). *Boots of leather, slippers of gold: The history of a lesbian community*. New York: Routledge.

Klein, F. (1993). *The bisexual option* (2nd ed.). New York: Harrington Park.

Lang, S. (1999). Lesbians, men-women and two-spirits: Homosexuality and gender in Native American cultures. In E. Blackwood & S. Wieringa (Eds.), *Female desires: Same-sex relations and transgender practices across cultures* (pp. 91–116). New York: Columbia University Press.

Levine, M. P. (1992). The life and death of gay clones. In G. Herdt (Ed.), *Gay culture in America: Essays from the field* (pp. 68–86). Boston: Beacon Press.

Lombardi, E. L. (1999). Integration within a transgender social network and its effect upon members' social and political activity. *Journal of Homosexuality, 37*, 109–126.

Lorber, J. (1998). Embattled terrain: Gender and sexuality. In M. M. Ferree, J. Lorber, & B. B. Hess (Eds.), *Revisioning gender* (pp. 416–448). Thousand Oaks, CA: Sage Publications.

Lynch, F. R. (1992). Nonghetto gays: An ethnography of suburban homosexuals. In G. Herdt (Ed.), *Gay culture in America: Essays from the field* (pp. 165–201). Boston: Beacon Press.

Marín, G., & Marín, B. V. (1991). *Research with Hispanic populations: Applied social research methods*. Newbury Park, CA: Sage Publications.

Marsiglia, F. F. (1998). Homosexuality and Latinos/as: Towards an integration of identities. *Journal of Gay & Lesbian Social Services, 8*, 113–125.

Martin, D., & Lyon, P. (1995). Lesbian liberation begins. *Harvard Lesbian & Gay Review, 2*, 15–18.

Maurer, L. (1999). Transgressing sex and gender: Deconstruction zone ahead? *Siecus Report, 28*, 14–21.

Mays, V. M. (1985). Black women working together: Diversity in same sex relationships. *Women's Studies International Forum, 8*, 67–71.

Mays, V. M., & Cochran, S. D. (1988). The black women's relationship project: A national survey of black lesbians. In M. Shernoff & W. Scott (Eds.), *The sourcebook on lesbian/gay health care* (2nd ed., pp. 54–62). Washington, DC: National Lesbian and Gay Health Foundation.

Miller, N. (1990). *In search of gay America.* New York: Harper & Row.

Mohr, J. J., & Rochlen, A. B. (1999). Measuring attitudes regarding bisexuality in lesbian, gay male, and heterosexual populations. *Journal of Counseling Psychology, 46*, 353–369.

Morales, E. S. (1990). Ethnic minority families and minority gays and lesbians. *Marriage and Family Review, 14*, 217–239.

Morales, E. S. (1992). Counseling Latino gays and Latina lesbians. In S. Dworkin & F. Gutiérrez (Eds.), *Counseling gay men and lesbians: Journey to the end of the rainbow* (pp. 125–139). Alexandria, VA: American Association for Counseling and Development.

Murray, S. O. (1992). Components of gay community in San Francisco. In G. Herdt (Ed.), *Gay culture in America* (pp. 107–146). Boston: Beacon Press.

Nakajima, G. A., Chan, Y. H., & Lee, K. (1996). Mental health issues for gay and lesbian Asian Americans. In R. P. Cabaj & T. S. Stein (Eds.), *Textbook of homosexuality and mental health* (pp. 563–581). Washington, DC: American Psychiatric Press.

Nakamura, K. (1997). Narrating ourselves: Duped or duplicitous? In B. Bullough, V. L. Bullough & J. Elias (Eds.), *Gender blending* (pp. 74–86). Amherst, NY: Prometheus Books.

Nakayama, T., & Corey, F. C. (1993). Homosexuality. In R. Kastenbaum (Ed.), *Encyclopedia of adult development* (pp. 208–215). Phoenix: Oryx.

National Gay and Lesbian Task Force. (2000). *GLBT civil rights laws in the U.S.* [Online]. Available: http://www.ngltf.org

Ochs, R. (1996). Biphobia: It goes more than two ways. In B. A. Firestein (Ed.), *Bisexuality: The psychology and politics of an invisible minority* (pp. 217–239). Thousand Oaks, CA: Sage Publications.

Ochs, R. (Ed.). (2001). *Bisexual resource guide* (4th ed.). Boston: Bisexual Resource Center.

Omoto, A., & Crain, A. (1995). AIDS volunteerism: Lesbian and gay community-based responses to HIV. In G. Herek & B. Greene (Eds.), *AIDS, identity and community: The HIV epidemic and lesbians and gay men* (pp. 187–209). Thousand Oaks, CA: Sage Publications.

Paul, J. P., Hays, R. B., & Coates, T. J. (1995). The impact of the HIV epidemic on U.S. gay male communities. In A. R. D'Augelli & C. J. Patterson (Eds.), *Lesbians, gay, and bisexual identities over the lifespan: Psychological perspectives* (pp. 347–397). New York: Oxford University Press.

Pearlman, S. F. (1987). The saga of continuing clash in lesbian community, or will an army of ex-lovers fail? In Boston Lesbian Psychologies Collective (Eds.), *Lesbian psychologies: Explorations and challenges* (pp. 313–326). Urbana: University of Illinois Press.

Pope, M. (1995). The "salad bowl" is big enough for us all: An argument for the inclusion of lesbians and gay men in any definition of multiculturalism. *Journal of Counseling & Development, 73,* 301–304.

Preves, S. E. (2002). Sexing the intersexed: An analysis of sociocultural responses to intersexuality. *Signs, 27,* 523–556.

Raymond, J. G. (1986). *A passion for friends: Toward a philosophy of female affection.* Boston: Beacon Press.

Rust, P. C. (1993). Neutralizing the political threat of the marginal woman: Lesbians' beliefs about bisexual women. *Journal of Sex Research, 30,* 214–228.

Rust, P. C. (1995). *Bisexuality and the challenge to lesbian politics: Sex, loyalty, & revolution.* New York: New York University Press.

Rust, P. C. (1996). Finding a sexual identity and community: Therapeutic implications and cultural assumptions in scientific models of coming out. In E. D. Rothblum & L. A. Bond (Eds.), *Preventing heterosexim and homophobia* (pp. 87–123). Thousand Oaks, CA: Sage Publications.

Saulnier, C. F. (1997). Alcohol problems and marginalization: Social group work with lesbians. *Social Work with Groups, 20,* 37–59.

Savin-Williams, R. C. (1996). Ethnic- and sexual-minority youth. In R. C. Savin-Williams & K. M. Cohen (Eds.), *The lives of lesbians, gay men, and bisexuals: Children to adults* (pp. 152–165). Fort Worth, TX: Harcourt Brace.

Schultz, G. (2001). Daughters of Bilitis: Literary genealogy and lesbian authenticity. *QLG: Journal of Lesbian and Gay Studies, 7*, 377–389.

Sears, J. T. (1989). The impact of gender and race on growing up lesbian and gay in the South. *National Women's Studies Association Journal, 1*, 422–457.

Stein, E. (1999). *The mismeasure of desire: The science, theory, and ethics of sexual orientation.* New York: Oxford University Press.

Stokes, J. P., & Peterson, J. L. (1998). Homophobia, self-esteem, and risk for HIV among African American men who have sex with men. *AIDS Education and Prevention, 10*, 278–292.

Stuart, K. E. (1991). *The uninvited dilemma: A question of gender.* Portland, OR: Metamorphous Press.

Tofoya, T. N. (1997). Native gay and lesbian issues: The two-spirited. In B. Greene (Ed.), *Ethnic and cultural diversity among lesbians and gay men* (pp. 1–10). Thousand Oaks, CA: Sage Publications.

Toledo, E. (1999, Spring). All feminists needed to make lesbian rights summit a success. *National NOW Times,* pp. 1, 16.

Weinberg, M. S., Williams, C. J., & Pryor, D. W. (1994). *Dual attraction: Understanding bisexuality.* New York: Oxford University Press.

Wight, E. (1996). A treasure hunt: Finding the dykes in Southwest Virginia. *Journal of Gay & Lesbian Social Services, 4*, 99–109.

Wilson, A. (1996). How we find ourselves: Identity development and two-spirit people. *Harvard Educational Review, 66*, 303–317.

Winnow, J. (1989, Summer). Lesbians working on AIDS: Assessing the impact on health care for women. *OUT/LOOK, 5*, 10–18.

Wooden, W. S., Kawasaki, H., & Mayeda, R. (1983). Lifestyles and identity maintenance among gay Japanese–American males. *Alternate Lifestyles, 5*, 236–243.

CHAPTER 2
CULTURAL, POLITICAL, LEGAL, AND SOCIAL ISSUES

What is heterosexism and how does it affect LGBT persons on cultural and individual levels?

How do the variables predicting heterosexist views engender prejudice and discrimination?

What is the status of public policy governing the rights of LGBT persons?

What is the status of marriage and civil unions for gay and lesbian persons?

What is the status of protections against discrimination in the workplace for LGBT persons on the federal, state, and local levels, and in the private sector?

How prevalent is violence against LGBT persons?

HETEROSEXISM AT THE CULTURAL LEVEL

Hetereosexism is an ideological system that dismisses and stigmatizes any form of behavior, identity, relationship, or community that does not comply with heterosexual norms. It operates at two levels: cultural and individual. Culturally, hetereosexism is the belief that affectional and sexual expression is only acceptable between men and women, and social customs and institutions constantly reinforce this belief. Cultural heterosexism is so pervasive and taken for granted that we rarely notice its existence or practices (Herek, 1995). This form of heterosexism erases the reality of persons who are not heterosexual so that heterosexuality appears as the only state of being. For example, the goal of research in the humanities and the social sciences is the pursuit of knowledge about humankind. Yet, until recent years, college textbooks did not mention LGBT persons except in sections on deviance and mental illness. Sometimes, even humanities research has neglected to enlighten students fully. For example, no one knew for a hundred years that, after her death, the family of Emily Dickinson changed the sex–gender (from female to male) of the persons to whom she wrote poetry and passionate love letters (Cruikshank, 1992).

HETEROSEXISM AT THE INDIVIDUAL LEVEL

Because heterosexism is pervasive in mainstream culture, it is not surprising to see it at the individual level in the behaviors and feelings directed at LGB persons (Herek, 1995), ranging from jokes and derogatory terms to physical attacks (McDougall, 1993; Neisen, 1990). Feelings include disgust and indignation (for example, Berrill, 1990; Herek, 1993). Lesbian and gay persons receive more negative responses on attitude scales than any other subordinated group (Yang, 1997). Because of their same sex–gender attractions, bisexual persons are also disliked (Istvan, 1983). Eliason (2001) found that the same variables are associated with negative attitudes about both bisexual persons and lesbian and gay persons, and about to the same degree.

The core factors contributing to heterosexism at the individual level are prejudice and stereotypes. Prejudice is a prejudgment or negative bias concerning a whole group based on limited or no experience with anyone in the group (DiAngelo, 1997; Johansson, 1990c). Stereotypes maintain prejudice (Herek, 1995) by overemphasizing certain characteristics of the target group (Yarhouse, 1999). Some stereotypes reflect general cultural ideologies about members of all subordinated groups that they are inferior or threatening to members of the dominant group. Other stereotypes are more specific such as believing that lesbian and gay adults can influence the sexual orientation of children (Herek, 1995). A stereotype about gay men recently in the news is that they are child molesters. This has been evident in the connection that many Americans and some church officials are making in the child sexual abuse crisis in the Catholic Church. They see it as a "homosexual" problem. Suggestions have been made to eliminate all gay priests. Yet, no evidence exists to support these views about gay men—most child sexual abusers are heterosexual men (Birch, 2002; Elias, 2002).

Negative stereotypes are not present in young children (Johansson, 1990c), but as they move into adolescence, children show adultlike negative reactions to certain groups (Bozett, 1987). Once children learn the stereotypes, popular culture (for example, the media) continually reinforce them (Herek, 1995). Various factors that have been associated with holding negative attitudes toward LGB persons are listed below—most likely negative attitudes result from an interaction of several of these variables rather than only one (Eliason, 1997).

Being Male

These people are going to ruin our children. We [White men] need your money to support the cause of the radical right of not letting them have any special rights.

Studies generally show that men, most often White men, hold more heterosexist beliefs and attitudes than women (for example, Burn, 2000; Herek, 2002; LaMar & Kite, 1998). Fathers, brothers, and sons react more harshly than female family members to another member's disclosure of a gay or lesbian identity (Herek, 1988; Kite, 1984). On college campuses, male students hold more negative attitudes about gay persons than do female college students; male students also perceive lesbians as a threat to society's basic institutions (D'Augelli & Rose, 1990). Heterosexual men not only express less comfort around gay and lesbian persons than do heterosexual women but also are less willing to support human rights for these groups. Heterosexual men are more likely to believe that "homosexuality" is a choice that can be altered through "therapy" (Johnson, Brems, & Alford-Keating, 1997).

Conservatism, Authoritarianism, Traditionalism, and Religiosity

That girl got raped because of her disgusting flaunting of "not needing any man" and saying that she "would never be submissive to any man." My church expects women to be subservient and when they are not they deserve to get what is coming to them. My parents think this way too.

College students who are more negative about gay persons are more often from conservative families instead of moderate or liberal families. Both men and women with negative attitudes toward lesbian and gay persons express conservative political views (for example, Seltzer, 1992; Waldo, 1998) and display high levels of sexual conservatism (Ficarrotto, 1990). In addition, they exhibit authoritarian thinking (for example, "I'm right, you're wrong") and intolerance for ambiguity (see Herek, 1988; Obear, 1991). Traditionalism, as investment in traditional sex–gender roles, is also associated with negative attitudes (Schope & Eliason, 2000; Stark, 1991). In particular, men dislike sex–gender role nonconformity. Lesbians receive negative ratings when they seem less traditionally "feminine" (Laner & Laner, 1980) and gay men who display "femininity" may receive negative responses from heterosexual men (Parrott, Adams, & Zeichner, 2002). Persons with more negative beliefs are also more likely to subscribe to a conservative or fundamentalist religious ideology (Schope & Eliason, 2000; Seltzer, 1992) and believe that religious authority backs their negative beliefs and supports their expressions of bigotry (Johansson, 1990a). Many religious persons feel greater discomfort around gay and lesbian persons and are less willing to support granting them human rights (Johnson et al., 1997). Self-identified Christians on college campuses are among the groups with the most negative attitudes and are the least sympathetic toward LGB students (Waldo, 1998).

Low Empathy

I do not understand those people and I have no sympathy for them. I will demonstrate against voting for that ridiculous ordinance against discrimination in city jobs.

Less empathic persons are more likely to discriminate against gay and lesbian persons. Those with higher levels of both empathic concern (affective form of empathy) and perspective (cognitive form of empathy) are significantly less likely to have negative attitudes and more likely to favor granting human rights. Being able to understand another's viewpoint is also associated with higher levels of comfort when around lesbian and gay persons (Johnson et al., 1997).

Certain Coping Styles

I refuse to speak to that gay man on my office floor. He tries to be friendly but I snub him every time. I am not at all happy either about having to attend that sensitivity program about "homos."

Coping styles also play a role in negative attitudes. Persons who tend to use denial, isolate or turn from others, or look for blame outside themselves are likely to respond to gay and lesbian persons in more prejudicial and discriminatory ways (Johnson et al., 1997).

Older Age and Less Educated

I am too old to change now. I heard about those people when I was younger but never met any of them. Just because you are one of the few family members getting an education, don't go getting any ideas of bringing one of those perverts home as your friend.

Persons with extreme negative attitudes and beliefs about LGB persons tend to be older (see Eliason, 1995; Simoni, 1996). Yet those who grew up with the "sexual revolution" and in the post-Stonewall era (the period following the 1969 riot instigated by LGBT patrons at the Stonewall Bar in Greenwich Village, New York) may eventually hold more positive attitudes than the current population of older persons. Persons with more negative attitudes and beliefs also have less education (Serovich, Skeen, Walters, & Robinson, 1993; Simoni, 1996).

Bigoted Peers and Residential Areas

Even though it is a small town, there is one of those gay bars here. My friends and I drive by on weekend nights and throw things at the queers walking in or out of the place. One night we got out of the truck and chased a bunch of them. They probably won't be back.

The peers of persons with negative attitudes tend to also oppose homosexuality (Franklin, 2000). These persons also tend to live in geographical and residential areas where negative attitudes about same sex–gender sexual orientations are the norm (for example, the midwestern and southern United States, rural areas, or small towns). Those who are more tolerant tend to live in suburbs and other urban areas; the most tolerant tend to live in large cities (Hong, 1984).

No Contact with Lesbian and Gay Persons

I do not believe there are any gay and lesbian persons that work here. If there are, I never met one and never want to or even be in the same room with one of them.

Most students in a college sample reported that they did not know a lesbian (94 percent) or a gay (92 percent) person (D'Augelli & Rose, 1990). In the general population of American adults, Herek and Glunt (1993) found that only about one-third reported that they knew a lesbian or gay person. Many studies reported that heterosexuals who have experienced no personal contact with gay or lesbian persons hold negative attitudes and beliefs about them (for example, Cotten-Huston & Waite, 2000; Herek & Glunt, 1993). Both men's and women's attitudes about potential contact with a gay or lesbian person of their sex–gender were more negative than their attitudes toward gay or lesbian persons not of their sex–gender (LaMar & Kite, 1998).

Heterosexual persons who have LGB family members or friends have the lowest levels of prejudice. Those with demographics associated with less prejudice, such as women and well-educated persons, are also more likely to experience contact with LGB persons (Herek & Capitanio, 1996). Yet, interaction with gay and lesbian persons did not influence self-reported discriminatory behavior in one study of students on a college campus (Rey & Gibson, 1997). Among college students who had a gay or lesbian friend, 79 percent had laughed at an antigay joke and about 40 percent had told antigay jokes, made fun of gay and lesbian persons, and had called someone "fag," "queer," or "dyke" (Schope & Eliason, 2000).

EFFECTS OF HETEROSEXISM IN POLITICAL AND LEGAL CONTEXTS

Three categories of basic rights for LGBT persons, identified by E. Stein (1999), include:

- decriminalization of sexual activity between adults of the same sex–gender involving mutual consent and no physical harm

- protection against discrimination because of sexual orientation

- positive rights or recognition of LGBT organizations, relationships, and families, including marriage, filing joint income tax returns, domestic partnerships, custody of one's children, becoming foster and adoptive parents, visitation rights when partners are hospitalized, and official status of LGBT organizations in schools, universities, and professional associations.

The status of the first two categories is discussed here, plus some of the positive rights. The status of other positive rights will be addressed in Chapters 6 and 7.

Because of the negative attitudes toward LGB persons in the United States, the legal system disentitles them; in most civil rights legislation, these persons are not included in the lists of protected categories (Byrne, 1993; Rivera, 1991). Except for a handful of statewide laws and a few dozen municipal laws, LGB persons have no legal protection from overt discrimination in areas such as employment, housing, services, and access to public accommodations (D'Augelli & Garnets, 1995; Herek, 1995). Only about 11 states prohibit employment discrimination in both public and private arenas; about 10 states prohibit it in only the public sector (http://www.–lambdalegal.org/cgi-in/iowa/states/antidiscrimi-map; see also the Lambda Legal Web site for a summary of states, cities, and counties that prohibit discrimination based on sexual orientation: http://www.lambdalegal.org/cgi-bin/iowa/ documents/record?record=217). Transgender persons also experience discrimination in employment and housing as well as in medical treatment, social services, the military, and sports competitions (Green & Brinkin, 1994). An exception is in San Francisco, which has a progressive city ordinance prohibiting discrimination because of gender expression. The city also provides a range of programs that address the needs of transgender persons. Recently the mayor approved $50,000 in health benefits to cover some of the costs of hormone treatment and sexual reassignment surgery for city workers who are transgender (Tarver, 2002).

Since LGB persons are not a protected class in the U.S. Constitution, they generally cannot rely on the Constitution or the courts to shield them from discrimination (Byrne, 1993). Even if they were a protected class, they would not be protected in private circles. For example, in October 1998, Bob Jones University, the fundamentalist Christian college, would not allow former gay and lesbian students on campus for a student reunion. School police threatened these alumnae with arrests if they attempted to enter the campus. As a private institution, with a tax-exempt status, the university is not subject to the civil rights legislation that applies to public institutions ("Christian School," 1998). A college student was suspended by Brigham Young University in 2001 for "homosexual conduct." Another student at the same university was given the choice of withdrawing from the university or face a two-year suspension because he held another man's hand ("News of the Year," 2002).

The Equal Protection Clause of the Fourteenth Amendment of the U.S. Constitution requires that states provide equal protection for all residents, but court cases determine what this means for LGB persons. In 1996, the U.S. Supreme Court ruled that lesbian and gay persons could not be singled out for official discrimination because of their sexual orientation (Savage, 1996). This was a momentous decision, but it does not guarantee protection for LGB persons from discrimination. In 40 states, it is still legal to deny housing and jobs because of sexual orientation (Hartman, 1999; Stein, 1999), and no federal law bans discrimination (Jost, 2000).

The historic source of all legal discrimination against LGB persons lies in sodomy laws (Johansson, 1990b). All 50 states once had these laws that criminalized (as a felony offense) private and consensual sexual behavior between adults of the same sex–gender. These laws still exist in 13 states (Lambda Legal, 2002: http://www.lambdalegal.org/cgi-bin/iowa/states/sodomy-map) and, though not often invoked, the symbolic message conveyed is that the state should punish same sex–gender sexual involvements and that LGB persons do not merit fair and nondiscriminatory treatment. They do not have rights for private choices in their intimate associations (D'Augelli & Garnets, 1995; Wolfson, 1994).

Almost all European countries no longer have such repressive criminal laws related to lesbian and gay persons, and only a few Western nations still have them. In the United States, 33 states and the District of Columbia have eliminated their sodomy laws, following enactment of the Model Penal Code in 1962 (Vetri, 1998). The most recent state to do away with a law barring sex acts between consenting adults of the same sex–gender was Arkansas; in July 2002 the state supreme court ruled this law unconstitutional (Vercher, 2002). So progress on this front is happening. The Lambda Legal Defense and Education Fund, a New York based gay legal rights organization, is working state by state to challenge the remaining sodomy laws (Copeland, 1998). For example, this organization asked the U.S. Supreme Court to review the constitutionality of the case of two men convicted in 1998 of violating the Texas "homosexual conduct" law (Lamda Legal, 2002; Vercher, 2002). On June 26, 2003, the U. S. Supreme Court voted six to three to strike down laws in Texas and 12 other states that criminalized sex between persons of the same sex–gender (Pusey, 2003).

Marriage

One of the "hot" civil right issues in the 1990s and the current decade centers on marriage (see the Lambda Legal Web site for its marriage project: http://www.lambdalegal.org/cgi-bin/iowa/issues/record2?record=9). The ancient Romans and early Christians recognized same sex–gender unions. It appears, however, that no gay or lesbian couple in the United States requested a marriage license or filed a case demanding the right to one until the 1990s. Feminists rejected marriage as an oppressive institution, and in the gay and lesbian community, same sex–gender marriage was a low priority because of other more pressing issues (Eskridge, 1996). By the early 1990s, though, gay and lesbian persons became more insistent about state recognition of their relationships. When denied marriage licenses in Hawaii, Alaska, New York, the District of Columbia, and Vermont, they filed cases in state courts to try to attain equal rights. The first of the state court cases to get major attention in the United States was in Hawaii because the appellate court decided that same sex–gender couples could marry. Following appeal, the Hawaii Supreme Court ruled that the state would have to demonstrate a compelling reason for limiting marriage to heterosexual persons. This case bounced between state interests and court decisions with the state wanting marriage to apply only to the union of a man and a woman and the courts declaring no compelling reason existed for the ban on gay and lesbian marriages. In 1998, however, 70 percent of voters approved an amendment that gave the legislature the power to limit marriage to a man and a woman (Chambers & Polikoff, 1999).

Several other countries have rectified the denial of equal rights in this area. Earlier, the Netherlands changed its laws to allow gay and lesbian marriages (Chambers & Polikoff, 1999), and Belgium followed suit in January 2003 (Asher, 2003). On June 10, 2003, the appeals court in Ontario, Canada, ruled that the right to marry should extend to same sex–gender couples (Oh, Canada!, 2003). The first legal same sex–gender marriages (a lesbian couple and three gay couples) took place in Amsterdam in April 2001 ("News of the Year," 2002).

In Vermont, the governor signed the civil unions bill for that state in April 2000. This gives gay and lesbian couples in Vermont the same rights as married couples. In the same month, the highest court in the Presbyterian Church ruled that local congregations could provide ceremonies for same sex–gender unions (but not marriages). In March 2000, the Central Conference of American Rabbis, the largest group of American clergy, declared that its members could conduct gay and lesbian unions (Delgado, 2000). In 1997, Hawaii was the first state to adopt partner registration (called reciprocal beneficiaries). Registered gay and lesbian couples in Hawaii now receive many rights that married couples receive under state law (Chambers & Polikoff, 1999).

Some newspapers announce same sex–gender unions or let same sex–gender couples take out advertisements to announce their unions. Notably, because of its reputation and large circulation, the New York Times began in September 2002 to print announcements of same sex–gender unions celebrated in a public ceremony and some types of formal registrations for domestic partnerships. These announcements are printed under the weddings and celebrations listings in the Sunday Style section ("N.Y. Times to Print," 2002).

Although progress continues, defeats on the marriage front continue as well. In November 2000, voters in Nebraska banned recognition of same sex–gender marriage, civil unions, and domestic partnerships ("Year in Review," 2001). In addition, at the prompting of conservative groups, more than 30 states have now adopted nonrecognition (of gay and lesbian unions) legislation with bills or referenda pending in eight other states. In 1996, the U.S. Congress passed the Defense of Marriage Act of 1996 that limits the aplication of any state's decision on same-sex marriage. This means that states do not have to recognize unions legalized in another state. In addition, all federal legislation and regulations that mention married persons or spouses must indicate this applies only to marriage of a man and a woman (Chambers & Polikoff, 1999).

Not all lesbian and gay persons support the pursuit of legal marriage, because most of the benefits of marriage go to White and upper class persons. Marriage is less attractive and less financially advantageous for women, poor persons, and racial and ethnic persons in the LGBT community. Achieving the right to marry one's same sex–gender partner will not place these persons in the mainstream; they will still experience subordination due to sexual orientation, race, ethnicity, or poverty (Ettelbrick, 1993; Hutchinson, 2000).

The Workplace

Job discrimination with its potential economic ruin is one of the most severe threats to the civil rights of LGBT persons (Byrne, 1993; Gonsiorek, 1993). Termination is the harshest form of discrimination in the workplace, but discrimination can take other forms, for example, not being hired or not being granted promotions. Mentoring and the support needed for advancement may also not be forthcoming (Goldman, 1992). In addition, few employers provide benefits such as health insurance for same sex–gender partners (Sussal, 1994; Woods & Lucas, 1993). Some companies wanting to provide this coverage are pressured by local governments not to do so. Government-sponsored benefits such as the Family and Medical Leave Act of 1993 also exclude employees with same sex–gender partners (Landau, 1994).

Explicit employment discrimination against lesbian and gay persons is most prominent and controversial in the current policy of the military. Two studies by the Department of Defense (McDaniel, 1989; Sarbin & Karols, 1988) showed that the service records of these persons were, on average, superior in comparison to the records of heterosexuals (also see Dyer, 1990). But, the current policy, which became effective on February 28, 1994, states that a member of the U.S. Armed Forces who engages in homosexual acts or states that he or she is homosexual will be separated from the armed forces (10 U.S.C.A. §654) (Landau, 1994). This policy reinforces continued secrecy, pretense, and silence. Yet gay and lesbian persons are speaking out, and the number of them forced out of the military is rising. In 1999, the Pentagon discharged persons for being gay, lesbian, or bisexual at a rate of three per day (Service Members Legal Defense Network, 2000). In 2001, the discharge rate was similar (Maines, 2002). Also investigations, threats, and interrogations are increasing (Hartman, 1999). Incidents of antigay harassment (968) reported by the Service Members Legal Defense Network in 1999 ranged from verbal bashing to murder. As reported by the Defense Department's Office of Inspector General, 37 percent of 71,500 services members had witnessed or experienced harassment because of sexual orientation; 80 percent had heard offensive speech or jokes, derogatory names, or remarks about gay and lesbian persons in the past year. Admitting for the first time that harassment because of sexual orientation was a problem, in July 2000 the Pentagon published an antiharassment action plan (Service Members Legal Defense Network, 2000). But a recent report from the Service Members Legal Defense Network indicates that the military has basically ignored this order, as training is sporadic and not taken seriously (Maines, 2002).

Another example of workplace discrimination happened in the private sector when, in 1991, the Cracker Barrel restaurants established a policy of not employing lesbian or gay persons. Employees identified as lesbian or gay were also terminated no matter how long they had worked for these restaurants (Kaupman, 1991). Because of considerable adverse publicity and protests outside the restaurants as customers were entering or leaving, Cracker Barrel stated that it would follow a nondiscrimination policy. But it never formally adopted such a policy or rehired the fired employees (Noble, 1992).

In most private companies, lesbian and gay persons can only rely on what their workplace is willing to do. Many companies hold explicit or implicit policies against employing and keeping LBGT workers (Hays, 1991). Workers who are fired from private companies have challenged discriminatory practices with varying outcomes (Landau, 1994). An executive fired from Shell Oil was awarded $5.3 million in a California court (Collins v. Shell Oil Co., 1991). Following this result, California enacted legislation providing more protection against discrimination because of sexual orientation (Gross, 1992). Employees terminated by

Cracker Barrel, however, had no legal recourse, as the restaurant did not operate in any state where protection was guaranteed (Landau, 1994).

Lesbian and gay employees may attempt to manage discrimination at work through four strategies which follow a progressive order: quit, but not give the reason of work discrimination; silence, or tolerate discrimination and keep it to oneself; social support, attempt to gain support from others through sharing one's experience; confrontation, or openly address discrimination with one's supervisor or the perpetrator demanding the end of harassment (Chung, 2001).

In contrast to the discriminatory work situations identified above, since the 1970s, various other private companies (as well as universities, professional organizations, and unions) developed and follow explicit policies to prohibit discrimination based on sexual orientation (Kronenberger, 1991). Universities and companies associated with high technology and the entertainment industries have led the way in adopting equal treatment for all employees. Examples include MCA Inc., Warner Bros., Walt Disney, Microsoft Corp., Apple Computer, Lotus Development Corp., Columbia University, and Stanford University (Dodge, 1993; Jones & Willette, 1995). In 2000, 41 of the top 50 U.S. companies prohibited discrimination based on sexual orientation (Good, 2000).

Eleven states and the District of Columbia have also enacted legislation to prohibit discrimination in private companies (Van der Meide, 2000). Yet in 40 states one can be fired in the private sector simply because of sexual orientation (Good, 2000). Some counties, cities, and the state of Minnesota provide legal protection from discrimination in private employment for transgender persons (Van der Meide, 2000) as do some major corporations (Maurer, 1999).

A resolution at the 1984 U.S. Conference of Mayors recommended a national end to discrimination based on sexual orientation, including in one's employment (National Gay Task Force, 1984). As a result, mayors of large cities began appointing lesbian and gay persons to influential positions in local government (Schneider, 1984). Domestic partnership benefits began to increase in cities, states, companies, and colleges ("Domestic-Partner Benefits," 1991; National Gay and Lesbian Task Force, 2000a). Particularly notable was the announcement in June 2000 that three U.S. automakers (DaimlerChrysler, General Motors, and Ford) would offer these benefits to more than 400,000 employees. One hundred and two Fortune 500 companies offer or plan to offer domestic benefits, a 30 percent increase between August 1999 and September 2000 (Good, 2000).

Federal law does not provide specific protections for LGB workers. Yet a bill introduced in Congress, the Employment Non-Discrimination Act of 1994, could potentially be a landmark bill that will change workplace discrimination with the exception of the armed forces and religious organizations (Zavos, 1995). The proposed bill "prohibits any 'different standards or treatment' in employment for persons based upon their sexual orientation" (Tafel, 1994, p. 19). In 1966, the bill was defeated in the Senate by one vote and although it has been reintroduced in the House and the Senate, it has not yet been approved (Hartman, 1999). Over half of Fortune 500 companies already have policies consistent with the proposed bill, and many other businesses endorse it along with civil rights organizations, religious organizations, labor unions, and women's organizations (Religious Action Center of Reform Judaism, 2000).

THE CHALLENGE OF QUEER POLITICS

The political and legal situation for LGB persons is better but still not good. Sexual acts between persons of the same sex–gender are still criminalized in some states and LGB persons continue to be subject to many discriminatory practices in the basic areas of justice, rights, privacy, equality, and liberty (Stein, 1999). The political strategies used to overcome these practices such as the push for civil rights have been challenged in recent years by "queer politics," a more radical activism including demonstrations by ACT UP (AIDS Coalition to Unleash Power, begun in 1987 in New York City) and Queer Nation (begun in 1990 in New York City).

In the early 1990s, the queer movement began offering a queer politics, a radical alternative to conventional gay and lesbian politics (Alexander, 1999). The politics of convention holds that once heterosexuals recognize that gay and lesbian persons are "just like us," they will grant them civil liberties and civil rights (Tierney, 1997). Queer politics, however, defines itself largely by its stance against normalization and opposes both the heterosexual and gay and lesbian mainstreams (Epstein, 1994; Quinlivan & Town, 1999).

Queer politics is a politics of outsiderhood and difference from traditional heterosexuality (Jeffreys, 1994). It advocates an in-your-face difference, with an edge of defiant separation (Edwards & Brooks, 1999). For instance, lesbian and gay persons could enter a bar frequented by heterosexuals and kiss each other in front of the other patrons (Epstein, 1994). Another in-your-face scenario was suggested by Rofes (2000) who asked us to imagine the effect if same sex-gender couples throughout America appeared on the same day to fill out the forms to register for marriage. Imagine that the clerks refused their requests for marriage forms. Imagine if the couples knew how to contact local media, organize teams of supporters, and deliver an impact message about this closed institution. Imagine if these couples returned every day for a week or a month making the same statement. Or they could chain themselves to front doors of the offices of justices of the peace. They could appear outside churches where politicians or celebrities were getting married with signs exclaiming: "Saying 'I do' when we can't is bigotry." Or they could crash marriage ceremonies at the moment officiators ask for any objections and make speeches about the inequitable access to marriage.

Queer politics is confrontational, and the goal is to be disruptive (Tierney, 1997). Whether these strategies will become more dominant remains to be seen. For now, attempts to redress discrimination are most often done through conventional means. But as Duggan (2001) stated: "Queer politics, with its critique of the categories and strategies of liberal gay politics, keeps the possibility of radical change alive at the margins" (p. 228).

VIOLENCE OF HETEROSEXISM

The impact of heterosexism extends beyond the rhetoric and practices of politics and law. By far the more extreme consequence of heterosexist ideology is violence (for example, Berrill, 1990; Comstock, 1991; Herek, 1990, 1993). Lesbian and gay persons are the most frequent targets of bias violence (Dean, Wu, & Martin, 1992; Von Schulthess, 1992), with as many as half the population of gay and lesbian persons reporting violent incidents (Comstock, 1991).

Early in the 1990s, community and advocacy organizations (for example, National Gay and Lesbian Task Force, 1994) and academic researchers (for example, Comstock, 1991;

Herek, 1989; Herek & Berrill, 1992) began documenting the incidents of harassment and violence. Reviewing 24 local, regional, and national samples of LGB persons, Berrill (1992) reported the following incidents: assault with weapons (9 percent), physical assault (17 percent), vandalization of property (19 percent), threats of violence (44 percent), thrown objects (25 percent), spitting (13 percent), and verbal harassment (80 percent). Similar results came from a national telephone survey ("Results of Poll," 1989). Reviewed further below are assaults against LGB youth in the community, public schools, and colleges; the escalation of violence; and the most deadly form of violence—murder.

Youth as Targets of Assaults

Youth thought to be gay or lesbian can be a prime target for verbal and physical assault (D'Augelli & Dark, 1995; Dean et al., 1992). When open about their sexual identity, they face verbal harassment and physical attacks at home, in school, and in their local communities. A significant number of sexually subordinated youth reported they were verbally and physically assaulted, robbed, raped, or sexually abused by family members and peers (Hunter, 1990; Rotheram-Borus, Rosario, & Koopman, 1991). Most (80 percent) LGB youth studied by Pilkington and D'Augelli (1995) reported experiencing verbal abuse because of their sexual identity. Verbal abuse happened more than two times for 48 percent of these youth. Rates for other bias crimes (for the entire group) included: the threat of physical violence (44 percent—19 percent more than two times); damaged personal property (23 percent); thrown objects (33 percent); chased (30 percent—16 percent more than one time); spitting (13 percent); physical assault (that is, punched, kicked, or beaten; 17 percent); assault with a weapon (10 percent); and sexual assault (22 percent). Some reported fear of verbal (22 percent) or physical (7 percent) abuse at home; more reported fear of verbal (31 percent) or physical (26 percent) abuse at school. In studies conducted with ethnic and racial youth seeking the services of the Hetrick-Martin Institute in New York City, one-half of the youth reported teasing and humiliation because of their sexual identity (Rosario, Rotheram-Borus, & Reid, 1992), and close to one-half experienced violent physical attacks because of their sexual identity (Hunter & Schaecher, 1990).

Between 33 percent and 49 percent of lesbian and gay youth responding to community surveys reported being victimized in public schools (Berrill, 1990). A survey of the Los Angeles County school system showed that classmates perpetrate much of the abuse against LGB youth and that the incidence rates of this abuse are escalating dramatically (Peterson, 1989). Close to three-quarters of females (71 percent) and males (73 percent) studied by Telljohann and Price (1993) reported harassment at school because of their sexual orientation, including rude comments and jokes, profanities written on their lockers, threats of violence, and physical abuse. In Remafedi's (1987a) study of 29 gay youth, 30 percent reported that they were victims of physical assaults; half of these assaults occurred on school property. Most gay youth in this study reported regular verbal abuse from classmates, and almost 40 percent lost friends at school because of their sexual identity. Uribe and Harbeck (1991) met regularly with a group of 50 gay and lesbian students at a Los Angeles high school. Many of these students heard derogatory terms about themselves, even as early as the elementary school level. Low self-esteem, feelings of isolation, alienation, and inadequacy were common to these students, and most of them hid their sexual orientation. Pilkington and D'Augelli

(1995) found that 19 percent of racial and ethnic lesbian and gay youth reported being emo-tionally hurt by another student because of their sexual identity and 10 percent reported that this happened by a teacher. Over a quarter (28 percent) of these students reported that they feared being physically hurt by students or teachers if they disclosed their sexual identity. Almost all (97 percent) of a sample of LGB youth in high school recalled negative attitudes displayed by classmates at school, and more than half feared harassment, especially if they made disclosures (Sears, 1991).

The Safe Schools Anti-Violence Documentation Project in the State of Washington stud-ies antigay sexual harassment and violence in the public schools from kindergarten through high school. Information from this project, provided by Reis (1998), sums up the types of vio-lence perpetrated on gay and lesbian students while at school:

- gang rapes—including multiple assailants; some assailants also urinated on gay and lesbian students, ejaculated on them, vomited on them, or broke their hands

- physical assaults—including kicking, punching, and injuring gay and lesbian students with weapons, resulting in cuts, contusions, and broken bones

- physical harassment or sexual assault, lacking rape—including pushing, pulling, or brushing one's body against gay and lesbian students; spitting on students; hitting students with fly-ing objects; and pulling student's clothes up, down, or off

- verbal and other harassment—including repeated public humiliation of gay and lesbian stu-dents, vandalizing their property, spreading rumors about them, and making death threats toward them

- one-time, climate-setting incidents—including primarily name calling and offensive lan-guage directed at gay and lesbian students.

Failing grades, truancy, and dropping out of school are not uncommon among LGB stu-dents. Though many are exceedingly intelligent, few perform to their level of potential in school (Uribe & Harbek, 1991). Over half of the gay and bisexual male youth studied by Rotheram-Borus and colleagues (1991) failed a grade. Gay and bisexual male youth studied by Remafedi (1987a, 1987b) were often truant (nearly 40 percent) and 28 percent dropped out of school. In a proportional random sample of public high school students in Massachusetts, Faulkner and Cranston (1998) found that gay and lesbian students reported truancy at three times the rate of their heterosexual peers. They reported feeling unsafe, being picked on, and having their property deliberately damaged or stolen.

Only two out of 36 high school youth studied by Sears (1991) found a supportive group at school. Most passed as heterosexual until graduation, although some students dropped out before graduating. Only a quarter (25 percent) lesbian and gay youth 14 to 21 years old in another study felt they could talk with school counselors about their sexual identity. Fewer than one in five youth identified a person who was supportive of them in their school (Telljohann & Price, 1993). Lesbian or gay teachers, who may have been able to provide sup-port and role models for these students, usually felt they had to remain hidden. If open about their sexual identity, they could lose their jobs. Heterosexual teachers may fear that others would suspect them of being gay or lesbian if they befriended LGB students (Khayatt, 1994).

Transgender youth are abused in schools because they do not or refuse to conform to expectations of feminine or masculine behavior. They are often made scapegoats and verbally abused, and sometimes the harassment takes the form of physical violence (Mallon, 1997).

The situation seems no better on college campuses. About two-thirds (64 percent) of gay and lesbian college students studied by D'Augelli (1989a) felt their safety on campus was in jeopardy based on threats, verbal abuse, or property damage. Data collected by the National Gay and Lesbian Task Force (1991) on the campus climate at 40 colleges and universities showed that between 40 percent and 54 percent of the LGB respondents experienced verbal harassment or threats. Harassment on campus included demeaning remarks such as "faggot" or "bash them back into the closet" (Lopez & Chism, 1993).

Further substantiating the hostile climate on college campuses for gay and lesbian students are the views and behaviors of heterosexual students. Close to half of the first-year college students surveyed by D'Augelli and Rose (1990) thought that sex between same sex–gender partners was wrong and that gay persons were "disgusting"; more than a quarter (29 percent) felt the campus would be a better place without lesbian and gay students. Over 80 percent (men more often than women) made hostile remarks about these students. Most of the 226 college students (95 percent) surveyed by D'Augelli and Rose participated in some form of discriminatory behavior directed at LGB students such as laughing or agreeing with jokes or derogatory statements, making jokes or derogatory statements, and using derogatory terms such as fag. Most (90 percent) of 129 college students studied by Schope and Eliason (2000) reported having witnessed heterosexist acts in the last year, including verbal and written assaults and verbal threats against lesbian and gay persons. Over 90 percent of the respondents had themselves laughed at an antigay joke or remark. Slightly more than one-half had made an antigay joke, made fun of a lesbian or gay person, or called someone fag, queer, or dyke. Even liberal campuses, for example, Oberlin College, reported widespread harassment toward LGB students including hostile graffiti and verbal insults (Norris, 1992). Negative attitudes about LGB students also happened in university housing where the resident assistants (especially if male) were likely to reinforce these attitudes by making negative comments about lesbian and gay students (D'Augelli, 1989b).

In the sample of college students studied by Schope and Eliason (2000), over half had participated once or twice in progay helping behaviors over the last year such as challenging an antigay joke. Progay behaviors, however, were rare when compared to heterosexist actions. In addition, only 20 percent of the respondents had defended a gay or lesbian person they observed being harassed or threatened.

Some instructors on campus also made deprecating remarks about gay and lesbian persons. In addition, many instructors did not address gay and lesbian issues in their classes but instead discussed topics such as families and couples purely from only a heterosexual point of view (Lopez & Chism, 1993).

Escalating Violence

Violence directed at lesbian and gay persons is escalating. In just a couple of years after 1988, it increased 161 percent in five major U.S. cities: New York, San Francisco, Chicago,

Boston, and Minneapolis–St. Paul (Berrill, 1990). The National Coalition of Anti-Violence Programs (2000) reported violent incidents directed at LGBT persons in 1999 for 13 cities, states, and regions across the United States. The National Coalition is a voluntary network composed of 25 community-based programs that monitors and responds to anti-LGBT violence nationwide. Compared to 1998, the total number of reported anti-LGBT incidents of violence declined slightly (3 percent) in 1999 (2,017 versus 1,965). The decline in reported incidents, however, was confined to only four of the 13 reporting regions. In the other nine regions, the number of incidents between 1998 and 1999 increased at a mean rate of 40 percent. The rate gains ranged from 7 percent in Columbus, Ohio, to 116 percent in Chicago. According to the FBI (reporting is voluntary), 1,229 hate crimes against LGBT persons occurred in 2000 (http://www.ngltf.org/issues/-issue.cfm?issueID=12). Hate crimes or bias crimes are crimes that target persons because of their sexual orientation. Herek, Cogan, and Gillis (2002) found in a study of LGB victims of hate crimes that they could easily recognize when a crime was based on their sexual orientation because the perpetrators knew what it was (through means such as gay-identified symbols or locations such as gay bars) and made anti-LGB statements while committing the crimes.

Most states do not collect information on bias violence. Only 23 states and the District of Columbia have some way to record information about bias or hate crimes related to sexual orientation. Only the District of Columbia and four states include this information on transgender persons (National Gay and Lesbian Task Force, 2000b, 2001). The federal Hate Crimes Statistics Act of 1990 requires the U.S. Department of Justice to collect and report hate crimes related to sexual orientation, but because the department does not have to record information on these crimes from all police agencies, the full scope of bias crimes remains unknown (National Gay and Lesbian Task Force, 2000b; Van der Meide, 2000). If passed, the Local Law Enforcement Enhancement Act will grant the federal government additional authority to respond to hate crimes based on race, religion, national origin, sexual orientation, gender, and disability (http://www.ngltf.org/issues/issue.cfm?-issueID=12).

Even if data were collected on bias crimes from all police departments, the estimates would be inaccurate because of many unreported cases, estimated as high as 85 percent (Berrill, 1992). Many victims of bias crimes do not report them because of the stigma (Waldo, Hesson-McInnis, & D'Augelli, 1998). They fear of being "outed" or losing control of the management of their identities (Tewksbury, Grossi, Suresh, & Helms, 1999). They fear further harassment at the hands of police or others (Herek, 1995; Murphy, 1994). Instances of verbal harassment and abuse by police officers perpetrated on these crime victims increased by 155 percent and reports of physical abuse by police grew by 866 percent between 1977 and 1998 (National Coalition of Anti-Violence Programs, 1999). In addition, authorities often blame the crime victims themselves for their attacks, and rationalize or excuse the violent behavior of the perpetrators (Martin & Hetrick, 1988).

From interviews with a convenience sample of 450 LGB adult victims of hate crimes, Herek and colleagues (2002) reported that the physical and psychological brutality of the crimes was striking. Following the crimes, compared to victims of nonbias crimes, the victims of bias or hate crimes experienced greater and prolonged psychological distress. But there are also consequences for the LGB communities as these crimes represent terrorism and send messages that LGB persons are not safe. For the victims, even a minor incident of harassment can now be more frightening because they never know where it will lead.

Deadly Violence

The perpetrators of bias violence are becoming bolder (advancing from drive-by verbal slurs to use of bats, ropes, and knives), and their actions are more premeditated (Ilnytzky, 1999). The most brutal violence is murder. In 1992, Allen Schindler was beaten and stomped to death on a U.S. naval ship because he was gay. These actions destroyed every organ in his body (Service Members Legal Defense Network, 1999). Another gay man in the military, Barry Mitchell, was also killed because of his sexual orientation. The assailants shattered his skull with a baseball bat. Before his murder in June 1999, he experienced four months of taunting and harassment by other soldiers at Fort Campbell in Kentucky (Jost, 2000). In October 1998, two men abducted 21-year-old Mathew Shepard, beat him, and tied him to a fence in Wyoming. After 18 hours, he looked like a scarecrow to the person who found him. While Mathew lay dying in a hospital, a scarecrow that mocked gays was in a homecoming parade at Colorado State University ("Gay Victim of Beating," 1998). What is also stunning is that 68 percent of the North American population think the same thing that happened to Mathew could happen in their community ("Time/CNN Poll," 1998). Also in March 1999, Billy Jack Gaither was murdered in a small town in Alabama because he was gay (Herek, 2000). In July 2000, Arthur "J. R." Warren, Jr., a gay African American, was murdered in West Virginia by two teenagers. They not only beat this young man but ran over him with their vehicle. In September 2000, a gay student, Eric Plunkett, was murdered at Gallaudet University in Washington, DC ("Year in Review," 2001). On September 22, 2000, an assailant shot seven patrons in a gay bar in Roanoke, Virginia. One of them died (Laris, 2000). Juama Vega, a Latino lesbian activist in Milwaukee, was shot repeatedly in the chest and face in November 2001. She died a few days later (National Gay and Lesbian Task Force, 2001).

One estimate shows that more than 80 percent of transgender persons experience physical assaults because of their sex–gender expression (GenderPAC, 1998). Transgender persons are also murdered, including the brutal rape and killing of Brandon Teena at age 21. Biologically female, she wanted to be a man and was living as one in Nebraska before being discovered and murdered on New Year's Eve 1993 (Kirp, 1999; Thomas, 1999). In the year 2001, the 17th murder case of a transgender person on October 21 happened when Ana Melisa Cortez was stabbed to death in Nashville, Tennessee (Remember Our Dead, 2000). In 2002, two transgender teenagers were murdered with at least 10 bullet wounds each in southeast Washington, DC (National Gay and Lesbian Task Force, 2002).

A 13 percent increase in murder occurred between 1998 and 1999, with a large increase in violent incidents by groups of 10 or more. In 1999, as in 1998, most offenders (87 percent) were male, and two-thirds were under age 30 (National Coalition of Anti-Violence Programs, 2000). Often, the perpetrators of the most vicious attacks are teenagers (Savin-Williams, 1994), some of whom are members of organized hate groups (Berrill, 1990), including the Ku Klux Klan, Aryan Nation, and other White supremacist groups. Membership in these groups is expanding, as is activity directed at targeted groups including LGBT persons (Cruikshank, 1992).

Summary

- Societies establish rules and expectations for their members to create order, but rigid cultural mandates can also produce an atmosphere of intolerance, and even hatred, for those who are different. Heterosexism is an ideological system that rejects any form of behavior, identity, relationship, or community that does not comply with heterosexual norms. At the cultural level, heterosexism or the expectation that all members of society are heterosexual "erases" LGBT members by failing to recognize them or their experiences as legitimate. At the individual level, heterosexism results in prejudice about LGBT persons and stereotypes about them. These results are accompanied by negative feelings about LGBT persons and, at times, physical attacks.

- Although research studies are inconclusive about the exact profile of persons who perpetuate prejudice or negative attitudes toward gay and lesbian persons, some common characteristics recur in the literature. Being male, conservative, religious, and having limited empathy predispose persons to support traditional social imperatives for sexual behavior. In addition, age, education level, and geographic location influence a person's tolerance for differences in others, particularly gay and lesbian persons. In almost all cases, persons who have no personal acquaintance with gay and lesbian persons are more prone to negative beliefs and negative actions against these groups.

- Generally, social policy perpetuates discrimination against LGBT persons. Lack of federal legislation leaves state and local governments to establish their own regulations and laws, resulting in varying degrees of protection and discrimination across the country. Antidiscrimination laws in a few states are evidence of strides in public policy, but widespread opposition continues.

- In the early 1990s, gay and lesbian persons started pushing for marriage licenses. Although this appeared possible in Hawaii, it never materialized. Conservative groups, alarmed by the possibility of gay and lesbian marriages, prompted most states to adopt legislation for nonrecognition of these marriages. The Defense of Marriage Act of 1996 passed through Congress and permits states to not have to recognize a marriage that happened in another state. This would be the case for the civil unions bill signed by the Governor of Vermont in April 2000. In 1997, Hawaii adopted partner registration through which gay and lesbian couples could receive many rights that married couples receive. In November 2000, however, voters in Nebraska banned recognition of same sex–gender marriages, civil unions, and domestic partnerships.

- No federal policy standardizes hiring practices in the private workplace sector. These controls remain the province of state and local governments; only 10 states have formally adopted antidiscrimination policies for the workplace. Yet, slowly, some cities are beginning to include LGBT partners in benefit packages for employees, and some large private sector employers, the U.S. automakers for one, are following suit. Eleven states and the District of Columbia have codified antidiscrimination policies in the private sector. Yet, many private businesses continue to discriminate against LGBT persons. The proposed Employment Non-Discrimination Act of 1994 could lay the foundation for a shift in federal policy on sexual orientation but to date this law has yet to be passed.

- Despite modest gains in policy, violence against LGBT persons is rising in cities across the United States. The reports of violence against gay and lesbian persons are staggering; these groups are the most frequent targets of bias crimes. As many as 95 percent of sampled gay and lesbian respondents report some level of violence, with as many as 64 percent of college students stating that they do not feel safe on their campuses. Reports of violence perpetrated by the police have increased by as much as 866 percent between 1977 and 1998. Although all forms of violence are on the rise, deadly violence continues to escalate with a 13 percent increase in murder victims between 1998 and 1999. More troubling, murderers are acting with greater boldness and premeditation. Twenty-three states and the District of Columbia record bias crimes. The federal Hate Crimes Statistics Act of 1990 mandates the recording of such data but the complete scope of violence remains unknown.

CHAPTER 2
REFERENCES

Alexander, J. (1999). Beyond identity: Queer values and community. *Journal of Gay, Lesbian, and Bisexual Identity, 4*, 293–326.

Asher, J. B. (2003, January 31). *Belgium approves gay marriage* [Online]. Retrieved from http://www.equality.org.za/news/2003/01/31bmar.htm on July 3, 2003.

Berrill, K. T. (1990). Anti-gay violence and victimization in the United States. *Journal of Interpersonal Violence, 5*, 274–294.

Berrill, K. T. (1992). Organizing against hate on campus: Strategies for activists. In G. M. Herek & K. T. Berrill (Eds.), *Hate crimes: Confronting violence against lesbians and gay men* (pp. 259–269). Newbury Park, CA: Sage Publications.

Birch, E. (2002, June 10). Priest abuse problem isn't a gay issue. *Dallas Morning News*, p. 17A.

Bozett, F. W. (1987). Children of gay fathers. In F. W. Bozett (Ed.), *Gay and lesbian parents* (pp. 39–57). New York: Praeger.

Burn, S. M. (2000). Heterosexuals' use of "fag" and "queer" to deride one another: A contributor to heterosexism and stigma. *Journal of Homosexuality, 40*, 1–11.

Byrne, J. S. (1993). Affirmative action for lesbians and gay men: A proposal for true equality of opportunity and work force diversity. *Yale Law & Policy Review, 11*, 47–108.

Chambers, D. L., & Polikoff, N. D. (1999). Family law and gay and lesbian family issues in the twentieth century. *Family Law Quarterly, 33*, 523–542.

Christian school warns gay alumni not to visit. (1998, October 24). *Dallas Morning News*, p. A5.

Chung, Y. B. (2001). Work discrimination and coping strategies: Conceptual frameworks for counseling lesbian, gay, and bisexual clients. *Career Development Quarterly, 50*, 33–44.

Collins v. Shell Oil Co., 56 Fair Empl. Prac. Cas. (BNA) 440, No. 610983-5 (Alameda County Super. Ct., June 13, 1991).

Comstock, G. D. (1991). *Violence against lesbians and gay men*. New York: Columbia University Press.

Copeland, L. (1998, November 24). Georgia's sodomy law overturned. *USA Today*, p. A1.

Cotten-Huston, A. L., & Waite, B. M. (2000). Anti-homosexual attitudes in college students: Predictors and classroom and classroom interventions. *Journal of Homosexuality*, *38*, 117–133.

Cruikshank, M. (1992). *The gay and lesbian liberation movement*. New York: Routlege.

D'Augelli, A. R. (1989a). Gay men's and lesbians' experiences of discrimination, harassment, and indifference in a university community. *American Journal of Community Psychology*, *17*, 317–321.

D'Augelli, A. R. (1989b). Homophobia in a university community: Views of prospective resident assistants. *Journal of College Student Development*, 30, 546–552.

D'Augelli, A. R., & Dark, L. J. (1995). Vulnerable populations: Lesbian, gay, and bisexual youth. In L. D. Erong, J. H. Gentry, & P. Schlegel (Eds.), *Reason to hope: A psychosocial perspective on violence and youth* (pp. 177–196). Washington, DC: American Psychological Association.

D'Augelli, A. R., & Garnets, L. D. (1995). Lesbian, gay, and bisexual communities. In A. R. D'Augelli & C. J. Patterson (Eds.), *Lesbians, gay, and bisexual identities over the lifespan* (pp. 293–320). New York: Oxford University Press.

D'Augelli, A. R., & Rose, M. L. (1990). Homophobia in a university community: Attitudes and experiences of heterosexual freshmen. *Journal of College Student Development*, *31*, 484–491.

Dean, L., Wu, S., & Martin, J. L. (1992). Trends in violence and discrimination against gay men in New York City: 1984–1990. In G. M. Herek & K. T. Berrill (Eds.), *Hate crimes: Confronting violence against lesbians and gay men* (pp. 46–64). Newbury Park, CA: Sage Publications.

Delgado, B. (2000, March 30). Reform rabbis OK blessing gay unions. *Dallas Morning News*, p. A5.

DiAngelo, R. (1997). Heterosexism: Addressing internalized dominance. *Journal of Progressive Human Services*, 8, 5–21.

Dodge, R. (1993, December 2). Fed accused of bias in job promotions. *Dallas Morning News*, pp. D1–D2.

Domestic-partner benefits. (1991, June). *HR Magazine*, *36*, 125–126.

Duggan, L. (2001). Making it perfectly queer. In A. J. Stewart (Ed.), *Theorizing feminism: Parallel trends in the humanities and social sciences* (pp. 215–231). Boulder, CO: Westview Press.

Dyer, K. (Ed.). (1990). *Gays in uniform: The Pentagon's secret report*. Boston: Alyson Publications.

Edwards, K., & Brooks, A. K. (1999). The development of sexual identity. *New Directions for Adult and Continuing Education, 84*, 49–57.

Elias, M. (2002, July 16). Is homosexuality to blame for the child sexual abuse crisis now plaguing the Catholic church? *USA Today*, p. 6D.

Eliason, M. J. (1995). Accounts of sexual identity formation in heterosexual students. *Sex Roles, 32*, 821–834.

Eliason, M. J. (1997). The prevalence and nature of biphobia in heterosexual undergraduate students. *Archives of Sexual Behavior, 26*, 317–326.

Eliason, M. J. (2001). Bi-negativity: the stigma facing bisexual men. *Journal of Bisexuality, 1*, 139–154.

Epstein, S. (1994). A queer encounter: Sociology and the study of sexuality. *Sociological Theory, 12*, 188–202.

Eskridge, W. (1996). *The case for same-sex marriage: From sexual liberty to civilized commitment*. New York: Free Press.

Ettelbrick, P. (1993). Since when is marriage a path to liberation? In W. B. Rubenstein (Ed.), *Lesbians, gay men, and the law* (pp. 401–406). New York: W. W. Norton.

Faulkner, A. H., & Cranston, K. (1998). Correlates of same-sex sexual behavior in a random sample of Massachusetts high school students. *American Journal of Public Health, 88*, 262–266.

Ficarrotto, T. (1990). Racism, sexism, and erotophobia: Attitudes of heterosexuals toward homosexuals. *Journal of Homosexuality, 19*, 111–116.

Franklin, K. (2000). Antigay behaviors among young adults: Prevalence, patterns, and motivators in a noncriminal population. *Journal of Interpersonal Violence, 15*, 339–362.

Gay victim of beating in Wyoming dies. (1998, October 13). *Dallas Morning News*, p. A3.

GenderPAC. (1998). *First national study on transviolence*. Waltham, MA: Author.

Goldman, J. (1992, September). Coming out strong. *California Lawyer, 13*, 30–36, 86–67.

Gonsiorek, J. C. (1993). Threat, stress, and adjustment: Mental health and the workplace for gay and lesbian individuals. In L. Diamant (Ed.), *Homosexual issues in the workplace* (pp. 242–263). Washington, DC: Taylor & Francis.

Good, O. S. (2000, October 10). Benefits up for domestic partners. *Dallas Morning News*, p. C5.

Green, J., & Brinkin, L. (1994, September). *Investigation into discrimination against transgendered people*. San Francisco: San Francisco Human Rights Commission.

Gross, J. (1992, September 26). Governor, in reversal, signs a bill on gay rights in jobs. *New York Times*, p. A1.

Hartman, A. (1999). The long road to equality: Lesbians and social policy. In J. Laird (Ed.), *Lesbians and lesbian families* (pp. 91–120). New York: Columbia University Press.

Hays, J. (1991). Cracker Barrel comes under fire for ousting gays. *Nation's Restaurant News, 25*, 1.

Herek, G. M. (1988). Heterosexuals' attitudes toward lesbians and gay men: Correlates and gender differences. *Journal of Sex Research, 25*, 451–477.

Herek, G. M. (1989). Hate crimes against lesbian and gay men: Issues for research and social policy. *American Psychologist, 44*, 948–955.

Herek, G. M. (1990). The context of anti-gay violence: Notes on cultural and psychological heterosexism. *Journal of Interpersonal Violence, 5*, 316–333.

Herek, G. M. (1993). Documenting prejudice against lesbians and gay men on campus: The Yale sexual orientation survey. *Journal of Homosexuality, 25*, 15–30.

Herek, G. M. (1995). Psychological heterosexism in the United States. In A. R. D'Augelli & C. J. Patterson (Eds.), *Lesbian, gay, and bisexual identities over the lifespan: Psychological perspectives* (pp. 321–346). New York: Oxford University Press.

Herek, G. M. (2000). The psychology of sexual prejudice. *Current Directions in Psychological Science, 9*, 19–22.

Herek, G. M. (2002). Gender gaps in public opinion about lesbians and gay men. *Public Opinion Quarterly, 66*, 40–66.

Herek, G. M., & Berrill, K. T. (Eds.). (1992). *Hate crimes: Confronting violence against lesbians and gay men*. Newbury Park, CA: Sage Publications.

Herek, G. M., Cogan, J. C., & Gillis, J. R. (2002). Victim experiences in hate crimes based on sexual orientation. *Journal of Social Issues, 58*, 319–339.

Herek, G. M., & Capitanio, J. P. (1996). "Some of my best friends": Intergroup contact, concealable stigma, and heterosexuals' attitudes toward gay men and lesbians. *Personality and Social Psychology Bulletin, 22*, 412–424.

Herek, G. M., & Glunt, E. (1993). Interpersonal contact and heterosexuals' attitudes toward gay men: Results from a national survey. *Journal of Sex Research, 30,* 239–244.

Hong, S. M. (1984). Australian attitudes towards homosexuality: A comparison with college students. *Journal of Psychology, 117,* 89–95.

Hunter, J. (1990). Violence against lesbian and gay male youth. *Journal of Interpersonal Violence, 5,* 295–300.

Hunter, J., & Schaecher, R. (1990). Lesbian and gay youth. In M. J. Rotheram-Borus, J. Bradley, & N. Obolensky (Eds.), *Planning to live: Evaluating and treating suicidal teens in community settings* (pp. 297–316). Tulsa: University of Oklahoma Press.

Hutchinson, D. L. (2000). "Gay rights" for "gay whites"? Race, sexual identity, and equal protection discourse. *Cornell Law Review, 85,* 1358–1391.

Ilnytzky, U. (1999). '98 anti-gay attacks fewer but more violent. *Dallas Voice, 15,* 13–14.

Istvan, J. (1983). Effects of sexual orientation on interpersonal judgement. *Journal of Sex Research, 19,* 173–191.

Jeffreys, S. (1994). The queer disappearance of lesbians: Sexuality in the academy. *Women's Studies International Forum, 17,* 459–472.

Johansson, W. (1990a). Discrimination. In W. R. Dynes (Ed.), *Encyclopedia of homosexuality* (pp. 320–323). New York: Garland.

Johansson, W. (1990b). Law, United States. In W. R. Dynes (Ed.), *Encyclopedia of homosexuality* (pp. 692–698). New York: Garland.

Johansson, W. (1990c). Prejudice. In W. R. Dynes (Ed.), *Encyclopedia of homosexuality* (pp. 1031–1033). New York: Garland.

Johnson, M. E., Brems, C., & Alford-Keating, P. (1997). Personality correlates of homophobia. *Journal of Homosexuality, 34,* 57–69.

Jones, D., & Willette, A. (1995, October 19). Critics claim Disney's gay policy is anti-family. *USA Today,* p. B1.

Jost, K. (2000). Gay-rights update. *Congressional Quarterly Researcher, 10,* 307–327.

Kaupman, G. (1991, February 29). Cracker barrel waffles on anti-gay policy. *Southern Voice,* p. 1.

Khayatt, D. (1994). Surviving school as a lesbian student. *Gender and Education, 6,* 47–61.

Kirp, D. L. (1999). Martyrs and movies. *American Prospect*, *11*, 52–53.

Kite, M. E. (1984). Sex differences in attitudes towards homosexuals: A meta-analytic review. *Journal of Homosexuality*, *10*, 69–89.

Kronenberger, G. K. (1991). Out of the closet. *Personnel Journal*, *70*, 40–44.

LaMar, L., & Kite, M. (1998). Sex differences in attitudes toward gay men and lesbians: A multidimensional perspective. *Journal of Sex Research*, *35*, 189–196.

Lambda Legal. (2002, June 16). *State/by/state sodomy law update* [Online]. Available: http://www.lambdalegal.org/cgi-bin/iowa/issues

Landau, A. D. (1994). Employment discrimination against lesbians and gays: The incomplete legal response of the United States and the European Union. *Duke Journal of Comparative and International Law*, *4*, 335–361.

Laner, M. R., & Laner, R. H. (1980). Sexual preference or personal style? Why lesbians are disliked. *Journal of Homosexuality*, *5*, 339–356.

Laris, M. (2000, October 1). City examines its attitudes after shooting at gay bar. *Dallas Morning News*, p. A4.

Lopez, G., & Chism, N. (1993). Classroom concerns of gay and lesbian students. *College Teaching*, *41*, 97–103.

Maines, D. (2002, March 22). Military boots gays at record rate. *Dallas Voice: The Community Newspaper for Gay & Lesbian Dallas*, pp. 1, 18.

Mallon, G. (1997). When schools are not safe places: Gay, lesbian, bisexual, and transgendered young people in educational settings. *Reaching Today's Youth*, *2*, 41–45.

Martin, A. D., & Hetrick, E. S. (1988). The stigmatization of the gay and lesbian adolescent. *Journal of Homosexuality*, *15*, 163–183.

Maurer, L. (1999). Transgressing sex and gender: Deconstruction zone ahead? *Siecus Report*, *28*, 14–21.

McDaniel, M. A. (1989). *Preservice adjustment of homosexual and heterosexual military accessions: Implications for security clearance suitability* (Rep. No. PER-TR-89–04, 21). Monterey, CA: Defense Personnel Security Research and Education Center.

McDougall, G. J. (1993). Therapeutic issues with gay and lesbian elders. *Clinical Gerontologist*, *14*, 45–57.

Murphy, B. C. (1994). Difference and diversity: Gay and lesbian couples. *Social Services for Gay and Lesbian Couples, 1*, 5–31.

National Coalition of Anti-Violence Programs. (1999). Anti-lesbian, gay, transgender, and bisexual violence in 1999. *New York: Gay and Lesbian Anti-Violence Project* (New York chapter).

National Coalition of Anti-Violence Programs. (2000). Anti-lesbian, gay, transgender, and bisexual violence in 1999. *New York: Gay and Lesbian Anti-Violence Project* (New York chapter).

National Gay and Lesbian Task Force. (1991). *Anti-gay violence, victimization and defamation in 1990.* Washington, DC: Author.

National Gay and Lesbian Task Force. (1994). *Lesbian, gay and bisexual rights in the U.S.: A chart of states, cities, counties and federal agencies whose civil rights laws, ordinances, and policies bar discrimination based on sexual orientation.* Washington, DC: Author.

National Gay and Lesbian Task Force. (2000a). Eight states now offer domestic partner benefits [Online]. Available: http://www.ngltf.org

National Gay and Lesbian Task Force. (2000b). GLBT civil rights laws in the U.S. [Online]. Available: http://www.ngltf.org

National Gay and Lesbian Task Force. (2001). GLBT civil rights laws in the U.S. [Online]. Available: http://www.ngltf.org

National Gay and Lesbian Taks Force. (2002, August 14). *Task force calls for continued vigilance in solving murders of transgender women in SE Washington, DC* [Online]. Available: http://www.ngltf.org/news/release.cfm?releaseid=474

National Gay Task Force. (1984). U.S. mayors' conference endorses gay/lesbian rights. *NGTF Newsletter, 11*, 1.

Neisen, J. H. (1990). Heterosexism: Redefining homophobia for the 1990s. *Journal of Gay & Lesbian Psychotherapy, 1*, 21–35.

News of the year. (2002, January). *The Advocate*, pp. 13–18.

Noble, B. (1992, November 25). Gay group asks accord in job dispute. *New York Times*, p. 4.

Norris, W. P. (1992). Liberal attitudes and homophobic acts: The paradoxes of homosexual experience in a liberal institution. In K. Harbeck (Ed.), *Coming out of the classroom closet: Gay and lesbian students, teachers and curriculum* (pp. 81–120). Binghamton, NY: Harrington Park.

N.Y. Times to print same-sex unions. (2002, August 18). *Boston Sunday Globe*, p. A5.

Obear, K. (1991). Homophobia. In N. J. Evans & V. A. Wall (Eds.), *Beyond tolerance: Gays, lesbians, and bisexuals on campus* (pp. 39–78). Alexandria, VA: American College Personnel Association.

Oh, Canada! (2003). *Court ruling prompts gay couples to apply for marriage licenses* [Online]. Retrieved from http://www.echomag.com/news/news2.html on July 3, 2003.

Parrott, D. J., Adams, H. E., & Zeichner, A. (2002). Homophobia: Personality and attitudinal correlates. *Personality and Individual Differences*, *32*, 1269–1278.

Peterson, J. W. (1989, April 11). In harm's way: Gay runaways are in more danger than ever, and gay adults won't help. *The Advocate*, pp. 8–10.

Pilkington, N. W., & D'Augelli, A. R. (1995). Victimization of lesbian, gay, and bisexual youth in community settings. *Journal of Community Psychology*, *23*, 33–56.

Pusey, A. (2003, June 27). New day for gay Americans: Supreme Court overturns Texas sodomy law. *Dallas Morning News*, p. 1.

Quinlivan, K., & Town, S. (1999). Queer pedagogy, educational practice and lesbian and gay youth. *Qualitative Studies in Education*, *12*, 509–524.

Reis, B. (1998). Will you be there for every child? Reports violence against lesbians and gays. *Siecus Report*, *26*, 9.

Religious Action Center of Reform Judaism. (2000). *Issues: Gay and lesbian rights* [Online]. Available: http://www.rac.org/issuegl.html#status

Remafedi, G. (1987a). Adolescent homosexuality: Psychosocial and medical implications. *Pediatrics*, *79*, 331–337.

Remafedi, G. (1987b). Male homosexuality: The adolescent's perspective. *Pediatrics*, *79*, 326–330.

Remembering Our Dead. (2000, October). *Ana Melisa Cortez* [Online]. Available: http://www.gender.org/remember/about/core.html

Results of poll. (1989, June 6). *San Francisco Examiner*, p. A19.

Rey, A. M., & Gibson, P. R. (1997). Beyond high school: Heterosexuals' self-reported anti-gay/lesbian behaviors and attitudes. *Journal of Gay & Lesbian Social Services*, *7*, 65–84.

Rivera, R. R. (1991). Sexual orientation and the law. In J. C. Gonsiorek & J. D. Weinrich (Eds.), *Homosexuality: Research implications for public policy* (pp. 81–100). Newbury Park, CA: Sage Publications.

Rofes, E. (2000). After California votes to limit marriage: A call for direct action and civil disobedience. *Social Policy, 30,* 31–35.

Rosario, M., Rotheram-Borus, M. J., & Reid, H. (1992). *Personal resources, gay-related stress, and multiple problem behaviors among gay and bisexual male adolescents.* Unpublished manuscript, Columbia University, New York.

Rotheram-Borus, M. J., Rosario, M., & Koopman, C. (1991). Minority youths at high risk: Gay males and runaways. In M. E. Colten & S. Gore (Eds.), *Adolescent stress: Causes and consequences* (pp. 181–200). New York: Aldine de Gruyter.

Sarbin, T. R., & Karols, K. E. (1988). *Nonconforming sexual orientations and military suitability* (Rep. No. PERS-TR-89-002). Monterey, CA: Defense Personnel Security Research and Education Center.

Savage, D. G. (1996, May 21). Supreme Court strikes down law targeting gays. *Los Angeles Times,* pp. A1, A14.

Savin-Williams, R. (1994). Verbal and physical abuse as stressors in the lives of lesbian, gay male, and bisexual youths: Associations with school problems, running away, substance abuse, prostitution, and suicide. *Journal of Consulting and Clinical Psychology, 62,* 260–269.

Schneider, B. (1984). Peril and promise: Lesbian's workplace participation. In J. T. Darty & S. Potter (Eds.), *Women-identified women* (pp. 211–230). Palo Alto, CA: Mayfield.

Schope, R. D., & Eliason, M. J. (2000). Thinking versus acting: Assessing the relationship between heterosexual attitudes and behaviors toward homosexuals. *Journal of Gay & Lesbian Social Services, 11,* 69–92.

Sears, J. T. (1991). *Growing up gay in the South: Race, gender, and journeys of the spirit.* New York: Harrington Park.

Seltzer, R. (1992). The social location of those holding antihomosexual attitudes. *Sex Roles, 26,* 391–398.

Serovich, J. M., Skeen, P., Walters, L. H., & Robinson, B. E. (1993). In-law relationships when a child is homosexual. *Journal of Homosexuality, 26,* 57–75.

Service Members Legal Defense Network. (1999). *Clemency hearing for gay sailor's killer* [Online]. Available: http://www.sldn.org

Service Members Legal Defense Network. (2000). *The year in review* [Online]. Available: http://www.sldn.org

Simoni, J. M. (1996). Pathways to prejudice: Predicting students' heterosexist attitudes with demographics, self-esteem, and contact with lesbians and gay men. *Journal of College Student Development, 37*, 68–78.

Slater, B. R. (1993). Violence against lesbian and gay male college students. *Journal of College Student Psychotherapy, 8*, 177–202.

Stark, L. (1991). Traditional gender role beliefs and individual outcomes: An explanatory analysis. *Sex Roles, 24*, 639–650.

Stein, E. (1999). *The mismeasure of desire: The science, theory, and ethics of sexual orientation.* New York: Oxford University Press.

Sussal, C. M. (1994). Empowering gays and lesbians in the workplace. *Journal of Gay & Lesbian Social Services, 1*, 89–103.

Tafel, R. L. (1994, September 12). End job discrimination against homosexuals. *Insight, 10*, 18–20.

Tarver, D. E. (2002). Transgender mental health: The intersection of race, sexual orientation, and gender orientation. In B. E. Jones & M. J. Hill (Eds.), *Mental health issues in lesbian, gay, bisexual, and transgender communities* (pp. 93–108). Washington, DC: American Psychiatric Press.

Telljohann, S. K., & Price, J. H. (1993). A qualitative examination of adolescent homosexuals' life experiences: Ramifications for secondary school personnel. *Journal of Homosexuality, 26*, 41–55.

Tewksbury, R., Grossi, E. L., Suresh, G., & Helms, J. (1999). Hate crimes against gay men and lesbian women: A routine activity approach for predicting victimization risk. *Humanity and Society, 23*, 125–142.

Thomas, K. (1999, April 15). Anti-trans violence. *Worker's World Newspaper*, p. 1.

Tierney, W. G. (1997). *Academic outlaws: Queer theory and cultural studies in the academy.* Thousand Oaks, CA: Sage Publications.

Time/CNN poll. (1998, October 18). Poll: Gay attack could have happened anywhere. *Syracuse Herald American*, p. D10.

Uribe, V., & Harbeck, K. M. (1991). Addressing the needs of lesbian, gay, and bisexual youth: The origins of PROJECT 10 and school-based intervention. *Journal of Homosexuality, 22*, 9–28.

Van der Meide, W. (2000). *Legislating equality: A review of laws affecting gay, lesbian, bisexual, and transgendered people in the United States.* Washington, DC: Policy Institute of the National Gay and Lesbian Task Force.

Vercher, D. (2002, July 12). Arkansas sodomy law tossed out. *Dallas Voice: The Community Newspaper for Gay & Lesbian Dallas,* pp. 1, 23–24.

Vetri, D. (1998). Almost everything you always wanted to know about lesbians and gay men, their families, and the law. *Southern University Law Review, 26,* 1–68.

Von Schulthess, B. (1992). Violence in the streets: Anti-lesbian assault and harassment in San Francisco. In G. M. Herek & K. T. Berrill (Eds.), *Hate crimes: Confronting violence against lesbians and gay men* (pp. 65–75). Newbury Park, CA: Sage Publications.

Waldo, C. R. (1998). Out on campus: Sexual orientation and academic climate in a university context. *American Journal of Community Psychology, 26,* 745–774.

Waldo, C. R., Hesson-McInnis, M. S., & D'Augelli, A. R. (1998). Antecedents and consequences of victimization of lesbian, gay, and bisexual young people: A structural model comparing rural university and urban samples. *American Journal of Community Psychology, 26,* 307–334.

Wolfson, E. (1994, Summer). Fighting sodomy laws: Why the government shouldn't be in our bedrooms, *Lambda Update, 11,* 1, 28.

Woods, J. D., & Lucas, J. (1993). *The corporate closet: The professional lives of gay men in America.* New York: Free Press.

Yang, A. (1997). Trends: Attitudes toward homosexuality. *Public Opinion Quarterly, 61,* 477–507.

Yarhouse, M. A. (1999). Social cognition research on the formation and maintenance of stereotypes: Applications to marriage and family therapists working with homosexual clients. *American Journal of Family Therapy, 27,* 149–161.

Year in review. (2001, January 16). *The Advocate,* pp. 11–26.

Zavos, M. A. (1995). Sexual orientation law in the 1990s. *Trial, 31,* 27–32.

CHAPTER 3
SEXUAL ORIENTATION, SEXUAL IDENTITIES, AND EVOLVING IDENTIFICATIONS

What does "sexual orientation" mean?

How do we determine or measure sexual orientation?

How is sexual identity different from sexual orientation?

Why is it so difficult to determine who is lesbian, gay, or bisexual?

How do race and ethnicity, age, and sex–gender impact sexual identity?

How do bisexual persons identify their sexuality?

What are some examples that reflect the diversity of transgender persons?

SEXUAL ORIENTATION

Two important issues about sexual orientation are how to define it and the binary divisions usually applied to it. In an exploration of definitions of sexual orientation, Stein (1999) proposed that the disposition view is the most suitable one. This view incorporates the virtues of two alternative definitions: (a) *behavior* (sexual orientation represents a person's sexual behavior) and (b) *self-identification* (sexual orientation represents one's own assessment of one's sexual orientation). The disposition view suggests that sexual orientation represents one's sexual desires, sexual fantasies, and sexual behaviors. Following this view, then, one is gay or lesbian if one has desires and fantasies about having sex primarily with others of the same sex–gender and if one is likely to engage in sexual acts primarily with others of the same sex–gender. It helps to have appealing sexual partners available and no obstacles that prevent or discourage one from acting on one's desires.

In further defining sexual orientation, researchers and others typically dichotomize persons by sexual attractions (same sex–gender or other sex–gender), by sex–gender identity (male or female), and sex–gender role (masculine or feminine) (Firestein, 1996). Binary divisions such as these, however, do not accurately portray most of us (Stein, 1999; see Chapter 1). For example, Alfred A. Kinsey and his associates (Kinsey, Pomeroy, & Martin, 1948; Kinsey, Pomeroy, Martin, & Gebbard, 1953) discovered that there is often more a mix of "homosexual" and heterosexual sexual behavior than one or the other. It is impossible, therefore, to place persons into only one of the two categories. This prompted the Kinsey group to develop a seven-point bipolar continuum to rate sexual orientation, with heterosexual on one end and homosexual on the other end. Positioning on this continuum depends upon the proportion of a person's sexual behavior that is oriented to one or the other sex–gender. This proportion results in a score that ranges from 0 (exclusive heterosexual behavior), through a midpoint of 3 (equal heterosexual and homosexual behavior), to 6 (exclusive homosexual behavior). These scores, however, are not stable. Kinsey and colleagues (1948) noted that placement on the scale can vary at different times in a person's life.

The Kinsey scale revolutionized theories about sexual behavior by undermining traditional restrictive views about it (Bullough, 1994a; Dynes & Donaldson, 1992). Also some of the findings of the Kinsey studies were startling such as a greater incidence of same sex–gender sexual behavior than most persons formerly believed to exist. Substantial numbers of persons participated in both same sex–gender and other sex–gender sexual activity. About 50 percent of men and 28 percent of women reported some degree of same sex–gender sexual experience in their lives, although since adolescence only 4 to 5 percent of men and less than 3 percent of women reported exclusive same sex–gender sexual activity. Based on cross-cultural studies done about the same time, Ford (1948) and Ford and Beach (1951) found that same sex–gender sexual behavior of some degree was "normal" in 76 human societies.

Though the Kinsey studies were revolutionary (Bullough, 1994b), the studies were also controversial because of notable shortcomings such as (a) the reduction of sexual orientation to numerical categories leading to the presumption that all persons who attain the same number are of the same sexual type; (b) the difficulty in determining the relative importance to a person of heterosexual and same sex–gender interests; (c) the measurement of heterosexuality and "homosexuality" on the same scale, making them exclusive categories; and (d) a nonrandom sample (for example, Bullough, 1998; Laumann, Gagnon, Michael, & Michaels, 1994; Sell, 1996).

Although the Kinsey group (Kinsey et al., 1948; Kinsey et al., 1953) challenged the simple dichotomous view of sexuality, the seven-point scale essentially continued to divide persons into exclusive heterosexual or homosexual categories. This makes the scale problematic for respondents who reported that they could potentially become involved with either women or men or that they experienced former sexual relationships with both women and men (Stein, 1999). Because "homosexual" experiences were the main interest of the Kinsey group, the bisexual experiences of most of the Kinsey respondents composed a default category in the middle of the seven-point continuum (Guidry, 1999). The assumption was also made that the degree of attraction to men equals the degree of attraction to women. But, bisexual persons experience varying degrees of attraction to men and to women. Their attraction to women may or may not be as strong as their attraction to men (Stein, 1999).

Beginning in the 1970s, amendments to Kinsey's work started and have continued. Examples of changes in scale development include: (a) addition of factors, such as love and affection; (b) measurement of the intensity level of emotional and sexual attraction; and (c) development of two continuous scales with separate ratings, one for measurement of same sex–gender orientation, the other for measurement of other sex–gender orientation, instead of the one continuous scale used by Kinsey. Researchers found that same sex–gender and other sex–gender behaviors are independent; persons can show high levels of both same sex–gender and other sex–gender sexual behavior, low levels of both, or levels of each that vary in strength (Klein, Sepekoff, & Wolf, 1985; Shively & De Cecco, 1977; Storms, 1980).

One of the more influential advances was the Klein Sexual Orientation Grid (Klein et al. 1985). This scale assumes that sexual orientation is multivariate and dynamic and contains seven components: (a) sexual attraction; (b) sexual behavior; (c) sexual fantasies; (d) emotional preference; (e) social preference; (f) self-identification; and (g) living as a lesbian, gay man, heterosexual woman or man, or bisexual woman or man. Ratings on the seven components can be congruent or incongruent with each other. In addition, the Klein scale attempts to distinguish patterns of the scale components in three time periods: present, past, and ideal future. Although an advancement, this scale also assumes a binary view. Another scale, developed by Berkey, Perelman-Hall, and Kurdek (1990), is a more sophisticated version of the Klein scale and is not binary, but it has yet to attain the popularity of the Klein scale (Stein, 1999).

Other researchers have included more components than the Klein scale (for example, Coleman, 1978; Sell, 1996) but all of the existing scales have limitations such as no thorough factor analysis. They also do not accommodate multiple sex–genders. A question posed by Stein (1999), for example, is whether transgender or intersex persons constitute a second sex–gender or a third or a fourth? If so, where do we locate them on scales? And where do we locate men and women who experience attraction to intersex or transgender persons? Another question posed by Bockting (1999) is where do we locate transgender persons who experience attractions to men, women, or other transgender persons, and who may sexually interact with gay, lesbian, bisexual, and heterosexually identified others? And what about some persons who may adopt a political gender of male or female even though they do not identify with that gender biologically, psychologically, or in any other way (Tarver, 2002)?

Where does all this leave sexual orientation? Although we know more post-Kinsey, many questions about sexual orientation remain unanswered. For example, because persons can be sorted into many groups by virtue of their sexual interests, the question arises why include only a narrow range of sexual interests under the heading of sexual orientation? Persons differ vastly in their sexual interests, including body type, hair color, personality, profession, sex–gender, types of sexual acts, locations for engaging in sexual acts, and entities engaged (for example, humans, animals, inanimate objects) (Stein, 1999).

SEXUAL IDENTITY

Whereas sexual orientation has to do with sexual dispositions, sexual desires, and sexual behaviors, sexual identity has to do with how one identifies oneself (for example, "I am gay" or "I am heterosexual"). One chooses a sexual identity from a given pool of culturally created sexual identities, and the cultural and historical contexts of one's life give meaning to the selected sexual identity (Ellis & Mitchell, 2000). We typically expect that this identity (heterosexual, lesbian, gay, or bisexual) is concordant with certain components such as one's sexual desire, affectional desire, sexual behavior, and community participation (Firestein, 1996; Golden, 1987; Laumann et al., 1994; Rothblum, 1994; Shively, Jones, & De Cecco, 1983–1984; Stein, 1999). Yet, we cannot infer anything this certain. Nothing is definite about the links between these components either, as they are independent of one another (see Hunter, Shannon, Knox, & Martin, 1998). These realities are shown in the following examples:

- *Sexual desire incongruent with sexual identity.* If persons experience same sex–gender sexual desire but never participate in same sex–gender sexual behavior, are they lesbian, gay, or bisexual? Certain psychological literature focuses only on sexual desire as the most basic indicator of sexual identity (Marmor, 1980). Yet, some persons who claim to experience sexual desire for others of the same sex–gender might not claim a lesbian, gay, or bisexual identity. Other persons can experience a different kind of incongruency—they self-identify as lesbian, gay, or bisexual but experience no sexual desire for their partner. Or sexual desire was present at one time but not now (Esterberg, 1997; Peplau & Cochran, 1990).

- *Affectional desire incongruent with sexual identity.* In contrast to women who self-identify as lesbians and are part of a lesbian culture, a broader category exists of women committed to women. These women experience a common bond with women on emotional and practical levels (Rupp, 1997). Sometimes the concepts of "romantic friendships" or "Boston marriages" apply to these relationships. The women are psychologically or emotionally passionate about each other but not sexually involved and do not self-identify as lesbian (for example, Faderman, 1981; Rothblum & Brehony, 1993; Rupp, 1997).

- *Sexual desire and sexual behavior incongruent with sexual identity.* Not all men and women who experience sexual desires for and sexual behavior with persons of the same sex–gender self-identify as lesbian, gay, or bisexual (Massey & Ouellette, 1996; Radonsky & Borders, 1995). In surveys on sexual behavior and mental (cognitive–affective) states, about one-third of men and women who in the past year desired same sex–gender partners and had sex with them did not identify themselves as gay, lesbian, or bisexual (Davis & Smith, 1993; Laumann et al., 1994). This circumstance also happens among persons in sex–gender segregated institutions such as prisons (Wooden & Parker, 1982).

- *Community participation incongruent with sexual identity and sexual desire.* Some persons who self-identify as lesbian or gay, and desire sex with persons of the same sex–gender, or who self-identify as bisexual and desire sex with persons of both sex–genders, do not participate in lesbian, gay, or bisexual social or political occasions. They may lack interest or time, or they may choose not to make public disclosures of their sexual identity (Herek, 1991).

- *Sexual behavior incongruent with community participation and with sexual identity.* Some persons who have no desire to participate in same sex–gender sexual behavior self-identify as lesbian or gay and participate in LGB communities for social or political purposes (Rothblum, 1994). Although men may identify as male lesbians for political reasons, most persons in this situation are women. Men tend to base their identities more directly on their sexual feelings and experiences, whereas women tend to base their identities more on social and political factors (Rust, 2000). Some women may prefer sex with men but adopt a lesbian identity to express emotional and political solidarity with the lesbian feminist community (for example, Faderman, 1984–1985; Golden, 1994). Women who adopt lesbian or bisexual identities for political or ideological reasons, however, are not always uninvolved sexually with women. The political pursuit of some women in Golden's sample seemed to be an erotic as well as a political choice.

Hence, each person experiences a unique combination of erotic and affectional identities, emotional attachments, behaviors, fantasies, relationships, and community ties (Rothblum, 2000). A set of discrete categories of sexual identities, therefore, is meaningless. A number of possible categories are available (Russell & Bohan, 1999). Self-imposed or externally imposed sexual identifications can also vary depending on group membership.

Racial and Ethnic Groups

Persons in various racial and ethnic cultures who have sex with same sex–gender persons may not identify as nonheterosexual. In East Asian cultures, no sexual identities are analogous to the modern Western constructs of lesbian and gay identities (Chan, 1997). Some African American women dislike the term lesbian because it is Eurocentric (Mason-John & Khambatta, 1993). In some cultures, it is not uncommon for men to engage in sex with same sex–gender persons without labeling themselves as gay. In Latino cultures, this is especially common with men who take the masculine active sexual role of inserter (Carballo-Diéguez, 1989; Espin, 1984). These men may also not identify as gay because they view this identity as part of the White gay political movement (Morales, 1990). They more easily view themselves as experiencing bisexual sexual experiences (but not the identity). Bisexual sexual practices are partly extensions of heterosexual machismo or masculine heterosexuality. For some Latino men, however, these practices also hide a same sex–gender sexual orientation (Manalansan, 1996). In some Native American communities, a masculine male who engages in the active role of inserter in sex with another male also is not labeled as "homosexual." If a male is masculine, the sex–gender of a sexual partner is irrelevant. But a male who takes the role of a passive, receptive partner while experiencing sex with another male gets labeled as "homosexual" (Tofoya, 1996).

Youth

Many youth who experience substantial and persistent sexual attractions for and fantasies about persons of the same sex–gender are usually not prepared to identify as lesbian, gay, or bisexual (Savin-Williams, 2001). Youths who engage in heterosexual sex will probably identify as gay, lesbian, or bisexual at some point (D'Augelli, 1991; Golden, 1997). In Savin-Williams' (1995, 1998) studies of boys, some had sex with other boys exclusively, or engaged in sex with both boys and girls, but did not acknowledge a gay or bisexual sexual identity. Other boys self-identified as gay but were celibate (see Chapter 13).

Women show striking variability in their combinations of sexual identity, sexual attractions, and sexual behaviors. This was demonstrated in Golden's (1996, 1997) sample of more than 100 women (primarily White, but of varying sexual orientations and social classes). Golden's sample developed over a decade. From the initial interviews with lesbian college students, she expanded the sample to include nonstudent lesbians in their 20s, 30s, and 40s as well as bisexual and heterosexual women of various ages. Some of these women reported they identified as lesbians but they only experienced sex with men; some women reported that they identified as heterosexual or bisexual but experienced sex only with women; some women reported that they identified as lesbian or heterosexual, but experienced sex with both women and men; some women experienced only heterosexual sex but identified as lesbian or bisexual; some women reported they identified as bisexual but only experienced sex with men. Some women experienced same sex–gender attractions but never acted on them sexually whereas other women seemed to make a conscious determination to pursue and act on the sexual part of their same sex–gender attractions.

Some bisexual women studied by Golden (1997) reported that although they did not fall in love with other women, they experienced sexual attraction to them; some heterosexual women reported they were in love with their girlfriends but not sexually aroused by them; some lesbians reported their relationships with other women, though loving, were asexual.

The remainder of this chapter focuses more attention to diversities among bisexual and transgender identifications. Only recently have identities and variations among these groups been the focus of empirical study.

Bisexual

The Kinsey studies (Kinsey et al., 1948; Kinsey et al., 1953) established that more men and women display bisexual rather than exclusively same sex–gender attraction or sexual behavior. More recent studies reported similar findings (for example, Laumann et al., 1994; Rogers & Turner, 1991). Yet, because of the prevailing assumption of sexual dualism, persons who claim a bisexual identity confront a number of myths that question their identity, such as "there is no such thing as a bisexual sexual identity" (Guidry, 1999; Rust, 1996). These persons often seem to others as refusing to admit their real sexual orientation (heterosexual, lesbian, or gay); they are viewed as indecisive or covering up what they really are (Firestein, 1996; Pope & Reynolds, 1991). Although they do not want to adopt a heterosexual or gay or lesbian identity, many bisexual persons feel forced to choose one of these identities, and to repress or distort their bisexual behaviors, feelings, and fantasies (Paul, 1992; Rust, 1996).

Another myth is that "bisexual attractions are temporary." Some argue that persons who claim a bisexual identity are in a phase adopted when either coming out as lesbian or gay or returning to a heterosexual sexual orientation. When bisexual persons accomplish coming out or choose a single partner, it is assumed that their real sexual orientation will show itself, and they will no longer identify as bisexual (Rust, 1996; Udis-Kessler, 1996). Because of this myth, persons who claim a bisexual identity may themselves think that their dual attractions are temporary (Rust, 1996). Another myth is that "persons who think that they are bisexual are really heterosexual" but currently only experimenting with the same sex–gender or trying to act cool, trendy, or liberated (Udis-Kessler, 1996).

Although the facts of bisexual experiences counter the myths cited here, several studies (Stokes & Damon, 1995; Stokes, Miller, & Mundhenk, 1998) found variations of sexual contact among men with male and female partners. The researchers developed four categories for these men—men in transition, experimenters, opportunity-driven men, and men with dual involvement:

- *Men in transition.* Men in this category use the label "bisexual" to mediate their anxiety and the isolation they may experience while in the "coming-out" process as gay. This label can lessen the sense of being different and help one retain feelings of commonality with heterosexual peers. Given the stigma attached to same sex–gender sexual involvements, men in this group often are probably the most likely to seek counseling because they are troubled by their sexual behavior with other men (Stokes & Damon, 1995). When more comfortable with their gay identity, however, these men may become behaviorally gay. Previous longitudinal research with men who were behaviorally bisexual showed that over the course of one year, about one-third of these men moved to the gay end of a dichotomous scale of self-rated sexual orientation (Stokes, Damon, & McKirnan, 1997).

Bisexual sexual behavior as part of a transition may be more common in African American and Latino men than among men in other racial and ethnic groups (Doll & Beeker, 1996; Stokes, Taywaditep, Vanable, & McKirnan, 1996). In contrast to White men, African American men are more likely to remain in this state and never declare a gay identity or reveal their same sex–gender sexual experiences. Often they marry or maintain close, romantic relationships with women (Stokes et al., 1998).

- **Experimenters.** Men in this category experience isolated incidents of same sex–gender sexual experience. Typically these incidents involve alcohol or other drug use and happen with friends who initiate the sexual activity. Some situations involve younger men who desire to participate in a different kind of sexual experience. Though experimenters can tolerate diverse sexualities, their self-identity and future behavior are usually consistent with their basic heterosexual sexual orientation (Stokes & Damon, 1995). Although they experience sex with both men and women, they do not identify as bisexual (Stokes et al., 1998).
- **Opportunity-driven men.** Men in this category usually self-identify as heterosexual; sex with other men is associated with availability or access. Factors such as the partner's sex–gender and emotional involvement are not relevant, so repeated sexual contacts with the same man either do not happen or happen outside the context of a "relationship." This category is to some degree a catchall one because it includes a variety of experiences, including: (a) men who seek sexual experiences in anonymous or casual-contact settings like public parks or rest rooms or though media outlets like telephone lines or personal ads; (b) men in transition to a gay identification; (c) men who seek sexual contact with men outside a relationship with a woman; (d) male prostitutes who limit their sexual activity with men to those who pay for sex; and (e) men who have same sex–gender sexual experiences only in prison (Stokes & Damon, 1995).
- **Men with dual involvement.** Men in this category experience emotional and sexual attraction to both men and women, and they are likely to experience serial or concurrent relationships with both men and women. They may or may not be interested in sex without commitment. Most often they identify as bisexual and their bisexual attractions usually persist (Stokes & Damon, 1995; Stokes et al., 1998).

Transgender

Sex–gender identity is one's psychological sense of what one's sex–gender is; it is independent of one's sexual orientation (Stein, 1999). The internal sex–gender identity of transgender persons does not match their genital sex (Maurer, 1999). For example, some persons who have XY chromosomes and male-typical internal and external genitalia have the feeling that they are female (Stein, 1999). Other transgender persons do not share this feeling but may cross-dress.

Cross-dressers (formerly called "transvestites" or "fetishistic cross-dressers") are usually heterosexual men (in a few instances bisexual); their sex–gender identity during childhood was masculine (Bailey, 1996; Talamini, 1982). In adulthood, they usually marry and become fathers. They differ from other heterosexual men because of their compulsive desire to cross-dress. They attain sexual gratification from this behavior (Bailey, 1996).

Persons who feel their sex–gender identity does not match their biological sex, usually still called "transsexual," also often cross-dressed throughout childhood and adolescence. Later they attempt to pass as a member of the sex–gender they wish to be (Seil, 1996). In their sample of men who wished for their biological sex to match their sex–gender, Gagné, Tewksbury, and McGaughey (1997) found that most of the respondents (13) began to cross-dress in childhood, but a few (four) began this behavior in adolescence. These men wore women's clothing to relax and to express their "feminine" selves. Although the motivation for cross-dressing for many of these men was erotic, for others this was not the case, or the erotic quality dissipated over time.

Not everyone who experiences a discrepancy between sex–gender and biological sex in childhood will experience this in adulthood (Green, 1987; Zuger, 1984). But, adults who wish for their sex to match their gender report that they always felt that nature assigned them the wrong body (Seil, 1996). From as early as three years to about 10 years of age, they reported strong feelings that they belonged to the other sex–gender and felt comfortable with the corresponding behavioral manifestations (for example, Gagné et al., 1997; Seil, 1996). In the Gagné and colleagues sample of men, about a third (16) felt a strong desire to become a girl or felt that they were female during childhood (before age 10). About the same number (15) first felt this way in adolescence, and fewer first felt this way in adulthood (10).

Some adults who experienced a discrepancy between their sex–gender and biological sex did not experience a wish to change their sexual anatomy until their 30s (Blanchard, Clemmensen, & Steiner, 1987). Before that time, they were often so successful in performing the expected sex–gender role that the announcement of their desired sex–gender identity astounded their family and friends. Many lost marriages, and jobs, and experienced rejection from their children. These outcomes often resulted in isolation and loneliness (Seil, 1996).

SEXUAL REASSIGNMENT SURGERY

Although the feeling that one's sex–gender does not match one's biological sex is agonizing, the situation is usually more stressful for feminine males because they are often the targets of teasing and rejection by families and peers. Without understanding and support in the family, feminine adolescent males tend to drop out of school and run away from home. On the streets, they are vulnerable to involvement with drugs and prostitution, and to HIV/AIDS. Usually, they live in poverty and, therefore, cannot procure treatment, if desired, such as sexual reassignment surgery (SRS) (Seil, 1996). Some of these persons mutilate their genitals in a futile effort to reconcile their sex–gender and biological sex (Anderson, 1998). Others who can finance it are willing to go through SRS (Bailey, 1996).

In 1930, the first known SRS occurred, a reassignment from male to female (Tarver, 2002). SRS cannot change a person's chromosomal sex, but can remove internal genital structures, alter external genitalia, and, combined with hormone treatments, dramatically affect a person's secondary sex characteristics. A person who has undergone successful surgery will seem to most persons to be a member of the sex–gender this person wants to be. Intersex persons who have ambiguous genitals at birth also often undergo surgery, usually in infancy, but later in life they may discover that the surgically assigned sex–gender does not match their desired sex–gender identity (Maurer, 1999; Stein, 1999).

Persons reassigned from male to female (MF) were usually distinctly *feminine boys* in child-hood whereas those reassigned from female to male (FM) were usually distinctly *masculine girls* (Bailey, 1996). Rehman, Lazer, Benet, Schaefer, and Melman (1999) and Stein, Tiefer, and Melman (1990) reported three years of follow-up studies for 28 persons who experienced MF surgery. All the respondents were at least 21 years of age at the time of surgery. All underwent one to two years of preparatory psychotherapy. Following surgery, the study respondents felt generally satisfied with the results both cosmetically (normal-appearing genitalia) and func-tionally (ability to experience orgasms). Most returned to their jobs and lived satisfactory social and personal lives. Support from friends and family was strong, and intimate relation-ships were more stable. Additionally, they reported a marked decrease in suicide attempts, criminal activity, and drug use.

No MF person studied by Rehman and colleagues (1999) and Stein and colleagues (1990) regretted SRS, but some respondents reported that the surgery did not solve all their "issues." They experienced difficulties in assuming their new sex–gender role and functioning as women. They felt unpracticed in how to live their lives as women—ranging from how to shop for women's clothes to how to respond sexually as a woman. It was not easy to form inter-personal and intimate sexual relations with men; some worried that intercourse would dam-age their new vaginal entrance. Although these respondents received some emotional and mental preparation, they had not tried to live as women before surgery. For those experienc-ing difficulties after surgery, more counseling was necessary.

Five years after surgery about 70 percent of adult respondents studied by Bodlund and Kullgren (1996) in Sweden improved in social, psychological, and psychiatric areas. Yet, about a third or more did not seem to benefit from SRS, and 16 percent experienced an unsatis-factory result. MF adults experienced a slightly better result than did FM adults. The discrep-ancy between these two groups was especially notable in establishing and maintaining part-nerships and improving socioeconomic status.

Adolescents Who Experience SRS

Persons who undergo SRS usually do so in young adulthood. Especially during their early 30s, candidates are young enough and also mature enough to cope with new life stressors (Rehman et al., 1999; Stein et al., 1990). Professionals are reluctant to recommend SRS to persons younger than 18 to 21 years of age, and parents may not grant consent for minor children. Yet, researchers have reported advantages to beginning the SRS procedure earlier than adulthood. Adolescents who evidenced an extreme pattern of cross sex–gender identifi-cation from their earliest years and suffered from the inability to be open about their feelings or self-concept are good candidates for early intervention. Waiting many years for treatment can evoke a sense of hopelessness in such youth. Another advantage to early intervention con-cerns physical appearance. Especially for those experiencing MF transitions, they do not have to live the rest of their lives with a deep voice and facial scaring from electrical epilation. Hence, they can more easily pass as female (Cohen-Kettenis & van Goozen, 1997).

In their sex clinic in Amsterdam, Cohen-Kettenis and van Goozen (1997) evaluated the outcomes of 22 adolescents who underwent SRS (not less than one year before the study). Twelve of these youth began hormone treatment between the ages of 16 and 18. All were functioning quite well socially and did not express feelings of regret about their reassignment. From one to five years after SRS, they rated their reassignment as "therapeutic" and beneficial. They had resolved issues with sex–gender identity and were living inconspicuously in their new sex–gender roles. Socially and psychologically they did not function differently from peers who never experienced sex–gender identity issues.

In a follow-up study of carefully selected adolescents who underwent SRS (from one to four years prior to follow-up), Smith, van Goozen, and Cohen-Kettenis (2001) reported that no one felt any regrets about electing SRS. All of these youth were functioning well socially and psychologically.

In a study of Dutch adults and adolescents undergoing SRS (Kuiper & Cohen-Kettenis, 1988), sex–gender reassignment was an effective treatment for adults, but not as effective as it was for adolescents in the study. Adults experienced more social issues and received less support from their families and friends. The adults also did not experience as much of a realistic appearance after surgery, which made passing in the desired sex–gender role more difficult. The voices of all except one MF adolescent were *not* noticeably male sounding, and beard growth on all adolescent MFs was only sparse at the time of hormonal treatment.

The positive results of SRS for adolescents may also be associated with the criteria for treatment eligibility. A careful assessment by a specialized team is made to determine if an early start is warranted. Strong determination by these youth is essential. They must also be psychologically stable, except for the depression that is often a consequence of living in the unwanted sex–gender role. They must also function well socially, have a supportive family, and perform well at school. Youth who meet the criteria for surgery undergo partial hormone treatment while also experiencing a real-life diagnostic test where they live full time in the desired sex–gender role. They encounter the advantages and disadvantages of the new situation and discover if they can pass as someone of the other sex–gender. The minimal duration of the real-life test is one year for FMs and one-and-a-half years for MFs. The reason for the longer real-life time for MFs is that sex–gender change seems to affect their lives more than the lives of FMs, and they need more time to adjust to the new situation (Cohen-Kettenis & van Goozen, 1997).

Adolescents who experienced SRS also express fewer regrets following surgery than persons who experienced a much longer and more inconsistent history of untreated sex–gender issues; longer periods of trying to live in the original sex–gender role tended to result in stronger ties to the original role (as a partner, a parent, or a colleague) (Kuiper & Cohen-Kettenis, 1988). The adults, in contrast to adolescents, experience more psychological differences (at least before SRS); experience more psychological difficulties from the enduring stress of coping with their cross sex–gender identity, including social stigmatization and isolation; experience educational and career arrest; and experience intrapsychic stress resulting from the escalating discrepancy between sex–gender role expectations and sex–gender identity as these persons move through developmental life phases (Cohen, de Ruiter, Ringelberg, & Cohen-Kettenis, 1997).

Though sex–gender reassignment for adolescents is a matter of considerable debate, it seems reasonable to conclude that youth treated during late adolescence, or shortly after, may function as well as persons treated later, especially if they have been properly screened and counseled, and have family support.

The Evolving Transgender Umbrella

The transgender "umbrella" increasingly includes more diversity. In recent times, for example, SRS is less inevitable. Biological changes may not be as desirable a goal (Bullough & Bullough, 1997). Although some persons experience selected medical and cosmetic procedures such as breast implants and electrolysis (Coombs, 1998; Tewksbury & Gagné, 1996), more and more persons realize that they can live as transgender men or women without altering their genitals (Bockting, 1999; Denny, 1997). The goal most commonly discussed now is the ability to "pass" as the other sex–gender (Gagné & Tewksbury, 1999). Without surgery, transgender persons can view themselves as the other sex–gender and publicly present themselves as such (Coombs, 1998). Cross-dressers also often dress in whatever way they want (Denny, 1997).

Many others are now under the transgender umbrella, including: *bigender persons* (who identify as both men and women); *drag queens and kings* (usually gay and lesbian persons who "do drag" and dress, respectively, in women's and men's clothes); and *female and male impersonators* (who impersonate women or men, usually for entertainment). Another group of transgender persons include those called *gender blender, gender bender, gender outlaw, and genderfree* (Bockting, 1999). Others who identify as *radical transgender, ambigenderist,* and *third sex* are viewed as *sex radicals* because they challenge not just their own sex–gender but also the existing sex–gender system (Gagné et al., 1997).

SUMMARY

- Definitions for sexual orientation have been elusive. Efforts to categorize people's sexual desires and behaviors had led to a limited understanding of highly variable attractions and sexual behaviors. Stein's "dispositional view" is the most flexible and inclusive as it defines sexual orientation according to a person's desires, fantasies, and behaviors under "ideal circumstances." Circumstances are ideal if there is sexual freedom, availability of attractive sexual partners, and no obstacles to prevent the desired sexual behaviors.
- Kinsey and colleagues were the first to measure sexual orientation; this group established a seven-point continuum ranging from exclusively heterosexual to exclusively homosexual. Although revolutionary for its time, more recent scales have attempted to capture the multivariate and temporal aspects of sexuality. Yet, no scales to date encompass the full range of sexual desires and behaviors.
- Sexual identity is distinguished from sexual orientation; persons label their identities according to social constructs of sexual classifications. In contrast, sexual orientation is most often viewed as more associated with one's biology.
- Self-identification may also depend on race and ethnicity. Some racial and ethnic groups, for example, disavow the terms gay and lesbian as constructs of the White, Eurocentric culture and so reject those labels despite clear attractions and activity with same sex–gender partners.
- Sexual activity can change across the life course so that declarations of sexual identity in adolescence may not continue throughout adulthood. Sexual identity for women seems especially fluid. Women report a range of emotions and attractions to other women, but

these reports do not necessarily reflect sexual orientation or identity. Essential to women, it seems, is the freedom to choose their partners, whatever their sex–gender.

- Bisexual identity may generate even more confusion as a concept since it challenges the bedrock notion of sexual orientation as dichotomous and because of numerous myths about this sexual orientation. Nevertheless, the label "bisexual" is more acceptable for some persons than gay or lesbian; it seems fashionable and avant-garde. As with all persons, bisexual persons experience a range of emotions, attractions, and behaviors. The defining characteristic for this group is that sexual attraction is not dependent on the sex–gender of the other person.

- Transgender persons represent the broadest spectrum of all. Transgender is not a sexual orientation; it is a form of sex–gender expression. Some transgender persons experience intense dissonance with their biological sex during childhood whereas others do not desire to live as a different gender until young adulthood. Some of these persons, including adolescents, undergo radical or modified sexual reassignment surgery but increasingly transgender persons are living without surgically induced changes. Transgender persons are pursuing unique and diverse identities such as sex–gender radicals.

CHAPTER 3
REFERENCES

Anderson, B. F. (1998). Therapeutic issues in working with transgendered clients. In D. Denny (Ed.), *Current concepts of transgendered identity* (pp. 215–226). New York: Garland.

Bailey, J. M. (1996). Gender identity. In R. C. Savin-Williams & K. M. Cohen (Eds.), *The lives of lesbians, gays, and bisexuals: Children to adults* (pp. 71–93). Fort Worth, TX: Harcourt Brace.

Berkey, B. R., Perelman-Hall, T., & Kurdek, L. A. (1990). The multidimensional scale of sexuality. *Journal of Homosexuality, 19*, 67–87.

Blanchard, R., Clemmensen, L. H., & Steiner, B. W. (1987). Heterosexual and homosexual gender dysphorias. *Archives of Sexual Behavior, 16*, 139–152.

Bockting, W. O. (1999). From construction to context: Gender through the eyes of the trans gendered. *Siecus Report, 28*, 3–7.

Bodlund, O., & Kullgren, G. (1996). Transsexualism—General outcome and prognostic factors: A five-year follow-up study of nineteen transsexuals in the process of changing sex. *Archives of Sexual Behavior, 25*, 303–316.

Bullough, B., & Bullough, V. (1997). Are transvestites necessarily heterosexual? *Archives of Sexual Behavior, 26*, 1–12.

Bullough, V. L. (1994a). Foreword. In D. Denny (Ed.), *Gender dysphoria: A guide to research* (pp. xv–xix). New York: Garland.

Bullough, V. L. (1994b). *Science in the bedroom: A history of sex research*. New York: Basic Books.

Bullough, V. L. (1998). Alfred Kinsey and the Kinsey report: Historical overview and lasting contributions. *Journal of Sex Research, 35*, 127–131.

Carballo-Diéguez, A. (1989). Hispanic culture, gay male culture, and AIDS: Counseling implications. *Journal of Counseling and Development, 68*, 26–30.

Chan, C. S. (1997). Don't ask, don't tell, don't know: The formation of a homosexual identity and sexual expression among Asian American lesbians. In B. Greene (Ed.), *Ethnic and cultural diversity among lesbians and gay men* (pp. 240–248). Thousand Oaks, CA: Sage Publications.

Cohen, L., de Ruiter, C., Ringelberg, H., & Cohen-Kettenis, P. T. (1997). Psychological functioning of adolescent transsexuals: Personality and psychopathology. *Journal of Clinical Psychology, 53,* 187–198.

Cohen-Kettenis, P. T., & van Goozen, S.H.M. (1997). Sex reassignment of adolescent trans sexuals: A follow up study. *Journal of the American Academy of Adolescent Psychiatry, 36,* 263–271.

Coleman, E. (1978). Toward a new model of treatment of homosexuality: A review. *Journal of Homosexuality, 3,* 345–359.

Coombs, M. (1998). Sexual dis-orientation: Transgendered people and same-sex marriage. *UCLA Women's Law Journal, 8,* 217–266.

D'Augelli, A. R. (1991). Gay men in college: Identity processes and adaptations. *Journal of College Student Development, 32,* 140–146.

Davis, J. A., & Smith, T. W. (1993). General social surveys, 1972–1993: *Cumulative codebook.* Chicago: National Opinion Research Center.

Denny, D. (1997). Transgender: Some historical, cross-cultural, and contemporary models and methods of coping and treatment. In B. Bullough, V. L. Bullough, & J. Elias (Eds.), *Gender blending* (pp. 33–47). Amherst, NY: Prometheus Books.

Doll, L., & Beeker, C. (1996). Male bisexual behavior and HIV risk in the United States: Synthesis of research with implications for behavioral interventions. *AIDS Education and Prevention, 8,* 205–225.

Dynes, W. R., & Donaldson, S. (1992). General introduction. In W. R. Dynes & S. Donaldson (Eds.), *Homosexuality and psychology, psychiatry, and counseling* (pp. v–xx). New York: Garland.

Ellis, A. L., & Mitchell, R. W. (2000). Sexual orientation. In L. T. Szuchman & F. Muscarella (Eds.), *Psychological perspectives on humans sexuality* (pp. 196–231). New York: John Wiley & Sons.

Espin, O. M. (1984). Cultural and historical influences on sexuality in Hispanic/Latin women: Implications for psychotherapy. In. C. Vance (Ed.), *Pleasure and danger: Exploring female sexuality* (pp. 149–163). London: Routledge & Kegan Paul.

Esterberg, K. G. (1997). Lesbian and bisexual identities: *Constructing communities, constructing selves.* Philadelphia: Temple University Press.

Faderman, L. (1981). *Surpassing the love of men: Romantic friendship and love between women from the Renaissance to the present.* New York: Morrow.

Faderman, L. (1984–1985). The new "gay" lesbians. *Journal of Homosexuality, 10,* 85-95.

Firestein, B. A. (1996). Bisexuality as paradigm shift: Transforming our disciplines. In B. A. Firestein (Ed.), *Bisexuality: The psychology and politics of an invisible minority* (pp. 263–303). Thousand Oaks, CA: Sage Publications.

Ford, C. S. (1948). Sexual behavior among primitive peoples. In D. P. Geddes & E. Currie (Eds.), *About the Kinsey report: Observations by 11 experts* (pp. 26–35). New York: New American Library.

Ford, C. S., & Beach, F. A. (1951). *Patterns of sexual behavior.* New York: Harper & Row.

Gagné, P., & Tewksbury, J. R. (1996). Transgenderists: Products of non-normative intersections of sex, gender, and sexuality. *Journal of Men's Studies, 5,* 105–130.

Gagné, P., & Tewksbury, J. R. (1999). Knowledge and power, body and self: An analysis of knowledge systems and the transgendered self. *Sociological Quarterly, 40,* 59–83.

Gagné, P., Tewksbury, R., & McGaughey, D. (1997). Coming out and crossing over: Identity formation and proclamation in a transgender community. *Gender & Society, 11,* 478-508.

Golden, C. (1987). Diversity and variability in women's sexual identities. In Boston Lesbian Psychologies Collective (Eds.), *Lesbian psychologies: Explorations and challenges* (pp. 19–34). Urbana: University of Illinois Press.

Golden, C. (1994). Our politics, our choices: The feminist movement and sexual orientation. In B. Greene & G. M. Herek (Eds.), *Lesbian and gay psychology: Theory, research, and clinical application* (pp. 54–70). Thousand Oaks, CA: Sage Publications.

Golden, C. (1996). What's in a name? Sexual self-identification among women. In R. C. Savin-Williams & K. M. Cohen (Eds.), *The lives of lesbians, gays, and bisexuals: Children to adults* (pp. 229–249). Fort Worth, TX: Harcourt Brace.

Golden, C. (1997, Winter). Do women choose their sexual identity? *Harvard Gay & Lesbian Review,* 8–20.

Green, R. (1987). *"Sissy boy syndrome" and the development of homosexuality.* New Haven, CT: Yale University Press.

Guidry, L. L. (1999). Clinical intervention with bisexuals: A contextualized understanding. *Professional Psychology: Research and Practice, 30,* 22-26.

Herek, G. M. (1991). Myths about sexual orientation: A lawyer's guide to social science research. *Law and Sexuality: Review of Lesbian and Gay Legal Issues, 1,* 133–172.

Hunter, S., Shannon, C., Knox, J., & Martin, J. I. (1998). *Lesbian, gay, and bisexual youths and adults: Knowledge for human services practice.* Thousand Oaks, CA: Sage Publications.

Kinsey, A. C., Pomeroy, W. B., & Martin, C. E. (1948). *Sexual behavior in the human male.* Philadelphia: W. B. Saunders.

Kinsey, A. C., Pomeroy, W. B., Martin, C. E., & Gebbard, P. H. (1953). *Sexual behavior in the human female.* Philadelphia: W. B. Saunders.

Klein, F., Sepekoff, B., & Wolf, T. J. (1985). Sexual orientation: A multi-variable dynamic process. *Journal of Homosexuality, 11,* 35–49.

Kuiper, A. J., & Cohen-Kettenis, P. T. (1988). Sex reassignment surgery: A study of 141 Dutch transsexuals. *Archives of Sexual Behavior, 17,* 439–457.

Laumann, E. D., Gagnon, J. H., Michael, R. T., & Michaels, S. (1994). *The social organization of sexuality: Sexual practices in the United States.* Chicago: University of Chicago Press.

Manalansan, M. F., IV. (1996). Double minorities: Latino, black, and Asian men who have sex with men. In R. C. Savin-Williams & K. M. Cohen (Eds.), *The lives of lesbian, gay men, and bisexuals: Children to adults* (pp. 393–425). Fort Worth, TX: Harcourt Brace.

Marmor, J. (1980). Overview: The multiple roots of homosexual behavior. In J. Marmor (Ed.), *Homosexual behavior: A modern reappraisal* (pp. 3–22). New York: Basic Books.

Mason-John, V., & Khambatta, A. (1993). *Making black waves: Lesbians talk.* London: Scarlett Press.

Massey, S. G., & Ouellette, S. C. (1996). Homosexual bias in the identity self-portraits of gay men, lesbians, and bisexuals. *Journal of Homosexuality, 32,* 57–76.

Maurer, L. (1999). Transgressing sex and gender: Deconstruction zone ahead? *Siecus Report, 28,* 14–21.

Morales, E. S. (1990). Ethnic minority families and minority gays and lesbians. *Marriage and Family Review, 14,* 217–239.

Paul, J. P. (1992). "Biphobia" and the construction of a bisexual identity. In M. Shernoff & W. A. Scott (Eds.), *The sourcebook on lesbian/gay health care* (2nd ed., pp. 259–264). Washington, DC: National Lesbian/Gay Health Foundation.

Peplau, L. A., & Cochran, S. D. (1990). A relational perspective on homosexuality. In D. P. McWhirter, S. A. Saunders, & J. M. Reinisch (Eds.), *Homosexuality/heterosexuality: Concepts of sexual orientation* (pp. 321–349). New York: Oxford University Press.

Pope, R. L., & Reynolds, A. L. (1991). Including bisexuality: It's more than just a label. In N. J. Evans & V. A. Walls (Eds.), *Beyond tolerance: Gays, lesbians and bisexuals on campus* (pp. 205–212). Alexandria, VA: American College Personnel Association.

Radonsky, V. E., & Borders, L. D. (1995). Factors influencing lesbian's direct disclosures of their sexual orientation. *Journal of Gay & Lesbian Psychotherapy, 213*, 17–37.

Rehman, J., Lazer, S., Benet, A. E., Schaefer, L. C., & Melman, A. (1999). The reported sex and surgery satisfactions of 28 postoperative male-to-female transsexual patients. *Archives of Sexual Behavior, 28*, 71–89.

Rogers, S. M., & Turner, C. F. (1991). Male-male sexual contact in the U.S.A.: Findings from five sample surveys, 1970–1990. *Journal of Sex Research, 48*, 491–519.

Rothblum, E. D. (1994). "I only read about myself on bathroom walls": The need for research on the mental health issues of lesbians and gay men. *Journal of Consulting and Clinical Psychology, 2*, 213–220.

Rothblum, E. D. (2000). Sexual orientation and sex in women's lives: Conceptual and methodological issues. *Journal of Social Issues, 56*, 193–204.

Rothblum, E. D., & Brehony, K. A. (1993). *Boston marriages: Romantic but asexual relationships among contemporary lesbians.* Amherst: University of Massachusetts Press.

Rupp, L. J. (1997). "Imagine my surprise": Women's relationships in historical perspective. *Journal of Lesbian Studies, 1*, 155–175.

Russell, G. M., & Bohan, J. S. (1999). Implications for clinical work. In J. S. Bohan & G. M. Russell (Eds.), *Conversations about psychology and sexual orientation* (pp. 31–56). New York: New York University Press.

Rust, P. C. (1996). Finding a sexual identity and community: Therapeutic implications and cultural assumptions in scientific models of coming out. In E. D. Rothblum & L. A. Bond (Eds.), *Preventing heterosexim and homophobia* (pp. 87–123). Thousand Oaks, CA: Sage Publications.

Rust, P.C.R. (2000). Bisexuality: A contemporary paradox for women. *Journal of Social Issues, 56*, 205–221.

Savin-Williams, R. (1995). An exploratory study of pubertal maturation timing and self-esteem among gay and bisexual male youths. *Developmental Psychology, 31*, 56–64.

Savin-Williams, R. C. (1998). *". . . and then I became gay": Young men's stories.* New York: Routledge.

Savin-Williams, R. C. (2001). A critique of research on sexual-minority youth. *Journal of Adolescence, 24*, 5–13.

Seil, D. (1996). Transsexuals: The boundaries of sexual identity and gender. In R. P. Cabaj & T. S. Stein (Eds.), *Textbook of homosexuality and mental health* (pp. 743–762). Washington, DC: American Psychiatric Press.

Sell, R. L. (1996). The Sell assessment of sexual orientation: Background and scoring. *Journal of Gay, Lesbian, and Bisexual Identity, 1*, 295–310.

Shively, M. G., & De Cecco, J. P. (1977). Components of sexual identity. *Journal of Homosexuality, 3*, 41–48.

Shively, M. G., Jones, C., & De Cecco, J. (1983–1984). Research on sexual orientation: Definition and methods. *Journal of Homosexuality, 9*, 127–136.

Smith, Y.L.S., van Goozen, S.H.M., & Cohen-Kettenis, P. T. (2001). Adolescents with gender identity disorder who were accepted or rejected for sex reassignment surgery: A prospective follow-up study. *Journal of the American Academy of Child Adolescent Psychiatry, 40*, 472–481.

Stein, E. (1999). *The mismeasure of desire: The science, theory, and ethics of sexual orientation.* New York: Oxford University Press.

Stein, M., Tiefer, L., & Melman, A. (1990). Follow up observations of operated male-to-female transsexuals. *Journal of Urology, 143*, 1188–1192.

Stokes, J., & Damon, W. (1995). Counseling and psychotherapy for bisexual men. *Directions in Mental Health Counseling, 5*, 4–15.

Stokes, J. P., Damon, W., & McKirnan, D. J. (1997). Predictors of movement toward homosexuality: A longitudinal study of bisexual men. *Journal of Sex Research, 34*, 304–312.

Stokes, J. P., Miller, R. L., & Mundhenk, R. (1998). Toward an understanding of behaviorally bisexual men: The influence of context and culture. *Canadian Journal of Human Sexuality, 7*, 1–12.

Stokes, J. P., Taywaditep, K., Vanable, P., & McKirnan, D. J. (1996). Bisexual men, sexual behavior, and HIV/AIDS. In B. A. Firestein (Ed.), *Bisexuality: The psychology and politics of an invisible minority* (pp. 149–168). Thousand Oaks, CA: Sage Publications.

Storms, M. D. (1980). Theories of sexual orientation. *Journal of Personality and Social Psychology, 38*, 783–792.

Talamini, J. T. (1982). *Boys will be girls: The hidden world of the heterosexual male transvestite.* Washington, DC: University Press of America.

Tarver, D. E. (2002). Transgender mental health: The intersection of race, sexual orientation, and gender orientation. In B. E. Jones & M. J. Hill (Eds.), *Mental health issues in lesbian, gay, bisexual, and transgender communities* (pp. 93–108). Washington, DC: American Psychiatric Publishing.

Tewksbury, R., & Gagné, P. (1996). Transgenderists: Products of non-normative intersections of sex, gender, and sexuality. *Journal of Men's Studies, 5,* 105–129.

Tofoya, T. N. (1996). Native two-spirit people. In R. P. Cabaj & T. S. Stein (Eds.), *Textbook of homosexuality and mental health* (pp. 603–617). Washington, DC: American Psychiatric Press.

Udis-Kessler, A. (1996). Challenging the stereotypes. In S. Rose & C. Stevens (Eds.), *Bisexual horizons: Politics, histories, lives* (pp. 45–57). London: Lawrence & Wisehart.

Wooden, W. S., & Parker, J. (1982). *Men behind bars: Sexual exploitation in prison.* New York: Plenum Press.

Zuger, B. (1984). Early effeminate behavior in boys: Outcome and significance for homosexuality. *Journal of Nervous and Mental Disorders, 172,* 90–97.

PART II
KNOWLEDGE AND THEORY

CHAPTER 4
INDIVIDUALS: COMING OUT AND IDENTITY DEVELOPMENT

What is coming out?

What are the distinctions or shared characteristics among models of coming out?

What are the experiences of coming out for adolescents?

How do coming-out experiences differ for men and women?

What is the impact of race or ethnicity on the coming-out process?

What is the process of coming out for bisexual persons?

What is the process of coming out for transgender persons?

What are the critiques of coming-out models and missing pieces?

COMING OUT AND STAGES OF THE PROCESS

Different phrases such as "coming out," "identity development," or "sexual questioning" signify that one is going through a process of recognition that one's sexual orientation may be lesbian, gay, or bisexual (Savin-Williams & Diamond, 1999). This recognition entails assuming a sexual identity previously regarded as unacceptable or irrelevant (Fassinger & Miller, 1996; McCarn & Fassinger, 1996). A person is challenged to overcome internalized oppression (Gonsiorek, 1993), declare a sexual identity in defiance of social values (Ponse, 1980), and reconstruct devalued parts of oneself (Stein & Cohen, 1984). Without heterosexism, none of these processes would be necessary. Instead, engaging in same sex–gender relationships and sexual behaviors would just be something persons do (Russell & Bohan, 1999).

Coming out seems to most theorists, researchers, and LGBT persons themselves to follow a developmental process in which one redefines one's sexual identity over time. It ends when one attains a positive lesbian, gay, or bisexual identity (Gonsiorek, 1993; Levine & Evans, 1991). All coming-out models follow a linear sequence of stages with variations in the number of stages (from three to seven) and in the order and importance of various stages and substages (for example, Cohen & Savin-Williams, 1996).

Most coming-out models link stages with chronological ages. Over the several decades of research on the coming-out process, the data showed that most persons come out during the teenage years and early 20s (for example, Chapman & Brannock, 1987; Harry, 1993; Rosario et al., 1996). Earlier age trends as well as an abbreviation of the whole coming-out process may be more prevalent among urban, collegiate, and media-saturated communities (for example, D'Augelli & Hershberger, 1993; Savin-Williams, 1998). In addition, in a study of 164 sexually subordinated young adults (78 women, 86 men; from

17 to 25 years of age), men reached all coming-out milestones earlier than women except for disclosure (Savin-Williams & Diamond, 2000).

Two empirically based coming-out models will be presented in detail, including the six-stage psychosocial model developed by Cass (1979, 1984, 1996) that is the foundation for much of the later contemporary work on identity formation. Second, as an illustration of the later work, the four-stage model developed by Fassinger and associates is presented (Fassinger & Miller, 1996; McCarn & Fassinger, 1996).

SEXUAL IDENTITY FORMATION MODEL

The Cass model, called Sexual Identity Formation, is the most well known of the coming-out models. It is also the most extensively studied model and has both theoretical and empirical validity (for example, Brady & Busse, 1994; Degges-White, Rice, & Myers, 2000; Levine, 1997; Whitman, Cormier, & Boyd, 2000). It offers a particularly comprehensive description of lesbian and gay identity development by addressing cognitive, emotional, and behavioral changes over six stages and integrating both social and psychological factors.

After a prestage in which one views oneself as heterosexual and does not think of oneself as lesbian or gay, one begins to question if a same sex–gender sexual orientation is possible for oneself. This questioning begins Stage 1 of the model.

Stage 1—Identity Confusion ("Who am I?")

In this stage, one begins to wonder if the information one hears about a gay or lesbian identity pertains to oneself. One of three alternative pathways is taken: (a) accept the relevance and desirability of the meaning of lesbian or gay; (b) accept the relevance but not the desirability of the meaning, try to remove all undesirable elements from one's life (identity foreclosure or no advancement to a new stage); or (c) refuse to accept one's behavior as relevant or desirable, stop behaviors viewed as lesbian or gay, halt access to information about being gay or lesbian, and avoid any provocative situations (identity foreclosure). If one cannot suppress the applicability of the meaning of lesbian or gay to oneself, or one accepts it, Stage 2 commences.

Stage 2—Identity Comparison ("I am different")

In this stage, a person experiences attraction to others of the same sex–gender. One of four pathways is taken: (a) develop a positive evaluation of self and anticipate high rewards versus costs; (b) develop a positive evaluation of self but perceive low rewards, which can lead to rejection of the relevance of the meaning of lesbian or gay (identity foreclosure) or, if these actions fail, a conclusion that one is probably lesbian or gay; (c) develop a negative evaluation of self but perceive high rewards which can lead to the desire to assess oneself as heterosexual, not lesbian or gay; or (d) develop a negative evaluation of self and perceive low rewards which can lead to devaluation of a lesbian or gay self-identification and a positive evaluation of a heterosexual self-identification (identity foreclosure). If one acknowledges a lesbian or gay identity at this stage but it is accompanied by a negative self-evaluation, it can result for some persons in self-hatred and possibly self-destructive behaviors such as self-mutilation or suicide attempts.

Stage 3—Identity Tolerance ("I am probably lesbian or gay")

In this stage, a person moves in the direction of greater commitment to a lesbian or gay identity and is likely to seek out a lesbian or gay community. One of six pathways is taken: (a) develop a positive view of self as probably lesbian or gay and experience positive contacts with other lesbian and gay persons; (b) develop a positive view of self but experience negative contacts with other lesbian and gay persons; these persons are devalued and contact with them reduced (identity foreclosure); the conception of oneself as lesbian or gay is reevaluated as less positive; (c) develop a negative view of self, but experience positive contacts with lesbian and gay persons that can lessen one's negative evaluation of self as lesbian or gay; (d) develop a negative evaluation of self and experience negative contacts with lesbian and gay persons that can lead to avoidance of contacts (identity foreclosure); a negative evaluation of self is modifiable if future positive contacts occur; (e) develop a positive evaluation of self and experience positive contacts with lesbian and gay persons that can lead to greater commitment as lesbian or gay, with no qualifiers; or (f) develop a positive evaluation of self as partly lesbian or gay and experience negative contacts with lesbian and gay persons that can lead to a devaluation of lesbian and gay persons (identity foreclosure) or the adoption of a somewhat negative evaluation of self as lesbian or gay.

Stage 4—Identity Acceptance ("I am lesbian or gay")

At this stage, a person begins to feel that being gay or lesbian is a valid self-identity and may prefer being around other gay and lesbian persons. The new identity is disclosed to more persons, decreasing the incongruence between one's self-perceptions and the perceptions of others or between one's positive evaluation of self and the negative evaluations of others. Continued "passing" as heterosexual at this stage is seen as identity foreclosure.

Stage 5—Identity Pride ("My sexual orientation is part of me")

At this stage, disclosures of one's sexual orientation are made in all, or most, areas of one's life. One may also further resolve the incongruence between self-acceptance and the devaluation by others through disregarding negative opinions. In this stage, everything that is heterosexual is devalued, and everything that is lesbian or gay is valued.

Stage 6—Identity Synthesis ("I am lesbian or gay!")

The ultimate goal for a person at this stage is to experience psychological integration or congruence between perceptions of one's self and one's behavior and between one's private and public identities. One gradually modifies the "us versus them" stance of the previous stage and increases contact with supportive heterosexual persons.

Dual-Branch Model

The second identity model to be described is the dual-branch model. The developers of this model (Fassinger & Miller, 1996; McCarn & Fassinger, 1996) proposed two separate trajectories of identity development: sexual identity development and group identity development. Earlier models focused on the internal developmental tasks in the early stages of coming out and on developing a public and politicized identity in the later stages. These models were heavily influenced by the politics of the Stonewall riots (see Chapter 1), the gay rights movement, and the women's movement. The separation of these two developmental trajectories in the dual-branch model seems now to better fit the diverse lives of lesbian and gay persons.

The first branch of the dual-branch model (sexual identity development) focuses on the internal process of confirming same sex–gender emotional and sexual wishes and incorporating them into one's identity. The second branch (group membership identity) focuses on the context in which the internal processes happen, and on one's attitudes and feelings about lesbian and gay persons, nonlesbian and gay persons, and oneself. Initially, empirical validation of the dual-branch model was based on the experiences of lesbians, but the model has evolved to fit the diverse population of gay persons in its reflection of greater sexual exploration and activity. Although persons do not progress through the two branches simultaneously, addressing developmental tasks in one branch can trigger movement in the other branch (McCarn & Fassinger, 1996). The model has four phases, each with a dual branch—awareness, exploration, deepening commitment, and internalization/synthesis.

Phase 1—Awareness

Individual sexual identity. One is cognizant of feeling or being different from the heterosexual norm and from what one predicted for oneself. Affective states may include confusion, bewilderment, and fear.

Group membership identity. One becomes aware of heterosexism and the gay and lesbian community. Falling in love with a person of the same sex–gender (an individual identity process) may trigger these realizations, producing bewilderment and confusion.

Phase 2—Exploration

Individual sexual identity. One experiences strong feelings, often sexual, for others of the same sex–gender or for a particular person of the same sex–gender. Despite these feelings, one may not explore sexual involvements. Affective states may include wonderment, ebullience, and longing.

Group membership identity. One explores knowledge about lesbian and gay persons as a group and one's attitudes about this group and one's possible membership in this group. Clarity about one's attitudes, however, can be difficult to attain because of one's previous heterosexist attitudes or limited access to correct information. Anger, anxiety, and guilt may emerge because of one's own participation in heterosexism, but one can also experience exhilaration, curiosity, and joy in becoming acquainted with other lesbian and gay persons. Progress in group membership identity does not imply simultaneous progress in individual sexual identity. For example, a woman developing a feminist consciousness may develop a positive view of lesbians but not yet (and maybe never) identify herself as a member of this reference group (see Chapter 3).

Phase 3—Deepening/Commitment

Individual sexual identity. One experiences a deepened commitment to self-knowledge, solidification of sexual identity, and a sense of self-fulfillment. Not every woman or man at this phase, however, will commit to only women or men as sexual partners. Instead, some may commit to both men and women. Affective states may include anger and sadness and, in addition, acceptance and self-assurance.

Group membership identity. One experiences a deepened commitment to personal involvement with the gay and lesbian community as a reference group. Awareness of oppression increases, as does the awareness of consequences of involvement in an oppressed group. Not every lesbian or gay person, however, will experience the same intensity of commitment to the lesbian or gay culture or deprecation of heterosexist society. Yet many will likely share some affective states such as excitement and pride as well as rage and internal conflict.

Phase 4—Internalization/Synthesis

Individual sexual identity. One experiences a deepened self-acceptance of sexual desire for and love of a person of the same sex–gender as part of one's identity, along with the development of a sense of internal consistency and an unwillingness to change course. Affective states can include contentment and pride. The reformulation of public identity and the meaning of being a lesbian or gay person in one's society are also likely to surface in this phase.

Group membership identity. One fully internalizes one's identity as a member of an oppressed group. One also distinguishes individual gay and lesbian persons from stereotypes. The affective states of rage, anxiety, and insecurity turn into directed anger, dedication, fulfillment, comfort, security, and self-love. One also develops a sense of oneself as gay or lesbian across contexts. Though it is likely that some disclosures will happen, one may or may not make public disclosures or become politicized.

COMING OUT IN ADOLESCENCE

Although coming out may involve similar processes for persons at all ages, significant distinctions emerge for adolescents who are developing in so many other ways. In addition, while developing a personal sense of self, they are usually living at home with parents and are not financially independent.

Many youth may experience confusion while trying to discover the meaning of their emotional and sexual feelings and experiences, and most of those who question their sexual identity will eventually define themselves as heterosexual (Fontaine & Hammond, 1996). Others, however, who experience intense emotional or sexual attractions to the same sex–gender will move beyond the initial awareness of "feeling different" from other adolescents to claim a gay, lesbian, or bisexual identity (Savin-Williams & Diamond, 1999).

Although many LGB youth try to deny that their same sex–gender attractions are sexual, the onset of puberty provides new meaning to these attractions (Hunter & Schaecher, 1987). These youth also recognize that they do not experience the sexual interest in the other sex–gender that their peers boast about (Savin-Williams, 1995). The development of more complex cognitive abilities and an increasingly autonomous social life facilitate the process of self-awareness and self-identity (D'Augelli, 1996). When youth distance themselves from family and the hometown community, they often swiftly recognize their sexual identity (Savin-Williams, 1998).

COMING OUT LATER IN LIFE

For a variety of reasons, some LGB persons come out later in life. Many have been in heterosexual marriages. In a Chicago sample of older gay and lesbian persons, Herdt, Beeler, and Rawls (1997) found that those who married came out an average of 10 years later (usually after age 30) than those who did not marry. For a quarter of this group coming out was delayed until after age 40. About one-quarter to over one-half of women in other studies who came out in midlife or later did so after years of marriage and rearing children (for example, Bradford & Ryan, 1991; Sang, 1991). Many committed themselves as wives and mothers and never questioned their heterosexuality until midlife (Lander & Charbonneau, 1990; Sang, 1991). Among both lesbian and gay persons, some who married were aware of same sex–gender attractions and experienced same sex–gender sexual relations before becoming married (Isay, 1998).

Other variations of delayed coming out among women include: (a) those who experienced same sex–gender attractions earlier in life but did not self-identify as lesbian until midlife (for example, Kirkpatrick, 1989a, 1989b); (b) those who never married and did not experience any same sex–gender behaviors earlier but later identified as lesbian because of fantasies about intimate relationships with women (Ponse, 1980); and (c) those who felt they had always been lesbians but did not realize it until midlife. For women who were previously unaware of same sex–gender attractions, no single event precipitated the shift in identity. Instead, a combination of events provided the context for change. Once same sex–gender sexual experiences happened, they felt immediately satisfying and natural (Charbonneau & Lander, 1991).

For gay persons, Kimmel and Sang (1995) identified two basic patterns of coming out. In the first pattern, men recognized their desire for same sex–gender identification early in life and began to follow this path at that time. In the second pattern, men did not come out as gay until midlife and may have welcomed a new search for identity and sexuality in this life period. Herdt and colleagues (1997) found differences in the degree to which gay persons acknowledged their identity to themselves and acted on it before divorce. Some of them always knew they were gay or at least felt captivated by men. Some reported illicit encounters with other men while still married. Some reported that they were not really aware of being gay until after their divorce.

Coming Out in a Racial or Ethnic Context

The eventual acceptance and integration of sexual identity may vary because of numerous social and environmental factors including the effects of race and ethnicity. When already marginalized, LGB persons may not choose to openly identify with another oppressed group (Martinez & Sullivan, 1998). Because of their different reference groups, many Latino, African American, and Asian American youth struggle with who they are and who they feel others in their cultures want them to be. Many feel that they must lead a double life or establish a dual identity. They face not only a hostile heterosexist world but also a hostile White gay and lesbian world. If they declare their sexual attractions, they also will most likely face a hostile ethnic community (Savin-Williams, 1998). Stereotypes, if accepted and internalized, can create strong negative feelings about one's sexual identity and exacerbate internalized oppression. For example, African American lesbians are portrayed as man-hating "masculine" butches (Jones & Hill, 1996). African American women are held to standards of physical appearance based on the White female ideal, so African American lesbians may experience shame about their physical appearance (West, 1995). Asian Americans are also often considered as sexually unattractive in lesbian and gay communities (Chung & Katayama, 1998). The dilemmas for ethnic and racial persons are addressed further in the discussion in Chapter 5 on disclosing one's sexual identity to one's family.

Coming Out as Bisexual

As with gay and lesbian persons, the coming-out process is happening earlier for bisexual persons because of changes in cultural attitudes, more access to affirmative information, and more visible and supportive bisexual communities (Fox, 1995). Self-identity as bisexual often occurs in the early to middle 20s; women tend to adopt a bisexual identity sooner than do men (Fox, 2000). Yet the coming-out process for bisexual persons holds additional complications, such as not always having a community or subculture for support (Klein, 1993). Also, bisexual identity may seem a more ambiguous status than a gay or lesbian identity (Matteson, 1996).

Persons who have dual heterosexual and same sex–gender attractions may not have accurate role models. For example, the media portrays bisexual men and women as experiencing sex with both men and women, usually in short-term liaisons. Men and women who are coming out as bisexual may think that this pattern is fundamental to a bisexual identity, although no particular pattern of behaviors is essential to this identity (Ochs, 1996; Rust, 1996).

Whereas bisexual men and women may feel pressured to play out the hybrid conceptualization of bisexual identity, they rarely report (less than one in four) feeling equal attraction to men and women. Their attractions range across a full spectrum of attraction to men and women. A person may also feel closer emotionally to women and more sexually attracted to men (Rust, 1996).

Based on longitudinal data from a sample of bisexual men and women in San Francisco, Weinberg, Williams, and Pryor (1994, 1998) proposed broad stages of bisexual identity development based on the most common experiences of their bisexual respondents: (a) initial confusion; (b) finding and applying the label; (c) settling into the identity or a more complete self-labeling, and (d) continued uncertainty about one's sexual identity because of the lack of social validation and support, and the absence of bisexual role models and community. These stages may not apply to all bisexual persons (Rust, 1992, 1993).

Coming Out as Transgender

Even if transgender persons do not adopt lesbian, gay, or bisexual identifications, they still personally experience coming out as transgender and later disclosing this identity to others. Coming out for these persons is a process of experimenting with various identities until they discover the most comfortable "fit" (Gagné, Tewksbury, & McGaughey, 1997).

Coming out as transgender after sexual reassignment surgery (SRS) is even more complicated because of the changes in sex–gender and genital composition and because of the subjective and social meanings of sexual interactions (Gagné et al., 1997). Research on the coming-out experiences of these persons, however, is almost nonexistent. An exception is the findings reported by Gagné and colleagues (1997) and Gagné and Tewksbury (1999) from a volunteer sample of 65 male–female persons. Coming out for these persons was defined as "crossing over" from one sex–gender category to the other. Three factors were involved in this transition: (a) dealing with the struggles that resulted from society's negative sanctions of what felt natural; (b) discovering names for their feelings; and (c) finding others who were experiencing equivalent feelings, the most common factor leading to acceptance of their identity.

Medical and media portrayals of transgender identity have evoked increased consciousness about sex–gender choices and have countered the confusion and shame often experienced by transgender persons. Those who feel they are in the wrong body have often reported thinking of themselves only as a medical condition in need of a cure. Just learning about the possibilities of SRS resulted, for some, in a reassessment of their identities and in a feeling that they had a place in the world. Not all identity symbols are positive, however, such as those that imply that transgender persons are "freaks." And, although transgender magazines and online computer services are useful for finding role models and mentors, these mediums sometimes raise more issues than they resolve. One can discover, for example, that one is quite different from others who label themselves in the same way (Gagné & Tewksbury, 1999; Gagné et al., 1997).

When they decided to move into public arenas, the transgender persons studied by Gagné and colleagues (1997) carefully thought through their initial public excursions, choosing safe places where disapproval was unlikely and where they could make a quick entry and exit. Most often, they first went to gatherings specifically for transgender persons. They also went to gay community events, bars, or other locations although they did not want to be perceived as gay. Although they were probably viewed as marginal members of the gay community, they could experiment both with sex–gender identity and sex. They could work on perfecting a feminine persona. They might experience for the first time responses to themselves as "women" or "ladies," which was an overwhelming desire. They might also experience opportunities for sexual exploration, some of which might occur with "punters"—men who do not want to participate in sex with either a man or a woman but who might agree to participate in sex with a man attired as a woman (Woodhouse, 1989).

CRITIQUES OF COMING-OUT MODELS

All coming-out models have limitations. Most evolved from clinical and anecdotal data; few were adequately tested (Fassinger, 1994); and the stages were usually conceptualized after data collection (Gruskin, 1999). Research samples were small or unrepresentative, and the measures unsound or undeveloped (Fassinger, 1994). Early models may not generalize beyond the cohorts that entered adolescence in the 1960s and 1970s. In addition, the models address only certain areas such as the cognitive category of identity development (Herdt, 1992). Several additional concerns about these models will be mentioned here; more detailed critiques exist in others sources (for example, McCarn & Fassinger, 1996).

Smooth Stages or Disorder?

As mentioned before, coming-out models are linear. Yet, the researchers and theorists who developed these models typically observed that all persons do not proceed through every stage or in the predicted sequence. Persons can experience stages in different orders, skip stages, repeat stages, remain in one stage indefinitely, backtrack, or abort the coming-out process and retain a heterosexual identity (for example, Rust, 1993; Savin-Williams & Diamond, 1999). In addition, some youth never been experience a gestalt shift to a new identity. Some have no memory of any coming-out process. They have never been in doubt about who and what they are; they have always been "out" to themselves and others. Other youth experience a sudden revelation of their sexual orientation but become comfortable with it overnight (Savin-Williams, 1998).

Ended Process or Continuing One?

Linear models suggest that once one reaches the end stage, identity development ends. This idea, however, does not fit the reality for most persons who experience coming out as a lifelong process (for example, Esterberg, 1997). Even persons who are certain about their identity and feel comfortable may experience changes in their sexual feelings and behaviors over the course of their lives (Rosario and colleagues, 1996; Rust, 1996). Some researchers described identity development as a repeating spiral. At each turn, with the introduction of new perspectives, identity is reworked and reframed (Olson & King, 1995), and new identity concepts develop (Rust, 1996). The coming-out process has also been described as circular because of changing life situations (Fassinger & Miller, 1996; McCarn & Fassinger, 1996). Instead of proceeding through a single linear process and stopping at an endpoint, a fluid conceptualization of identity development seems a better fit for many persons.

Description Becomes Prescription

Another issue with linear developmental models is that they assume that sexual orientation is a core trait to be discovered, acknowledged, and accepted. But, this description of what happens can become a prescription of what is supposed to happen (Gruskin, 1999). This makes coming-out models judgmental because they define a specific goal and how to make progress to reach this goal (acknowledging no optional paths). When progress is arrested, one is in a state of regression and immaturity (Rust, 1996). Persons who adopt a bisexual identity instead of a gay or lesbian identity are also considered immature (Rust, 1996; Vargo, 1998). Yet, "therapy" is always available to "help" persons in the "immature" states to advance through the other stages (Kitzinger & Perkins, 1993).

Politicalization and Mandatory Disclosure

Activism and a politicized public identity signify developmental maturity to some scholars who developed coming-out models (Esterberg, 1997; Rust, 1996). These models presume widespread public disclosure in the final stage; the lack of disclosure or activism signals developmental arrest (McCarn & Fassinger, 1996). Expectations for disclosure and activism, however, do not recognize the social realities of diverse groups or contexts (for example, work settings, family situations, racial and ethnic groups, geographical locations) or other realities including legal and economic situations and the availability of support systems (Fassinger, 1991; Fassinger & Miller, 1996).

MISSING PIECES OF COMING-OUT MODELS

The research supporting stage models of coming out used primarily White, middle-class, self-identified samples of lesbian and gay persons. None of the models adequately addressed or explained the interaction of sexual identity with other identifications, including social class, race and ethnicity, bisexual orientation, transgender identity, adolescence, and older persons. Other missing pieces are discussed in more detail here including social contexts and constructs, historical effects, sex–gender, immigration and acculturation, and disabilities and chronic illnesses.

Social Contexts and Constructs

The social constructionist perspective challenges the essentialist perspective typical of coming-out models. It creates space for continuing exploration and fluidity of identity and does not dictate that one must lock into a life script prematurely (Bohan & Russell, 1999). Instead of being an intrinsic quality, sexual identity is seen as a social construction or an interpretation of personal and sociopolitical experiences. Examples of these experiences are sociopolitical factors (for example, the lesbian and gay rights movement), new romantic or sexual relationships with same sex–gender persons, or the introduction of a bisexual person into one's life, which evokes awareness of bisexuality (Rust, 1996). Through interaction with our environment or social contexts, we take an active role in constructing our sexual identity. We have some choice in our development of an identity and how we express it. In addition, because the identity we construct is not an underlying essence in us, both the identity and its expression may vary over time as our social contexts change (Horowitz & Newcomb, 2002).

The fixed, essentialist perspective of identity is only one among many possible scripts. The constructionist perspective does not reject the benefits provided by the essentialist perspective on coming out but rather expands our understandings of other influential experiences on coming out both at the individual and collective levels (Russell & Bohan, 1999).

Historical Effects

As noted earlier, our historical location can also influence coming out by opening up or suppressing one's awareness of and access to others like oneself. For example, from interviews with lesbians born between 1917 and 1972, Parks (1999) concluded that the internal progression from self-awareness to self-identification across three generations (the pre-Stonewall era, age 45 and older; the gay liberation era, ages 30 to 44; and the gay rights era, age 30 and younger) was linked to each respondent's awareness of and access to other lesbians and lesbian-identified events. Women in the gay rights era, for example, did not experience the severe isolation and silence that characterized women in the pre-Stonewall era or the condemnation that characterized women in the liberation era. In another study that compared historical periods, Stein (1997) found that in the "old dyke world" being a lesbian involved developing a social identity or living as a lesbian by focusing on sex–gender roles. But women in the newer lesbian–feminist culture rejected the emphasis on sex–gender roles for lesbians.

Sex–Gender

The stage models that address lesbians (for example, Chapman & Brannock, 1987; Faderman, 1984–1985; Sophie, 1985–1986) do not express the variation in the identity development we now know exists (Esterberg, 1997). Even less fitting for women are the models developed from samples of gay persons (Savin-Williams, 1998).

Only a few young lesbian and bisexual persons were discovered by Diamond (1996) to follow the male-oriented "master narrative" of identity development. Few recalled childhood behavioral predictions of same sex–gender sexual orientation characterized as "typical" development for all sexually subordinated groups. Lesbian and bisexual women are more likely than gay persons to be influenced by current circumstances and choices instead of by early-life predictors. Other researchers (for example, Gonsiorek, 1993, 1995; Stein, 1993) also reported that the identity process for lesbians is more fluid and ambiguous than the more abrupt process reported by gay persons.

Males and females also differ in the contexts in which they become aware of same sex–gender attractions. This tends to happen for females (both lesbian and bisexual) in an affectionate link with another female, but before sexual involvement (Esterberg, 1994; Weinberg and colleagues, 1994). Nearly one-third of young sexually subordinated women studied by Diamond (1998) questioned their sexual identity before experiencing same sex–gender attractions. For males, this awareness more often happens after sexual experiences and not necessarily in the context of a close link (Nichols, 1990). Females may also delay identifying as lesbian or bisexual because expressions of affection between females are customary behaviors among them. To interpret their sexual feelings and take on a lesbian or bisexual identity, females may need certain interpersonal situations often found in a community of females (Savin-Williams & Diamond, 2000).

For gay persons, cohort changes may modify their identity development. Dubé (1997) showed that although many older White gay persons followed the male-oriented master narrative, younger cohorts of White gay and bisexual men were less likely to follow it. Many post-Stonewall youth identified themselves as gay or bisexual before engaging in same sex–gender sexual encounters. This change was less prevalent, however, among Latino, Asian American, and African American gay and bisexual youth. The classical ordering of developmental milestones also fit only two of the gay youth studied by Savin-Williams (1998). In this study, nearly 40 percent of the youth did not engage in same sex–gender sex until after they labeled their sexual identity as gay or bisexual. For 30 percent, disclosure of their sexual identity to another person happened before experiencing same sex–gender sexual encounters; 15 percent reported feeling good about their sexual identity before experiencing same sex–gender sexual encounters. Some of these youth, then, did not engage in same sex–gender sex until after reaching many other developmental milestones.

Immigration and Acculturation

Beginning with the Immigration Act of 1917, lesbian and gay persons were not permitted to enter the United States because of the belief that "homosexuality" was a disease. Although the American Psychiatric Society removed "homosexuality" from its categories of mental disorders in 1979, it took until 1990 for this exclusion of lesbian and gay persons from entering the

United States to end. Asylum is also permitted when gay and lesbian persons fear persecution in their country of origin. (Bennett, 1999).

Immigration from other countries to the United States or crossing borders can create issues that coming-out models rarely consider. Acculturation issues can be central to how identity issues are negotiated. In studies of immigrant lesbians, for example, it was observed that even if a woman were a lesbian before migration, she must ascertain how to be a lesbian in the new cultural context (Espin, 1997). She will have to reorganize her identity in terms of new societal expectations (González & Espin, 1996). In addition, if a woman is from a background other than European, she will also acculturate as a "subordinated" person from another background (Espin, 1997).

Even if one's entire family immigrates voluntarily, strong ties to one's homeland are likely to remain. If immigration is recent, there may also be a dependence on family members and one's racial or ethnic community for emotional and possibly economic support. If not acculturated, a new immigrant also may not have contact with lesbian and gay communities or lesbian and gay persons even in one's own community (Espin, 1987).

Disabilities and Chronic Illnesses

Disabilities and chronic illnesses are also rarely addressed in coming-out models or in LGBT literature generally. An exception is the work of Axtell (1999) who interviewed 20 lesbian and bisexual women with disabilities or chronic illnesses. Some viewed their conditions as part of their multiple identities whereas others did not. Although the disability or chronic illness identity was fluid for some, for others it was constant.

Disabilities and chronic illnesses cannot only further stigmatize LGBT persons but also interfere with their identity development. LGBT usually move outside of their families to meet others in LGBT communities. Access to these communities, however, may be limited if one must depend on family members for care and mobility. Opportunities for these persons to make contact with LGBT communities or develop friendships may be severely hampered, and even more so if families do not approve of their sexual orientation. Inconsistent or no transmission of LGBT culture creates difficulties in the development of identity, a sense of group cohesion, and a sense of culture (Linton, 1998).

SUMMARY

- Coming out is a process of realizing that one's sexual orientation is lesbian, gay, or bisexual. This process includes questioning one's sexual orientation; considering that options besides heterosexuality exist; imagining oneself as something other than heterosexual; and learning how to "be" lesbian, gay, or bisexual, including behavior and establishing relationships. This process may happen quickly or take a lifetime to complete. The end of the process may include disclosing one's sexual identity to others although many persons may not choose to do this.

- Researchers have endeavored to explain the coming-out process by interviewing LGB persons to determine how and when they knew they were different. This type of questioning is flawed since it assumes that the pathway to sexual identity is clearly marked and universally followed. Yet, these assumptions create the common ground of many models: that sexual self-identification occurs in discrete steps, that the steps follow a certain sequence, and that all persons go through all steps. "Maturity" means public disclosure and political activism in most models. Critiques of these typical assumptions of coming-out models suggest that these steps are not universal.

- Information about how adolescents explore and discover their sexual identity is varied. Confounded by the complex physiological and psychological processes of puberty, adolescents are fraught with ambivalence, experimentation, and vacillation about their sexuality. In many studies, adolescents reported that they "always felt different," yet they did not always act on these feelings. Some easily accepted that they might be gay or lesbian whereas others might not confront this possibility until well into their adulthood, despite their early desires. More recent studies of current adolescents revealed less ambivalence toward same sex–gender identities, as evidenced by their disclosing lesbian, gay, or bisexual identities at earlier ages.
- Overall, women self-identify as lesbian about a year later than men self-identify as gay; and women engage in same sex–gender sexual relationships, on average, about a year later than men. Women, also, are more likely to identify as lesbian only during or after an affectionate link with another woman whereas men may identify as gay outside the context of an intimate relationship. Many women contend that they did not know that they were lesbian until midlife whereas men, even those who married and only admitted to themselves or others in midlife that they were gay, maintain that they always knew that they felt attracted to men. Some women also knew from adolescence that they experienced attractions to women.
- Race and ethnicity can confound the coming-out process. Some ethnic and racial persons find acknowledging yet another subordinated status in their lives more than they are willing to do. Others, because of their close and supportive family relationships, more easily acknowledge their sexual orientation. Many other ethnic and racial LGB persons experience conflicts of allegiance between identifying with their sexual orientation or their ethnicity or race; often, they choose to maintain loyalty to their culture and family.
- Sexual identity of bisexual persons is complicated by several factors: lack of information, little community support, and confusion about what bisexuality entails. These factors predispose persons to identify as bisexual at later ages than persons identify as either lesbian or gay. Bisexual persons may not have role models for their feelings and behaviors, and they are sometimes pressured by gay and lesbian communities to choose a gay or lesbian identity. No empirically established models for coming out have been identified, although some researchers characterize the process as having four stages ranging from initial confusion to self-labeling (but with continued confusion).
- The range of experiences for transgender persons spans those who enjoy cross-dressing to those who want SRS. Many face the ridicule and rejection of their peers and family as they themselves try to understand their feelings and behaviors. As with other groups, transgender persons are more likely to identify as transgender once they meet others involved in similar journeys.
- The models for coming out are laudable for their focus on the developmental process in the lives of lesbian and gay persons. But the models were established with small samples

and other limitations and, for the most part, address only the cognitive processes of coming out. Only a couple of the models have had gone through any empirical assessments.

- The coming-out models have essential missing pieces such as social class, race, and ethnicity; bisexual orientation; transgender identity; adolescence and older age; social contexts and constructs; historical effects; sex–gender; immigration and acculturation; and disabilities and chronic illnesses.

CHAPTER 4
REFERENCES

Axtell, S. (1999). Disability and chronic illness identity: Interviews with lesbians and bisexual women and their partners. *Journal of Gay, Lesbian, and Bisexual Identity, 4,* 53–72.

Bennett, A. G. (1999). The "cure" that harms: Sexual orientation-based asylum and the changing definition of persecution. *Golden Gate University Law Review, 29,* 279–309.

Bohan, J. S., & Russell, G. M. (1999). Conceptual frameworks. In J. S. Bohan & G. M. Russell (Eds.), *Conversations about psychology and sexual orientation* (pp. 11–30). New York: New York University Press.

Bradford, J., & Ryan, C. (1991). Who we are: Health concerns of middle-aged lesbians. In B. J. Warshow & A. J. Smith (Eds.), *Lesbians at midlife: The creative transition* (pp.147–163). San Francisco: Spinsters.

Brady, S., & Busse, W. J. (1994). The gay identity questionnaire: A brief measure of homosexual identity formation. *Journal of Homosexuality, 26,* 1–22.

Cass, V. C. (1979). Homosexual identity formation: A theoretical model. *Journal of Homosexuality, 4,* 219–235.

Cass, V. C. (1984). Homosexual identity formation: Testing a theoretical model. *Journal of Sex Research, 20,* 143–167.

Cass, V. C. (1996). Sexual orientation identity formation: A western phenomenon. In R. P. Cabaj & T. S. Stein (Eds.), *Textbook of homosexuality and mental health* (pp. 227–251). Washington, DC: American Psychiatric Press.

Chapman, B. E., & Brannock, J. C. (1987). Proposed model of lesbian identity development: An empirical examination. *Journal of Homosexuality, 14,* 69–80.

Charbonneau, D., & Lander, P. (1991). Redefining sexuality: Women becoming lesbian in midlife. In B. Sang, J. Warshow, & A. Smith (Eds.), *Lesbians at midlife: The creative transition* (pp. 35–43). San Francisco: Spinsters.

Chung, Y. B., & Katayama, M. (1998). Ethnic and sexual identity development of Asian American lesbian and gay adolescents. *Professional School Counseling, 1,* 21–25.

Cohen, K. M., & Savin-Williams, R. C. (1996). Developmental perspectives on coming out to self and others. In R. C. Savin-Williams & K. M. Cohen (Eds.), *The lives of lesbians, gays, and bisexuals children to adults* (pp. 113–151). Fort Worth, TX: Harcourt Brace.

D'Augelli, A. R. (1996). Lesbian, gay, and bisexual development during adolescence and young adulthood. In R. P. Cabaj & T. S. Stein (Eds.), *Textbook of homosexuality and mental health* (pp. 267–287). Washington, DC: American Psychiatric Press.

D'Augelli, A. R., & Hershberger, S. L. (1993). Lesbian, gay, and bisexual youth in community settings: Personal challenges and mental health problems. *American Journal of Community Psychology, 21*, 421–448.

Degges-White, S., Rice, B., & Myers, J. E. (2000). Revisiting Cass' theory of sexual identity formation: A study of lesbian development. *Journal of Mental Health Counseling, 22*, 318–333.

Diamond, L. M. (1996). Attraction and identity: Evidence for sexual fluidity among young lesbian, bisexual, and heterosexual women. *Unpublished master's thesis*, Cornell University, Ithaca, NY.

Diamond, L. M. (1998). Development of sexual orientation among adolescent and young adult women. *Developmental Psychology, 34*, 1085–1095.

Dubé, E. M. (1997). *Sexual identity and intimacy development among two cohorts of sexual minority men.* Unpublished master's thesis, Cornell University, Ithaca, NY.

Espin, O. M. (1987). Issues of identity in the psychology of Latina lesbians. In Boston Lesbian Psychologies Collective (Eds.), *Lesbian psychologies: Explorations and challenges* (pp. 35–51). Urbana: University of Illinois Press.

Espin, O. M. (1997). Crossing borders and boundaries: The life narratives of immigrant lesbians. In B. Greene (Ed.), *Ethnic and cultural diversity among lesbians and gay men* (pp. 191–215). Thousand Oaks, CA: Sage Publications.

Esterberg, K. G. (1994). Being a lesbian and being in love: Constructing identity through relationships. *Journal of Gay & Lesbian Social Services, 1*, 57–82.

Esterberg, K. G. (1997). *Lesbian and bisexual identities: Constructing communities, constructing selves.* Philadelphia: Temple University Press.

Faderman, L. (1984–1985). The new "gay" lesbians. *Journal of Homosexuality, 10*, 85–95.

Fassinger, R. E. (1991). The hidden minority: Issues and challenges in working with lesbians and gay men. *Counseling Psychologist, 19*, 157–176.

Fassinger, R. E. (1994, February). *Sexual orientation and identity development: Human dignity for all?* Invited address at the 20th annual Maryland Student Affairs Conference, University of Maryland, College Park.

Fassinger, R. E., & Miller, B. A. (1996). Validation of an inclusive model of sexual minority identity formation on a sample of gay men. *Journal of Heterosexuality, 32,* 53–78.

Fontaine, J. H., & Hammond, N. L. (1996). Counseling issues with gay and lesbian adolescents. *Adolescence, 31,* 817-830.

Fox, R. C. (1995). Coming out bisexual: Identity, behavior, and sexual orientation self-disclosure (Doctoral dissertation, California Institute of Integral Studies, 1993). *Dissertation Abstracts International, 55*(12), 5565B.

Fox, R. C. (2000). Bisexuality in perspective: A review of theory and research. In B. Greene & G. L. Croom (Eds.), *Education, research, and practice in lesbian, gay, bisexual, and transgendered psychology* (Vol. 5, pp. 161–206). Thousand Oaks, CA: Sage Publications.

Gagné, P., & Tewksbury, J. R. (1999). Knowledge and power, body and self: An analysis of knowledge systems and the transgendered self. *Sociological Quarterly, 40,* 59–83.

Gagné, P., Tewksbury, R., & McGaughey, D. (1997). Coming out and crossing over: Identity formation and proclamation in a transgender community. *Gender & Society, 11,* 478–508.

Gonsiorek, J. C. (1993). Threat, stress, and adjustment: Mental health and the workplace for gay and lesbian individuals. In L. Diamant (Ed.), *Homosexual issues in the workplace* (pp. 242–263). Washington, DC: Taylor & Francis.

Gonsiorek, J. C. (1995). Gay male identities: Concepts and issues. In A. R. D'Augelli & C. J. Patterson (Eds.), *Lesbian, gay, and bisexual identities over the life span* (pp. 24–47). New York: Oxford University Press.

González, F. J., & Espin, O. M. (1996). Latino men, Latino women, and homosexuality. In R. P. Cabaj & T. S. Stein (Eds.), *Textbook of homosexuality and mental health* (pp. 583–601). Washington, DC: American Psychiatric Press.

Gruskin, E. P. (1999). *Treating lesbians and bisexual women: Challenges and strategies for health professionals.* Thousand Oaks, CA: Sage Publications.

Harry, J. (1993). Being out: A general model. *Journal of Homosexuality, 26,* 25–39.

Herdt, G. H. (1992). "Coming out" as a rite of passage: A Chicago study. In G. H. Herdt & A. Boxer (Eds.), *Gay culture in America: Essays from the field* (pp. 29–65). Boston: Beacon Press.

Herdt, G. H., Beeler, J., & Rawls, T. W. (1997). Life course diversity among older lesbians and gay men: A study in Chicago. *Journal of Gay, Lesbian, and Bisexual Identity, 2*, 231–246.

Horowitz, J. L., & Newcomb, M. D. (2002). A multidimensional approach to homosexual identity. *Journal of Homosexuality, 42*, 1–19.

Hunter, J., & Schaecher, R. (1987). Stresses on lesbian and gay adolescents in schools. *Social Work in Education, 9*, 180–189.

Isay, R. A. (1998). Heterosexually married homosexual men: Clinical and developmental issues. *American Journal of Orthopsychiatry, 68*, 424–432.

Jones, B. E., & Hill, M. J. (1996). African American lesbians, gay men, and bisexuals. In R. P. Cabaj & T. S. Stein (Eds.), *Textbook of homosexuality and mental health* (pp. 549–561). Washington, DC: American Psychiatric Press.

Kimmel, D. C., & Sang, B. E. (1995). Lesbians and gay men in midlife. In A. R. D'Augelli & C. J. Patterson (Eds.), *Lesbian, gay, and bisexual identities over the lifespan: Psychological perspectives* (pp. 190–214). New York: Oxford University Press.

Kirkpatrick, M. (1989a). Lesbians: A different middle-age? In J. Oldham & R. Liebert (Eds.), *New psychoanalytic perspectives: The middle years* (pp. 135–148). New Haven, CT: Yale University Press.

Kirkpatrick, M. (1989b). Middle age and the lesbian experience. *Women's Studies Quarterly, 17* 1–2, 87–96.

Kitzinger, C., & Perkins, R. (1993). *Changing our minds: Lesbian feminism and psychology.* New York: New York University Press.

Klein, F. (1993). *The bisexual option* (2nd ed.). New York: Harrington Park.

Lander, P. S., & Charbonneau, C. (1990). The new lesbian in midlife: Reconstructing sexual identity. In J. Hurtig, K. Gillogly, & T. Gulevich (Eds.), *Gender Transformations, Michigan Discussions in Anthropology, 9*, 1–14.

Levine, H. (1997). A further exploration of the lesbian identity developmental process and its measurement. *Journal of Homosexuality, 34*, 67–78.

Levine, H., & Evans, N. J. (1991). The development of gay, lesbian, and bisexual identities. In N. J. Evans & V. A. Wall (Eds.), *Beyond tolerance: Gays, lesbians, and bisexuals on campus* (pp. 1–24). Alexandria, VA: American College Personnel Association.

Linton, S. (1998). *Claiming disability: Knowledge and identity*. New York: New York University Press.

Martinez, D. G., & Sullivan, S. C. (1998). African American gay men and lesbians: Examining the complexity of gay identity development. *Journal of Human Behavior and the Social Environment, 1,* 243–264.

Matteson, D. R. (1996). Counseling and psychotherapy with bisexual and exploring clients. In B. A. Firestein (Ed.), *Bisexuality: The psychology and politics of an invisible minority* (pp. 185–213). Thousand Oaks, CA: Sage Publications.

McCarn, S. R., & Fassinger, R. E. (1996). Revisioning sexual minority identity formation: A new model of lesbian identity and its implications for counseling and research. *Counseling Psychologists, 24,* 508–534.

Nichols, M. (1990). Lesbian relationships: Implications for the study of sexuality and gender. In D. P. McWhirter, S. A. Sanders, & J. M. Reinisch (Eds.), *Homosexuality/heterosexuality: Concepts of sexual orientation* (pp. 350–364). New York: Oxford University Press.

Ochs, R. (1996). Biphobia: It goes more than two ways. In B. A. Firestein (Ed.), *Bisexuality: The psychology and politics of an invisible minority* (pp. 217–239). Thousand Oaks, CA: Sage Publications.

Olson, E. D., & King, C. A. (1995). Gay and lesbian self-identification: A response to Rotheram-Boras and Fernandez. *Suicide and Life-Threatening Behavior, 25,* 35–39.

Parks, C. (1999). Lesbian identity development: An examination of differences across generations. *American Journal of Orthopsychiatry, 69,* 347–361.

Ponse, B. (1980). Lesbians and their worlds. In J. Marmor (Ed.), *Homosexual behavior: A modern reappraisal* (pp. 157–175). New York: Basic Books.

Rosario, M., Meyer-Bahlburg, H.F.L., Hunter, J., Exner, T. M., Gwadz, M., & Keller, A. M. (1996). The psychosexual development of urban lesbian, gay, and bisexual youths. *Journal of Sex Research, 35,* 113–126.

Russell, G. M., & Bohan, J. S. (1999). Implications for clinical work. In J. S. Bohan & G. M. Russell (Eds.), *Conversations about psychology and sexual orientation* (pp. 31–56). New York: New York University Press.

Rust, P. C. (1992). The politics of sexual identity: Sexual attraction and behavior among lesbian and bisexual women. *Social Problems, 39,* 366–387.

Rust, P. C. (1993). "Coming out" in the age of social constructionism: Sexual identity formation among lesbian and bisexual women. *Gender & Society, 7,* 50–77.

Rust, P. C. (1996). Finding a sexual identity and community: Therapeutic implications and cultural assumptions in scientific models of coming out. In E. D. Rothblum & L. A. Bond (Eds.), *Preventing heterosexim and homophobia* (pp. 87–123). Thousand Oaks, CA: Sage Publications.

Sang, B. (1991). Moving toward balance and integration. In B. Sang, J. Warshow, & A. Smith (Eds.), *Lesbians at midlife: The creative transition* (pp. 206–214). San Francisco: Spinsters.

Savin-Williams, R. C. (1995). Lesbian, gay male, and bisexual adolescents. In A. R. D'Augelli & C. J. Patterson (Eds.), *Lesbian, gay, and bisexual identities over the lifespan* (pp. 165–189). New York: Oxford University Press.

Savin-Williams, R. C. (1998). ". . . and then I became gay": Young men's stories. New York: Routledge.

Savin-Williams, R. C., & Diamond, L. M. (1999). Sexual orientation. In W. K. Silverman & T. H. Ollendick (Eds.), *Developmental issues in the clinical treatment of children* (pp. 241–258). Boston: Allyn & Bacon.

Savin-Williams, R. C., & Diamond, L. M. (2000). Sexual identity trajectories among sexual-minority youths: Gender comparisons. *Archives of Sexual Behavior, 29,* 607–627.

Sophie, J. (1985-1986). A critical examination of stage theories of lesbian identity development. *Journal of Homosexuality, 12,* 39–51.

Stein, A. (1997). Difference, desire, and the self. In A. Stein (Ed.), *Sex and sexuality: Stories of a lesbian generation* (pp. 47–57). Berkeley: University of California Press.

Stein, T. S. (1993). Overview of new developments in understanding homosexuality. *Review of Psychiatry, 12,* 9–40.

Stein, T. S., & Cohen, C. J. (1984). Psychotherapy with gay men and lesbians: An examination of homophobia, coming-out, and identity. In E. S. Hetrick & T. S. Stein (Eds.), *Innovations in psychotherapy with homosexuals* (pp. 60–73). Washington, DC: American Psychiatric Press.

Vargo, M. E. (1998). *Acts of disclosure: The coming-out process of contemporary gay men.* New York: Harrington Park.

Weinberg, M. S., Williams, C. J., & Pryor, D. W. (1994). *Dual attraction: Understanding bisexuality.* New York: Oxford University Press.

Weinberg, M. S., Williams, C. J., & Pryor, D. W. (1998). Becoming and being "bisexual." In E. J. Haeberle & R. Gindorf (Eds.), *Bisexualities: The ideology and practice of sexual contact with both men and women* (pp. 169–181). New York: Continuum.

West, C. M. (1995). Mammy, Sapphire, and Jezebel: Historical images of black women and their implications for psychotherapy. *Psychotherapy, 32,* 458–466.

Whitman, J. S., Cormier, S., & Boyd, C. J. (2000). Lesbian identity management at various stages of the coming out process: A qualitative study. *International Journal of Sexuality and Gender Studies, 5,* 3–18.

Woodhouse, A. (1989). *Fantastic women: Sex, gender, and transvestism.* New Brunswick, NJ: Rutgers University Press.

CHAPTER 5
INDIVIDUALS: DISCLOSURES

What prevents LGBT persons from disclosing their sexual identity or sex–gender identification?

What are the processes of disclosure?

What are the likely reactions of parents?

How does ethnicity or culture impact the reactions of parents and other family members?

How do siblings react to disclosure?

How do marital partners and children react to disclosure?

How to friends react to disclosure?

Do most LGBT persons disclose at work? Why or why not?

What does disclosure management entail?

HIDING AND NOT HIDING

Lesbian, gay, and bisexual (LGB) persons are "in the closet" when they hide their sexual identity—to "come out of the closet" is to be open about their sexual identity (Gagné, Tewksbury, & McGaughey, 1997; Garnets, Herek, & Levy, 1990). As noted in Chapter 4, most coming-out models include the act of disclosure as an important step to finalizing the identity development process. Although this expectation for openness is not always realistic, the post-Stonewall philosophy (developed after the riots against police raids at the Stonewall Bar in Greenwich Village, NY, in 1969) is that invisibility reinforces negative stereotypes and, by that, perpetuates social oppression (D'Augelli & Garnets, 1995). Furthermore, it is argued that pretenses of heterosexuality support the notion that it is bad or wrong to be gay, lesbian, or bisexual (for example, Healy, 1993; Herek, 1991). In some communities, tension exists between those who agree with this post-Stonewall philosophy and those who do not. For example, Whittier (1997) reported disunity and animosity between "secretive" versus "open" gay persons in a small town in the southeastern United States.

Some LGB persons hide their sexual identity because of insecurities or negative feelings about themselves. They hide the private self they view as bad and unlovable (Grace, 1992). More often, though, LGB persons hide their sexual identity for other reasons (Cain, 1991a, 1991b). Many persons have not yet adjusted to their new identity and the related personal and social consequences (Williamson, 1998). Early in their development, LGB persons internalized the negative images of their sexual orientations (Borhek, 1988). They heard frequent heterosexist comments from family and peers, and they saw what happened to LGB persons who made disclosures (Martin, 1982). These persons may fear that openness about their sexual identity will lead to rejection by family and friends; religious condemnation; discrimination; and, possibly, verbal, emotional, physical, or other forms of harm (Remafedi, 1987b; Uribe &

Harbeck, 1991). Just as in the past, LGB persons can lose child custody (for example, Falk, 1989), jobs, and job promotions (for example, Hall, 1989; Levine & Leonard, 1984). If these persons live in small towns or rural areas, they may experience even more negative attitudes and reprisals (Hanley-Hackenbruck, 1989). Adolescents who are or think they might be gay or lesbian soon recognize that they are part of a stigmatized group. They hear name calling directed toward them or others and see malicious words scrawled on lockers and school walls about gay and lesbian persons. They know that disclosures are not safe, and they may live in fear of exposure (Hunter, 1995). Bisexual persons who acknowledge same sex–gender attractions risk negative responses and loss of support in the heterosexual as well as in lesbian and gay communities (Bohan, 1996). Racial and ethnic LGB persons who disclose their sexual identities are also vulnerable to rejection and loneliness in their families and communities (Espin, 1987; Loiacano, 1989).

As with the various milestones of coming out, disclosure happens at varying times for different persons (Radonsky & Borders, 1995; Savin-Williams, 1998a). Yet, despite the disincentives to disclose, the age of first disclosure has sharply declined since the 1970s (Savin-Williams, 1998a).

RANGE OF DISCLOSURES AND MOTIVATIONS FOR DISCLOSURES

From interviews with gay and lesbian educators, Griffin (1992) identified varying degrees of disclosure, ranging from no disclosure to complete openness: (a) totally closeted or telling no one; (b) passing or giving the impression that one is heterosexual; (c) covering or omitting information; (d) implicit disclosure or giving information but no label for one's sexual identity; (e) explicit disclosure or open information about one's sexual identity; and (f) public disclosure or openness with an entire group such as work associates.

LGB persons who make disclosures do so because of various motivations. Some of these motivations, identified by Cain (1991b), include

- relationship-building disclosures (trying to improve relationships with others, especially through increased closeness)
- problem-solving disclosures (trying to end constant questioning about one's private life or why one was never married)
- preventative disclosures (avoiding anticipated difficulties with friends and employers, telling them before they discover the information from someone else)
- political or ideological disclosures (making disclosures to promote political benefits through greater visibility of LGB persons).

LGB persons weigh choices regarding disclosures to multiple, sometimes overlapping, audiences including family (parents, siblings, extended family); friends (ranging from casual acquaintances to close friends); and persons in their social networks (for example, coworkers, religious leaders, teachers) (D'Augelli, 1996). The ramifications of disclosures to selected audiences are the focus of the remainder of this chapter. These audiences include the family of origin, marriage partners, children, friends, college settings, and work settings.

THE FAMILY

Disclosure to parents is the most difficult for LGB persons and probably evokes the greatest fear. In several studies of youth, fewer than 10 percent made the first disclosure to parents (for example, D'Augelli & Hershberger, 1993; Savin-Williams, 1998a). Transgender children also anticipate negative reactions from parents who assume not only that their children are heterosexual but also that their sex–gender identification matches their biological sex (Gagné et al., 1997). Fears of negative reactions can delay disclosures to parents by children of any age.

Brown (1989) identified several patterns of keeping one's sexual orientation hidden from the family, including distancing or maintaining a rigid emotional and geographical distance from the family. Another pattern, "I know you know," involves an unspoken accord not to discuss a family member's sexual orientation even though everyone knows it. This pattern provides stability in the family, but the price for the lesbian, gay, or bisexual person is a lack of acknowledgement of one's life. The family will probably also not acknowledge the partner or invite this person to family events. Another pattern, "don't tell your father," involves disclosure to a supportive sibling or mother. Thereafter, all agree not to tell other family members, especially the father.

Various researchers and writers who focus on LGB youth recommend that they carefully ponder whether or not to disclose to parents. Those who are not yet self-sufficient depend on their parents for financial support and other resources. If parents object to their child's sexual identify, the child could lose these resources (Bales, 1985; Hersch, 1988). Parents, Families, and Friends of Lesbians and Gays (PFLAG) groups encourage youth not to disclose to their families unless they are sure of a positive reaction or have secure alternatives if expelled from the family. Few youth have access to needed alternatives—an optional place to live, financial and emotional support, and a means for continuing their education (Henderson, 1998).

Even though they are independent from their families, some adult lesbian and gay persons still do not disclose to parents because they want to avoid conflict or reprisal for themselves (for example, Whittlin, 1983) and hurt or disappointment for their parents (Cramer & Roach, 1988). They want to continue to show deference to or respect for their parents' feelings or beliefs (Cain, 1991a).

Many LGB persons finally disclose their sexual identity to their families because of discomfort and guilt about misleading them (for example, Leaveck, 1994; Strommen, 1990). In addition, they may feel unhappy with the impersonal distance between themselves and their families and with their inner sense of isolation (for example, Brown, 1989; Cramer & Roach, 1988).

The early effects of disclosure to parents vary but often are negative. In a study of LGB youth, D'Augelli and Hershberger (1993) found that only 11 percent received a positive response from parents after disclosure. Other studies reported that 43 percent of gay youth (Remafedi, 1987b) and 42 percent of lesbian youth (Telljohann & Price, 1993) indicated that their parents reacted in a negative manner.

LGB persons generally anticipate a more negative response from their fathers than from their mothers. The young adult lesbian and gay persons studied by Ben-Ari (1995) usually told their mothers about their sexual orientation in a face-to-face meeting but told their fathers in a letter. In a sample of 194 youth, D'Augelli and Hershberger (1993) found that only two respondents first disclosed to their fathers. Other studies showed that most lesbian and gay persons are out only to their mothers (62 to 69 percent) whereas fewer are out to their fathers (39 to 55 percent) (Boxer, Cook, & Herdt, 1991; Savin-Williams, 1998b). In a sample of older lesbian and gay persons, Beeler, Rawls, Herdt, and Cohler (1999) discovered that 45 percent were out to their mothers and fewer (28 percent) were out to their fathers. The strong preference of the 506 African American lesbian and 673 African American gay persons studied by Mays, Chatters, Cochran, and Mackness (1998) was to make disclosures to women in their families (both mothers and sisters) instead of to men.

LGB persons may more often disclose to their mothers because they more often display unconditional acceptance of their children than do fathers. Most studies show that mothers are perceived as more supportive than fathers (55 percent versus 37 percent, D'Augelli & Hershberger, 1993; 90 percent versus 75 percent, D'Augelli, Hershberger, & Pilkington, 1998; 21 percent versus 10 percent, Remafedi, 1987a). Of the ethnic and racial youth studied by Pilkington and D'Augelli (1995), 25 percent experienced their father's reactions as rejective compared to 22 percent of their mothers' reactions. Nevertheless, Cramer and Roach (1988) reported initial negative responses from 55 percent of men's mothers compared to 42 percent of fathers. In their sample of LGB youth, D'Augelli and Hershberger (1993) found that 36 percent of fathers were tolerant compared to 25 percent of mothers.

Rarely are parents unaffected upon first learning of their child's LGB identity. They may experience considerable inner turmoil (DeVine, 1983–1984) including shock, devastation, humiliation, denial, and anger. Some parents who feel responsible for their child's sexual orientation feel guilt and a sense of failure as parents (Bernstein, 1990; Griffin, Wirth, & Wirth, 1986; Robinson, Walters, & Skeen, 1989). Parents who feel this way still believe older theories that blamed the mother primarily and the father secondarily for "homosexuality" in children (Scasta, 1998). Parents of transgender children may also express guilt over what they did or did not do to "cause this" to happen to their children (Rosenfeld & Emerson, 1998).

Though parents may display similar initial reactions to their children's disclosures, the range and intensity of these reactions can vary (Greene & Herek, 1994). They can involve one or more of these typical responses:

- *Estrangement.* Parents often feel estranged from their child; this person is a stranger or someone they no longer know. Some of their questions reflect this reaction, for example, "How should we act with our child now?" (Bernstein, 1990).
- *Rejection of the family role of the child.* Some parents claim that their child no longer has a role or identity as a family member (Collins & Zimmerman, 1983; DeVine, 1983–1984). Some of them experience profound grief as if their child were dead (Robinson et al., 1989).
- *Lost hopes and dreams.* Another question parents often have is, "What will happen to the hopes and dreams we had for this child?" (Bernstein, 1990). Before parents knew that their child was lesbian, gay, or bisexual, they assumed a heterosexual orientation and typically anticipated that their child would experience a traditional family life and provide grandchildren and continuation of the family lines. The parents may now feel that these dreams are gone forever (Bernstein, 1990; Scasta, 1998).
- *Concealment of shameful knowledge.* When parents experience distress about a child, they often turn to family and friends for advice, physicians or mental health professionals for physical or psychological aid, and their church for moral and spiritual guidance. Parents of a LGB child, however, usually feel that they cannot use these sources of support. They are ashamed

Affirmative Practice: Understanding and Working with Lesbian, Gay, Bisexual, and Transgender Persons

of their child's sexual orientation or sex–gender expression and do not want to expose themselves to possible rejection from others who may also disapprove. Parents sometimes distance themselves from close friends if they predict rejection from them (Bernstein, 1990; Rosenfeld & Emerson, 1998).

- *Perpetuation of violence.* Parents and other family members may perpetrate verbal and physical violence on LGBT youth in the home (Durby, 1994; Savin-Williams, 1994). Almost half (49 percent) of the lesbian and gay youth studied by Martin and Hetrick (1988) were physically assaulted at home, either by parents or siblings. More than one-third (36 percent) of the gay and lesbian youth in support groups studied by Pilkington and D'Augelli (1995) reported that family members verbally assaulted them and one in 10 was physically assaulted. Older males in the family most often perpetrated the violence, usually the father (D'Augelli, 1991b) but sometimes an uncle or a brother (Martin & Hetrick, 1988). The most abused youth were those with a history of childhood "femininity" and poor relationships with their fathers (Harry, 1989) or those who were transgender and did not meet cultural ideals of suitable behaviors and roles for their sex–gender (Savin-Williams & Cohen, 1996).

- *Cast the child out of the home.* Aside from verbally and physically abusing the child, parents who are extremely rejective might cast out their "unacceptable" child, including putting the child out on the street (Hersch, 1988; Martin & Hetrick, 1988). Males are at greater risk for expulsion from the home, whereas females may face more physical and emotional abuse (Hunter & Martin, 1984). Bales (1985) attributed at least part of teenage male prostitution in the United States to the banishment of gay adolescents from the home.

RACIAL AND ETHNIC FAMILIES

Several racial and ethnic youth identified by Savin-Williams (1998a) believed that they could not successfully negotiate the development of a positive gay or bisexual identity until they disclosed to their parents. For most racial and ethnic lesbian and gay youth and adults, however, the particular needs and values of their racial and ethnic groups present obstacles for both their identity development and their disclosures (Smith, 1983).

Most ethnic and racial persons feel inextricably tied to their racial or ethnic communities because of oppression and the consequent need for group bonds (Kanuha, 1990). Their communities and extended families, often the main reference groups for these persons, provide most of their social networks and support. In addition, because the family in most racial and ethnic communities provides the basic means of survival for the culture, family expectations take precedence over individual wishes (for example, Chan, 1992; Wooden, Kawasaki, & Mayeda, 1983).

Disclosures of same sex–gender or bisexual sexual orientation by racial or ethnic children is equivalent to putting themselves before their racial or ethnic groups, thereby threatening survival of the culture (Kanuha, 1990). Disclosure risks disgrace not only for themselves but also for their families, including their ancestors. These children are to accept, without question, the cultural obligations of marriage and perpetuation of the family name (Savin-Williams, 1998b). So, LGB members feel that they must conform to acceptable outward roles (Chan, 1992).

These themes appear in all family-centered cultures. Unique issues also exist, though, among different racial and ethnic groups (Rust, 1996).

African American Families

Five basic reasons may influence African American gay and lesbian persons to hide their same sex–gender attractions from their families (Stokes & Peterson, 1998). First, conservative Christian religiosity dominates African American communities (Bonilla & Porter, 1990; Greene, 1996). Their Christian churches (often called "Black churches") claim that the Bible forbids sex between two persons of the same sex–gender (Crisp, Priest, & Torgerson, 1998; Peterson, 1992). Second, African American heterosexual men and women who ardently want "normalcy" in their communities may feel embarrassed about gay and lesbian members (Poussaint, 1990). Third, strong pressures enforce sex–gender role conformity (Icard, 1985–1986). Young African American males are particularly likely to label any male a "sissy" who does not conform to expected sex–gender role behaviors, mannerisms, and gestures (Jones & Hill, 1996). Fourth, negative reactions to gay persons result from a perceived shortage of marriageable African American men and the implications for the continuation of the race (Dyne, 1980). Fifth, African American women may disapprove of lesbians because their status is lower than the status associated with heterosexual sexual orientation and privilege (Greene, 1997).

Although these beliefs have propagated rejection from African American families, in recent years, ambivalence, tolerance, and acceptance have emerged. Family norms of "Don't ask so they won't tell" or "Be silent and invisible" may also allow the family to accept a lesbian, gay, or bisexual family member without directly dealing with the reality of their sexual identity and the conflicts associated with it (Manalansan, 1996; Smith, 1997). Gay African American men are more accepted when they focus on their accomplishments within the African American community instead of their sexual activities or sexual identity (Hawkeswood, 1990).

African American LGB persons are pushing for more openness and acceptance in their communities. The increase in HIV/AIDS has forced communities to confront their existence more directly. Some political leaders now include open lesbian and gay persons in political coalitions. Most civil rights organizations support civil rights for these persons and in their bylaws oppose discrimination directed at LGBT persons. Open groups also now exist in a few African American churches. Still, these persons may experience considerable stress about living openly in lesbian and gay communities. They also may have concerns about their personal safety, HIV/AIDS, and whether they can be successful in relationships (Jones & Hill, 1996).

Latino Families

Overt acknowledgment and disclosure of a gay or lesbian identity will likely meet with disapproval in Latino families (for example, Espin, 1984, 1987; Morales, 1992). These families are less outspoken about moral disapproval of same sex–gender sexual orientation than are African American families (Bonilla & Porter, 1990), but they maintain strong conservative attitudes, cultivated by Catholicism (Carballo-Diéguez, 1989; Rodriguez, 1996). The Catholic Church also prescribes family and sex–gender roles. Men, for example, must provide for, protect, and defend the family. If gay, men are viewed as deserting these obligations (Morales, 1992).

Additionally, the Latino culture rigidly adheres to the traditions and practices of *machismo* and *marianismo* in the socialization of males and females. Males are expected to become dominant and independent, characteristics of machismo, whereas females are expected to model behaviors that manifest marianismo or represent the virtues of the Virgin Mary (Reyes, 1992). Males who do not model machismo are tagged with various negative labels such as: (a) "alien," "odd," "of another way," and "broken"; (b) "inferior" or *joto* (meaning of no significance or worth); and (c) "feminine," "butterflies," or "not masculine" (Morales, 1996). Some Latino families think that gay persons are nonmen or that they are feminine-identified drag queens (Moraga & Hollibaugh, 1985).

Unless openly "butch," lesbians are more invisible in Latino communities than are gay persons. Families may even encourage single women to participate in emotionally close friendships with other women with no presumption that these might be lesbian relationships (Espin, 1984, 1987). If, however, it becomes known that a daughter is linked with a lesbian partner, she may pay an even higher price than a gay son because the violation of her prescribed sex–gender role threatens the preservation of cultural continuity (Espin, 1997). Latino lesbians also violate *etiquela* or the proper sex–gender role for Latino females that mandates patience, nurturance, passivity, and subservience (for example, Ramos, 1994). Latino women must remain virtuous, hence, some women may live with their parents until marriage (Morales, 1992). Abandoning these sex–gender role expectations is tantamount to trying to overthrow men or threaten men's dominance and the masculine Latino cultural heritage. Such women are labeled *macho* or man haters (for example, Ramos, 1994). Latino lesbians also threaten the cultural norms of their community because they may encourage other Latino women to question their status in their families and to imagine possibilities for their independence (Trujillo, 1991). Moreover, they also force the culture to confront the sexuality of women (Espin, 1987; González & Espin, 1996). Good Latino women are not viewed as sexual. Single lesbians are more acceptable than those with sexual partners and viewed as promiscuous and unchaste (Espin, 1984, 1987; Ramos, 1994).

Some open lesbian and gay family members maintain a place in the family and experience quiet tolerance. This does not mean, however, that the family approves of their sexual orientation but instead that they most likely deny it (Morales, 1996). Yet, increasingly, families display varying levels of acceptance because of dissimilarities in national origin, acculturation and assimilation statuses, socioeconomic status, educational level, and geographical residence. Traditional Latino conceptions of manhood and womanhood are moving to a more egalitarian model. This is attributed mostly to expanded education, exposure to American culture, and the influence of feminism (Marsiglia, 1998).

Asian American Families

The family and its heritage loom large in the lives of Asian American youth (Savin-Williams, 1998b). The family dictates the behavior of the children, if not always their attitudes (Savin-Williams, 1998b). Parents may regard same sex–gender sexual identity as an act of treason against the family and the culture (Greene, 1997). If children make disclosures, parents may refuse to discuss their new identity with them and may build a wall of silence around them (Liu & Chan, 1996; Savin-Williams, 1996).

The most notable expectations in Asian families for children are unquestioned obedience and unending demand for conformity (Chan, 1992). Obedience is to be shown through respect and loyalty to parents and other elders (for example, Liu & Chan, 1996; Lopez & Lam, 1998) followed by loyalty to one's siblings and then to one's marital partner (Liu & Chan, 1996). The demand for conformity in the Asian American family centers around expected sex–gender roles. Rejection of these roles threatens the continuation of the family line (Chan, 1992; Wooden et al., 1983). Asian sons are the carriers of the family name, linkage, and heritage. They are expected, therefore, to marry, provide heirs (Chan, 1989), and care for older parents (Lopez & Lam, 1998). Women are obligated to fulfill the roles of dutiful daughter, wife, and mother (Chan, 1992).

The tight restrictions in the Asian American family can seem oppressive, but the family also bestows support, affection, and security. Gay and lesbian children, therefore, may not be willing to risk losing their family bond by disclosure, especially to their parents (Chan, 1989). Others, more assimilated into Western culture, are more open about their sexual identity, albeit often only in non-Asian contexts (Chan, 1997; Nakajima, Chan, & Lee, 1996) and seldom to their parents (Chan, 1989).

A large number of Vietnamese families immigrated to the United States as refugees following the Vietnam War. The children strive for perfection and want to conform to the Asian traditions maintained by their parents. The fear of discovery becomes a source of mental pressure and anguish for gay and lesbian children in Vietnamese families. Sons, especially, experience considerable difficulty in attempting to reconcile cultural and sexual identity conflicts (Lopez & Lam, 1998; Timberlake & Cook, 1984). The Vietnamese culture morally and socially condemns "homosexuality." Vietnamese families often castigate and abandon gay sons (Lopez & Lam, 1998) and label them *lai cai*, meaning "half man and half woman" ("Dong," 1992).

Native American Families

In contrast to other ethnic groups, Native American lesbian and gay persons do not anticipate disapproval by the traditional Indian community. Few Native American families repudiate relatives because of a disclosure of "difference" (Brown, 1997) or pressure them to be other than who they are (Jacobs & Brown, 1997). Despite sexual orientation, the membership of Native Americans in a clan, an extended family, a tribe, or a nation never changes (Tofoya, 1996). Yet, in contrast to other ethnic and racial groups, the attitudes of more acculturated Native Americans (for example, third and fourth generations) are often more negative. This is attributed in large part to their adoption of Western Christian religions (Walters, 1997).

Many Native American lesbian and gay persons living on rural reservations move to larger urban areas and join Native American lesbian and gay communities in these locations. There they can be more open about their sex–gender relationships. They also find more opportunities for work and education (Lang, 1999). To attain these benefits, however, they lose support from their culture and family (Greene, 1997; Williams, 1986).

Greek American Families

Greek American families usually avoid talking about same sex–gender sexual orientation altogether. Whether adolescents or adults, gay and lesbian persons often collude with their families' wishes and do not share their feelings or concerns. Bonded by love and loyalty, these families maintain a link with their LGB children, albeit, at times, a superficial one depending on assimilation of the family into the dominant American culture. But, many Greek Americans who are several generations removed from immigration continue to identify strongly with their Greek heritage (Fygetakis, 1997).

PARENTS' PROGRESSION OVER TIME

Though families and their gay, lesbian, or bisexual member(s) can experience considerable distress, they can also move beyond it. Parents must come to terms with their gay, lesbian, or bisexual child (Strommen, 1990), but they need time to adapt (Scasta, 1998). They must identify and reevaluate previous negative attitudes, move from stigmatized to nonstigmatized beliefs, revise their dreams for their child, construct a new identity for their child, and come to accept the new identity (for example, Brown, 1989; Strommen, 1989, 1990). Several theorists categorized into stages various challenges that White parents confront (for example, McCubbin & Patterson, 1983; Neisen, 1987; Robinson et al., 1989).

The stage approach of Savin-Williams and Dubé (1998) is summarized here. First, parents may experience an initial reaction of shock, followed by *denial* and *isolation*. At some level, parents may already know of their child's LGB orientation but refuse to believe it, refuse to discuss it, try to convince their child that it is not real, or dismiss it as a temporary phase, experimentation, or rebellion. Parents may feel isolated if they think they are in a unique situation. Second, parents may react with *anger, agitation*, or even *rage*. Third, parents may *bargain* or try to make various exchanges—for instance, not throwing a child out of the house or ending an allowance if the child agrees to "convert" back to being heterosexual. Or, they may bargain for the child to tell no one else. Fourth, anger evolves into *depression*. If others discover the facts about their child, parents may feel humiliated and ashamed. The final stage is *acceptance*, often facilitated by education and support groups. In this stage, parents no longer see their child's same sex–gender or bisexual sexual orientation as temporary—nor is it kept a secret. Only a few parents, however, become proud of a gay, lesbian, or bisexual child.

The reactions of families with a transgender member seem comparable to those in families with a gay, lesbian, or bisexual member. A family who discovers a member's cross sex–gender behavior often experiences *shock* and *denial*. If the person does not assume a full-time cross sex–gender role or lives away from home, the family may be able to maintain denial. If this is not the case, eventually the shock and denial diminish and the predominant feeling becomes *anger*. Often, frustration and scapegoating are directed at the transgender person for upsetting the family with "crazy" ideas or behaviors. All the family's difficulties are blamed on this member. During the next phase, *bargaining*, family members may threaten the transgender member with disinheritance if this person will not behave "normally" or at least keep cross-dressing or sexual reassignment surgery secret. Parents may offer money for the child to go to college or begin a business. But, as reality sets in, family members often experience depression, weeping, physical illness, or suicide. The transgender member may also experience these reactions. Sometimes family members withdraw, use drugs, and if the discord escalates, the parents may divorce. Family members reach the *acceptance* phase when they confront the loss of the person they once knew and no longer try to force the person to change. The family shifts from its own concerns to concerns about the welfare of the transgender member (Emerson & Rosenfeld, 1996; Rosenfeld & Emerson, 1998).

Parents Who Make No Progress and Those Who Do

Parents who do not progress to more acceptance of their LGB or T child subscribe to the negative stereotypes about these persons and apply them to their child. They blame the child for causing disruption in the family (Strommen, 1990) and use other ineffective coping strategies such as scapegoating and avoidance (Collins & Zimmerman, 1983; DeVine, 1983–1984). Due to inflexible rules and norms (Laird, 1996), they tend to get stuck at the initial point of conflict and fail to move away from their stereotypes, negative thinking, and feelings of anger and disappointment. Consequently, the hostile, strained family situation does not improve (Strommen, 1990). Parents who are disparaging and offensive may later blame themselves for family rifts that may take years to repair, if they can be repaired at all (Mattison & McWhirter, 1995).

A good result in families of LGB or T persons requires a strong affectional bond (Williamson, 1998). Transgender persons who make disclosures to parents often believe that the relationship bond will weather the strain. Given time and space to adjust to the information, responses from parents are mostly accepting, tolerant, and supportive (Gagné et al., 1997). Williamson pointed out that the best outcomes for LGBT persons require parents to tolerate different values and lives, but it is equally important for children to understand and support their parents.

Parents who make a positive adaptation eventually accept the new identity of their child. They eventually acknowledge loss of the child's former identity and grieve over the loss (Collins & Zimmerman, 1983; DeVine, 1983–1984). They also renounce negative stereotypes associated with lesbian and gay persons (Strommen, 1990) and develop new values that do not stigmatize them (Bernstein, 1990). Accepting parents also gain the perspective that sexuality is only one part of the total child they love (Strommen, 1990). Although the expected time for parents to accept their child's same sex–gender sexual orientation is about two years (Robinson et al. 1989), the time needed for any particular parent is likely to vary from months to many years (Sauerman, 1984). In ethnic and racial families, rigid attitudes and stereotypes about same sex–gender sexual orientation may change when the family no longer feels bound by traditional religion and culture (Tremble, Schneider, & Appathurai, 1989).

DISCLOSURE TO OTHER FAMILY MEMBERS

Siblings

A sibling is often the first person in the family who gay or lesbian persons tell about their sexual orientation, especially if a significant link exists between the siblings (DeVine, 1983–1984). Several studies reported that many lesbian and gay persons are out to their siblings (62 to 72 percent) (Green, Bettinger, & Zacks, 1996; Savin-Williams, 1998b). Sometimes another relative (for example, grandmother, aunt, uncle, cousin) is the first person told if, again, a particularly significant bond is present (D'Augelli & Hershberger, 1993).

For Asian Americans, a sister is often a source of support, and disclosures happen more often with sisters than with parents (Chan, 1989). Urban African American and Latino gay and bisexual male youth, however, are less likely to disclose to siblings (30 percent) than to peers (90 percent) or mothers (50 percent). Yet, disclosures to siblings happen somewhat more often than to fathers (20 percent) (Murray, 1994).

Siblings generally are more accepting than rejecting (D'Augelli, 1991a; Savin-Williams, 1995). But when they are the only family members who know the sexual identity of a brother or sister, they may feel awkward and uncomfortable as a co-conspirator in the cover-up. This may lead to their disclosing the information to the parents (Murray, 1994). When a transgender person discloses to a younger sibling, this family member does not typically view a transgender brother or sister as any different than before and does not go through a grieving process. Older siblings, however, experience a sense of loss, as do their parents (Rosenfeld & Emerson, 1998).

Marital Partners

Most men who identify as bisexual following marriage soon tell their partners (Weinberg, Williams, & Pryor, 1994) but gay persons married to women rarely disclose their sexual orientation because they fear the reaction of their wives and children. They also want to preserve job security and social status (Strommen, 1989, 1990). Lesbian wives do not often make disclosures to marital partners either. Upon disclosure, the partners may react in a severe and angry manner, sometimes including physical violence. Lesbian mothers fear custody battles especially when their partners express extreme animosity toward them (Hanscombe & Forster, 1982).

Some gay and lesbian persons disclose to their marriage partners because of guilt about living a double life and anxiety about hiding their same sex–gender sexual desires (Strommen, 1989). Since the partners most likely never thought of them as anything other than heterosexual, they understandably feel astounded upon hearing the disclosure. Data on these disclosures, largely based on indirect anecdotal accounts, suggest that a partner's reactions are similar to those of parents (for example, Hanscombe & Forster, 1982; Kirkpatrick, Smith, & Roy, 1981). Initially, marital partners experience shock, sense of estrangement, confusion, guilt, stigma, and sense of loss. They may feel that they failed as wives or husbands (Gochros, 1985). A forced or unwanted disclosure, as from a husband who discovers that he is HIV+, can cause an explosive crisis. A wife does not just confront a partner's bisexual or gay sexual orientation and marital infidelity but the possibility of being HIV+ also. This situation can lead to feelings of loss, betrayal, vulnerability, and uncertainty about the future (Paul, 1996).

When a male partner in a heterosexual marriage acknowledges bisexuality, he must prepare for a variety of reactions from his wife. She may react with confusion, hurt, rage, grief, disgust, shame, resentment, betrayal, loss, confusion, inadequacy, powerlessness, or any combination of these feelings. If she cannot accept his bisexuality, he must decide either to suppress his same sex–gender attractions or lose his marital partner (Paul, 1992; Stokes & Damon, 1995).

Once a lesbian, gay, or bisexual person makes a disclosure to a marital partner, the final resolution is usually divorce (Coleman, 1985a, 1985b; Gochros, 1985). The divorce rates reported by Wyers (1987) were high for both lesbian (97 percent) and gay (78 percent) persons. In the sample of married gay persons studied by Scott and Ortiz (1996), divorce typically occurred for 73 percent of the sample and typically between the self-acceptance and disclosure phases of coming out.

Lesbian and bisexual women end marriages more quickly; their lack of sexual desire for the heterosexual partner, their husbands' disparagement of their sexual orientation, and a dislike of open marriages or secret extramarital relationships are often the reasons (Coleman, 1985a; Matteson, 1987). Although a husband's revelation of a gay or bisexual sexual orientation also can lead to separation or divorce, these outcomes happen more often from a wife's disclosure (Bozett, 1982).

Sometimes partners restructure their marital arrangements to adjust to a same sex–gender or bisexual sexual orientation with an open or semi-open marriage or an "asexual" friendship between the marital partners. But integrating a lesbian, gay, or bisexual partner with a heterosexual partner is not an easy endeavor (Gochros, 1989; Stokes & Damon, 1995; Whitney, 1990).

Marriages with a Transgender Partner

Partners of transgender persons also experience a variety of reactions. Some wives of transgender persons who cross-dress express confusion about these activities of their husbands. Other wives find sex–gender confused men appealing (Hunt & Main, 1997). Generally, however, the reaction of wives to the revelation of the partner's transgender identity is negative. They feel betrayed and wonder what other secrets their partner is hiding (Anderson, 1998; Emerson & Rosenfeld, 1996). Some partners feel abandoned, left out, used, and no longer needed. Partners just recognizing that they are transgender may become increasingly absorbed in cross-dressing, and their wives may become secondary to this activity (Hunt & Main, 1997). If a wife discovers the partner's transgender identity before the partner reveals it, she may experience more intense feelings of betrayal and possibly will want to abandon the relationship. Because of rage, she may disclose the transgender identity of her partner to others. Studies on other partnerships such as those involving a wife who is transgender (or partnerships with two transgender persons) are rare (Cole, Denny, Eyler, & Samons, 2000).

One of the largest studies reported to date on women in relationships with transgender men is a six-year longitudinal study on 106 pairs. The men were predominantly cross-dressers. The women, who were members of informal discussion groups throughout the country, reported that issues of betrayal and lost trust were major obstacles to intimacy with a cross-dressing partner. Yet, divorce was not prevalent; over two-thirds of the wives never seriously thought about divorce or separation (Brown, 1998).

Children

The question of when to disclose to children remains unanswered (Scasta, 1998). Relationships between transgender parents and their children are often strained because of the distance parents create to try to keep their children from discovering their identity (Anderson, 1998). Whereas some of these parents may struggle with hiding their identity, those who cross-dress struggle with hiding clothing and makeup. Because disclosure to children is a central issue in families with gay and lesbian parents, this issue is addressed further in Chapter 7.

Friends

Disclosures are most often first made to one's friends as the safest and most supportive group (for example, Herdt & Boxer, 1993; Savin-Williams, 1990). Close to three-quarters (73 percent) of gay and lesbian youth studied by D'Augelli and Hershberger (1993) first told a friend about their same sex–gender sexual attractions. In samples of gay youth studied by Savin-Williams (1995, 1998a), the first person told was usually a best friend or the person they were dating. Bisexual men and women disclosed more to friends (and to partners, including their marital partners, or practitioners) than to others, including family members and work colleagues (for example, Fox, 1995; Weinberg et al., 1994). A large percentage (83 percent) of a sample of older lesbian and gay persons studied by Beeler et al. (1999) reported that most of their friends knew of their sexual identities.

Most of the gay youth studied by Savin-Williams (1998a) reported that responses from friends following disclosure were variable, but the vast majority of both male and female friends expressed support, acceptance, and encouragement. Gay and bisexual African American and Latino male youth from the Hetrick-Martin Institute in New York City were surprised when disclosure to friends turned out as a positive event (Rotheram-Borus, Rosario, & Koopman, 1991). But, in another sample of gay youth studied by Remafedi (1987b), 41 percent reported negative reactions from friends. In the Weinberg et al. (1994) study of bisexual persons, responses by friends to the disclosure of a person's bisexual sexual orientation were benign.

Other Arenas: The Workplace Example

Every arena that LGB persons enter raises the question of whether to make disclosures. They may be open about their sexual identity in every area of their lives except work. This lack of openness at work is not startling as discrimination is rampant in the workplace as are potential harassment and other abuses (for example, Croteau & Lark, 1995; Woods & Lucas, 1993). Just the thought of disclosure at work typically creates considerable anxiety (Jordan & Deluty, 1998). No matter how competent and adept they are, LGB employees still anticipate devaluation by their coworkers and their employers if their sexual identity is revealed (Levine & Leonard, 1984). Transgender persons also receive negative reactions at work—harassment from other workers and demotion, termination, or pressures to resign (Gagné et al., 1997).

Often, secrecy at work is an adaptive stance (D'Emilio, 1983; Hetherington & Orzek, 1989). To try to avoid detection, various strategies include:

- maintaining firm boundaries between personal and work life (Hall, 1986, 1989; Kitzinger, 1991)
- conforming to expected sex–gender role dress, appearance, and hairstyles (Kitzinger, 1991)
- avoiding situations and conversations where hints of one's sexual identity can occur (Levine & Leonard, 1984; Shachar & Gilbert, 1983)
- hiding one's discomfort with heterosexist comments and jokes (Byrne, 1993)
- directing attention from oneself (Hall, 1989; Levine & Leonard, 1984)
- presenting a "heterosexual front" with made-up heterosexual dates, fiancées, and marital partners (Byrne, 1993; Peters & Cantrell, 1993)
- changing the pronoun of a same sex–gender partner in conversations with work associates or referring to the partner as a "friend" at social gatherings (Byrne, 1993).

Although the strategies identified here may be successful, separation between one's private life (sexual orientation) and public life (employee) can be costly. To pass, gay and lesbian persons do not place pictures of partners on office desks and rarely take partners to office functions (Byrne, 1993). Unlike heterosexual coworkers, they do not discuss their home life or what they do on weekends. Positive events such as engagements or anniversaries are not celebrated at work. Even painful breakups cannot be shared (Kitzinger, 1991). Workers who "pass" at work report experiencing depression, hostility, anxiety, low self-esteem, ill health, and high rates of substance misuse (Brooks, 1991; Triandis, Kurowski, & Gelfand, 1994).

Living a double life can also place a person in an ethical conflict (Levine & Leonard, 1984), for example, saying nothing when one hears antilesbian or gay jokes at work (Croteau & Hedstrom, 1993). In a sample of lesbians, 30 to 45 years of age, Boatwright, Gilbert, Forrest, and Ketzenberger (1996) found that though they feared that discovery at work would lead to the loss of respect from coworkers, they also feared that they would hate themselves for not being honest. Even when secrecy seems right or sensible, disclosure can become more of an issue of emotion than of logic. Values and meaning can override "objective success" (Gonsiorek, 1993). Honesty is so important for some workers that even negative reactions do not deter their commitment to be open (Shallenberger, 1994).

DISCLOSURE MANAGEMENT

Disclosure is the "end stage" of most coming-out models, but this can lead to a misconception that disclosure is a one-time event. Instead, it is a complex, grueling, and never finished endeavor (Gonsiorek, 1993; Kitzinger, 1991). As shown throughout this chapter, LGBT persons must constantly weigh when to disclose, to whom, and possible consequences (Walters & Phillips, 1994). Some persons may disclose to coworkers on a particular job but revert to the closet if they change jobs. Returning to the closet may also happen when moving from a large city to a small town (Cruikshank, 1992). In late life, persons may decide to close the door on the closet—possibly for good—if, for example, they must enter a predominantly heterosexual and likely heterosexist nursing home.

In a study of gay persons, Cain (1991a) found that respondents did a cost–benefit analysis to determine whether to make a disclosure. Some felt that disclosure was not worth the costs or the risks outweighed the costs of remaining hidden. Without a beneficial return such as more honesty and self-respect, or a closer link, disclosure was not worth the risks. Gonsiorek (1993) recommended rational "outness," or being as open as possible but closed if necessary to protect oneself from discrimination. If one wants to be honest, Gartrell (1984) recommended presenting one's sexual identity in a direct, factual, and calm manner with no invitation for detailed or intimate discussion. For example, when answering an intrusive question such as "Are you married?" the response could be "No, I'm a lesbian and involved in a relationship." Some LGB persons, however, do not weigh costs and benefits of disclosure or strategize how to deliver them.

In a qualitative study of lesbians and identity management, Whitman, Cormier, and Boyd (2000) discovered that some of these are in a "living out" mode. They live outside the closet in everything they do and no matter whom they are interacting with. These women are no longer managing their identity.

SUMMARY

- Like all subordinated groups, LGBT persons understand the heterosexism of the mainstream culture. They understand that they may not only be the targets of discrimination but also the targets of repudiation, rejection, and even violence. They may be hesitant to disclose their sexual orientation to friends, family members, or society at large.

- Some LGBT persons disclose early in their coming-out process though most models of coming out indicate that disclosure occurs later. Some disclose totally to all family members, coworkers, and friends; they participate openly in political and social events and encourage others to do the same. Others disclose along a continuum of possibilities; they may disclose only to a few trusted friends; only to family; only to family and friends but to no one at work. Disclosures may occur at any phase of life, although the age of disclosure is decreasing.

- The reactions of parents are eventually generally positive, especially among mothers; most parents go through stages of reactions from shock to acceptance. Few parents expel children from their homes or abandon them for life, although these reactions are documented and prevalent in families where relationships have always been strained and coping mechanisms limited. Siblings are usually the most accepting and, frequently, the first family members trusted with disclosure.

- Generally, racial and ethnic parents react according to their cultural backgrounds. Many racial and ethnic LGBT children experience angry rejection from their parents following disclosure. The parents feel betrayed that their children are not living up to the cultural mandates for sex–gender roles. African American parents are, typically, religious conservatives and rebuff their children for "choosing" a sinful life. Latino families operate under the machismo and marianismo traditions and are scornful of children who do not conform to these traditions. Asian, including Vietnamese, parents have a strong sense of respect for elders and consider disclosure an act of rebellion. Native American parents who remain immersed in their tribal traditions are less likely to judge their LGBT children, although the more acculturated they are, the more rejecting. In Greek families, LGBT children feel pressured to cover up their identities in order to conform to their parent's wishes to avoid the topic. Facing these cultural constraints, many ethnic or racial LGBT persons choose not to tell their families about their sexual identity or do so knowing they are at the risk of breaking family ties.

- Disclosing a LGB sexual identity to a marriage partner most often results in the dissolution of the marriage, although this is more common for women than for men. Some gay persons are able to remain in marriages after disclosing to their partners; the couple renegotiates boundaries and rules and remains together congenially. The same is often true for bisexual persons married to heterosexual persons.

- Most LGB persons report that their friends are their primary resources for support. They hope to increase closeness when they make disclosures to their friends. They feel that these disclosures are the safest, yet they are still monumental. Whereas some friends may experience the same continuum of feelings as parents, most continue close relationships with their LGB friends.

- Work may present the most difficult venue for disclosure. Termination, demotion, and discrimination may ensue and can force LGBT persons to work in lower paying positions with fewer benefits. One must decide for oneself whether disclosure is prudent or safe. Some prefer to keep their personal lives separate from their work lives even though that may mean never sharing significant events with coworkers; others feel compelled to disclose at work to promote psychological congruence and honesty.

- Most LGBT persons participate in disclosure management of weighing when to disclose, to whom, and the possible consequences. Rational outness is perhaps the best strategy. One can be not only open but also protect oneself from discrimination by being closed in certain situations and with certain persons.

CHAPTER 5
REFERENCES

Anderson, B. F. (1998). Therapeutic issues in working with transgendered clients. In D. Denny (Ed.), *Current concepts of transgendered identity* (pp. 215–226). New York: Garland.

Bales, J. (1985, December). Gay adolescents' pain compounded. *APA Monitor, 16,* 21.

Beeler, J. A., Rawls, T. W., Herdt, G. H., & Cohler, B. J. (1999). Needs of older lesbians and gay men in Chicago. *Journal of Gay and Lesbian Social Services, 9,* 31.

Ben-Ari, A. (1995). The discovery that an offspring is gay: Parents', gay men's, and lesbians' perspectives. *Journal of Homosexuality, 30,* 89–112.

Bernstein, B. E. (1990). Attitudes and issues of parents of gay men and lesbians and implications for therapy. *Journal of Gay & Lesbian Psychotherapy, 1,* 37–53.

Boatwright, K. J., Gilbert, M. S., Forrest, L., & Ketzenberger, K. (1996). Impact of identity development upon career trajectory: Listening to the voices of lesbian women. *Journal of Vocational Behavior, 48,* 210–228.

Bohan, J. S. (1996). *Psychology and sexual orientation: Coming to terms.* New York: Routledge.

Bonilla, J., & Porter, J. (1990). A comparison of Latino, Black, and non-Hispanic White attitudes toward homosexuality. *Hispanic Journal of Behavioral Sciences, 12,* 437–452.

Borhek, M. V. (1988). Helping gay and lesbian adolescents and their families. *Journal of Adolescent Health Care, 9,* 123–128.

Boxer, A. M., Cook, J. A., & Herdt, G. (1991). Double jeopardy: Identity transitions and parent-child relationships among gay and lesbian youth. In K. Pillemer & K. McCartney (Eds.), *Parent-child relations throughout life* (pp. 59–92). Hillsdale, NJ: Lawrence Erlbaum.

Bozett, F. W. (1982). Heterogeneous couples in heterosexual marriages: Gay men and straight women. *Journal of Marital and Sexual Therapy, 8,* 81–89.

Brooks, S. E. (1991). Resources. In N. J. Evans & V. A. Walls (Eds.), *Beyond tolerance: Gays, lesbians, and bisexuals on campus* (pp. 213–232). Alexandria, VA: American College Personnel Association.

Brown, G. R. (1998). Women in the closet: Relationships with transgendered men. In D. Denny (Ed.), *Current concepts of transgendered identity* (pp. 353–371). New York: Garland.

Brown, L. B. (1997). Women and men, not-men and not-women, lesbians and gays: American Indian gender-style alternatives. *Journal of Gay & Lesbian Social Services, 6*, 5–20.

Brown, L. S. (1989). Lesbians, gay men and their families: Common clinical issues. *Journal of Gay & Lesbian Psychotherapy, 1*, 65–77.

Byrne, J. S. (1993). Affirmative action for lesbians and gay men: A proposal for true equality of opportunity and work force diversity. *Yale Law & Policy Review, 11*, 47–108.

Cain, R. (1991a). Relational contexts and information management among gay men. *Families in Society, 72*, 344–352.

Cain, R. (1991b). Stigma management and gay identity development. *Social Work, 36*, 67–73.

Carballo-Diéguez, A. (1989). Hispanic culture, gay male culture, and AIDS: Counseling implications. *Journal of Counseling and Development, 68*, 26–30.

Chan, C. S. (1989). Issues of identity development among Asian-American lesbians and gay men. *Journal of Counseling and Development, 68*, 16–20.

Chan, C. S. (1992). Cultural considerations in counseling Asian American lesbians and gay men. In S. Dworkin & F. Gutiérrez (Eds.), *Counseling gay men and lesbians* (pp. 115–124). Alexandria, VA: American Association for Counseling and Development.

Chan, C. S. (1997). Don't ask, don't tell, don't know: The formation of a homosexual identity and sexual expression among Asian American lesbians. In B. Greene (Ed.), *Ethnic and cultural diversity among lesbians and gay men* (pp. 240–248). Thousand Oaks, CA: Sage Publications.

Cole, S. S., Denny, D., Eyler, A. E., & Samons, S. L. (2000). Issues of transgender. In L. T. Szuchman & F. Muscarella (Eds.), *Psychological perspectives on human sexuality* (pp. 149–195). New York: John Wiley & Sons.

Coleman, E. (1985a). Bisexual women in marriages: Conflicts and resolutions in therapy. *Journal of Homosexuality, 11*, 87–99.

Coleman, E. (1985b). Integration of male bisexuality and marriage. *Journal of Homosexuality, 11*, 189–207.

Collins, L. E., & Zimmerman, N. (1983). Homosexual and bisexual issues. In J. C. Hansen, J. D. Woody, & R. H. Woody (Eds.), *Sexual issues in family therapy* (pp. 82–100). Rockville, MD: Aspen.

Cramer, D. W., & Roach, A. J. (1988). Coming out to mom and dad: A study of gay males and their relationships with their parents. *Journal of Homosexuality, 15*, 79–91.

Crisp, D., Priest, B., & Torgerson, A. (1998). African American gay men: Developmental issues, choices, and self-concept. *Family Therapy, 25*, 161–168.

Croteau, J. M., & Hedstrom, S. M. (1993). Integrating commonality and difference: The key to career counseling with lesbian women and gay men. *Career Development Quarterly, 41*, 201–209.

Croteau, J. M., & Lark, J. S. (1995). A qualitative investigation of biased and exemplary student affairs practice concerning lesbian, gay, and bisexual issues. *Journal of College Student Development, 36*, 472–482.

Cruikshank, M. (1992). *The gay and lesbian liberation movement.* New York: Routlege.

D'Augelli, A. R. (1991a). Gay men in college: Identity processes and adaptations. *Journal of College Student Development, 32*, 140–146.

D'Augelli, A. R. (1991b). Teaching lesbian and gay development: A pedagogy of the oppressed. In W. G. Tierney (Ed.), *Culture and ideology in higher education: Advancing a critical agenda* (pp. 213–233). New York: Praeger.

D'Augelli, A. R. (1996). Enhancing the development of lesbian, gay, and bisexual youths. In E. D. Rothblum & L. A. Bond (Eds.), *Preventing heterosexism and homophobia* (pp. 124–150). Thousand Oaks, CA: Sage Publications.

D'Augelli, A. R., & Garnets, L. D. (1995). Lesbian, gay, and bisexual communities. In A. R. D'Augelli & C. J. Patterson (Eds.), *Lesbian, gay, and bisexual identities over the lifespan* (pp. 293–320). New York: Oxford University Press.

D'Augelli, A. R., & Hershberger, S. L. (1993). Lesbian, gay, and bisexual youth in community settings: Personal challenges and mental health problems. *American Journal of Community Psychology, 21*, 421–448.

D'Augelli, A. R., Hershberger, S. L., & Pilkington, B. A. (1998). Lesbian, gay, and bisexual youth and their families: Disclosure of sexual orientation and its consequences. *American Journal of Orthopsychiatry, 68*, 361–371.

D'Emilio, J. (1983). *Sexual politics, sexual communities: The making of a homosexual minority in the United States*, 1940–1970. Chicago: University of Chicago Press.

DeVine, J. L. (1983-1984). A systematic inspection of affectional preference orientation and the family of origin. *Journal of Social Work and Human Sexuality, 2*, 9–17.

Dong tinh luyen ai co phai la can benh hay khong? [Is homosexuality a disease?] (1992, January 31). [Orange County, CA] *Vietnamese Weekly Newspaper*, pp. 4–5.

Durby, D. D. (1994). Gay, lesbian, and bisexual youth. *Journal of Gay and Lesbian Social Services, 1*, 1–37.

Dyne, L. (1980, September). Is DC becoming the gay capitol of America? *Washingtonian*, pp. 96-101, 133–141.

Emerson, S., & Rosenfeld, C. (1996). Stages of adjustment in family members of transgender individuals. *Journal of Family Psychotherapy, 7*, 1–12.

Espin, O. M. (1984). Cultural and historical influences on sexuality in Hispanic/Latin women: Implications for psychotherapy. In C. Vance (Ed.), *Pleasure and danger: Exploring female sexuality* (pp. 149–163). London: Routledge and Kegan Paul.

Espin, O. M. (1987). Issues of identity in the psychology of Latina lesbians. In Boston Lesbian Psychologies Collective (Eds.), *Lesbian psychologies: Explorations and challenges* (pp. 35–51). Urbana: University of Illinois Press.

Espin, O. M. (1997). Crossing borders and boundaries: The life narratives of immigrant lesbians. In B. Greene (Ed.), *Ethnic and cultural diversity among lesbians and gay men* (pp. 191–215). Thousand Oaks, CA: Sage Publications.

Falk, P. J. (1989). Lesbian mothers: Psychosocial assumptions in family law. *American Psychologist, 44*, 941–947.

Fox, R. C. (1995). Coming out bisexual: Identity, behavior, and sexual orientation self-disclosure (Doctoral dissertation, California Institute of Integral Studies, 1993). *Dissertation Abstracts International, 55*(12), 5565B.

Fygetakis, L. M. (1997). Greek American lesbians: Identity odysseys of honorable good girls. In B. Greene (Ed.), *Ethnic and cultural diversity among lesbians and gay men* (pp.152–190). Thousand Oaks, CA: Sage Publications.

Gagné, P., Tewksbury, R., & McGaughey, D. (1997). Coming out and crossing over: Identity formation and proclamation in a transgender community. *Gender & Society, 11*, 478–508.

Garnets, L. D., Herek, G. M., & Levy, B. (1990). Violence and victimization of lesbians and gay men: Mental health consequences. *Journal of Interpersonal Violence, 5*, 366–383.

Gartrell, N. (1984). Combating homophobia in the psychotherapy of lesbians. *Women & Therapy, 3*, 13–29.

Gochros, J. S. (1985). Wives' reactions to learning that their husbands are bisexual. *Journal of Homosexuality, 11*, 101–113.

Gochros, J. S. (1989). *When husbands come out of the closet.* New York: Haworth Press.

Gonsiorek, J. C. (1993). Threat, stress, and adjustment: Mental health and the workplace for gay and lesbian individuals. In L. Diamant (Ed.), *Homosexual issues in the workplace* (pp. 242–263). Washington, DC: Taylor & Francis.

González, F. J., & Espin, O. M. (1996). Latino men, Latino women, and homosexuality. In R. P. Cabaj & T. S. Stein (Eds.), *Textbook of homosexuality and mental health* (pp. 583–601). Washington, DC: American Psychiatric Press.

Grace, J. (1992). Affirming gay and lesbian adulthood. In N. J. Woodman (Ed.), *Lesbian and gay lifestyles: A guide for counseling and education* (pp. 33–47). New York: Irvington.

Green, R.-J., Bettinger, M., & Zacks, E. (1996). Are lesbian couples fused and gay male couples disengaged? Questioning gender straight jackets. In J. Laird & R.-J. Green (Eds.), *Lesbians and gays in couples and families* (pp. 185–231). San Francisco: Jossey-Bass.

Greene, B. (1996). Lesbians and gay men of color: The legacy of ethnosexual mythologies in heterosexism. In E. D. Rothblum & L. A. Bond (Eds.), *Preventing heterosexism and homophobia* (pp. 59–70). Thousand Oaks, CA: Sage Publications.

Greene, B. (1997). Ethnic minority lesbians and gay men: Mental health and treatment issues. In B. Greene (Ed.), *Ethnic and cultural diversity among lesbians and gay men* (pp. 216–239). Thousand Oaks, CA: Sage Publications.

Greene, B., & Herek, G. M. (Eds.). (1994). *Lesbian and gay psychology: Theory, research, and clinical applications.* Thousand Oaks, CA: Sage Publications.

Griffin, C., Wirth, M., & Wirth, A. (1986). *Beyond acceptance: Parents of lesbians and gays talk about their experiences.* Englewood Cliffs, NJ: Prentice Hall.

Griffin, P. (1992). Lesbian and gay educators: Opening the classroom closet. *Empathy, 3,* 25–28.

Hall, M. (1986). The lesbian corporate experience. *Journal of Homosexuality, 12,* 59–75.

Hall, M. (1989). Private experiences in the public domain: Lesbians in organizations. In J. Hearn, D. L. Sheppard, P. Tancred-Sheriff, & G. Burrell (Eds.), *The sexuality of organization* (pp. 125–138). Newbury Park, CA: Sage Publications.

Hanley-Hackenbruck, P. (1989). Psychotherapy and the "coming out" process. *Journal of Gay & Lesbian Psychotherapy, 1,* 21–39.

Hanscombe, G., & Forster, J. (1982). *Rocking the cradle.* Boston: Alyson Press.

Harry, J. (1989). Parental physical abuse and sexual orientation. *Archives of Sexual Behavior, 18*, 251–261.

Hawkeswood, W. G. (1990, November). *I'm a black man who just happens to be gay: The sexuality of black gay men.* Paper presented at the American Anthropological Association Annual Meeting, New Orleans.

Healy, T. (1993). A struggle for language: Patterns of self-disclosure in lesbian couples. *Smith College Studies in Social Work, 63*, 247–263.

Henderson, M. G. (1998). Disclosure of sexual orientation: Comments form a parental perspective. *American Journal of Orthopsychiatry, 68*, 372–375.

Herdt, G. H., & Boxer, A. (1993). *Children of the horizons: How gay and lesbian teens are leading a way out of the closet.* Boston: Beacon Press.

Herek, G. M. (1991). Myths about sexual orientation: A lawyer's guide to social science research. *Law and Sexuality: Review of Lesbian and Gay Legal Issues, 1*, 133–172.

Hersch, P. (1988, January). Coming of age on city streets. *Psychology Today*, pp. 28–32.

Hetherington, C., & Orzek, A. (1989). Career and life planning with lesbian women. *Journal of Counseling and Development, 68*, 52–57.

Hunt, S., & Main, T. L. (1997). Sexual orientation confusion among spouses of transvestites and transsexuals following disclosure of spouse's gender dysphoria. *Journal of Psychology and Human Sexuality, 9*, 39–52.

Hunter, J. (1995). At the crossroads: Lesbian youth. In K. Jay (Ed.), *Dyke life: A celebration of the lesbian experience.* New York: Basic Books.

Hunter, J., & Martin, A. D. (1984). *A comparison of presenting problems of homosexually and non-homosexually oriented young people at a student run health service.* New York: Hetrick Martin Institute.

Icard, L. D. (1985–1986). Black gay men and conflicting social identities: Sexual orientation versus racial identity. *Journal of Social Work and Human Sexuality, 4*, 83–93.

Jacobs, M. A., & Brown, L. B. (1997). American Indian lesbians and gays: An exploratory story. *Journal of Gay and Lesbian Social Services, 6*, 29–41.

Jones, B. E., & Hill, M. J. (1996). African American lesbians, gay men, and bisexuals. In R. P. Cabaj & T. S. Stein (Eds.), *Textbook of homosexuality and mental health* (pp. 549–561). Washington, DC: American Psychiatric Press.

Jordan, K. M., & Deluty, R. H. (1998). Coming out for lesbian women: Its relation to anxiety, positive affectivity, self-esteem, and social support. *Journal of Homosexuality*, *35*, 41–63.

Kanuha, V. (1990). Compounding the triple jeopardy: Battering in lesbian of color relationships. *Women and Therapy*, *9*, 169–184.

Kirkpatrick, M., Smith, C., & Roy, R. (1981). Lesbian mothers and their children: A comparative survey. *American Journal of Orthopsychiatry*, *51*, 545–551.

Kitzinger, C. (1991). Lesbian and gay men in the workplace: Psychosocial issues. In M. J. Davidson & J. Earnshaw (Eds.), *Vulnerable workers: Psychosocial and legal issues* (pp. 223–257). New York: John Wiley & Sons.

Laird, J. (1996). Family-centered practice with lesbian and gay families. *Families in Society: Journal of Contemporary Human Services*, *77*, 559–572.

Lang, S. (1999). Lesbians, men-women and two-spirits: Homosexuality and gender in Native American cultures. In E. Blackwood & S. Wieringa (Eds.), *Female desires: Same-sex relations and transgender practices across cultures* (pp. 91–116). New York: Columbia University Press.

Leaveck, A. (1994). *Perceived parental reactions to same-sex sexual orientation disclosure: A search for predictors*. Unpublished doctoral dissertation, Central Michigan University, Mount Pleasant.

Levine, M. P., & Leonard, R. (1984). Discrimination against lesbians in the work force. *Signs*, *9*, 700–710.

Liu, P., & Chan, C. C. (1996). Lesbian, gay, and bisexual Asian Americans and their families. In J. Laird & R.-J. Green (Eds.), *Lesbians and gays in couples and families: A handbook for therapists* (pp. 137–152). San Francisco: Jossey-Bass.

Loiacano, D. K. (1989). Gay identity issues among black Americans: Racism, homophobia, and the need for validation. *Journal of Counseling and Development*, *68*, 21-25.

Lopez, R. A., & Lam, B. T. (1998). Social supports among Vietnamese American gay men. *Journal of Gay & Lesbian Social Services*, *8*, 29–50.

Manalansan, M. F., IV. (1996). Double minorities: Latino, black, and Asian men who have sex with men. In R. C. Savin-Williams & K. M. Cohen (Eds.), *The lives of lesbian, gay men, and bisexuals: Children to adults* (pp. 393–425). Fort Worth, TX: Harcourt Brace.

Marsiglia, F. F. (1998). Homosexuality and Latinos/as: Towards an integration of identities. *Journal of Gay & Lesbian Social Services*, *8*, 113–125.

Martin, A. D. (1982). Learning to hide: Socialization of the gay adolescent. *Adolescent Psychiatry*, *10*, 52–64.

Martin, A. D., & Hetrick, E. S. (1988). The stigmatization of the gay and lesbian adolescent. *Journal of Homosexuality*, *15*, 163–183.

Matteson, D. R. (1987). The heterosexually married gay and lesbian parent. In F. W. Bozett (Ed.), *Gay and lesbian parents* (pp. 138–161). New York: Praeger.

Mattison, A. M., & McWhirter, D. P. (1995). Lesbians, gay men, and their families: Some therapeutic issues. *Psychiatric Clinics of North America*, *18*, 123–137.

Mays, V. M., Chatters, L. M., Cochran, S. D., & Mackness, J. (1998). African American families in diversity: Gay men and lesbians as participants in family networks. *Journal of Comparative Family Studies*, *29*, 73–87.

McCubbin, H., & Patterson, J. (1983). The family stress process: The double ABCX model of adjustment and adaptation. *Marriage and Family Review*, *6*, 7–37.

Moraga, C., & Hollibaugh, A. (1985). What we're rolling around in bed with. In A. Snitow, C. Stansell, & S. Thompson (Eds.), *Powers of desire: The politics of sexuality* (pp. 394–405). New York: Monthly Review.

Morales, E. S. (1992). Counseling Latino gays and Latina lesbians. In S. Dworkin & F. Gutiérrez (Eds.), *Counseling gay men and lesbians: Journey to the end of the rainbow* (pp. 125–139). Alexandria, VA: American Association for Counseling and Development.

Morales, E. S. (1996). Gender roles among Latino gay and bisexual men: Implications for family and couple therapy. In J. Laird & R.-J. Green (Eds.), *Lesbians and gays in couples and families: A handbook for therapists* (pp. 272–297). San Francisco: Jossey-Bass.

Murray, C. I. (1994, November). *Siblings of gay and lesbian people: Coming out, identity, and caregiving issues.* Paper presented at the annual meeting of the National Council on Family Relations, Minneapolis.

Nakajima, G. A., Chan, Y. H., & Lee, K. (1996). Mental health issues for gay and lesbian Asian Americans. In R. P. Cabaj & T. S. Stein (Eds.), *Textbook of homosexuality and mental health* (pp. 563–581). Washington, DC: American Psychiatric Press.

Neisen, J. H. (1987). Resources for families with a gay/lesbian member. In E. Coleman (Ed.), *Integrated identities for gay men and lesbians: Psychotherapeutic approaches for emotional well-being* (pp. 239–251). New York: Harrington Park.

Paul, J. P. (1992). "Biphobia" and the construction of a bisexual identity. In M. Shernoff & W. A. Scott (Eds.), *The sourcebook on lesbian/gay health care* (2nd ed., pp. 259–264). Washington, DC: National Lesbian/Gay Health Foundation.

Paul, J. P. (1996). Bisexuality: Exploring/exploding the boundaries. In R. C. Savin-Williams & K. M. Cohen (Eds.), *The lives of lesbian, gay men, and bisexuals: Children to adults* (pp. 436–461). Fort Worth, TX: Harcourt Brace.

Peters, D. K., & Cantrell, P. J. (1993). Gender roles and role conflict in feminist lesbian and heterosexual women. *Sex Roles, 28,* 379–392.

Peterson, M. R. (1992). *At personal risk: Boundary violations in professional-client relationships.* New York: W. W. Norton.

Pilkington, N. W., & D'Augelli, A. R. (1995). Victimization of lesbian, gay, and bisexual youth in community settings. *Journal of Community Psychology, 23,* 33-56.

Poussaint, A. (1990, September). An honest look at black gays and lesbians. *Ebony,* pp. 124,126,130–131.

Radonsky, V. E., & Borders, L. D. (1995). Factors influencing lesbian's direct disclosures of their sexual orientation. *Journal of Gay & Lesbian Psychotherapy, 213,* 17–37.

Ramos, J. (1994). *Companeras: Latina lesbians.* New York: Routledge.

Remafedi, G. (1987a). Adolescent homosexuality: Psychosocial and medical implications. *Pediatrics, 79,* 331–337.

Remafedi, G. (1987b). Male homosexuality: The adolescent's perspective. *Pediatrics, 79,* 326–330.

Reyes, M. (1992). Women's studies programs in Latin America: A source of empowerment. (Doctoral dissertation, University of Massachusetts, 1992). *Dissertation Abstracts International, 53*(6–A), 1819.

Robinson, B. E., Walters, L. H., & Skeen, P. (1989). Response of parents to learning that their child is homosexual and concern over AIDS: A national study. *Journal of Homosexuality, 18,* 59–80.

Rodriguez, F. I. (1996). Understanding Filipino male homosexuality: Implications for social services. *Journal of Gay & Lesbian Social Services, 5,* 93–113.

Rosenfeld, C., & Emerson, S. (1998). A process model of supportive therapy for families of transgender individuals. In D. Denny (Ed.), *Current concepts of transgender identity* (pp. 391–400). New York: Garland.

Rotheram-Borus, M. J., Rosario, M., & Koopman, C. (1991). Minority youths at high risk: Gay males and runaways. In M. E. Colten & S. Gore (Eds.), *Adolescent stress: Causes and consequences* (pp. 181–200). New York: Aldine de Gruyter.

Rust, P. C. (1996). Finding a sexual identity and community: Therapeutic implications and cultural assumptions in scientific models of coming out. In E. D. Rothblum & L. A. Bond (Eds.), *Preventing heterosexim and homophobia* (pp. 87–123). Thousand Oaks, CA: Sage Publications.

Sauerman, T. H. (1984). *Coming out to your parents.* Los Angeles: Federation of Parents & Friends of Lesbians and Gays.

Savin-Williams, R. (1990). *Gay and lesbian youth: Expressions of identity.* New York: Hemisphere.

Savin-Williams, R. (1994). Verbal and physical abuse as stressors in the lives of lesbian, gay male, and bisexual youths: Associations with school problems, running away, substance abuse, prostitution, and suicide. *Journal of Consulting and Clinical Psychology, 62,* 260–269.

Savin-Williams, R. C. (1995). Lesbian, gay male, and bisexual adolescents. In A. R. D'Augelli & C. J. Patterson (Eds.), *Lesbian, gay, and bisexual identities over the lifespan* (pp. 165–189). New York: Oxford University Press.

Savin-Williams, R. C. (1996). Ethnic-and sexual-minority youth. In R. C. Savin-Williams & K. M. Cohen (Eds.), *The lives of lesbians, gay men, and bisexuals: Children to adults* (pp. 152–165). Fort Worth, TX: Harcourt Brace.

Savin-Williams, R. C. (1998a). *". . . and then I became gay": Young men's stories.* New York: Routledge.

Savin-Williams, R. C. (1998b). Lesbian, gay, and bisexual youths' relationships with their parents. In C. J. Patterson & A. R. D'Augelli (Eds.), *Lesbians, gay, and bisexual identities in families: Psychological perspectives* (pp. 75–98). New York: Oxford University Press.

Savin-Williams, R., & Cohen, K. M. (1996). Psychosocial outcomes of verbal and physical abuse among lesbian, gay, and bisexual youths. In R. C. Savin-Williams & K. M. Cohen (Eds.), *The lives of lesbians, gays, and bisexuals: Children to adults* (pp. 181–200). Fort Worth, TX: Harcourt Brace.

Savin-Williams, R., & Dube, E. M. (1998). Parental reactions to their child's disclosure of a gay/lesbian identity. *Family Relations, 47,* 7–13.

Scasta, D. (1998). Issues in helping people come out. *Journal of Gay & Lesbian Psychotherapy, 2,* 87–98.

Scott, R. R., & Ortiz, E. T. (1996). Marriage and coming out: Four patterns in homosexual males. *Journal of Gay & Lesbian Social Services, 4*, 67–79.

Shachar, S. A., & Gilbert, L. A. (1983). Working lesbians: Role conflicts and coping strategies. *Psychology of Women Quarterly, 7*, 272–284.

Shallenberger, D. (1994). Professional and openly gay: A narrative study of the experience. *Journal of Management Inquiry, 3*, 119–142.

Smith, A. (1997). Cultural diversity and the coming-out process: Implications for clinical practice. In B. Greene (Ed.), *Ethnic and cultural diversity among lesbians and gay men* (pp. 279–300). Thousand Oaks, CA: Sage Publications.

Smith, B. (Ed.). (1983). *Home girls: A black feminist anthology.* New York: Kitchen Table.

Stokes, J., & Damon, W. (1995). Counseling and psychotherapy for bisexual men. *Directions in Mental Health Counseling, 5*, 4–15.

Stokes, J. P., & Peterson, J. L. (1998). Homophobia, self-esteem, and risk for HIV among African American men who have sex with men. *AIDS Education and Prevention, 10*, 278–292.

Strommen, E. F. (1989). "You're a what?": Family members' reactions to the disclosure of homosexuality. *Journal of Homosexuality, 18*, 37–58.

Strommen, E. F. (1990). Hidden branches and growing pains: Homosexuality and the family tree. *Marriage & Family Review, 14*, 9–34.

Telljohann, S. K., & Price, J. H. (1993). A qualitative examination of adolescent homosexuals' life experiences: Ramifications for secondary school personnel. *Journal of Homosexuality, 26*, 41–55.

Timberlake, E. M., & Cook, K. O. (1984). Social work and the Vietnamese refugee. *Social Work, 29*, 108–113.

Tofoya, T. N. (1996). Native two-spirit people. In R. P. Cabaj & T. S. Stein (Eds.), *Textbook of homosexuality and mental health* (pp. 603–617). Washington, DC: American Psychiatric Press.

Tremble, B., Schneider, M., & Appathurai, C. (1989). Growing up gay or lesbian in a multi cultural context. *Journal of Homosexuality, 17*, 253–267.

Triandis, H. C., Kurowski, L. L., & Gelfand, M. J. (1994). Workplace diversity. In H. C. Triandis, M. D. Dunnette, & L. M. Housh (Eds.), *Handbook of industrial and organizational psychology* (2nd ed., Vol. 4, pp. 769–827). Palo Alto, CA: Consulting Psychologists.

Trujillo, C. (Ed.). (1991). *Chicana lesbians: The girls our mothers warned us about.* Berkeley, CA: Third Woman.

Uribe, V., & Harbeck, K. M. (1991). Addressing the needs of lesbian, gay, and bisexual youth: The origins of PROJECT 10 and school-based intervention. *Journal of Homosexuality, 22,* 9–28.

Walters, A. S., & Phillips, C. P. (1994). Hurdles: An activity for homosexuality education. *Journal of Sex Education & Therapy, 20,* 198–203.

Walters, K. L. (1997). Urban lesbian and gay American Indian identity: Implications for mental health service delivery. *Journal of Gay & Lesbian Social Services, 6,* 43–65.

Weinberg, M. S., Williams, C. J., & Pryor, D. W. (1994). *Dual attraction: Understanding bisexuality.* New York: Oxford University Press.

Whitman, J. S., Cormier, S., & Boyd, C. J. (2000). Lesbian identity management at various stages of the coming out process: A qualitative study. *International Journal of Sexuality and Gender Studies, 5,* 3–18.

Whitney, C. (1990). *Uncommon lives: Gay men and straight women.* New York: Plume.

Whittier, D. K. (1997). Social conflict among "gay" men in a small(er) southern town. *Journal of Gay & Lesbian Social Services, 7,* 53–71.

Whittlin, W. (1983). Homosexuality and child custody: A psychiatric viewpoint. *Conciliation Courts Review, 21,* 77–79.

Williams, W. L. (1986). *The spirit and the flesh: Sexual diversity in American Indian culture.* Boston: Beacon Press.

Williamson, D. S. (1998). An essay for practitioners: Disclosure is a family event. *Family Relations, 47,* 23–25.

Wooden, W. S., Kawasaki, H., & Mayeda, R. (1983). Lifestyles and identity maintenance among gay Japanese-American males. *Alternate Lifestyles, 5,* 236–243.

Woods, J. D, & Lucas, J. (1993). *The corporate closet: The professional lives of gay men in America.* New York: Free Press.

Wyers, N. L. (1987). Homosexuality in the family: Lesbian and gay spouses. *Social Work, 32,* 143–148.

CHAPTER 6
FRIENDS AND PARTNERS

What role do friends play in the lives of LGB persons?

How do LGB persons meet prospective partners or dates?

What are some of the scripts for LGB partnerships?

What factors are associated with satisfaction and longevity for LGB couples?

What factors are associated with breakups for LGB couples?

What is the impact of breaking up for LGB couples?

CHOSEN FAMILIES

Gay and lesbian persons are members of not only families of origin and extended families but also families made up of friends and partners. These other families are "created families" (Weinstock, 1998) or "chosen families" (Weston, 1991) that develop through choice and love, and are the major support networks for most gay and lesbian persons (for example, Weinstock, 1998; Weston, 1991). Lesbian and gay support networks usually contain more friends compared with the support networks of heterosexual persons although fewer kin (Julien, Chartrand, & Begin, 1999). In these networks, friends generally provide more social support than family-of-origin members, work colleagues, or partners (Kurdek, 1988), and support from friends is associated significantly with the psychological adjustment, functioning, and quality of life for gay and lesbian persons and couples (Kurdek, 1988; Oetjen & Rothblum, 2000). Racial and ethnic group members may not place as much value on persons outside their biological families (D'Augelli & Garnets, 1995), yet in Latino gay and lesbian samples, social support from friends rather than families was associated with increased psychological well-being (Zea, Reisen, & Poppen, 1999).

Aside from linking with friends, LGB persons also want to link with a partner. When these persons are in a relationship, the central focus of their chosen family is the primary partner (James & Murphy, 1998). Yet gay and lesbian couples are diverse. For example, some partners commit to each other but do not live with each other; some partners see each other as a couple but have more than one significant partner; and some partners coexist in heterosexual marriages (Hostetler & Cohler, 1997; James & Murphy, 1998). Some persons who have only casual relationships with several others may not identify themselves as single. Asking LGB persons to define their situations is the best way to understand the nature and significance of their relationships (Cabaj & Klinger, 1996; Hostetler & Cohler, 1997).

Another source of diversity lies in what gay and lesbian couples label themselves. In a national survey of mostly White lesbian (560) and gay (706) couples together an average of six years, several terms were most often and about equally used—lover and partner or life partner. Whereas more men (40 percent) than women (30 percent) preferred the term lover, more women (37 percent) than men (27 percent) preferred the terms partner or life partner (Bryant & Demian, 1994). Partner, however, can imply a business association and lover can imply a main interest in sex (Berger, 1990; Murphy, 1994). It is best to ask the members of couples what they prefer to call themselves (Berger, 1990).

FINDING DATES AND PARTNERS

The pool of potential partners for LGB persons is smaller than for heterosexual persons and even smaller for racial, ethnic, and other subgroups of LGB persons (Greene, 1995). The fear of HIV/AIDS also decreases the dating pool, especially for gay persons (Linde, 1994). Another limiting factor is that gay and lesbian persons are often invisible (Rutter & Schwartz, 1996). Because rural lesbian and gay persons usually live in isolation from each other, it is also difficult for them to meet potential partners (Moses & Buckner, 1986).

Bars are still the only public places where many gay and lesbian persons feel they can be themselves (James & Murphy, 1998; Weinberg, Williams, & Pryor, 1994). Gay and bisexual men are more likely to meet partners in bars than are lesbian and bisexual women (Thorne & Coupland, 1998; Weinberg et al., 1994). In large urban areas, many mainstream locations and resources are also available for meeting others, including organized sports groups, singles cruises, book groups, and political groups; singles social groups and dances; and ads in the singles pages of newspapers and magazines (James & Murphy, 1998). One-third of the sample of lesbian and gay persons studied by Weinberg and colleagues (1994) reported that they use mainstream connections for meeting partners and friends such as work or conventional parties to name a few. Black gay persons also use mainstream venues such as private house parties and friendship networks (Peterson, 1992). Active LGB groups are growing in high schools and on college and university campuses; after graduation, alumni groups are available. Some churches and concerned citizens sponsor community groups for gay and lesbian youth (James & Murphy, 1998). The Internet also provides opportunities to meet other LGBT persons for electronic friendships or courtships (Diamond, Savin-Williams, & Dubé, 1999).

Meeting may lead to dating, but there is little known about the dating process among gay and lesbian persons. In one of the rare studies on this topic, Klinkenberg and Rose (1994) discovered that cultural and interpersonal scripts for same sex–gender dating paralleled heterosexual scripts during all stages of a first date. In comparing gay persons with lesbians in first-date behaviors, gay persons followed traditional male roles wherein one person arranges a date and other activities; more often lesbians negotiated their dating activities.

COUPLES SCRIPTS

According to the 2000 census data, about one in 200 couples in U.S. households are gay or lesbian and in some cities the proportion is as large as one in 40 couples, such as in Dallas (Gillman & Langford, 2001). A lesbian or gay pair who declares couplehood, however, may not know exactly what to do at least in the beginning since the models for couples that dominate all cultures only portray heterosexual couples (Blumstein & Schwartz, 1983; McWhirter & Mattison, 1984). A prevalent belief is that partners in same sex–gender couples mimic traditional heterosexual couples, meaning that these couples adopt the role of either husband or wife, or one plays a masculine–dominant role and the other a feminine–submissive role (Peplau, 1982–1983; Weitz, 1989). This pattern, known as *butch–femme* (Laird, 2000), was dominant in the United States from the 1920s to the early 1960s (Davis & Kennedy, 1986; Faderman, 1992) and was especially prevalent among lesbian couples during the 1950s (Nestle, 1992). In their study of working-class lesbians between the mid-1930s and early 1960s in Buffalo, NY, Kennedy and Davis (1993) found that butch–femme roles were primarily enacted through appearance and sexual expression. Butches constructed a masculine appearance in clothes and haircuts whereas femmes constructed a feminine or even glamorous appearance. The butch was also the doer and the giver whereas the femme was the receiver.

Given that heterosexuality was the only visible source of modeling, it does not seem unusual that lesbians would draw ideas from it for use in their relationships (Laird, 2000). This did not mean, however, that butches imitated heterosexual men or that femmes imitated heterosexual women (Weston, 1996). Butch and femme are complex metaphors rather than just an imitation of heterosexual models, and the meanings attached to these metaphors change in different cultural and historical contexts (Laird, 2000).

Generally, the butch–femme roles have not endured (Weston, 1996). Starting in the 1970s, it became difficult for lesbians to imagine any social imperative to take on a butch or femme role. The feminist and lesbian feminist movements also rejected these roles as they reflected the patriarchal system (Kennedy & Davis, 1993). This is not to say that no one in lesbian and gay communities plays traditional roles. Some persons may feel comfortable with these roles and may play out some version of them (Weber, 1996).

Another somewhat traditional pattern, mentor–apprentice, is still characteristic among a small minority of gay persons. The partners are usually separated in age by five to 10 years. The older partner is the mentor or leader who dominates decision making (Harry, 1982, 1984). Lesbians are less likely than men to follow this pattern (Reilly & Lynch, 1990).

Most contemporary lesbian and gay couples do not adopt any type of dichotomous roles such as wife–husband, butch–femme, dominant–submissive, active–passive, or powerful–less powerful (for example, Murphy, 1994; Peplau, 1991, 1993). Even in couples where one partner looks stereotypically masculine and the other feminine, stereotypic roles are seldom evident in actual behaviors (Nichols, 1989). Typically, contemporary gay and lesbian couples try to find roles that will meet both individual and couple needs (Blumstein & Schwartz, 1983; McWhirter & Mattison, 1984). The most prevalent couple pattern is one of best friends (Peplau, 1983a, 1983b). This pattern reflects the general social shift to more flexible and egalitarian roles (Faderman, 1991), assuming a relative similarity in age, status, dominance, interests, resources, and skills (Peplau, 1993) and promoting equality, sharing, reciprocity, companionship, and role flexibility (Kurdek & Schmitt, 1986b; Lynch & Reilly, 1986). Many couples develop innovative rules, expectations, and divisions of labor (Peplau & Cochran, 1990) even though this process can cause stress and conflict (Patterson & Schwartz, 1994).

BISEXUAL RELATIONSHIPS

Relationships among bisexual persons are complex as they often seek several different relationship arrangements to meet their sexual, romantic, and emotional needs, including a partner who meets many needs but is not solely responsible for all needs; different partners, each of whom meet some particular need; partners who are friends and sexual partners, but not romantic partners; and acquaintances and strangers who provide purely sexual encounters (Rust, 1996a). Some bisexual persons who have secondary sexual relationships also have close, nonsexual friendships with persons of the other sex–gender. Sometimes two gay husbands link up while remaining committed to their wives as their primary partners. These strategies may stabilize marriages with bisexual husbands. Occasionally, three persons live together in a satisfying and stable arrangement (Matteson, 1996).

Bisexual men and women prefer simultaneous primary and secondary links (Rust, 1996b; Weinberg et al., 1994). The most frequent ideal arrangement involves two core relationships, one heterosexual and one same sex–gender. Variations of this arrangement, from most prevalent to least prevalent, include an open link with no boundaries regarding other possible sexual partners; a primary heterosexual link (often a marriage) and secondary same sex–gender links; and a primary same sex–gender link and one or more secondary heterosexual links (Weinberg et al., 1994). Women want a person of each sex–gender to meet different emotional needs (Nichols, 1988) whereas men want each sex–gender primarily to meet sexual needs (Matteson, 1987). Yet, many bisexual persons may never fulfill their ideal arrangements (Weinberg et al., 1994).

TRANSGENDER RELATIONSHIPS

Much of the current literature on relationships involving transgender persons focuses on situations such as wives finding out that their partners are transgender. Sometimes wives eventually accept that their former husbands are now women, and perhaps some lesbians may eventually accept that their partners are now men (Cooper, 1999).

Transgender persons want partners who understand and support them. More often now, they are forming relationships with other transgender persons. Yet, hardly anything is known about these relationships (Cooper, 1999).

COMMITTED RELATIONSHIPS

Most lesbian (92 percent) and gay (96 percent) persons in couples studied by Bryant and Demian (1994) wanted to be together for life or for "a long time." Close to one-half of lesbian (48 percent) and more gay (80 percent) persons studied by Rust (1996b) indicated that they wanted a lifetime monogamous link with one partner; 30 percent of bisexual women and 15 percent of bisexual men expressed this wish. An increasing number of gay and lesbian couples are using ceremonies and rituals to reflect their long-term commitments (Bryant & Demian, 1994).

In a study of 15 gay and 15 lesbian persons, all of whom reported that they were in committed relationships, Haas and Stafford (1998) found that the couples used relationship maintenance behaviors comparable to those used by heterosexual couples. The three most often reported behaviors were shared tasks (70 percent), metarelational communication (for example, discussing difficulties; 57 percent), and sharing time together (50 percent). Three behaviors tied for fourth place (47 percent) were reactive prosocial, overt assurances, and having social networks (public). Two social network subcategories—family and coworkers—tied for fifth place (43 percent).

The gay and lesbian couples studied by Haas and Stafford (1998) also sought gay/lesbian supportive environments to live in, work in, and socialize in. Being out or open as a couple within their network seemed to function as a relationship-strengthening behavior for these couples. Within their home, sharing in tasks such as household duties, home maintenance, and child care were also significantly associated with maintenance as well as working on the establishment of equity.

SATISFACTION IN LESBIAN AND GAY COUPLES

Two findings have emerged about the outcomes of being in same sex–gender couples. First, many studies reported positive benefits. Gay and lesbian youth in love partnerships experience high levels of self-esteem and self-acceptance (Savin-Williams, 1990). Women in couples, no matter what their sexual orientation, score higher on measures of well-being than single women (Wayment & Peplau, 1995). Gay persons in primary relationships experience less depression and greater well-being (O'Brien, 1992). Second, comparing lesbian and gay couples with heterosexual couples, many studies reported no discrepancies in quality (Kurdek, 1994b, 1995a), cohesion (Green, Bettinger, & Zacks, 1996), closeness (Peplau & Cochran, 1990), adjustments (Kurdek, 1995b), or satisfaction (for example, Kurdek, 1994b, 1995b; Peplau & Cochran, 1990).

If perceived costs decrease and perceived rewards and emotional investment increase, satisfaction with one's relationship is likely to increase over time (Kurdek, 1992, 1995a). Specific factors that may operate as rewards or costs are discussed here.

COMMITMENT, EQUITY, EQUAL INVOLVEMENT, AND POWER

When both partners experience equal involvement in and commitment to their link, satisfaction tends to be high (Kurdek, 1988; Schneider, 1986). Lesbian partners strongly value equity, believing that partners should be equal in every way (for example, Blumstein & Schwartz, 1983). They want fairness in decision making about roles, finances, and household responsibilities (Caldwell & Peplau, 1984; Reilly & Lynch, 1990), whereas two men in a couple may both want to play the dominant role in decision making (James & Murphy, 1998).

Power tends to be equal if partners are evenly interested, committed, and in love and if their resources are equivalent (Burgess & Huston, 1979). More than half of lesbian (59 percent) partners and more than a third of gay (38 percent) partners were found not to believe that their partnerships are "exactly equal" (Peplau & Cochran, 1990).

CONFLICT RESOLUTION

Unhappy couples exhibit more negative behaviors than satisfied couples. Their arguments involve destructive characteristics such as criticism, contempt, blame, and stonewalling. These behaviors negatively correlate with couple satisfaction for all couples (Kurdek, 1991a, 1993). Several other researchers reported that gay and lesbian persons do not show differences from heterosexual couples in the way they handle negative affect (Arellano, 1993; Julien, Gagnon, Hamelin, & Belanger, 1995). *Hostile/withdrawn, withdrawn/withdrawn,* or *hostile/hostile* behaviors occur across heterosexual, gay, and lesbian couples and are more intense in distressed couples. Yet, some differences emerge among these groups. The hostile/withdrawn responses are much stronger in the heterosexual group than in the gay group; lesbians are less hostile and withdraw less than either of the other groups. Heterosexual wives are more hostile and confronting than all other partners (Julien, Arellano, & Turgeon, 1997; Julien, Pizzamiglio, Chartrand, & Begin, 1995). Among partners in gay and lesbian couples, those who are feminine also display the highest levels of negative conflict behavior, including hostility and confrontation (Arellano, 1993).

Gay and lesbian partners are also similar to married heterosexual partners in constructive problem solving (Kurdek, 1998). Satisfied partners are more likely to use positive problem-solving methods, for example, focusing on the specific current issue. They are less likely to use negative approaches such as personal attacks, defensiveness, or withdrawal from interaction (Kurdek, 1991a). Lesbian couples studied by Metz, Simon Rosser, and Strapko (1994) showed a more positive pattern of conflict management than gay or heterosexual couples in several significant ways. They felt greater optimism about conflict resolution, made a greater effort to resolve conflict, and engaged in assertiveness more than in physical aggression.

INTIMACY AND CLOSENESS

Couple-centered partners are the happiest and the most committed (Blumstein & Schwartz, 1983). Participants in lesbian couples more than those in any other type of couple are coupled centered, caring, nurturing, and express their feelings (Kurdek, 1989). They report that emotional intimacy is the strongest contributor to their satisfaction (Eldridge & Gilbert, 1990).

Several factors discovered by Mackey, Diemer, and O'Brien (2000) predict psychological intimacy including minimal levels of relational conflict; use of a confrontational conflict management style by the partners of the respondents or dealing with conflicts by initiating face-to-face discussions; a sense of equity or fairness about the link; and physical affection between the partners, such as touching and hugging. In 108 same sex–gender and heterosexual couples (216 partners) together an average of 30 years, Mackey and colleagues defined psychological intimacy as "the sense that one could be open and honest in talking with a partner about personal thoughts and feelings not usually expressed in other relationships" (p. 201). More lesbian partners reported that their relationships were psychologically intimate than did gay and heterosexual partners.

Although some studies (for example, Patterson & Schwartz, 1994) reported that gay persons may express too much individuation and not enough intimacy, Kurdek (1991a) concluded from a review of other studies (Deenen, Gijs, & van Naerssen, 1994; Peplau & Cochran, 1990) that altogether lesbian and gay couples are more comparable than different from each other in their desire for intimacy. Communication styles and means used to attain intimacy may differ, but both men and women desire love and closeness (Gottman, 1994). In the sample of African American lesbian and gay persons studied by Peplau, Cochran, and Mays (1997), both groups reported high levels of closeness though the levels were somewhat higher for lesbians.

DURATION OF LESBIAN, GAY, AND BISEXUAL COUPLES

Almost half (47 percent) of heterosexual marriages break up by their fifth anniversary (Bumpass & Sweet, 1989). The average length of time together for the sample of gay and lesbian couples studied by Haas and Stafford (1998) was five and one-half years. Yet several studies found lesbian and gay couples remained together 10 years or longer (for example, Bryant & Demian, 1994; Johnson, 1990; McWhirter & Mattison, 1984). In anecdotal accounts, older lesbian and gay persons reported that relationships of 20 to 30 years in duration or longer were common (for example, Adelman, 1986; Clunis & Green, 2000; Kehoe, 1989; McWhirter & Mattison; 1984; Silverstein, 1981). In a study of older lesbians, it appeared that longevity in itself may lead to continued longevity (Kehoe, 1989). Breakups are rare in couples together for more than 10 years (Blumstein & Schwartz, 1983). Without marriage and divorce records for lesbian and gay couples, however, longevity of their relationships is not determinable on any large scale (Peplau, 1993).

Changes in Satisfaction

In four annual assessments, Kurdek (1989, 1992, 1995b, 1998) compared heterosexual married couples and gay and lesbian couples in relationship satisfaction and relationship stability over time. Changes in the quality of the relationship were appraised for both partners on five dimensions—intimacy, autonomy, equality, constructive problem solving, and barriers to leaving. In the initial sample, lesbian and gay partners reported levels of satisfaction similar to heterosexual partners but over time their levels of satisfaction decreased.

Every couple experiences conflict. In another study of 51 lesbian, 75 gay, and 108 heterosexual couples who lived together without children over a one-year period, Kurdek (1994a) identified six areas of conflict: power (for example, overly critical); social issues (for example, politics); personal flaws (for example, smoking); distrust (for example, lying); intimacy (for example, sex); and personal distance (for example, job commitments). Frequent arguing over power resulted in decreased satisfaction with one's relationship. Couples also confronted challenges related to identity management and disclosure issues, work, family of origin, interracial differences, sex–gender role complications, and the balance between attachment and autonomy.

Identity Management and Disclosure Issues

Couples often experience conflicts about identity management issues, especially disclosure to others (Roth, 1989; Smith, 1997). The partners can be at different places in decisions about disclosure (Roth & Murphy, 1986) and unable to negotiate acceptable levels of openness or secrecy (Murphy, 1994; Roth, 1985). One partner may feel that it is mandatory to be secretive with work associates, parents, and children—the other partner may want to make disclosures because of a political commitment to openness (Rutter & Schwartz, 1996). The more open partner may also want to be involved with the other partner's family. If this does not happen, tensions can emerge because of feelings of exclusion from the family. The more closeted partner, though, may experience considerable anxiety about the relationship being exposed to the family (Okun, 1996).

Work

Most gay and lesbian couples experience the same dual-career issues faced by many heterosexual couples (for example, Eldridge, 1987; Hall & Gregory, 1991). The basic issues between these partners center on the allocation of time and energy (Patterson & Schwartz, 1994; Shachar & Gilbert, 1983) and how to distribute household tasks (Kurdek, 1993).

Gay couples may experience additional conflicts regarding work because of competition between partners. Power struggles can result from discrepancies in income (Berger, 1990; Blumstein & Schwartz, 1983). If the income discrepancy is extensive and the resultant power discrepancy clear, the less powerful partner may harbor resentment, and he may not easily capitulate independence and influence in decision making (Blumstein & Schwartz, 1983; Huston & Schwartz, 1995).

Family-of-Origin Issues

For many couples, conflicts involving family of origin are one of the most frequent sources of difficulty (Berger, 1990). For example, split loyalties between one's partner and one's family can create a volatile couple relationship (Kurdek & Schmitt, 1987). In addition, a partner's parents may support their child but not the partner who they may see as responsible for their child's "deviant" sexual identity. The unsupported partner is unlikely to be invited to family events (Rutter & Schwartz, 1996). LaSala (2002) found, however, that among 20 lesbian and 20 gay couples, most of the couple members were not affected by parental disapproval and were assertive in establishing intergenerational boundaries around their partnerships. Yet, whereas gay members were more interested in being independent of their families, lesbian members wanted intergenerational connections and ones that were harmonious and supportive. Although this difference could be sex–gender based, it could also result from the different cities represented. The gay couples lived in Albany, New York, whereas the lesbian couples lived in New York City where there is more open knowledge about lesbian and gay persons. The New York parents of lesbian couples may know more about lesbians and thereby be more accepting and supportive.

INTERRACIAL ISSUES

Cross-cultural and mixed race lesbian and gay couples experience unique issues (McWhirter & Mattison, 1996). In these relationships, the partners often deal with racism, misunderstandings, miscommunications, and possibly loss of support from families or racial and ethnic communities (Browning, Reynolds, & Dworkin, 1991; Greene, 2000). Furthermore, they may be targets of harassment and violence.

Confrontation with racial or ethnic discrimination is probably a new experience for a White partner in a link with a non-White partner. This partner may not recognize racist subtleties and think that the other partner's anger is inappropriate. Or a White partner who recognizes the situation for what it is may castigate the partner for not reacting to it. In addition, a White partner may assume the role of rescuer or, if feeling guilty about racism, may attempt to compensate the partner. But compensation cannot really succeed and the White partner may end up feeling angry and frustrated.

A White partner may also feel guilty about membership in a privileged group. Some White women seek out African American lesbians for partners to diminish their guilt about being White or as proof of their liberal attitudes. A person's politics or intentions, however, cannot free one from racial, nor can one understand what the experience of racism is like for one's ethnic or racial partner on any consistent basis. The ethnic or racial partner may never completely feel that the White partner is free from racism and may experience feelings of jealousy or resentment about the partner's privileged status in both the mainstream and the gay and lesbian communities (Clunis & Green, 2000; Greene, 1994c, 1995).

Both partners' ethnic and racial groups may perceive these partners as lacking in loyalty, and both partners may experience shame about their involvement with a person who is not of the same culture or race (Clunis & Green, 2000; Greene, 1994a, 1995). Some partners, however, refuse to acknowledge accusations of betrayal to their ethnic and racial groups (Leslie & Mac Neill, 1995).

Ethnic and racial lesbians linked with lesbians of other ethnic and racial backgrounds may presume greater similarities than actually exist. For example, although African American lesbians share oppression with other racial and ethnic women, they may confront differences in culture and values regarding their couple roles and the roles of other family members in their lives. In addition, they may have conflicts concerning food, religion, child-rearing behavior, and maintaining a household (Greene, 1994a, 1995; Leslie & Mac Neill, 1995).

Increased visibility of these couples may also engender heterosexist reactions toward them (Greene, 1994c, 1995). Yet these couples may actively resist and subvert heterosexism. Many of them fight back, survive, and create their own families and communities (Robinson, 1997).

SEX–GENDER ROLE ISSUES

Couples seem more satisfied when both members adhere to the roles associated with their sex–gender. When one partner in a gay or lesbian couple adheres to a feminine sex–gender role and the other a masculine sex–gender role, Julien and colleagues (1997) discovered that negative behaviors increased. In addition, the negative effects of the feminine–masculine pair are stronger in lesbian than in gay couples. Lesbian couples in this type of pairing reported the highest levels of destructive communication and conflict management; the lowest levels of constructive conflict management; the lowest levels of satisfaction with their link and relationship efficacy; and the highest levels of problem intensity and verbal and physical aggression.

When two women are together, each may expect from her partner nurturing and emotional support. If one of the partners subscribes to a traditionally masculine sex–gender role, however, she may not fulfill these expectations but instead pull away from these demands, escalating a demand–withdrawal pattern. The same situation can happen in heterosexual couples.

Lesbian, gay, and heterosexual members of distressed couples display more rigid sex–gender stereotypic behaviors, experience fewer similarities in emotional expressions and behaviors, and lack basic communication skills for managing differences (Julien et al., 1997). Couples who are comparable in sex–gender roles may understand each other better and communicate with each other better, but they must also counterbalance the similarities (Rutter & Schwartz, 1996). For example, high levels of emotion can become claustrophobic, leading to avoidance behaviors (Gottman, 1994). A high level of emotion, however, is not always an issue in lesbian couples. The dilemma for gay couples with a low level of communication is they may not openly identify relationship issues. When issues are finally addressed, an explosion of pent up negative feelings can erupt (Rutter & Schwartz, 1996).

ISSUES RELATED TO BALANCING ATTACHMENT AND AUTONOMY

Partners in close relationships try to balance attachment and autonomy. Attachment reflects emotional closeness, sharing, exclusiveness, commitment, and security in a link with another person. Autonomy reflects independence, separation, and boundaries between the partners. These orientations are independent but not polar opposites. Some partners prefer a combination of both high attachment and high autonomy whereas other partners emphasize one variable but not the other. For example, some partners want to maintain a high degree of personal independence including separate interests and friends. Other partners do everything together and develop few boundaries between them; they seek no outside interests and activities (Peplau, 1993).

In reports on lesbian couples, more emphasis is placed on dyadic attachment than on autonomy (for example, Burch, 1997; Kaufman, Harrison, & Hyde, 1984; Toder, 1992). Writers on this topic use analogous concepts such as fusion (Bowen, 1966), enmeshment (Minuchin, 1974), or merger (Krestan & Bepko, 1980) to imply a sense of oneness (Burch, 1986), intense intimacy, pursuit of the same activities, blurring of identities, and over identification with each other (Mencher, 1997). Many researchers concluded that these factors explain the genesis of both intimacy and conflict in lesbian relationships (for example, Greene, Causby, & Miller, 1999).

Fusion is typically attributed to the differences in male and female socialization. Whereas socialization of females leads them to seek connection rather than autonomy and relational distance, socialization of males leads them to seek separation (Krestan & Bepko, 1980). Yet, no strong evidence supports the notion that female socialization makes women predisposed to fusion in relationships (Green et al., 1996).

Particularly when referring to subordinate populations, it is also problematic to generalize between clinical and nonclinical groups (Green et al., 1996). Fusion was not discernible by Kurdek (1991b) in nonclinical samples of lesbian couples. Several other researchers found that their lesbian respondents did not think that fusion characterized their relationships, nor did they desire it. They wanted both attachment and autonomy in their partnerships (Hill, 1999; Mackey, O'Brien, & Mackey, 1997). Probably an accurate description of lesbian couples in general is that they are close instead of fused or, as Surrey (1985) suggested, they are both exceedingly close and exceedingly differentiated. Balance between attachment and autonomy is the ideal in contrast especially to greater attachment than autonomy (Kelley, 1983; Rusbult, 1983).

BROKEN COMMITMENTS

Although the desire may be strong for lasting relationships, many couples do not stay committed probably in large part due to changes in satisfaction. Exchange theory attempts to explain what seems to happen on the way to broken commitments. Commitment can rise or fall in any couple depending on two factors: (a) positive attractions associated with the partner and the relationship, such as love or satisfaction, or decline in these attractions; and (b) barriers that make a termination costly, such as investments in the relationship or financial costs of termination or low barriers (Levinger, 1982). Lesbian and gay couples and married heterosexual couples generally do not differ in levels of positive attractions over time. Studies show, however, that married heterosexual partners have stronger barriers to leaving their linkups than either gay or lesbian partners. Joint investments, the cost of divorce, possible negative effects on children, and less earning power of wives can be formidable obstacles to separation (Kurdek & Schmitt, 1986c). Because lesbian and gay couples do not have socially sanctioned public events to mark their union—an engagement or a wedding—they use other symbols and behaviors to symbolize confirmation (for example, moving in together, participating in commitment ceremonies, registering for shower and wedding presents, wearing rings, choosing a new common name). But, these confirmations are less formal and often less binding (James & Murphy, 1998; Murphy, 1994).

Every couple is vulnerable to broken commitments because of the decline in positive attractions. Internal factors that can play a role in this decline can happen for every couple. External factors also can play a role, especially for gay and lesbian couples.

Internal Factors

Two categories of internal factors that may be associated with broken commitments are individual and interpersonal.

Individual factors. Individual factors identified in various studies include younger age; less satisfaction with the link; negative affectivity (for example, depression, anxiety); less investment in the link; lack of love; nonresponsiveness (for example, no communication or support); emotional distance; higher value placed on personal autonomy (Kurdek, 1991a; 1992; Rusbult, 1983); desire to be independent (Peplau, Padesky, & Hamilton, 1982); expectation of perfection in sexual relations (Blumstein & Schwartz, 1983); dissatisfaction with sex (Blumstein & Schwartz, 1983; Kurdek, 1991b); sexual nonexclusivity (Bell & Weinberg, 1978); work ambitions; time spent at work (Blumstein & Schwartz, 1983); unfulfilled expectations (Rutter & Schwartz, 1996); and unrealistic standards and destructive problem-solving methods that can wear down the other partner's positive evaluation of the link and personal dedication to the link (Kurdek, 1997b). Personal difficulties of a partner can also be contributors such as drug or alcohol addiction, mental cruelty, and frequent absences (Kurdek, 1991c).

Interpersonal factors. Interpersonal factors include connecting too quickly with partners; mismatches between partners (Rutter & Schwartz, 1996); decline in positivity (satisfaction, personal commitment, intimacy, and equality); elevation in relationship conflicts (Kurdek, 1996); discrepancies between partners in interests (36 percent), attitudes about sex (24 percent), background (17 percent), political views (7 percent) (Peplau et al., 1982); not spending time together (Blumstein & Schwartz, 1983); sexual incompatibility (Kurdek, 1991c); arguments about sex, money, family, friends, unequal power (Blumstein & Schwartz, 1983; Kurdek, 1991b, 1993); not pooling incomes; financial management difficulties (Blumstein & Schwartz, 1983); less endorsement of monogamy as a relationship value (Andrews, 1990); nonmonogamy (Rutter & Schwartz, 1996); communication difficulties (for example, lack of open communication, not talking things out, experiencing thoughts about the partner or the link but not expressing them; Alexander, 1997); and boundary struggles (Rutter & Schwartz, 1996). Some lesbian and gay persons studied by Weinberg and colleagues (1994) identified the absence of certain interpersonal factors as contributors to their breakups, including "shared values, common interests, communication, emotional compatibility, mutual determination, trust, the desire to share, love, basic respect, finding time for each other, and the willingness to make adjustments" (p. 183).

External Factors

A wider social context also affects the formation and maintenance of linkups (Kitzinger & Coyle, 1995). Certain external factors may negatively affect any couple, such as the intrusion of work responsibilities, but lesbian and gay couples also face distinct external challenges to their relationships because of their sexual orientation. Although external to couples, these challenges can create internal difficulties that interfere with or destroy happiness with each other.

Cultural heterosexism. Lesbian and gay couples exist in a climate of cultural heterosexism (Herek, 1995; see Chapter 2). Society condemns their love for each other, their sexuality, and their partnerships (Kitzinger & Coyle, 1995). If their affection for each other is open, they risk harassment ranging from minor but humiliating insults such as name calling to major threats such as death (Huston & Schwartz, 1995).

Lack of binding social arrangements. Without institutional frameworks like legal marriage (Rutter & Schwartz, 2000), lesbian and gay couples do not have the recognitions and rights that heterosexual couples enjoy (Fajer, 1992; Huston & Schwartz, 1995). This includes institutional policies such as insurance regulations, inheritance laws, tax regulations, and hospital visitation rights (D'Augelli & Garnets, 1995).

Lack of support from families of origin and heterosexual friends. Married heterosexual couples can usually count on congratulations, blessings, presents, and other tangible and intangible support from the time they declare themselves to be a serious couple. Lesbian and gay couples rarely receive anything close to this extent of support (Bryant & Demian, 1994). If a lesbian or gay couple is in trouble, families or heterosexual friends may not encourage "working out the difficulties" (Greene, 1994b). If the link ends, family members and heterosexual friends often do not understand or empathize with the emotional impact of the loss (Greene & Boyd-Franklin, 1996).

IMPACT OF EXTERNAL OBSTACLES ON COUPLES

External obstacles, especially heterosexism, can create negative effects for lesbian and gay couples such as hiding and passing and internalization of negative beliefs and images.

Hiding and passing. Many lesbian and gay couples do not make public disclosures because of anticipated hostile responses. Yet relationship quality is higher when both partners are open about their link, especially with their families of origin (Caron & Ulin, 1997). Closeting limits the potential social support available from one's family as well as from friends and work associates (Krestan & Bepko, 1980). It also intensifies the couple's dependency on each other (Patterson & Schwartz, 1994) so that any move to individuation by the other partner is viewed as a threat to the security of the link (Roth, 1989; Roth & Murphy, 1986). Isolation from other lesbian and gay persons also eliminates observable models for alternative and, possibly, more satisfying couple and maintenance behaviors. Partners can also experience a sense of unreality about their couple status because their link is only real to them (Patterson & Schwartz, 1994).

Internalization of negative beliefs and images. Negative cultural beliefs and images so saturate the lives of lesbian and gay persons that they may think that they cannot form enduring happy linkups (Bryant & Demian, 1994). Guilt, fear, self-hatred, or hatred of the partner, resulting from acceptance of society's negative attitudes, can also interfere with satisfaction in one's link (Murphy, 1994).

SEVERING OF COUPLES

As do most other persons, lesbian and gay persons begin their linkups with high hopes for a lifetime of love and closeness but often end up with dissolved linkups. Difficulties that can challenge couples are probably more troublesome in their second and third years of being together. During the first year together when couples are still in the throes of romantic love, they may overlook issues that can be "problematic" later. In the second and third years, or the "nesting stage," couples studied by Kurdek and Schmitt (1986a) noticed more differences and made more adjustments and compromises. If the partners were comfortable with these resolutions, the following years could bring renewed satisfaction. Many couples, however, did not survive beyond the early years.

In their landmark study of 3,574 married couples, 642 cohabiting couples, 957 gay couples, and 772 lesbian couples, Blumstein and Schwartz (1983) offered a glimpse of the breakup rates among different groups. When the survey began, all groups predicted comparable expectations of staying together over the 18 months of the study. Yet, by the end of the study, one in five couples had broken up. The proportion of breakups was highest among lesbian couples (22 percent), compared to gay (16 percent), cohabiting (17 percent), and married (4 percent) couples. Findings for the longevity of lesbian and gay couples were also reported by the Teichner poll: a median length of 1.8 years for lesbian couples compared to 2.5 years for gay couples ("Results of Poll," 1989). In another longitudinal study (5 years), Kurdek (1997a, 1998) reported breakup rates comparable to those found by Blumstein and Schwartz: 7 percent for heterosexual couples, 14 percent for gay couples, and 16 percent for lesbian couples. Yet, 86 percent of gay couples and 84 percent of lesbian couples were still together. This stability might result from attempts of lesbian and gay persons to make their relationships work despite a hostile social environment.

About one-third of the bisexual women and about one-quarter of the bisexual men studied by Weinberg and colleagues (1994) reported that their longest link lasted four years or less (compared to one-quarter of heterosexual women and men and about one-half of lesbian and gay persons). About one-third of the bisexual women and 40 percent of the bisexual men reported a longer link, for 10 or more years, compared to nearly half of heterosexual women and men, 20 percent of gay persons, and 12 percent of lesbian persons. Both bisexual men and women studied by Matteson (1996) fell in love with women more than with men, and both experienced longer lasting relationships with women than with men.

EMOTIONAL IMPACT OF BREAKUPS

The major difficulties of breakups are the emotional ones that usually accompany the breakups of any close couple (Kurdek, 1991c; Marcus, 1988). Gay, lesbian, and heterosexual persons separated from their partners for about 6 months showed no differences in the reasons they gave for the ending of their relationships. Nor did they recount differences in distress accompanying the breakups (Kurdek, 1997a).

Gay, lesbian, and heterosexual couples studied by Blumstein and Schwartz (1983) recalled their breakups as involving sadness, regrets, and anger. In a study of lesbian and heterosexual women who had lost partners, depression was common for both groups. Depression was especially typical for lesbians not connected to a lesbian network (Rothblum, 1990). Some racial and ethnic lesbians may feel more hurt if the failed relationship involved a person of their own ethnic group instead of a White person (Greene, 1995). Certain factors associated with severe emotional reactions for both lesbian and gay persons were a link of long duration, pooled finances, strong emphasis on attachment, and greater love for the partner (Kurdek, 1991c).

If closeted, lesbian and gay persons who are grieving their lost relationships may disclose their sexual orientation for the first time to receive support from others in their community (Browning et al., 1991). Often, however, they grieve the loss by themselves. Even if family and heterosexual friends know about the breakup, they may not show support and sympathy (Becker, 1988).

Addressing and preparing for a separation can affect post-separation adjustment in a positive way (Lazarus & Folkman, 1984). The contemplation of separation decreases the distress, maybe because one starts to gather psychological and social resources to cope with the pending dissolution. When one feels a sense of self-efficacy and control, one can contain the stress of separation (Kurdek, 1997a). Lesbian, gay, and heterosexual persons who experience severe emotional reactions to dissolution are also likely to experience positive outcomes over time such as personal growth and relief from conflict (Kurdek, 1991c).

SUMMARY

- Finding someone to date or to partner with is not easy because of the secrecy that often surrounds the same sex–gender or bisexual sexual identity of LGB persons. Many persons meet each other in bars, although there are increasingly alternative places for meeting.
- Many LGB single persons and those in couples live without the emotional support of their families of origin. Sometimes, families live too far away; in other cases, family members are angry with their LGB family members for "choosing" to be lesbian, gay, or bisexual. So, LGB persons and couples learn to search out supportive communities of friends.

- LGB persons understand the value of surrounding themselves with persons who care about them and offer them nurturance and, sometimes, role models for behavior.
- A primary issue facing LGB couples is the lack of role models. The most obvious scripts for dating and couple behavior are the heterosexual images promoted through the media.
- In the past, LGB couples tried to follow these scripts, creating relationships based on the male-dominant/female-submissive roles. Although this "butch–femme" model remains a useful metaphor for some, increasingly LGB couples, particularly lesbian couples, are establishing more egalitarian relationships.
- Generally, lesbians report more relationship satisfaction than other groups, but some variables increase the likelihood of satisfaction for all, including commitment, equal involvement, and equity. When communication remains open, intimacy is high, and persons feel the right balance between attachment and independence; couples may remain committed to one another for a longer time.
- Whereas marriage and other legal complications of financial interdependence may pressure heterosexual couples to remain together, LGB couples may feel freer to leave an unsatisfying relationship. Like heterosexual couples, LGB couples begin to experience some dissatisfaction in their relationships after one year, and many are not together after five years. Some of the factors that exacerbate conflict after the first year are work issues such as inequitable salaries, interracial differences, sex–gender role complications, and the balancing of attachment and autonomy. One underlying issue facing all LGB couples is the subtle, but wearing influence of heterosexism. Trying to maintain intimate relationships in a persistently hostile environment would challenge even the closest of partners. When couples have to hide their real lives or their real selves from the external world, the pressure on their intimate world can be overwhelming, especially if couples are isolated.
- The emotional effects of breaking up for LGB partners are no different than for heterosexual partners with one confounding feature: LGB couples rarely find support and empathy among their families of origin or heterosexual friends, or even among gay and lesbian persons, if they had kept the relationship closeted.
- Usually a breakup results in distress including regret, sorrow, and a sense of isolation that may increase depression.
- Preparing for a breakup may modify the emotional distress if one can develop supportive psychological and social resources.

CHAPTER 6
REFERENCES

Adelman, M. (1986). *Long time passing*. Boston: Alyson Press.

Alexander, C. J. (1997). Factors contributing to the termination of long-term gay male relationships. *Journal of Gay and Lesbian Social Services, 7*, 1–12.

Andrews, C. (1990). *Closeness and satisfaction in lesbian relationships.* Unpublished master's thesis, University of Washington, Seattle.

Arellano, C. M. (1993). *The role of gender in handling negative affect in same-sex couples.* Unpublished doctoral dissertation, University of Denver.

Becker, C. S. (1988). *Broken ties: Lesbian ex-lovers.* Boston: Alyson Press.

Bell, A. P., & Weinberg, M. S. (1978). *Homosexualities: A study of diversity among men and women.* New York: Simon & Schuster.

Berger, R. M. (1990). Men together: Understanding the gay couple. *Journal of Homosexuality, 19*, 31–49.

Blumstein, P., & Schwartz, P. (1983). *American couples.* New York: William Morrow.

Bowen, M. (1966). The use of family theory in clinical practice. *Comprehensive Psychiatry, 7*, 345–374.

Browning, C., Reynolds, A. L., & Dworkin, S. H. (1991). Affirmative psychotherapy for lesbian women. *Counseling Psychologist, 19*, 177–196.

Bryant, S., & Demian. (1994). Relationship characteristics of American gay and lesbian couples: Findings from a national survey. *Journal of Gay and Lesbian Social Services, 1*, 101–117.

Bumpass, L. L., & Sweet, J. (1989). National estimates of cohabitation: Cohort levels and union stability. *Demography, 26*, 615–625.

Burch, B. (1986). Psychotherapy and the dynamics of merger in lesbian couples. In T. S. Stein & C. J. Cohen (Eds.), *Contemporary perspectives on psychotherapy with lesbians and gay men* (pp. 57–71). New York: Plenum Press.

Burch, B. (1997). *Other women: Lesbian/bisexual experience and psychoanalytic views of women.* New York: Columbia University Press.

Burgess, R. L., & Huston, T. L. (Eds.). (1979). *Social exchange in developing relationships*. New York: Academic Press.

Cabaj, R. P., & Klinger, R. L. (1996). Psychotherapeutic interventions with lesbian and gay couples. In R. P. Cabaj & T. S. Stein (Eds.), *Textbook of homosexuality and mental health* (pp. 485–502). Washington, DC: American Psychiatric Press.

Caldwell, M. A., & Peplau, L. A. (1984). The balance of power in lesbian relationships. *Sex Roles, 10*, 587–600.

Caron, S. L., & Ulin, M. (1997). Closeting and the quality of lesbian relationships. *Families in Society: Journal of Contemporary Human Services, 78*, 413–419.

Clunis, D. M., & Green, G. D. (2000). *Lesbian couples: A guide to creating healthy relationships*. Seattle: Seal Press.

Cooper, K. (1999). Practice with transgendered youth and their families. *Journal of Gay & Lesbian Social Services, 10*, 111–129.

D'Augelli, A. R., & Garnets, L. D. (1995). Lesbian, gay, and bisexual communities. In A. R. D'Augelli & C. J. Patterson (Eds.), *Lesbian, gay, and bisexual identities over the lifespan* (pp. 293–320). New York: Oxford University Press.

Davis, D., & Kennedy, E. L. (1986). Oral history and the study of sexuality in the lesbian community: Buffalo, New York, 1940–1960. *Feminist Studies, 12*, 7–26.

Deenen, A. A., Gijs, L., & van Naerssen, A. X. (1994). Intimacy and sexuality in gay male couples. *Archives of Sexual Behavior, 23*, 421–431.

Diamond, L. M., Savin-Williams, R. C., & Dubé, E. M. (1999). Sex, dating, passionate friendships, and romance. In W. Furman, B. B. Brown, & C. Feiring (Eds.), *The development of romantic relationships in adolescence* (pp. 175–210). New York: Cambridge University Press.

Eldridge, N. S. (1987). Correlates of relation satisfaction and role conflict in dual-career lesbian couples. *Professional Psychology: Research and Practice, 18*, 567–572.

Eldridge, N. S., & Gilbert, L. A. (1990). Correlates of relationship satisfaction in lesbian couples. *Psychology of Women Quarterly, 14*, 43–62.

Faderman, L. (1991). *Odd girls and twilight lovers: A history of lesbian life in twentieth century America*. New York: Columbia University Press.

Faderman, L. (1992). The return of butch and femme: A phenomenon in lesbian sexuality of the 1980s and 1990s. *Journal of the History of Sexuality, 2*, 578–596.

Fajer, M. A. (1992). Can two real men eat quiche together? Storytelling, gender-role stereotypes, and legal protection for lesbians and gay men. *University of Miami Law Review, 46,* 511–651.

Gillman, T. J., & Langford, T. (2001, August 22). Gays stand out in census. *Dallas Morning News,* pp. A25, A30.

Gottman, J. M. (1994). *What predicts divorce? The relationship between marital processes and marital outcomes.* Hillsdale, NJ: Lawrence Erlbaum.

Green, R.-J., Bettinger, M., & Zacks, E. (1996). Are lesbian couples fused and gay male couples disengaged? Questioning gender straight jackets. In J. Laird & R.-J. Green (Eds.), *Lesbians and gays in couples and families* (pp. 185–231). San Francisco: Jossey-Bass.

Greene, B. (1994a). Ethnic minority lesbians and gay men: Mental health and treatment issues. *Journal of Consulting and Clinical Psychology, 62,* 243–251.

Greene, B. (1994b). Lesbian and gay sexual orientations: Implications for clinical training, practice, and research. In B. Greene & G. M. Herek (Eds.), *Lesbian and gay psychology: Theory, research, and clinical applications* (pp. 1–24). Thousand Oaks, CA: Sage Publications.

Greene, B. (1994c). Lesbian women of color: Triple jeopardy. In L. Comas-Diaz & B. Greene (Eds.), *Women of color* (pp. 389–427). New York: Guilford Press.

Greene, B. (1995). Lesbian couples. In K. Jay (Ed.), *Dyke life: From growing up to growing old-A celebration of the lesbian experience* (pp. 97–106). New York: Basic Books.

Greene, B. (2000). African American lesbian and bisexual women. *Journal of Social Issues, 56,* 239–249.

Greene, B., & Boyd-Franklin, N. (1996). African American lesbian couples: Ethnocultural considerations in psychotherapy. *Women & Therapy, 19,* 49–60.

Greene, K., Causby, V., & Miller, D. H. (1999). The nature and function of fusion in the dynamics of lesbian relationships. *Affilia, 14,* 78–97.

Haas, S. M., & Stafford, L. (1998). An initial examination of maintenance behaviors in gay and lesbian relationships. *Journal of Social and Personal Relationships, 15,* 846–855.

Hall, M., & Gregory, A. (1991). Subtle balances: Love and work in lesbian relationships. In B. Sang, J. Warshow, & A. Smith (Eds.), *Lesbians at midlife: The creative transition* (pp. 122–133). San Francisco: Spinsters.

Harry, J. (1982). Decision making and age differences among gay couples. *Journal of Homosexuality, 8,* 9–21.

Harry, J. (1984). *Gay couples*. New York: Praeger.

Herek, G. M. (1995). Psychological heterosexism in the United States. In A. R. D'Augelli & C. J. Patterson (Eds.), *Lesbian, gay, and bisexual identities over the lifespan: Psychological perspectives* (pp. 321–346). New York: Oxford University Press.

Hill, C. A. (1999). Fusion and conflict in lesbian relationships? *Feminism & Psychology, 9*, 179–185.

Hostetler, A. J., & Cohler, B. J. (1997). Partnership, singlehood, and the lesbian and gay life course: A research agenda. *Journal of Gay, Lesbian, and Bisexual Identity, 2*, 199–230.

Huston, M., & Schwartz, P. (1995). The relationships of lesbians and gay men. In J. Wood & S. Duck (Eds.), *Under-studied relationships: Off the beaten track* (pp. 89–121). Thousand Oaks, CA: Sage Publications.

James, S. E., & Murphy, B. C. (1998). Gay and lesbian relationships in a changing social con text. In C. J. Patterson & A. R. D'Augelli (Eds.), *Lesbian, gay, and bisexual identities in families: Psychological perspectives* (pp. 99–121). New York: Oxford University Press.

Johnson, B. (1990). Survey reveals male and female differences in sexual behaviors of older adults. *Contemporary Sexuality, 24*, 3.

Julien, D., Arellano, C., & Turgeon, L. (1997). Gender issues in heterosexual, gay and lesbian couples. In W. K. Halford & H. J. Markman (Eds.), *Clinical handbook of marriage and couples intervention* (pp. 107–127). New York: John Wiley & Sons.

Julien, D., Chartrand, E., & Begin, J. (1999). Social networks, structural interdependence, and conjugal adjustment in heterosexual, gay, and lesbian couples. *Journal of Marriage and the Family, 61*, 516–530.

Julien, D., Gagnon, I., Hamelin, M., & Belanger, I. (1995). *A comparison of conflict issues in gay, lesbian and heterosexual couples.* Unpublished manuscript, University of Quebec, Montreal.

Julien, D., Pizzamiglio, M. T., Chartrand, E., & Begin, J. (1995). An observational study of com munication in gay, lesbian and heterosexual couples. *Unpublished manuscript*, University of Quebec, Montreal.

Kaufman, P. A., Harrison, E., & Hyde, M. L. (1984). Distancing and intimacy in lesbian relationships. *American Journal of Psychiatry, 141*, 530–533.

Kehoe, M. (1989). *Lesbians over 60 speak for themselves*. New York: Harrington Park.

Kelley, H. H. (1983). Love and commitment. In H. H. Kelley, E. Berscheid, A. Christensen, J. H. Harvey, T. L. Huston, G. Levinger, E. McClintock, L. A. Peplau, & D. R. Peterson (Eds.), *Close relationships* (pp. 265–314). New York: W. H. Freeman.

Kennedy, E. L., & Davis, M. D. (1993). *Boots of leather, slippers of gold: The history of a lesbian community.* New York: Routledge.

Kitzinger, C., & Coyle, A. (1995). Lesbian and gay couples: Speaking of difference. *Psychologist, 8,* 64–69.

Klinkenberg, D., & Rose, S. (1994). Dating scripts of gay men and lesbians. *Journal of Homosexuality, 26,* 23–35.

Krestan, J., & Bepko, C. (1980). The problem of fusion in the lesbian relationship. *Family Process, 19,* 277–290.

Kurdek, L. A. (1988). Relationship quality of gay and lesbian cohabiting couples. *Journal of Homosexuality, 15,* 93–118.

Kurdek, L. A. (1989). Relationship quality in gay and lesbian cohabiting couples: A 1-year fol low-up study. *Journal of Social and Personal Relationships, 6,* 39–59.

Kurdek, L. A. (1991a). Correlates of relationship satisfaction in cohabiting gay and lesbian couples: Integration of contextual, investment, and problem-solving models. *Journal of Personality and Social Psychology, 61,* 910–922.

Kurdek, L. A. (1991b). The dissolution of gay and lesbian couples. *Journal of Social and Personal Relationships, 8,* 265–278.

Kurdek, L. A. (1991c). Sexuality in homosexual and heterosexual couples. In K. McKinney & S. Sprecher (Eds.), *Sexuality in close relationships* (pp. 177–191). Hillsdale, NJ: Lawrence Erlbaum.

Kurdek, L. A. (1992). Relationship stability and relationship satisfaction in cohabiting gay and lesbian couples: A prospective longitudinal test of the contextual and interdependence models. *Journal of Social and Personal Relationships, 9,* 125–142.

Kurdek, L. A. (1993). *The assessment of destructive arguing and personal conflict resolution styles in gay, lesbian, heterosexual nonparent and heterosexual parent couples.* Unpublished manuscript, Wayne State University, Dayton, OH.

Kurdek, L. A. (1994a). Areas of conflict for gay, lesbian, and heterosexual cohabiting couples: What couples argue about influences relationship satisfaction. *Journal of Marriage and the Family, 56,* 923–934.

Kurdek, L. A. (1994b). Conflict resolution styles in gay, lesbian, heterosexual nonparent, and heterosexual parent couples. *Journal of Marriage and the Family, 56*, 705–722.

Kurdek, L. A. (1995a). Assessing multiple determinants of relationship commitment in cohabitating gay, cohabitating lesbian, dating heterosexual, and married heterosexual couples. *Family Relations, 44*, 261–266.

Kurdek, L. A. (1995b). Developing changes in relationship quality in gay and lesbian cohabiting couples. *Developmental Psychology, 31*, 86–94.

Kurdek, L. A. (1996). The deterioration of relationship quality for gay and lesbian cohabitating couples: A five-year prospective longitudinal study. *Personal Relationships, 3*, 417–442.

Kurdek, L. A. (1997a). Adjustment to relationship dissolution in gay, lesbian, and heterosexual partners. *Personal Relationships, 4*, 145–161.

Kurdek, L. A. (1997b). Relation between neuroticism and dimensions of relationship commitment: Evidence from gay, lesbian, and heterosexual couples. *Journal of Family Psychology, 11*, 109–124.

Kurdek, L. A. (1998). Relationship outcomes and their predictors: Longitudinal evidence from heterosexual married, gay cohabiting, and lesbian cohabiting couples. *Journal of Marriage and the Family, 60*, 553–568.

Kurdek, L. A., & Schmitt, J. P. (1986a). Early development of relationship quality in hetero sexual cohabiting, gay, and lesbian couples. *Developmental Psychology, 22*, 305–309.

Kurdek, L. A., & Schmitt, J. P. (1986b). Interaction of sex role self-concept with relationship quality and relationship beliefs in married, heterosexual cohabiting, gay and lesbian relationships. *Journal of Personality and Social Psychology, 51*, 365–370.

Kurdek, L. A., & Schmitt, J. P. (1986c). Relationship quality of partners in heterosexual married, heterosexual cohabiting, and gay and lesbian relationships. *Journal of Personality and Social Psychology, 51*, 711–720.

Kurdek, L. A., & Schmitt, J. P. (1987). Perceived emotional support from family and friends in members of homosexual, married, and heterosexual cohabiting couples. *Journal of Homosexuality, 14*, 57–68.

Laird, J. (2000). Gender in lesbian relationships: Cultural, feminist, and constructionist reflections. *Journal of Marital and Family Therapy, 26*, 455–467.

LaSala, M. C. (2002). Walls and bridges: How coupled gay men and lesbians manage their intergenerational relationships. *Journal of Marital and Family Therapy, 28*, 327–339.

Lazarus, R. S., & Folkman, S. (1984). *Stress, appraisal, and coping.* New York: Springer-Verlag.

Leslie, D., & Mac Neill, L. (1995). Double positive: Lesbians and race. In J. Adelman & G. M. Enguidanos (Eds.), *Racism in the lives of women: Testimony, theory, and guides to antiracist practices* (pp. 161–169). New York: Harrington Park.

Levinger, G. C. (1982). A social exchange view of the dissolution of pair relationships. In F. L. Nye (Ed.), *Family relationships: Rewards and costs* (pp. 97–112). Beverly Hills, CA: Sage Publications.

Linde, R. (1994). Impact of AIDS on adult gay male development: Implications for psychotherapy. In S. A. Cadwell, R. A. Burnhan, & M. Forstein (Eds.), *Therapists on the frontline: Psychotherapy with gay men in the age of AIDS* (pp. 25–31). Washington, DC: American Psychiatric Press.

Lynch, J. M., & Reilly, M. E. (1986). Role relationships: Lesbian perspectives. *Journal of Homosexuality*, *12*, 53–69.

Mackey, R. A., Diemer, M. A., & O'Brien, B. A. (2000). Psychological intimacy in the lasting relationships of heterosexual and same-gender couples. *Sex Roles*, *43*, 201–227.

Mackey, R. A., O'Brien, B. A., & Mackey, E. F. (1997). *Gay and lesbian couples: Voices from lasting relationships.* Westport, CT: Praeger.

Marcus, E. (1988). *The male couple's guide to living together.* New York: Harper & Row.

Matteson, D. R. (1987). Counseling bisexual men. In M. Scher, M. Stevens, G. Good, & G. A. Eichenfield (Eds.), *Handbook of counseling and psychotherapy with men* (pp. 232–249). Newbury Park, CA: Sage Publications.

Matteson, D. R. (1996). Psychotherapy with bisexual individuals. In R. P. Cabaj & T. S. Stein (Eds.), *Textbook of homosexuality and mental health* (pp. 433–449). Washington, DC: American Psychiatric Press.

McWhirter, D. P., & Mattison, A. M. (1984). *The male couple.* Englewood Cliffs, NJ: Prentice Hall.

McWhirter, D. P., & Mattison, A. W. (1996). Male couples. In R. P. Cabaj & T. S. Stein (Eds.), *Textbook of homosexuality and mental health* (pp. 819–837). Washington, DC: American Psychiatric Press.

Mencher, J. (1997). Intimacy in lesbian relationships: A critical reexamination of fusion. In N. V. Jordan (Ed.), *Women's growth in diversity: More writings from the Stone Center* (pp. 311–332). Wellesley, MA: Wellesley College.

Metz, M. E., Simon Rosser, B.R.S., & Strapko, N. (1994). Differences in conflict-resolution styles among heterosexual, gay, and lesbian couples. *Journal of Sex Research, 31,* 293–308.

Minuchin, S. (1974). *Families and family therapy.* Cambridge, MA: Harvard University Press.

Moses, A. E., & Buckner, J. A. (1986). The special problems of rural gay clients. In A. Moses & R. O. Hawkins (Eds.), *Counseling lesbian women and gay men: A life issues approach* (pp. 173–180). St. Louis: C.V. Mosby.

Murphy, B. C. (1994). Difference and diversity: Gay and lesbian couples. *Social Services for Gay and Lesbian Couples, 1,* 5–31.

Nestle, J. (1992). *The persistent desire: A femme-butch reader.* Boston: Alyson Press.

Nichols, M. (1988). Bisexuality in women: Myths, realities, and implications for therapy. *Women & Therapy, 7,* 235–252.

Nichols, M. (1989). Sex therapy with lesbians, gay men, and bisexuals. In S. R. Leiblum & R. C. Rosen (Eds.), *Principles and practice of sex therapy: Update for the 1990s* (2nd ed., pp. 269–297). New York: Guilford Press.

O'Brien, K. (1992). Primary relationships affect the psychological health of men at risk for AIDS. *Psychological Reports, 71,* 147–153.

Oetjen, H., & Rothblum, E. D. (2000). When lesbians aren't gay: Factors affecting depression among lesbians. *Journal of Homosexuality, 39,* 49–73.

Okun, B. F. (1996). *Understanding diverse families: What practitioners need to know.* New York: Guilford Press.

Patterson, D. G., & Schwartz, P. (1994). The social construction of conflict in intimate same-sex couples. In D. D. Cahn (Ed.), *Conflict in personal relationships* (pp. 3–26). Hillsdale, NJ: Lawrence Erlbaum.

Peplau, L. A. (1982–1983). Research on homosexual couples: An overview. *Journal of Homosexuality, 8,* 3–21.

Peplau, L. A. (1983a). What homosexuals want. In O. Pocs (Ed.), *Human sexuality* (pp. 201–207). New York: Guilford Press.

Peplau, L. A. (1983b). Roles and gender. In H. H. Kelly, E. Berscheid, A. Christensen, J. H. Harvey, T. L. Huston, G. Levinger, E. McClintock, L. A. Peplau, & D. R. Peterson (Eds.), *Close relationships* (pp. 220–264). San Francisco: Freeman.

Peplau, L. A. (1991). Lesbian and gay relationships. In J. C. Gonsiorek & J. D. Weinrich (Eds.), *Homosexuality: Research findings for public policy* (pp. 177–196). Newbury Park, CA: Sage Publications.

Peplau, L. A. (1993). Lesbian and gay relationships. In L. D. Garnets & D. C. Kimmel (Eds.), *Psychological perspectives on lesbian & gay male experiences* (pp. 395–419). New York: Columbia University Press.

Peplau, L. A., & Cochran, S. D. (1990). A relational perspective on homosexuality. In D. P. McWhirter, S. A. Saunders, & J. M. Reinisch (Eds.), *Homosexuality/heterosexuality: Concepts of sexual orientation* (pp. 321–349). New York: Oxford University Press.

Peplau, L. A., Cochran, S. D., & Mays, V. M. (1997). In B. Greene (Ed.), *Ethnic and cultural diversity among lesbians and gay men* (pp. 11–38). Thousand Oaks, CA: Sage Publications.

Peplau, L. A., Padesky, C., & Hamilton, M. (1982). Satisfaction in lesbian relationships. In D. Perlman & S. Duck (Eds.), *Intimate relationships: Development, dynamics and deterioration* (pp. 13–42). Newbury Park, CA: Sage Publications.

Peterson, M. R. (1992). *At personal risk: Boundary violations in professional-client relationships.* New York: W. W. Norton.

Reilly, M. E., & Lynch, J. M. (1990). Power-sharing in lesbian relationships. *Journal of Homosexuality, 19*, 1–30.

Results of poll. (1989, June 6). *San Francisco Examiner, p. A19.*

Robinson, C. H. (1997). Everyday (hetero)sexism: Strategies of resistance and lesbian couples. In C. R. Ronai, B. A. Zsembik, & J. R. Feagan (Eds.), *Everyday sexism in the third millennium* (pp. 33–50). New York: Routledge.

Roth, S. (1985). Psychotherapy issues with lesbian couples. *Journal of Marital and Family Therapy, 11*, 273–286.

Roth, S. (1989). Psychotherapy with lesbian couples: Individual issues, female socialization and the social context. In M. McGoldrick, C. Anderson, & F. Walsh (Eds.), *Women in families: A framework for family therapy* (pp. 286–307). New York: W. W. Norton.

Roth, S., & Murphy, B. C. (1986). Therapeutic work with lesbian clients: A systematic therapy view. In M. Ault-Riche (Ed.), *Women and family therapy* (pp. 78–89). Rockville, MD: Aspen Press.

Rothblum, E. D. (1990). Depression among lesbians: An invisible and unresearched phenomenon. *Journal of Gay & Lesbian Psychotherapy, 1*, 67–87.

Rusbult, C. E. (1983). A longitudinal test of the investment model: The development (and deterioration) of satisfaction and commitment in heterosexual involvements. *Journal of Personality and Social Psychology, 45,* 101–117.

Rust, P. C. (1996a). Finding a sexual identity and community: Therapeutic implications and cultural assumptions in scientific models of coming out. In E. D. Rothblum & L. A. Bond (Eds.), *Preventing heterosexism and homophobia* (pp. 87–123). Thousand Oaks, CA: Sage Publications.

Rust, P. C. (1996b). Monogamy and polyamory: Relationship issues for bisexuals. In B. A. Firestein (Ed.), *Bisexuality: The psychology and politics of an invisible minority* (pp. 127–148). Thousand Oaks, CA: Sage Publications.

Rutter, V., & Schwartz, P. (1996). Same-sex couples: Courtship, commitment, context. In A. W. Auhagen (Ed.), *The diversity of human relationships* (pp. 197–226). New York: Cambridge University Press.

Rutter, V., & Schwartz, P. (2000). Gender, marriage, and diverse possibilities for cross-sex and same-sex pairs. In D. H. Demo, K. R. Allen, & M. A. Fine (Eds.), *Handbook of family diversity* (pp. 59–81). New York: Oxford University Press.

Savin-Williams, R. (1990). *Gay and lesbian youth: Expressions of identity.* New York: Hemisphere.

Schneider, M. S. (1986). The relationships of cohabitating lesbian and heterosexual couples: A comparison. *Psychology of Women Quarterly, 10,* 234–239.

Shachar, S. A., & Gilbert, L. A. (1983). Working lesbians: Role conflicts and coping strategies. *Psychology of Women Quarterly, 7,* 272–284.

Silverstein, C. (1981). *Man to man: Gay couples in America.* New York: William Morrow.

Smith, A. (1997). Cultural diversity and the coming-out process: Implications for clinical practice. In B. Greene (Ed.), *Ethnic and cultural diversity among lesbians and gay men* (pp. 279–300). Thousand Oaks, CA: Sage Publications.

Surrey, J. (1985). *Self-in-relation: A theory of women's development* (Work in Progress No. 13). Wellesley, MA: Wellesley College, Stone Center for Women's Development.

Thorne, A., & Coupland, J. (1998). Articulations of same-sex desire: Lesbian and gay male dating advertisements. *Journal of Sociolinguistics, 2,* 233–237.

Toder, N. (1992). Lesbian couples in particular. In B. Berzon & R. Leighton (Eds.), *Positively gay* (pp. 50–63). Berkeley, CA: Celestial Arts.

Wayment, H., & Peplau, L. A. (1995). Social support and well-being among lesbian and heterosexual women: A structural modeling approach. *Personality and Social Psychology Bulletin, 21,* 1189–1199.

Weber, J. C. (1996). Social class as a correlate of gender identity among lesbian women. *Sex Roles, 35,* 271–280.

Weinberg, M. S., Williams, C. J., & Pryor, D. W. (1994). *Dual attractions: Understanding bisexuality.* New York: Oxford University Press.

Weinstock, J. S. (1998). Lesbian, gay, bisexual, and transgendered friendships in adulthood. In C. J. Patterson & A. R. D'Augelli (Eds.), *Lesbian, gay, and bisexual identities in families: Psychological perspectives* (pp. 122–153). New York: Oxford University Press.

Weitz, R. (1989). Uncertainty and the lives of persons with AIDS. *Journal of Health and Social Behavior, 30,* 270–281.

Weston, K. (1991). *Families we choose: Lesbians, gays, kinship.* New York: Columbia University Press.

Weston, K. (1996). *Render me, gender me: Lesbians talk sex, class, color, nation, studmuffins.* New York: Columbia University Press.

Zea, M. C., Reisen, C. A., & Poppen, P. J. (1999). Psychological well-being among Latino lesbians and gay men. *Cultural Diversity & Ethnic Minority Psychology, 14,* 371–379.

CHAPTER 7
PARENTING

*What are the proportions of gay and lesbian parents and of the children
of these parents?*

Under what circumstances do gay and lesbian persons become parents?

*What stressors do gay and lesbian persons face in the process
of becoming parents or when sharing parenting with a coparent?*

What does research report about lesbian mothers and gay fathers?

What stressors do lesbian and gay parents face in raising their families?

*Are children of gay and lesbian parents different from peers raised in homes
of heterosexual parents?*

DEMOGRAPHICS OF LESBIAN AND GAY FAMILIES

Many lesbian and gay persons desire to be parents and to raise children. Some are the
biological parents of children conceived in previous heterosexual marriages; some are the
biological parents of children conceived outside heterosexual marriages; some are the partners of biological parents; and some are adoptive and foster care parents (National Gay and
Lesbian Task Force, 2000). Although precise statistics are not available, estimates indicate that
between 2 and 8 million gay and lesbian persons are parents in the United States; of this
group, it is estimated that about 1.5 to 5 million are lesbians (Hare, 1994; Lott-Whitehead &
Tully, 1993).

Approximations of the total number of children of lesbian and gay persons range from 4
to 14 million (Hare, 1994; Patterson & Chan, 1996). Data from the 1990 census indicated
that about 21.1 percent of lesbian couples and 5.2 percent of gay couples have children in
their homes. About three-quarters of the children (71 percent in lesbian households, 76 percent in gay households) are under 18 years of age. The data from the 2000 census showed
that gay and lesbian families live in 99.3 percent of all counties in the United States ("News
of the Year," 2002). The General Social Survey (GSS) and the National Health and Social Life
Survey (NHSLS) also collected national data on gay and lesbian parents indicating that about
28 percent of lesbian and 14 percent of gay persons have children in their households. Many
children in gay and lesbian households were probably born in previous marriages since,
according to the census sample, about 20 percent of gay persons in couples and about 30
percent of lesbians in couples had been in heterosexual marriages. In the combined GSS-
NHSLS data, the marriage rate was higher: about 30 percent of gay and 46 percent of lesbian persons (Black, Gates, Sanders, & Taylor, 2000).

WAYS OF HAVING CHILDREN

Despite adverse social and legal circumstances, gay and lesbian persons find ways to have children. Some of these ways are the same as in traditional heterosexual families whereas others are less traditional.

CHILDREN FROM PRIOR MARRIAGES

Formerly, children were most often born to gay and lesbian persons through heterosexual marriages (Allen, 1997; Parks, 1998). The parents of these children quietly suppressed their own sexual identities for the sake of family unity or, upon disclosing their sexual identities, ended their marriages and risked losing custody of their children (Fredriksen, 1999; Friedman, 1997; Nations, 1997). Often in divorce hearings, they were granted only limited visitation rights, specifically ordered to occur outside the presence of a same sex–gender partner (Patterson & Redding, 1996). The courts enforced the illusion of heterosexuality despite the parents' sexual orientation (Allen, 1997). Even so, many children live with their biological mothers or fathers and their same sex–gender partners. Some children live in the homes of these mothers or fathers full time and others part time as permitted in divorce custody agreements.

Gay fathers are less likely to have any custody arrangements with their children from a prior marriage. Most of these men do not even attempt to gain custody because the likelihood of success is low, not only because they are gay but also because they are male. These men may have little contact with their children during their formative years (Golombok, 2000).

GAY AND LESBIAN COUPLES HAVING CHILDREN

Advances in medical fertility research now afford gay and lesbian couples new opportunities to raise children from infancy. Couples may choose to bear children through donor sperm insemination or surrogacy. For example, one of the partners in a lesbian couple can bear a baby through donor sperm insemination contributed by a friend, relative, acquaintance, or an unknown person through a sperm bank. Lesbians can also conceive a child through planned sexual intercourse with a consenting male who may or may not play a part in the child's upbringing. Gay persons can become fathers through means such as paid surrogacy arrangements, sexual intercourse with a woman, or providing sperm to a lesbian friend. Sometimes joint parenting arrangements are created such as between a lesbian and gay person or a lesbian couple and a gay couple. Gay persons also can also make paid surrogacy arrangements (McLeod & Crawford, 1998; Shernoff, 1996).

CHILDREN OBTAINED THROUGH ADOPTION OR FOSTER CARE

Lesbian and gay persons also become parents through adoption or foster care (Patterson, 1992) and have done so for many years (Arnup, 1999). There is considerable variation in statutes, guidelines, and practices across and within states regarding sexual orientation and child welfare issues, ranging from no mention of sexual orientation in foster care or adoption policies to those that forbid gay and lesbian parenting (Dudley, 2002; Leiter, 1997). Legal barriers also complicate the adoption and foster care process. Lambda Legal provides a review of adoption laws across the country that are favorable or not favorable to adoptions by lesbian and gay persons (see http://www.lambdalegal.org/cgi-bin/iowa/documents/record?record=399).

In 38 states, the county, not the state, administers the department of social services. This can lead to huge variations across these states in decisions on adoption and foster parenting for same sex–gender couples (Arnup, 1999). In addition, individual agency policy can either complicate or facilitate adoptions and foster care. If the agency allows placement, usually accompanying requirements ensue such as granting adoption or foster care to only one of the partners in a couple or requiring the couple members to hide their sexual orientation. Or agencies may place only adolescents identified as gay or lesbian with gay or lesbian couples (Ariel & McPherson, 2000; Hartman, 1999).

Although lesbian and gay couples experience some of the same issues that heterosexual couples experience when pursuing the various options of having children, they also face a different set of issues because of their sexual orientation. These issues can lead to unique stressors for gay and lesbian families—the overriding obstacle being heterosexism, which affects both bearing and raising children.

STRESSORS FACED BY LESBIAN AND GAY PARENTS

Heterosexism

Once lesbian or gay couples decide to have children, they receive little or no validation for their desired families because of disapproval of their sexual orientation and same sex–gender coupling. They often face beliefs that they should have no association with children and that they are unfit to raise children. Another belief is that any children these parents raise will be psychologically and socially maladjusted, will suffer social stigmatization (Matthews, & Lease, 2000), will experience negative development in sex–gender identity, and will become gay or lesbian themselves (Shapiro, 1996).

Dilemmas about Pregnancy, Donors, and Surrogates

Once a lesbian couple decides to have a child, the issue arises about which partner will become pregnant and what the role will be of the partner who does not. An issue for gay persons can be who will do the "mothering" tasks. The next big issue is how to achieve a pregnancy. The heterosexual sex way? The gay friend donor way? The medical system way? If the latter, it may not be easy to find affirmative health care providers in many parts of the country. If a couple uses donor sperm insemination, questions arise such as: Will the sperm donor be anonymous? What might be the future legal or social connection with the donor? Other questions concern sperm bank policies: Who controls them? What are the standards? What information is open? What are the rights of donors? Gay persons who use surrogate pregnancy arrangements know the women giving birth from the beginning of these arrangements, but this route can also entail legal and moral dilemmas (Hartman, 1999; Patterson & Chan, 1997).

Fears of Losing Custody

For gay and lesbian persons who have custody of their children from a previous heterosexual marriage, one of the biggest stressors is the fear that because of their sexual orientation, they will lose custody of or contact with their children (Bigner, 1996; Patterson, 1995). This is a realistic fear since many gay and lesbian parents are denied custody or visitation rights of their biological children (Patterson, 1992). In states with sodomy laws, lesbian and gay sexual partners are in violation of these laws and vulnerable to negative court rulings if custody of their children is challenged (Segal-Sklar, 1996). In many jurisdictions, court decisions have awarded custody to the heterosexual parent or even to other persons in the extended family, for example, biological grandparents (Benkov, 1994; Patterson, 1995).

The general assumption underlying much of the judicial decision making regarding custody is the belief that gay and lesbian parents have adverse effects on the social and psychological development of their children (Patterson, 1992). An automatic judicial assumption is that the best interests of a child mean being reared by heterosexual parents. Some of the cases have become highly publicized as in the case of the biological mother in Virginia, Sharon Bottoms, who lost custody of her son because of her sexual orientation (*Bottoms v. Bottoms*, 1995). Mary Ward, a biological mother in Florida, lost custody to her ex-husband because she was a lesbian. The husband had been convicted of murdering his first wife reportedly in the in the midst of another custody battle. Apparently, however, this was better in the judge's view than continued placement with a "sex deviate" (*Ward v. Ward*, 1996).

Court decisions on custody issues are changing. The legal position of lesbian and gay parents has improved since the appearance in courts of the first lesbian custody cases several decades ago (Arnup, 1999). Some judges now take the stance that same sex–gender sexual orientation alone does not necessarily render a parent unfit to raise children (Rosenblum, 1991). The National Association of Social Workers, the American Psychological Association, and other professional and human services organizations and associations support the position that a person's sexual orientation should have no effect on child custody decisions or in determining whether a person qualifies to be a foster or adoptive parent (Benkov, 1994). This thinking has evolved from consistent research findings that the developmental outcomes for children reared by lesbian or gay parents are as good or better than children reared in comparable heterosexual households.

Coparents

The presence of a coparent in a gay or lesbian family (the nonbiological parent of a child born into a lesbian link or the nonadoptive parent in a gay or lesbian couple) can result in both support and stress. A partner who is a coparent in a lesbian couple can provide considerable support as a full partner in parenting, especially with a child born or adopted into their relationship. With blended families or those in which a partner takes a parenting role in a relationship with a person who was already a parent, the coparent's role may be more variable across couples (Appleby & Anastas, 1998). Yet in a study of 25 adult children raised by lesbian mothers, the children formed positive bonds with their mothers' partners (Tasker & Golombok, 1997).

Gay fathers with partners may also gain more support and experience fewer difficulties in the parenting role than when they are without partners (Harris & Turner, 1985–1986). When the father's partner is supportive and participates in child care, the father feels more secure in his parental role, and the couple's relationship also benefits. When gay partners mutually decide to adopt, commitment to the parental role increases (Bozett, 1993). Both partners devote more time and effort to child care than typical heterosexual fathers, although partners of gay fathers are somewhat less involved in child care than partners of lesbian mothers (Patterson, 1996).

A stressor in gay and lesbian families with coparents is that usually only one person is the legal parent or parent of record, although this is changing in a few states such as New Jersey (Mallon, 2000). This creates an unequal balance of power in the couple (Rutter & Schwartz, 1996). Usually, the biological parent is the legal parent, and the coparent has no legal rights regarding the child. Rarely are both parents' names on the birth certificate, and rarely does the nonbiological parent win the right to adopt the child (Burke, 1993; Segal-Sklar, 1996). With no legal claim to the child, the coparent receives no recognition from social institutions such as schools or medical systems (Reimann, 1997). Nor are legal protections afforded by the courts to the link between the nonbiological or nonlegal parent and the child if the partners separate. The breakup may sever the coparent's relationship with the child, or if the relationship continues, it happens only at the discretion of the biological mother. If a custody fight ensues with the biological mother, the coparent has no legal ground for attaining custody or even visiting rights (Arnup, 1999). If the biological parent becomes incapacitated or dies, custody may be granted to the biological father, to other relatives (perhaps even those who are strangers to the child), or to the state (Allen, 1997; Arnup, 1999). Whoever receives custody can take the child out of state and deny visitation to the nonbiolgical parent (Kuehlwein & Gottschalk, 2000).

One solution to the coparent dilemma is taking turns in childbearing if the couple wants several children (Appleby & Anastas, 1998). Another solution is for the coparent to adopt a child born to or adopted by the other (Benkov, 1994; Shernoff, 1996). Second-parent adoption can be a strong means to strengthen and legitimize lesbian and gay families. For example, in families with two mothers, it can remove the vagueness about the status of the "other mother" (McClellan, 2001).

Second-parent adoptions have been used for lesbian or gay couples after the dissolution of the original heterosexual marriage, allowing the "new" parent to assume rights and responsibilities without necessitating that the original parent forfeit parenting status (Arnup, 1999). This legal recourse has seldom been granted to gay and lesbian couples in the United States or Canada until recently (Segal-Sklar, 1996). The availability in some parts of the country of joint and second-parent adoption was the greatest legal accomplishment for gay and lesbian parents in the 1990s. The first reported second-parent adoption by a lesbian couple occurred in 1991 in the District of Columbia. Trial courts in more than a dozen other states have since granted these adoptions. They are granted under the best-interests-of-the-child standard used in all other adoptions (American Civil Liberties Union, 1999).

But, from the mid-1990s, the high profile of gay and lesbian families evoked escalating efforts to prevent them from adopting children and serving as foster parents. Several states (Missouri, Oklahoma, South Carolina, Tennessee, and Washington) introduced legislation between 1995 and 1997 proposing statewide bans on adoption and foster parenting, but none of the legislation passed. Also in 1999, an amendment that would have prohibited a joint adoption by unmarried gay and heterosexual couples was defeated in the District of Columbia. Three other states (Arkansas, Texas, and Utah) proposed prohibitions in 1998. Restrictions passed in Utah and Arkansas in 1999 (Chambers & Polikoff, 1999). In April 2000, the Mississippi legislature passed a bill that bars gay and lesbian persons from adopting or becoming foster parents ("Year in Review," 2001). Yet New Hampshire repealed its ban on adoption and foster parenting in 1999.

LESBIAN MOTHERS

Generally, the lives of lesbian mothers are similar to the lives of heterosexual mothers (McNeill, Rienzi, & Kposowa, 1998; Parks, 1998). They manage jobs, relationships, car pools, school, homework, and a myriad of other activities associated with raising a family (Muzio, 1999). Yet, for lesbians, bearing children means crossing the line from invisibility to visible participation in some of society's most conservative institutions—school, church, day care, and the various family-oriented organizations like parent–teacher groups (Friedman, 1997; Morningstar, 1999). This participation and the attendant scrutiny place stress on these mothers that heterosexual mothers do not have to endure (Friedman, 1997; Gartrell et al., 1999).

Even so, lesbian mothers deeply commit themselves to their children and to rearing them in safe, nurturing environments, sometimes creating supportive networks of friends and other lesbian families (Johnson & Keren, 1998; Morningstar, 1999). Successful lesbian partners negotiate the division of their labor at home and structure leisure time for themselves individually and as a couple to cope with the stresses of family life (Bialeschki & Pearce, 1997; Reimann, 1997). The couple must decide who will be the primary caregiver and how to divide the multiple tasks involved in family life, including financial and domestic responsibility. Among lesbians, the resulting family structure does not follow sex–gender prescribed roles. These couples are typically egalitarian in dividing the tasks of raising and caring for a family. They negotiate tasks, share responsibilities, and work together to support their family in all ways (Gartrell et al., 1999; Reimann, 1997). In addition, lesbian mothers are knowledgeable about effective parenting skills, able to identify critical issues in child care situations, and able to formulate suitable solutions to the difficulties encountered with their children (Bigner & Jacobson, 1992).

Quality of Life in Lesbian Families

In the National Lesbian Family Study, Gartrell and colleagues (1999) used semistructured interviews to gather information from 156 mothers of 85 two-year-old children (43 girls and 42 boys) all conceived through donor sperm insemination. The respondents lived in areas around Boston, Washington, DC, and San Francisco; most were White (93 percent) with a median household income of $60,000. Sixty-five of the 80 families represented couples with active comothers; the remainder involved single mothers. The findings indicated that most of the mothers and children in the sample were healthy and accessed traditional medical services for routine care. Additionally, most had sought the support of mental health services to cope with the demands of motherhood, although couples reported generally egalitarian division of labor in the home. Most mothers had to reduce their work hours to spend time with their children. All mothers reported some fear about the effects of heterosexism on their children.

Even so, all the children were presently thriving and developing normally, and the mothers reported profound joy in their roles as mothers.

In a subsequent report of the National Lesbian Family Study (Gartrell et al., 2000), interviews with mothers of five-year-old children indicated that 87 percent related well to peers but that 18 percent had experienced heterosexism from peers or teachers. The mothers described their own lives as child focused, leaving little time and energy for their adult relationships, sometimes resulting in sexual infrequency and relationship conflict. About a third (31 percent) of the original couples had separated. Yet many mothers reported feeling that having a child strengthened their relationships. Coparents maintaining a relationship with the biological mother were sharing child rearing and feeling less jealous of the bonding between the birth mother and child. In 43 percent of these cases, the children spent equal time with both mothers. Coparents reported that the child was bonded to both mothers.

The quality of intrafamily relationships was studied by McNeill and colleagues (1998) in a snowball sample of 24 lesbian and 35 heterosexual mothers. Comparing the scores on four inventories, the authors found no significant discrepancies in the mean scores between the groups. The relationships between the couple members, the competence of the families, intrafamilial stress, and how the parents viewed their children were all below clinically problematic ranges. The only discrepancy to emerge was a higher variance in scores among the lesbian mothers, indicating more diversity within that group.

From interviews with 34 lesbian mothers in the Boston area, Mitchell (1998) reported that two-thirds conceived their children though donor sperm insemination, half of those from an unknown donor; one-fourth conceived their children through heterosexual contact; and the remainder adopted their children. The researcher reported that parental behavior and responses regarding sex education were about the same for all parents despite the parents' sexual orientation although some differences emerged when children were conceived by anonymous donor sperm insemination. Parents in this study were particularly careful to be truthful with their children about how they were born, using correct anatomical labels and clear-cut descriptions of conception. Having such discussions meant disclosing to their children, using the terms "gay" or "lesbian" to identify themselves, and explaining their reasons for having children. Overall, the mothers endeavored to make their children feel good about their families.

CONTACTS BEYOND THE FAMILY

A concern that researchers and courts express about lesbian (and gay) parents is that these parents isolate their children from other persons, especially male or female role models. Research findings clearly dispute this assumption. For example, lesbian mothers acknowledge the need for diverse adult influences for their children. Many lesbian mothers arrange for their children to experience the caring support of grandfathers, uncles, male cousins, and male friends (Morningstar, 1999; Nations, 1997). African American lesbians commonly have children from prior relationships and are rearing their children in the cultural tradition of extended family care for children (Greene & Boyd-Franklin, 1996). The 28 lesbian mothers studied by Hare and Richards (1993) who conceived their children in heterosexual marriages maintained better relationships with the fathers of the children than heterosexual women did. A by-product for the children of lesbian mothers was greater contact with their fathers.

The contact between children of lesbian mothers with grandparents and other family members was examined by Patterson, Hurt, and Mason (1998). Respondents included 37 families from the San Francisco Bay area: 26 families involved lesbian couples and seven families single lesbian mothers. These families were predominantly White, educated, and middle class with 34 (92 percent) of the children born to lesbian mothers and three adopted by lesbian mothers. The remaining four families in the sample were no longer together, and the children were in de facto joint custody (or living with each mother part time). In this study, the mothers reported the contacts their children had with all adults (and who they were) and completed a behavior checklist. The children participated in structured interviews to determine their self-concepts. The study revealed that most of the children experienced regular contact with grandparents, and a few experienced contacts with the parents of their biological fathers. Thirty-two percent had at least annual contact with other relatives of the biological mother, and 33 percent had at least annual contact with other relatives of the nonbiological mother. Almost all the children were in regular contact with a variety of other adults, male and female. Mothers rated those children in frequent contact with grandparents and other adults as experiencing fewer behavior difficulties than children who did not have such contact. Moreover, the children themselves reported feeling greater well-being than children who did not experience as much contact with grandparents or other adults. Fulcher, Chan, Raboy, and Patterson (2002) also reported that most children of lesbian parents had regular contact with grandparents and other important relatives, especially those related to the biological mother.

GAY FATHERS

Gay fathers share many of the same concerns that all parents express, and like lesbian mothers, they live and parent in a social climate that not only does not legitimize their sexual orientation but also does not respect their right, desire, or competency to raise children (Shernoff, 1996). Gay parents surveyed by Fredriksen (1999) differed from lesbian parents in several ways: first, they earned higher incomes; second, they were less likely to be in permanent relationships with partners; and third, they were more likely to experience difficulties with child custody. If they are not granted custody, they parent their children as part-time custodial parents. These fathers make special efforts to be available to their children (Gottman, 1990) and they characterize themselves as warm and nurturing (Bigner & Jacobson, 1989).

Studies comparing the attitudes and parenting styles of gay and heterosexual fathers uncovered few dissimilarities (Bigner & Jacobson, 1992). No discrepancies between these two father groups were evident in involvement in their children's activities, intimacy with their children, or problem solving around child-rearing issues. The one difference was that gay fathers were more likely to set limits on the behavior of their children (Bigner & Jacobson, 1989).

Forty-eight gay stepfamilies (that is, gay couples) were studied by Crosbie-Burnett and Helmbrecht (1993). One partner had a child or children who either lived with the couple or had regular visitation. Comparing the association between family functioning and family happiness, the researchers found that the children and their biological fathers were generally happier when the stepparents, or gay partners, involved themselves in an integral way in family activities and decision making. The stepparents' happiness, however, did not correlate with the level of integration. In a study of 110 gay (91 percent) and bisexual (8.9 percent) fathers in the United Kingdom and Eire, the men who lived with male partners reported that they were successfully meeting parenting challenges (Barrett & Tasker, 2001).

As observed earlier, some gay couples are choosing to have children in less traditional ways. Sbordone (1993) compared 78 gay persons who were parents through either surrogacy or adoption with 83 gay persons who did not have children. The gay fathers displayed higher self-esteem and fewer difficulties with negative attitudes about their sexual orientation than did the nonfathers. Many men without children expressed a desire to have them; generally the men in this group were younger and comparable to the other nonparents in income, race, education, and self-esteem.

To define more clearly how gay fathers function in the home, McPherson (1993) assessed how gay couples divided household labor, how satisfied they were with these arrangements, and how satisfied they were with their partner relationships. Studying 28 gay and 27 heterosexual couples, McPherson discovered that, like lesbian mothers, gay fathers developed a more egalitarian division of family responsibilities than their heterosexual counterparts. Generally, gay couples were more content with the distribution of household maintenance tasks and with the quality of their relationships. Possibly, without the constraints of socially prescribed sex–gender roles, couples are freer to split child rearing and domestic chores by more realistic criteria, such as time, opportunity, and talent. This freedom may lead to greater satisfaction for parents.

Generally, research on gay fathers is sparse, but what little there is provides evidence that, although they experience concerns regarding heterosexism in society and about the legal system, they are parenting their children with care and nurturing attention. Parenting seems to bring these men considerable satisfaction as fathers and as partners.

STRESSORS FOR MOTHERS AND FATHERS

Lesbian and gay parents experience similar stressors in raising their families: ambiguity of parenting roles, disclosures to children, and lack of support from others.

Ambiguity of Parenting Models

A lack of parenting models for gay and lesbian families can create difficulties. A family with one legal parent and a coparent with no legal rights can especially create questions about how to define parenting roles in a couple (Kirkpatrick, 1996; Patterson, 1995, 1996). What are the parents of the same sex–gender to be called? Will "mom" only refer to the birth mother? Will the names be the same inside and outside the home? Will the child use only one surname or both? (see Appleby & Anastas, 1998; Martinez, 2002) These families create new parenting models, but experimenting to find comfort with a particular model can be stressful (Crawford, 1987; Laird, 1994, 1996).

Disclosures to Children and Others

Most lesbian and gay parents report that openness with their children improves their relationships in the long term. Gay fathers, however, are not as open with their children as lesbian mothers (Hanscombe & Forster, 1982). These fathers fear that disclosure of their sexual orientation will damage their relationships with their children. Yet, children seldom reject their fathers because they are gay (Golombok, 2000). Also, gay fathers who are out in their family life experience better relationships with their partners, their children, and their extended families, including the relatives of their former wives (Bozett, 1993). In a study of bisexual men and women conducted by Weinberg, Williams, and Pryor (1994), positive results from disclosures included better communication and greater closeness between parents and children. Some children, however, never talked with their parents about the disclosed knowledge and some found it difficult to explain bisexuality to their friends.

Secrecy with children limits intimacy (Rohrbaugh, 1992) and openness in addressing family issues (Patterson & Chan, 1997). It also limits support from others. Secrecy can also contribute to relationship difficulties; for example, if partners disagree about the need for secrecy (Matthews & Lease, 2000). Nevertheless, because of the fear of losing custody and other potential harms, both gay and lesbian parents may keep their sexual orientation secret (Patterson & Chan, 1996). Three-quarters of the gay and lesbian persons with children studied by Fredriksen (1999) had experienced harassment because of their sexual orientation: verbal (88 percent), emotional (50 percent), physical (9 percent), and sexual (9 percent).

Many partners will have to negotiate disclosure of their sexual orientations to children (Bigner, 1996) including whether to do it, how, and when. If they do disclose, it may involve a complex and delicate discussion of conception, such as donor sperm insemination, or why the child does not have a dad or a mom (Segal-Sklar, 1996). If a partner enters a family where the other partner already has children, the presence, role, and meaning of the new same sex–gender partner also requires an explanation. Many LGB parents who do not live with or have custody of their biological children may also face disclosure issues. They may decide not to make disclosures to placate the custodial parent or members of the child's extended family who may control continued contact with the child (Appleby & Anastas, 1998).

Generally, gay and lesbian parents should not tell children about their sexual orientations until they are old enough to understand and ask questions. Then, parents should feel confident about their sexual orientations and sex–gender expressions before they make disclosures, and they should be willing to speak candidly about themselves and educate their children (Scasta, 1998).

Generally, the reactions of children to their parent's disclosures are positive (Bigner, 1996; Lott-Whitehead & Tully, 1993). They may respond with a sense of protectiveness toward their parents (O'Connell, 1993) or they may indicate that the information makes no difference or that they already knew it (Turner, Scadden, & Harris, 1990). This does not mean, however, that these children will have no more questions. Children often need continued discussions about the situation (Patterson, 1992).

Children first told of their parent's gay or lesbian sexual orientation in early adolescence might have a more difficult time adjusting than either younger or older children. Younger children are usually unaware of the associated stigma (Patterson, 1992). Children between five and 12 years of age studied by Dundas and Kaufman (2000) were content with and did not feel stigmatized by their family makeup of two mothers. They seemed to understand that their two mothers lived together because they loved each other. Most of the mothers in this study (27) intended to be honest with their children about their situations and believed that it was essential to avoid secrets.

Older children, especially adolescents who are aware of the stigma associated with same sex–gender or bisexual sexual orientations, express more resentment (Bozett, 1987; Scasta, 1998). Initially, they may react with distress, anxiety, anger, and sorrow, and may make deprecating statements to the parents. They may be angry not only about the disclosure but also about divorce or other family changes (Appleby & Anastas, 1998).

In particular, male adolescents who are trying to assert masculine characteristics can be deeply troubled by a parent's announcement of a same sex–gender sexual orientation (Scasta, 1998). Older adolescents who came from heterosexual marriages and are now living with lesbian and gay parents may suddenly worry about being seen as different by their peers (Hargaden & Llewellin, 1996). Peers most likely hold prejudices about same sex–gender relationships and may taunt them (Sears, 1993–1994) or harm them in other ways (Scasta, 1998). These children may not make any disclosures because they do not want to risk being singled out; they may not even bring friends and dates home (Matthews & Lease, 2000). If they can keep their sex–gender expressions private, transgender parents sometimes decide to wait until all the children are older before disclosing their sex–gender expressions. Others decide to be open so that all the family, including the partner, can develop understanding and coping skills together (Cole, Denny, Eyler, & Samons, 2000).

When peers know about the parents' sexual orientation, Cramer (1986) reported that younger children of lesbian mothers rarely recall facing harassment from peers. Other studies reported that younger children are just as popular and have no more difficulty making friends than do younger children with heterosexual parents (Golombok, Spencer, & Rutter, 1983). Yet adolescent children are more likely to receive negative messages from peers about their parents' sexual orientation (Matthews & Lease, 2000). Other researchers have reported, however, that although incidents of peer group teasing are recorded, relationships with peers are generally good (Tasker & Golombok, 1977).

Parents should help children decide whom they can tell. To avoid harassment, children should use discretion in disclosures. Parents may need to intervene in school and other arenas if harassment occurs (Scasta, 1998). Although some parents may caution their children to keep their sexual orientation secret and the children may want to keep the information to themselves, the secrecy about disclosure can create anxiety for the both the parents and the children (Crawford, 1987). Parents also have to make decisions about disclosures to a variety of persons involved in a child's life—medical staff, child care workers, and school officials, to name a few. Are they going to cross out "father" or "mother" on forms and put in "other mother" or "other father" or "parent–parent" (Segal-Sklar, 1995). Many gay and lesbian parents studied by Fredriksen (1999) were open in some settings: 51 percent were out to all coworkers, 58 percent to medical services providers, 65 percent to school personnel, and 34 percent to neighbors. Parents must also make decisions about how to handle ordinary encounters and questions when out in the world such as when grocery shopping with their children (Martin, 1993).

Another disclosure issue involves donor identification. In a study of 41 children, from seven to 17 years of age, and 45 lesbian parents, Vanfraussen, Ponjaert-Kristoffersin, and Brewaeys

(2001) found that the majority of mothers preferred that donors remain unknown. Over half (54 percent) of the children also preferred donor anonymity but 46 percent wanted to know more about their donors. More boys than girls wanted to know the donor's identity and to meet the donor.

Not Enough Support from Others

Lesbian and gay persons are also raising families with varying levels of support from their extended families and their communities. Even when one's family of origin is somewhat accepting or tolerant of one's sexual orientation and even of the couple's relationship, reactions may change if the couple decides to raise children. Members of one's family of origin may act on the myths about psychological and social difficulties the children are thought to experience (Ariel & Stearns, 1992; Matthews & Lease, 2000). Some family members think it is wrong for a gay or lesbian couple to bring a child into what they see as a sinful relationship (Muzio, 1999). Yet having children for some gay and lesbian couples brings them closer to their extended families, because having children may afford them more mainstream status. Family members sometimes rally to support the couple and are available for and attentive to the children (Gartrell et al., 1999; Hequembourg & Farrell, 1999). Two-thirds of a sample of 31 lesbian women studied by Nations (1997) rated family support moderately high to high.

Gay and lesbian parents also face lack of support from formalized support systems that assist heterosexual couples during parenthood (for example, Patterson, 1994, 1995; Ricketts & Achtenberg, 1990). Communities offer different levels of support. Whereas few communities openly endorse gay and lesbian families, some extend less hostility and fewer obstacles, permitting families to flourish without harassment. Urban settings are more tolerant than rural ones (Friedman, 1997). Yet gay and lesbian families usually have less support from their own communities than heterosexual families receive. Gay and lesbian communities are not as structured around children as are heterosexual communities. When heterosexual mothers experience the arrival of a child, they feel more integrated into their communities and more satisfied with emotional support from family members, whereas lesbian mothers feel more isolated or more like a "separate" family (Stiglitz, 1990). Because of the increased rate of lesbian and gay couples who are parents, however, support systems for them are expanding (Scrivner & Eldridge, 1995).

THE CHILDREN

In a study of 23 lesbian and gay stepfamilies, Lynch (2000) concluded that they show unique strengths and flexibility in discovering creative ways to be families that nourish and support all members. The parents were child centered and strongly committed to maintaining the family unit. Opponents to the parenting of children by lesbian and gay persons, however, proclaim that the children will suffer social stigma, that they will experience confusion about their own sexual orientation, and that they will be traumatized psychologically by their parents' sexual orientations. Some children can experience the same heterosexism that affects their parents. Revealing the sexual orientation of their parents can set children up for castigation, ridicule, and ostracism among their friends. Additionally, they are at the mercy of courts in custody disputes that base decisions on heterosexist ideology instead of on the best interests of the child (Stacy, 1998). Yet the other side of this story is much more positive.

Research focusing on the children of lesbian and gay persons disputes assertions that children of gay and lesbian parents display aberrant behavior or psychological damage. Though the research samples are small and nonrepresentative, interviews with and psychosocial measures of children from lesbian and gay families do not reveal significant discrepancies in personality and social, sexual, or emotional development. The children studied to date report healthy relationships with their parents and with their peers (Eliason, 1996).

Children of Lesbian Mothers

The San Francisco Bay Area study (Patterson, 1996) reported on various aspects of development for children of lesbian mothers. The 37 children (19 girls and 18 boys) studied demonstrated no more behavior difficulties than children from normative samples; children of lesbian mothers were normal in social competence and self-concept; and their sex–gender role behavior was typical of children in the age range studied. These findings supplemented the 25 years of research that shows that a mother's sexual orientation is not an important factor in determining the psychological well-being or sex–gender development of her children. Parents, whether heterosexual, or gay, or lesbian, have little influence on sex–gender development of their children (Mooney-Somers & Golombok, 2000). The only distinction to emerge between the lesbian and heterosexual mothers studied by Patterson (1996) was that children of lesbian mothers seemed to experience more stress. But, they also experienced a greater sense of well-being. Whether these children were more stressed or simply more adept at expressing feelings was ambiguous. What was clearer was that in this sample no findings indicated that they were suffering because of their family environment.

Comparing 30 lesbian mother families and 42 families headed by single, heterosexual mothers (previously divorced) Golombok, Tasker, and Murray (1997) sought to assess various facets of the development of the children. The study found no distinctions among the children on psychological adjustment, development of emotional or behavioral difficulties, and social adjustment. Children raised by heterosexual mothers, however, were lower in cognitive and physical competence than children with fathers. The children of lesbian mothers in this study generally displayed no large negative effects. In some respects, the children of lesbian mothers were better off than children of divorce since they did not have to separate from a parent they loved; they did not experience as much parental conflict; they did not experience their mothers' emotional distress about divorce; and they did not experience the downturn in financial assets that children of divorce often do.

The method of conception has little bearing on how children function socially and emotionally. Children of gay and lesbian parents who take advantage of current reproductive technologies are developing well. Looking specifically at psychosocial adjustment in children conceived through donor sperm insemination by lesbian and heterosexual mothers, Chan, Raboy, and Patterson (1998) studied 80 families: lesbian couples headed 34 of the families; single lesbians headed 21 of the families; heterosexual couples headed 16 of the families; and heterosexual mothers headed nine of the families. The sample included 169 children, 108 boys and 61 girls, with an average age of seven. Reviewing scores on standardized measures for child adjustment, parent adjustment, and parent relationship satisfaction, the researchers discovered strong correlations between parents' adjustment and the adjustment of their children, despite the parents' sexual orientation. Similarly, parents who were happier in their relationships with their partners rated their children as better adjusted than did parents who were less happy in their relationships with their partners. No association emerged between family structure and child adjustment; that is, children in single mother households were comparable to children in two-parent families regarding their behavior and adjustment. Both parents and school-teachers rated children in the sample as having good behavior without obvious difficulties.

In a longitudinal study of 25 adult children raised in lesbian mother families, Tasker and Golombok (1997) found that the children experienced no more mental health difficulties in adulthood than children of heterosexual mothers. In addition, they were no more likely to identify as lesbian, gay, or bisexual than children of heterosexual mothers. Mooney-Somers and Golombok (2000) reported from a review of studies over the previous 25 years that it seemed what mattered most for children's psychological adjustment was not whether mothers were lesbians but the quality of relationships in the family home.

Children of Gay Fathers

Although more studies have addressed lesbian mothers than gay fathers (Golombok, 2000), the findings are similar. The children of gay fathers report positive relationships with their fathers, and although these children socially face some stigmatizing situations because of their fathers' sexual orientation, they depict their relationships with their fathers as warm and caring. Adolescents reported some worry about what others would think of their sexual orientation if their father's sexual orientation were known. Some of these children were selective about confiding in others, and some tried to limit the exposure of their fathers' sexual orientation by not bringing friends into the home or by asking their fathers to change some of their overt behaviors. Generally, the parent and child negotiated how to resolve these issues (Bigner, 1996).

Studies on children of gay fathers report that the sex–gender development of sons and daughters is no different from that of other children. Sons of gay fathers are just as masculine and daughters just as feminine when compared with other boys and girls their age (Golombok & Tasker, 1994). For children who remain in contact with their gay fathers following the parents' divorce, emotional and behavioral difficulties appear to be more associated with the divorce than with having gay fathers (Golombok, 2000).

Moreover, research on the children of gay persons disputes one of the most fearful arguments about gay persons raising children—that their sons will turn out gay (Patterson & Chan, 1996). In a study of 82 adult sons of 55 gay fathers, Bailey, Bobrow, Wolfe, and Mikach (1995) determined that the fathers' sexuality did not correlate with the sexual orientation of the sons. Despite arguments to the contrary, sons of gay persons are overwhelmingly heterosexual and no more likely to be gay than sons of heterosexual fathers.

In a critique of the research on comparing children raised by heterosexual parents and children raised by lesbian and gay parents (21 studies), Stacy and Biblarz (2001) pointed out that most researchers downplay differences in their findings regarding sexual orientation, gender, and heterosexism. Some of the issues of heterosexism have been discussed above. As an example related to gender, children, especially those with comothers, may develop less gender stereotypes than children raised with heterosexual parents. In terms of sexual orientation of the parents, there appears to be an effect (but not large) on children. Limited data suggest that the parent's sexual orientation appears to be positively associated with children being more open to alternatives to heterosexual relationships. So these children may be less sex–gender typed and more open to same sex–gender relationships. The latter findings, however, do not mean that these children are more likely than children raised by heterosexual parents to self-identify as lesbian, gay, or bisexual.

If some children raised either by gay or lesbian parents turn out to be gay, lesbian, or bisexual, many heterosexuals will disparage this, but other persons might respond, "So what."

SUMMARY

- Gay and lesbian persons have raised children throughout history, but they have typically done so without disclosing their sexual orientation; if they have made disclosures, they often lose custody and, sometimes, contact with their children. Most gay and lesbian parents conceived their children in heterosexual marriages, some before they realized their same sex–gender sexual orientation and others because they were willing to marry to have children. As society and technology afford, however, more gay and lesbian persons are choosing to have children outside traditional marriage, through adoption, foster parenting, surrogacy, or donor sperm insemination.

- Gay and lesbian parents wishing to become parents face a variety of obstacles, including lack of support from extended family members, social obstacles, and legal obstacles. Custody of children is denied to many parents because of their sexual orientation, and many must choose between their same sex–gender partner and their children when courts rule that they cannot have contact with their children if they live "open" lives. Others who wish to adopt or have foster children run into institutional obstacles to placing children with them. When gay and lesbian couples find ways to have children (donor sperm insemination, private adoption, surrogacy), they still face legal obstacles in achieving equal custodial rights for both parents. Although some states provide for second-parent adoptions, most do not, leaving coparents without legal rights to the children.

- Families of lesbian and gay persons are sometimes more supportive with the birth of children in their partnerships. Other families, however, regard the decision to have children as sinful. In addition, gay and lesbian persons may experience a lack of support from their own communities.

- Without role models, gay and lesbian parents create their own systems for parenting and family structures. Sometimes, these structures mirror those of society at large, wherein one parent assumes a more active parenting role than the other, but generally these families develop a more egalitarian structure, wherein the parents share parenting and household responsibilities. Children from these homes are less likely to have stereotypical views of family roles.

- Gay and lesbian parents face the same obstacles that heterosexual parents face: balancing responsibilities of home, work, and children. Moreover, they meet these challenges in the face of an often hostile and heterosexist environment. Parents worry about losing their children through custody disputes, and all parents worry about the impact of social prejudice on their children.

- Most researchers agree that honesty about the parents' sexual orientation is advisable when children are old enough to understand and ask questions. Most young children accept this knowledge without incident, but young adolescents may react negatively because they are, themselves, sorting out their own sexual issues and are aware of the public consequences of espousing something other than a heterosexual orientation—they may fear taunting by their peers. Usually, the parents negotiate openness with the child, sometimes encouraging the child not to be open about the same sex–gender relationship. Yet, when others know about their parents, relationships between adolescent children and their peers are generally good.

- Community support for gay and lesbian parents and their children fluctuates according to location and links with other lesbian and gay families. Generally, the lesbian and gay community is not as structured around children as is the heterosexual community. As parenting becomes more common among younger gay and lesbian persons, however, the support among gay and lesbian organizations is likely to increase as well.

- Research on the children of gay and lesbian parents shows few significant distinctions between these children and peers reared by heterosexual parents. In numerous studies, the children of gay and lesbian parents score well on indexes of self-esteem, prosocial behavior, and psychological adjustment. These children experience no significant disadvantages compared to children raised by heterosexual mothers and fathers.

CHAPTER 7
REFERENCES

Allen, K. R. (1997). Lesbian and gay families. In T. Arndell (Ed.), *Contemporary parenting: Challenges and issues* (pp. 196–218). Thousand Oaks, CA: Sage Publications.

American Civil Liberties Union. (1999). *Gay rights project* [Online]. Available: http://www.aclu.org

Appleby, G. A., & Anastas, J. W. (1998). *Not just a passing phase: Social work with gay, lesbian, and bisexual people*. New York: Columbia University Press.

Ariel, J., & McPherson, D. W. (2000). Therapy with lesbian and gay parents and their children. *Journal of Marital and Family Therapy, 26,* 421–432.

Ariel, J., & Stearns, S. M. (1992). Challenges facing gay and lesbian families. In S. H. Dworkin & F. J. Gutiérrez (Eds.), *Counseling gay men and lesbians: Journey to the end of the rainbow* (pp. 95–112). Alexandria, VA: American Association for Counseling and Development.

Arnup, K. (1999). Out in the world: The social and legal context of gay and lesbian families. *Journal of Gay & Lesbian Social Services, 10,* 1–25.

Bailey, J. M., Bobrow, D., Wolfe, M., & Mikach, S. (1995). Sexual orientation of adult sons of gay fathers. *Developmental Psychology, 31,* 124–129.

Barrett, H., & Tasker, F. (2001). Growing up with a gay parent: Views of 101 gay fathers on their son's and daughter's experiences. *Educational and Child Psychology, 18,* 62–77.

Benkov, L. (1994). *Reinventing the family: The emerging story of lesbian and gay partners*. New York: Crown.

Bialeschki, M., & Pearce, K. (1997). I don't want a lifestyle—I want a life: The effect of role negotiations on the leisure of lesbian mothers. *Journal of Leisure Research, 29,* 113–131.

Bigner, J. (1996). Working with gay fathers. In J. Laird & R. Green (Eds.), *Lesbians and gays in couples and families* (pp. 370–403). San Francisco: Jossey-Bass.

Bigner, J. J., & Jacobson, R. B. (1989). Parenting behaviors of homosexual and heterosexual fathers. *Journal of Homosexuality, 18,* 173–186.

Bigner, J. J., & Jacobson, R. B. (1992). Adult responses to child behavior and attitudes toward fathering: Gay and nongay fathers. *Journal of Homosexuality*, *23*, 99-112.

Black, D., Gates, G., Sanders, S., & Taylor, L. (2000). Demographics of the gay and lesbian population in the United States: Evidence from available systematic data sources. *Demography*, *37*, 139–154.

Bottoms v. Bottoms, 457 S.E. 2d 102 (Va. 1995). Supreme Court of Virginia No. 94–1166 [Online]. Available: http://www.psyclaw.org/bottomsbrief.html

Bozett, F. W. (1987). Children of gay fathers. In F. W. Bozett (Ed.), *Gay and lesbian parents* (pp. 39–57). New York: Praeger.

Bozett, F. W. (1993). Gay fathers: A review of the literature. In L. D. Garnets & D. C. Kimmel (Eds.), *Psychological perspectives on lesbian and gay male experiences* (pp. 437–457). New York: Columbia University Press.

Burke, P. (1993). *Family values: Two moms and their son.* New York: Random House.

Chambers, D. L., & Polikoff, N. D. (1999). Family law and gay and lesbian family issues in the twentieth century. *Family Law Quarterly*, *33*, 523–542.

Chan, R., Raboy, B., & Patterson, C. (1998). Psychosocial adjustment among children conceived via donor insemination by lesbian and heterosexual mothers. *Child Development*, *69*, 443–457.

Cole, S. S., Denny, D., Eyler, A. E., & Samons, S. L. (2000). Issues of transgender. In L. T. Szuchman & F. Muscarella (Eds.), *Psychological perspectives on human sexuality* (pp. 149–195). New York: John Wiley & Sons.

Cramer, D. (1986). Gay parents and their children: A review of research and practical implications. *Journal of Counseling and Development*, *64*, 504–507.

Crawford, S. (1987). Lesbian families: Psychosocial stress and the family-building process. In Boston Lesbian Psychologies Collective (Eds.), *Lesbian psychologies* (pp. 195–214). Urbana: University of Illinois Press.

Crosbie-Burnett, M., & Helmbrecht, L. (1993). A descriptive empirical study of gay male step families. *Family Relations*, *42*, 256–262.

Dudley, R. G. (2002). Offering psychiatric opinion in legal proceedings when lesbian or gay sexual orientation is an issue. In B. J. Jones & M. J. Hill (Eds.), *Mental health issues in lesbian, gay, bisexual, and transgender communities* (pp. 37–70). Washington, DC: American Psychiatric Press.

Dundas, S., & Kaufman, M. (2000). The Toronto lesbian family study. *Journal of Homosexuality*, *40*, 65–79.

Eliason, M. (1996). Lesbian and gay family issues. *Journal of Family Nursing*, *2*, 10–29.

Fredriksen, K. I. (1999). Family caregiving responsibilities among lesbians and gay men. *Social Work*, *44*, 142–155.

Friedman, L. (1997). Rural lesbian mothers and their families. *Journal of Gay & Lesbian Social Services*, *7*, 73–82.

Fulcher, M., Chan, R. W., Raboy, C., & Patterson, C. J. (2002). Contact with grandparents among children conceived via donor insemination by lesbians and heterosexual mothers. *Parenting: Science and Practice*, *2*, 61–76.

Gartrell, N., Banks, A., Hamilton, J., Reed, N., Bishop, H., & Rodas, C. (1999). The national lesbian family study. *American Journal of Orthopsychiatry*, *69*, 362–369.

Gartrell, N., Banks, A., Reed, N., Hamilton, J., Rodas, C., & Deck, A. (2000). The national lesbian family study: 3. Interviews with mothers of five-year-olds. *American Journal of Orthopsychiatry*, *70*, 542–549.

Golombok, S. (2000). Parents' sexual orientation: Heterosexual or homosexual? In S. Golombok (Ed.), *Parenting: What really counts?* (pp. 45–60). Philadelphia: Routledge.

Golombok, S., Spencer, A., & Rutter, M. (1983). Children in lesbian and single-parent house holds: Psychosexual and psychiatric appraisal. *Journal of Child Psychology*, *24*, 551–572.

Golombok, S., & Tasker, F. (1994). Children in lesbian and gay families: Theories and evidence. *Annual Review of Sex Research*, *5*, 73–100.

Golombok, S., Tasker, F., & Murray, C. (1997). Children raised in fatherless families from infancy: Family relationships and the socioemotional development of children of lesbians and single heterosexual mothers. *Journal of Child Psychology and Psychiatry*, *38*, 783–791.

Gottman, J. S. (1990). Children of gay and lesbian parents. In F. W. Bozett & M. B. Sussman (Eds.), *Homosexuality and family relations* (pp. 177–196). New York: Harrington Press.

Greene, B., & Boyd-Franklin, N. (1996). African American lesbians: Issues in couples therapy. In J. Laird & R.-J. Green (Eds.), *Lesbians and gays in couples and families: A handbook for therapists* (pp. 251–271). San Francisco: Jossey-Bass.

Hanscombe, G., & Forster, J. (1982). *Rocking the cradle*. Boston: Alyson Press.

Hare, J. (1994). Concerns and issues faced by families headed by a lesbian couple. *Families in Society, 75,* 27–35.

Hare, J., & Richards, L. (1993). Children raised by lesbian couples: Does context of birth affect father and partner involvement? *Family Relations, 42,* 249–255.

Hargaden, H., & Llewellin, S. (1996). Lesbian and gay parenting issues. In D. Davies & C. Neal (Eds.), *Pink therapy: A guide for counselors and therapists working with LGB clients* (pp. 116–130). Philadelphia: Open University Press.

Harris, M. B., & Turner, P. H. (1985–1986). Gay and lesbian parents. *Journal of Homosexuality, 12,* 101–113.

Hartman, A. (1999). The long road to equality: Lesbians and social policy. In J. Laird (Ed.), *Lesbians and lesbian families* (pp. 91–120). New York: Columbia University Press.

Hequembourg, A., & Ferrell, M. P. (1999). Lesbian motherhood: Negotiating marginal–main stream identities. *Gender and Society, 13,* 540–557.

Johnson, T., & Keren, M. (1998). The families of lesbian women and gay men. In M. McGoldrich (Ed.), Re-visioning family therapy: *Race, culture, and gender in clinical practice* (pp. 320–329). New York: Guilford Press.

Kirkpatrick, M. (1996). Lesbians as parents. In R. P. Cabaj & T. S. Stein (Eds.), *Textbook of homo sexuality and mental health* (pp. 353–370). Washington, DC: American Psychiatric Press.

Kuehlwein, K. T., & Gottschalk, D. I. (2000). Legal and psychological issues confronting lesbian, bisexual, and gay couples and families. *Handbook of couples and family forensic: A source-book for mental health and legal professionals* (pp. 164–187). New York: John Wiley & Sons.

Laird, J. (1994). Lesbian families: A cultural perspective. In M. P. Mirkin (Ed.), *Women in context: Toward a feminist reconstruction of psychotherapy* (pp. 118–148). New York: Guilford Press.

Laird, J. (1996). Invisible ties: Lesbians and their families of origin. In J. Laird & R.-J. Green (Eds.), *Lesbians and gays in couples and families* (pp. 89–122). San Francisco: Jossey-Bass.

Leiter, R. A. (1997). *National survey of state laws.* Detroit: Gale Research.

Lott-Whitehead, L., & Tully, C. T. (1993). The family lives of lesbian mothers. *Smith College Studies in Social Work, 63,* 266–280.

Lynch, J. M. (2000). Considerations of family structure and gender composition: The lesbian and gay stepfamily. *Journal of Homosexuality, 40,* 81–95.

Mallon, G. P. (2000). Gay men and lesbians as adoptive parents. *Journal of Gay & Lesbian Social Services, 11*, 1–22.

Martin, A. (1993). *The lesbian and gay parenting handbook.* New York: HarperCollins.

Martinez, B. E. (2002, May 30). Naming the baby was the easy part: As same sex–gender households raise children, parents ponder what kids will call them. *Washington Post, p. C10.*

Matthews, C. R., & Lease, S. H. (2000). Focus on lesbian, gay, and bisexual families. In R. M. Perez, K. A. DeBord, & K. J. Bieschke (Eds.), *Handbook of counseling and psychotherapy with lesbian, gay, and bisexual clients* (pp. 249–273). Washington, DC: American Psychological Association.

McClellan, D. L. (2001). The "other-mother" and second parent adoption. *Journal of Gay & Lesbian Social Services, 13*, 1-21.

McLeod, A., & Crawford, I. (1998). The postmodern family: An examination of the psychosocial and legal perspectives of gay and lesbian parenting. In G. M. Herek (Ed.), *Stigma and sexual orientation: Understanding prejudice against lesbians, gay men, and bisexuals* (pp. 211–222). Thousand Oaks, CA: Sage Publications.

McNeill, K., Rienzi, B., & Kposowa, A. (1998). Families and parenting: A comparison of lesbian and heterosexual mothers. *Psychological Reports, 82*, 59–62.

McPherson, D. (1993). Gay parenting couples: Parenting arrangements, arrangement satisfaction, and relationship satisfaction (Doctoral dissertation, Pacific Graduate School of Psychology, 1993). *Dissertation Abstracts International, 54*, 3859B.

Mitchell, V. (1998). The birds, the bees . . . and the sperm banks: How lesbian mothers talk with their children about sex and reproduction. *American Journal of Orthopsychiatry, 68*, 400–419.

Mooney-Somers, J., & Golombok, S. (2000). Children of lesbian mothers: From the 1970s to the new millennium. *Sexual and Relationship Therapy, 15*, 121–126.

Morningstar, B. (1999). Lesbian parents: Understanding developmental pathways. In J. Laird (Ed.), *Lesbians and lesbian families: Reflections on theory and practice* (pp. 213–241). New York: Columbia University Press.

Muzio, C. (1999). Lesbian co-parenting: On being/being with the invisible (m)other. In J. Laird (Ed.), *Lesbians and lesbian families: Reflections on theory and practice* (pp. 197–211). New York: Columbia University Press.

National Gay and Lesbian Task Force. (2000). *Families* [Online]. Available: http://www.ngltf.org

Nations, L. (1997). Lesbian mothers: A descriptive study of a distinctive family structure. *Journal of Gay and Lesbian Social Services, 7,* 23–47.

News of the year. (2002, January). *The Advocate,* pp. 13–18.

O'Connell, A. (1993). Voices from the heart: The developmental impact of a mother's lesbianism on her adolescent children. *Smith College Studies in Social Work, 63,* 281–299.

Parks, C. (1998). Lesbian parenthood: A review of the literature. *American Journal of Orthopsychiatry, 68,* 376–389.

Patterson, C. (1996). Lesbian mothers and their children: Findings from the Bay area families study. In J. Laird & R.-J. Green (Eds.), *Lesbians and gays in couples and families* (pp. 420–437). San Francisco: Jossey-Bass.

Patterson, C., & Chan, R. (1997). Gay fathers and their children. In R. P. Cabaj & T. S. Stein (Eds.), *Textbook of homosexuality and mental health* (pp. 371–393). Washington, DC: American Psychiatric Press.

Patterson, C. J. (1992). Children of lesbian and gay men. *Journal of Sex Research, 30,* 62–69.

Patterson, C. J. (1994). Lesbian and gay families. *Current Directions in Psychological Science, 3,* 62–64.

Patterson, C. J. (1995). Lesbian mothers, gay fathers, and their children. In A. R. D'Augelli & C. J. Patterson (Eds.), *Lesbian, gay, and bisexual identities over the lifespan: Psychological perspectives* (pp. 262–290). Oxford: Oxford University Press.

Patterson, C., Hurt, S., & Mason, C. (1998). Families of the lesbian baby boom: Children's contact with grandparents and other adults. *American Journal of Orthopsychiatry, 68,* 390–399.

Patterson, C., & Redding, R. (1996). Lesbian and gay families with children: Implications of social science research for policy. *Journal of Social Issues, 52,* 29–50.

Reimann, R. (1997). Does biology matter? Lesbian couples' transition to parenthood and their division of labor. *Qualitative Sociology, 20,* 153–185.

Ricketts, W., & Achtenberg, R. (1990). Adoption and foster parenting for lesbians and gay men: Creating new traditions in families. *Marriage & Family Review, 14,* 83–118.

Rohrbaugh, J. B. (1992). Lesbian families: Clinical issues and theoretical implications. *Professional Psychology: Research and Practice, 23,* 467–473.

Rosenblum, D. M. (1991). Custody rights of gay and lesbian parents. *Villanova Law Review, 36,* 1665–1696.

Rutter, V., & Schwartz, P. (1996). same sex–gender couples: Courtship, commitment, context. In A. W. Auhagen (Ed.), *The diversity of human relationships* (pp. 197–226). New York: Cambridge University Press.

Sbordone, A. (1993). *Gay men choosing fatherhood.* Unpublished doctoral dissertation, City University of New York.

Scasta, D. (1998). Issues in helping people come out. *Journal of Gay & Lesbian Psychotherapy, 2,* 87–98.

Scrivner, R., & Eldridge, N. S. (1995). Lesbian and gay family psychology. In R. H. Mikesell, D. D. Lusterman, & S. H. McDaniel (Eds.), *Integrating family therapy: Handbook of family psychology and systems theory* (pp. 327–345). Washington, DC: American Psychological Association.

Sears, J. T. (1993–1994). Challenges for educators: Lesbian gay, and bisexual families. *High School Journal, 77,* 138–156.

Segal-Sklar, S. (1996). Lesbian parenting: Radical or retrograde? In K. Jay (Ed.), *Dyke life: A celebration of the lesbian experience* (pp. 174–191). New York: Basic Books.

Shapiro, J. (1996). Custody and conduct: How the law fails lesbian and gay parents and their children. *Indiana Law Journal, 71,* 623–621.

Shernoff, M. (1996). Gay men choosing to be fathers. In M. Shernoff (Ed.), *Human services for gay people: Clinical and community practice* (pp. 41–54). Binghampton, NY: Harring-ton Park.

Stacy, J. (1998). Gay and lesbian families: Queer like us. In M. A. Mason, A. Skolnick, & S. D. Sugarman (Eds.), *All our families: New politics for a new century* (pp. 117–143). New York: Oxford University Press.

Stacy, J., & Biblarz, T. J. (2001). (How) does the sexual orientation of parents matter? *American Sociological Review, 66,* 159–183.

Stiglitz, E. (1990). Caught between two worlds: The impact of a child on a lesbian couple's relationship. *Women & Therapy, 10,* 99–116.

Tasker, F. L., & Golombok, S. (1997). *Growing up in a lesbian family: Effects on child development.* New York: Guilford Press.

Turner, P. H., Scadden, L., & Harris, M. B. (1990). Parenting in gay and lesbian families. *Journal of Gay and Lesbian Psychotherapy*, *1*, 55–66.

Vanfraussen, K., Ponjaert-Kristoffersin, I., & Brewaeys, A. (2001). An attempt to reconstruct children's donor concept: A comparison between children's and lesbian parents' attitudes towards donor anonymity. *Human Reproduction*, *16*, 2019–2035.

Ward v. Ward, No. 95–4184, 1996 Fla. App. LEXIS 9130 (D.C. Fla. Aug. 30, 1996).

Weinberg, M. S., Williams, C. J., & Pryor, D. W. (1994). *Dual attraction: Understanding bisexuality*. New York: Oxford University Press.

Year in review. (2001, January 16). *The Advocate*, pp. 11–26.

PART III
PRACTICE: HISTORY AND
AFFIRMATIVE PRACTICE REQUIREMENTS

CHAPTER 8
TRANSFORMATION FROM OPPRESSIVE DIAGNOSES AND INTERVENTIONS TO AFFIRMATIVE APPROACHES

Are LGBT persons more psychologically disturbed than their heterosexual peers?

What are oppressive interventions?

What are its consequences?

What are affirmative interventions?

Although secular and religious conversion interventions are still around, are they ethical?

What are the effects of these interventions on clients?

What are the experiences of lesbian and gay persons in practice situations today?

What are the drawbacks of practice?

CHALLENGES TO OPPRESSIVE LABELS AND PRACTICE

After being viewed as a sin during much of the 19th century (Gonsiorek, 1982a), "homosexuality" became medicalized and labeled a disease (Bérubé, 1990; Rosenberg & Golden, 1992) By the early part of the 20th century it was viewed as a mental illness (Morin, 1977). Based on psychoanalytic theories, mainstream psychological practice equated "homosexuality" with pathology (Lewes, 1988). Sigmund Freud (1949), however, argued that "homosexuality" occurred in persons who were not only unimpaired but also of high intellectual and ethical development. But, these observations were incongruent with the views of many of his earlier and later followers. Not only did other psychoanalysts view "homosexuality" as a pathological and serious deviation that negatively affects one's total social functioning (Bayer, 1987), but many of them reacted to "homosexual" patients with "anger, revulsion, and distaste" (Johansson, 1990, p. 448). Such views and attitudes were not based on dispassionate scientific research on "homosexuality," as it was nonexistent until the second half of the 20th century (Herek, 1991). Only in the late 1940s and early 1950s did empirically based research emerge that challenged the connection between "homosexuality" and mental illness. As noted in Chapter 3, the Kinsey studies revealed a wide range of same sex–gender sexual behaviors among humans (Kinsey, Pomeroy, & Martin, 1948; Kinsey, Pomeroy, Martin, & Gebbard, 1953). In most societies (64 percent) studied by Ford and Beach (1951), not only was homosexual behavior widespread, but it was not stigmatized or linked to mental illness or to deviance. In societies where this behavior was stigmatized, value judgments of the culture, not empirical evidence of psychopathology or deviance, were the source of these prejudicial views.

Sensational results also appeared in two other studies reported in the 1950s. First, a special committee of the British legislature investigating "homosexual" offenses and prostitution concluded that "homosexual" persons were well adjusted. The committee recommended the repeal of British laws that prohibited same sex–gender sexual behavior between consenting adults (Wolfenden, 1963). Second, psychologist Evelyn Hooker (1957) did a pioneering study on gay persons at the University of California at Los Angeles. After developing a friendship with some gay persons when a young psychologist, Hooker realized that little research was available on this group. She sought and received a grant from the National Institute of Mental Health for a longitudinal study to compare the personality structure and adjustment of 30 heterosexual and 30 gay persons. They were matched for age, intelligence, and educational level. In contrast with the samples of gay persons in earlier studies that included either patients in psychoanalysis or prisoners, Hooker's sample of gay persons came from community organizations. At the time of the study, none of the men in either group were in "therapy." For the assessment of personality and adjustment, Hooker used the standard battery of tools available to American psychologists in the 1950s: projective techniques (the Rorschach Ink Blot Test, Thematic Apperception Test, and Make-a-Picture-Story Test), attitude scales, and intensive life history interviews (Bullough, 1994).

Clinicians, unaware of any respondent's sexual orientation, were trained by Hooker (1957) to assess the personality and adjustment of the respondents. Using a five-point scale, they classified two-thirds of each group as in the three highest categories of adjustment (average or better). Men with same sex–gender sexual orientations were equivalent to the heterosexual men in psychological health. When asked to identify which profiles were those of the gay persons, the trained clinicians could not identify them on projective test data. Most of the gay persons were happy and productive; some of them functioning at superior levels. Hooker concluded that same sex–gender sexual orientation was not inherently pathological.

Before Hooker's report in 1957, it was unthinkable that a "homosexual" could be "healthy," but the research she did provided empirical evidence that "homosexuality" was not indicative of psychological disturbance. This work was followed by more than 100 additional empirical studies focused on the mental health of both gay and lesbian persons (for example, Adelman, 1977; Freedman, 1971; Thompson, McCandless, & Strickland, 1971). Almost every study confirmed the basic finding of Hooker's research that few significant differences in mental health existed between lesbian and gay samples and samples of heterosexual women and men. The psychological adjustment of lesbian and gay persons was consistently within normal ranges. Enough studies have been done with acceptable designs and samples to show a clear and consistent pattern: "homosexuality" in and of itself is unrelated to maladjustment or psychopathology (Gonsiorek, 1982c). Other researchers (for example, Masters & Johnson, 1979; Nurius, 1983; Zinik, 1984, 1985) also demonstrated that bisexual women and men are not pathological or psychologically maladjusted when compared to heterosexual women and men. As reported by Fox (1995), bisexual women and men are characteristically self-confident, independent, and demonstrate high levels of self-esteem, cognitive flexibility, and positive sense of self.

Overturn of Mental Illness Diagnosis

After two decades of struggle and three years of intense challenge by activists in the Gay Liberation Movement and allies in the American Psychiatric Association (APA) to eliminate the classification of "homosexuality" as a mental illness, the battle was won (for example, Barr & Catts, 1974; Green, 1972; Marmor, 1972). On December 15, 1973, the APA board of trustees voted unanimously to remove "homosexuality" from its official list of psychiatric disorders (see Adam, 1987). Hence, the diagnostic category of "homosexuality" was not present in the 1980 edition of APA's *Diagnostic and Statistical Manual of Mental Disorders* (DSM-III), but a new diagnostic category appeared—"sexual orientation disturbance" (later called "ego-dystonic homosexuality"). This category was supposedly applicable to persons who felt upset with their same sex–gender sexual orientation and wanted to change it. Pressured by lesbian and gay psychiatrists, psychologists, and social workers, APA fully eradicated this final remnant of "homosexuality" from the revised edition of DSM-III in 1987 (Morin & Rothblum, 1991; Stein, 1993).

Recent research also demonstrates that transgender behavior and identity do not directly impair people's lives (Lombardi, 1999). Transgender persons are no more likely to be severely impaired than anyone else who seeks mental health services (Cole, Denny, Eyler, & Samons, 2000). Nevertheless, these persons are still fighting the DSM battles that lesbian and gay persons fought in the 1970s (Gagné, Tewksbury, & McGaughey, 1997). In the 1994 DSM-IV there is no mention of transgender or transsexual, but the diagnostic category "sex-identity disorder" (GID) does appear (Denny, 1999). The GID category applies to persons who experience "cross-sex identification, feelings of discomfort and inappropriateness in one's assigned sex–gender role, the absence of a physical intersex condition, and impairment in social, occupational, or other arenas of living" (Anderson, 1998, p. 222). In some areas of the country, transgender youth have been forced into psychiatric hospitals in order to "correct" their GID condition. The real "problem" is society's refusal to expand beyond rigid sex–gender roles. Cross-dressing (by heterosexual or bisexual males who obtain erotic gratification from this activity) remains in the category of "transvestic fetishism" although a growing body of evidence shows that cross-dressing is not a mental disorder (Cole et al., 2000; Denny, 1997, 1999).

Transgender activists want to reduce the domination of mental health professionals over the lives of transgender persons (International Conference on Transgender Law, 1994). They advocate for the removal of both GID and "transvestic fetishism" from the DSM. The GID category is especially a target because of its use in the institutionalization of children and adolescents (Cole et al., 2000). Harry Benjamin and his associates provided groundbreaking arguments for sex–gender reassignment for persons who desired it. But the updated 1998 Standards of Care by the Harry Benjamin International Gender Dysphoria Association narrowed the definition of "transsexualism" and thereby restricted those who could qualify for sexual reassignment surgery (SRS). The Benjamin model also acknowledges only two sex–genders, saying that in SRS, one changes to the other sex–gender, leaving out anyone who chooses to live outside these binary roles (Levine et al., 1998).

Persons who feel that their sex–gender identity does not match their biological sex began to disclose to each other at meetings during the 1985 International Foundation for Gender Education forum in Boston that they did not conform to the Benjamin criteria for transsexuals or transvestites. This led to the development of the transgender model in the 1990s and to transgender community development (Cole et al., 2000). The transgender model is now the most accepted model in the transgender community and encourages openness to an infinite number of sex–gender identities and ways of life. The Standards of Care are being revised to reflect this new way of thinking (Denny, 1999).

The genitals of many intersex persons were altered at birth to fit either a male or female sex–gender identity. The majority (over 90 percent) of these persons were assigned female because a fully functioning penis cannot be reproduced through surgery (Intersex Society of North America, 1996). Intersex persons, however, are now speaking out about this practice of assigning gender, and physicians are urged not to take this action until these persons identify their internal sex–gender themselves (Israel & Tarver, 1997). The Intersex Society of North America (ISNA) is helping parents and intersex persons formulate these new positions (Cooper, 1999). The Web site for the ISNA is: http://www.isna.org

Oppressive Treatments

Aside from diagnostic categories, the other central issue for lesbian and gay persons was the prescribed treatments to cure persons classified as "homosexual." Treatments were frequently punitive and coercive and usually ignored the will of the patients. Included among these treatments were various biological therapies such as induced seizures, nausea–inducing drugs, electric shock, covert sensitization, masturbation while viewing pictures of a nude woman, lobotomy, castration, implantation of "normal" testes, and supplementation of various hormones. Psychotherapy was the most humane form of treatment. Yet the goal of any treatment was the same—to cure the "homosexual" patient of the disease of "homosexuality" (Haldeman, 1994; Silverstein, 1991, 1996).

Psychoanalysis and behavior modification were the most common psychotherapy approaches used but the outcome of these interventions did not show any "cures" (for example, Curran & Parr, 1957; Freund, 1977; Mayerson & Lief, 1965). Psychoanalysts reported a 27 percent success rate of converting "homosexual" persons to heterosexuality (Bieber et al., 1962), but these results were dubious because the analysts (who were the researchers as well as the practitioners) "expected" success. In addition, only 18 percent of the treatment group was exclusively "homosexual"; about half of the so-called successes were bisexual. Methodological flaws were widespread in all of the psychoanalysis studies. For example, in some studies, the assessment method was "clinical impressions" of conversions to heterosexuality. In other studies, success of the treatment was evaluated predominantly by self-reports by the clients (for example, Hadden, 1966; Mintz, 1966). Especially in groups, self-reports are susceptible to social influences (Haldeman, 1994).

Programs using the behavioral approach operated on the premise that "homosexuality" resulted from faulty learning; therefore, one could unlearn it. In one of the behaviorist studies, Freund (1977) used aversion therapy and positive conditioning to increase attraction to women as a behavioral treatment for male "homosexuality." Following this treatment, 20 percent of the men eventually married and had children. Yet, in follow-up studies, Freund concluded that none of the cures lasted. The marriages were full of conflict because of the husband's "homosexuality." Other behaviorist studies confirmed these findings. Behavioral approaches were no more successful at curing "homosexuality" than were the analytic approaches (for example, Conrad & Wincze, 1976; Rangaswami, 1982).

No treatment can change persons who have exclusive attractions to others of the same sex–gender (Isay, 1990). Even when a person claimed to be cured from "homosexuality," this usually meant only control of sexual behavior. Persons sexually attracted to others of the same sex–gender still reported these attractions. Behavioral conditioning did not develop hetero-sexual interest (Conrad & Wincze, 1976; Rangaswami, 1982) although some clients reported additional contact with heterosexual persons (Haldeman, 1994). Experiencing heterosexual sex did not mean a change in sexual orientation. Even for those who reported happy marriages, same sex–gender fantasies persisted (Birk, 1980).

None of the so-called treatments to cure a person from "homosexuality" worked and the methodologies of these treatments were problematic (Haldeman, 1994). Eventually, adverse pub-licity about the treatments, and the research showing that same sex–gender sexual orientation was not pathological, led to the reduction of conversion attempts (Dynes & Donaldson, 1992).

NEW AFFIRMATIVE APPROACHES

Professional organizations representing human services practitioners no longer endorse the prejudicial treatments reviewed above. One by one, these organizations passed resolutions declaring that "homosexuality" was no longer to be labeled a mental illness. In 1975, the American Psychological Association adopted an official policy statement: "homosexuality per se implies no impairment in judgment, stability, reliability, or general social or vocational capa-bilities" (Conger, 1975, p. 633). The National Association of Social Workers also issued a state-ment at about the same time in support of removing the link between "homosexuality" and pathology. Every other major human services profession eventually adopted similar statements and directed their members to stop treating lesbian and gay persons as if they were mentally ill.

Beginning in the early 1970s, one of the most significant steps in providing an alternative form of treatment was the creation of gay and lesbian counseling centers in major urban areas, such as New York and Seattle. These centers were staffed only with peer counselors or both peer and professional counselors, and the services provided were "gay affirmative" in contrast with the oppressive or pathology-focused practice in traditional agencies (Malyon, 1981–1982). New approaches to treatment developed with the goal of supporting gay and lesbian persons to accept and value their sexual identities and their sexual attractions. An affirmative focus also developed for bisexual persons (for example, Matteson, 1996a; Nichols, 1988) and is evolving for transgen-der persons (for example, Emerson & Rosenfeld, 1996; Rosenfeld & Emerson, 1998). The affir-mative approach to practice is not a technique but a frame of reference (Malyon, 1981). It sig-nifies a moral practice that challenges injustices (Hartman & Laird, 1998).

In an active affirmative approach, practitioners tell a client their position on heterosexism and promote a "healthy" view of LGB sexual orientations and overcoming internalized oppression (Mair & Izzard, 2001). An affirmative approach has also evolved for transgender persons: "transpositive" or "transaffirmative." In this approach, transgender persons are affirmed as to whatever unique identity they want to develop. In addition, there is the call to educate others about transgender persons and advocate for their political, social, and economic rights (Carroll, Gilroy, & Ryan, 2002).

Affirmative practitioners reinforce the naturalness of living with the sexual orientation or sex–gender expression that clients identify as their own (Matteson, 1996b). This approach is similar to the concept of "nurturance," suggested by Schreier and Werden (2000), or a healing practice with LGBT persons. Malyon (1981–1982) applied Alexander's model of the "corrective emotional experience" (Alexander & French, 1946) to alleviate internalized heterosexist oppression and to affirm one's sexual identity.

Affirmative practice is also closely linked to other concepts that help move practitioners away from focusing on the deficits of clients and helping them overcome weaknesses (Longres, 2000). Longres pointed to three related and overlapping concepts. The first concept is *resistance*, which recognizes that subordinated persons and communities actively struggle against oppressive circumstances. The second concept is *resilience* or the positive, self-directed adaptive capacities shown by subordinated persons even in the face of great adversity (Fraser, 1997). "Exceptionality" is a concept that D'Augelli (1992) applied to gay and lesbian persons who, given their hostile environments, can develop adaptive coping skills to negotiate these environments. The third concept is *strengths* or the personal and environmental resources that serve to protect persons and provide the base for their resistance and resilience (Saleebey, 1997b).

The concepts of resistance and resilience perhaps most directly relate to the oppressive ideology of heterosexism that LGB persons struggle with daily. Yet, they usually manage to live positive lives in the face of this oppression. The *strengths* perspective (for example, Hall & Fradkin, 1992; Saleebey, 1997a; Wormer, Wells, & Boes, 2000) takes a developmental, nonpathological approach by building upon a person's existing strengths and abilities (Hershenson, Power, & Seligman, 1989). Like all persons, LGBT persons can call upon many untapped reserves of mental, physical, and emotional resources to help them meet the challenges in their lives. Instead of searching for their "problems," their "pathology," or their "deficits," the clients are guided to find ways to take advantage of their capacities to grow, develop, and reformulate directions in their lives (Saleebey, 1997b). With LGBT clients, instead of diagnosing, attempting to determine causative factors, or attempting to change their sexual orientation, practitioners help them to become self-actualized and lead fulfilling lives in their relationships, their families, their jobs, and their communities (Garnets, Hancock, Cochran, Goodchilds, & Peplau, 1991; Graham, Rawlins, Halpern, & Hermes, 1984). The emphasis is on using clients' resilience and capacity to overcome difficulties in their lives (Laird, 1996). Strengths are identified through listening to clients' views of the world, themselves and others, their talents, what makes them feel good about themselves, how they survive, and where they get support (Saleebey, 1997a). Cowger (1997) identified in detail how to assess strengths in three areas: environmental, psychological, and physiological. Obstacles that may occur in these three areas are also assessed.

Other affirming approaches for practice with LGBT persons include practices with empowerment, ecological, and feminist focuses. The *empowerment approach* focuses on clients' gaining mastery or control over their lives, handling difficulties on their own, and seeing that institutional structures respond humanely and equitably to their needs. It focuses on clients' identifying and developing their strengths, working in collaboration with others, and linking personal and political power. The basic goal is to modify environments for a better person-in-environment fit (Dubois & Miley, 1996; Schriver, 1998; Tully, 2000). Basic characteristics of the empowerment approach for practitioner behaviors are summarized as follows: collaborate and share power with clients; establish trust; accept clients' definitions of the reasons they are seeing a practitioner; identify and build on clients' strengths; raise clients' consciousness of issues of class and power; involve clients in the change process; teach clients specific skills; use small groups that emphasize mutual aid, self-help, and support; mobilize resources for clients; and advocate on behalf of clients (Gutierrez, Delois, & Linnea, 1995).

The *ecological approach* (see Chapter 12) emphasizes enhancing and restoring the psychosocial functioning of persons and changing the oppressive or destructive social conditions that negatively affect the interaction between persons and their environments. The ultimate goal of this approach is the best person-in-environment "fit." Both the ecological and empowerment frameworks address issues and needs at all system levels (for example, Compton & Galaway, 1984; Germain, 1981, 1991; Hepworth & Larsen, 1993; Meyer, 1988, 1993). An adequate understanding of the lives of LGBT persons requires consideration of biological, psychological, social, political, economic, spiritual, and environmental influences (James & Murphy, 1998).

One of the themes of the *feminist approach* is the recognition that persons and their difficulties are political. The reality of pervasive societal oppression, first addressed with women, is also a significant issue with LGBT clients (for example, Browning, Reynolds, & Dworkin, 1991; Neisen, 1993). Practitioners who operate from an affirmative practice perspective understand that cultural, social, and psychological heterosexism aggravates the difficulties these clients experience. In addition, feminist practice also emphasizes that race, ethnicity, class, and sex–gender all interact to produce multiple levels of discrimination. Affirmative practice must address these complex sociocultural issues in making an assessment and developing an intervention strategy for LGBT clients. Feminist practice also encourages clients to become involved in political action so that they can become empowered to influence political and social change. As does the empowerment approach, the feminist approach also strives to establish practice relationships based on equal power between practitioners and clients in contrast to traditional practice relationships based on an inequitable power arrangement. The practitioner attempts to equalize the link with the client through forming a collaborative or partnership interaction with negotiated goals (Brown, 1988).

UNRELENTING OPPONENTS: CONVERSION PRACTITIONERS

Even with the complete removal of homosexuality from the revised edition of the DSM-III (APA, 1987) and the overwhelming evidence of positive mental health among lesbian and gay persons, many human services professionals continue to mirror outdated attitudes both in their conceptualization of these persons and their practice with them (Rothblum, 1989). Some physicians, psychiatrists, psychologists, nurses, counselors, and social workers refuse to surrender the illness-oriented, and for some, sin-oriented perspective on same sex–gender sexual orientation and they attempt to cure a gay, lesbian, or bisexual person (Kelly, 1994). This continued focus on cure also meshes with the desire of social conservatives who do not want gay and lesbian persons to have any legal protections. To them if the sexual orientation of only one person changed, this would make the case for no entitlements for protection (Drescher, 2002).

Modern-Day Secular Conversion Practitioners

Conservative psychoanalytic psychiatrists such as Socarides (1978, 1992, 1995) claim that the changes in the DSM were political actions, and they want "homosexuality" reinstated as a mental illness. Psychotherapists such as Nicolosi (1991) and Socarides continue to present "homosexuality" as pathological and recommend treatment methods for conversion to heterosexuality. These practitioners cannot, however, present any evidence that their so-called conversion therapies are effective (for example, Fernandez, 1990; Haldeman, 1991). Nor do they discuss any of the harmful effects of these therapies such as guilt, anxiety, depression, and abandoned same sex–gender partners. In addition, many persons are coerced into these treatments, pressured to stay if they want to leave, and they experience violations of confidentiality when discussions with their therapists are reported to family members and school personnel (Drescher, 2002; Haldeman, 2001; Schroeder & Shidlo, 2001).

This is not to say that spontaneous shifts in sexual practices or identity do not occur over a person's life (Haldeman, 1995). In the best survey to date, because of both sample size and methodological rigor (Laumann, Gagnon, Michael, & Michaels, 1994), most young persons who at some point adopted same sex–gender sexual practices gave them up later. Some women, as noted in Chapter 3, experience fluidity in sexual identity. Yet, spontaneous shifts are one thing, attempts by practitioners to force change are another (Haldeman, 1995). Nor can persons will themselves to change their sexual orientation (Schneider, Brown, & Glassgold, 2002).

Secular Conversion Interventions

Typically, secular conversion therapy is focused on the behavior of gay clients and the practitioner attempts to evoke attraction to women and heterosexual sexual fantasies by showing them heterosexual pornographic magazines and X-rated movies. In one particular case, reported by Markowitz (1998), homework included taking pornographic magazines home between sessions and masturbating while looking at the pictures. When the client reported that none of this interested him, the practitioner became cold, aloof, and disapproving. The client, who felt ashamed and humiliated, was told to invest more effort in this endeavor. On one occasion, the client reported that his favorite fantasy was kissing his best male friend. The practitioner told him to never be alone with this friend again and to imagine that feces and vomit covered this person.

Another component of the conversion therapy described here was "educating" the client about the detrimental realities of "homosexuality," including, for example, the claim that gay persons are sexual predators. The practitioner also told the client that he would end up alone, unloved, and persecuted. The client left therapy after fabricating heterosexual fantasies. He also reported that he took a girl to his senior prom. His parents felt relieved that he was now living a normal life. Four months later, however, he attempted suicide and checked himself into a psychiatric hospital. There, an affirmative practitioner helped him come to terms with his sexual orientation as a positive one (Markowitz, 1998).

In a study of the treatments used by 139 psychologists with lesbian and gay clients, Jordan and Deluty (1995) reported that though 6 percent supported use of aversion techniques to try to change sexual orientation, none claimed to use such techniques themselves. Nevertheless, some (11 percent) reported the use of other methods, such as psychoanalytic techniques, for the same purpose. Practitioners who viewed same sex–gender sexual orientation as unacceptable would likely support aversion techniques and the use of alternative conversion techniques.

Modern-Day Religious Conversion Practitioners

Fundamentalist religious groups also apply conversion therapy to mostly gay persons, but Christian theorists and psychotherapists (for example, Jones & Workman, 1989) claim they want to cure "homosexuality" not because it is "sick" but because it is "immoral." "Homosexuals" must convert to heterosexuality to be saved from this immorality and sin (Haldeman, 1994). Some church-affiliated practitioners attempt to coerce gay persons to sublimate their same sex–gender sexual attractions through programs that combine religious exhortation that condemns "homosexuality," prayer, Bible study, group pressure, brainwashing, and corrective sexual experiences. These interventions are often intermixed with elements of 12-step self-help programs (Drescher, 2002; Haldeman, 1994; Rosenberg, 1994).

Among the religious groups are the Exodus Movement with over 100 chapters in the United States, Asia, and Europe; Courage, a Roman Catholic group with about 15 U.S. centers; Evergreen International, Inc., a Mormon treatment center with 13 branches in the United States, Canada, and Australia; Homosexuals Anonymous with chapters throughout the United States; and Parents and Friends of Ex-Gays, which supports the family and friends of persons who claim they were once gay but no longer (Markowitz, 1998). Some of the groups provide live-in programs where one can spend up to a year trying to change (Rosenberg, 1994).

Religious conversion practitioners usually claim that their successes "choose" to replace their immoral "homosexual life" with a moral heterosexual life, but they never report any research or scientific data of actual cure from same sex–gender sexual attractions (Gonsiorek, 1996; Haldeman, 1995). In one program reviewed by Rosenberg (1994), some men who converted reported that they "became heterosexual," married, and had children. Many became celibate and dedicated their lives to God. Most acknowledged, though, that they still experienced same sex–gender sexual fantasies (Gonsiorek, 1996; Haldeman, 1994). Some transgender persons also hope that marriage and children will cure them, but this can lead to multiple marriages and divorces in search of the illusory "right medicine" (Anderson, 1998).

Conclusions about Conversion Interventions

Conversion therapy is not only scientifically unproven but serious ethical questions arise about using any form of therapy that causes harm to clients. Many clients of conversion therapy experience depression or severe anxiety, shame, and conflict about their sexual orientation (Gonsiorek, 1996; Haldeman, 1994; Isay, 1990). In December 1998, board members of the American Psychiatric Association voted unanimously to repudiate any therapy with the sole goal of turning gay and lesbian persons into heterosexual persons. The board emphasized that these therapies can cause depression, anxiety, and self-destructive behavior (American Psychiatric Association, 1999). Attempts to change same sex–gender sexual orientation are also ethically irresponsible since this orientation is not a psychiatric disorder (Gonsiorek, 1982b, 1982c). Later in 2000, the Commission of Psychotherapy by Psychiatrists of the American Psychiatric Association elaborated on the 1998 statement by recommending that ethical psychiatrists not attempt to change any one's sexual orientation (American Psychiatric Association, 2000).

But, what about the values of autonomy or self-determination? Given the fear of damnation that some persons experience it may seem difficult to oppose the right of practitioners to attempt to practice conversion therapy. This therapy, however, is blatantly prejudicial, and a request for this therapy is not alone a justification for providing it (Halpert, 2000).

Gay affirmative theorists and practitioners assert that persons who desire to change their sexual orientation are going through a stage in the coming-out process and have yet to reach a positive gay or lesbian identity (Atkinson & Hackett, 1998). Shernoff (1998) worked with profoundly depressed or anxious gay persons following failed psychotherapeutic attempts to change their sexual orientation. The initial intervention was to help them understand that nothing is intrinsically wrong with their sexual orientation and that society's heterosexism and intolerance are the causes of their distress. One way of accomplishing this goal is through bibliotherapy or assignments of gay affirmative readings for discussions during sessions. Sometimes just the assignment of going to a lesbian or gay bookstore and browsing through the books can be enlightening to these clients. They will see many affirmative titles. But, as noted by Clay (1996), clients have to reach their own conclusions about what to do after examining the literature on conversion and the affirmative literature on gay and lesbian persons.

LGB PERSONS SEEKING HUMAN SERVICES TODAY

LGB persons show no greater "maladjustment" than heterosexual persons and they show social, psychological, and political resiliency while living in oppressive societies (Appleby & Anastas, 1998). Nevertheless, they seek services in every helping field (Brown, 1996).

Both gay and lesbian persons who use "therapy" do so more often and are in "therapy" for longer periods of time compared to heterosexual persons (Liddle, 1997). In a national sample of 1,633 lesbians surveyed by Sorensen and Roberts (1997), most (80 percent) reported having seen a practitioner at some time and about 50 percent more than twice. When compared with heterosexual women, lesbians show much higher rates of being in "therapy." Compared to 29 percent of heterosexual women, 78 percent of lesbians saw a mental health professional in samples studied by Morgan (1992). In another survey by Bernhard and Applegate (1999), lesbians were significantly more likely (86 percent) to report seeing a practitioner at some time than were heterosexual women (54 percent).

Services for gay and lesbian clients have greatly improved over recent years (Liddle, 1999). An upswing in satisfaction with services began in the late 1980s, or about 15 years after many professional organizations passed resolutions supporting the removal of homosexuality from the DSM (Adam, 1987; Morin & Rothblum, 1991). A greater amount of research and writing on same sex–gender and bisexual sexual orientation during the subsequent years also played a role, as did the AIDS crisis and gay and lesbian activism.

Most lesbian and gay clients (86 percent) studied by Jones and Gabriel (1999) reported that "therapy" had a positive effect on their lives; 50 percent felt "very positive" about "therapy"; and 33 percent felt that "therapy" had "saved their lives." In ratings on a 10-point scale, respondents reported that they felt liked by the practitioner (7.8), felt respected by the practitioner (7.8), felt understood by the practitioner (7.2), and felt accepted by the practitioner (7.9). Lesbians studied by Liddle (1997) held more positive attitudes about seeking professional help than heterosexual persons did.

In a study of the experiences of transgender persons in therapy, Rachlin (2001) discovered that they also (more than 87 percent of the respondents) reported that positive changes in their lives resulted from "therapy." When asked what was most helpful, four things stood out: acceptance, respect for their sex–gender expression, flexibility in interventions, and connection to the transgender community. They also appreciated experience with and knowledge of sex–gender issues.

Based on a study of the experiences of lesbians with mental health and health providers, Saulnier (2002) suggested that each new cohort of mental (and health) providers needs training in affirmative services delivery and exposure to pertinent new knowledge. This suggestion applies to those working with gay, bisexual, and transgender persons as well.

LESBIANS, THERAPY, AND THE OPPOSITION

Therapy and lesbian communities almost seem to go together. As noted above, many lesbians participate in individual "therapy." They also attend "therapy" workshops and read self-help books (Perkins, 1996). Possible reasons for this phenomenon include oppression that creates more stress; fewer resources for social support; the difficulties in coming out that may require help; more willingness of lesbians to engage in introspective therapy to address difficult personal issues; and the modeling of and acceptance of therapy and personal growth experiences in the lesbian community (Morgan, 1992).

Lesbians also report positive experiences with their practitioners and with their "therapy." They say that "therapy" helps them because someone attends to them, listens to them, does not dismiss their feelings, and validates their experiences (Kitzinger & Perkins, 1993). In a sample of 247 lesbians studied by Morgan and Eliason (1992), 43.5 percent reported that they experienced a safe and supportive environment when in "therapy." Helpful "therapy" experiences included clarification of problems (34.8 percent); getting information or new ways to think about things (26 percent); receiving objective feedback (21.7 percent); facilitation of change (21.7 percent); focus on self and finding one's own answers (17.4 percent); being challenged (11.3 percent); experiencing a good relationship with the practitioner (8.7 percent); use of alternate techniques including meditation and massage therapy (8.7 percent); and finding out that one was not alone (4.3 percent).

Is there a downside to all this therapy for lesbians? Even though the experiences are positive, Kitzinger and Perkins (1993) opposed seeking these experiences with a therapist instead of with friends. Friendship behaviors such as trust, listening, understanding, encouragement, protection, healing, and practical help are now the province of therapeutic experts as treatment or "therapy." Perkins (1996) cautioned that the extensive use of "therapy" in lesbian communities creates the risk of destroying genuine lesbian friendship.

Psychological "therapy" for women, including lesbians, is also opposed by Kitzinger and Perkins (1993) because it makes their difficulties private and individual, even pathological, rather than clarifying their difficulties as consequences of societal oppression. Even severe difficulties, for example, extreme anxiety, depression, or suicidal thoughts, are more often "social disabilities" or difficulties for all women instead of private and personal issues. Practitioners usually ignore the political implications of clients' issues such as patriarchal society and male supremacy. Kitzinger and Perkins advocate that lesbians spend their time and energy on political solutions to their issues and reduce their reliance on psychological approaches that take time and energy away from the political realm.

Most (78 percent) of the lesbians surveyed by Eliason and Morgan (1996) who had been in "therapy" agreed that it tends to put the focus on the individual instead of on society. Surprisingly, however, those who had been in "therapy" were somewhat more politically oriented than those who had not been in "therapy." Over half of those who had been in "therapy" thought that it made them more aware of their oppression as lesbians and as women, and 62 percent developed more awareness of how oppression affected their daily lives. Yet, most of them engaged in introspective and private endeavors more often than they engaged in public or political work; only 29 percent were politically active. Those who had been in "therapy" and were also politically active. They invested time more often in feminist causes than in specifically lesbian or AIDS-related work. They might have felt more oppressed as women than as lesbians.

SUMMARY

- In the early 20th century, "homosexuality" was considered a mental illness or disorder, and was cataloged by the American Psychiatric Association as such in their comprehensive manual of mental disorders. Cataloguing sexual orientation as a disorder placed it alongside other deviant behaviors such as sociopathology. In 1957, Evelyn Hooker provided the first empirical evidence that gay persons were no more likely to have mental disturbances than heterosexual men. Her work and subsequent work of others, including lesbians in some samples, resulted in the removal of this category from the Association's Diagnostic and Statistical Manual of Mental Disorders in 1973; and all remaining references to "homosexuality" were eliminated by 1987, including "ego-dystonic homosexuality," a diagnostic category supposedly applicable to persons upset by their same sex–gender sexual orientation and seeking change. Professional organizations representing human services professionals now declare that a same sex–gender sexual orientation is not a mental illness. Research has shown as well that a bisexual sexual orientation and transgender expressions do not impair people's lives. However, several diagnostic categories are still listed, referring to transgender statuses; transgender activists are working for removal of these categories from the manual.

- Oppressive treatment results from the medical model view that same sex–gender sexual orientation is a pathological disorder. Rooted in the belief that gay and lesbian persons are "diseased," oppressive treatment models emerged to convert these persons to "normal" thoughts, feelings, and behaviors. This type of treatment is harmful because participants cannot achieve the practice goal of heterosexuality and, therefore, experience shame, a sense of hopelessness, and ostracism. Although some participants report success, they also report continued attractions to and fantasies about same sex–gender partners, and few maintain their heterosexuality over the long term.

- Although not a technique but a frame of reference, affirmative approaches reinforce practices with LGBT clients that do not diagnose them, determine what causes their sexual orientation or sex–gender expression, or attempt to change them. Instead, these approaches guide practice along the lines of helping these clients lead happy and fulfilling lives. Other perspectives, including strengths, empowerment, and feminist, add to affirmative approaches through, for example, emphasizing strengths of clients instead of deficits, helping clients take control of their lives, helping clients understand the influences of various systems on their lives, and helping clients to understand that persons and their concerns are political, not just personal. Interventions at all levels are necessary and the practitioner and client work in collaboration with each other to determine assessments, goals, and interventions.

- Both secular and religious conversion interventions continue to be offered and the practitioners claim conversion successes. Yet, the success reported from these treatments is dubious self-reporting that cannot withstand rigorous evaluation.
- The gay and lesbian population seeks professional help that today is notably more affirmative than in the past, and at rates higher than most heterosexuals. Particularly, lesbians seek out therapy for help with issues regarding relationships, work, family of origin, parenting, and finances. In short, these persons seek services for many of the same reasons that any other person does, although they may also seek the support of practitioners when experiencing some of the painful processes of coming out or disclosure.
- Lesbian and gay persons report that they like the services and support they now receive. Lesbians report that they enjoy the focused attention and encouragement of those persons who seems to care about them. Others caution, however, that using therapists as "friends" replaces friendships from the lesbian community. These critics of "therapy" also argue that most therapists do not emphasize the role of society in the lives of lesbians and seek, instead, to find the source of difficulties within the clients. Affirmative forms of practice consider the person-in-environment and emphasize strengths and supports available to clients. Affirmative practitioners can also encourage clients to find strengths and supports in their communities.

CHAPTER 8
REFERENCES

Adam, B. D. (1987). *The rise of the gay and lesbian movement*. Boston: Twayne.

Adelman, M. (1977). A comparison of professionally employed lesbians and heterosexual women on the MMPI. *Archives of Sexual Behavior, 6,* 193–201.

Alexander, F., & French, T. (1946). *Psychoanalytic therapy*. New York: Ronald Press.

American Psychiatric Association. (1980). *Diagnostic and statistical manual of mental disorders* (3rd ed.). Washington, DC: Author.

American Psychiatric Association. (1987). *Diagnostic and statistical manual of mental disorders* (3rd ed., rev.). Washington, DC: Author.

American Psychiatric Association. (1999). Position statement on psychiatric treatment and sexual orientation, 1998. *American Journal of Psychiatry, 156,* 1131.

American Psychiatric Association, Commission on Psychotherapy by Psychiatrists. (2000). Position statement on therapies focused on attempts to change sexual orientation (reparative or conversion therapies). *American Journal of Psychiatry, 157,* 1719–1721.

Anderson, B. F. (1998). Therapeutic issues in working with transgendered clients. In D. Denny (Ed.), *Current concepts of transgendered identity* (pp. 215–226). New York: Garland.

Appleby, G. A., & Anastas, J. W. (1998). *Not just a passing phase: Social work with gay, lesbian, and bisexual people*. New York: Columbia University Press.

Atkinson, A. D., & Hackett, G. (1998). *Counseling and diverse populations* (2nd ed.). Boston: McGraw-Hill.

Barr, R. F., & Catts, S. V. (1974). Psychiatry opinion and homosexuality: A short report. *Journal of Homosexuality, 1,* 213–215.

Bayer, R. (1987). *Homosexuality and American psychiatry: The politics of diagnosis* (2nd ed.). Princeton, NJ: Princeton University Press.

Bernhard, L. A., & Applegate, J. M. (1999). Comparison of stress and stress management strategies between lesbian and heterosexual women. *Health Care for Women International, 20,* 355–347.

Bérubé, A. (1990). *Coming out under fire: The history of gay men and women in World War II*. New York: Free Press.

Bieber, I., Dain, H. J., Dince, P. R., Drellich, M. G., Grand, H. G., Gundlach, R. H., Kremer, M. W., Rifkin, A. H., Wilbur, C. B., & Bieber, T. B. (1962). *Homosexuality: A psychoanalytic study*. New York: Basic Books.

Birk, L. (1980). The myth of classic homosexuality: Views of a behavioral psychotherapist. In J. Marmor (Ed.), *Homosexual behavior: A modern reappraisal* (pp. 376–390). New York: Basic Books.

Brown, L. S. (1988). Feminist therapy with lesbians and gay men. In M. A. Dutton-Douglas & L.E.A. Walker (Eds.), *Feminist psychotherapies: Integrating therapeutic and feminist systems* (pp. 206–227). Norwood, NJ: Ablex.

Brown, L. S. (1996). Ethical concerns with sexual minority patients. In R. P. Cabaj & T. S. Stein (Eds.), *Textbook of homosexuality and mental health* (pp. 897–916). Washington, DC: American Psychiatric Press.

Browning, C., Reynolds, A. L., & Dworkin, S. H. (1991). Affirmative psychotherapy for lesbian women. *Counseling Psychologist, 19*, 177–196.

Bullough, V. L. (1994). *Science in the bedroom: A history of sex research*. New York: Basic Books.

Carroll, L., Gilroy, P. J., & Ryan, J. (2002). Counseling transgendered, transsexual, and gender-variant clients. *Journal of Counseling & Development, 80*, 131–139.

Clay, R. A. (1996, September). What to do when a patient wants to become heterosexual? *APA Monitor, 27*, 49.

Cole, S. S., Denny, D., Eyler, A. E., & Samons, S. L. (2000). Issues of transgender. In L. T. Szuchman & F. Muscarella (Eds.), *Psychological perspectives on human sexuality* (pp. 149–195). New York: John Wiley & Sons.

Compton, B. R., & Galaway, B. (1984). *Social work processes*. Homewood, IL: Dorsey.

Conger, J. J. (1975). Proceedings of the American Psychological Association for the year 1974: Minutes of the annual meeting of the Council of Representatives. *American Psychologist, 30*, 620–651.

Conrad, S., & Wincze, J. (1976). Orgasmic reconditioning: A controlled study of the effects upon the sexual arousal and behavior of male homosexuals. *Behavior Therapy, 7*, 155–166.

Cooper, K. (1999) Practice with transgendered youth and their families. *Journal of Gay & Lesbian Social Services, 10*, 111–129.

Cowger, C. (1997). Assessing client strengths: Assessment for client empowerment. In D. Saleebey (Ed.), *The strengths perspective in social work practice* (2nd ed., pp. 59–73). White Plains, NY: Longman.

Curran, D., & Parr, D. (1957). Homosexuality: An analysis of 100 male cases. *British Medical Journal, 1,* 797–801.

D'Augelli, A. R. (1992). Teaching lesbian/gay development: From oppression to exceptionality. In K. M. Harbeck (Ed.), *Coming out of the classroom closet: Gay and lesbian students, teachers, and curricula.* New York: Haworth Press.

Denny, D. (1997). Transgender: Some historical, cross-cultural, and contemporary models and methods of coping and treatment. In B. Bullough, V. L. Bullough, & J. Elias (Eds.), *Gender blending* (pp. 33–47). Amherst, NY: Prometheus Books.

Denny, D. (1999). Transgender in the United States: A brief discussion. *Siecus Report, 28,* 8–13.

Drescher, J. (2002). Sexual conversion ("reparative") therapies: History and update. In B. E. Jones & M. J. Hill (Eds.), *Mental health issues in lesbian, gay, bisexual, and transgender communities* (pp. 71–91). Washington, DC: American Psychiatric Press.

Dubois, B., & Miley, K. K. (1996). *Social work: An empowering profession* (2nd ed.). Boston: Allyn & Bacon.

Dynes, W. R., & Donaldson, S. (1992). General introduction. In W. R. Dynes & S. Donaldson (Eds.), *Homosexuality and psychology, psychiatry, and counseling* (pp. v–xx). New York: Garland.

Eliason, M. J., & Morgan, K. S. (1996). The relationship between therapy usage and political activity in lesbians. *Women & Therapy, 19,* 31–45.

Emerson, S., & Rosenfeld, C. (1996). Stages of adjustment in family members of transgender individuals. *Journal of Family Psychotherapy, 7,* 1–12.

Fernandez, E. (1990, February 4). This ministry works to put gays straight. *San Francisco Examiner,* p. A1.

Ford, C. S., & Beach, F. A. (1951). *Patterns of sexual behavior.* New York: Harper & Row.

Fox, R. C. (1995). Bisexual identities. In A. R. D'Augelli & C. J. Patterson (Eds.), *Lesbians, gay, and bisexual identities over the lifespan* (pp. 48–86). New York: Oxford University Press.

Fraser, M. W. (Ed.). (1997). *Risk and resilience in childhood: An ecological perspective.* Washington, DC: NASW Press.

Freedman, M. (1971). *Homosexuality and psychological functioning.* Belmont, CA: Brooks/Cole.

Freud, S. (1949). *Three essays on a theory of sexuality.* London: Imago Publishing.

Freund, K. (1977). Should homosexuality arouse therapeutic concern? *Journal of Homosexuality, 2,* 235–249.

Gagné, P., Tewksbury, R., & McGaughey, D. (1997). Coming out and crossing over: Identity formation and proclamation in a Transgender community. *Gender & Society, 11,* 478–508.

Garnets, L. D., Hancock, K. A., Cochran, S. D., Goodchilds, J., & Peplau, L. A. (1991). Issues in psychotherapy with lesbians and gay men: A survey of psychologists. *American Psychologist, 46,* 964–972.

Germain, C. B. (1981). The ecological approach to people-environment transactions. *Social Casework, 62,* 323–331.

Germain, C. B. (1991). *Human behavior and the social environment.* New York: Columbia University Press.

Gonsiorek, J. C. (1982a). Introduction to mental health issues and homosexuality. *American Behavioral Scientist, 25,* 267–383.

Gonsiorek, J. C. (1982b). Introduction: Present and future directions in gay/lesbian mental health. *Journal of Homosexuality, 7,* 5–20.

Gonsiorek, J. C. (1982c). Results of psychological testing on homosexual populations. *American Behavioral Scientist, 25,* 385–396.

Gonsiorek, J. C. (1996). Mental health and sexual orientation. In R. C. Savin-Williams & K. M. Cohen (Eds.), *The lives of lesbian, gay men, and bisexuals: Children to adults* (pp. 462–478). Fort Worth, TX: Harcourt Brace.

Graham, D., Rawlins, E. I., Halpern, H. S., & Hermes, J. (1984). Therapists' needs for training in counseling lesbians and gay men. *Professional Psychology, 15,* 482–496.

Green, R. (1972). Homosexuality as a mental illness. *International Journal of Psychiatry, 10,* 77–128.

Gutierrez, L., Delois, K., & Linnea, G. (1995). Understanding empowerment practice: Building on practitioner-based knowledge. *Families in Society, 76,* 534–543.

Hadden, S. (1966). Treatment of male homosexuals in groups. *International Journal of Group Psychotherapy, 16,* 13–22.

Haldeman, D. C. (1991). Sexual orientation conversion therapy for gay men and lesbians: A scientific examination. In J. C. Gonsiorek & J. D. Weinrich (Eds.), *Homosexuality: Research implications for public policy* (pp. 149–160). Newbury Park, CA: Sage Publications.

Haldeman, D. C. (1994). The practice and ethics of sexual orientation conversion therapy. *Journal of Consulting and Clinical Psychology, 62,* 221–227.

Haldeman, D. C. (1995, April). *Sexual orientation conversion therapy update* (Society for the Psychological Study of Lesbian and Gay Issues, Division of the American Psychological Association). Division 44 Newsletter, 4–6.

Haldeman, D. C. (2001). Therapeutic antidotes: Helping gay and bisexual men recover from conversion therapies. *Journal of Gay & Lesbian Psychotherapy, 5,* 119–132.

Hall, A. S., & Fradkin, H. R. (1992). Affirming gay men's mental health: Counseling with a new attitude. *Journal of Mental Health Counseling, 14,* 362–374.

Halpert, S. C. (2000). "If it ain't broke, don't fix it": Ethical considerations regarding conversion therapies. *International Journal of Sexuality and Gender Studies, 5,* 19–35.

Hartman, A., & Laird, J. (1998). Moral and ethical issues in working with lesbians and gay men. *Families in Society: Journal of Contemporary Human Services, 79,* 163–276.

Hepworth, D. H., & Larsen, J. A. (1993). *Direct social work practice.* Pacific Grove, CA: Brooks/Cole.

Herek, G. M. (1991). Myths about sexual orientation: A lawyer's guide to social science research. *Law and Sexuality: Review of Lesbian and Gay Legal Issues, 1,* 133–172.

Hershenson, D. B., Power, P. W., & Seligman, L. (1989). Counseling theory as a projective test. *Journal of Mental Health Counseling, 76,* 273–279.

Hooker, E. (1957). The adjustment of the male overt homosexual. *Journal of Projective Techniques, 211,* 18–31.

International Conference on Transgender Law and Employment Policy. (1994). *Health law standards of care for transsexualism.* Houston: Author.

Intersex Society of North America. (1996). *Intersexuality—Frequently asked questions* [Online]. Available: http://www.sexuality.org/l/transgen/intefaq.html

Isay, R. A. (1990). Psychoanalytic theory and the therapy of gay men. In D. P. McWhirter, S. A. Sanders, & J. M. Reinisch (Eds.), *Homosexuality/heterosexuality: Concepts of sexual orientation* (pp. 283–303). New York: Oxford University Press.

Israel, G. E., & Tarver, D. E. (1997). *Transgender care: Recommended guidelines, practical information & personal accounts*. Philadelphia: Temple University Press.

James, S. E., & Murphy, B. C. (1998). Gay and lesbian relationships in a changing social context. In C. J. Patterson & A. R. D'Augelli (Eds.), *Lesbian, gay, and bisexual identities in families: Psychological perspectives* (pp. 99–121). New York: Oxford University Press.

Johansson, W. (1990). Functioning. In W. R. Dynes (Ed.), *Encyclopedia of homosexuality* (pp. 448–451). New York: Garland.

Jones, M. A., & Gabriel, M. A. (1999). Utilization of psychotherapy by lesbians, gay men, and bisexuals: Findings from a nationwide survey. *American Journal of Orthopsychiatry, 69,* 209–219.

Jones, S. L., & Workman, D. E. (1989). Homosexuality: The behavioral sciences and the church. *Journal of Psychology and Theology, 17,* 213–225.

Jordan, K. M., & Deluty, R. H. (1995). Clinical interventions by psychologists with lesbians and gay men. *Journal of Clinical Psychology, 51,* 448–456.

Kelly, G. F. (1994). *Sexuality today: The human perspective* (4th ed.). Guilford, CT: Dushkin Publishing Group.

Kinsey, A. C., Pomeroy, W. B., & Martin, C. E. (1948). *Sexual behavior in the human male.* Philadelphia: W. B. Saunders.

Kinsey, A. C., Pomeroy, W. B., Martin, C. E. & Gebbard, P. H. (1953). *Sexual behavior in the human female.* Philadelphia: W. B. Saunders.

Kitzinger, C., & Perkins, R. (1993). *Changing our minds: Lesbian feminism and psychology.* New York: New York University Press.

Laird, J. (1996). Family-centered practice with lesbian and gay families. *Families in Society: Journal of Contemporary Human Services, 77,* 559–572.

Laumann, E. D., Gagnon, J. H., Michael, R. T., & Michaels, S. (1994). *The social organization of sexuality: Sexual practices in the United States.* Chicago: University of Chicago Press.

Levine, S. B., Brown, G. B., Coleman, E., Hage, J. J., Cohen-Kettenis, P., Van Maasdam, J., Petersen, M., Pfafflin, F., & Schaefer, L. (1998, April to June). Harry Benjamin International Gender Dysphoria Association's standards of care for gender identity disorders. *International Journal of Transgenderism, 2,* 2.

Lewes, K. (1988). *The psychoanalytic theory of male homosexuality.* New York: Simon & Schuster.

Liddle, B. J. (1997). Gay and lesbian clients' selection of therapists and utilization of therapy. *Psychotherapy, 34,* 11–18.

Liddle, B. J. (1999). Recent improvement in mental health services to lesbian and gay clients. *Journal of Homosexuality, 37,* 127–137.

Lombardi, E. L. (1999). Integration within a transgender social network and its effect upon members' social and political activity. *Journal of Homosexuality, 37,* 109–126.

Longres, J. F. (2000). *Human behavior and the social environment* (3rd ed.). Itasca, IL: F. E. Peacock.

Mair, D., & Izzard, S. (2001). Grasping the nettle: Gay men's experiences in therapy. *Psychodynamic Counseling, 7,* 475–490.

Malyon, A. K. (1981). The homosexual adolescent: Development issues and social bias. *Child Welfare, 60,* 321–330.

Malyon, A. K. (1981–1982). Psychotherapeutic implications of internalized homophobia in gay men. *Journal of Homosexuality, 7,* 56–59.

Markowitz, L. M. (1998). Dangerous practice: Inside the conversionist therapy controversy. *In the Family, 4,* 10–13, 25.

Marmor, J. (1972). Homosexuality: Mental illness or moral dilemma? *International Journal of Psychiatry, 10,* 114–117.

Masters, W., & Johnson, V. (1979). *Homosexuality in perspective.* Boston: Little, Brown.

Matteson, D. R. (1996a). Counseling and psychotherapy with bisexual and exploring clients. In B. A. Firestein (Ed.), *Bisexuality: The psychology and politics of an invisible minority* (pp. 185–213). Thousand Oaks, CA: Sage Publications.

Matteson, D. R. (1996b). Psychotherapy with bisexual individuals. In R. P. Cabaj & T. S. Stein (Eds.), *Textbook of homosexuality and mental health* (pp. 433–449). Washington, DC: American Psychiatric Press.

Mayerson, P., & Lief, H. (1965). Psychotherapy of homosexuals: A follow-up study of nine teen cases. In J. Marmor (Ed.), *Sexual inversion* (pp. 302–344). New York: Basic Books.

Meyer, C. H. (1988). The eco-systems perspective. In R. Dorfman (Ed.), *Paradigms of clinical social work* (pp. 275–294). New York: Brunner/Mazel.

Meyer, C. H. (1993). *Assessment in social work practice.* New York: Columbia University Press.

Mintz, E. (1966). Overt male homosexuals in combined group and individual treatment. *Journal of Counseling Psychology, 20*, 193–198.

Morgan, K. S. (1992). Caucasian lesbians' use of psychotherapy: A matter of attitude? *Psychology of Women Quarterly, 16*, 127–130.

Morgan, K. S., & Eliason, M. J. (1992). The role of psychotherapy in Caucasian lesbian's lives. *Women & Therapy, 13*, 27–52.

Morin, S. F. (1977). Heterosexual bias in research on lesbianism and male homosexuality. *American Psychologist, 32*, 629–637.

Morin, S. F., & Rothblum, E. D. (1991). Removing the stigma: Fifteen years of progress. *American Psychologist, 46*, 947–949.

Neisen, J. H. (1993). Healing from cultural victimization: Recovery from shame due to heterosexism. *Journal of Gay & Lesbian Psychotherapy, 2*, 49–63.

Nichols, M. (1988). Bisexuality in women: Myths, realities, and implications for therapy. *Women & Therapy, 7*, 235–252.

Nicolosi, J. (1991). *Reparative therapy of male homosexuality: A new clinical approach.* Northvale, NJ: Jason Aronson.

Nurius, P. S. (1983). Mental health implications of sexual orientation. *Journal of Sex Research, 19*, 119–136.

Perkins, R. E. (1996). Rejecting therapy: Using our communities. In E. D. Rothblum & L. A. Bond (Eds.), *Preventing heterosexism and homophobia* (pp. 71–83). Thousand Oaks, CA: Sage Publications.

Rachlin, K. (2001, August 20-24). *Transgender individuals' experiences of psychotherapy.* Paper presented at the 109th annual convention of the American Psychological Association, San Francisco.

Rangaswami, K. (1982). Difficulties in arousing and increasing heterosexual responsiveness in a homosexual: A case report. *Indian Journal of Clinical Psychology, 9*, 147–151.

Rosenberg, C. E., & Golden, J. (Eds.). (1992). *Framing disease: Studies in cultural history.* New Brunswick, NJ: Rutgers University Press.

Rosenberg, K. P. (1994). Notes and comments: Biology and homosexuality. *Journal of Sex & Marital Therapy, 20*, 147–151.

Rosenfeld, C., & Emerson, S. (1998). A process model of supportive therapy for families of transgender individuals. In D. Denny (Ed.), *Current concepts of transgender identity* (pp. 391–400). New York: Garland.

Rothblum, E. D. (1989). Introduction: Lesbianism as a model of a positive lifestyle for women. In E. D. Rothblum & E. Cole (Eds.), *Lesbianism: Affirming nontraditional roles* (pp. 1–12). New York: Haworth Press.

Saleebey, D. (1997a). The strengths approach to practice. In D. Saleebey (Ed.), *The strengths perspective in social work practice* (2nd ed., pp. 49–57). New York: Longman.

Saleebey, D. (1997b). *The strengths perspective in social work practice* (2nd ed.). New York: Longman.

Saulnier, C.F. (2002). Deciding who to see: Lesbians discuss their preferences in heath and mental health care providers. *Social Work, 47,* 355–365.

Schneider, M. S., Brown, L. S., & Glassgold, J. M. (2002). Implementing the resolution on appropriate therapeutic responses to sexual orientation: A guide for the perplexed. *Professional Psychology: Research and Practice, 33,* 265–276.

Schreier, B. A., & Werden, D. L. (2000). Psychoeducational programming: Creating a context of mental health for people who are lesbian, gay, or bisexual. In R. M. Perez, K. A. DeBord, & K. J. Bieschke (Eds.), *Handbook of counseling and psychotherapy with lesbian, gay, and bisexual clients* (pp. 359–382). Washington, DC: American Psychological Association.

Schriver, J. M. (1998). *Human behavior and the social environment* (2nd ed.). Needham Heights, MA: Allyn & Bacon.

Schroeder, M., & Shidlo, A. (2001). Ethical issues in sexual orientation conversion therapies: An empirical study of consumers. *Journal of Gay & Lesbian Psychotherapy, 5,* 133–168.

Shernoff, M. (1998). Individual practice with gay men. In G. P. Mallon (Ed.), *Foundations of social work practice with lesbian and gay persons* (pp. 77–103). New York: Haworth Press.

Silverstein, C. (1991). Psychological and medical treatments of homosexuality. In J. C. Gonsiorek & J. D. Weinrich (Eds.), *Homosexuality: Research implications for public policy* (pp. 101–114). Newbury Park, CA: Sage Publications.

Silverstein, C. (1996). History of treatment. In R. P. Cabaj & T. S. Stein (Eds.), *Textbook of homosexuality and mental health* (pp. 3–16). Washington, DC: American Psychiatric Press.

Socarides, C. W. (1978). *Homosexuality*. New York: Jason Aronson.

Socarides, C. W. (1992). Sexual politics and scientific logic: The issue of homosexuality [Special issue: America after the Thomas-Hill hearings]. *Journal of Psychohistory, 19*, 307–329.

Socarides, C. W. (1995). *Homosexuality; a right too far: A psychoanalyst answers 1000 questions about causes and cure and the impact of the gay rights movements on American society.* Phoenix, AZ: Adam Margrave.

Sorensen, L., & Roberts, S. J. (1997). Lesbian uses of and satisfaction with mental health services: Results from Boston lesbian health project. *Journal of Homosexuality, 33*, 35–49.

Stein, T. S. (1993). Overview of new developments in understanding homosexuality. *Review of Psychiatry, 12*, 9–40.

Thompson, N. L., McCandless, B. R., & Strickland, B. (1971). Personal adjustment of male and female homosexuals and heterosexuals. *Journal of Abnormal Psychology, 76*, 237–240.

Tully, C. (2000). *Lesbians, gays, and the empowerment perspective.* New York: Columbia University Press.

Wolfenden, J. (1963). *Reports of the committee on homosexual offenses and prostitution.* New York: Stein & Daly.

Wormer, K. V., Wells, J., & Boes, M. (2000). *Social work with lesbians, gays, and bisexuals: A strengths perspective.* Boston: Allyn & Bacon.

Zinik, G. (1984). The relationship between sexual orientation and eroticism, cognitive flexibility, and negative affect (Doctoral dissertation, University of California, Santa Barbara, 1983). *Dissertation Abstracts International, 45*(8-B), 2707–2708.

Zinik, G. (1985). Identity conflict or adaptive flexibility? Bisexuality reconsidered. *Journal of Homosexuality, 11*, 7–19.

CHAPTER 9
REQUIREMENTS OF PRACTITIONERS
AND SOCIAL SERVICE AGENCIES

What is heterosexist practice?

What is emotional and intellectual competence in practice?

How can practitioners create welcoming environments for LGBT clients?

How can practitioners serve as advocates and allies for LGBT clients?

How do the practitioner's sex–gender and sexual orientation impact client satisfaction?

How does the practitioner's sexual orientation impact the effectiveness of practice?

What are the special boundary issues for LGBT practitioners working with LGBT clients?

HETEROSEXIST ATTITUDES IN PRACTICE AND CLIENT DISSATISFACTION

As discussed in Chapter 8, practice with gay and lesbian clients has greatly improved although some practitioners still view and denigrate LGBT clients as abnormal, make incorrect assumptions about their sexual orientation (for example, that they can change it), lack knowledge about their issues of concern, and lack recognition of the negative effects of heterosexist oppression (for example, Berkman & Zinberg, 1997; Cramer, 1997). Heterosexism can affect every aspect of the practice process including referral, history taking and assessment, and the intervention process (McHenry & Johnson, 1993). The American Psychological Association Task Force Report on Heterosexual Bias in Psychotherapy (Garnets, Hancock, Cochran, Goodchilds, & Peplau, 1991) surveyed 2,500 clinical psychologists and found frequent biased, inappropriate, or inadequate practices in the assessment of gay and lesbian clients and the interventions recommended. Bisexual clients also experience these kinds of practices because of their attractions to persons of the same sex–gender. In addition, they may be misunderstood because of the typical either/or or dichotomous view of sexuality (heterosexuality versus homosexuality) or not accepted because of the view that bisexuality is not a stable or legitimate sexual orientation (Mohr, Israel, & Sedlacek, 2001; see Chapter 3). Mohr and colleagues found that counselors who had low scores on tolerance for bisexuality (thinking that their sexual orientation is deviant and pathological) and stability (thinking that their sexual orientation is temporary) were more likely to have negative reactions to bisexual clients.

Heterosexist attitudes displayed in practice can range from overt to liberal. Any of these attitudes along the entire continuum are hurtful and unacceptable. Riddle (1996) identified several overt levels and a liberal level of heterosexist attitudes. She called the most extreme overt level *repulsion*. At this level, practitioners view same-sex sexual orientation as a "crime versus nature," and LGB persons as sick, sinful, and immoral. Based on an attitude of superiority, these practitioners are judgmental, condescending, and disrespectful to these persons in general and as clients (Donaldson, 1998). Practitioners at this level use anything to try to change a client's same-sex sexual orientation, including conversion therapies. Clearly, these practitioners are harmful to gay and lesbian clients. Unless they can abandon their own prior assumptions and myths about lesbian and gay persons (Laird, 1995, 1996), and comply with standards of ethical practice with these clients, such practitioners should never perform any services for LGB populations (for example, DiAngelo, 1997; Sears & Williams, 1997).

Several other overt levels of heterosexist attitudes displayed in practice include:
- *Pity.* At this level, practitioners view heterosexuality as preferable to any other sexual orientation. In their view, persons who cannot change their lesbian, gay, or bisexual sexual orientation or seem born that way should be pitied.
- *Tolerance.* At this level, practitioners tolerate same sex–gender or bisexual sexual orientation as just a phase of adolescent development that many will go through but will eventually outgrow. These practitioners treat those who do not outgrow this phase or are "immature" in their development with the protectiveness and indulgence one might apply to a young child.
- *Acceptance.* At this level, practitioners say they accept LGB persons. Yet, thinking that they have to accept something implies that these clients have a problem (Riddle, 1966).

So-called liberal practitioners who see themselves as amicable with sexually subordinated persons also seem to accept them (Brown, 1995). But, even though these practitioners endorse positive or at least neutral attitudes, they display heterosexist bias when they take for granted the privilege associated with heterosexual status. In addition, although they disapprove of overt bias and prejudice they feel uncomfortable with overt displays of affection between same sex–gender persons or with the ambiguity of transgender or bisexual identifications.

Four working models of heterosexual identity were developed by Mohr (2002) for use in understanding the diversity in heterosexual practitioners' understanding of sexual orientation issues and why they presents obstacles to affirmative practice with LGB clients. Two of the models fit with the pity, acceptance, and liberal stances discussed above. For example, Mohr's *compulsory heterosexuality* model fits with the pity level. Borrowing the phrase from Rich (1980) for a title for this model, Mohr explained that practitioners who follow it believe that heterosexuality is the only morally and socially acceptable sexual orientation. They probably hold negative views of LGB persons and think of their interactions with them as distasteful. They tend to avoid contact with LGB persons so they are vulnerable to stereotypes about them. These practitioners are likely to try to get LGB clients to "choose" a heterosexual sexual orientation.

A second model developed by Mohr (2002) is called *democratic heterosexuality* and fits with the acceptance and liberal perspectives discussed above. Practitioners subscribing to this model view persons of all sexual orientations as essentially the same. Hence, sexual orientation is not viewed as an important area of focus because there are no meaningful differences in the life experiences of persons due to their sexual orientations. LGB clients will essentially be invisible to these practitioners and they may assume that all of their clients are heterosexual. They are unlikely to recognize the effects of heterosexism on LGB persons or recognize their own heterosexism, their subscription to heterosexual privilege, or their stereotypes about persons with different sexual orientations.

A third model developed by Mohr (2002) of heterosexual identity is the reverse of the democratic heterosexuality model. Followers of this model, *politicized heterosexuality*, overfocus on sexual orientation and encourage their clients to make disclosures to significant persons in their lives but with no regard for the possible negative consequences. They view LGB persons as oppressed but also as survivors of a hostile sociopolitical culture. They may experience anger, guilt, and self-criticism about their contributions to heterosexism, including living with the privileges of heterosexuality. The fourth model of heterosexual identity, which is the most affirmative model, will be discussed below along with other affirmative views (Mohr, 2002).

Institutional denial of the specific needs of LGBT clients also occurs. Many social services agencies appear to deny that LGBT persons have specific needs, and administrators often resist developing affirmative programs specifically for LGBT clients. They may argue, for example, that these clients can explore their relationship and family issues in any of the agency's dating, relationship, or family groups although these groups are geared toward heterosexuals (Ball, 1994; Hancock, 1995).

Most LGB clients are well aware of institutional denials of their needs and the negative attitudes held by health and mental health professionals, as well as those of the general public (Rothblum, 1994). These clients assess external environments all their lives for signs of prejudice, rejection, hatred, or violence, including voice or mannerism, awkwardness, defensiveness, hesitancy, hostility, distance, disapproval, and contempt (Brown, 1989; Pope, 1997). Because of rigid heterosexist views of sexuality or hostility about LGBT persons, these clients are probably harmed daily. When they perceive that practitioners hold negative views of them, they can experience greater psychological distress following social services than they experienced before services began (Fassinger, 1991). In the practice setting, the openness and trust of LGBT clients in their practitioners will likely diminish, a situation that is difficult to correct later (Messing, Schoenberg, & Stephens, 1983–1984; Pope, 1997). Some of these clients in traditional social services agencies anticipate outright rejection. Some prematurely terminate because they think that the practitioner will terminate services with them (Alexander, 1998). Others terminate after one session because of unhelpful behaviors by the practitioner (Liddle, 1996).

Unfortunately, practitioners in all disciplines receive little or no education about issues pertinent to LGBT populations (Buhrke & Douce, 1991; Mackelprang, Ray, & Hernandez-Peck, 1996), much less assistance in changing their attitudes. This is often the case even though codes of ethics of human services professions now endorse training and other requirements regarding same sex–gender and bisexual sexual orientations. For example, the code of ethics of the National Association of Social Workers (1999) states the following requirements:

- Social workers *should obtain education about and seek to understand* the nature of social diversity and oppression with respect to…sexual orientation. (p. 9)
- Social workers *should not practice, condone, facilitate, or collaborate* with any form of discrimination on the basis of…sexual orientation. (pp. 22–23)
- Social workers *should act to prevent and eliminate domination of, exploitation of, and discrimination against* any person or group on the basis of…sexual orientation. [italics added] (p. 27)

If practitioners in human services agencies adhere to a professional code of ethics, they must be affirmative, not oppressive, with LGBT clients. They must serve all clients equitably. As human services organizations provide most of the counseling, case management, and other services for these persons, it is crucial that these organizations insist upon nonjudgmental, affirmative attitudes by their staffs. Practitioners are called upon not only to proclaim accurate views of the mental health of LGBT persons but also to provide compassionate and affirmative services to these populations (Downey & Friedman, 1996; Hall & Fradkin, 1992).

Trainees, practitioners, and administrators in social services agencies must deal with their heterosexist biases (Hancock, 1995; McHenry & Johnson, 1993). They must continually examine how their biases, beliefs, preferences, and convictions shape their attitudes and beliefs—do they harm others (Hartman & Laird, 1998)? Once practitioners know that they hold heterosexist biases and how they display these biases, they must change their attitudes. No practitioner at any of the hetereosexist levels discussed above should work with LGB clients or attend training sessions on heterosexisms. Transformations can occur as explained below, but students and practitioners must motivate themselves to be open to the process (for example, DiAngelo, 1997; Sears & Williams, 1997).

TRANSFORMATION TO THE AFFIRMATIVE STANCE

Social services agencies should create a nonjudgmental atmosphere for staff to talk about differences, biases, and lack of knowledge about LGBT persons. It should be clear to the staff that agencies will not tolerate discrimination based on sexual orientation or sex–gender expression (Humphreys & Quam, 1998). Novices also need to seek regular consultation from a practitioner who has the necessary experience and can point out subtle expressions of bias (Brown, 1995). It would help all practitioners to seek supervision from any educated, enlightened affirmative practitioner, but procuring supervision from an openly LGB or T practitioner may be the most beneficial educational experience, especially if the student or professional has not earlier been acquainted with a lesbian, gay, bisexual, or transgender person (Buhrke, 1989). Practitioners must also take responsibility for attaining both emotional competency and intellectual competency in their work with these clients. Ethical dilemmas result if either type of competency is deficient or missing (Brown, 1996).

Emotional Competency

Emotional competency involves awareness of attitudes and feelings about LGBT persons and the continual examination of one's biases and prejudices as these can impair both one's capacity to effectively and compassionately offer services and one's ability to assess emotional readiness to practice with LGBT clients (Brown, 1996). Beyond identifying biases and stereotypes it is also necessary to examine their deeper personal effects (Markowitz, 1991). A useful check for these effects is to ask oneself certain questions such as: What messages do I communicate to LGBT clients about their worth and value? (Brown, 1995). What assumptions do I make about a client's sexual orientation? Why do I make these assumptions? (Eldridge, 1987). If one is heterosexual, one can imagine that one's partner is of the same sex–gender. What feelings does this arouse? Fear? Shame? (Hartman & Laird, 1998). For another check, Hall and Fradkin (1992) posed these questions: "Would I feel very comfortable if a son of mine were gay? Would I feel very comfortable participating in a gay rights march? Will I confront heterosexist jokes when I hear them?" (p. 364).

Maybe even more disturbing to most heterosexual practitioners is another question posed by Hall and Fradkin (1992): "Am I as comfortable with my [homosexual] feelings as my heterosexual feelings?" (p. 364). As discussed in Chapter 3, Kinsey and his colleagues confirmed that persons are rarely exclusively heterosexual. Moreover, many persons go through a transient period after puberty when they engage in same sex–gender sexual behavior (Kinsey, Pomeroy, & Martin, 1948). In their studies on sexuality, Masters and Johnson (1979) found that same sex–gender erotic imagery was one of the most frequent fantasies reported by the heterosexual group. For the courageous practitioner, Hall and Fradkin (1992) posed the following question: "What homoerotic fantasies, feelings, or behaviors have I had or do I have, and can I appreciate and enjoy these parts of me?" (p. 364). Heterosexual practitioners may not participate in same sex–gender sexual behaviors or fantasize about them, but they still may fear that they are not exclusively heterosexually oriented. It is essential for all practitioners to feel comfortable with their own sexuality and sexual orientation and with sexual issues that LGBT clients may present (Cabaj, 1988; Fassinger, 1991).

Several educational and practice models delineate the transformation process to reach emotional competency (for example, Bruss, Brack, Brack, Glickauf-Hughes, & O'Leary, 1997; Chojnacki & Gelberg, 1995; Gelberg, Chojnacki, Gibson, Benn, & Holahan, 1992). Using four stages of a model developed by Prochaska and DiClemente (1986), Tyler, Jackman-Wheitner, Strader, and Lenox (1997) identified interventions to match the stages of the process. The following discussion describes this model and includes interventions that trainers can use.

Precontemplative stage. At this stage, trainees are unaware of a need to change. They do not understand or acknowledge the negative effects of their current behavior and attitudes on persons who are not heterosexual. They do not experience emotional reactions to the negative aspects of their attitudes and behaviors, and they have no motivation to make any attempts to change them (for example, Berkman & Zinberg, 1997; Black, Oles, & Moore, 1996). At this stage, trainees may be most affected by experiential activities that force them to modify their existing heterosexist schema. The intent is to help trainees identify with the struggles and prejudices that LGBT persons face daily in a heterosexist society so that they can develop empathy and sensitivity.

Suggested interventions include interacting with LGBT persons on speaker panels; discussing books, articles, and films about LGBT persons; role playing in which trainees can assume the roles of LGBT persons in various scenarios; using guided imagery such as waking up one morning as a lesbian, gay, bisexual, or transgender person and imagining the fears that arise as result of this "discovery" (Emert & Milburn, 1997); filling out the reverse questionnaire (Rochlin, 1992) that may prompt trainees to begin to think about the type of questioning that LGBT persons are frequently confronted with but heterosexual persons are not; or imagining how their immediate environment would be different if heterosexuals were the subordinated group.

Trainees should increase contact with LGBT persons beyond clinical populations. Contact with nonclinical members of these groups helps reduce stereotypes (Yarhouse, 1999).

Contemplative stage. At this stage, trainees are aware that their biases and behaviors are problematic and may be open to questioning themselves about where they stand on LGBT persons. Interventions to facilitate self-questioning include (a) a continuum activity where trainees create a scale of one to 10 on the floor of a room and choose a place on the scale to match their personal reactions to a series of questions that evaluate their values, beliefs, and behaviors regarding LGBT persons; and (b) a modified think-aloud protocol that involves reading brief vignettes to participants about a situation which an LGBT person might encounter, then assessing their first thoughts as evaluative, information seeking, or emotional, thus identifying automatic thoughts that may not be in the trainees' awareness.

Action stage. This is probably the most difficult stage because it involves attempts at new behaviors, attitudes, and commitments to action. First, trainees identify action goals such as specific changes they desire in their personal cognitions and behaviors or changes in their educational or work environments. Then they develop action plans with follow-up practice. It can be useful for trainees working on comparable goals to work together to generate action plans. Another action strategy is to systematically identify (a) desired behaviors; (b) environmental factors that will support the desired behaviors, for example, becoming allies and advocates for LGBT persons; and (c) environmental factors that are obstacles such as pressures to maintain old attitudes and behaviors by families, work associates, and others.

Maintenance stage. This stage involves maintaining a consistent sense that behavior, thoughts, and feelings are congruent or moving toward this goal (Prochaska, Norcross, & DiClemente, 1994). It is crucial for trainees to experience a personal sense that they are developing into the type of person they want to be. They may experience a greater sense of personal value as well as more respect from others. Various community groups can provide support for maintaining new attitudes and behaviors, such as Parents and Friends of Lesbians and Gays (PFLAG), LGBT student groups, metropolitan community churches, and other groups and organizations in LGBT communities. Students can also volunteer in programs such as the buddy program for persons with AIDS. Within the social work profession, trainees and practitioners can attend meetings of the LGBT committees of NASW and the Council on Social Work Education.

Trainees and future practitioners should engage themselves in an evaluation process in which they compare their earlier beliefs, values, and actions related to LGBT persons with their current beliefs, values, and actions. Awareness of successful growth experiences can generate further growth (Tyler and colleagues, 1997).

Selecting applicable interventions for trainees depends on the individual development of each trainee; yet it may be possible to address a group of persons who are not at the same stage. For example, self-reflective activity, or the self-evaluation that occurs at the maintenance level, may also affect persons at earlier stages. Similarly, persons at all levels can develop action plans although they will contain quite different goals. Because the model is dynamic and cyclical, persons may move through all of the stages many times depending on specific issues (Tyler and colleagues, 1997).

The main factor predicting whether interventions will affect students, trainees, and persons who are already practitioners is a person's level of change readiness. Change will occur with some persons and not with others. It also may not be possible to observe what really happens with trainees except in field placements and human services jobs (Prochaska & DiClemente, 1986). A significant change may occur only in a trainee's life outside the educational or training experience (Bruss and colleagues, 1997).

Emotional competence also involves understanding the affirmative stance on practice and integrating it into one's attitudes and behaviors. Identified by Riddle (1996), the attitudes of affirmative practice include:

- *Support.* At this level, practitioners work to safeguard the rights of LGBT persons. They are aware of the heterosexist climate and the irrational unfairness of it. They support LGBT persons in their efforts to live fuller lives and to experience pride in who they are.
- *Admiration.* At this level, practitioners admire the courage and strength it takes to declare oneself LGBT in our society.
- *Appreciation.* At this level, practitioners value the diversity of persons and see LGBT persons as a valid part of that diversity.

Intellectual Competency

Intellectual competency includes attaining accurate and scientifically sound information and professional training regarding LGBT persons (Brown, 1996). For bisexual persons, this includes learning more about the alternative views to the dichotomous model of sexual orientation as well as specific information about bisexual persons (Mohr and colleagues, 2001). Practitioner knowledge of issues specific to lesbian and gay persons is associated with the satisfaction of gay and lesbian clients (Liddle, 1996). Practitioners must become aware of the gaps in their knowledge and seek further training, supervision, and consultation (Brown, 1996). More specifically, required knowledge includes (a) unique issues in the lives of LGBT persons such as the coming-out process, identity management, family of origin, internalized oppression, couples, parenting, and career (for example, Brown, 1995; Liddle, 1996; Mallon, 1994); (b) basics about HIV/AIDS and where clients who are HIV-positive can get support and assistance with medication, health care expenses, financial management, job security, school issues, relationship issues, sexuality issues, and legal issues (Kus & Smith, 1995); (c) LGBT culture such as history, major holidays, Pride Day/Week (late June), and National Coming Out Day (October 11); and (d) general resources such as LGBT community centers, help lines, support groups, bookstores, health and mental health services, educational opportunities, and colleagues to consult (Garnets and colleagues, 1991; Hardman, 1997). Aside from knowledge about lesbian and gay persons from literature, practitioners need to let clients tell their story. Literature can help guide questions and exploration of a client's story, but it will not provide information about the unique experiences and meanings of a client's life (Hartman & Laird, 1998). For example, transgender persons want someone who will hear their stories and validate their feelings (Carroll, Gilroy, & Ryan, 2002). Practitioners must also actively attain information on suitable and unsuitable practices with LGBT clients (Garnets and colleagues, 1991).

Other affirmative applications focus on the practice environment and the language and questions used with clients.

AFFIRMATIVE ENVIRONMENT, LANGUAGE, AND QUESTIONS

Environment

It is difficult for LGBT clients to ask for help if the environment is not affirmative (Appleby & Anastas, 1998). Social services agencies should, therefore, provide positive, affirmative environments that communicate a supportive and appreciative atmosphere so that clients will feel that they can discuss feelings, experiences, and ideas in a free and open manner (Radkowsky & Siegel, 1997). Affirmative environments include positive written acknowledgment of LGBT persons such as client information forms that offer categories other than single, married, and divorced; the mention of sexual orientation in statements about working with diverse groups; visible resources such as a pamphlet that addresses concerns of these persons; a logo to indicate that this agency welcomes LGBT clients and that LGBT persons work in the agency (Gruskin, 1999); posters placed on the walls from local or national LGBT organizations; affirmative books, articles, periodicals, and other items focused on LGBT persons displayed on shelves and tables (Barrett, 1998; Croteau & Theil, 1994; Mallon, 1999); affirmative symbols on clothing such as pins or other jewelry (Gruskin, 1999); and staff who know about community resources (Eldridge & Barnett, 1991).

Language

Respectful, inclusive, and gender-neutral language should be used (Croteau & Morgan, 1989; Croteau & von Destinon, 1994), for example, *sexual activity* versus sexual intercourse; *relationship status* versus marital status; *partner* versus spouse; and *couples practice* versus marital practice (Bernstein, 1992). Marital status should not be asked for on client forms and brochures but instead clients can be asked whom they view as their family. This allows clients to state what they choose (Deevey, 1990; Gruskin, 1999; Kelly, 1998). Using gender-neutral language indicates that one is open to hear about same sex–gender relationships (Scrivner & Eldridge, 1995).

Questions

Open-ended and neutral questions are best: Who is essential to you? and not Are you married, widowed, or divorced? What can you tell me about your relationships? What can you tell me about the persons who are significant in your life? (see McAllan & Ditillo, 1994). Would you like to include someone in discussions about your treatment? Would you like to bring someone with you to your next appointment? (see Gruskin, 1999; McAllan & Ditillo, 1994). It is important not to ask questions that assume a client's heterosexuality, now or anytime in the past, or questions about heterosexual relationships. Lesbian and gay clients may interpret such questions as value judgments about the primacy of heterosexuality (Gartrell, 1984).

Practitioners should never search for causes of a person's sexual orientation or ask questions about etiology. Seeking answers to these questions implies that these sexual orientations are pathological (Gartrell, 1984). For clients searching for causes, the practitioner should acknowledge the importance of this quest to the client but acknowledge that there is no certainty about causes.

THE ULTIMATE GOAL: ALLY/ADVOCATE OF LGBT PERSONS

The highest affirmative level identified by Riddle (1996) is *nurturance*. At this level, practitioners assume that LGBT persons are indispensable to our society. They feel genuine affection and delight about these persons, and they are allies and advocates for them. Mohr (2002) portrayed practitioners who follow the *integrative heterosexuality* model as affirmative. They do not see themselves as fundamentally different from LGB persons and consider sexual orientation as only one important part of a person. Yet, they acknowledge differences such as their own more privileged positions in society. They understand the complexity of sexual orientations and that they are multidimensional. They have LGB-affirming beliefs and opinions. Raup (1995) and others (Barrett, 1998; Crumpacker & Vander Haegen, 1993; Mallon, 1994, 1998; Scrivner & Eldridge, 1995; Simoni, 1996; Stokes, Miller, & Mundhenk, 1998) defined requirements for a practitioner who wants to transcend heterosexism to the extent of becoming an ally/advocate:

- Take responsibility to continually pursue experiences and contact with and getting to know LGBT persons and not just those who are clients
- Acknowledge that it may take months or years of personal experience and education to begin to understand what it means to be an ally/advocate
- Work continually to end oppression in one's personal and professional life and to be an advocate with and for oppressed populations
- Make a personal commitment to personal growth and self-responsibility for change, no matter what others do
- Recognize the consequences of complicity in any statements or acts of heterosexism
- Confront anti-LGBT jokes and conversation, understanding that this may alienate friends, family, and colleagues
- Challenge stereotypes and detrimental generalizations about LGBT persons
- Learn about local support networks and positive LGBT role models for clients
- Call on others for answers, more information, or other types of support when needed
- Keep updates on information and resources in the local LGBT community
- Know the right resource for a specific issue
- Learn of local attorneys, physicians, dentists, and other health professionals competent in addressing LGBT needs in their respective fields
- Read LGBT newspapers and other related materials to keep updated on what is going on in LGBT communities
- Start a chapter of PFLAG if one does not exist in the community
- Start other support groups where needed
- Help publicize and celebrate events significant to LGBT persons
- March in gay pride events and participate in public protests against anti-LGBT efforts
- Join organizations and commissions within organizations that address LGBT issues
- Advocate for LGBT issues in schools, group homes, and foster homes
- Assist in the training of other professionals by providing them with accurate information and affirmative perspectives
- Speak to political, religious, educational, and civic groups as an advocate for human rights for all persons and about the need for more inclusive policies

- Speak at city, county, and state official meetings when antigay issues arise
- Advocate for inclusion of material on LGBT persons in undergraduate and graduate programs
- Encourage libraries to carry affirmative books and journals
- Join the LGBT divisions of one's professional organization (also, a good source for information and networking)
- Work for affirmative policies in one's place of employment and for inclusion of LGBT persons as employees.

For heterosexual practitioners who invest themselves in becoming knowledgeable and affirmative, working with LGBT clients can be rewarding. These clients are often high functioning, motivated, and often make more progress than other clients. For the most part they are trying to manage stress or developmental issues instead of trying to cope with psychopathology (Liddle, 1999b). If no LGBT practitioners are available in the local area, heterosexual practitioners who are affirmative should make themselves known. If they want potential LGBT clients, they can offer support groups or workshops for LGBT persons, advertise in LGBT newspapers or directories, or let local professionals know they offer affirmative services (Liddle, 1997).

RATING HUMAN SERVICES PROFESSIONALS

Psychiatrists, psychologists, counselors, and social workers are generally helpful to the population at large. But their affirmative ratings with gay and lesbian clients vary by group. Liddle (1999a) asked about the helpfulness of these practitioners in a study of 367 gay and lesbian volunteers. The respondents rated their practice experiences with 110 psychiatrists, 332 psychologists, 151 social workers, and 130 counselors.

Psychiatrists were rated as much less helpful than social workers, psychologists, and counselors. Forty-five percent of the respondents rated psychiatrists as either not at all helpful or as destructive. Psychiatrists were about half as likely to not help clients feel good about themselves as gay or lesbian and three times as likely to convey a belief that a gay or lesbian identity is bad, sick, or inferior; blame clients' difficulties on their sexual orientation; or insist on focusing on sexual orientation when it is not relevant. Only 23 percent of psychiatrists demonstrated knowledge of gay and lesbian communities or resources compared to 51 percent of other practitioners (Liddle, 1999a).

Social workers were the most likely to exhibit exemplary practices—for example, being knowledgeable about lesbian and gay communities and other resources; not making an issue of a client's sexual orientation when not relevant; willingness to deal with a client's sexual orientation when relevant; and helping a client feel good about being gay or lesbian. In their sample of gay and lesbian persons, Jones and Gabriel (1998) also found that they attained a significantly greater benefit from social workers (8.0), than from psychologists (7.6) or psychiatrists (6.4). The rankings represent the mean scores on a 10-point scale, ranging from 10 (very beneficial) to 1 (very destructive).

Practitioner–Client Matchup on Sexual Orientation and Sex–Gender

It seems important for clients and practitioners to feel that they are more alike than different. Jones and Gabriel (1998) found that the ratings on a 10-point scale by gay and lesbian clients on benefits of practice associated with the sex–gender and sexual orientation of the practitioner included gay, 8.4 (significantly greater benefit than from heterosexual male or female practitioners); lesbian, 8.0; heterosexual female, 7.6; and heterosexual male, 6.2 (significantly lower benefit than the other three groups). LGB practitioners of both sex–genders and heterosexual female practitioners in Liddle's (1996) study also received ratings as more helpful than heterosexual male practitioners. Yet some (30 percent) of the heterosexual male practitioners and males with an unidentified sexual orientation were rated as "very helpful."

Gay and lesbian clients usually prefer working with a gay or lesbian practitioner, and they tend to rate a practitioner perceived as gay or lesbian as more expert, knowledgeable, understanding, empathic, and trustworthy (for example, Ryan, Bradford, & Honnold, 1999). Matching the "therapist's" sexuality with that of the client may facilitate rapport and a deeper understanding of the client, but matching in and of itself will not necessarily prevent an unsatisfactory situation (Liddle, 1996; Malley & Tasker, 1999).

Most practitioners who are affirmative and prepared to work with gay and lesbian clients can be effective. Gay and lesbian persons studied by Moran and Moore (1993) did not rate heterosexual practitioners less favorably than gay or lesbian practitioners when the practice issue was not sexual in nature. In a study of gay and lesbian clients, Lease, Cogdal, and Smith (1995) found that the sexual orientation of the practitioner had no impact on satisfaction. The sample of gay and lesbian clients surveyed by Jones and Gabriel (1998) was asked if a practitioner must be a lesbian or gay person to provide affirmative practice. About a quarter (26 percent) responded "definitely to probably yes," but almost three-quarters (73 percent) responded "probably not to definitely not." Gay and lesbian clients studied by Liddle (1999b) rated 75 percent of their nongay practitioners "very helpful," and another 19 percent "fairly helpful," compared to the ratings of heterosexual clients at 62 percent and 24 percent.

Although many gay and lesbian clients see heterosexual practitioners, there are still many clients that prefer to see LGB practitioners. Nearly half of the gay and lesbian respondents studied by McDermott, Tyndall, and Lichtenberg (1989) preferred to see a gay or lesbian practitioner. Whereas the sexual orientation of the professional was not a significant factor for most of the gay and lesbian respondents (60 percent) studied by Modcrin and Wyers (1990), 40 percent would only seek professional help from someone of the same sexual orientation. In a national sample, Sorensen and Roberts (1997) found that lesbians across all ages gave higher satisfaction ratings to lesbian practitioners than to heterosexual practitioners. Therefore, if requested by LGB clients, heterosexual practitioners need to refer these clients to available gay, lesbian, or bisexual practitioners.

Sex–gender of the practitioner was an issue for 68 percent of the lesbians studied by Modcrin and Wyers (1990), who indicated that they would only see a woman. In contrast, only 24 percent of gay persons would only see a man. Most (89 percent) of the lesbian respondents studied by Bradford, Ryan, and Rothblum (1994) preferred to see a woman; a similar proportion of lesbians (80 percent) studied by Brooks (1981) also preferred to see a woman. Lesbians were significantly more likely than heterosexual women to prefer a woman who was feminist or pro-woman, lesbian, and held similar political views (Bernhard & Applegate, 1999).

Selection Process

From research on the selection of practitioners by 392 gay and lesbian clients, Liddle (1997) concluded that heterosexual practitioners can anticipate encountering many of these clients in their practice. Only 41 percent of the practitioners selected were gay, lesbian, or bisexual. The findings also indicated that heterosexual practitioners should anticipate that some potential clients might interview them about their attitudes regarding gay and lesbian persons. Two-thirds (63 percent) of the practitioners surveyed by Liddle were screened for gay-affirmative attitudes and prescreening was associated with higher practitioner ratings. Clients who did not prescreen for affirmative attitudes (37 percent) may confront an unpleasant situation with a heterosexist or poorly prepared practitioner.

Special Issues for Gay and Lesbian Practitioners

Gay and lesbian practitioners must contend with several issues before providing services to LGB clients. For example, if some of these practitioners have not reached self-acceptance, they should abstain from working with gay and lesbian clients. Without self-acceptance, practitioners may ask clients to take actions that they, themselves, have yet to accomplish. For example, a lesbian or gay practitioner who has made no disclosures at work or to family may cajole or insist on such actions by gay and lesbian clients. The practitioner may vicariously experience disclosure through clients, but without the personal risk and without regard for the risks of such a course of action for the clients. For other practitioners who accept themselves and involve themselves in political activity within their communities, an unintended consequence may be the confusion of some of their political ideals with practice goals. They may believe, for example, that disclosure is a political agenda and that all gay and lesbian persons should disclose their sexual orientation. Politics, however, should not be confused with practice. Following the value of self-determination, practitioners should encourage clients to explore and follow their own reasons for disclosing or not (Brown, 1996).

PRACTICING AND LIVING IN GAY AND LESBIAN COMMUNITIES

When practicing and living in the same communities as their clients, particularly small communities, practitioners may find privacy elusive. Clients may observe a practitioner in various settings in the community and know other persons who are acquaintances, friends, colleagues, or lovers (past or present) of the practitioner. If practitioners are out in public with a partner, clients might observe them and critique the partner. If single, finding dates can be problematic if clients live in the same community (Kranzberg, 1998).

If practitioners and clients live in the same communities, the possibility of seeing each other in public should be addressed in a session. For example, if they see each other, will they acknowledge each other and if so who will initiate contact? What are the expectations for handling personal introductions? Is the encounter to be seen as a topic for discussion in a practice session or not? Some practitioners constrict their actions to avoid contact with clients; they may not attend parties (for example, if they have previously checked guest lists and find clients included). Some may even choose to live several hours outside the city in which clients live, particularly if it is a small town (Hanson & Weeks, 1998).

Client and Practitioner Overidentification

Gay and lesbian clients often intentionally seek out a gay or lesbian practitioner with the expectation that this person will model a positive identity for them (Kranzberg, 1998; Ramirez Barranti, 1998). LGB practitioners are esteemed as leaders and teachers (Brown, 1988). Lesbian clients particularly may idealize their lesbian "therapists" or have fantasies about their power, superior knowledge, and interpersonal adeptness (Dillon, 1999). Gay and lesbian practitioners may see themselves as the best or only persons to serve as role models for their LGB clients and think that clients should follow their recommendations because of their particular experiences and perceptions as gay or lesbian persons. What practitioners recommend, however, may or may not fit well for individual clients (Kranzberg, 1998) and may stop further exploration by clients for their own best fit (Greene, 1994). Clients may not share the "therapist's" vision about what is or is not necessary for happiness or well-being (Kranzberg, 1998). If practitioners project their own experiences and perceptions onto clients, they will not hear or see clients as they are or what they want for their lives. Prescriptions and interventions that gay and lesbian practitioners recommend to their clients are best presented as suggestions (Nichols, 1982). Practitioners can share their opinions about issues, provide education, and recommend the most suitable interventions. They should not, however, become overly responsible for the client's choices and outcomes (Stein, 1988).

Boundary Issues

Boundaries and roles can become confused in practice. This is most likely to happen when practitioners become involved in multiple roles such as practitioner, friend, and mentor (Cabaj, 1996). In their survey of practitioners and clients, Jones and Gabriel (1998) found both social and sexual boundary violations. The rates of social boundary violations among different groups of practitioners included 8.8 percent for the aggregate sample; 11.7 percent for gay; 12.2 percent for lesbian; 6.4 percent for heterosexual male; and 7.8 percent for heterosexual female. Rates of these violations among the specific profession of the practitioners included 10.2 percent for social worker; 6.7 percent for psychologist; 4.0 percent for psychiatrist; 9.6 percent for psychoanalyst; 21.1 percent for clergy; 6.1 percent for marital/family practitioner; and 23.3 percent for other categories. Sex–gender of the clients who experienced social boundary violations by their practitioners were 9.5 percent for males and 8.5 percent for females.

The rates of *sexual* boundary violations among the different groups of practitioners included 2.4 percent for the aggregate sample of practitioners; 3.9 percent for gay; 2.8 percent for lesbian; 3.4 percent for heterosexual male; and .6 percent for heterosexual female. The profession of the practitioners included 2.4 percent for social worker; 2.7 percent for psychologist; 2.5 percent for psychiatrist; 4.0 percent for psychoanalyst; 2.5 percent for clergy; 1.0 percent for marital/family practitioner; and 2.1 percent for other categories. Sex–gender of the clients who experienced sexual boundary violations was 1.8 percent for males and 2.6 percent for females.

Practitioners can lose perspective if they are too active in a client's life, too protective, or experience too much intimacy with a client (Cadwell, 1994). To gratify one's personal needs through clients abdicates the practitioner's primary role and responsibility to the client and is unethical as well. Even if a client requests such contacts or relationships, practitioners must refuse. Practitioners must never use clients for personal benefit (Greene, 1994). It is in the best interests of both client and practitioner for the practitioner to eliminate potential boundary conflicts (Kranzberg, 1998). This is another reason why it is important for practitioners to develop support networks of peers and colleagues that offer social and emotional supports. Without these various connections, practitioners may seek to meet social and intimacy needs with their clients by viewing them as social acquaintances, friends, or lovers (Greene, 1994).

Other recommendations regarding boundary issues for practitioner issues include (a) talk to other professionals about boundary issues; (b) participate in a support group for practitioners; (c) discuss issues on professional internet lists; (d) get involved in outside activities; (e) procure competent supervision with more experienced practitioners; and (f) participate in peer supervisory sessions to discuss ethical issues and ensure responsible behavior. The goal is for these supports to lead to reliance on one's own ability to set up proper boundaries (Fickey & Grimm, 1998).

Extraordinary Situations

Sometimes the boundaries between practitioners and clients get blurred because of extraordinary situations. For a gay practitioner who works with gay persons with HIV/AIDS, for example, many factors can affect the boundaries between them: the practitioner's HIV status, the number of persons in his life lost to AIDS, and the grief he experienced over these loses. The practitioner might visit a client with HIV/AIDS in the hospital or at home. Especially with a client in the final stages of the disease, boundaries can become ambiguous if the client needs and wants touching and other forms of physical closeness. It may not be necessary to maintain a professional distance as long as these behaviors involve nonsexual comfort to the client. In addition, because of extended work with the client and development of a strong attachment, it is not unusual for the practitioner to feel strong emotion as the client's health declines. It is not, however, the client's role to care for the practitioner even if this person is expressing strong emotions (Fickey & Grimm, 1998).

In all cases, LGB practitioners must surround themselves with reliable personal and social networks. As with all professionals, they need the support of their peers as well as satisfying lives beyond their practice environments (Brown, 1996).

SUMMARY

- Heterosexist practice describes practitioners and agencies that create either overtly hostile or vaguely oppressive environments for LGBT clients. This includes the practice of conversion therapies as well as the perpetuation of anti-LGBT beliefs, attitudes, and policies. It also includes practitioners or agencies that do nothing to accommodate diverse populations in their work. The codes of ethics for most human services professionals prohibit heterosexist practice.
- Practitioners who take responsibility for affirmative practice with LGBT clients develop emotional competence. These professionals are aware that everyone grows up exposed to, and acclimated to, heterosexist attitudes and beliefs. These professionals monitor themselves closely to ensure that they do not discriminate against clients because of sexual orienta-

tion or display any behaviors that would make their clients feel uncomfortable or unwelcome. Emotionally competent practitioners are willing to examine their own belief systems, to practice empathic exercises, and to continue their emotional growth until they can work with LGBT clients without prejudicial judgments or behaviors. Practitioners must also develop intellectual competence through thorough knowledge about LGBT issues and resources.

- Practitioners can make their LGBT clients feel welcome by using nonheterosexist intake forms, that is, forms that do not display assumptions of marital status or other heterosexual linkups. Waiting areas might display signs stating that everyone is welcome in this office regardless of their sex–gender, race, sexual orientation, or sex–gender expression. Offices might also display literature advertising community resources for LGBT clients.

- Practitioners can advocate for their clients by establishing a "nurturing" point of view about their LGBT clients and recognizing them as valuable members of society. Practitioners should also maintain relationships with community support systems for LGBT clients by clearly advertising their support of these groups, by participating in public events, and by endorsing civil rights for all.

- Most studies demonstrate that lesbians and gay persons prefer to work with practitioners of the same sexual orientation, but both groups prefer working with women, of all sexual orientations, as opposed to working with heterosexual men. Despite the many difficulties LGBT clients face in searching for a competent practitioner, most report satisfaction with their practitioner even if this person is heterosexual.

- Although LGBT practitioners may more clearly understand the social obstacles facing LGBT clients, heterosexual practitioners who are affirmative can provide effective services to these client populations if they maintain high levels of emotional and intellectual competence.

- LGBT practitioners confront some unique issues when working with LGBT clients. First, they may "overidentify" with their clients; that is, they may confuse their own issues with those of their clients around certain topics, such as coming out or AIDS. Second, practitioners may have little privacy from clients; LGBT communities can be small and cohesive, and practitioners and clients may find themselves in social gatherings more often than they would like. Third, LGBT practitioners may feel pressure to serve as role models; they may feel the need to be perfect both in personal and political arenas. Like all practitioners, LGBT practitioners must carefully monitor their affections for clients and not violate social or sexual boundaries. In codes of ethics of the helping professions these boundary crossings are ethical violations

CHAPTER 9
REFERENCES

Alexander, C. J. (1998). Treatment planning for gay and lesbian clients. *Journal of Gay & Lesbian Social Services, 8,* 95–106.

Appleby, G. A., & Anastas, J. W. (1998). *Not just a passing phase: Social work with gay, lesbian, and bisexual people.* New York: Columbia University Press.

Ball, S. (1994). A group model for gay and lesbian clients with chronic mental illness. *Social Work, 39,* 109–115.

Barrett, B. (1998). Gay and lesbian activism: A frontier in social advocacy. In C. C. Lee (Ed.), *Social action: A mandate for counselors* (pp. 84–98). Alexandria, VA: American Counseling Association.

Berkman, C., & Zinberg, J. G. (1997). Homophobia and heterosexism in social workers. *Social Work, 42,* 319–331.

Bernhard, L. A., & Applegate, J. M. (1999). Comparison of stress and stress management strategies between lesbian and heterosexual women. *Health Care for Women International, 20,* 355–347.

Bernstein, G. S. (1992). How to avoid heterosexual bias in language. *Behavior Therapist, 15,* 161.

Black, B., Oles, T. P., & Moore, L. (1996). Homophobia among students in social work programs. *Journal of Baccalaureate Social Work, 2,* 23–41.

Bradford, J., Ryan, C., & Rothblum, E. D. (1994). National lesbian health care survey: Implications for mental health care. *Journal of Consulting and Clinical Psychology, 62,* 228–242.

Brooks, V. R. (1981). Sex and sexual orientation as variables in therapists' biases and therapy outcomes. *Clinical Social Work Journal, 9,* 198–210.

Brown, L. S. (1988). Beyond thou shalt not: Thinking about ethics in the lesbian therapy community. *Women & Therapy, 8,* 13–25.

Brown, L. S. (1989). New voices, new visions: Toward a lesbian/gay paradigm for psychology. *Psychology of Women, 13,* 445–458.

Brown, L. S. (1995). Therapy with same-sex couples: An introduction. In N. S. Jacobson & A. S. Guttman (Eds.), *Clinical handbook of couple therapy* (pp. 274–291). New York: Guilford Press.

Brown, L. S. (1996). Ethical concerns with sexual minority patients. In R. P. Cabaj & T. S. Stein (Eds.), *Textbook of homosexuality and mental health* (pp. 897–916). Washington, DC: American Psychiatric Press.

Bruss, K. V., Brack, C. J., Brack, G., Glickauf-Hughes, C., & O'Leary, M. (1997). A developmental model for supervising therapists treating gay, lesbian, and bisexual clients. *Clinical Supervisor, 15,* 61–73.

Buhrke, R. (1989). Female student perspectives on training in lesbian and gay issues. *Counseling Psychologist, 17,* 629–636.

Buhrke, R., & Douce, L. (1991). Training issues for counseling psychologists in working with lesbian women and gay men. *Counseling Psychologist, 19,* 216–234.

Cabaj, R. P. (1988). Homosexuality and neurosis: Considerations for psychotherapy. *Journal of Homosexuality, 15,* 13–23.

Cabaj, R. P. (1996). Gay, lesbian, and bisexual mental health professionals and their colleagues. In R. P. Cabaj & T. S. Stein (Eds.), *Textbook of homosexuality and mental health* (pp. 33–39). Washington, DC: American Psychiatric Press.

Cadwell, S. A. (1994). Over-identification with HIV clients. *Journal of Gay & Lesbian Psychotherapy, 2,* 77–99.

Carroll, L., Gilroy, P. J., & Ryan, J. (2002). Counseling transgendered, transsexual, and gender-variant clients. *Journal of Counseling & Development, 80,* 131–139.

Chojnacki, J. T., & Gelberg, S. (1995). The facilitation of a gay/lesbian/bisexual support-therapy group by heterosexual counselors. *Journal of Counseling & Development, 73,* 352–354.

Cramer, E. P. (1997). Strategies for reducing social work students' homophobia. In J. T. Sears & W. L. Williams (Eds.), *Overcoming heterosexism and homophobic: Strategies that work* (pp. 287–298). New York: Columbia University Press.

Croteau, J. M., & Morgan, S. (1989). Combating homophobia in AIDS education. *Journal of Counseling and Development, 68,* 86–97.

Croteau, J. M., & Theil, M. J. (1994). Facing gay issues in counseling. *Education Digest, 59,* 25–28.

Croteau, J. M., & von Destinon, M. (1994). A national survey of job search experiences of lesbian, gay and bisexual student affairs professionals. *Journal of College Student Development, 35,* 40–45.

Crumpacker, L., & Vander Haegen, E. M. (1993). Pedagogy and prejudice: Strategies for con fronting homophobia in the classroom. *Women's Studies Quarterly, 21*, 94–105.

Deevey, S. (1990). Older lesbian women: An invisible minority. *Journal of Gerontological Nursing, 16*, 35–37, 39.

DiAngelo, R. (1997). Heterosexism: Addressing internalized dominance. *Journal of Progressive Human Services, 8*, 5–21.

Dillon, C. (1999). A relational perspective on mutuality and boundaries in clinical practice with lesbians. In J. Laird (Ed.), *Lesbians and lesbian families: Multiple reflections on theory and practice* (pp. 48–89). New York: Columbia University Press.

Donaldson, S. M. (1998). Counselor bias in working with gay men and lesbians: A commentary on Barret and Barzan (1996). *Counseling and Values, 42*, 88–91.

Downey, J. I., & Friedman, R. C. (1996). The negative therapeutic reaction and self-hatred in gay and lesbian patients. In R. P. Cabaj & T. S. Stein (Eds.), *Textbook of homosexuality and mental health* (pp. 471–484). Washington, DC: American Psychiatric Press.

Eldridge, N. S. (1987). Gender issues in counseling same-sex couples. *Professional Psychology: Research and Practice, 18*, 567–572.

Eldridge, N. S., & Barnett, D. C. (1991). Counseling gay and lesbian students. In N. J. Evans & V. A. Walls (Eds.), *Beyond tolerance: Gays, lesbians, and bisexuals on campus* (pp. 147–178). Alexandria, VA: American College Personnel Association.

Emert, T., & Milburn, L. (1997). Sensitive supervisors, prepared practicum, and "queer" clients: A training model for beginning counselors. In J. T. Sears & W. L. Williams (Eds.), *Overcoming heterosexism and homophobia* (pp. 272–286). New York: Columbia University Press.

Fassinger, R. E. (1991). The hidden minority: Issues and challenges in working with lesbians and gay men. *Counseling Psychologist, 19*, 157–176.

Fickey, J., & Grimm, G. (1998). Boundary issues in gay and lesbian psychotherapy relationships. *Journal of Gay & Lesbian Social Services, 8*, 77–93.

Garnets, L. D., Hancock, K. A., Cochran, S. D., Goodchilds, J., & Peplau, L. A. (1991). Issues in psychotherapy with lesbians and gay men: A survey of psychologists. *American Psychologist, 46*, 964–972.

Gartrell, N. (1984). Combating homophobia in the psychotherapy of lesbians. *Women & Therapy, 3*, 13–29.

Gelberg, J. S., Chojnacki, J., Gibson, S., Benn, M., & Holahan, W. (1992, March). *Coming out as gay-affirmative: Developmental transitions of heterosexual therapists.* Paper presented at the 1992 Annual American College Personnel Association convention, San Francisco.

Greene, B. (1994). Lesbian and gay sexual orientations: Implications for clinical training, practice, and research. In B. Greene & G. M. Herek (Eds.), *Lesbian and gay psychology: Theory, research, and clinical applications* (pp. 1–24). Thousand Oaks, CA: Sage Publications.

Gruskin, E. P. (1999). *Treating lesbians and bisexual women: Challenges and strategies for health professionals.* Thousand Oaks, CA: Sage Publications.

Hall, A. S., & Fradkin, H. R. (1992). Affirming gay men's mental health: Counseling with a new attitude. *Journal of Mental Health Counseling, 14,* 362–374.

Hancock, K. A. (1995). Psychotherapy with lesbians and gay men. In A. R. D'Augelli & C. J. Patterson (Eds.), *Lesbian, gay, and bisexual identities over the lifespan* (pp. 398–432). New York: Oxford University Press.

Hanson, P., & Weeks, P. (1998). Lesbian therapists and lesbian clients: Therapeutic and practical considerations, with implications for private practice. *Journal of Gay & Lesbian Social Services, 8,* 43–57.

Hardman, K. L. (1997). Social worker's attitudes to lesbian clients. *British Journal of Social Work, 21,* 545–563.

Hartman, A., & Laird, J. (1998). Moral and ethical issues in working with lesbians and gay men. *Families in Society: Journal of Contemporary Human Services, 79,* 163–276.

Humphreys, N. A., & Quam, J. K. (1998). Middle-aged and old gay, lesbian, and bisexual adults. In G. A. Appleby & J. W. Anastas (Eds.), *Not just a passing phase: Social work with gay, lesbian, and bisexual people* (pp. 245–267). New York: Columbia University Press.

Jones, M. A., & Gabriel, M. A. (1998, March). *The experience of gay men and lesbians in psychotherapy: Results from a nationwide survey.* Paper presented at the 44th annual program meeting, Council on Social Work Education, Orlando, FL.

Kelly, M. (1998). View from the field out in education: Where the personal and political collide. *Siecus Report, 26,* 14–15.

Kinsey, A. C., Pomeroy, W. B., & Martin, C. E. (1948). *Sexual behavior in the human male.* Philadelphia: W. B. Saunders.

Kranzberg, M. B. (1998). Comments on "countertransference considerations." *International Journal of Group Psychotherapy, 48,* 25–38.

Kus, R. J., & Smith, G. B. (1995). Referrals and resources for chemically dependent gay and lesbian clients. *Journal of Gay and Lesbian Social Services, 2,* 91–107.

Laird, J. (1995). Family-centered practice in the postmodern era. *Families in Society: Journal of Contemporary Human Services, 76,* 150–162.

Laird, J. (1996). Family-centered practice with lesbian and gay families. *Families in Society: Journal of Contemporary Human Services, 77,* 559–572.

Lease, S. H., Cogdal, P. A., & Smith, D. (1995). Counseling expectations related to counselors' sexual orientation and clients' internalized homophobia. *Journal of Gay & Lesbian Psychotherapy, 2,* 51–65.

Liddle, B. J. (1996). Therapist sexual orientation, gender, and counseling practices as they relate to ratings of helpfulness by gay and lesbian clients. *Journal of Counseling Psychology, 41,* 394–401.

Liddle, B. J. (1997). Gay and lesbian clients' selection of therapists and utilization of therapy. *Psychotherapy, 34,* 11–18.

Liddle, B. J. (1999a). Gay and lesbian clients' ratings of psychiatrists, psychologists, social workers, and counselors. *Journal of Gay & Lesbian Psychotherapy, 3,* 81–93.

Liddle, B. J. (1999b). Recent improvement in mental health services to lesbian and gay clients. *Journal of Homosexuality, 37,* 127–137.

Mackelprang, R. W., Ray, J., & Hernandez-Peck, M. (1996). Social work education and sexual orientation: Faculty, student, and curriculum issues. *Journal of Gay & Lesbian Social Services, 5,* 17–31.

Malley, M., & Tasker, F. (1999). Lesbians, gay men, and family therapy: A contradiction in terms? *Journal of Family Therapy, 21,* 3–29.

Mallon, G. (1998). Knowledge for practice with gay and lesbian persons. In G. P. Mallon (Ed.), *Foundations of social work practice with lesbian and gay persons* (pp. 1–30). New York: Haworth Press.

Mallon, G. (1999). A call for organizational trans-formation. *Journal of Gay & Lesbian Social Services, 10,* 131–142.

Mallon, G. P. (1994). Counseling strategies with gay and lesbian youth. In T. De Crescenzo (Ed.), *Helping gay and lesbian youth* (pp. 75–91). New York: Haworth Press.

Markowitz, L. M. (1991, January/February). Homosexuality: Are we still in the dark? *Family Therapy Networker, 15*(1), 26–29, 31–35.

Masters, W., & Johnson, V. (1979). *Homosexuality in perspective*. Boston: Little, Brown.

McAllan, L. D., & Ditillo, D. (1994). Addressing the needs of lesbian and gay clients with disabilities. *Journal of Applied Rehabilitation Counseling, 25*, 26–35.

McDermott, D., Tyndall, L., & Lichtenberg, J. W. (1989). Factors related to counselor preference among gays and lesbians. *Journal of Counseling & Development, 68*, 31–35.

McHenry, S. S., & Johnson, J. W. (1993). Homophobia in the therapist and gay or lesbian client: Conscious and unconscious illusions in self-hate. *Psychotherapy, 30*, 141–151.

Messing, A. E., Schoenberg, R., & Stephens, R. K. (1983–1984). Confronting homophobia in health care settings: Guidelines for social work practice. *Journal of Social Work & Human Sexuality, 2,* 65–74.

Modcrin, M. J., & Wyers, N. L. (1990). Lesbian and gay couples: Where they turn when help is needed. *Journal of Gay & Lesbian Psychotherapy, 1*, 89–104.

Mohr, J. J. (2002). Identity and the heterosexual therapist: An identity perspective on sexual orientation dynamics in psychotherapy. *Counseling Psychologist, 30*, 532–566.

Mohr, J. J., Israel, T., & Sedlacek, W. E. (2001). Counselor's attitudes regarding bisexuality as predictors of counselor's clinical responses: An analogue study of a female bisexual client. *Journal of Counseling Psychology, 48*, 212–222.

Moran, M. J., & Moore, K. K. (1993). Effects of sexual orientation similarity and counselor expertise on gay men's and lesbians' perceptions of counselors. *Journal of Counseling Psychology, 39*, 247–251.

National Association of Social Workers. (1999). *NASW code of ethics*. Washington, DC: NASW Press.

Nichols, M. (1982). The treatment of inhibited sexual desire (ISD) in lesbian couples. *Women & Therapy, 1*, 49–66.

Pope, M. (1997). Sexual issues for older lesbians and gays. *Topics in Geriatric Rehabilitation, 12*, 53–60.

Prochaska, J. O., & DiClemente, C. C. (1986). The transtheoretical approach. In J. Norcross (Ed.), *Handbook of eclectic psychotherapy* (pp. 163–199). New York: Brunner/Mazel.

Prochaska, J. O., Norcross, J. C., & DiClemente, C. C. (1994). *Changing for good: The revolutionary program that explains the six stages of change and teaches you how to free yourself from bad habits.* New York: William Morrow.

Radkowsky, M., & Siegel, L. J. (1997). The gay adolescent: Stressors, adaptations, and psychosocial interventions. *Clinical Psychology Review, 17,* 191–216.

Ramirez Barranti, C. C. (1998). Social work practice with lesbian couples. In G. P. Mallon (Ed.), *Foundations of social work practice with lesbian and gay persons* (pp. 183–207). New York: Haworth Press.

Raup, G. (1995). From the heart: Being an ally to the gay, lesbian, and bisexual community. *Campus Activities Programming, 28,* 33–36.

Riddle, D. (1996). Riddle homophobia scale. In M. Adams, P. Brighham, P. Dalpes, & L. Marchesani (Eds.), *Social diversity and social justice: Gay, lesbian, and bisexual oppression* (p. 31). Dubuque, IA: Kendall/Hunt Publishing.

Rochlin, M. (1992). Heterosexual questionnaire. In W. J. Blumenfeld (Ed.), *Homophobia: How we all pay the price* (pp. 203–204). Boston: Beacon Press.

Rothblum, E. D. (1994). Introduction to the special section: Mental health of lesbians and gay men. *Journal of Consulting and Clinical Psychology, 67,* 211–212.

Ryan, C., Bradford, J. B., & Honnold, J. A. (1999). Social workers' and counselors' understanding of lesbian needs. *Journal of Gay & Lesbian Social Services, 9,* 1–26.

Scrivner, R., & Eldridge, N. S. (1995). Lesbian and gay family psychology. In R. H. Mikesell, D. D. Lusterman, & S. H. McDaniel (Eds.), *Integrating family therapy: Handbook of family psychology and systems theory* (pp. 327–345). Washington, DC: American Psychological Association.

Sears, J. T., & Williams, W. L. (Eds.). (1997). *Overcoming heterosexism and homophobia.* New York: Columbia University Press.

Simoni, J. M. (1996). Confronting heterosexism in the teaching of psychology. *Teaching of Psychology, 23,* 220–225.

Sorensen, L., & Roberts, S. J. (1997). Lesbian uses of and satisfaction with mental health services: Results from Boston lesbian health project. *Journal of Homosexuality, 33,* 35–49.

Stein, T. S. (1988). Theoretical considerations in psychotherapy with gay men and lesbians. *Journal of Homosexuality, 15,* 75–95.

Stokes, J. P., Miller, R. L., & Mundhenk, R. (1998). Toward an understanding of behaviorally bisexual men: The influence of context and culture. *Canadian Journal of Human Sexuality, 7,* 1–12.

Tyler, J. M., Jackman-Wheitner, L., Strader, S., & Lenox, R. (1997). A change-model approach to raising awareness of gay, lesbian, and bisexual issues among graduate students in counseling. *Journal of Sex Education and Therapy*, *22*, 37–43.

Yarhouse, M. A. (1999). Social cognition research on the formation and maintenance of stereotypes: Applications to marriage and family therapists working with homosexual clients. *American Journal of Family Therapy*, *27*, 149–161.

PART IV
PRACTICE WITH INDIVIDUALS, COUPLES, FAMILIES, AND LARGER SYSTEMS

CHAPTER 10
PRACTICE WITH INDIVIDUALS

How can practitioners help LGBT clients through the coming-out process?

What special considerations arise when working with LGBT youth?

How can practitioners help LGBT clients with disclosure?

How can practitioners help families of LGBT persons after disclosure?

What are the special considerations for ethnic families in dealing with disclosure?

What are the special considerations for transgender persons and their families after disclosure?

What are the special considerations following disclosure of a bisexual partner in a marriage?

What are some of the issues concerning disclosure in the workplace?

COMING OUT

Clients may seek services at any stage of the coming-out process (Gonsiorek, 1982) or to ascertain whether they even have a same sex–gender or bisexual sexual identity. The main task for affirmative practitioners is to assist clients in exploring and discovering whatever self-identification they feel is "their own." Until and unless clients are ready to self-identify with a label, it is important not to mention one or assign a category to them.

Although many practitioners may be familiar with Kinsey and his colleagues' seven-point bipolar scale rating sexual orientation—from heterosexual to "homosexual"—they may not be familiar with the many revisions of it (Kinsey, Pomeroy, & Martin, 1948; Kinsey, Pomeroy, Martin, & Gebbard, 1953). Though none of the existing scales are yet satisfactory, some of the multidimensional scales, for example, the Klein Sexual Orientation Grid (Klein, Sepekoff, & Wolf, 1985), can be useful in assisting clients who feel confused about their sexual identity. Chapter 3 addresses sexual orientation and sexual identity and various combinations of how lesbian, gay, bisexual, and transgender persons identify themselves. For some clients, however, it may be advisable to avoid using any sexual identity labels at all. Instead, practice can focus on the various aspects of attraction to men and to women, including sexual behavior, fantasy, and emotional or affectional intimacy. If clients use categorical labels like bisexual or gay, practitioners can help them explore what these labels mean to them (Stokes, Miller, & Mundhenk, 1998).

Use of Developmental Models

Sequential identity development models are both useful and problematic for practitioners. They are useful because they (a) provide clues of what to look for in a client's identity development; (b) aid a client to understand possible pathways to identity development, (c) normalize a client's feelings and experiences, (d) provide tasks for a client to anticipate, and (e) suggest interventions.

These models are problematic because they (a) represent the way in which only some persons experience the coming-out process and (b) obscure or invalidate issues unique to some persons (Rust, 1996). It is best to inquire what the client's actual experiences are because these experiences may vary from the established models, and a client may provide coming-out stories not addressed in the models. Clients will also vary in the timing of moving from initial discovery of same sex–gender sexual orientation to other stages. Many variables in one's social context will also affect the coming-out process and the timing of reaching the various stages or stopping and not going further.

Identity development models most often imply a stable resolution to identification when one reaches the final stages, but some clients may not experience this stability. The practitioner's task is not to help clients arrive at a firm and fixed identity but instead to support flexibility in exploring sexual identity. A complication in assessment is determining what might be genuine fluidity for one person and the need for another person to reach a definitive and essentialist understanding of his or her sexual orientation that matches traditional models of identity development. The complexity of these issues suggests the need for the adoption of a constructionist stance in addition to the essentialist stance (Bohan, 1996). Also, LGB identities are not universal or fixed concepts (Cass, 1996). Yet clients often wish to hold on to their essentialist beliefs about their identities and this should be respected.

Suggested Interventions Based on Coming-Out Models

The coming-out models for lesbian and gay persons referred to here are presented in Chapter 4. Using Cass's (1996) sexual identity formation (SIF) model, Rust (1996) discussed ideas that may be useful to practitioners to consider with clients at any of the six stages of this model.

1. *Identity confusion.* This is probably the most difficult stage for many clients as they begin to think they might be lesbian, gay, or bisexual, but they still present a heterosexual identity. The practitioner can encourage clients who feel confused about their sexual identity or are just beginning to explore it to discover their own needs and desires without pressure or censorship (Matteson, 1996a). One can express to confused clients that it is all right to declare that they are gay, lesbian, or bisexual, or not; to feel confused; to go back and forth; and to change their minds. We accept clients as they are, no matter where this process takes them (Drescher, 1998; Mallon, 1998a).

Several other issues that may arise for clients at this stage were identified by Levy (1995), including validating a new self-concept resulting from the changes in self-concept that often happen during coming out and challenging negative thoughts about themselves if internalized oppression surfaces. Because of the many difficult issues clients confront at this stage, supportive groups and educational approaches can be useful (Guidry, 1999). Some clients will experience conflict between religion and thinking they might be lesbian, gay, or bisexual. They may experience guilt, shame, depression, and isolation. If clients bring up conflicts with religion, practitioners can help them talk their conflicts through as well as refer them to affirmative ministers and congregations, and supportive groups and organizations such as Dignity (for Catholics), Integrity (for Episcopalians), and gay and lesbian churches such as MCC. Bibliotherapy is also useful including books such as Helminiak's (1995) *What the Bible Really Says about Homosexuality* (Schuck & Liddle, 2001).

2. *Identity comparison.* Clients at this stage want to see and interact with other LGB persons. This can be facilitated in local support groups (Degges-White, Rice, & Myers, 2000).

3. *Identity tolerance.* Clients are likely to want seek out LGB communities. If they do not know locations, they can be directed to community centers, bookstores, special-interest groups, and a variety of other places where LGB persons congregate. Also, there are LGB newspapers and phone books (listed under gay or lambda) that list LGB organizations.

4. *Identity acceptance.* At this stage, clients begin to make disclosures of their sexual orientation to others. Interventions related to preparing for disclosures are discussed later in this chapter.

5. *Identity pride.* A client may experience conflict at this stage with a desire to be completely out but anticipating that this will create difficulties in some situations. Interventions related to making the best judgments about disclosures are discussed later in this chapter.

6. *Identity synthesis.* Clients have worked through much of the coming-out process by this stage. They are often preparing to terminate services, as they may no longer feel a need for a practitioner.

Cass (1996) also provided various suggestions about using her SIF model in practice:

- *Use terms that fit the client's stage of identity development.* Describing someone as lesbian, gay, or bisexual, for example, is inappropriate when that person is actually saying, "I am confused about what I'm doing" (Stage 1) or "I might be gay, lesbian, or bisexual" (beginning of Stage 2).
- *Identify the stage where the client is.* This can facilitate a focus on the particular issues of that stage instead of on same sex–gender sexual orientation generally. Talking about the ideological aspects of oppression, for example, may be inappropriate when someone's current desire is to meet other lesbian and gay persons (Stage 3).
- *Accept the stage location identified by the client.* An 18-year-old person who happily says, "I am a lesbian" (end of stage 3 and onward) should not hear, "You're too young to know that." Instead, the practitioner should recognize that identity formation for this person is already in progress.
- *Avoid judgment of one stage as better than another.* Judgment should also be withheld regarding one person as more advanced than another because one's feelings and behaviors correspond or do not correspond with any particular stage. Care should be taken not to impose clinical judgments on clients who are in any of the stages.

Following their dual-branch model, McCarn and Fassinger (1996) proposed that practitioners use interventions such as individual and couple counseling, psychoeducation, group treatment, bibliotherapy, and referral to LGB community resources. The decision about intervention, though, comes after accurate assessment of the distinct developmental issues and the personal and social needs of clients, including their awareness of and desire to be involved in the larger gay and lesbian community.

Coming-Out Issues for Bisexual Persons

Bisexual clients may seek assistance for and express both identity concerns (how to handle difficulties and complications of adopting a bisexual identity) and system concerns (how to handle multiple relationships if desired and how to find supports for bisexual relationships). Potential issues identified by Matteson (1996b) and others include:

Exploration of bisexuality and coming out to self. Because of prevalent dichotomized conceptions of sexual orientation, persons with sexual attractions to both sex–genders may self-identify as gay or lesbian or as heterosexual. As it often is for gay and lesbian persons, confusion about sexual orientation is especially intense during the early stages of bisexual identity development. Practitioners can help these clients reframe their confusion as a response to society's heterosexism and to simplistic dichotomous views of sexuality (Stokes & Damon, 1995). These clients can also read autobiographical accounts of what other bisexual men and women experienced and how they successfully moved through the coming-out process, such as accounts published by the Off Pink Collective (1988). Practitioners can provide locations of organizations for bisexual persons and additional ways for clients to meet other bisexual persons. These contacts can help clients who are still working out their identities to sort out the direction of their sexual feelings and behaviors (Matteson, 1996b).

Life decisions. Practitioners can assist clients to make realistic assessments of the life decisions they are contemplating. Assessment areas identified by Matteson (1996b) include:

- *Personal and social risk taking.* Is the client willing to take personal and social risks? Personal risks include both psychological risks such as internalized oppression and physical risks such as HIV/AIDS and harassment or bashing. An example of a social risk is being fired from a job.
- *Link between sex and intimacy.* Are sex and intimacy viewed as occurring together or as separate processes? Are they associated with one or both sex–genders? How significant is each of these factors to clients? Are clients open to recreational sex?
- *Importance of the sex–gender of a partner.* Are one's attractions more for women or men? Or is the sex–gender of a partner not a significant determinant of partner choice?
- *Desire for monogamous relationships or concurrent partners.* Is monogamy preferred or does the client seek more than one partner?
- *Ambiguity, confusion, and complexity accompanying concurrent, multiple relationships with each sex–gender.* Can clients tolerate these experiences accompanying their relationships? Conclusions about this can be sorted out by fantasy alone by some clients whereas for others real-life experience is necessary.

Fluidity. Even when they acknowledge attractions to both sex–genders, women's sexual identity may remain fluid and more defined by particular relationships or social settings (Rust, 1993; Savin-Williams & Diamond, 1999).

Lack of social confirmation for bisexual experience. Because of the stereotypes and myths associated with bisexual persons, they may have trouble attaining social validation from heterosexual and gay and lesbian persons. Practitioners can facilitate comfort with bisexual attractions by affirming that attraction to persons of both sex–genders is legitimate and acceptable. This may be the only "therapy" these clients need (Fox, 1991; Stokes & Damon, 1995).

Overcoming self-oppression. Bisexual persons struggle with heterosexism because of their attractions to persons of their own sex–gender. They are also at odds with taboos about extramarital sex or multiple relationships (Matteson, 1996b). It is important for them to become acquainted with persons who are comfortable with their bisexual sexual orientation. Coming-out groups and affirmative readings are also helpful (Lourea, 1985; Paul, 1988).

Guilt. If clients who are exploring coming out as bisexual are presently in a committed heterosexual link, they may feel guilty if they break the expectation of sexual exclusivity. Support networks can be helpful for these persons and for their partners who are coping with this news (Matteson, 1995).

Grief. Whether gay, lesbian, or bisexual, coming out often involves grief (for example, Barron, 1996; Thompson, 1992) as persons recognize that dreams and desires they pursued earlier no longer work for them. These dreams and desires may have included monogamy and a traditional life of heterosexual marriage with children. These persons may also grieve the loss of support from some heterosexual friends and relatives.

Finding support networks. It is essential for bisexual clients to interact with positive models of bisexual identity. If clients are unaware of resources, practitioners can help them identify places where they can meet others with the same sexual orientation and common interests.

Issues for previously gay- or lesbian-identified persons. Lesbian and gay persons are often surprised when they become captivated with some one of the other sex–gender. Reentry into the world of heterosexual relations can create social difficulties for them (Matteson, 1995). Women who identified as lesbian before realizing that they were bisexual may particularly experience little support in the lesbian community (Nichols, 1988). They need support groups specifically for women like them who have been exclusively lesbian for an extended period and are now aware of heterosexual attractions—as do gay persons in the same situations (Lourea, 1985).

Coming-Out Issues for Transgender Persons

Transgender persons may seek a practitioner because of a need to understand a compulsive desire to cross-dress; the belief that they are different from others or perverted, mentally ill, or sinful; the belief that they are in the wrong body; and the strong dislike of their genitals. Common issues in the transgender client population also include shame, depression, guilt, low self-esteem and low sense of competence, social isolation, substance misuse, and suicidal behaviors. They are also dealing with secretiveness about their feelings about being in the wrong body (Anderson, 1998). An extensive list of assessment factors for use with transgender persons, including those related to health history, mental health history, legal history, sexual history, sex–gender continuum placement-is provided in the work of Cole, Denny, Eyler, and Samons (2000).

Most transgender persons studied by Gagné, Tewksbury, & McGaughey (1997) were active in counseling. Support groups are of particular help for testing out their identities. As practitioners, we must communicate to these clients that whatever they present about themselves is totally acceptable. We must communicate that we value and appreciate diversity (Gagné et al., 1997). Another major task for the practitioner is to provide accurate and meaningful information for transgender clients (Anderson, 1998). In these groups, transgender persons studied by Gagné felt full acceptance and freedom to be themselves for the first time. If others in these groups accepted them, they often felt that they were truly transgender. Organizations, publications, and online services that focus on transgender persons were also helpful.

Another concern for transgender clients is sexual reassignment surgery (SRS), if they decide to pursue this course. If persons are thinking about SRS but do not know much about it, they need information about requirements to become a candidate for the surgery, where to obtain electrolysis, hormonal intervention, cosmetic surgery, and other community resources. Reality testing and examination of future expectations are important. Work with these clients usually takes a minimum of six months before surgery and then for a continued time following surgery (Anderson, 1998). Centers should be recommended that do not coerce clients into specific outcomes or exclude persons deemed too young, too old, or who will not "pass" well in the new sex–gender. These centers also should not require clients to cross live full time as a condition for initiating hormone therapy. This requirement creates a dangerous situation for hate crimes because prior to hormone treatment, these persons can be easily noticed. Only a few SRS centers exist in the United States: the University of Michigan Comprehensive Gender Services Program and the University of Minnesota Program in Human Sexuality (Cole et al., 2000).

Some transgender persons have no preparation for the period following SRS and do not know the locations of needed services. Others who relocate to "start a new life" may feel isolated and lonely. The practitioner can be most helpful in a supportive role, helping to bolster coping skills and furnishing information about community services. These clients also need assistance in coping with discrimination and victimization in society at large. They need an accurate assessment of how well they pass as the new sex–gender and must prepare to cope if identified by others as transgender if this matters to them. Practitioners can address needed modifications in appearance and behavior. They may also need to address relationship stress or specific transition periods such as when children mature or when partners enter or leave their lives (Anderson, 1998).

Persons who want SRS but cannot attain it because of health or financial reasons may require considerable support. They must come to terms with the lack of fulfillment of their dreams of matching their bodies with their sex–gender. Practitioners can help them to cross live successfully without surgical modification of their bodies. The primary goals with all transgender clients are experiencing relief of painful feelings and self-assessments, making informed decisions, and living productive and fulfilling lives (Anderson, 1998).

Special Issues with Youth and Sexual Identification

Adolescents and their parents may want to know how to predict LGB sexual identities. Few reliable indictors predict which youth will take this road, but one's identity may shift from mere consideration of a nonheterosexual identity to certainty when (a) sexual activity happens with a same sex–partner, (b) thoughts happen that one might be lesbian, gay, or bisexual, and (c) one's attractions and fantasies about the same sex–gender persist and intensify (Rosario et al., 1996). Youth who might later define themselves as gay are more likely than others to engage in same sex–sexual behavior as teens and to do so for a longer time (Savin-Williams, 1990). But, many youth who identity or eventually identify as gay, lesbian, or bisexual also engage in heterosexual sex during their childhood and adolescence (for example, Diamond, 1998; Rotheram-Borus, Hunter, & Rosario, 1994). With age, however, the meaning of sexual attractions, fantasies, and behaviors becomes clearer to them. A high correspondence also increasingly emerges among desires, sexual behavior, and identity (Savin-Williams, 1995b). The data of Rosario and colleagues and Savin-Williams (1995a) indicate that once sexual identity becomes certain to a lesbian or gay youth, sexual activity happens primarily with same sex–gender partners, with corresponding decreases of sexual activity with other sex–gender partners.

LGB youth negotiate developmental transitions when their adaptive skills can meet the demands of the transition (Herdt, 1989). If, during a sexual identity transition, confusion continues regarding same sex–gender sexual fantasies, attractions, or incidents of same sex–gender sexual contact, young persons can explore the meanings of their attractions and fantasies with a practitioner. Practitioners can provide information to help these youth differentiate among sexual orientation, sexual identity, and sexual behavior using scales such as the Klein Sexual Orientation Grid (Klein et al., 1985).

PREPARING FOR DISCLOSURE

As disclosure is a never-ending process, most GLB or T persons assess every new person or situation (for example, Cain, 1991; Pope, 1996). When clients determine that they want to make disclosures, practitioners can help them assess these situations for costs and benefits. (Browning, Reynolds, & Dworkin, 1991). Clients, however, must decide what to do about disclosures. Practitioners should never impose their views about this issue on clients, with one exception. When clients are HIV positive or have AIDS and have not disclosed this information to their partners, practitioners must encourage them to make this information known (Shernoff, 1998).

One of the aspects of disclosures that practitioners can help clients realistically assess is whether they can handle the repercussions in their interpersonal lives. One way to do this is to ask clients to envision the reactions of others through questions such as: If you make disclosures, how would your mother/father; best friend/girlfriend/boyfriend; wife or husband; children; religious leader; and/or employer react and how would you respond? Which friends would be supportive? If married, what would be the implications for your marriage and how would you feel about that? (Rust, 1996).

If clients feel they can handle the repercussions of disclosures, they can be helped to make thoughtful choices about who, when, where, and how (Williamson, 1998). *Who* involves which persons to tell. Clients have an uncanny ability to predict responses to startling information and can anticipate the best and worst situations (Kuehlwein, 1992; Williamson, 1998). Because it often takes weeks or months to work through feelings about a particular disclosure, it is best not to disclose to everyone in their lives simultaneously. Instead, it is useful to develop a ranked order of persons to tell (Gartrell, 1984).

When involves timing or when to make disclosures and when one should not disclose (Williamson, 1998). In her job as a nurse, Deevey (1993) reported her thoughts about the timing of disclosures:

> I chose the timing carefully, when privacy was available. I determined that extreme loneliness or anger in response to homophobic remarks could trigger my self-disclosure. Because both these feelings expanded my vulnerability, I tried to postpone self-disclosure until I felt reasonably secure. (p. 22)

Clients should make disclosures when they are feeling positive about themselves rather than when they are feeling vulnerable. They should feel prepared instead of making impulsive or reactive disclosures (Gartrell, 1984).

Where involves the locations for disclosures as well as the numbers of persons in the location. For example, should one tell one person at a time or several persons in a group? If a group, what type of group? Family, work, recreational (Williamson, 1998)?

How involves the style of disclosure such as a subtle statement, a strong statement, or a matter-of-fact statement (Williamson, 1998). The strongest or the most forward type of disclosure is the "Queer Nation" approach in which persons announce their sexual orientation publicly by every act they do, with the accompanying attitude that it is unimportant whether other persons like them or not (Esterberg, 1996). Most persons are subtler than this, just making matter-of-fact disclosures (for example, "I went out with a woman last weekend") (Pope, 1995).

The *how* or the methods for making disclosures may take the most attention. What "disclosure skills" do one's clients have? Are they up to the task or do they need further coaching and time to prepare? (see Williamson, 1998). If clients need coaching, the practitioner can first apprise them of various ways to make disclosures such as those used by Deevey (1993) at her job as a hospital nurse:

- I know you know this already, but I wanted to bring it out in the open. I think that you know that my sexual orientation is lesbian. (This approach implies circumspection and sensitivity from the listener.)
- You are an open-minded person, so I know you will not have a problem with this. I've decided to be more open about my lesbian relationship with Lana. (Here, one appeals to strengths in the recipient such as maturity. These are also persons one wants to keep as friends or colleagues.)
- I need your support for a risk I want to take. I'm starting to tell people about the lesbian community that I am part of. (This approach enlists assistance from the listener after unexpected information.)
- I want to share something with you, since you have talked so openly with me about your life. I have been shy to talk openly about my lesbian life. (This approach fits when one desires to build friendships based on honesty and equality in self-disclosures. It is most effective with peers.) (p. 22)

Role play is useful for rehearsing various approaches to telling others and practicing a projected disclosure conversation (Gartrell, 1984; Mallon, 1998b). The practitioner and client can play both sides of an interchange, and the role play can be audio taped and played back for critique and revision (Kuehlwein, 1992).

The options for disclosure and the outcomes may vary depending on the context. Discussed here are two contexts—family of origin and work.

DIFFERENT CONTEXTS: FAMILY OF ORIGIN

Clients may worry most about a negative response from their families. But, generalizations are impossible to make about their responses (Green, 2000). The relationship with parents must be secure or strong enough to tolerate disclosure. It is especially important for parents to feel strong attachment and affection for their child (Boxer, Cook, & Herdt, 1991). In addition, parents who are flexible in religious and moral values adjust better than parents who have more rigid values (Boxer et al., 1991). With parents who are more rigid, clients need to avoid putting themselves in the position of having to defend their sexual identity or defer to heterosexist remarks (Gartrell, 1984). The practitioner can model a steady and resilient response to intense reactions (Williamson, 1998).

Clients may decide that positive consequences from disclosures to family will be few and that many negative consequences will happen, such as protracted conflict with the family or a permanent state of distance from the family (Green, 2000). If anticipating rejection, clients may decide not to make disclosures to their families, but if they decide to go ahead with them, they should prepare for rejection by developing sufficient resources (for example, support systems) to help deal with the situation (Scasta, 1998).

Parent reactions to youths' sexual orientation were found by D'Augelli (2002) to be significantly associated with the youths' mental health, especially if both parents are rejecting. In addition, living with rejecting parents creates distress because there is no support at home and usually no one to talk to there. Even if they have not disclosed to parents, youths can live in fear of their finding out, rejecting them, verbally or physically attacking them, or forcing them out of the home. Unless one of the parents is accepting, youths should be advised not to make disclosures to the parents because of possible verbal and physical harm. Because they are also still financially dependent on parents, they may want to wait until they are in a more favorable financial (as well as emotional) position (D'Augelli, Hershberger, & Pilkington, 1998). If, however, they insist on making a disclosure, they should develop a safety plan before the disclosure. If parents throw them out of the house, whom can they contact for emotional and financial support? Where can they live? A list of contact persons, locations, phone numbers, and local services and emergency assistance is essential (Vargo, 1998).

Practitioners can facilitate clients' understanding that future relationships with rejecting parents are largely dependent upon the parent's willingness to expunge themselves of heterosexism though self-examination and education (Gartrell, 1984). Empathy and patience may diffuse angry responses to those who are rejecting by placing their negative reactions into context—for example, by exploring how long it took oneself to accept one's sexual orientation and by recognizing the false beliefs that family members and others are likely to hold that prevent a positive response (Kuehlwein, 1992). Still, rejecting parents are difficult to contend with.

Even if clients decide to make disclosures to families they do not think will be severely rejecting, they may still have fears about possible negative results. In this situation, it is helpful for these clients to make explicit in words their strongest fears. They may discover that they can live through the realization of these fears or desensitize them. Parents may also react with less anger if the disclosure is not sudden or if they have already formed an impression on their own that their child is probably lesbian or gay (Hammersmith, 1987). This provides a mild anesthetic or time to become emotionally prepared to face the news (Williamson, 1998). Parents are also likely to respond more positively if they feel that their children desire to be honest. Under these circumstances, they are more likely to acknowledge and accept their children's sexual orientation and are less likely to experience anger, shock, and denial following disclosure (Ben-Ari, 1995).

Prior to the real event, clients can develop greater confidence and skill at handling difficult situations through repeated practice with standard communication and assertion techniques. Different styles of delivery and word choices can also be practiced and modified before the real event (Kuehlwein, 1992). For example, clients can learn to make disclosures in a proud, affirmative, and direct manner. This communicates that they feel good about themselves and their lives. When lesbian or gay children use positive words in their initial disclosure to parents (for example, "I am lesbian and happy"), both they and their parents adjust more easily. An adjustment is more difficult when the first disclosure contains negative information (for example, "I have a problem because I am gay") or even a neutral statement (for example, "I am gay"). Also, disclosures should not be equivocal such as "Mom, I think I am gay" (Ben-Ari, 1995). Equivocation fosters denial in parents and can lead to demands for their children to change their minds or get "fixed" through "therapy" (Scasta, 1998).

Helping Parents

Parents who are distressed following a child's disclosure may turn to human services professionals for assistance. Various challenges and themes associated with practice with parents are reviewed here. First, the practitioner is likely to confront a conflicted emotional atmosphere in the initial meeting with parents and, possibly, their lesbian or gay child (Bernstein, 1990). The parents and their child may be quite angry with one another. Williamson (1998) observed that anger/rejection is one of five dominant patterns of emotional response displayed by parents. The other patterns include *shock/disbelief/embarrassment*; *fear/worry/anxiety*; *sadness/sorrow*; and *hopefulness/acceptance*. Moments of each of these responses may occur at different points in the emotional process, and more than one pattern may occur simultaneously. If a practitioner meets parents in any of the patterns of emotional response except the hopefulness/acceptance pattern, attention needs to focus on this state before moving on. Parents need time to express their feelings about the situation.

Families usually also make large adjustments when a family member is transgender. Following recognition or disclosure of the transgender identity of a family member, others in the family appear to go through overlapping, nondiscrete stages, depending on their relationship with the transgender person. These stages, identified by Rosenfeld and Emerson (1998), are similar to those developed by Kübler-Ross (1969): denial, bargaining, depression, and anger. Ellis and Eriksen (2002) also identified stages following the themes that families of a transgender person experience.

Sometimes parents require additional help with their emotions. For example, anger control sessions may be necessary if parents are experiencing severe anger. Families can also join groups to learn skill-building techniques for resolving disputes and communication impasses (Coenen, 1998). Once emotions cool, practitioners should encourage parents to not trivialize what their children tell them because they risk hearing nothing more from them. Parents should be asked to respect the courage needed to disclose difficult information. They should also strive to understand same sex–gender sexual orientation and unlearn misconceptions, stereotypes, and negative attitudes about LGBT persons. They should convey love for their children (Vargo, 1998) and help them create a positive identity (Hammersmith, 1987).

The practitioner can encourage the parents to grieve the loss of their presumed heterosexual child and begin to create a new role for this child. The practitioner also may want to encourage "regrieving" which involves discussing the disclosure event in more detail (Coenen, 1998). Parents also may have to realize that part of the contention with their children is what happens in any family as the children begin to show value differences, develop autonomy, and change their relationships (Brown, 1989). This also results in new roles for their children and the parents. If parents have trouble allowing their children to develop in their own way, they may insist on loyalty to their social, religious, or political ideas. They do not offer support for their children's personal development that necessitates exploration of alternative ideas (Laird, 1996).

Answering Questions

Parents will likely ask many questions about same sex–gender sexual orientation. How does it happen? Is it permanent? What are the consequences in the long run? What about disclosures outside of the family?

How did it happen? Critical and painful questions for most parents are "how" or "why." They try to find causes in an apparent attempt to make sense of something they do not understand. Some parents may review their performance as parents and their mistakes and shortcomings in ways they have never done before (Williamson, 1998). The practitioner should inform the parents that little or no association exists between family background and sexual orientation (Bell, Weinberg, & Hammersmith, 1981). Also, parents cannot be given an answer about why their child is lesbian or gay because no one knows the etiology of sexual orientation (Bernstein, 1990).

Is it permanent? Most parents want to know whether the expressed sexual orientation or sex–gender is a permanent situation. Can their child change? Isn't this just a passing phase? (see Bernstein, 1990; Emerson & Rosenfeld, 1996). Parents may try to get someone to "change" their child's sexual orientation or sex–gender expression. Some parents seek psychiatric intervention or institutionalization whereas others seek pastoral counseling in the hope that divine intervention will return their children to heterosexuality or to the former sex–gender expression. Other parents resort to actions such as verbal harassment, physical violence, or throwing children out of the home if they refuse to recant their sexual orientation or their sex–gender expression (Anderson, 1987; Brown, 1989).

Parents need to conquer false hopes for change even though they do not surrender these hopes easily (Mallon, 1998b). Sexual identity can be fluid, and persons can modify their same sex–gender sexual behavior, but a well-integrated sexual orientation in an adult is unlikely to be changed by any strategy (see Chapter 8). If the child is transgender, the practitioner must help family members to realize that this child is not sick, crazy, or going through a phase, and that the child is unlikely to quit pursuing strong desires for changes in their sex–gender expression. Practitioners also need to establish or reestablish contact between the child and the family, to assist with the family's adjustment to the change, and to help family members normalize what first seems incomprehensible (Rosenfeld & Emerson, 1998).

What kind of future is there for my child? Parents tend to believe that their gay or lesbian child cannot be happy without marriage and children. They envision their child living a lonely life and never having stable relationships. Even if daughters plan children, parents worry about a child raised by a lesbian parent or the daughter's ability to support a child financially. Parents also worry about prejudice and violence against their child (Bernstein, 1990). If the child is male, the greatest concern is HIV/AIDS (Robinson, Walters, & Skeen, 1989).

What about disclosures outside of the family? Not only are the parents questioning their child's sexual identity or sex–gender expression, but they also are adjusting to a new identity of themselves as parents of a lesbian, gay, bisexual, or transgender child. They are unsettled to think that others know of their situation (Bernstein, 1990). Their child's disclosure and their new identity may seem to them as unsharable secrets (Savin-Williams, 1996). But, if they decide others should know, the issue arises of who should make these disclosures. Should the parents tell others? Or is this an action for the child to take? (See Bernstein, 1990.) The practitioner should inform parents about the issue of "outing" or when someone else announces a person's sexual orientation or sex–gender expression without permission. When this happens, the person may not be able to handle the public disclosure. It should always be the person's choice to make disclosures, and parents should honor this (Cabaj, 1996).

Providing Information

Parents need accurate, unbiased information about same sex–gender sexual orientation, sex–gender expression, and HIV/AIDS (Williamson, 1998). Assigning readings, or "bibliotherapy," to educate and inform them about a wide variety of issues pertaining to LGBT persons is a useful strategy (Neisen, 1987). Many affirmative books now exist, some written by parents (for example, Griffin, Wirth, & Wirth, 1986; Muller, 1987; Rafkin, 1987). Books by other parents provide views of affirmative family settings for LGBT members (Brown, 1989). The understanding of general reactions by parents may provide other parents hope that they can also reach acceptance and that they will not always feel as they did at first. It can help to know that other parents struggled in similar ways. Parents can also be assigned readings from the professional literature, such as the findings of Beeler and DiProva (1999) that identified 12 themes in family stories. These themes reflected how families responded to disclosures over time and how they integrated a lesbian or gay child into the family after they reached acceptance of their sexual orientation.

Parents need a vision of a positive outcome and understanding that other families have met the same challenge successfully. Parents also need to know that they will require time as well as stamina for their adjustment to the new realities they face (Hammersmith, 1987). For families with a transgender member, a family ceremony can help all members accept the "rebirth" and a new beginning for the family (Rosenfeld & Emerson, 1998). Part of the new realities may include changes in names, pronouns, and clothing.

For eventual acceptance and inner peace, parents of LGBT children need to find acceptable meaning in this life development (Williamson, 1998). If religion is a barrier to acceptance of their child, the practitioner should recommend a referral to sympathetic and affirmative clergy. Also affirmative material from some mainline denominations is available on same sex–gender sexual orientation and religion (Hammersmith, 1987).

Support Groups for Families

When families are in crisis, those who can develop sources of social support are better able to recover and regain stability (McCubbin & Patterson, 1983). It is important, therefore, for practitioners to help families with LGBT children expand their sources of support. Extended family members and friends can help parents adapt to their new status, especially if they can offer a different and needed perspective (Savin-Williams, 1996). In support groups of families with LGBT children, they can share information about how they are succeeding (McCubbin & Patterson, 1983; Williamson, 1998).

Practitioners should have available the support resources available in their area such as Parents, Families, and Friends of Lesbians and Gays (PFLAG). PFLAG groups often include transgender members and can also provide support for families of transgender children. Networking with other parents and siblings can be effective in helping the family gain more understanding, greater comfort with transgender or LGB family members, and more practice in developing coping strategies. The family members need love and support (Cole et al., 2000). PFLAG subscribes to the view that same sex–gender sexual orientation and sex–gender expression are not choices or sins. It challenges parents to examine their values regarding same sex–gender sexual orientation and sex–gender expression and to empathize with their lesbian or gay child's stigmatized situation (Strommen, 1990). What is best about support groups such as PFLAG is that they help parents overcome the barriers preventing them from loving their child unconditionally (Savin-Williams, 1998; Savin-Williams & Dubé, 1998).[1] Wren (2002) also recommended that parents of transgender children develop an empathetic approach to them and listen to their stories in order to try to make sense of them. Parents, however, cannot be moved further than they are ready to move. For example, intellectual acceptance may happen, but emotional acceptance may take much longer.

Disclosures in Ethnic and Racial Families

Facilitating the disclosure process in persons from different ethnic and racial groups requires an understanding of their cultures (Rust, 1996) and what may happen following disclosure. This process is particularly difficult, for example, for Asian gay and lesbian persons in their families. They may also be reluctant to seek out practitioners or support groups because of the stigma associated with seeking mental health services and the possible loss of confidentiality (Nakajima, Chan, & Lee, 1996). In a study of Asian American lesbian and gay persons who were seeing practitioners, Chan (1992) found that the most common themes about these clients identified by the practitioners were the fear of rejection from families and the anticipation of a complete lack of understanding from parents. These clients need to be supported throughout the long process of gaining understanding and acceptance by their parents. Another task is to help them modify feelings of guilt for choosing a desired life that meets their own needs instead of what their parents want. The dilemma is how to be an adult with one's own needs and yet continue as a part of the family.

Latino lesbian and gay persons must prepare for the possibility that their families may never understand their lives and that many of them, particularly gay persons, will feel alienated within the Latino community. The practitioner in contact with the family can emphasize the Latino value of respecting all family members and the family's dedication to loyalty (Morales, 1996).

---

[1] There are several Web sites that can be helpful: *Parents, Families and Friends of Lesbians and Gays*. Available: www.pflag.org; and *My Child Is Gay! Now What Do I Do?* Available: www.pe.net/~bidstrup/parents.htm

When working with gay and lesbian Native Americans, the level of acculturation and the corresponding cultural values and conflict in allegiances need to be addressed. If these clients are having trouble coping with conflicts in allegiances, finding ways in which they can begin to integrate their disparate worlds may help. Native American organizations and support groups can assist with this goal. Additional sources of assistance are usually necessary if clients are not acculturated. This involves drafting other members of their families or tribes as well as elders or medicine persons to help them integrate a positive identity. Other significant interventions include access to positive Native American role models specific to clients' Native American culture and tribe and involvement with more gay and lesbian contacts. It is crucial for Native American clients to find culturally relevant ways to come out and make disclosures that do not deny the gay or lesbian and Native American aspects of themselves (Walters, 1997).

African American LGB persons may not disclose to their families because their families tend to discourage disclosure of a nonheterosexual sexual identity. Chapter 5 presents many reasons that underlie the negative responses to disclosures in African American families and communities. Yet not all families are rejecting if, for example, LGB family members do not make an issue of their sexual orientation (Jones & Hill, 1996). African American LGB persons, who face decisions similar to other ethnic and racial LGB persons, should weigh the pros and cons of making disclosures and what they can negotiate between their parents' desires and their own desires to not deny who they are.

Ethnic and racial persons must contend with the external systemic factors of heterosexism and racism and the internal issues of resolving conflicting allegiances. Practitioners should focus on the resilience and positive coping of these persons and reinforce a positive sense of an integrated self. These and other LGB persons need to be reminded of their strengths (Walters, 1997).

Disclosures by Bisexual Marital Partners

Most data on disclosures by bisexual persons focus on the context of marriage. As noted in Chapter 5, the acknowledgement of bisexuality to a marriage partner usually results in serious changes in the marriage. Guidry (1999) recommended the following guidelines for marriage partners after disclosure: (a) pursue direct and honest communication; (b) acknowledge and support earlier established feelings of love and attachment to the partner; (c) use positive qualities in the relationship to sustain the difficult work of adjusting to the disclosure; and (d) take the necessary time to resolve and reconcile disclosure issues. Other suggestions proposed by Matteson (1999) include: (a) try to hear each other's perspectives and respond with understanding; (b) decide boundaries for what information will be shared and what will be private; and (c) if maintenance of the marriage is a goal, provide the partner assurance of his or her primacy as a partner. Similar to work with couples on any issue, the practitioner should evaluate the general strength and flexibility of the relationship, patterns of interaction and roles, the partners' satisfaction with the relationship, communication skills, conflict-resolution skills and deficits, and the presence of other or unresolved couple issues or stressors. Other considerations, suggested by Paul (1992), include the heterosexism or biphobia of each partner, the quality of the couple's sexual life, and the supports available to both partners.

Commitment of the couple members and their satisfaction with their relationship can empower the couple to act on pertinent issues. But, doing so demands honest communication about any sources of dissatisfaction in the link without blaming the bisexual partner. Couples may need help in slowing down and reducing the pressure for an instantaneous resolution of all the complications; a moratorium period permits necessary communication, reflection, education, and moving beyond the initial emotional upset (Paul, 1992).

DIFFERENT CONTEXTS: WORK

Discrimination in the workplace, discussed in Chapter 2, makes disclosure of a LGB sexual orientation difficult. Cost–benefit analyses of disclosures can be useful in most contexts, including work settings. One compares the likely benefits of disclosure (for example, honesty, support, preventing any possibility of blackmail, bringing partners to work events) to the possible costs (for example, lost income, demotions, job loss, no promotions, deprecation, gossip, social isolation, excessive energy to monitor cues of sexual orientation, harassment) (Pope, 1996; Vargo, 1998). A person with a larger income may think the costs of disclosure are high compared to the benefits of no disclosure. A person with a lower income may think that the costs of disclosure are lower when compared to the benefits (Badgett, 1996), unless they are the sole source of their income or do not have a good chance of getting another job.

Before she began making disclosures on her job, Deevey (1993) wrote a plan using the assessment and planning skills she learned in nursing school. She identified plus factors for disclosure such as nurses whose support she could seek and potential areas of difficulty such as a lack of positive role models and potential condemnation from closeted lesbian friends. Following disclosure in the workplace, Vargo (1998) cautioned that one must prepare for the possibility of being treated differently than other workers. If mistreatment is possible, one should learn in advance the protections and nondiscrimination policies of the workplace.

Transgender persons may particularly have a hard time holding jobs (Anderson, 1998). Disclosures at work are usually a last step for transgender persons, following their having taken hormones for a long time, living most of their time outside the workplace in the sex–gender they are adopting, and desiring a legal name change. It is best to deal with many other issues before addressing work issues resulting from disclosure. Hormonal intervention, however, can have rapid effects in some persons. A beard or breasts may develop so quickly that a faster outing at work may occur. A lower dosage of hormones may slow down this development (Cole et al., 2000).

SUMMARY

• Practitioners can help gay and lesbian clients in the coming-out process by providing a safe, nonjudgmental place for them to explore their feelings, thoughts, and desires. Practitioners should guarantee complete confidentiality and allow for exploration without themselves prescribing outcomes for clients. Practitioners should be aware of the developmental models of coming out (for example, SIF and the dual branch models) but realize that not everyone follows all the steps in sequence or moves through them in a linear fashion; some clients may cycle through certain phases more than once. Practitioners can provide information on community services and support groups.

- The same guidelines apply for practitioners who are working with bisexual clients. Additionally, however, practitioners must be aware that these persons may experience confusion because they have earlier identified as gay, lesbian, or exclusively heterosexual. Other groups who regard bisexual persons as ambivalent or as betraying their prior commitments may spurn them. Balancing relationships with more than one person requires honesty and clarity that clients may need to help develop.

- Transgender clients require the same sorts of support as other groups. They also need accurate information. These clients may come into a practitioner's office with misconceptions about what their feelings and desires mean. Information can normalize their inner experiences and reduce negative feelings as well as offer hope for reconciling the life they want to live with the life they have now.

- Some youth clearly know what their lifelong sexual identity is, and some do not. Practitioners can provide a nonjudgmental environment for youth to explore and understand themselves. Yet, practitioners must guard against guiding youth in their decisions about identity.

- Practitioners can explore with their clients the best contexts and timing for disclosing their sexual identities. Practitioners can help clients decide who will be more inclined to accept the information well and suggest that disclosures happen with them first. Practitioners can teach clients how to present the information positively and unequivocally, using words and phrases that are most likely to elicit a positive response. Practitioners can role play disclosure speeches, tape them, and allow clients to develop the most useful strategy for family and friends.

- Families react in different ways to the disclosure of a family member of a lesbian, gay, or bisexual sexual identity or sex–gender expression, but most go through grieving and reappraisal of their family member, mourning the loss of certain expectations, and determining the implications of this new knowledge. Parents and other family members may be shocked, angry, sad, and ultimately hopeful and accepting. Practitioners can be a source of comfort and information as they support the process toward acceptance. Practitioners can help families focus on their affection for their children. Furthermore, practitioners can provide information to dispel myths about LGBT persons and provide referrals to community support systems and organizations.

- Practitioners must be sensitive to the unique cultural beliefs of racial and ethnic families and the difficulties these beliefs create for a lesbian, gay, or bisexual family member to disclose. They must also respect the decision of the client and encourage the client to integrate his or her disparate identifications instead of fragmenting them into separate racial–ethnic and sexual identities.

- The adjustments of a transgender child and the family are difficult ones. The family may go through stages ranging from denial to acceptance. Before reaching acceptance, much of the family's energy is focused on trying to get the child to change and the family may experience many negative emotions and behaviors. Practitioners can aid these families with accurate information about transgender sex–gender expression, help to normalize the transgender person, help keep communications open, and help encourage family support and acceptance of "what is." PFLAG groups can be useful supports for the whole family.

Affirmative Practice: Understanding and Working with Lesbian, Gay, Bisexual, and Transgender Persons

- Practitioners can provide guidelines for the bisexual client in dealing with the effects of disclosure for a marriage partner, such as direct and honest communication, and in allowing the necessary time to resolve the issues resulting from the disclosure. If the link contains common values and intimacy, it is possible that once a heterosexual partner deals with the shock of the disclosure, the couple can work out new contracts and agreements that will allow continuation of the marriage. The relationship's future depends primarily on the commitment of the couple members and their satisfaction with the link.
- As in other settings, a cost–benefit analysis of disclosures is useful in the workplace. It is important to carefully weigh the costs; the benefits may not outweigh heavy costs. For example, if losing a job is a possibility, this cost may be too high to pay. Several versions of cost–benefit approaches exist that can be used in the workplace, including the investment model that addresses the risks of disclosure at different points in time.

CHAPTER 10
REFERENCES

Anderson, B. F. (1998). Therapeutic issues in working with transgendered clients. In D. Denny (Ed.), *Current concepts of transgendered identity* (pp. 215–226). New York: Garland.

Anderson, D. (1987). Family and peer relations of gay adolescents. *Adolescent Psychiatry, 14*, 162–178.

Badgett, M.V.L. (1996). Employment and sexual orientation: Disclosure and discrimination in the workplace. *Journal of Gay & Lesbian Social Services, 4*, 29–52.

Barron, J. (1996). Some issues in psychotherapy with gay and lesbian clients. *Psychotherapy, 33*, 611–616.

Beeler, J., & DiProva, V. (1999). Family adjustment following disclosure of homosexuality by a member: Themes discerned in narrative accounts. *Journal of Marital and Family Therapy, 25*, 443–459.

Bell, A. P., Weinberg, M. S., & Hammersmith, S. K. (1981). *Sexual preference: Its development in men and women.* Bloomington: Indiana University Press.

Ben-Ari, A. (1995). The discovery that an offspring is gay: Parents', gay men's, and lesbians' perspectives. *Journal of Homosexuality, 30*, 89–112.

Bernstein, B. E. (1990). Attitudes and issues of parents of gay men and lesbians and implications for therapy. *Journal of Gay & Lesbian Psychotherapy, 1*, 37–53.

Bohan, J. S. (1996). *Psychology and sexual orientation: Coming to terms.* New York: Routledge.

Boxer, A. M., Cook, J. A., & Herdt, G. (1991). Double jeopardy: Identity transitions and parent–child relationships among gay and lesbian youth. In K. Pillemer & K. McCartney (Eds.), *Parent–child relations throughout life* (pp. 59–92). Hillsdale, NJ: Lawrence Erlbaum.

Brown, L. S. (1989). Lesbians, gay men and their families: Common clinical issues. *Journal of Gay & Lesbian Psychotherapy, 1*, 65–77.

Browning, C., Reynolds, A. L., & Dworkin, S. H. (1991). Affirmative psychotherapy for lesbian women. *Counseling Psychologist, 19*, 177–196.

Cabaj, R. P. (1996). Sexual orientation of the therapist. In R. P. Cabaj & T. S. Stein (Eds.), *Textbook of homosexuality and mental health* (pp. 513–524). Washington, DC: American Psychiatric Press.

Cain, R. (1991). Relational contexts and information management among gay men. *Families in Society, 72,* 344–352.

Cass, V. C. (1996). Sexual orientation identity formation: A western phenomenon. In R. P. Cabaj & T. S. Stein (Eds.), *Textbook of homosexuality and mental health* (pp. 227–251). Washington, DC: American Psychiatric Press.

Chan, C. S. (1992). Cultural considerations in counseling Asian American lesbians and gay men. In S. Dworkin & F. Gutiérrez (Eds.), *Counseling gay men and lesbians* (pp. 115–124). Alexandria, VA: American Association for Counseling and Development.

Coenen, M. E. (1998). Helping families with homosexual children: A model for counseling. *Journal of Homosexuality, 36,* 73–85.

Cole, S. S., Denny, D., Eyler, A. E., & Samons, S. L. (2000). Issues of transgender. In L. T. Szuchman & F. Muscarella (Eds.), *Psychological perspectives on human sexuality* (pp. 149–195). New York: John Wiley & Sons.

D'Augelli, A. R. (2002). Mental health problems among lesbian, gay, and bisexual youths ages 14 to 21. *Clinical Child Psychology and Psychiatry, 7,* 433–456.

D'Augelli, A. R., Hershberger, S. L., & Pilkington, N. W. (1998). Lesbian, gay, and bisexual youths and their families: Disclosure of sexual orientation and its consequences. *American Journal of Orthopsychiatry, 68,* 361–371.

Deevey, S. (1993). Lesbian self-disclosure: Strategies for success. *Journal of Psychosocial Nursing, 31,* 21–26.

Degges-White, S., Rice, B., & Myers, J. E. (2000). Revisiting Cass' theory of sexual identity formation: A study of lesbian development. *Journal of Mental Health Counseling, 22,* 318–333.

Diamond, L. M. (1998). Development of sexual orientation among adolescent and young adult women. *Developmental Psychology, 34,* 1085–1095.

Drescher, J. (1998). Contemporary psychoanalytic psychotherapy with gay men: With a commentary on reparative therapy of homosexuality. *Journal of Gay & Lesbian Psychotherapy, 2,* 51-74.

Ellis, K. M., & Eriksen, K. (2002). Transsexual and transgenderist experiences and treatment options. *Family Journal, 10,* 289–299.

Emerson, S., & Rosenfeld, C. (1996). Stages of adjustment in family members of transgender individuals. *Journal of Family Psychotherapy*, 7, 1–12.

Esterberg, K. G. (1996). Gay cultures, gay communities: The social organization of lesbians, gay men, and bisexuals. In R. C. Savin-Williams & K. M. Cohen (Eds.), *The lives of lesbians, gay men, and bisexuals: Children to adults* (pp. 377–391). Fort Worth, TX: Harcourt Brace.

Fox, R. C. (1991). Development of a bisexual identity: Understanding the process. In L. Hutchins & L. Kaahumanu (Eds.), *Bi any other name: Bisexual people speak out* (pp. 29–36). Boston: Alyson Press.

Gagné, P., Tewksbury, R., & McGaughey, D. (1997). Coming out and crossing over: Identity formation and proclamation in a transgender community. *Gender & Society*, 11, 478–508.

Gartrell, N. (1984). Combating homophobia in the psychotherapy of lesbians. *Women & Therapy*, 3, 13–29.

Gonsiorek, J. C. (1982). Introduction to mental health issues and homosexuality. *American Behavioral Scientist*, 25, 267–383.

Green, R.-J. (2000). "Lesbians, gay men, and their parents": A critique of LaSala and the prevailing clinical wisdom. *Family Process*, 39, 257–266.

Griffin, C., Wirth, M., & Wirth, A. (1986). *Beyond acceptance: Parents of lesbians and gays talk about their experiences*. Englewood Cliffs, NJ: Prentice Hall.

Guidry, L. L. (1999). Clinical intervention with bisexuals: A contextualized understanding. *Professional Psychology: Research and Practice*, 30, 22–26.

Hammersmith, S. K. (1987). A sociological approach to counseling homosexual clients and their families. *Journal of Homosexuality*, 14, 173–190.

Helminiak, D. A. (1995). *What the Bible really says about homosexuality*. San Francisco: Alamo Square Press.

Herdt, G. H. (1989). Gay and lesbian youth, emergent identities, and cultural scenes at home and abroad. *Journal of Homosexuality*, 17, 1–42.

Jones, B. E., & Hill, M. J. (1996). African American lesbians, gay men, and bisexuals. In R. P. Cabaj & T. S. Stein (Eds.), *Textbook of homosexuality and mental health* (pp. 549–561). Washington, DC: American Psychiatric Press.

Kinsey, A. C., Pomeroy, W. B., Martin, C. E., & Gebbard, P. H. (1948). *Sexual behavior in the human male.* Philadephia: W. B. Saunders.

Kinsey, A. C., Pomeroy, W. B., Martin, C. E., & Gebbard, P. H. (1953). *Sexual behavior in the human female.* Philadelphia: W. B. Saunders.

Klein, F., Sepekoff, B., & Wolf, T. J. (1985). Sexual orientation: A multi-variable dynamic process. *Journal of Homosexuality, 11,* 35–49.

Kübler-Ross, E. (1969). *On death and dying.* New York: Macmillan.

Kuehlwein, K. T. (1992). Working with gay men. In A. M. Freeman & F. M. Dattilio (Eds.), *Comprehensive casebook of cognitive therapy* (pp. 249–255). New York: Plenum Press.

Laird, J. (1996). Family-centered practice with lesbian and gay families. *Families in Society: Journal of Contemporary Human Services, 77,* 559–572.

Levy, E. F. (1995). Feminist social work practice with lesbian and gay clients. In N. Van Den Bergh (Ed.), *Feminist practice in the 21st century* (pp. 278–294). Washington, DC: NASW Press.

Lourea, D. N. (1985). Psycho-social issues related to counseling bisexuals. *Journal of Homosexuality, 11,* 51–62.

Mallon, G. (1998a). Knowledge for practice with gay and lesbian persons. In G. P. Mallon (Ed.), *Foundations of social work practice with lesbian and gay persons* (pp. 1–30). New York: Haworth Press.

Mallon, G. P. (1998b). Social work practice with gay men and lesbians within families. In G. P. Mallon (Ed.), *Foundations of social work practice with lesbian and gay persons* (pp. 145–180). New York: Haworth Press.

Matteson, D. R. (1995). Counseling with bisexuals. *Individual Psychology, 51,* 144–159.

Matteson, D. R. (1996a). Counseling and psychotherapy with bisexual and exploring clients. In B. A. Firestein (Ed.), *Bisexuality: The psychology and politics of an invisible minority* (pp. 185–213). Thousand Oaks, CA: Sage Publications.

Matteson, D. R. (1996b). Psychotherapy with bisexual individuals. In R. P. Cabaj & T. S. Stein (Eds.), *Textbook of homosexuality and mental health* (pp. 433–449). Washington, DC: American Psychiatric Press.

Matteson, D. R. (1999). Intimate bisexual couples. In J. Carlson & L. Sperry (Eds.), *The intimate couple* (pp. 439–459). Philadelphia: Brunner/Mazel.

McCarn, S. R., & Fassinger, R. E. (1996). Revisioning sexual minority identity formation: A new model of lesbian identity and its implications for counseling and research. *Counseling Psychologists, 24*, 508–534.

McCubbin, H., & Patterson, J. (1983). The family stress process: The double ABCX model of adjustment and adaptation. *Marriage and Family Review, 6*, 7–37.

Morales, E. S. (1996). Gender roles among Latino gay and bisexual men: Implications for family and couple therapy. In J. Laird & R.-J. Green (Eds.), *Lesbians and gays in couples and families: A handbook for therapists* (pp. 272–297). San Francisco: Jossey-Bass.

Muller, A. (1987). *Parents matter.* New York: Naiad.

Nakajima, G. A., Chan, Y. H., & Lee, K. (1996). Mental health issues for gay and lesbian Asian Americans. In R. P. Cabaj & T. S. Stein (Eds.), *Textbook of homosexuality and mental health* (pp. 563–581). Washington, DC: American Psychiatric Press.

Neisen, J. H. (1987). Resources for families with a gay/lesbian member. In E. Coleman (Ed.), *Integrated identities for gay men and lesbians: Psychotherapeutic approaches for emotional well-being* (pp. 239–251). New York: Harrington Park.

Nichols, M. (1988). Low sexual desire in lesbian couples. In S. Leiblum & R. C. Rosen (Eds.), *Sexual desire disorders* (pp. 387–412). New York: Guilford Press.

Off Pink Collective. (1988). *Bisexual lives.* London: Off Pink Publishing.

Paul, J. P. (1988). Counseling issues in working with a bisexual population. In M. Shernoff & W. A. Scott (Eds.), *The sourcebook on lesbian/gay health care* (2nd ed., pp. 142–150). Washington, DC: National Lesbian/Gay Health Foundation.

Paul, J. P. (1992). "Biphobia" and the construction of a bisexual identity. In M. Shernoff & W. A. Scott (Eds.), *The sourcebook on lesbian/gay health care* (2nd ed., pp. 259–264). Washington, DC: National Lesbian/Gay Health Foundation.

Pope, M. (1995). Gay/lesbian career development research: Career counseling interventions. *Career Development Quarterly, 44*, 178–190.

Pope, M. (1996). Gay and lesbian career counseling: Special career counseling issues. *Journal of Gay & Lesbian Social Services, 4*, 91–105.

Rafkin, L. (Ed.). (1987). *Different daughters: A book by mothers of lesbians.* Pittsburgh: Cleis.

Remafedi, G., Farrow, J. A., & Deisher, R. W. (1991). Risk factors for attempted suicide in gay and bisexual youth. *Pediatrics, 87*, 869–875.

Robinson, B. E., Walters, L. H., & Skeen, P. (1989). Response of parents to learning that their child is homosexual and concern over AIDS: A national study. *Journal of Homosexuality, 18,* 59–80.

Rosario, M., Meyer-Bahlburg, H.F.L., Hunter, J., Exner, T. M., Gwadz, M., & Keller, A. M. (1996). The psychosexual development of urban lesbian, gay, and bisexual youths. *Journal of Sex Research, 35,* 113–126.

Rosenfeld, C., & Emerson, S. (1998). A process model of supportive therapy for families of transgender individuals. In D. Denny (Ed.), *Current concepts of transgender identity* (pp. 391–400). New York: Garland.

Rotheram-Borus, M. H., Hunter, J., & Rosario, M. (1994). Suicidal behavior and gay-related stress among gay and bisexual male adolescents. *Journal of Adolescent Research, 9,* 498–508.

Rust, P. C. (1993). "Coming out" in the age of social constructionism: Sexual identity formation among lesbian and bisexual women. *Gender & Society, 7,* 50–77.

Rust, P. C. (1996). Finding a sexual identity and community: Therapeutic implications and cultural assumptions in scientific models of coming out. In E. D. Rothblum & L. A. Bond (Eds.), *Preventing heterosexim and homophobia* (pp. 87–123). Thousand Oaks, CA: Sage Publications.

Savin-Williams, R. C. (1990). Youth. In W. R. Dynes (Ed.), *Encyclopedia of homosexuality* (pp. 1409–1415). New York: Garland.

Savin-Williams, R. C. (1995a). An exploratory study of pubertal maturation timing and self-esteem among gay and bisexual male youths. *Developmental Psychology, 31,* 56–64.

Savin-Williams, R. C. (1995b, June). *Parents' reactions to the discovery of a child's sexual orientation.* Paper presented at the Lesbian, Gay, and Bisexual Identities and the Family: Psychological Perspectives Conference, Pennsylvania State University, University Park.

Savin-Williams, R. C. (1996). Ethnic-and sexual-minority youth. In R. C. Savin-Williams & K. M. Cohen (Eds.), *The lives of lesbians, gay men, and bisexuals: Children to adults* (pp. 152–165). Fort Worth, TX: Harcourt Brace.

Savin-Williams, R. C. (1998). The disclosure to families of same–sex attractions by lesbian, gay, and bisexual youths. *Journal of Research on Adolescence, 8,* 49–68.

Savin-Williams, R. C., & Diamond, L. M. (1999). Sexual orientation. In W. K. Silverman & T. H. Ollendick (Eds.), *Developmental issues in the clinical treatment of children* (pp. 241–258). Boston: Allyn & Bacon.

Savin-Williams, R. C., & Dubé, E. M. (1998). Parental reactions to their child's disclosure of a gay/lesbian identity. *Family Relations, 47,* 7–13.

Scasta, D. (1998). Issues in helping people come out. *Journal of Gay & Lesbian Psychotherapy, 2,* 87–98.

Schuck, K. D., & Liddle, B. J. (2001). Religious conflicts experienced by lesbian, gay, and bisexual individuals. *Journal of Gay & Lesbian Psychotherapy, 5,* 63–82.

Shernoff, M. (1998). Individual practice with gay men. In G. P. Mallon (Ed.), *Foundations of social work practice with lesbian and gay persons* (pp. 77–103). New York: Haworth Press.

Stokes, J., & Damon, W. (1995). Counseling and psychotherapy for bisexual men. *Directions in Mental Health Counseling, 5,* 4–15.

Stokes, J. P., Miller, R. L., & Mundhenk, R. (1998). Toward an understanding of behaviorally bisexual men: The influence of context and culture. *Canadian Journal of Human Sexuality, 7,* 1–12.

Strommen, E. F. (1990). Hidden branches and growing pains: Homosexuality and the family tree. *Marriage & Family Review, 14,* 9–34.

Thompson, C. A. (1992). Lesbian grief and loss issues in the coming out process. *Women & Therapy, 12,* 175–185.

Vargo, M. E. (1998). *Acts of disclosure: The coming-out process of contemporary gay men.* New York: Harrington Park.

Walters, K. L. (1997). Urban lesbian and gay American Indian identity: Implications for mental health service delivery. *Journal of Gay & Lesbian Social Services, 6,* 43–65.

Williamson, D. S. (1998). An essay for practitioners: Disclosure is a family event. *Family Relations, 47,* 23–25.

Wren, J. (2002). "I can accept my child is transsexual but if I ever see him in a dress I'll hit him": Dilemmas in parenting a transgendered adolescent. *Clinical Child Psychology and Psychiatry, 7,* 377–397.

CHAPTER 11
PRACTICE WITH COUPLES AND FAMILIES

What is the impact of internalized oppression on lesbian and gay couples?

What types of issues do lesbian and gay couples encounter?

How can practitioners assist gay and lesbian persons who are experiencing breakups?

What specific interventions can practitioners use with bisexual persons and their partners?

What are some of the issues that practitioners will likely address

when working with lesbian and gay families with children?

Competent practice with lesbian and gay couples and families begins with accurate knowledge. Same-sex couples and families are similar to heterosexual couples and families. Yet, they experience unique obstacles because of heterosexism (Hunt, 1993), including bias, stereotypes, discrimination, stigmatization, and sometimes violence. In addition, they often experience difficult processes such as coming out and disclosure (for example, Murphy, 1994; Peplau, 1993). Unfortunately, practitioners may exhibit heterosexual bias in how they approach these couples and families, for example, by asking members in a couple which one plays the male role and which one plays the female role. Clients generally respond to such questions with disbelief (Gonsiorek & Weinrich, 1991; Markowitz, 1991).

Another result of heterosexual bias is that some practitioners do not support the maintenance of gay and lesbian relationships and even encourage dissolution. Such practitioners do not provide or recommend any services. The Committee on Lesbian and Gay Concerns of the American Psychological Association (APA) reported that practitioners often are biased and do not value the couple members' commitment, including not valuing the couple members' commitment to each other, telling a couple to view their difficulties as insurmountable, and presuming their families are inappropriate (Garnets, Hancock, Cochran, Goodchilds, & Peplau, 1991).

Work with gay and lesbian couples should follow the guidelines of exemplary practice expressed by the Committee on Lesbian and Gay Concerns (APA, 1991): (a) have knowledge about the diverse nature of lesbian and gay relationships and validate their importance; (b) recognize the effects of prejudice and discrimination on lesbian and gay relationships and parenting; and (c) recognize the importance of alternative families for lesbian and gay persons (Garnets et al., 1991).

COUPLES AND ISSUES

Lesbian, gay, and bisexual couples can experience various issues for which they may seek help from a human services practitioner. Examples of these issues are discussed here.

Issues Involving Internalized Oppression

When a practitioner first sees a gay or lesbian couple, the members will probably seem, on the surface, affirmative about their sexual orientation (APA, 1991). The oppression of heterosexism, however, can operate in subtle and nonconscious ways, and even persons with a positive self-image are not totally shielded from this oppression (Brown, 1996). Several practitioners (Brown, 1996; McVinney, 1998) identified ways that internalized oppression can affect gay and lesbian couples. For example, some persons in these couples devalue same-sex intimacy, setting themselves up for failure in relationships. Some partners think that since they will eventually break up, they should never combine anything. For the same reason, some partners may establish loose boundaries for their links. Other couples may tighten their boundaries and become closed systems. Closed systems, however, put pressure on the partners to fulfill most of each other's needs.

If internalized oppression is an issue for one or both partners, this obstacle should be the first focus for intervention. Practitioners need to challenge these couples' assumptions and their expectations for failure (Okun, 1996). They need to communicate to these couples that the choice of a gay or lesbian partner is as natural as the choice of a heterosexual partner (Igartua, 1998). Practitioners can connect couples with support groups to meet other gay and lesbian couples who overcame issues associated with internalized oppression. If such groups are not available, affirmative and educational books and videos are useful (MacDonald, 1998). Groups are preferable, however, because they will help these couples to build social networks (Laird, 1996).

Issues Involving Identity Development and Disclosure

Issues here include the extent of coming out and disclosure of each partner and the couple as a unit. The couple members may be at different stages in identity development and at different levels of comfort with disclosures. Questions to consider include: How "out" is each partner? How out is the couple? Who are they out to, or not out to, and in what contexts? (Cabaj & Klinger, 1996). Couples may fight over whether to disclose to parents or at work, or to consider the exclusion of one partner from family and work social events (Brown, 1996).

The partner who has made more progress in identity development and disclosure may be patient and tolerant or impatient and frustrated about the other partner's "immaturity." Practitioners can provide each partner a clearer view of the other's own unique experiences (Brown, 1996) by challenging the notion that one partner's desire for openness or secrecy is symbolic of love, or not, for the other partner (Roth, 1985). Love and disclosure are independent of one another. A partner who wants to be more open must understand the other partner's fear of possibly losing friends, job, and family. Reluctance to disclose has nothing to do with ambivalence about the relationship (MacDonald, 1998).

Issues Concerning Sex–Gender Roles in Gay and Lesbian Couples

Competition and power. For gay couples, relationship patterns characterized by power imbalance, unilateral decision making, inequitable distribution of labor, and role inflexibility are likely to lead to conflict, hostile feelings, relationship dissatisfactions, and, sometimes, low self-esteem for the disadvantaged partner (Granvold & Martin, 1999). Men in Western cultures equate their value with power, prestige, and income (Brown, 1996), and conflict in gay couples can occur over perceived inequities in finances, power, and the status or influence each partner holds (for example, Brown, 1994, 1996; McVinney, 1998). The partner with more assets usually has more influence (Reilly & Lynch, 1990).

With inequities of power, prestige, and income in a gay couple, the partner who is on the low end may see the other partner as a competitor or enemy (Brown, 1996). Competition may also result from insecurity about the relationship, with each trying to prove that he is worthy of love (MacDonald, 1998). Yet, worth is hard to attain when partners devalue and insult each other (Brown, 1996; MacDonald, 1998).

Practitioners can probe for the effects of occupational and income discrepancies in gay couples and explore symbolic meanings and cultural messages regarding money, status, and power. This may help partners comprehend why one partner may feel demeaned or that he is "losing" in the competition (Brown, 1996). Exposing patterns of aggression and competitiveness and the underlying reasons may help gay couples reduce or eliminate power struggles (MacDonald, 1998). Males often have to work extra hard to surrender ingrained assumptions about masculinity and rigid stereotypical "masculine" roles, so that they can develop the collaborative communication and negotiating skills required for more satisfying linkups (Okun, 1996).

Overseparation. Social expectations for men also emphasize independence and differentiation (Cabaj & Klinger, 1996). Instead of overattachment that may characterize some lesbian couples, some gay couples may experience overseparation, including nonacknowledgment of emotional needs, emotional distance, and physical distance (for example, excessive travel and avoidance of affectionate behavior; see Colgan, 1988). The goal of overseparation is to preserve independence, which makes forming and maintaining intimate bonds difficult (Cabaj & Klinger, 1996). Once the sexual attraction fades, men may be at a loss for how to proceed (Brown, 1996). Traditional marital practice may help with the expression of feelings and vulnerability (MacDonald, 1998), learning how to listen, to empathize, and how to state what one wants from a partner. Goals for these clients include developing more emotional involvement and negotiating solutions instead of arguing (Gray & Isensee, 1996).

Women's relationship visions and devaluation. Women are generally more relational than men (for example, Chodorow, 1978; Gilligan, 1982). They define morality as responsibility and care; they respond to and empathize with the needs of others; and they suppress competitive and aggressive drives (Goodrich, 1988). Whereas men may use shared activities to establish intimacy and sexual activity, women establish intimacy through shared feelings, secrets, and insights (Wood & Inman, 1993). Lesbians in couples hold a vision of their relationships as based not on power politics but on intimacy, mutuality, interdependence, and equality (Goodrich, 1988). These "feminine" behaviors, however, are not generally valued in our society.

Growing up in a sexist cultural context, women learn to place little value on feminine stereotypical behaviors such as their nurturance, empathy, relational orientation, or themselves as women. This devaluation of women may lead women in couples to devalue each other. They may hold perfectionist standards for their partners to compensate for the deficiency of not being male. Partners expect each other to be endlessly available, always listening, and always interested. Yet, the partners must also be independent, individuated, and able to take care of their own needs. The practitioner must challenge each woman to overcome the deval-uation of women so that each one values the partner and reduces perfectionist standards (Brown, 1996).

Intimacy and autonomy. Maintaining a comfortable level of intimacy while retaining one's independence is a difficult task in any close relationship. Although the nurturance and empa-thy that women learned from childhood may facilitate the development of intimate relation-ships, these qualities may also predispose lesbians to "fusion"(sometimes referred to as "merg-er")—in other words, difficulties with maintaining autonomy within their relationships (MacDonald, 1998).

The concept of fusion dominates both common lore and the clinical literature about les-bian couples. Much of the literature suggests that an excessively high level of relatedness is the primary cause of difficulties in lesbian couples (for example, Krestan & Bepko, 1980; Roth, 1985). Fusion is blamed for distancing, diminishing sexual interest, and other relational difficulties (Laird, 1996). Yet, little evidence substantiates a problematic degree of fusion in lesbian couples (Zacks, Green, & Morrow, 1988). Fusion and differentiation also are not polar opposites; persons can experience both (Laird, 1996). It is important, therefore, for profes-sionals not to impose their own ideas of a suitable balance between autonomy and intimacy or to succumb to the over individualist bias of Western culture (Matteson, 1996b; McCandlish, 1982).

Given that satisfaction is high in lesbian couples, closeness, even if experienced as fusion, may not be at all distressing. In some couples, however, excessive mutual dependency can be an obstacle to asserting needs or acting with autonomy (Roth, 1989; Schreurs & Buunk, 1996). Because women learn to deny self or to place the needs of others before their own needs, in lesbian couples neither woman may be skilled in self-definition or autonomy (Kleinberg & Zorn, 1995; Krestan & Bepko, 1980). The identities of the couple members can be so undifferentiated that they see themselves as part of the other or even the same as the other. They may not tolerate distance from their partners and may experience separation anxiety when apart (Clunis & Green, 2000). One partner may view any desires for autono-my by her partner, such as having her own friends, as a step to end the link instead of as a move toward balance. Difficulties become acute if one partner becomes more autonomous as the other becomes more dependent. The autonomy-desiring person will likely feel trapped by the other person who is pushing for more emotional and behavioral fusion (Okun, 1996).

ISSUES INVOLVING PROBLEMATIC FUSION-INTERVENTIONS FOR LESBIAN COUPLES

Some lesbians (and presumably some gay persons) can be so close emotionally that they ask for help in negotiating distance (Igartua, 1998). It is important, however, not to identify the cou-ple's difficulties as pathological deviations—describing these experiences as normative is more useful to clients. Practitioners can also rename the issue as connectedness or commitments instead of fusion (Green, Bettinger, & Zacks, 1996). Giving a nonpathological theoretical expla-nation for what is happening can be a critical element of intervention (Brown, 1996).

The California Inventory for Family Assessment (Werner & Green, 1989) was recommended by Green and colleagues (1996) as a way to identify couples' interactional difficulties with closeness, their strengths, and to determine focused goals. The model assesses each partner's functioning in three domains: (1) *closeness-caregiving* ("warmth, time together, nurturance, physical intimacy, and consistency"); (2) *openness of communication* ("self-disclosure and decreased conflict avoidance"); (3) *intrusiveness* ("separation anxiety, possessiveness/jealousy, emotional interactivity, projection/mystification, anger/aggression, and dominance") (Green et al., 1996, p. 205). If, based on this assessment, couple members do not experience enough autonomy, Matteson (1996b) recommended assisting partners to develop a fuller sense of self and more autonomous expression. These interventions include teaching partners to speak from the "I" position (Bowen, 1978) and helping them become more sensually grounded, using focusing techniques (Gendlin, 1981), body workouts (for example, Pesso, 1969), or both. Differentiation models of couples' treatment (for example, Buxton, 1994; Schnarch, 1991) are also useful because they emphasize a self-validating stance instead of a fusion (or other-validating) stance for members of a couple.

The fusion literature also offers prescriptions for expanding the distance and differentiation between the partners (Krestan & Bepko, 1980). The concept of "distancing for intimacy" (Burch, 1986; Kaufman, Harrison, & Hyde, 1984) can help the partners achieve both intimacy and independence while maintaining strong boundaries (Cabaj & Klinger, 1996). They can have individual friends and spend regular time with them, find times to be alone, and decrease life-maintenance time together, such as grocery shopping (Gray & Isensee, 1996). Couple members who are afraid to ask for what they desire can benefit from books that emphasize more precise communications (for example, Berzon, 1988) and from role playing more direct requests (Cabaj & Klinger, 1996).

Lesbians in couples may also benefit from expanded knowledge of identity formation, women's psychology, and heterosexism (Igartua, 1998). Interventions can focus on reducing the pressures of internalized oppression and female socialization. One condition for overcoming these pressures includes group work to validate and support the couple. Group work can encourage couple members to establish pride in their identities and to identify and express their own needs. Another condition that can help is the "couples dialogue," a communication tool for resolving conflicts. This intervention requires both couple members to experiment with two roles (sender and receiver) and the three processes of mirroring, validation, and empathy. Mirroring allows the receiver to be more open to the other partner's (the sender's) spoken message through reflecting back what the other partner just said. The message can be paraphrased or repeated word by word. This process goes back and forth until each partner (as the sender) expresses what she wants to say and feels that the receiver genuinely has heard her and without judgment. This process reveals that two points of view are always operating, a threatening revelation for the partner who believes that being close means sharing the same thoughts and feelings. The receiver can express empathy while listening to the sender without sharing the feelings or denying her own feelings. The goal is to understand the partner's desires and tell the partner that she understands them (Kleinberg & Zorn, 1995).

As a couple, sometimes fusion spontaneously decreases as the excitement of new love and the desire to be together lessen. Eventually, some degree of individuation will occur for all couples (Greene, Causby, & Miller, 1999; Okun, 1996).

ISSUES INVOLVING SEXUALITY

Lesbian and gay couples can experience sexual issues comparable to those of heterosexual couples: frequency, discrepancies in the partner's level of sexual desire, and differences in sexual behavior preferences. Lesbian couples, however, do not seem to experience pervasive sexual difficulties (for example, Burch, 1982; Nichols, 1995). Generally, these couples feel satisfied with their sex lives though they experience less genital sex than other couples at all stages of their link (Blumstein & Schwartz, 1983). Some lesbian couples engage in no sexual behavior at all (Loulan, 1984, 1987).

The relationships of lesbians may be mostly affectionate (Nichols, 1982) with more emphasis on kissing and caressing than on genital sex (Blumstein & Schwartz, 1983; Clunis & Green, 2000). Not all lesbian partners, however, are happy about their sexual situation; they may complain about either desire discrepancy or low desire (Hall, 1987; Nichols, 1982, 1995). An absence of sexual desire or the avoidance of all sex may be the most frequent sexual situation in lesbian couples (Hall, 1987; Roth, 1985). Power imbalances can also lead to sexual difficulties. The low-influence partner may withhold sex as a way to maintain some control (Burch, 1987). In addition, women seldom learn to initiate sex, so they may be uncomfortable in the initiator role (Blumstein & Schwartz, 1983; Roth, 1985). Lesbians also may not like performing what they see as a masculine role such as initiating sex or pressuring the partner for sex. Other reasons for avoiding sex include negative cultural messages about women's sexuality (Loulan, 1984, 1987); internalized oppression (MacDonald, 1998); and shame, anxiety, or guilt about sex (Loulan, 1987). Some women who began same-sex sexual relationships in adolescence experienced chastisement and ridicule and, therefore, guilt about these past relationships may affect their adult relationships (Sang, 1992).

Practitioners can address these issues directly with clients. Interventions focused on increasing sexual pleasure can include anxiety reduction and improving sensory awareness and communication. Sensate-focus exercises (Hall, 1987; Nichols, 1982), successive development of sexual skill and comfort using in vivo homework assignments (Granvold & Martin, 1999), and self-help books are useful interventions (for example, Loulan, 1984, 1987). These couples are also likely to be helped by support groups with other lesbian couples so they can see that their sex lives are not unusual (MacDonald, 1998).

In contrast to lesbians, many gay persons learn to take an active, ready, and willing role in sex (Okun, 1996). Still, they may also experience sexual issues when in couples, such as inhibited sexual desire, inhibited orgasm, and inhibited sexual excitement. Inhibited sexual desire can result from internalized oppression or aversion to sex. Inhibited orgasm may result from internal conflicts due to internalized oppression or the fear of loss of control. Inhibited sexual excitement can result from the belief that the partner grades performance (George & Behrendt, 1987). Iasenza (1999), a practitioner with lesbian couples, reported that she tries to normalize these situations such as helping partners to acknowledge their different levels of sexual desire and sexual differences. She also helps them adjust to changing levels of sexual desire in long-term relationships. It can also be helpful to discuss the need to be more responsible for one's own sexual pleasure through masturbation. Iasenza also recommends the concept, introduced by Loulan (1984), of "willingness" to have sex.

Desire discrepancy is also a commonly reported dilemma among gay partners (Reece, 1987) because of (a) fear of HIV and AIDS (Forstein, 1994); (b) aversions to particular sexual acts

(McWhirter & Mattison, 1984); (c) power differences so that the partner with less power withholds sex whereas the other partner may make demands for sex (Blumstein & Schwartz, 1983); and (d) the fear of dependency or giving oneself completely to the other (MacDonald, 1998). The same kinds of interventions discussed for lesbian couples can be used for gay couples.

ISSUES INVOLVING SAFE SEX

Any recommendations regarding sexual involvements must occur in the context of safe-sex practices (MacDonald, 1998). Safe sex should be directly addressed in practice. Fear of AIDS is a primary motivator to use safe-sex practices (Appleby, Miller, & Rothspan, 1999). Especially if sex occurs outside the primary link, both partners should be committed to safe-sex practices with a written accord specifying what those practices are (Granvold & Martin, 1999). For gay couples in which one or both are not monogamous, interventions can include explorations of the meaning and expectations of safe sex. For example, does it mean no oral sex or no anonymous sexual encounters? Both gay and lesbian couples have access to safe-sex programs, videos, and books that encourage more open and direct discussion about sexuality and provide ideas of more creative and experimental sexual activities (for example, Loulan, 1984, 1987). Health clinics distribute condoms, spermicidal jellies, and other safety devices (Appleby & Anastas, 1998). Practitioners can offer referrals to AIDS services organizations that provide gay persons ways to eroticize safe-sex techniques and help create contact with other men committed to safe sex (Brown, 1996).

ISSUES INVOLVING EFFECTS OF HIV/AIDS ON GAY COUPLES

In some couples, both partners become infected with HIV or AIDS. Where only one couple member is HIV positive, the disclosure of this status by the infected partner can lead to reactions by the uninfected partner ranging from increased intimacy with the infected partner to recriminations and breakup (McWhirter & Mattison, 1996; Paradis, 1991). Usually the disclosure of HIV/AIDS status destabilizes the couple's arrangements (Rutter & Schwartz, 1996). The balance of power can be affected if one partner must care for the other partner, so that the growing dependency of the ill partner can have an oppressive effect on the link (Paradis, 1991). An approach-avoidance situation may develop similar to couples who have been together for many years and are facing natural deaths; a partner may want to get close to the dying partner but also may want to avoid the partner as a protection against the anticipated pain of losing the partner (McWhirter & Mattison, 1996).

Practitioners can assist partners to discuss their fears and concerns with each other. For example, discussion of the relative safety of sexual techniques may help alleviate some of the fear associated with sexual contact. These couples may also need assistance with working their way through various options within the medical system and the different community resources. If couples are feeling isolated, practitioners can encourage them to join support groups and to become involved with AIDS organizations.

Practitioners require knowledge about HIV and AIDS, knowledge of resources, and knowledge of how these diseases affect individuals, couples, and communities (Appleby & Anastas,

1998). A considerable amount of material on these topics is available, and many communities have agencies that specialize in assisting individuals, couples, and families affected by a member with HIV or AIDS.

ISSUES INVOLVING COUPLE STAGES

Though stage models do not always fit couples, they can be useful in elucidating potential relationship issues. A stage model for gay couples, developed by McWhirter and Mattison (1996), notes potential difficulties they may experience at each stage. Several examples of the potential difficulties are presented here:

Stage 1. Because love, blending, and togetherness characterize the first year, partners may view any change in this scenario as ending the link. They may withdraw from each other and eventually end their link.

Stage 2. The typical issue here involves differences and disagreements between partners. The decline in passion results in realism wherein the partners no longer ignore the perceived shortcomings of each other. They may pursue outside sexual interests.

Stage 3. In this stage, a greater development of individuation emerges (including desire for sex with others), resulting in new anxieties, fears of loss, and anger from a partner who is not individuating in this way. .

Stage 4. Fear of loss is prevalent at this stage also because of considerable distancing from each other. Eventually, however, the relationship may experience greater consolidation.

Stage 5. Issues here include aging, routine, and monotony.

Stage 6. Stage 5 issues continue along with restlessness and possible withdrawal and aimlessness.

Most likely, couples will not experience a simultaneous progression through these stages. McWhirter and Mattison (1996) observed in their practice with gay couples that more than half experienced some degree of stage discrepancy (couple members were at different stages) but also experienced considerable relief when presented with the discrepancy concept. They could reframe their difficulties from flaws in themselves and their partners to discrepancies in developmental progression (McWhirter & Mattison, 1996).

Recognizing each other's stage needs lays a basis for negotiation (Butler & Clarke, 1991). For example, one partner may be ready to pursue more individuation whereas the other partner may still want to nest or blend (Cabaj & Klinger, 1996). Partners can negotiate how they can meet each other's different needs.

Also important are the transitions such as moving from blending in the early phases to the reemergence of individuality in the later stages. At the early stages, the intense feelings, romance, and sexual drive lead persons to blend or merge. The partners may seem ideal to each other during this period. As time passes, though, and intensity fades, they will see each other more realistically. Individual needs and desires will reemerge, and because of this development, differences and conflicts will surface too. Some partners may view this transition as the loss of love or the ending of the link. The challenge is to find reasons to stay together such as companionate love and a life together instead of intense sex and passion. Each person's level of maturity, life stage, and ability to function as an independent person influence how smoothly this and other transitions go (Cabaj & Klinger, 1996).

The stage model presented here is useful because it normalizes the difficulties of gay couples. The stages can also apply, with some alterations, to lesbian couples and to bisexual relationships (Cabaj, 1988; MacDonald, 1998). This education may reduce the partners' conflicts by removing the anxiety about changes in the relationship and blaming of each other for the difficulties (MacDonald, 1998). Instead of the partners viewing their difficulties as personal they can see them as typical hurdles in the progression of the relationship. The couple members can also clarify their expectations and assumptions about their link (Butler & Clarke, 1991).

Though the staging concept is a reassuring cognitive framework for couples, it is only intuitively applicable (MacDonald, 1998). No empirical account supports the clinical effectiveness of the McWhirter and Mattison (1996) stage model or another model developed for lesbian couples by Clunis and Green (2000).

BENEFITS OF SOCIAL SUPPORT FOR COUPLES

As discussed in Chapter 6, social support can be essential for gay and lesbian couples. In a sample of 156 cohabiting gay couples, Smith and Brown (1998) found that social support for the couples was significantly associated with the quality of their linkups and the strengthening commitment of the partners. Persons in the social network may encourage the couple to stay together through stressful times. Formal groups can also provide opportunities for gay and lesbian couples to meet and offer each other support, practical as well as emotional.

Other researchers (for example, Kurdek, 1988; Kurdek & Schmitt, 1987; Blumstein & Schwartz, 1983) also observed the importance of social support from friends in relational adjustments and in the reduction of relational distress in gay and lesbian couples (Greene, 1994; Kurdek, 1988). Practitioners should emphasize the benefits of social support and encourage couples to participate in interactions with friends, as well as family.

LEGAL PROTECTIONS FOR COUPLES

Gay and lesbian couples may need to protect themselves from heterosexist family members or social institutions. For example, if one of the partners dies, the surviving partners may think that because of the other partners' desires, assets of that partner will be theirs. Families of the deceased partner, however, often intervene and even overturn wills that left property to the partner (Vetri, 1998).

Practitioners need to discuss with couples the need for written documents, recently identified by Kuehlwein and Gottschalk (2000), that will allow the partners to (a) create joint financial arrangements; (b) inherit the house if the other partner dies; (c) design a will with the partner as chief beneficiary; (d) allow the partner to make medical decisions if a crisis situation arises with the other partner; (e) allow the partner to make financial decisions if a crisis occurs; (f) create an accord that the partners are equal coparents of the children; (g) allow the partner to be the guardian to the children; (h) designate another guardian if both partners die; (i) develop instructions for what should happen to a partner's body in case of death; and (j) develop instructions for medical intervention in the event of irreversible coma or terminal illness of a partner. The idea here is to ensure that a couple has made the legal and economic provisions they desire in the face of future difficulties.

Several more specific examples of protections include (a) *a contract of love* that covers the joint payment of outstanding debts and distribution of personal and real property acquired during and before the link (Robson, 1995); (b) *a medical directive/living will* that allows a person to determine desires about medical treatment in advance (Gruskin, 1999); (c) *a health care power of attorney* that alleviates heartaches such as being barred from hospital access to one's partner, becoming prohibited from involvement in medical decisions for an incapacitated partner, and having no rights to be the guardian for an incapacitated partner (Vetri, 1998); (d) *a conservatorship/guardianship* that allows a person to specify wishes for the partner to make personal and business decisions in the event of incapacitation; (e) *a last will and testament* that allows a person to choose what happens to property and children in the event of death (without a will all property and sometimes joint property goes to relatives); (f) if available, *a stand-by guardian* appointed by a terminally ill patient that allows the patient to assign someone to decide under what circumstances and by whom any children will be cared for upon death; and (g) *a revocable living trust* that provides a way to avoid probate (a court proceeding) (Gruskin, 1999). Although practitioners cannot give legal counsel, they need to know about these various legal protections. They should know the legal terms and what each addresses. They should also have a list of legal resources available for clients, as well as Web sites and books (Kuehlwein & Gottschalk, 2000). One of the recommended books is *A Legal Guide for Lesbian and Gay Couples* by Curry, Clifford, and Hertz (2002).

BREAKUPS

Separation distress is the same for all couples (Kurdek, 1997; see Chapter 6). Interventions for grieving heterosexual partners, then, are applicable to gay and lesbian couples. The differences are that when gay and lesbian partnerships dissolve, no legal guidelines govern the division of property. Resolution of disputes depends upon on the goodwill of the partners though partners in dissolved relationships may not have goodwill (Hartman, 1996). Same–sex gender couples should prepare an accord in advance of separation. This agreement can include how the couple will divide property that they buy together and their other merged assets. With a formal financial strategy to specify how to divide property and other resources, couples are less likely to experience an acrimonious dispute (Chambers, 1998). Without prior agreements in the event of separation, mediation is an alternative (Hartman, 1996).

ISSUES EXPERIENCED BY COUPLES WITH BISEXUAL MEMBERS

When one or both members of a couple identifies as bisexual, practice becomes even more complex (Guidry, 1999; Rust, 1996). Following Deacon, Reinke, and Viers (1998), the issues that bisexual clients and their heterosexual partners might want to work on can be divided into behavioral, cognitive, and affective categories. In the *behavioral* category, potential issues include alteration of the family structure; disclosure to children, family, and friends; integration of a gay or lesbian partner into the marriage; feelings of rejection and betrayal by one's marital partner; and the use of money for outside relationships (Buxton, 1994). Couples may need to learn problem-solving skills to work out a new structure and set of rules (Deacon et al., 1998). Once a bisexual partner begins experiencing sex outside the primary link, sexual difficulties may arise within the primary link that may also need to be addressed (Coleman, 1985). In the *cognitive* category, issues can include perceptions of sexual identity, assumptions regarding discrimination and internalized oppression, standards regarding monogamy and multiple partners, and attributions and automatic thoughts such as blaming relationship difficulties on a partner's bisexual orientation. In the *affective* category, issues include depression and anger over unfulfilled desires and jealousy over outside relationships (Deacon et al., 1998). Examples of interventions for several of these issues appear below.

Handling jealousy. A key issue in working with mixed-orientation couples is the jealousy of the monogamous partner. Jealousy is rooted in a sense of insecurity or fear of losing the link (Matteson, 1996a). Bisexual attractions in one of the partners raise understandable issues of insecurity in the other partner, even when the underlying relationship is strong (Stokes & Damon, 1995). A constructive focus would be to explore what the bisexual partner can do to clarify his or her commitment to the primary link (Matteson, 1996a).

Contracts and rules. In the context of a link that includes any nonmonogamous partners, the couple should develop ground rules together to provide explicit guidelines for what the partners can and cannot do with relationships outside the marriage. Practitioners can assist with contract writing and negotiating what to include. Mixed-orientation partnerships usually require detailed and individually tailored contracts. They must also elucidate safe-sex practices. These rules should be readily open to discussion and revision (Matteson, 1995; Paul, 1992). Another negotiable accord is how much a heterosexual partner knows or wishes to know about the bisexual partner's sexual activities with others. Sometimes an accord develops during explicit negotiations between the two parties whereas other couples participate in no explicit discussion of this issue, maintaining secrets about outside sexual activities. Practitioners should challenge unilateral secrets (Matteson, 1995).

Many couples can develop stable, satisfying relationships with relationship contracts (Matteson, 1995). Couples may need to learn problem-solving skills to work out a new structure and rules. This includes training in identifying and clarifying the issues, identifying possible solutions, negotiating and agreeing on a solution, using a trial period for trying out the solution, assessing the result, and making alterations (Deacon et al., 1998). As previously indicated, rarely can a couple with a bisexual member shift the marriage from a traditional one to an open relationship without agreements that the marital partner will remain primary to the bisexual partner (for example, Weinberg, Williams, & Pryor, 1994). The couple members should discuss the primacy of the marriage and their commitment to it (Coleman, 1985). Still, open relationships are difficult to maintain and often falter because of the couple's inability to handle the complexity of demands, jealousy issues, and the lack of social support (Matteson, 1995).

Balancing act. Often, when a bisexual person seeks a practitioner, balance is destabilized by internal or external processes (Matteson, 1996a). Practitioners may need to assist a bisexual marriage partner in balancing multiple partners. No matter what the arrangement between the partners, however, this not an easy task. It requires communication skills, trust between partners, and the ability of the heterosexual partner to handle jealousy. It also requires skill in time management (Paul, 1992).

HIV/AIDS

The discussion here applies to both bisexual and gay persons especially if they are not committed to monogamy (Stokes, Miller, & Mundhenk, 1998). Some HIV-positive men do not always disclose their status to sexual partners, including steady ones. Some think that disclosure is unnecessary because they use condoms. Practitioners should take strong exception to this practice because all partners, whether bisexual, heterosexual, gay, or lesbian, have the right to decide for themselves if the risk is acceptable for them. If regular intercourse occurs without a condom or without disclosure, the practitioner should insist that the client inform partners. If the client refuses, "duty-to-protect" laws in some states require practitioners to notify persons who unknowingly are at physical risk by the client's behavior (Matteson, 1996a). Yet, these laws may be ambiguous about their applicability to the practice of safe sex. Before informing partners, therefore, practitioners should consult other practitioners and attain legal counsel (Hughes & Friedman, 1994; Marks, 1993).

FAMILIES

Generally, practitioners will intervene with gay and lesbian families as they do with all families. Yet, practitioners must keep some special issues in mind when working with gay and lesbian parents. Although they have as many social skills and psychological strengths as heterosexual parents, they live in an environment hostile to them and they do not have suitable legal protection for themselves or their families (Gonsiorek, 1996).

Some lesbian and gay parents are also still working on their own identity and disclosure issues, especially those whose families started out in heterosexual marriages. They may be struggling about how to tell former marital partners about their sexual identity and their children who assumed that both of their parents were heterosexual (Martin, 1998). Having children can serve as an "outing" for lesbian or gay parents to their extended family members and society at large. Such exposure can provoke anxiety, to say the least (Rothberg & Weinstein, 1996). If involved in custody battles, this can also strain couples (Rutter & Schwartz, 1996; see Chapter 7 for further discussion of disclosure and custody issues).

Practitioners need to be knowledgeable about information that can help lesbian and gay families chart new territory. Martin's (1993) *The Lesbian and Gay Parenting Handbook* is an excellent resource, offering extensive lists of resources across the nation as well as practical advice about adoption, disclosure, and family life. This detailed guide can help both practitioner and client. Other useful resources include *For Lesbian Parents* (Johnson & O'Connor, 2001) and *The Queer Parent's Primer* (Brill, 2001). It is helpful to provide children with a general explanation about two persons of the same sex–gender caring for each other. Various books are also useful to educate them, for example, *Daddy's Roommate* (Willhoite, 2000).

Practitioners must also be able to help these parents develop constructive coping mechanisms for themselves and for helping their children cope with stress and other challenges (Baum, 1996; Bigner, 1996). Children may fear embarrassment and ridicule or stigmatization and repudiation by peers (Rothschild, 1991). Often teenagers are able to identify other teenagers who are "gay friendly" and get some support and friendship from them. It is also helpful to know other children who have lesbian or gay parents. A support group for children in this situation can provide friendships and stress relief (Martin, 1998; Tasker & Golombok, 1997). There may be local support groups of this type. If a child of a lesbian, gay, bisexual, or transgender parent cannot find friends in the same situation locally, he or she may be able to connect with a pen pal on the Children of Lesbians and Gays Everywhere Web site at: http://www.colage.org/ or join one or more of the recommended e-mail lists on this site. This site also provides various activities going on in certain cities for children of lesbian and gay parents. James (2002) suggested that another benefit of support groups of children of lesbian and gay parents is learning how to face social injustice. They can learn ways to identify and to confront prejudice and discrimination.

Because society does not generally recognize gay and lesbian families, it is especially important for them to develop rituals, traditions, and other ways to celebrate their family successes (Laird, 1994). It is also important for them to seek out other gay and lesbian families so they and their children can feel that their family is not unusual. Practitioners should emphasize the need for both celebrations and interchanges with other gay and lesbian families.

School Systems

Lesbian, gay, and bisexual parents are often invisible or not served well by the school systems their children attend. Ryan and Martin (2000) made numerous recommendations for ways these systems can meet the needs of families with sexually subordinated parents. First, school personnel must discard traditional ideas about family structures and accept that a child's parents meet two criteria: they intend to be parents and they intend to take on the responsibilities and functions of parents. Other recommendations include:

- antibias training for school personnel that challenges prejudice about sexually subordinated persons with educational and experiential material
- specific education about the issues LGB facing families with sexually subordinated parents
- establishment, dissemination, and discussion of administrative policy that affirms LGB sexual orientation, sex–gender expression, and diverse family structures
- training in how to talk with the children of these families (useful video materials are available such as "Both of My Mom's Names Are Judy," distributed by the Lesbian and Gay Parents Association in San Francisco)
- curricula that include education on family diversity and sexual orientation starting as early as prekindergarten
- discussions among professionals and parents in which they report and address concerns
- use of inclusive language in the school environment such as lesbian- or gay-parented families

- statements welcoming all family structures and parents of all sexual orientations and sex-gender expressions in school brochures and on information sheets
- replace "mother's name" and "father's name" with "parent's name" on all school forms
- information forms and school interviews should ask the question, "Is there anyone else involved in your child's life regularly who assumes a role similar to a parent?"
- recognition of parent's different comfort levels with disclosures; school personnel working with them should assure confidentiality in terms of employers, other parents in the school, other teachers in the school, and ex-partners.

If the first best step has yet to be made (a districtwide policy affirming these families), the next best beginning step is diversity awareness programs. Eventually, more schools will realize that diversity is an educational strength. Practitioners can participate in advocacy in schools and in training school personnel. In addition, practitioners can help parents be assertive in seeking support from teachers and administrators.

Community Resources for Parents

Practitioners need to know the resources for parent support in the lesbian and gay community (Hess & Hess, 1998). Support groups for parents can help them feel less isolated and provide social and psychological validation, and benefits from the experiences of others (Kuehlwein & Gottschalk, 2000). Many communities provide social and support groups for gay and lesbian parents and their children (Baum, 1996). An example is Family Pride Coalition (formerly Gay and Lesbian Parents Coalition International) that is an international advocacy and support organization for gay, lesbian, and bisexual parents, their partners, and their children, with over 100 local chapters across the United States and in several other countries.[1] This organization provides information on health care, legal, and other resources for each state. Patterson (2002) also recommended the expansion of services to public libraries that can build collections of materials on lesbian and gay parenting, educational institutions that can include accurate information in curriculums, and religious groups that can educate members of their congregations about lesbian and gay parenting.

Legal Issues

Practitioners must be aware of all the legal challenges facing lesbian and gay parents. Custody is the most common legal challenge—but practitioners must bear in mind that custody disputes arise not only from heterosexual divorce but also from the separation of lesbian and gay couples (Chambers, 1998). Other legal issues include adoption law (Connolly, 1998; Reilly, 1996), inheritance law for the partners and coparents (Katzen, 1997), and civil rights and hate

---

[1] The Family Pride Coalition is available online at: http://www.familypride.org. Also, Children of Lesbians and Gays Everywhere (COLAGE), mentioned above, is a project of the Family Pride Coalition. In addition to the services it provides for children of lesbian and gay parents, COLAGE provides information that challenges the myths held by the courts, media, and the general public about gay and lesbian families. Parents, Families, and Friends of Lesbians and Gays (PFLAG) is also a community resource available in many communities for families and children. PFLAG is available online at http://www.pflag.org. Another web site for LGBT couples and families that provides information about services and resources is Alternative Family Institute at: http/www.altfamily.org

crime legislation (Hartman, 1996). Currently partners are not eligible for insurance benefits (Hixson, 1997), and rarely can partners and coparents adopt the children that couples are raising together. Practitioners need to know the legal status of LGB families in their community and state, as well as have available a list of attorneys who are knowledgeable and affirmative.[2]

Practitioners must also stay up-to-date with pertinent policies and legislation to counsel their clients and advocate for policy changes that will strengthen these families (Hess & Hess, 1998). They can advocate for the rights of nonlegal parents within as well as outside their agencies, such as lobbying legislators to pass laws that will accord these parents legal rights (McClellan, 2001). Recently, several professional organizations, including NASW, filed friend-of-the court briefs, involving three cases focused on child welfare and the rights of lesbian and gay parents to attain, for example, second-parent adoptions. NASW is acting on a new policy statement pressing the association to participate in coalitions to get legal rights for LGB couples and parents (Vallianatos, 2002). This is one of the greatest needs of lesbian and gay families: activism to promote social and political change that include the same legal rights as heterosexual families, equal access to medical care, and protection from hate crimes and other forms of harassment (Patterson, 2002).

In February 2002 a significant policy statement was issued by the American Academy of Pediatricians, the largest organization of pediatricians. It strongly favored adoption of one's partner's children in gay and lesbian couples and urged courts to stop using sexual orientation as grounds to deny such adoptions. The benefits of these adoptions were listed as protecting the custody rights of the second parent if the first parent becomes ill or dies; protecting the custody and visitation rights of the second parent if the couple breaks up; provision of eligibility of health benefits for the child from both parent's workplaces; provision of legal grounds for important consents such as medical services by both parents; and provision of eligibility for entitlements such as social security survivor benefits. Several other organizations have already adopted this position on adoption including the American Psychological Association, the American Academy of Child and Adolescent Psychiatry (Hausman, 2002), and the National Association of Social Workers (Vallianatos, 2002).

SUMMARY

- Internalized oppression resulting from the pervasiveness of heterosexism can affect couples in several ways: devaluing of same sex–gender relationships, thinking that same sex–gender relationships cannot last, and tightening the boundaries around a couple so that the partners are the only ones meeting each other's needs.
- Gay and lesbian partners must negotiate similar tasks faced by heterosexual couples of living together and, sometimes, raising a family together. Often, practitioners can employ the same techniques. Yet, certain practice issues are unique to gay and lesbian couples, such as coming out, disclosure, and sex–gender roles.

---

[2] The National Gay and Lesbian Task Force provides an overview of state laws as well as assistance in reaching LGB-affirmative lawyers and lawmakers (Matthews & Lease, 2000). It is available online at http://www.ngltf.org. Other legal resources include Lambda Legal Defense at http://www.lambdalegal.org/cgi-bin/iowa/issues and the National Center for Lesbian Rights at: http://www.nclrights.org/

- Breaking up is the same painful process for all. Many gay and lesbian persons endure this process alone because no one else in their lives knows of their link or understands its profound nature. Sometimes, practitioners are the only persons gay and lesbian persons can turn to. Practitioners can support, educate, and encourage problem solving and closure for persons devastated by the loss of a partner.
- Practice with bisexual partners often focuses on complex issues including negotiating the rules accompanying bisexuality in a marriage and the roles of multiple partners. Practitioners must teach, role play, and model communication and boundary settings that will allow couples to create rewarding relationships. Bisexual partners must also reassure their mates of their loyalty and their devotion to the primary link.
- Practice with gay and lesbian families with children will often focus on issues related to blended families, internalized oppression, school systems, community resources, legal issues, and how to help the children understand their family. One of the major roles practitioners can take with these families is that of an advocate in heterosexist institutions.

CHAPTER 11
REFERENCES

American Psychological Association, Committee on Lesbian and Gay Concerns. (1991). Avoiding heterosexist bias in language. *American Psychologist, 46*, 937–974.

Appleby, G. A., & Anastas, J. W. (1998). *Not just a passing phase: Social work with gay, lesbian, and bisexual people.* New York: Columbia University Press.

Appleby, P. R., Miller, L. C., & Rothspan, S. (1999). The paradox of trust for male couples: When risking is a part of loving. *Personal Relationships, 6*, 81–93.

Baum, M. I. (1996). Gays and lesbians choosing to be parents. In C. J. Alexander (Ed.), *Gay and lesbian mental health: A sourcebook for practitioners* (pp. 113–126). New York: Haworth Park Press.

Berzon, B. (1988). *Permanent partners.* New York: E. P. Dutton.

Bigner, J. (1996). Working with gay fathers. In J. Laird & R. Green (Eds.), *Lesbians and gays in couples and families* (pp. 370–403). San Francisco: Jossey-Bass.

Blumstein, P., & Schwartz, P. (1983). *American couples.* New York: William Morrow.

Bowen, M. (1978). *Family therapy in clinical practice.* New York: Aronson.

Brill, S. A. (2001). *The queer parent's primer: A lesbian and gay families' guide to navigating the straight world.* Oakland, CA: New Harbinger.

Brown, L. S. (1994). *Subversive dialogues: Theory in feminist therapy.* New York: Basic Books.

Brown, L. S. (1996). Ethical concerns with sexual minority patients. In R. P. Cabaj & T. S. Stein (Eds.), *Textbook of homosexuality and mental health* (pp. 897–916). Washington, DC: American Psychiatric Press.

Burch, B. (1982). Psychological merger in lesbian couples: A joint ego psychological and systems approach. *Family Therapy, 9*, 201–208.

Burch, B. (1986). Psychotherapy and the dynamics of merger in lesbian couples. In T. S. Stein & C. J. Cohen (Eds.), *Contemporary perspectives on psychotherapy with lesbians and gay men* (pp. 57–71). New York: Plenum Press.

Burch, B. (1987). Barriers to intimacy: Conflicts over power, dependency, and nurturing in lesbian relationships. In Boston Lesbian Psychologies Collective (Eds.), *Lesbian psychologies: Explorations and challenges* (pp. 127–141). Chicago: University of Illinois Press.

Butler, M., & Clarke, J. (1991). Couple therapy with homosexual men. In D. Hooper & W. Dryder (Eds.), *Couple therapy: A handbook* (pp.196–216). Philadelphia: Open University.

Buxton, A. P. (1994). *The other side of the closet: The coming-out crisis for straight spouses and families.* New York: John Wiley & Sons.

Cabaj, R. P. (1988). Gay and lesbian couples: Lessons on human intimacy. *Psychiatric Annals, 18,* 21–25.

Cabaj, R. P., & Klinger, R. L. (1996). Psychotherapeutic interventions with lesbian and gay couples. In R. P. Cabaj & T. S. Stein (Eds.), *Textbook of homosexuality and mental health* (pp. 485–502). Washington, DC: American Psychiatric Press.

Chambers, D. (1998). Lesbian divorce: a commentary on legal issues. *American Journal of Orthopsychiatry, 68,* 420–423.

Chodorow, N. (1978). *The reproduction of mothering: Psychoanalysis and the sociology of gender.* Berkeley: University of California Press.

Clunis, D. M., & Green, G. D. (2000). *Lesbian couples: A guide to creating healthy relationships.* Seattle: Seal Press.

Coleman, E. (1985). Integration of male bisexuality and marriage. *Journal of Homosexuality, 11,* 189–207.

Colgan, P. (1988). Treatment of identity and intimacy issues in gay males. In E. Coleman (Ed.), *Integrated identity for gay men and lesbians: Psychotherapeutic approaches for emotional well-being* (pp. 101–123). New York: Harrington Park.

Connolly, C. (1998). The description of gay and lesbian families in second-parent adoptions cases. *Behavioral Sciences and the Law, 16,* 225–236.

Curry, H., Clifford, D., & Hertz, F. (2002). *A legal guide for lesbian and gay couples* (11th ed.). Berkeley, CA: Nolo Press.

Deacon, S. A., Reinke, L., & Viers, D. (1998). Cognitive-behavioral therapy for bisexual couples: Expanding the realms of therapy. *American Journal of Family Therapy, 24,* 242–258.

Forstein, M. (1994). Psychotherapy with gay male couples: Loving in the time of AIDS. In S. A. Caldwell, R. A. Burnham, & M. Forstein (Eds.), *Therapists in the front line: Psychotherapy with gay men in the age of AIDS.* Washington, DC: American Psychiatric Press.

Garnets, L. D., Hancock, K. A., Cochran, S. D., Goodchilds, J., & Peplau, L. A. (1991). Issues in psychotherapy with lesbians and gay men: A survey of psychologists. *American Psychologist, 46,* 964–972.

Gendlin, E. (1981). *Focusing.* New York: Bantam Books.

George, K. D., & Behrendt, A. E. (1987). Therapy for male couples experiencing relationship problems and sexual problems. *Journal of Homosexuality, 14,* 77–88.

Gilligan, C. (1982). *In a different voice: Psychological theory and women's development.* Cambridge, MA: Harvard University Press.

Gonsiorek, J. C. (1996). Mental health and sexual orientation. In R. C. Savin-Williams & K. M. Cohen (Eds.), *The lives of lesbian, gay men, and bisexuals: Children to adults* (pp. 462–478). Fort Worth, TX: Harcourt Brace.

Gonsiorek, J. C., & Weinrich, J. D. (1991). The definition and scope of sexual orientation. In J. C. Gonsiorek & J. Weinrich (Eds.), *Homosexuality: Research implications for public policy* (pp. 1–12). Newbury Park, CA: Sage Publications.

Goodrich, T. J. (1988). *Feminist family therapy: A case book.* New York: W. W. Norton.

Granvold, D. K., & Martin, J. I. (1999). Family therapy with gay and lesbian clients. In C. Franklin & C. Jordan (Eds.), *Family practice: Brief and systemic methods* (pp. 299–320). Pacific Grove, CA: Brooks/Cole.

Gray, D., & Isensee, R. (1996). Balancing autonomy and intimacy in lesbian and gay relationships. In C. J. Alexander (Ed.), *Gay and lesbian mental health: A sourcebook for practitioners* (pp. 95–114). Binghamton, NY: Harrington Park Press.

Green, R.-J., Bettinger, M., & Zacks, E. (1996). Are lesbian couples fused and gay male couples disengaged? Questioning gender straight jackets. In J. Laird & R.-J. Green (Eds.), *Lesbians and gays in couples and families* (pp. 185–231). San Francisco: Jossey-Bass.

Greene, B. (1994). Lesbian women of color: Triple jeopardy. In L. Comas-Diaz & B. Greene (Eds.), *Women of color* (pp. 389–427). New York: Guilford Press.

Greene, K., Causby, V., & Miller, D. H. (1999). The nature and function of fusion in the dynamics of lesbian relationships. *Affilia, 14,* 78–97.

Gruskin, E. P. (1999). *Treating lesbians and bisexual women: Challenges and strategies for health professionals.* Thousand Oaks, CA: Sage Publications.

Guidry, L. L. (1999). Clinical intervention with bisexuals: A contextualized understanding. *Professional Psychology: Research and Practice, 30*, 22–26.

Hall, M. (1987). Sex therapy with lesbian couples: A four stage approach. *Journal of Homosexuality, 14*, 137–156.

Hartman, A. (1996). Social policy as a context for lesbian and gay families: The political is personal. In J. Laird & R.-J. Green (Eds.), *Lesbians and gays in couples and families* (pp. 69–85). San Francisco: Jossey-Bass.

Hausman, K. (2002). Pediatricians support adoption by gay partners. *Psychiatric News, 37*, 4.

Hess, P., & Hess, H. (1998). Values and ethics in social work practice with lesbian and gay persons. In G. P. Mallon (Ed.), *Foundations of social work practice with lesbian and gay persons* (pp. 31–46). New York: Haworth Press.

Hixson, T. (1997). Public and private recognition of the families of lesbians and gay men. *Journal of Gender and the Law, 5*, 501–523.

Hughes, R. B., & Freidman, A. L. (1994, October). AIDS-related ethical and legal issues for mental health professionals. *Journal of Mental Health Counseling, 16*, 445–458.

Hunt, B. (1993). What counselors need to know about counseling gay men and lesbians. *Counseling and Human Development, 26*, 1–12.

Iasenza, S. (1999). The big lie: Debunking lesbian bed death. *In the Family, 4*, 8–11, 20.

Igartua, K. J. (1998). Therapy with lesbian couples: The issues and the interventions. *Canadian Journal of Psychiatry, 43*, 391–396.

James, S. E. (2002). Clinical themes in gay- and lesbian-parented adoptive families. *Clinical Child Psychology and Psychiatry, 7*, 475–486.

Johnson, S. M., & O'Connor, E. (2001). *For lesbian parents: Your guide to helping your family grow up happy, healthy, and proud.* New York: Guilford Press.

Katzen, H. (1997). Valuing our differences: The recognition of lesbian and gay relationships. *Australian & New Zealand Journal of Family Therapy, 18*, 1–9.

Kaufman, P. A., Harrison, E., & Hyde, M. L. (1984). Distancing and intimacy in lesbian relationships. *American Journal of Psychiatry, 141*, 530–533.

Kleinberg, S., & Zorn, P. (1995). Rekindling the flame: A therapeutic approach to strengthening lesbian relationships. In J. M. Glassgold & S. Iasenza (Eds.), *Lesbians and psychoanalysis:*

Revolutions in theory and practice (pp. 125–143). New York: Free Press.

Krestan, J., & Bepko, C. (1980). The problem of fusion in the lesbian relationship. *Family Process, 19,* 277–290.

Kuehlwein, K. T., & Gottschalk, D. I. (2000). Legal and psychological issues confronting lesbian, bisexual, and gay couples and families. In F. W. Kaslow (Ed.), *Handbook of couples and family forensic: A sourcebook for mental health and legal professionals* (pp. 164–187). New York: John Wiley & Sons.

Kurdek, L. A. (1988). Perceived social support in gays and lesbians in cohabiting relationships. *Journal of Personality and Social Psychology, 54,* 504–509.

Kurdek, L. A. (1997). Adjustment to relationship dissolution in gay, lesbian, and heterosexual partners. *Personal Relationships, 4,* 145–161.

Kurdek, L. A., & Schmitt, J. P. (1987). Perceived emotional support from family and friends in members of homosexual, married, and heterosexual cohabitating couples. *Journal of Homosexuality, 14,* 57–68.

Laird, J. (1994). Lesbian families: A cultural perspective. In M. P. Mirkin (Ed.), *Women in context: Toward a feminist reconstruction of psychotherapy* (pp. 118–148). New York: Guilford Press.

Laird, J. (1996). Family-centered practice with lesbian and gay families. Families in Society: *Journal of Contemporary Human Services, 77,* 559–572.

Lesbian and Gay Parents' Association, San Francisco. (1994). *Both of my mom's names are Judy.* San Diego: Family Pride Coalition.

Loulan, J. (1984). *Lesbian sex.* San Francisco: Spinsters Ink.

Loulan, J. (1987). *Lesbian passion: Loving ourselves and each other.* San Francisco: Spinsters/Aunt Lute.

MacDonald, B. J. (1998). Issues in therapy with gay and lesbian couples. *Journal of Sex & Marital Therapy, 24,* 165–190.

Markowitz, L. M. (1991, January/February). Homosexuality: Are we still in the dark? *Family Therapy Networker,* 26–29, 31–35.

Marks, R. (Ed.). (1993, April). Focus: *A guide to AIDS research and counseling* (Publication of AIDS Health Project, No. 8). San Francisco: University of California.

Martin, A. (1993). *The lesbian and gay parenting handbook.* New York: HarperCollins.

Martin, A. (1998). Clinical issues in psychotherapy with lesbian-, gay-, and bisexual-parented families. In C. J. Patterson & A. R. D'Augelli (Eds.), *Lesbian, gay, and bisexual identities in families: Psychological perspectives* (pp. 270–291). London: Oxford University Press.

Matteson, D. R. (1995). Counseling with bisexuals. *Individual Psychology, 51,* 144-159.

Matteson, D. R. (1996a). Counseling and psychotherapy with bisexual and exploring clients. In B. A. Firestein (Ed.), Bisexuality: *The psychology and politics of an invisible minority* (pp. 185–213). Thousand Oaks, CA: Sage Publications.

Matteson, D. R. (1996b). Psychotherapy with bisexual individuals. In R. P. Cabaj & T. S. Stein (Eds.), *Textbook of homosexuality and mental health* (pp. 433–449). Washington, DC: American Psychiatric Press.

Matthews, C. R., & Lease, S. H. (2000). Focus on lesbian, gay, and bisexual families. In R. M. Perez, K. A. DeBord, & K. J. Bieschke (Eds.), *Handbook of counseling and psychotherapy with lesbian, gay, and bisexual clients* (pp. 249–273). Washington, DC: American Psychological Association.

McCandlish, B. (1982). Therapeutic issues with lesbian clients. *Journal of Homosexuality, 7,* 71–78.

McClellan, D. L. (2001). The "other-mother" and second parent adoption. *Journal of Gay & Lesbian Social Services, 13,* 1–21.

McVinney, L. D. (1998). Social work practice with gay male couples. In G. P. Mallon (Ed.), *Foundations of social work practice with lesbian and gay persons* (pp. 209–227). New York: Haworth Press.

McWhirter, D. P., & Mattison, A. M. (1984). *The male couple.* Englewood Cliffs, NJ: Prentice Hall.

McWhirter, D. P., & Mattison, A. W. (1996). Male couples. In R. P. Cabaj & T. S. Stein (Eds.), *Textbook of homosexuality and mental health* (pp. 819–837). Washington, DC: American Psychiatric Press.

Murphy, B. C. (1994). Difference and diversity: Gay and lesbian couples. *Social Services for Gay and Lesbian Couples, 1,* 5–31.

Nichols, M. (1982). The treatment of inhibited sexual desire (ISD) in lesbian couples. *Women & Therapy, 1,* 49–66.

Nichols, M. (1995). Sexual desire disorder in lesbian-feminist couples: The intersections of therapy and politics. In R. C. Rosen & S. R. Leiblum (Eds.), *Case studies in sex therapy* (pp. 161–175). New York: Guilford Press.

Okun, B. F. (1996). *Understanding diverse families: What practitioners need to know*. New York: Guilford Press.

Paradis, B. A. (1991). Seeking intimacy and integration: Gay men in the era of AIDS. *Smith College Studies in Social Work, 61*, 260–274.

Patterson, C. L. (2002). Lesbian and gay parenting. In M. H. Bornstein (Ed.), *Handbook of parenting* (2nd ed., pp. 317–338). Mahwah, NJ: Lawrence Erlbaum.

Paul, J. P. (1992). "Biphobia" and the construction of a bisexual identity. In M. Shernoff & W. A. Scott (Eds.), *The sourcebook on lesbian/gay health care* (2nd ed., pp. 259–264). Washington, DC: National Lesbian/Gay Health Foundation.

Peplau, L. A. (1993). Lesbian and gay relationships. In L. D. Garnets & D. C. Kimmel (Eds.), *Psychological perspectives on lesbian & gay male experiences* (pp. 395–419). New York: Columbia University Press.

Pesso, A. (1969). *Movement in psychotherapy: Psychomotor techniques and training*. New York: New York University Press.

Reece, R. (1987). Causes and treatments of sexual desire discrepancies in male couples. *Journal of Homosexuality, 14*, 157–172.

Reilly, M. E., & Lynch, J. M. (1990). Power-sharing in lesbian relationships. *Journal of Homosexuality, 19*, 1–30.

Reilly, T. (1996). Gay and lesbian adoptions. *Journal of Sociology and Social Welfare, 23*, 94–115.

Robson, R. (1995). Our relationships and their laws. In K. Jay (Ed.), *Dyke life: From growing up to growing old, a celebration of the lesbian experience* (pp. 127–140). New York: Basic Books.

Roth, S. (1985). Psychotherapy issues with lesbian couples. *Journal of Marital and Family Therapy, 11*, 273–286.

Roth, S. (1989). Psychotherapy with lesbian couples: Individual issues, female socialization and the social context. In M. McGoldrick, C. Anderson, & F. Walsh (Eds.), *Women in families: A framework for family therapy* (pp. 286–307). New York: W. W. Norton.

Rothberg, B., & Weinstein, D. L. (1996). A primer on lesbian and gay families. *Journal of Gay & Lesbian Social Services, 4*, 55–68.

Rothschild, M. (1991). Life as improvisation. In B. Sang, J. Warshow, & A. Smith (Eds.), *Lesbians at midlife: The creative transition* (pp. 91–98). San Francisco: Spinsters.

Rust, P. C. (1996). Finding a sexual identity and community: Therapeutic implications and cultural assumptions in scientific models of coming out. In E. D. Rothblum & L. A. Bond (Eds.), *Preventing heterosexim and homophobia* (pp. 87–123). Thousand Oaks, CA: Sage Publications.

Rutter, V., & Schwartz, P. (1996). Same-sex couples: Courtship, commitment, context. In A. W. Auhagen (Ed.), *The diversity of human relationships* (pp. 197–226). New York: Cambridge University Press.

Ryan, D., & Martin, A. (2000). Lesbian, gay, bisexual, and transgender parents in the school systems. *School Psychology Review, 29,* 207–216.

Sang, B. E. (1992). Psychotherapy with lesbians: Some observations and tentative generalizations. In W. R. Dynes (Ed.), *Encyclopedia of homosexuality* (pp. 260–269). New York: Garland.

Schnarch, D. M. (1991). *Constructing the sexual crucible.* New York: W. W. Norton.

Schreurs, K.M.G., & Buunk, B. P. (1996). Closeness, autonomy, equity, and relationship satisfaction in lesbian couples. *Psychology of Women Quarterly, 20,* 577–592.

Smith, R. G., & Brown, R. A. (1998). The impact of social support on gay male couples. *Journal of Homosexuality, 33,* 39–61.

Stokes, J., & Damon, W. (1995). Counseling and psychotherapy for bisexual men. *Directions in Mental Health Counseling, 5,* 4–15.

Stokes, J. P., Miller, R. L., & Mundhenk, R. (1998). Toward an understanding of behaviorally bisexual men: The influence of context and culture. *Canadian Journal of Human Sexuality, 7,* 1–12.

Tasker, F., & Golombok, S. (1997). *Growing up in a lesbian family.* New York: Guilford Press.

Vallianatos, C. (2002, January). Gay parents' rights backed. *NASW News, 47,* 5.

Vetri, D. (1998). Almost everything you always wanted to know about lesbians and gay men, their families, and the law. *Southern University Law Review, 26,* 1–68.

Weinberg, M. S., Williams, C. J., & Pryor, D. W. (1994). *Dual attraction: Understanding bisexuality.* New York: Oxford University Press.

Werner, P. D., & Green, R.-J. (1989). *California inventory for family assessment* (CIFA). Unpublished manuscript, California School of Professional Psychology, Alameda.

Willhoite, M. (2000). *Daddy's roommate*. Los Angeles: Alyson Wonderland.

Wood, J. T., & Inman, C. C. (1993). In a different mode: Masculine styles of communicating closeness. *Journal of Applied Community Research, 2*, 279–295.

Zacks, E., Green, R., & Morrow, J. (1988). Comparing lesbian and heterosexual couples on the circumplex model: An initial investigation. *Family Process, 27*, 471–484.

CHAPTER 12
PRACTICE AT THE INSTITUTIONAL, COMMUNITY, AND MACROCULTURAL LEVELS

What can be done in workplaces to make them safe for and supportive of LGBT workers?

What can be done on college campuses to provide safety for LGBT students and a welcoming environment for them?

How can an affirmative environment for LGBT students in public schools be created?

What are important guidelines for working with LGBT persons in their communities?

What are the obstacles for combating heterosexism at the macro level?

CHANGE AT THE INSTITUTIONAL LEVEL

Workplace

True equality for LGBT persons in the workplace requires an atmosphere where they can be open with no fear of discrimination, harassment, or violence (Byrne, 1993; Kitzinger, 1991). Top management's commitment to affirmative actions as well as positive attitudes from supervisors, managers, and coworkers are needed to ensure a supportive work environment (Ankeny, 1991; Lee & Brown, 1993). Numerous actions can contribute to an affirmative workplace (Brooks, 1991; Byrne, 1993; Jacobs, 1994; Kitzinger, 1991; Kronenberger, 1991; Lee & Brown, 1993; Levine & Leonard, 1984; Mickens, 1994; Woolsey, 1991), including those listed below:

- Follow a goals and timetables model—goals include numerical targets for hiring or promotion of qualified LGBT workers, and timetables represent the deadlines for achieving the goals.
- Develop an explicit policy prohibiting discrimination based on sexual orientation or sex–gender expression.
- Establish zero tolerance for heterosexism in the workplace, including antilesbian and gay jokes and derogatory comments and assumptions.
- Intervene when difficulties arise such as verbal harassment from heterosexual workers because of the perception that LGBT workers receive special treatment.
- Conduct and require participation in diversity training programs and workshops to change attitudes and sensitize employees to others' perspectives and concerns.
- Foster contact between lesbian, gay, bisexual, transgender, and heterosexual coworkers, which can be one of the most powerful means of reducing heterosexist prejudice in the workplace.
- Include lesbian and gay domestic partnerships and nonbiological children in employee benefit packages and family leave policies.

- Implement strong employment policies and practices that encourage closeted employees to make disclosures while at the same time respecting their privacy rights.
- Provide LGBT affirmative contacts in the organization.
- Talk with open LGBT workers to identify their concerns.
- Actively encourage support groups for LGBT workers.
- Provide information on organizations helpful to LGBT workers (for example, Gay Teachers Association, Lesbian and Gay People in Medicine, High Tech Gays).

Although protective legislation at the national level is critical to reducing discrimination in workplaces, even more important is a supportive or LGBT-friendly workplace. Ragins and Cornwell (2001) reported that this factor was key to whether or not discrimination was perceived in their national sample of 534 lesbian and gay employees. Particularly important were written policies that included sexual orientation in definitions of diversity, forbade discrimination because of sexual orientation, and provided same sex–gender domestic partner benefits. Also standing out among policies and practices that showed movement beyond slogans or just talking about nondiscrimination was the inclusion of same sex–gender partners in company social events.

Some organizations are now rating companies on their nondiscrimination policies. The National Gay and Lesbian Task Force (NGLTF) maintains a list of companies that have a stated position on the sexual orientation of employees (NGLTF, 1991). Between 1976 and 1981, this organization surveyed more than 850 firms including the top 500 American industrial corporations (*Fortune 500*) and more than 350 leading nonindustrial firms involved in areas such as finance, insurance, and retail sales. Of the original number of firms, 238 (28 percent) responded. Ratings of personnel policies ranged from 1 (specific statements regarding nondiscrimination because of sexual orientation) to 6 (policies do not address the issue). Of those companies that responded, 61 percent scored 1 or 2 on the scale. Companies in these categories were mostly the largest firms in the country. About half (51 percent) of the top 100 firms reported nondiscrimination policies for gay and lesbian employees as did the top 10 *Fortune 500* companies. Only 30 percent of all *Fortune 500* companies, however, reported similar policies regarding sexual orientation (NGLTF, 1991). The reasons that 72 percent of the organizations did not respond are unknown, but possibly these workplaces are not supportive of gay and lesbian employees (Elliott, 1993). Other resources include Mickens' (1994) assessment of the 100 best companies for lesbian and gay persons and Chojnacki and Gelberg's (1995) methodology for assessing workplace positions on discrimination.

If management has yet to propose affirmative changes, individuals or small groups within an organization can start an employee resource group. Generally, these resource groups provide some or all the following functions: (a) personal support for isolated LGBT employees; (b) safety in numbers for taking some actions such as pointing out biased behaviors in the organization when too risky to do alone; (c) expansion of potential solutions through the diverse perspectives of a group such as creating a nondiscrimination policy; (d) financial resources through dues for group events, conferences, or producing written materials; (e) diverse talents for the many group responsibilities; (f) legitimacy of being an organizational group; (g) alliances with other groups with "diversity" goals such as those representing women or racial and ethnic persons; and (h) developing a critical mass necessary for influencing the organizational culture (Gore, 2000).

The downside of making workplaces affirmative is that they become a target of bigoted groups in the United States. These groups spend enormous energy and resources on countering affirmative actions. As an example, a coalition of conservative religious groups may regularly protest against diversity training and partner benefits and call for boycotts of companies that they believe promote "homosexuality." During the late 1990s, religious and social conservatives branded American Airlines as among the "worst offenders," and persons were cajoled to not fly on this airline. Because of the "immoral ideologies" of Disney, by offering medical benefits to partners of lesbian and gay employees, the Southern Baptist Convention passed a resolution calling on its membership to stop patronizing the Walt Disney Company and its subsidiaries, including Disney World and Disney Land (Caldwell, 1997).

College Campus

LGBT college students often experience harassment or worse on college campuses (see Chapter 2). Colleges and universities should act to ensure that these students accomplish their educational goals without fear, harassment, discrimination, or violence by taking affirmative action (D'Augelli, 1989; D'Emilio, 1990; Herek, 1994; Obear, 1991; Schoenberg, 1989; Slater, 1993; Tierney, 1992; Waldo, 1998). This action can include:

- Include sexual orientation in the mission of the college or university and the nondiscrimination policy statements; verify that the whole campus is aware of such policies and that students understand intolerable behaviors.
- Provide intellectual leadership from the president, other administrators, and faculty in learning more about diversity.
- Encourage faculty and staff networks of "allies" to demonstrate their support and respect for LGBT students by wearing buttons and hanging posters in their offices to reflect their affirmative views.
- Do not allow organizations that discriminate against LGBT students to operate on campus.
- Promote interactions between heterosexual and LGBT students.
- Refuse to tolerate hate-motivated attacks on LGBT students and have the highest officers of the institution correct underlying difficulties associated with such attacks.
- Sponsor and closely monitor programs in which LGBT victims of campus violence and harassment are paired with a perpetrator, as this type of interpersonal interaction may reduce prejudice in the perpetrator.
- Challenge students to develop the building blocks for valuing diversity, such as relativistic thinking, openness to new ideas, and a belief in civil rights for all persons.
- Sponsor educational panels of LGBT students in residence halls, classrooms, fraternities, and sororities.
- Augment library materials on LGBT persons and their issues.
- Provide LGBT courses and scholarships to demonstrate the seriousness of the commitment of the academic community to LGBT persons and to the education of all students on campus about the lives of LGBT persons.

- Support LGBT student organizations in the college or university; help students with resources to procure speakers and to sponsor dances and other programs.
- Require the campus counseling center and health center to have staff who specialize in the difficulties experienced by LGBT persons.

Programs such as Safe Zone and similar initiatives are now available on many college campuses to provide a more positive campus climate for LGBT students and employees. As an example, as part of the Safe Zone program at the University of Wyoming, students, staff, and faculty volunteers provide training in two-hour sessions on LGBT topics, including myths and stereotypes; definitions and terminology; resources to help participants better understand sexual orientation; and ways to support LGBT students and promote a positive campus environment for everyone. Aside from educating the program participants, other goals include modeling nonheterosexist behavior and attitudes; confronting overt heterosexist incidents; and advocating social change (Conklin, 1999). Evans (2002) reported the results of an exploratory, qualitative study of a newly established Safe Zone project at Iowa State University (ISU). The study was focused on whether or not the project changed oppressive social structures affecting LGBT persons on the campus. A key part of the project involved providing a Safe Zone sticker for any faculty, staff, or student who wanted to wear one. It included a pink triangle and the words "safe zone" around the triangle. The main positive changes included increased visibility of LGBT persons on campus and increased support of them. LGBT students overwhelmingly reported that they felt safer on campus and more affirmed. In addition, there was increased visibility of and increased discussion and communication about LGBT issues and concerns both generally and specifically at ISU. The overall conclusion was that as a result of the Safe Zone project, the culture of ISU was changed.

Public School

American public schools play a central role in the perpetuation of heterosexism (see Chapter 2). Many school personnel tolerate prejudice, discrimination, and violence perpetrated on LGBT youth (Herdt & Boxer, 1993); are often among the perpetrators; and some are as emotionally abusive as the students (Sanford, 1989). LGBT students not only hear anti-LGBT statements from principals, teachers, counselors, and coaches (Uribe & Harbeck, 1991) but also find teachers often fail to intervene or take a stance when these youths are physically and emotionally abused by peers. Teachers and other school personnel may pretend that the harassment does not exist (Sanford, 1989). When they do respond, they often "blame the victim" or the LGBT students themselves for the harassment and assaults they experience (McManus, 1991), thereby sanctioning the harassment (Rofes, 1993–1994).

Safe and affirmative schools. Schools must provide a safe environment for all students including those who are LGB or T; the U.S. Constitution requires schools to stop the harassment of these students. In 1996, the U.S. Court of Appeals for the Seventh Circuit ruled for Jamie Nabozny, a high school student who claimed that the school violated his guarantee of equal protection (*Nabozny v. Podlesny*, 1996) by not protecting him, even after persistent complaints to school personnel about antigay harassment and violence. Although the school provided other students protection from other forms of harassment and abuse, school personnel repeatedly ignored or dismissed Nabozny's complaints. The defendants (the school district, the district administrator, two principals, and one assistant principal) agreed to pay one million dollars for Nabozny's medical expenses and damages (Logue, 1997). See the following Web sites for descriptions of similar cases:

http://www.aclu.org/news/n111398a.html

http://www.sgn.org/archives/sgn.11.13.98/

http://www.postgazette.com/breaking/20020117gayp7.asp

Schools may not be able to promise full safety but still can do much more to protect these youth (D'Augelli, 1996). First, the school culture must change. The leadership must inspire a shared vision of a hostile-free or safe school and an inclusive school culture. The leadership must firmly insist that violence, harassment, hate, and ignorance are unacceptable because these behaviors are morally wrong. Inclusive schools provide more information about our diverse world and teach skills to manage differences. Inclusive schools are places of growth and possibilities for all students. These goals call for multiple levels of participation from the top leadership down (Camille, 2002; Chen-Hayes, 2001; Cook & Pawlowski, 1991; D'Augelli, 1996; Friend, 1998; Giorgis, Higgins, & McNab, 2000; Hollander, 2000; Safe Schools Coalition of Washington State, 1996; Taylor, 2000; Uribe, 1994). Affirmative actions can be taken by school officials to

- Establish policies that protect LGBT students from harassment, discrimination, or violence such as having zero tolerance for harassment, thoroughly investigating incidents of harassment, educating perpetrators, educating the parents of those involved, supporting and protecting those who were harassed, educating staff to prevent future incidents, and educating the student body.
- Develop systematic responses for students who demonstrate sex–gender or gender-variant behavior.
- Model affirmation of diversity and dignity and respect for all persons.
- Educate adults working in schools about diverse sexual orientations.
- Include opportunities for parents of all youth in schools to learn more about the diversity of sexual orientations.
- Use film series, lectures, and LGBT organizations as ways to increase knowledge about LGBT youth.
- Require stigma–free language, forbidding the use of terms such as "fag" or "dyke."
- Forbid jokes about LGBT persons.
- Avoid judgment of "normal–abnormal" or "good–bad."
- Use inclusive language such as "Whom are you dating?" rather than "Who is your boyfriend or girlfriend?"
- Affirm the identities of LGBT youth.
- Foster an environment where LGBT youth can be safely open.
- Provide strictest confidence to students who disclose a nonheterosexual sexual orientation.
- Create safe, harassment-free zones such as a classroom or counseling room; LGBT students can go into these zones if they are feeling unsafe; the eventual goal is for all school zones to be safe for these students.
- Designate certain staff to be available to share students' concerns around their sexual orientation; LGBT faculty and staff can serve as role models but will need formal protection from harassment or from losing their jobs.

- Establish affirmative peer support groups and counseling services, including semester-long coming-out groups.
- Provide peer support groups to any student who wants to learn more about heterosexism and sexual identity.
- Establish an alliance group as an opportunity for all students to work on common projects.
- Provide support groups for parents of LGBT students.
- Incorporate LGBT issues throughout the curriculum.
- Include in the curriculum accurate information about LGBT persons who contributed to the scientific, social, economic, political, and cultural richness of current and prior generations.
- Place educational materials, pamphlets, and posters on LGBT persons in visible locations.
- Include LGBT-affirming books in the school library and a list of supportive local resources that can include churches, mental health clinics, and LGBT community organizations.
- Make school-sponsored social functions such as proms and dances inclusive with invitations that make it clear that all individuals and couples are welcome.
- Provide activities just for LGBT youth such as dances and movies.

In 1985 in a Los Angeles high school the first specialized school-based program was developed—Project 10—to provide discussion, support, and advocacy for lesbian and gay students, as well as training and education for school personnel and administrators (Uribe, 1994). It also promoted a code of conduct for students and faculty to ensure safety for these students. Throughout the Los Angeles Unified School District, Project 10 is now in use and the district has formed a Gay and Lesbian Education Commission empowered to make recommendations to the Board of Education regarding gay and lesbian youth (Greeley, 1994). The Project 10 model is also in use in the San Francisco Unified School District, as well as several other schools in California and beyond (Rofes, 1989).

Henning-Stout, James, and Macintosh (2000) identified 14 model programs focusing on preventing harassment of subordinated youth in schools, including Project 10. All the programs have common elements that contribute to their success, organized by guiding ideas, goals, objectives, and processes:

Guiding Ideas
- Respond directly to harassment issues.
- Take a preventive approach for students at risk.

Goals
- Increase safety for all children and youth.
- Counter heterosexism in the school and community cultures.

Objectives
- Listen to everyone involved, including perpetrators and harassed students.
- Engage in program development, implementation, and maintenance persons who have referent and legitimate power, are trusted, and are likely to be followed.
- Provide what persons involved in the program need such as support and resources.

- Model and support dialogues on issues of difference, beliefs, and understandings.
- Provide training on conflict resolution and mediation, and the structure and space for practicing the training.
- Recognize the many paths to attain the goals.
- Evaluate systematically the effects of the program on creating a safe environment and countering heterosexist bias.

Processes

- Identify issues in the local community that emerge such as assaults on LGBT persons.
- Develop coalitions with allies.
- Gather information such as the history of harassment in the school and community, the political climate, pertinent laws, and potentials for backlash.
- Plan actions; present information and programs with confidence.
- Implement actions such as policy changes, nondiscrimination clauses, staff development programs, community education programs, curriculum supplements, and support groups.

Additional information to foster an understanding of heterosexism in schools and interventions to curb it is available from the Gay, Lesbian, and Straight Teachers Network, the largest national organization that addresses heterosexism in public schools.[1]

Many LGB youth may not seek out visible programs in schools such as Project 10 because they do not want to be visible (D'Augelli, 1996). But some of the indirect methods recommended in the above list for creating affirmative school environments and other methods can create a more hospitable environment for these students. This includes publishing articles about gay and lesbian adolescents in the school newspaper, providing books in the library, placing literature in waiting areas, providing in-service training for teachers and administrators, and developing policies that support teachers to challenge heterosexist remarks (Fontaine & Hammond, 1996).

Unfortunately, the affirmative initiatives discussed here are rare. Most schools deny the presence of and ignore the needs of their LGBT students. More programs (for example, support groups) in community settings are needed and, for some students, may be more comfortable places (Gerstel, Feraios, & Herdt, 1989; Greeley, 1994; Singerline, 1994). Several alternative schools are also now available. The Hetrick-Martin Institute, a private agency in New York, runs the Harvey Milk School, an alternative high school for LGBT youth. The first private high school for LGB students in the United States, the Walt Whitman Community School, began in Dallas in the fall of 1997 (Fowler, 1997).

Sources of opposition. Several scholars (for example, Fontaine & Hammond, 1996; Rofes, 1989) emphasized the challenges of those seeking to meet the needs of LGBT youth in mainstream schools, such as the frequent opposition of heterosexist parents, school boards, and others in the community. Teachers or administrators who advocate positive changes in their schools may confront attacks and pressures from parents and other community members to not encourage "the gay lifestyle."

---

[1]The Gay, Lesbian, and Straight Teachers netowrks is available at http://www.glstn.org/

An example of what can result from attempts to develop programs to benefit LGBT students happened in a suburb of Dallas. A workshop to train middle school counselors how to help gay and lesbian youth was cancelled by the school district after protests from local ministers and other Christian conservatives. A local resident who was also a state executive member of the Republican Party did not want the counselors trained by persons from a local gay and lesbian counseling center because these persons would not present a balanced view that "homosexuality" is sinful. Nor would they present information on religious-based counseling to change same sex–gender sexual orientation. A minister in the area claimed that religious conservatives have a right to declare that "homosexuality" is sinful and to counsel "homosexuals" to change (McCoy, 1999).

Reaching beyond schools. The challenges referred to above make it clear that ameliorating struggles for LGBT youth in schools calls for intervention at many different levels. This includes going well beyond the boundaries of the school campus. A strategic approach is needed that includes anticipating the opposition and building a broad base of support for inclusion. Also needed is active community support from teachers, unions, parents, alumni, religious organizations, and from a broad range of race, ethnic, and social class backgrounds. Other requirements are patience, perseverance, resources, and commitment (Friend, 1991, 1998).

CHANGE AT THE COMMUNITY LEVEL

Heterosexism is probably the most relevant environmental or structural issue affecting LGB persons. Compounded with racism and sexism, it generates barriers to the development and well-being of LGBT persons. The basic models used in social work address issues at the environmental or structural level. Appleby and Anastas (1998) identified these models as the general systems model (Hearn, 1969) and the ecological model (Germain, 1991; Germain & Gitterman, 1980). These models view clients as interdependent systems operating in larger systems, as persons-in-situations, or persons-in-environment (DeHoyos & Jensen, 1985) instead of as self-contained and isolated units. The ecological model of practice also addresses the processes of stress and the role of stress in the difficulties of living. Stress arises in three interrelated areas of living: life transitions, environmental pressures, and interpersonal processes. Environments can be the source of stress depending on whether they support or interfere with life transitions. Heterosexism, for example, is a social arrangement that is an interference for LGB persons. Focusing on this interference from the systems model allows us to see it as sourced not only in the more immediate environments of friends and families but in the larger environments of communities, organizations, cultures, and societies (Appleby & Anastas, 1998).

The ecological and system models both point to the importance of macrosystems or cultural systems within which individuals and families develop and function. Though micropractice has its place, practitioners must also understand environmental pressures such as discrimination and attend to the needs or concerns of LGBT communities (Appleby & Anastas, 1998). Macrointerventions recommended by Appleby and Anastas include community development, education and consciousness raising, self-help, political mobilization, and coalition building with other oppressed groups.

At a minimum, practitioners require knowledge about cultural and community resources for LGBT clients. They also need to know how to assess the communities of these clients, their cultural resources, and their connectivity and involvements (Appleby & Anastas, 1998; Hunter & Mallon, 1998). Furthermore, practitioners can teach community members how to make these assessments and changes. A workshop, described by Hollander (1989), taught lesbians in a midwest city how to analyze the structure of their social networks and how to develop plans to expand sources of social support. Following the workshop, more than half of the members (60 percent) indicated that their social networks expanded because of what they learned in the workshop. More accessible social support networks developed and modified the entire city's lesbian social system.

Macrosystem interventions, including educational and political strategies, create less oppressive and more nurturing social environments. One useful political strategy is to form coalitions with national advocacy groups such as the American Civil Liberties Union, Lambda Legal Defense and Education Fund, and the National Gay and Lesbian Task Force to pursue the promotion of civil rights legislation, to counter efforts to defeat or undo civil rights legislation, and to expand community-based institutions and services. More specific tasks include: *civil rights* (for example, appeal of state sodomy laws, passage of statutes on antidiscrimination and on protections against violence and hate crimes); *family rights* (for example, custody rights, foster care rights); *adult services* (for example, mental health, drug and alcohol, health care for AIDS and for women's health needs; *youth services* (for example, education, support services); *elder care services* (for example, social centers, retirement centers); *rights in the private sector* (for example, equitable employment rights, nondiscrimination and harassment policies, health and pension benefits, and marriage or domestic partnership entitlements) (Appleby & Anastas, 1998).

ILLUSTRATION OF COMMUNITY PRACTICE: NEEDS ASSESSMENT

As examples of community practice, results of several recently reported community assessments of the needs of older lesbian and gay persons are presented. The results of these assessments guided the development of social services programs for this population.

When asked what their greatest human need was, most of the gay persons reported in Brown, Sarosy, Cook, and Quarto (1997) indicated acceptance, validation, and love from others. In an assessment of needs among older lesbian and gay persons in Chicago, Beeler, Rawls, Herdt, and Cohler (1999) discovered that more opportunities to socialize with other older gay and lesbian persons was by far the most commonly expressed need. In addition, the respondents wanted social opportunities other than bars.

Expanded social opportunities might be an especially acute desire for gay persons who have lost many close friends and partners to AIDS, and for men and women who came out later in life and want to develop a network of lesbian and gay friends. Others who feel they will benefit from expanded social opportunities also want a focus on social activities and social interactions that are not age stratified. Some who do not yet think of themselves as the older generation want to meet retired persons so they can picture what retired life might eventually be like for them. They are hoping for reassurance that retirement will be a positive experience (Beeler et al., 1999). The Chicago sample of older lesbian and gay persons expressed these additional needs:

- *Giving back.* Respondents expressed a desire to give back to the lesbian and gay community and to become more involved in the community. This was also a way to meet others.
- *Volunteer registry.* Several respondents suggested a volunteer registry of older lesbian and gay adults.
- *Support groups.* Respondents expressed some interest in support groups for persons in similar situations such as gay fathers or those who were heterosexually married, divorced, and then came out. "Support" also overlapped with the desire for additional social opportunities. In a San Diego sample studied by Jacobs, Rasmussen, and Hohman (1999), both men and women used lesbian and gay social groups and support groups more often than other types of services provided by the lesbian and gay community.
- *Counseling services.* Respondents were interested in counseling services only when they focused on particular situations such as disclosure to one's children or developmental transitions in the life course such as retirement or the death of a partner. The respondents did not want "treatment." Mental health needs were the least indicated needs.
- *Information and education.* Respondents wanted more information and education on an array of topics.
- *Workshops and seminars.* Respondents expressed a desire for workshops and seminars on various topics of interest to this population such as estate planning, retirement finances, and legal issues (for example, wills and powers of attorney).
- *Advocacy.* Respondents saw a need for advocacy services including training and educating mainstream services providers to be sensitive to the needs of their LGB clients.
- *Referral network.* Respondents wanted a link to services, programs, and events through an information and referral system created specifically for older LBG persons. The focus of the referral network would be LGB-friendly providers for services used by older adults, such as health care facilities, attorneys, nursing homes, and in-home health care providers.
- *Basic needs.* Several respondents pointed out that some older gay and lesbian persons needed food, shelter, and medical care. Some also needed transportation to participate in programs for older lesbian and gay persons. Some might need help with basic household tasks to continue living independently. These various needs suggested the need for a case management program to assist these particular older gay and lesbian persons in procuring suitable services.
- *Outreach program.* Respondents recommended an outreach program targeted at isolated persons and those unable to locate human services agencies.

COMMUNITY ORGANIZING ON BEHALF OF OLDER LESBIAN AND GAY PERSONS

Traditional services for older persons are not an answer for the needs of older LGB persons. For example, openly gay and lesbian persons are not welcome in senior centers in New York (National Gay and Lesbian Task Force Policy Institute, 2000). So it is crucial to develop services for this population in LGB communities.

The population of older gay and lesbian persons is diverse and, as indicated above, presents a large range of needs and often would benefit from a variety of services. Goals identified by Beeler et al. (1999), based on the needs assessment presented above, are

- To provide *ongoing opportunities for social interaction and opportunities to build friendship networks and create or expand existing supports.* Expand involvement in the LGB community through social, educational, and fun activities structured so that persons can talk to each other before leaving the events. Social events can include dances, brunches, picnics, potluck lunches, day trips, workshops, and rap groups. Provide opportunities for some sex–gender specific or sex–gender segregated activities.
- To provide *information and discussion opportunities.* Include support groups and activity groups that encourage sharing of feelings, concerns, interests, and special issues. Educational workshops can be hosted on a variety of topics such as dating, starting a relationship, how to maintain relationships, how to end relationships, and how to get out of abusive relationships. Examples of the focus for other groups include coming out and bereavement. Groups can also focus on personal growth, creative writing, languages, history projects, and books.
- To create *an information and referral system of services and programs and events.* Tailor this specifically for older lesbian and gay persons and include information lines for resources, services, programs and events, referrals to legal services, and gay and lesbian physicians.
- To provide *a resource manual.* List services such as medical and legal, social programs, publications, churches and temples, and other resources. Update the manual on a monthly basis. Such a manual would be useful for all older lesbian and gay persons and for counselors, phone hotline volunteers, and crisis counselors. A monthly newsletter with a calendar of events and a schedule of support groups and activity groups can be sent to consumers and other agencies. Volunteers can fold newsletters and stuff envelopes at monthly "mailing parties."
- To provide *outreach services.* Maintain services for persons who are homebound or living in nursing homes, persons living in rural areas, and persons who feel isolated. Others are struggling with their identity and feel uncomfortable going to a center for subordinated groups; others are shy and withdrawn. Examples of outreach services include a "buddy system" visiting program for persons living on their own who are frail, ill, or otherwise housebound or socially isolated. These persons can receive LGB-oriented newspapers and opportunities to correspond with other LGB persons. Direct contact can be supplemented with telephone contact.
- To establish *a networking system.* Ensure accountability of services providers and quality of care and services by including other agencies.
- To provide *assistance in procuring fair and adequate services.* This would be applied to areas such as health care, legal, and financial services.

Comprehensive organizations that could meet such a large range of needs—for instance, Senior Action in a Gay Environment in New York City (see Chapter 14)—are not feasible in most locations. This array of services is beyond the capacity of any single agency or even several agencies that usually compete for limited resources. A community-based approach may be a more practical solution to this situation, as it would draw upon the substantial and varied resources of the target population itself. Time, energy, and funds would be directed toward organizing older gay and lesbian persons, hence enabling them to help one another and to provide needed services. In this study by Beeler et al. (1999), respondents expressed a willingness to dedicate themselves and some combination of their resources to helping others. This approach boosts the feasibility of developing extensive services in a tight economy and helps alleviate the most frequently cited need encountered: additional opportunities for meaningful community involvement and social interactions with other gay and lesbian persons.

CHANGE AT THE MACROCULTURE LEVEL

All persons experience similar stressors such as difficulties in relationships, coping with the death of someone close, or changing jobs. As noted throughout this book, however, LGB persons also experience a distinctive source of distress: the heterosexist oppression of the macroculture (Rothblum, 1990). LGB persons will not be liberated from heterosexism until mainstream society views them as full and equal citizens. Yet, this goal seems remote, if not unreachable, because curtailing heterosexism is no easy task.

Herek (1995) explained why stereotypes are so difficult to change. All of us use cognitive strategies to assist us in perceiving our environment as generally stable, predictable, and manageable (for example, Snyder, 1981). We view the world selectively with stereotypes and use illusory correlations (for example, conjecturing that a same sex–gender sexual orientation is associated with maladjustment, when no such association exists). But, persons who hold prejudices about LGB persons usually notice only the characteristics that match their stereotypes of these persons and ignore information that contradicts the match. Not only are one's current observations distorted, but stereotypes can also affect memory of past events. Only the past information that fits with one's stereotypes of LGB persons is recalled (Herek, 1995).

Negative stereotypes also fulfill certain psychological functions, identified by Herek (1995) as experiential, social identity, and ego defensive. The *experiential function* helps persons to make sense of their previous interactions with LGB persons. When interactions are amiable, they generally accept LGB persons whereas unpleasant experiences may lead to negative attitudes that are then generalized to all LGB persons. As most heterosexual men and women say they do not know any LGB persons, they probably view them as symbolic; generally representing the type of person one is not, does not want to be, and does not want in one's family. The negative symbol of LGB persons often results in distancing from them or attacking them.

The *social identity function* increases one's self-esteem through two interrelated components: *value expressive* and *social expressive*. First, significant values are usually tied to and affirm one's self-concept. For example, fundamentalist Christians may express hostile attitudes about lesbian and gay persons to affirm their self-concept as a good Christian. Violence directed at LGB persons is value expressive when certain values such as upholding moral authority reinforce the self-concepts of the perpetrators. Franklin (2000) identified a similar group she called "antigay ideology" perpetrators who think of themselves as social norms enforcers; they are punishing gay persons for moral transgressions.

Second, a person's sense of belonging to a significant reference group can strengthen certain social values. When one expresses values of the reference group, one gains acceptance, approval, and love from the group. Approval comes by regarding LGB persons either favorably or unfavorably, depending on the particular slant of the reference group. If the group favors violence toward these persons, the psychological benefit for members who are perpetrators of violence is social expressive because they maintain status and affiliation with their peer group. Franklin identified three groups of perpetrators that seemed driven by social functions: "peer dynamics" perpetrators who are trying to prove their "masculine" identity to their peers; "thrill-seeker" perpetrators who feel socially alienated and powerless; and "self-defense" perpetrators who attack someone who they interpret as flirting with them or propositioning them, suggesting that they think they have cultural permission for violence based on "homosexual innuendo."

The *ego defensive function* occurs when hostility about lesbian and gay persons represents an unconscious defensive strategy. This allows some persons to avoid internal conflict about unacceptable parts of themselves such as their own attraction to persons of their sex–gender. Violence is ego defensive when perpetrators attack or castigate someone because that person symbolizes the unacceptable parts of themselves. They are probably unaware, however, of the motivations that underlie their hostile and violent behaviors.

Perpetrators of violence may play out several or all the functions or act from multiple motives. It was observed in Chapter 2, for example, that usually groups physically attack LGBT persons; typically the group members are male juveniles or young adults. The victim is usually a gay man (for example, Kite & Deaux, 1986) who is a stranger (Berrill, 1990). The functions of the attack are to boost the cohesiveness among group members, show antagonism toward the sexual and sex–gender role violations of gay persons (social identity functions), and affirm for the attackers their own heterosexual orientation and masculine sex–gender role identity (ego defensive function) (Herek, 1992b). Attacks on gay persons provide the attackers a psychological reward. Particularly, if the attackers subordinate older, White men (assumed to be members of the dominant elite), they experience enhancement of their own masculinity and status (Connell, 1995).

For those who are attacked, the best types of social services response are mental health services, peer counselors, and advocacy. Wertheimer (1990) described the integrated services of the Anti-Violence Project in New York City. The core service is a telephone hotline that responds to assault victims around the clock. The location of the project in the New York Lesbian and Gay Community Services Center also makes the project accessible to many walk-in clients.

Every social services agency can train staff about the effects of assaults and the types of services and sensitivities needed for LGBT clients. Publications in social services agencies should explicitly state what services are provided for these persons if assaulted. Speakers from these agencies can inform LGBT organizations of their services for assault victims. Mainstream victim agencies can use outreach to inform the LGBT communities of their services. It is important for the policies of these agencies to be committed to nondiscrimination and that there are LGBT staff to assist LGBT victims of assaults.

What, if anything, can stop assaults on LGBT persons? Stopping assaults and other manifestations of heterosexism requires changes at both the institutional and individual levels. Change at the institutional level is difficult to achieve except through legal means (Rubenstein, 1996). Change at the individual level is far more difficult to attain because it necessitates a transformation in the consciousness of heterosexual persons.

Personal contact seems to be the most consistently influential factor in reducing prejudice (Herek & Glunt, 1993) because it challenges misconceptions that, in turn, can change cognitions. So, disclosure of one's identity to family members, friends, and coworkers is an important way to challenge heterosexism at the individual level (Herek, 1992a).

According to Herek (1995) it is necessary for change strategies to match the functions served by holding prejudicial attitudes. The contact strategy, for example, may work best with persons who hold heterosexist attitudes because they serve an experiential function. Their attitudes are shaped by experience. Attitudes may not change through personal contact if they serve a value expressive function. A strategy of creating dissonance between the person's prejudices and another significant value, such as personal freedom, may have a stronger influence in these situations. Attitudes supporting the value expressive function may also change if a respected authority, such as a minister, presents a more positive view of same sex–gender or bisexual sexual orientation, grounded in religious teachings. Close contact is also unlikely to have any positive influence on attitudes that serve an ego defensive function because it may arouse anxiety and heighten defensiveness. If one has fears about one's own sexual orientation, close contact is unlikely to result in positive responses. Attitudes that express a social expressive function may change if one's reference groups change (for example, from conservative to more liberal groups). If cultural norms about heterosexism change, the attitudes of reference groups and individuals are likely to shift accordingly. Yet, little evidence currently shows any significant shift in norms as heterosexism remains strongly entrenched in our culture. An array of other methods for attempting to change heterosexist attitudes are discussed by Sears and Williams (1997), including those suitable for different ethnic and racial groups. Not only should heterosexism be eradicated but so should all forms of social bigotry (Bohan & Russell, 1999).

SUMMARY

- Workplaces must clearly be defined as supportive of all employees regardless of sexual orientation. Any equivocation about this results in covert, and sometimes blatant, discrimination against LGBT employees. Workplaces can also institute many policies to advance an affirmative workplace environment, such as establishing zero tolerance for harassment in the workplace and immediately intervening when harassment emerges. These practices can ensure that the workplace is not only safe for but also supportive of LGBT employees.

- Colleges must also provide safety and inclusion for LGBT students. Colleges can take many actions, for example, by including LGBT students as part of the mission statement, establishing nondiscrimination policies for the college, and sponsoring LGBT organizations.

- Despite legal mandates to provide a safe environment for all public school students, some school officials turn away from teasing, ridicule, and physical assaults on LGBT students. To change these school settings into places where LGBT students can feel safe, schools have much to do both inside among students and staff and outside among parents and other invested groups. The insistence on creating an affirmative environment must start at the top levels. Many models now exist for creating affirmative school systems, and school districts should be urged to implement a model or be vulnerable to lawsuits brought by former students who experienced endless harassment.

- Community organizers and practitioners can improve community access and services by educating themselves about LGBT populations. A needs assessment of older lesbian and gay persons is the example provided in this chapter. Organizers and practitioners can call upon the wealth of resources and talents that LGBT persons have. Organizers should assume the position of "respectful outsider," tapping into the talents of the group and providing a venue for establishing and prioritizing the group's needs. Organizers and community practitioners can mobilize these groups through civil rights activities and by coordinating services desired by certain groups.
- Heterosexism is expressed at all levels. At the macro level, it is expressed in social values. LGBT persons will not be liberated from heterosexism until these values change and LGBT persons are full and equal citizens. These are distant goals, however, because moderating heterosexism is not easy. Negative stereotypes and attitudes about LGBT persons, for example, are difficult to change because for the persons who hold them, they provide various psychological functions or benefits.

CHAPTER 12
REFERENCES

Ankeny, D. C. (1991). Creating the statistical portion of an affirmative action plan. *Tulane Law Review, 65*, 1183, 1205.

Appleby, G. A., & Anastas, J. W. (1998). *Not just a passing phase: Social work with gay, lesbian, and bisexual people.* New York: Columbia University Press.

Beeler, J. A., Rawls, T. W., Herdt, G. H., & Cohler, B. J. (1999). Needs of older lesbians and gay men in Chicago. *Journal of Gay and Lesbian Social Services, 9*, 31.

Berrill, K. T. (1990). Anti-gay violence and victimization in the United States. *Journal of Interpersonal Violence, 5*, 274–294.

Bohan, J. S., & Russell, G. M. (1999). Afterword: The conversation continues. In J. S. Bohan & G. M. Russell (Eds.), *Conversations about psychology and sexual orientation* (pp. 183–209). New York: New York University Press.

Brooks, S. E. (1991). Resources. In N. J. Evans & V. A. Walls (Eds.), *Beyond tolerance: Gays, lesbians, and bisexuals on campus* (pp. 213–232). Alexandria, VA: American College Personnel Association.

Brown, L. B., Sarosy, S. G., Cook, T. C., & Quarto, J. G. (1997). *Gay men and aging.* New York: Garland Publishing.

Byrne, J. S. (1993). Affirmative action for lesbians and gay men: A proposal for true equality of opportunity and work force diversity. *Yale Law & Policy Review, 11*, 47–108.

Caldwell, D. K. (1997, June 19). Baptists vote to boycott Disney Co. *Dallas Morning News*, pp. A1, A16.

Camille, L. (2002). The impact of belonging to a high school gay/straight alliance. *High School Journal, 85*, 13–26.

Chen-Hayes, S. F. (2001). Counseling and advocacy with transgendered and gender-variant persons in schools and families. *Journal of Humanistic Counseling, Education, and Development, 40*, 34–48.

Chojnacki, J. T., & Gelberg, S. (1995). The facilitation of a gay/lesbian/bisexual support-therapy group by heterosexual counselors. *Journal of Counseling & Development, 73*, 352–354.

Conklin, S. C. (1999). Wyoming horror breaks dam of silence on violence based on sexual orientation. *Siecus Report*, *27*, 8–11.

Connell, R. W. (1995). *Masculinities*. Berkeley: University of California Press.

Cook, A. T., & Pawlowski, W. (1991). *Youth and homosexuality* (Issue Paper 3). Washington, DC: Parents and Friends of Lesbians and Gays.

D'Augelli, A. R. (1989). Lesbians and gay men on campus: Visibility, empowerment, and educational leadership. *Peabody Journal of Education*, *66*, 124–142.

D'Augelli, A. R. (1996). Enhancing the development of lesbian, gay, and bisexual youths. In E. D. Rothblum & L. A. Bond (Eds.), *Preventing heterosexism and homophobia* (pp. 124–150). Thousand Oaks, CA: Sage Publications.

DeHoyos, G., & Jensen, C. (1985). The systems approach in American social work. *Social Casework*, *66*, 490–497.

D'Emilio, J. (1990). The campus environment for gay and lesbian life. *Academe*, *76*, 16–19.

Elliott, J. E. (1993). Career development with lesbian and gay clients. *Career Development Quarterly*, *41*, 210–226.

Evans, N. J. (2002). The impact of an LGBT Safe Zone project on campus climate. *Journal of College Student Development*, *43*, 522–539.

Fontaine, J. H., & Hammond, N. L. (1996). Counseling issues with gay and lesbian adolescents. *Adolescence*, *31*, 817–830.

Fowler, J. (1997, November). School's out. *Dallas Observer*, pp. 17–18, 20–24, 27, 29, 31.

Franklin, K. (2000). Antigay behaviors among young adults: Prevalence, patterns, and motivators in a noncriminal population. *Journal of Interpersonal Violence*, *15*, 339–362.

Friend, R. A. (1991). Older lesbian and gay people: A theory of successful aging. *Journal of Homosexuality*, *20*, 99–118.

Friend, R. A. (1998). Heterosexism, homophobia, and the culture of schooling. In S. Books (Ed.), *Invisible children in the society and its schools* (pp. 137–166). Mahwah, NJ: Lawrence Erlbaum.

Germain, C. B. (1991). *Human behavior and the social environment*. New York: Columbia University Press.

Germain, C. B., & Gitterman, A. (1980). *The life model of social work practice*. New York: Columbia University Press.

Gerstel, C. J., Feraios, A. J., & Herdt, G. (1989). Widening circles: An ethnographic profile of a youth group. *Journal of Homosexuality, 17,* 75–92.

Giorgis, C., Higgins, K., & McNab, W. L. (2000). Continuing education health issues of gay and lesbian youth: Implications for school. *Journal of Health Education, 31,* 28–36.

Gore, S. (2000). The lesbian and gay workplace: An employee's guide to advancing equity. In B. Greene & G. L. Croom (Eds.), *Education, research, and practice in lesbian, gay, bisexual, and transgendered psychology* (Vol. 5, pp. 282–302). Thousand Oaks, CA: Sage Publications.

Greeley, G. (1994). Service organizations for gay and lesbian youth. *Journal of Gay and Lesbian Social Services, 1,* 111–130.

Hearn, G. (1969). Introduction. In G. Hearn (Ed.), *The general systems approach: Contributions toward an holistic conception of social work* (pp. 1–4). New York: Council on Social Work Education.

Henning-Stout, M., James, S., & Macintosh, S. (2000). Reducing harassment of lesbian, gay, bisexual, transgender, and questioning youth in schools. *School Psychology Review, 29,* 180–191.

Herdt, G. H., & Boxer, A. (1993). *Children of the horizons: How gay and lesbian teens are leading a way out of the closet.* Boston: Beacon Press.

Herek, G. M. (1992a). Homophobia. In W. R. Dynes (Ed.), *Encyclopedia of homosexuality* (pp. 552–555). New York: Garland.

Herek, G. M. (1992b). Psychological heterosexism and anti-gay violence: The social psychology of bigotry and bashing. In G. M. Herek & K. T. Berrill (Eds.), *Hate crimes: Confronting violence against lesbians and gay men* (pp. 149–169). Newbury Park, CA: Sage Publications.

Herek, G. M. (1994). Assessing heterosexuals' attitudes toward lesbian and gay men. In B. Greene & G. M. Herek (Eds.), *Lesbian and gay psychology: Theory, research, and clinical applications* (pp. 206–228). Thousand Oaks, CA: Sage Publications.

Herek, G. M. (1995). Psychological heterosexism in the United States. In A. R. D'Augelli & C. J. Patterson (Eds.), *Lesbian, gay, and bisexual identities over the lifespan: Psychological perspectives* (pp. 321–346). New York: Oxford University Press.

Herek, G. M., & Glunt, E. (1993). Interpersonal contact and heterosexuals' attitudes toward gay men: Results from a national survey. *Journal of Sex Research, 30,* 239–244.

Hollander, G. (2000). Questioning youth: Challenges to working with youths forming identities. *School Psychology Review, 29,* 173–179.

Hollander, J. (1989). Restructuring lesbian social networks: Evaluation of an intervention. *Journal of Gay & Lesbian Psychotherapy, 1,* 63–72.

Hunter, J., & Mallon, G. P. (1998). Social work practice with gay men and lesbians within communities. In G. P. Mallon (Ed.), *Foundations of social work practice with lesbian and gay persons* (pp. 229–247). New York: Haworth Press.

Jacobs, H. (1994). A new approach for gay and lesbian domestic partners: Legal acceptance through relational property theory. *Duke Journal of Gender Law & Policy, 1,* 159–172.

Jacobs, R. J., Rasmussen, L. A., & Hohman, M. M. (1999). The social support needs of older lesbians, gay men, and bisexuals. *Journal of Gay and Lesbian Social Services, 9,* 1–30.

Kite, M. E., & Deaux, K. (1986). Attitudes toward homosexuality: Assessment and behavioral consequences. *Basic and Applied Social Psychology, 7,* 137–162.

Kitzinger, C. (1991). Lesbian and gay men in the workplace: Psychosocial issues. In M. J. Davidson & J. Earnshaw (Eds.), *Vulnerable workers: Psychosocial and legal issues* (pp. 223–257). New York: John Wiley & Sons.

Kronenberger, G. K. (1991). Out of the closet. *Personnel Journal, 70,* 40–44.

Lee, J. A., & Brown, R. G. (1993). Hiring, firing, and promoting. In L. Diamant (Ed.), *Homosexual issues in the workplace* (pp. 45–62). Washington, DC: Taylor & Francis.

Levine, M. P., & Leonard, R. (1984). Discrimination against lesbians in the work force. *Signs, 9,* 700–710.

Logue, P. M. (1997). *Near $1 million settlement raises standard for protections of gay youth* [Online]. Available: http://www.lambdalegal.org/cgi-bin/pages/documents

McCoy, J. (1999, February 21). Workshop cancelled on gay, lesbian youths. *Dallas Morning News,* p. A35.

McManus, M. (1991). Serving lesbian and gay youth. *Focal Point, 5,* 1–4.

Mickens, E. (1994). *The 100 best companies for gay men and lesbians.* New York: Pocket Books.

Nabozny v. Podlesny, 92 F.3d 446 (7th Cir. 1996) [Online]. Available: http://www.kentlaw.edu/7circuit/1996/jul/95-3634.html

National Gay and Lesbian Task Force. (1991). *Anti-gay violence, victimization and defamation in 1990.* Washington, DC: Author.

National Gay and Lesbian Task Force Policy Institute. (2000). *Aging initiative* [Online]. Available: http://www.ngltf.org/pl/aging.htm

Obear, K. (1991). Homophobia. In N. J. Evans & V. A. Wall (Eds.), *Beyond tolerance: Gays, lesbians, and bisexuals on campus* (pp. 39–78). Alexandria, VA: American College Personnel Association.

Ragins, B. R., & Cornwell, J. M. (2001). Pink triangles: Antecedents and consequences of perceived workplace discrimination against gay and lesbian employees. *Journal of Applied Psychology, 86,* 1244–1261.

Rofes, E. (1989). Opening up the classroom closet: Responding to the educational needs of gay and lesbian youth. *Harvard Educational Review, 59,* 444–453.

Rofes, E. E. (1993-1994). Making our schools safe for sissies. *High School Journal, 77,* 37–40.

Rothblum, E. D. (1990). Depression among lesbians: An invisible and unresearched phenomenon. *Journal of Gay & Lesbian Psychotherapy, 1,* 67–87.

Rubenstein, W. B. (1996). Lesbians, gay men, and the law. In R. C. Savin-Williams & K. M. Cohen (Eds.), *The lives of lesbian, gay men, and bisexuals: Children to adults* (pp. 331–343). Fort Worth, TX: Harcourt Brace.

Safe Schools Coalition of Washington State. (1996, January). *A report on the five year anti-violence research project of the Safe Schools Coalition of Washington State* [Online]. Available: www.safeschools-wa.org

Sanford, N. D. (1989). Providing sensitive health care to gay and lesbian youth. *Nurse Practitioner, 14,* 30–47.

Schoenberg, R. (1989, April). *Unlocking closets in the ivory tower: Lesbian/gay identity formation and management in college.* Paper presented at the meeting of the American College Personnel Association, Washington, DC.

Sears, J. T., & Williams, W. L. (Eds.). (1997). *Overcoming heterosexism and homophobia.* New York: Columbia University Press.

Singerline, H. (1994). OutRight: Reflections on an out-of-school gay youth group. *High School Journal, 77,* 133–137.

Slater, B. R. (1993). Violence against lesbian and gay male college students. *Journal of College Student Psychotherapy, 8,* 177–202.

Snyder, M. (1981). On the self-perpetuating nature of social stereotypes. In D. Hamilton (Ed.), *Cognitive processes in stereotyping and intergroup behavior* (pp. 183-211). Hillsdale, NJ: Lawrence Erlbaum.

Taylor, H. E. (2000). Meeting the needs of lesbian and gay young adolescents. *The Clearing House, 73,* 221–224.

Tierney, W. G. (1992). *Enhancing diversity: Toward a better campus climate.* Report of the Committee on Lesbian and Gay Concerns, Pennsylvania State University, University Park. Available: http://www.lions.psu.edu/clgbte/hi/index2.htm

Uribe, V. (1994). The silent minority: Rethinking out commitment to gay and lesbian youth. *Theory into Practice, 33,* 168–172.

Uribe, V., & Harbeck, K. M. (1991). Addressing the needs of lesbian, gay, and bisexual youth: The origins of PROJECT 10 and school-based intervention. *Journal of Homosexuality, 22,* 9–28.

Waldo, C. R. (1998). Out on campus: Sexual orientation and academic climate in a university context. *American Journal of Community Psychology, 26,* 745–774.

Wertheimer, D. M. (1990). Treatment and service interventions for lesbian and gay male crime victims. *Journal of Interpersonal Violence, 5,* 384–400.

Woolsey, C. (1991, October 7). Digital pioneers program to fight AIDS, ignorance. *Business Insurance,* p. 80.

PART V
SPECIAL GROUPS AND PRACTICE

CHAPTER 13
YOUTH

What are the developmental tasks of LGBT youth?

What helps LGBT youth successfully negotiate their lives?

What are the obstacles for LGBT youth?

What are some examples of affirmative practice with LGBT youth?

What affirmative helping systems are available for LGBT youth?

When adolescents begin the transition from childhood to youth, they engage in two major developmental challenges: adapting to pubertal changes that transform their bodies, usually in early adolescence; and developing identities independent of their parents, usually in middle-to-late adolescence (for example, Turner & Helms, 1991). Exhibit 13.1 provides a list of many of the specific tasks to be accomplished in the context of adolescents' developmental challenges (Cranston, 1992; D'Augelli, Hershberger, & Pilkington, 1998; Davis, Anderson, Linkowski, Berger, & Feinstein, 1985; Dempsey, 1994; Hunter, 1995; Mallon, 1998a; McAnarney, 1985; Morrow, 1997; Offer, Ostrov, & Howard, 1981; Radkowsky & Siegel, 1997; Sullivan & Schneider, 1987).

EXHIBIT 13.1: DEVELOPMENTAL TASKS OF YOUTH

- Disengage from childhood patterns
- Integrate physical, emotional, and cognitive development
- Learn and practice social skills
- Create an expanding self-concept that usually evolves from identifications with one's sex–gender, family, and cultural group
- Develop a positive sense of self
- Develop a sense of one's own values and identity
- Integrate different parts of one's identity to attain a sense of wholeness
- Increase independence from parents
- Change major reference group from family to friends
- Build a social support network, including social and work relationships with peers
- Discover intimate and sexual selves
- Establish intimate and sexual linkups
- Prepare to pursue educational, career, vocational, or other life goals.

Ideally, most adolescents adjust to these various biological, cognitive, psychological, and social changes within a context of family stability (Germain, 1991) and without experiencing the "inevitable crisis" often associated with this stage of life (for example, Jackson &

Sullivan, 1994). The developmental tasks of this life period are transforming and often stressful (for example, Anderson, 1998; Fontaine & Hammond, 1996).

UNIQUE STRESSORS FOR LGBT YOUTH

Though LGBT adolescents share the same developmental concerns and processes of other adolescents (Savin-Williams, 1995b), they experience additional unique stressors (for example, D'Augelli, 1996a; Fontaine & Hammond, 1996). They often confront the daunting task of exiting from heterosexual socialization and creating a new "self," usually without available models for this process (for example, D'Augelli, 1996b; Mallon, 1998a). Often, these adolescents only have negative stereotypes and myths about being LGB or T, for instance, that they will never be happy. These youth may not know many LGB or T persons are successful, happy, and involved in long-term relationships (Sanford, 1989; Whitlock, 1989).

In childhood, transgender persons often are not unhappy, as they feel free to express behaviors and interests of the other sex–gender (Gagné & Tewksbury, 1996). But with puberty, many begin to experience unwanted and embarrassing physical changes in their bodies (Lee, 2001). In school, they often hide or repress their inclinations to be the other sex–gender and begin feeling more alienated and isolated (Gagné & Tewksbury, 1996). Adolescent peers are quick to make negative judgments of anyone who is different. So adolescents with desires to be the other sex–gender may attempt to not be themselves so that they will be like others. Later, when they decide to live authentically, they may decide to make disclosures of their desired sex–gender identity to others but not without the risk of ridicule and harassment from peers, families, and others. Families may pressure them to suppress their feelings and act "appropriately" (Ellis & Eriksen, 2002; Pela, 1997).

LGBT YOUTH WHO SUCCESSFULLY NEGOTIATE THEIR LIVES

Studies on LGBT youth usually focus on the hazards they face and the consequent difficulties in their lives (Savin-Williams, 1998; see a review of these difficulties under "Obstacles for LGBT Youth" in the next section). Yet, many LGBT youth move successfully through their adolescent years. They connect well with their families, complete school, get jobs, and live in every community across the United States (Mallon, 1998a; Olson & King, 1995). They do this though they face discrimination in almost every educational, work, and neighborhood setting (Gonsiorek & Rudolph, 1991).

Many LGBT youth exhibit unique skills that allow them to cope and even thrive in a culture that seldom recognizes them and actively attempts to suppress their identities and desires for same sex–gender relationships (Savin-Williams, 1998; Schneider, 1989). They often cope well because of internal and external resources that mediate the stressors and, thereby, diminish difficulties in their lives. Several factors that can mediate stressors when one is experiencing difficult life situations were identified by Anderson (1998): high levels of perceived social support, positive self-esteem, self-efficacy displayed through an internal locus of control, and average or above average cognitive abilities. In addition, resiliency can serve as a protection for children and adolescents, sourced in factors such as social skills, self-understanding, and a secure attachment in early childhood to at least one caring adult (not always a parent). In studies of other populations, persons who were resilient and had sufficient resources could cope well with many stressors and obstacles (Halpern, 1993).

Only a few studies address mediating factors for LGBT youth. In one of these studies, Friend (1998) discovered common themes for effective coping: (a) experiencing mentoring, love, and support from a caring adult or family member; (b) finding opportunities for socialization and support as a member of a peer group of LGBT youth; (c) helping others, which underlies the value of community responsibility; and (d) learning the skills of planning, decision making, and negotiation. Other findings from a study by Anderson (1998) showed that gay youth exhibit strengths attained from external and internal resources. These resources, some of which overlap those identified in other findings of researchers cited here, are listed below:

External Resources
- Loving and caring relationships with parents and others
- Availability of supportive persons and groups
- Gay, lesbian, and bisexual friends
- Receiving support when disclosing to parents and nongay peers
- Attaining unanticipated support

Internal Resources
- Seeking out and using available supportive persons and groups
- Positive self-esteem and sense of efficacy
- Higher levels of self-esteem in ethnic youth who reported that experiences with racism prepared them to confront heterosexism
- Increased cognitive competency
- Developing a sense of control over their lives
- Not applying the stigma of being LGB or T to their own identity until their cognitive abilities and social experiences allow them to cope with it
- Processing issues about their sexual orientation and sex–gender expression
- Making decisions about the management of their identities.

Another internal resource, delaying disclosure, can particularly benefit gay and lesbian youth by allowing them to experience psychosocial development in ways similar to their heterosexual peers. They can delay focusing on sexual orientation to a later time when they may have greater cognitive and emotional skills to cope with the realization of a nonheterosexual sexual orientation. The maturation of defensive strategies and coping skills can also help them manage conscious stressors as well as postpone thoughts and feelings that they are not yet ready to deal with. With these thoughts and feelings on hold, they can pursue academics, athletics, or social interactions (Anderson, 1998; Olson & King, 1995). Nonsuspecting parents also provide needed supports for accomplishing the developmental tasks of adolescence and for establishing strengths to cope with life (Anderson, 1998). Even if well-supported by their friends, gay youth may be less resilient if their relationships with significant family members, particularly their fathers, are poor (Nichols & Howard, 1998).

OBSTACLES FOR LGBT YOUTH

As indicated above, some LGBT youth navigate adolescence or young adulthood without serious difficulties, but a minority of this group does experience difficulties and are the ones human services practitioners are most likely to encounter. Without the supports needed for successful transformations from childhood, LGBT youth may fail in school, drop out of school, or run away. Many live on the streets and may survive by prostitution, making them vulnerable to violence, HIV infection, and conflicts with the law. Furthermore, they are at risk for anxiety, depression, chemical misuse, and suicide (for example, Patterson, 1994; Pazos, 1999; Proctor & Groze, 1994; Savin-Williams, 1994).

Explored here are selected troubles of LGBT youth who live on the street. Also examined are issues and controversies about LGBT youth and suicide. Although rarely mentioned in the studies, youth who identify as transgender or are questioning their sex–gender are also at risk for school drop out, misuse of chemicals, self-mutilation, and suicide. Their families may also ostracize and abuse them, prompting them to run from home and join the homeless (Brown & Rounsley, 1996).

Homelessness

Examined here are homelessness and several of its possible corollaries, including prostitution, chemical use, legal troubles, and health risks. LGBT youth may be homeless either temporarily or on a long-term basis. Parents may expel them from the home, or they may choose on their own to seek another environment (Mallon, 1998b). Bucy and Obolensky (1990), along with others, identified four categories of homeless youth as shown below:

- *Runaway youth.* These youth leave their families overnight without parental or caretaker permission. They often return home after one night, but for some this pattern is repeated often (Rotheram-Borus, Rosario, & Koopman, 1991). About half of runaway youth run from foster care placements, delinquent detention facilities, or group homes (Robertson, 1989).
- *Homeless or throw-away youth.* These youth also leave home but with the full acknowledgment of their parents or guardians. Some parents or guardians tell youth to leave home though they have nowhere to go (Rotheram-Borus et al., 1991).
- *Street youth.* These youth have been runaways or homeless for a long time. They fend for themselves on the streets, and are possibly participating in illegal, high-risk activities such as selling drugs or exchanging sex for money (Bucy & Obolensky, 1990).
- *System youth.* For their own protection (for example, from sexual abuse), these youth no longer live with their families. They often live in foster homes (Bucy & Obolensky, 1990).

Several sources reported that homeless youth represent as much as 20 percent to 60 percent of all street youth (Kunreuther, 1991; Savin-Williams, 1994). Little reliable data exist, however, on the actual proportion of homeless youth who identify themselves as LGB or T. Some estimates claim that these groups comprise as much as 20 percent to 47 percent of street youth (for example, Jackson, 1997; O'Brien, Travers, & Bell, 1993). Yet, the reported proportion in many studies was lower than 20 percent, ranging from 2 percent (U.S. General Accounting Office, 1989) to 13 percent (Yates, MacKenzie, Pennbridge, & Swofford, 1991).

The reported proportions of homeless youth who are LGBT, especially the low estimates, are probably large underestimations since many youth are not willing to reveal a nonhetero-sexual sexual identity to authorities, or they may feel unsure about what their sexual identifications are (Savin-Williams, 1994). When youth are asked whether they have ever run away from home, much higher proportions of LGBT youth answer yes. For example, nearly one-half of bisexual and gay youth in one study (Remafedi, 1987) reported that they had run away at least once; many had run away repeatedly. Investigations of runaways in specific locales also discovered a much larger proportion of runaway and homeless youth who were LGBT. Some studies in metropolitan areas, such as Los Angeles and Seattle, indicated that the proportion of runaway and homeless youth who were gay was between 25 percent and 40 percent (Los Angeles County Task Force on Runaway and Homeless Youth, 1988; Seattle Commission on Children and Youth, 1988).

Results from studies on these youth (for example, Coleman, 1989; Peterson, 1989; Rotheram-Borus et al., 1991) suggest that if they do not find programs to meet their needs within two weeks of their arrival on the street, they are likely to be overtaken by assaults and sexual exploitation, drug usage, prostitution, pregnancy, criminal activity, or HIV. Many homeless runaway and throwaway LGBT youth not from metropolitan areas gravitate to cities like New York, San Francisco, Seattle, San Diego, and Los Angeles. Street youth may think that these cities will provide a hospitable environment for them (Durby, 1994), but they are easy targets for assaults and sexual exploitation by adult males, many of whom are heterosexual (Whitlock, 1989). These youth are at risk for rape both on the streets and in some shelters, particularly those where younger adolescents are grouped with older youth (Durby, 1994).

USE OF CHEMICALS

LGBT youth often use chemicals. Of 191 male and 75 female adolescents seeking counseling at a New York City agency, 17 percent of males and 18 percent of females reported frequent chemical use; 19 percent of males and 17 percent of females reported problematic chemical use. The three most commonly used chemicals were alcohol, marijuana, and cocaine (Shifrin & Solis, 1992). Other studies reported higher rates of chemical use. In Hammelman's (1993) study of LGBT youth, 35 percent reported that they were misusing alcohol or drugs. Uribe and Harbeck (1991) found that 97 percent of gay adolescents acknowledged alcohol or drug use, whereas 54 percent of lesbian adolescents acknowledged use of alcohol. Over two-thirds (65 percent) of gay and bisexual males reported high rates of weekly alcohol consumption and 58 percent were using drugs in a study by Remafedi (1987). In a study of urban teenage lesbians, all had consumed alcohol and three-quarters had used drugs, including almost one-third who reported cocaine or crack use (Rosario, Rotherham-Borus, & Reid, 1992). The data on the number of black and Latino LGBT youth who used chemicals in New York City are similar to the data cited here (for example, Rosario et al., 1992; Rotheram-Borus et al., 1991; Rothram-Borus et al., 1992; Rotheram-Borus et al., 1994). Rosario, Hunter, and Gwadz (1997) found that the majority of ethnically diverse LGBT youth from various sites in New York City had a history of multiple substance misuse.

Based on data also collected in New York City, Rotheram-Borus and colleagues (1992) reported chemical abuse among young gay and bisexual male youth in their lifetimes: alcohol, 77 percent; marijuana, 42 percent; crack or cocaine, 23 percent; and hallucinogens, 15 percent. Compared to subjects in national surveys, the lifetime prevalence rates of these youth were 50 percent higher for alcohol, three times higher for marijuana, and eight times higher for cocaine or crack. Among young lesbians, rates in the three months preceding the study by Rosario and colleagues (1992) included: alcohol, 83 percent; drugs, 56 percent; and crack or cocaine, 11 percent. In the Rotheram-Borus and colleagues (1994) study of 131 predominantly ethnic and racial gay and bisexual males presenting at a social services agency for gay adolescents in New York City, high rates of lifetime substance misuse were reported that were well above national rates for male adolescents: alcohol, 76 percent versus 49 percent; marijuana, 42 percent versus 21 percent; cocaine or crack, 25 percent versus 2 percent.

Use of chemicals among homeless youth is almost routine (Whitlock, 1989). Among 72 homeless gay youth and three homeless lesbian youth served by the Hetrick-Martin Institute in New York City, 100 percent were addicted to crack or cocaine (Shifrin & Solis, 1992). High rates of chemical use are particularly high among homeless youth involved in prostitution. Coleman (1989) reported that 20 percent to 40 percent of young prostitutes use drugs (including heroin) and alcohol. They are likely to use the money they make from prostitution in order to support these habits. Yates and colleagues (1991) reported that 75 percent of homeless youth who engaged in prostitution had "diagnosable drug abuse problems" compared to 36 percent of homeless youth who did not acknowledge engaging in prostitution.

Many LGBT youth use drugs and alcohol to decrease or temporarily alleviate their emotional pain (Whitlock, 1989). Over half of the LGBT youth studied by Hammelman (1993) cited that their sexual orientation was partly or the main reason for misusing drugs or alcohol. Shifrin and Solis (1992) explained that chemical use is a strategy for coping with anxiety, depression, and low self-esteem. Chemicals numb anxiety and depression and act as an antidote to the pain of exclusion, ridicule, and rejection. They also provide a feeling of power rather than devaluation. Whitlock (1989) added that for youth on the streets, drugs and alcohol reduce inhibitions and guilt, thereby allowing them to engage in sexual activity for money.

The high use of chemicals among ethnic and racial groups may be indicative of the high stress that youth in these groups experience because of their sexual orientation, minority status, and poverty. Chemicals may temporarily muffle an increasing awareness of their non-heterosexual sexual orientation and the painful realization that being lesbian or gay means that a difficult life may lie ahead (Hammond, 1986).

CONFLICT WITH THE LAW

LGBT youth are at high risk for conflict with the law. This includes one-quarter to one-half of gay and bisexual male youth. Urban male youth experience trouble with the law largely because of substance use, prostitution, truancy, and running away (Remafedi, 1987; Rotheram-Borus et al., 1991). One in four gay and bisexual ethnic youth encounters trouble with the police and one in seven has been jailed (Rotheram-Borus et al., 1991). Along with behaviors to support chemical use such as prostitution and drug trafficking, impaired decision-making capabilities from chemical use probably also underlie some of the conflict with the law experienced by LGBT youth (Whitlock, 1989; Zenilman, 1988).

RISK FOR HIV/AIDS

LGBT youth are at risk for a variety of health difficulties that are sexually transmitted. Many of these difficulties are life threatening or potentially debilitating. Among them are chlamydia, gonorrhea, syphilis, yeast infections, hepatitis-B, HIV infection, and AIDS (Durby, 1994). Coleman (1989) found that one-half of gay and bisexual male prostitutes were treated for at least one sexually transmitted disease. The main focus here will be HIV/AIDS.

LGBT youth put themselves at risk for HIV/AIDS and other health difficulties in a number of ways. Because they often are not comfortable socializing in an open way, they may seek secretive and high-risk sexual contacts (Martin & Hetrick, 1988). About a quarter of HIV-infected youth studied by Remafedi (1988) acquired this disease through sexual activity with others of the same sex–gender. Many LGBT youth feel they have to directly experience sex with persons of the same sex–gender to prove to themselves that they are not heterosexual. This may put them at risk, however, for unsafe sex (Fontaine & Hammond, 1996).

Another contributor to health risks includes the impulsiveness of adolescents; they may not see that today's behavior will affect their future (Remafedi, 1990). They tend to think concretely and feel invulnerable. These characteristics result in denying the realities and risks of sexual experimentation or exploitative sexual relationships (Dempsey, 1994; Remafedi, 1988; Savin-Williams, 1994). Use of chemicals also diminishes their ability to make safe decisions about sexual encounters (Zenilman, 1988). Youth may also be trying to overcome feelings of isolation, alienation, and despair through these encounters (Grossman, 1994). Young gay males, in particular, may resort to transient, anonymous, and potentially abusive sexual contacts as their only sexual outlet. Yet, anonymous sex may be preferable to loneliness and isolation (Martin, 1982). Rosario, Hunter, Maguen, Gwadz, and Smith (2001) identified self-esteem and distress as associated with unprotected sex. For male youth they found a link between anxiety and a higher rate of unprotected anal sex. Also related was low self-esteem via anxiety. Female youth who had higher rates of unprotected oral and vaginal–digital sex had more conduct problems. Limited involvements with gay or lesbian activities and negative attitudes to same sex–gender sexual orientation were also found to be related to more unprotected sex for these lesbian and gay youth.

The National Coalition for the Homeless (1990) estimated that 12 percent to 20 percent of all homeless youth are HIV positive. Runaway and homeless youth are especially at risk for unsafe sex because they may engage in survival sex as well as alcohol and drug use (Durby, 1994). Their concerns for daily survival take priority over illness prevention (Remafedi, 1988). The risks also increase when youth engage in prostitution and in all youth when chemicals are used during sex (Durby, 1994). As noted earlier, youth living on the streets are often drinking alcohol and/or using drugs (Grossman, 1994).

Gay and bisexual male youth are at the greatest risk for HIV/AIDS. Six behavioral patterns put these youth at risk for HIV: many sexual partners, early age of initiation of sexual activity, receptive anal intercourse, bartering of sex for money or drugs, inconsistent condom use, and frequent use of drugs and alcohol during sex (Rotheram–Borus et al., 1994). Anal penetration and associated trauma during sex between males provide a portal of entry for diseases (Remafedi, 1990). Males who participate in receptive anal intercourse without a condom are at particular risk for HIV infection (D'Augelli, 1996a). In a sample of gay youth in Minnesota, 63 percent experienced unprotected anal intercourse or used intravenous drugs (Remafedi, 1994). Dean and Meyer (1995) found 37 percent of 18 to 24 year old gay youth in New York engaged in unprotected receptive anal intercourse over a two-year period. In a study of San Francisco gay males in 1989, Stall, Barrett, and Bye (1992) found that the youngest group (18 to 29 year olds) was at the highest risk. About 10 percent engaged in unprotected anal sex with multiple partners. Lemp and colleagues (1994) also found in a San Francisco sample that 4 percent of the 17 to 19 year olds and 12 percent of the 20 to 22 year olds were HIV positive and one-third had unprotected anal intercourse during the prior six months. Most (70 percent) HIV-positive males did not know their HIV status, despite prior HIV testing.

Monteiro and Fuqua (1994) claimed that young, African American gay males are at an even higher risk for HIV infection than similar European American males, but there are only limited data to support their claim. One study of gay and bisexual men in San Francisco revealed an infection rate of 14.3 percent among the participants who were 17 to 19 years old. Yet, African American participants, ages 17 to 25, had an infection rate of 22.9 percent (Lemp et al., 1994). In a study of predominantly ethnic and racial gay and bisexual males, a high prevalence of behaviors placed the respondents at risk for contracting and transmitting HIV. Sex was bartered for money or drugs by 22 percent, and this bartering was related to a high number of sexual partners (44 percent reported 11 or more lifetime male and female partners) (Rotheram-Borus et al., 1994). Some racial and ethnic youth who engage in sexual activities with others of the same sex–gender make a distinction between these sexual involvements and their sexual identities. Even though they participate in sex with others of the same sex–gender, they do not view themselves as gay. Consequently, they may not identify themselves at risk for HIV/AIDS (Grossman, 1997).

Those who self-identify as gay or bisexual are often unaware that they carry the AIDS virus. This was revealed at the 14th International AIDS Conference in Barcelona, Spain, from a survey of 5,719 gay or bisexual males ages 15 to 29 living in large cities: Baltimore, Dallas, Los Angeles, Miami, New York, and Seattle. Of this group, 573 tested positive for HIV and over three-quarters (77 percent) did not have prior knowledge they were HIV positive; among African American males, 91 percent of those infected did not have prior knowledge of their HIV status. During the prior six months, half of those unaware of their infection reported unprotected anal intercourse with one or more men and nearly half did not use condoms because they did not think their partners were at high risk of infecting them (Devlin & Lum, 2002). HIV/AIDS is also a serious issue among transgender persons (both female–male and male–female persons). Most of the transgender respondents studied by Kenagy (2002) also did not think they were vulnerable to infection and experienced at least one high-risk sexual encounter during the three months prior to the study (mean age: mid to late 20s). They also planned additional high-risk sex in the future.

Young lesbians are at high risk for HIV infection primarily if they or their partners participate in sex with men. Especially if their sexual encounters involve the use of alcohol or drugs and poor judgment, there may be outcomes such as pregnancy, HIV, and other sexually transmitted diseases. They may not insist upon the use of condoms or other preventive measures (Durby, 1994). Young lesbians participating in sex only with other women who likewise avoid sex with men are probably at low risk for HIV infection, but they are at as much risk as young gay males for other sexually transmitted diseases such as gonorrhea, syphilis, and hepatitis. Additional health risks for females include yeast infections and chlamydia (Durby, 1994). Chlamydia is now at epidemic levels among sexually active adolescent girls. Testing twice a year is recommended because early treatment can prevent long-term outcomes such as infertility (Painter, 1998).

An exception for lesbians and HIV involves incarceration. Morris, Baker, and Huscroft (1992) found that both gay and lesbian adolescents were among the groups at highest risk for HIV infection in their sample of incarcerated youth. Among these youth, those who experienced more than 25 sexual partners, prostituted, used intravenous drugs at least once a week, or were pregnant at least once were most likely to be infected.

SUICIDE ATTEMPTS AND COMPLETIONS

Aside from the potential troubles commented on above, some researchers report that LGBT youth also experience higher rates of depression, anxiety, and suicide attempts than do heterosexual youth (for example, Hetrick & Martin, 1987; Remafedi, 1987). Reports of suicide attempts among gay and lesbian adults are long-standing. According to Bagley and Tremblay (1997), the study that Bell and Weinberg executed for the Kinsey Institute is still one of the best general population studies available on suicidal risk among gay males. These researchers analyzed data from a 1969 sample of 575 White, predominantly gay males living in San Francisco. The mean age was 37 years. A stratified random sample of predominantly heterosexual males drawn from the same area provided a comparison group. Controlled variables included age, education, and occupational level. Results showed a suicide attempt rate of 9.6 percent among gay males and .07 percent among heterosexual males, making gay males 13.6 times more likely to attempt suicide by 20 years of age. In their studies of smaller samples of African American gay, lesbian, and heterosexual males and females, Bell and Weinberg also discovered higher attempted suicide rates among gay and lesbian respondents.

Researchers only recently began to acknowledge the risk of suicide among gay and lesbian youth, although these findings were not discrepant from those of the adult investigations. With a growing realization that adolescents were at high risk for suicide, the U.S. Department of Health and Human Services (1989) commissioned a task force to study youth suicide. The "Report of the Secretary's Task Force on Youth Suicide" concluded from a review of the limited empirical literature that gay and lesbian youth represented 30 percent of all adolescent suicides and that these youth were two to three times more likely to make a suicide attempt than were their heterosexual peers (Gibson, 1989). Many more recent studies using community-based samples of young gay youth, primarily ages 14 to 24, found the rate of attempted suicide at between 18 percent and 63 percent (for example, Bagley & Tremblay, 1997; D'Augelli & Hershberger, 1993; D'Augelli, Hershberger, & Pilkington, 2001; Hammelman, 1993; Remafedi, Farrow, & Deisher, 1991; Rotheram-Borus, Hunter, & Rosario, 1994). Studies of school populations estimated the attempted suicide rate among LGBT students at between 20 percent and

40 percent and up to six and a half times greater than rates for heterosexual youth (for example, DuRant, Krowchuk, & Sinal, 1998; Faulkner & Cranston, 1998; Garofalo, Wolf, Wissow, Woods, & Goodman, 1999; Remafedi, French, Story, Resnick, & Blum, 1998).

Predictors of Suicide Attempts. Though suicide attempts are typically linked to completed suicide, some researchers view attempters and completers as two distinct groups (for example, Andrews & Lewinsohn, 1992). Either way, the personal suffering of attempters (Garofalo et al., 1999; Hartstein, 1996) necessitates the identification of remediable predisposing factors (Remafedi et al., 1998). Running away from home, prostitution, and using drugs and alcohol all place LGB youth at risk for suicide or for becoming a casualty of homicide (Savin-Williams & Cohen, 1996). Other kinds of stressors that may provoke suicide attempts and accompanying depression or anxiety, identified by D'Augelli (1996b), include: (a) struggles in managing a stigmatized LGBT identity; (b) disruptions in peer relationships; (c) conflicts about disclosure to family and negative consequences of disclosure; (d) emotional reactions to progressions in close relationships; (e) isolation from LGBT-affirming contexts; (f) discrimination, harassment, and violence because of sexual orientation; and (g) anxieties associated with sexual health, especially threats of HIV infection.

Even though the factors cited above may play a role, factors unique to LGBT youth suicide attempts are not yet determined because studies of suicide among LGBT youth rarely use comparison groups of demographically analogous heterosexual youth. Without these kinds of comparisons, it is difficult to determine whether factors pertinent to sexual orientation or other sample characteristics play a role in suicide attempts for LGBT youth (Safren, 1998). Yet, the unique psychosocial stressors associated with membership in a stigmatized group are likely to contribute to the suicide risk of LGBT youth (Bagley & Tremblay, 1997; Garofalo et al., 1999). Even so, suicide attempts are most likely prompted by a complex interplay of multiple factors; LGBT suicide attempters are not all alike or easy to categorize (Hershberger, Pilkington, & D'Augelli, 1996; Waldo, Hesson-McInnis, & D'Augelli, 1998).

Suicide Completion Rates and Predictors. Estimates of suicide attempts are at 40 to 100 times more common than completed suicides (Shaffer, Garland, Gould, Fisher, & Trautman, 1988). Still, the incidence of completed suicide among LGBT youth is of utmost concern although the actual incident rates are unknown. Reported annual rates of suicide in this group range from as high as 30 percent (U.S. Department of Health and Human Services, 1989) to as low as 2.5 percent (Shaffer, Fisher, Hicks, Parides, & Gould, 1995).

Prior suicide attempts in the general adolescent populations are strongly predictive of eventual suicide (Low & Andrews, 1990). A report by Lewinsohn, Rohode, and Seeley (1996) found about one-third of males who completed suicide, and as many as 50 percent of females who completed suicide, made previous attempts. No one knows, however, whether LGBT attempters are generally more likely than heterosexual attempters to complete suicide (Remafedi et al., 1998). Several studies (for example, D'Augelli & Hershberger, 1993; Hammelman, 1993) suggested that lesbian and female bisexual youth had comparable or somewhat higher completion rates than gay and male bisexual youth. In another study, though, whereas generally young females (ages 13 to 24) attempted suicide two to nine times more often than young males, males were about six times more likely than the females to complete suicide (Rotheram-Borus & Bradley, 1990).

Controversy over Findings on Suicide. The findings on suicide among LGBT youth are controversial because of methodological issues and sampling limits. Methodological issues abound in the studies. Just a few are mentioned here, such as the lack of corroborating evidence of attempts, lack of detailed descriptions of attempts, and lack of standardized measures of suicidal ideation and intent (Remafedi et al., 1998). No uniform definitions exist of suicide, attempted suicide, or even sexual orientation (Herek, 1991). Other limitations are that none of the studies sampled unselected populations, none included matched heterosexual control respondents, and none compared LGBT youth with multiple difficulties to youth without these confounding difficulties (Meehan, Lamb, Saltzman, & O'Carroll, 1992).

Sampling a largely hidden population makes knowing the exact numbers of LGBT persons who commit suicide impossible. Reports of suicide may underestimate suicide among LGBT youth because of the difficulty after death in verifying the sexual orientation of those who committed suicide. Studies focused on identifying LGBT suicides use the psychological autopsy technique that relies on the testimony of others and data drawn from coroner reports (Nichols & Howard, 1998). But, coroners and medical examiners may not know about the gay, lesbian, or bisexual sexual orientation of the respondents, in the absence of prior self-disclosure, and families and friends may not know the person's non-heterosexual sexual orientation, or if they have such information or reasons to suspect it, they may suppress it (Bagley & Tremblay, 1997). Families of street youth may not even be contacted because researchers may not know where they are (Hartstein, 1996).

Because of the numerous issues associated with the studies of suicide attempts and completions among LGBT youth, it is premature to reach definite conclusions (Durby, 1994). Savin-Williams (2001) discovered in a study of lesbian and gay youth ages 18 to 25 that they reported higher rates of suicide attempts compared to heterosexual youth. But many of the attempt reports were false. In other words, claims were made of attempts that did not take place. Of the true attempts, many were not life threatening. The extent of true attempts that were life threatening did not vary by sexual orientation. This does not, however, negate the fact that some lesbian and gay youth are at risk and if they can be accurately identified, appropriate interventions are needed. But, as Savin-Williams emphasized, to target lesbian and gay youth as an at-risk category for such interventions may cause them harm, such as lending credence to arguments that being lesbian or gay results in a "deadly" life. What is not emphasized enough is that most LGBT youth cope with the stressors of their lives well and most of them do not attempt suicide.

PRACTICE WITH YOUTH

Although most LGBT youth manage their lives well, some may need help. Unfortunately many traditional helping systems fail these youth. The kinds of affirmative services and supports that LGBT youth need to meet the challenges of adolescence are emerging in the literature and are adaptable for many types of mainstream centers and agencies. Though most LGBT youth successfully mature into adulthood, many of them will also need some of the supports recommended in the following sections (Hunter, 1995).

Support Groups

Support groups are one of the essential resources for LGBT youth (Robinson, 1991) to decrease emotional and social isolation (Remafedi, 1990) and to provide a safe environment (Jackson & Sullivan, 1994). In a study of 542 LGB youth from community settings, D'Augelli (2002) found that one-third had lost friends because of their sexual orientation. Peer support groups are often crucial for socializing, sharing information, developing social skills, and discussing many topics about sexual identity development (Gonsiorek, 1988). In suburbs and rural areas, support groups may be the only safe place for these youth to make friends and talk openly about their lives (Peters, 1997). Several well-established support groups exist around the country, including OutRight in Durham, NC, OutYouth in Austin, TX, and the Horizons Youth Group, a program of Chicago's Horizons Community Services. Such support groups can be established anywhere to address challenges unique to LGBT adolescents.

Some topics for group discussions were identified by various scholars (for example, D'Augelli et al., 1998; Klein, 1999; Peters, 1997; Rotheram-Borus & Fernandez, 1995) including:

- Overcoming isolation
- Resolving issues related to coming out
- Meeting other LGBT youth
- Carrying on relationships
- Finding romantic partners
- Deciding when and with whom to become sexually active
- Knowing what safe-sex practices to follow
- Dealing with peer pressures for sex
- Passing, if desired, in one's preferred gender
- Deciding when and with whom to disclose
- Identifying risks and advantages of disclosure to certain audiences such as one's family
- Lessening negative responses from family
- Protecting oneself from harassment and potentially violent situations
- Managing conflict
- Coping with anxiety and depression
- Finding positive and successful gay and lesbian role models
- Becoming engaged in the LGBT community and using its resources such as bookstores, centers, and theaters
- Identifying resources for developing social networks
- Developing consciousness about heterosexism.

Adult Support

One organization, Parents, Families, and Friends of Lesbians and Gays (PFLAG), is instrumental in providing adult support for LGBT adolescents. Although originally established as a support group for parents with LGBT children, now the children themselves often attend meetings to get ideas on how best to disclose to their parents (Strommen, 1990; see Chapter 5).

Out-of-Home Care Settings

To improve the conditions for LGBT youth in out-of-home care settings, Mallon (1992) recommended the following actions: (a) provide accurate information about these youth for staff members and the heterosexual youth in these placements; (b) develop a code of conduct that strongly denounces harassment of any kind as intolerable; (c) help LGBT youth to cope with family and school difficulties pertinent to their sexual orientation; (d) help LGBT youth to develop coping skills for handling conflicts with others; and (e) provide opportunities for all youth served to discuss their sexuality with each other.

HIV Prevention Programs

Recently HIV emerged in epidemic proportions among young males who have sex with other males (Valleroy, Secura, MacKellar, & Behel, 2001). Hence, HIV/AIDS prevention programs targeting these youth are essential (Gonsiorek, 1988). Pederson (1994) cautioned, however, that treatment of youths infected with HIV is different from treatment for adults. Youth often lack the skills and experience needed to navigate the logistics of receiving suitable treatment, especially if services are fragmented. Even more problematic is that many agencies deny services to these young persons.

An ecological approach to HIV services for these youth may be helpful. Education about HIV and the methods by which youth can prevent infection are only part of such an approach. Coping skills training, case management, and support are other significant parts. Youth must understand the severity of AIDS, their own vulnerability, and use preventive measures such as safe sex to reduce risk (Pederson, 1994).

Peer education about HIV/AIDS that is empowering or helps youth gain control over their lives was recommended by Zibalese-Crawford (1997). Rotheram-Borus and Koopman (1991) supported this approach in their findings that the ability to avoid high-risk sexual behavior was associated with the perception of being in control of one's life. Though youth can learn the mechanics of safe sex, including condom use, they may lack self-efficacy or the belief that they than can used learned skills to promote their well-being. Enhanced self-efficacy and empowerment of youth must, then, go hand in hand with HIV education and prevention efforts if programs are to be effective. Kirby and DiClemente (1994) add that effectiveness of the programs depends on active learning methods; activities that focus on managing social pressures to participate in sex; and practicing communication skills, negotiation skills, assertiveness skills, and sexual risk refusal skills.

Small peer groups are preferred for information on HIV and prevention, and the material should be understandable and culturally sensitive (Zibalese-Crawford, 1997). Prevention programs are more likely to be effective if provided in the context of larger programs that focus on building social support networks, self-esteem, and positive identity. Additionally, prevention programs need to exist in a variety of settings for gay youth: schools, teen clinics, youth groups, detention centers, and homeless shelters (Cranston, 1992). More and extensive material on HIV counseling, testing, and care resources for adolescents is offered by Ryan and Futterman (1997).

The effects of a comprehensive HIV/AIDS risk reduction program on cognitive and behavioral changes in gay and bisexual adolescents were studied by Remafedi (1994).

Interventions included individualized risk education counseling as well as peer education in small groups. The adolescents received information about HIV transmission and prevention, effects of substance misuse on risky sexual behaviors, ways to avoid the use of chemicals in sexual situations, and HIV antibody testing and counseling. The program also provided methods to facilitate direct communication with sexual partners regarding risk reduction strategies—for example, consistent use of condoms and decreased risky sexual behaviors. Among the participants, this program resulted in a 60 percent reduction in high-risk behaviors such as drug use and unprotected anal intercourse.

Social Services Programs

Despite the particular troubles, most LGBT youth who seek professional social services are in need of someone to talk to, especially someone they can trust and who cares for them and accepts them. They also need resources and referrals to places where they can explore their sexual identity and practice social skills as well as find information, peer support, friendships, and positive role models (Gonsiorek, 1988). Peters (1997) identified the needs of LGBT youth that social services can address. These same goals can also apply to transgender youth (see Mallon, 1999). They are categorized in three categories in Exhibit 13.2.

EXHIBIT 13.2: SOCIAL SERVICES NEEDS OF GAY AND LESBIAN ADOLESCENTS

Normative
- Assistance to attain independence from family
- Opportunities to link with peers and develop friendships and romantic relationships
- Experiences to enhance self-esteem, coherent identity, and sense of competence
- Education about safe sex
- Education about the negative consequences of chemical usage
- Assistance in developing life goals.

Specific
- Information about same sex–gender sexual identity
- Opportunities to link with LGBT peers
- Information about what to anticipate in the coming-out process
- Assistance in deciding to whom and when to disclose
- Skills to initiate and maintain same sex–gender relationships.

Contextual
- Information about safety from physical and emotional harm
- Identification of safe places for social events
- Identification of available peer groups
- Identification of strategies to cope with stigma and other consequences of heterosexism and internalized oppression.

Some youth can benefit from focused programs around coping with disclosure to family and others, dating and intimacy, avoiding HIV infection, and educational/vocational development (D'Augelli, 1996a). Social groups can provide opportunities to meet others. Savin-Williams (1995a) pointed out that LGBT youth need ways to find each other to obtain affection, intimacy, and romance. If they do not find each other, they may experience encounters that are only sexual. If they cannot find peers, they may reach out to adults, leading to premature sexual experiences and unsafe sexual encounters. What they need more are affirming, safe atmospheres with opportunities for nonerotic socialization as well as opportunities to develop age-suitable intimate friendships and dating relationships.

Combating Isolation

Once youth acknowledge same sex–gender attractions and label themselves as LGBT, they usually have few resources for understanding their situations. Affirmative written material may not be available, or these young persons may not feel comfortable purchasing it (D'Augelli, 1996a). They also may not connect with others who have comparable feelings and identity concerns (D'Augelli, 1996a, 1996b; Martin & Hetrick, 1988). It is especially difficult for youth to find other LGBT peers if they do not appear to be "gay" or "lesbian" and are "passing" as heterosexual (Hammersmith, 1987). Even open youth may have a difficult time finding positive peer environments where they can meet other LGBT youth (Radkowsky & Siegel, 1997). Without peer groups, isolation can be especially intense (Hunter, 1995).

Isolation was the most frequently presented dilemma among 329 participants at a New York social services agency for gay and lesbian adolescents. From this group, researchers identified three forms of isolation: *cognitive*—the lack of access to accurate information about same sex–gender sexual orientation or role models; *emotional*—feelings of separateness, both affectionally and emotionally, from one's environments; and *social*—feelings of aloneness in all one's social contexts (that is, family, peers, school, religious institutions). Most of the participants (95 percent) reported that they often felt separated and emotionally isolated from their peers because of feelings of being different (Hetrick & Martin, 1987).

Most of the youth studied by Grossman and Kerner (1998) felt they did not have enough friends, a factor associated with loneliness and drug use. The combination of feeling that they did not have enough friends and feeling lonely was associated positively with suicide ideation and suicide attempts. These youth also often did not feel that they could approach most adults, including their parents and school personnel, because these adults may lack knowledge or be so ingrained with negative attitudes that they could not be supportive.

Telephone/counseling systems or helplines are sometimes available in certain urban areas. Youth can access these systems with relative anonymity; they can also access on-line computer resources and enjoy anonymous communication with other youth. This is often the sole source of affirmative links for isolated youth (Maynard, 2002; Olson & King, 1995).[1]

---

[1] Two examples of these helplines include the Gay and Lesbian Helpline at 888-340-GLBT, Monday to Friday, 6 P.M. to 11 P.M., Saturday and Sunday, 5 P.M. to 10 P.M.; Peer Listening Line at 800-399-PEER, Monday to Friday, 5 P.M. to 10 P.M.

Alleviating Depression and Hopelessness

Cognitive–behavioral interventions for LGBT youth experiencing depression and hopelessness can be useful. Cognitive restructuring may decrease negative attributions that may lead to depression. The hopelessness theory, a cognitive theory of depression, suggests that the cognitive tendency to attribute negative events to internal, global, and stable causes augments the risk for hopelessness and depression (Abramson, Metalksy, & Alloy, 1989). Such negative attributions can develop through cognitive interpretations of negative events that, for example, specifically result from one's sexual orientation. When open about their same sex–gender attractions, youth are likely to experience negative and castigating reactions that may reinforce their belief that they are worthless or unlovable. Even if not open, they observe what happens to others (Safren, 1998). The resulting negative beliefs may contribute to hopelessness about changing or coping with their life circumstances (for example, Cole, 1988). These negative events do not uniquely predict distress in LGBT youth, but a hopeless pathway to depression may develop if one conjectures that same sex–gender attractions are negative, internal, unchanging, and reflect a global sense of personal inadequacy (Safren & Heinberg, 1998). In line with behavioral theories of depression, hopelessness results from the absence of response-contingent positive reinforcement (Lewinsohn, 1974). Compared to heterosexual youth, LGBT youth experience fewer positive events (Safren & Heinberg, 1998).

In addition to cognitive-behavioral interventions (Safren & Heinberg, 1998), skills training approaches can teach adaptive coping techniques and problem-solving methods for meeting with, interacting with, and gaining positive reinforcement from peers. Finding positive social events and finding and associating with positive role models from a variety of sources can change one's pathway from depression toward more happiness (Safren, 1998). Reports on youth attending the Hetrick Martin Institute showed that they experienced high levels of various difficulties such as depression, underachieving in school, dropping out of school, conflicts with families, and high levels of attempted suicide (Hetrick & Martin, 1987; Martin & Hetrick, 1988). Once these youth had the opportunity to socialize with peers at the institute, however, many of their difficulties abated.

SUMMARY

- LGBT adolescents must achieve the same transition tasks to adulthood that all adolescents face. They must separate from their families, develop a sense of their own identity, find their own source of initiative, form intimate relationships and friendships with others, and prepare themselves for a career. Heterosexual youth are bombarded with positive media role models for their journey, but LGBT youth are not. Experiencing confusion about sexual orientation as well as major life decisions and transitions, LGBT youth frequently feel isolated and overwhelmed. Bisexual youth may self-identify as bisexual only as a transition into a gay or lesbian orientation, or they may recognize that they feel genuinely attracted to both sexes.
- Focusing on the strengths, or resilience, of LGBT youth can allow practitioners to find the internal and external resources that can help them not only survive but also thrive as they move toward maturity. Helping these youth discover their own positive self-esteem and a

sense of efficacy can empower them to make supportive contact with external resources like friends and support groups and organizations. As they develop an increasing sense of control, these teens can recognize heterosexism as something outside themselves that they can combat with assertiveness and self-advocacy instead of self-loathing. Generally, despite lack of support and even hostile forces, LGBT youth manage to mature emotionally, assert their identity, and find meaningful lives as they reach young adulthood. For those who are experiencing troubles of one kind or another and seek professional help, practitioners can help them to realize their own strengths and develop a healthy sense of self-reliance and competence in an antagonistic society.

- Troubled LGBT youth face compounded difficulties in development. They may find themselves homeless, either by running away or by being banished by their parents. They may misuse chemicals, experience conflicts with the law, and place themselves at risk for HIV/AIDS. Whereas adolescence is a time of upheaval for all young persons, it can be a deadly time for LGBT youth.

- Struggling with sexual identity issues, fighting with family, feeling isolated, and experiencing harassment and discrimination, LGBT youth may have higher rates of depression, anxiety, and suicide attempts than their heterosexual counterparts. Although research offers a wide range of statistics on this topic, samples indicate that about 30 percent of LGBT youth have attempted suicide; this figure is at least double that for heterosexual youth. Some samples indicated that 50 percent to 60 percent have contemplated suicide. All these statistics are suspect, however, because of nonrandom and small samples, although repeated studies continue to show about the same numbers. Methodological issues and other limitations in studies on completed suicides also make the conclusions of these studies suspect; thus the rate of suicides among LGBT youth is uncertain.

- Support groups, both locally generated and those with national affiliations, can provide information, role models, and support to LGBT youth as they navigate their teen years. Adult support is probably the most valuable resource for young persons. Support from parents is essential, although if parents withdraw support or refuse it, youth can join organizations like PFLAG to find adults for guidance and advice. Some youth will need out-of-home care settings to keep from living homeless. Foster homes or kinship care placements need to be prepared to offer more than a roof over these youth's heads; help with coping and support for emotional growth are crucial for these youth. In addition, youth need HIV prevention information. Because young persons think that they are invulnerable and because they are often woefully uninformed about HIV/AIDS, they need connections with programs that provide accurate, direct information about health and safety.

CHAPTER 13
REFERENCES

Abramson, L.Y., Metalsky, G. I., & Alloy, L. B. (1989). Hopelessness depression: A theory-based subtype of depression. *Psychological Review, 96*, 358–372.

Anderson, B. F. (1998). Therapeutic issues in working with transgendered clients. In D. Denny (Ed.), *Current concepts of transgendered identity* (pp. 215–226). New York: Garland.

Andrews, J. A., & Lewinsohn, P. M. (1992). Suicidal attempts among older adolescents: Prevalence and co-occurrence with psychiatric disorders. *Journal of the American Academy of Child and Adolescent Psychiatry, 31*, 655–662.

Bagley, C., & Tremblay, P. (1997). Suicidal behaviors in homosexual and bisexual males. Crisis: *International Journal of Suicide and Crisis Studies, 18*, 24–34.

Brown, M., & Rounsley, C. A. (1996). *True selves: Understanding transsexualism-For families, friends, coworkers, and helping professionals.* San Francisco: Jossey-Bass.

Bucy, L., & Obolensky, N. (1990). Runaways and homeless youth. In M. J. Rotheram-Borus, J. Bradley, & N. Obolensky (Eds.), *Planning to live: Evaluating and treating suicidal teens in community settings* (pp. 333–353). Tulsa: University of Oklahoma Press.

Cole, D. A. (1988). Psychopathology of adolescent suicide: Hopelessness, coping beliefs, and depression. *Journal of Abnormal Psychology, 98*, 248–255.

Coleman, E. (1989). The development of male prostitution activity among gay and bisexual adolescence. *Journal of Homosexuality, 17*, 131–149.

Cranston, K. (1992). HIV education for gay, lesbian, and bisexual youth: Personal risk, personal power, and the community of conscience. *Journal of Homosexuality, 22*, 247–259.

D'Augelli, A. R. (1996a). Enhancing the development of lesbian, gay, and bisexual youths. In E. D. Rothblum & L. A. Bond (Eds.), *Preventing heterosexism and homophobia* (pp. 124–150). Thousand Oaks, CA: Sage Publications.

D'Augelli, A. R. (1996b). Lesbian, gay, and bisexual development during adolescence and young adulthood. In R. P. Cabaj & T. S. Stein (Eds.), *Textbook of homosexuality and mental health* (pp. 267–287). Washington, DC: American Psychiatric Press.

D'Augelli, A. R. (2002). Mental health problems among lesbian, gay, and bisexual youths ages 14 to 21. *Clnical Child Psychology and Psychiatry*, 7, 433–456.

D'Augelli, A. R., & Hershberger, S. L. (1993). Lesbian, gay, and bisexual youth in community settings: Personal challenges and mental health problems. *American Journal of Community Psychology*, 21, 421–448.

D'Augelli, A. R., Hershberger, S. L., & Pilkington, B. A. (1998). Lesbian, gay, and bisexual youth and their families: Disclosure of sexual orientation and its consequences. *American Journal of Orthopsychiatry*, 68, 361–371.

D'Augelli, A. R., Hershberger, S. L., & Pilkington, B. A. (2001). Suicidality patterns and sexual orientation-related factors among lesbian, gay, and bisexual youths. *Suicide and Life-Threatening Behavior*, 3, 250–264.

Davis, S., Anderson, C., Linkowski, D., Berger, K., & Feinstein, C. (1985). Developmental tasks and transitions of adolescents with chronic illnesses and disabilities. *Rehabilitation Counseling Bulletin*, 29, 69–80.

Dean, L., & Meyer, I. (1995). HIV prevalence and sexual behavior in a cohort of New York City gay men (aged 18–24). *Journal of Acquired Immune Deficiency Syndromes and Human Retrovirology*, 8, 208–211.

Dempsey, C. (1994). Health and social issues of gay, lesbian, and bisexual adolescents. *Families in Society: Journal of Contemporary Human Services*, 75, 160–167.

Devlin, J., & Lum, M. (2002, July 11). Research shows 77 percent of young, gay men with HIV don't know they're infected. *The Texas Triangle*, p. 3.

DuRant, R., Krowchuk, D., & Sinal, S. (1998). Victimization, use of violence and drug use among male adolescents who engage in same-sex sexual behaviour. *Journal of Pediatrics*, 133, 113–118.

Durby, D. D. (1994). Gay, lesbian, and bisexual youth. *Journal of Gay and Lesbian Social Services*, 1, 1–37.

Ellis, K. M., & Eriksen, K. (2002). Transsexual and transgender experiences and treatment options. *Family Journal*, 10, 289–299.

Faulkner, A. H., & Cranston, K. (1998). Correlates of same-sex sexual behavior in a random sample of Massachusetts high school students. *American Journal of Public Health*, 88, 262–266.

Fontaine, J. H., & Hammond, N. L. (1996). Counseling issues with gay and lesbian adolescents. *Adolescence*, 31, 817–830.

Friend, R. A. (1998). Heterosexism, homophobia, and the culture of schooling. In S. Books (Ed.), *Invisible children in the society and its schools* (pp. 137–166). Mahwah, NJ: Lawrence Erlbaum.

Gagné, P., & Tewksbury, J. R. (1996). Transgenerists: Products of non-normative intersections of sex, gender, and sexuality. *Journal of Men's Studies, 5,* 105-130.

Garofalo, R., Wolf, R. C., Wissow, L. S., Woods, E. R., & Goodman, E. (1999). Sexual orientation and risk of suicide attempts among a representative sample of youth. *Archives of Pediatric and Adolescent Medicine, 153,* 487–493.

Germain, C. B. (1991). *Human behavior and the social environment.* New York: Columbia University Press.

Gibson, P. (1989). Gay male and lesbian youth suicide. In M. R. Feinberg (Ed.), *Prevention and intervention in youth suicide* (Report of the Secretary's task force on youth suicide, pp. 110–142). Washington, DC: U.S. Department of Health and Human Services.

Gonsiorek, J. C. (1988). Mental health issues of gay and lesbian adolescents. *Journal of Adolescent Health Care, 9,* 114–122.

Gonsiorek, J. C., & Rudolph, J. R. (1991). Homosexual identity: Coming out and other developmental events. In J. G. Gonsiorek & J. D. Weinrich (Eds.), *Homosexuality: Research implication for public policy* (pp. 161–176). Newbury Park, CA: Sage Publications.

Grossman, A. H. (1994). Homophobia: A cofactor of HIV disease in gay and lesbian youth. *Journal of the Association of Nurses in AIDS Care, 5,* 39–43.

Grossman, A. H. (1997). Growing up with a "spoiled identity": Lesbian, gay and bisexual youth at risk. *Journal of Gay & Lesbian Social Services, 6,* 45–55.

Grossman, A. H., & Kerner, M. S. (1998). Support networks of gay male and lesbian youth. *Journal of Gay, Lesbian, and Bisexual Identity, 3,* 27–46.

Halpern, D. (1993). Minorities and mental health. *Social Science and Medicine, 36,* 597–607.

Hammelman, T. L. (1993). Gay and lesbian youth: Contributing factors to serious attempts or considerations of suicide. *Journal of Gay & Lesbian Psychotherapy, 2,* 77–89.

Hammersmith, S. K. (1987). A sociological approach to counseling homosexual clients and their families. *Journal of Homosexuality, 14,* 173–190.

Hammond, N. (1986, May). *Chemical abuse in lesbian and gay adolescents.* Paper presented at the Symposium on Gay and Lesbian Adolescents, Minneapolis.

Hartstein, N. B. (1996). Suicide risk in lesbian, gay, and bisexual youth. In R. P. Cabaj & T. S. Stein (Eds.), *Textbook of homosexuality and mental health* (pp. 819–837). Washington, DC: American Psychiatric Press.

Herek, G. M. (1991). Myths about sexual orientation: A lawyer's guide to social science research. *Law and Sexuality: Review of Lesbian and Gay Legal Issues, 1,* 133–172.

Hershberger, S. L., Pilkington, N. W., & D'Augelli, A. R. (1996). Categorization of lesbian, gay, and bisexual suicide attempters. In C. J. Alexander (Ed.), *Gay and lesbian mental health: A sourcebook for practitioners* (pp. 39–59). New York: Haworth Park Press.

Hetrick, E. S., & Martin, A. D. (1987). Developmental issues and their resolution for gay and lesbian adolescents. *Journal of Homosexuality, 14,* 25–44.

Jackson, D., & Sullivan, R. (1994). Developmental implications of homophobia for lesbian and gay adolescents: Issues in policy and practice. *Journal of Gay & Lesbian Social Services, 1,* 93–109.

Jackson, T. (1997, March). *In Houston, most street teens are bisexual or gay* [Online]. Available: www.outline.com/triangle/features/houston teens11.html

Kenagy, G. P. (2002). HIV among transgendered people. *AIDS Care, 14,* 127–134.

Kirby, D., & DiClemente, R. J. (1994). School-based behavior interventions to prevent unprotected sex and HIV among adolescents. In R. J. DiClemente & J. C. Peterson (Eds.), *Preventing AIDS: Theories and methods of behavioral interventions* (pp. 117–139). New York: Plenum Press.

Klein, R. (1999). Group work practice with transgendered male-to-female sex workers. *Journal of Gay & Lesbian Social Services, 10,* 95–109.

Kunreuther, F. (1991). The Hetrick-Martin Institute: Services for youth. *Focal Point, 5,* 10–11.

Lee, T. (2001). Trans(re)lations: Lesbian and female to male transsexual accounts of identity. *Women's Studies International Forum, 24,* 347–357.

Lemp, G. F., Hirozawa, A. M., Givertz, D., Nieri, G. N., Anderson, L., & San Francisco Department of Public Health AIDS Office. (1994). Seroprevalence of HIV and risk behaviors among young homosexual and bisexual men: The San Francisco/Berkeley young men's survey. *Journal of the American Medical Society, 272,* 449–454.

Lewinsohn, P. M. (1974). A behavioral approach to depression. In R. J. Friedman & M. M. Katz (Eds.), *The psychology of depression: Contemporary theory and research* (pp. 157–178). Washington, DC: V. H. Winston.

Lewinsohn, P. M., Rohode, P., & Seeley, J. R. (1996). Adolescent suicidal ideation and attempts: Prevalence, risk factors, and clinical implications. *Clinical Psychological Science Practice, 3*, 25–46.

Los Angeles County Task Force on Runaway and Homeless Youth. (1988). *Report and recommendations of the task force.* Los Angeles: Author.

Low, B. T., & Andrews, S. F. (1990). Adolescent suicide. *Medical Clinics of North America, 74*, 1251–1264.

Mallon, G. P. (1992). Gay and no place to go: Assessing the needs of gay and lesbian adolescents in out-of-home settings. *Child Welfare, 71*, 547–556.

Mallon, G. P. (1998a). Lesbian, gay, and bisexual orientation in childhood and adolescence. In G. A. Appleby & J. W. Anastas (Eds.), *Not just a passing phase: Social work with gay, lesbian, and bisexual people* (pp. 123–144). New York: Columbia University Press.

Mallon, G. P. (1998b). Social work practice with gay men and lesbians within families. In G. P. Mallon (Ed.), *Foundations of social work practice with lesbian and gay persons* (pp. 145–180). New York: Haworth Press.

Mallon, G. P. (Ed.). (1999). Practice with transgendered children. *Journal of Gay & Lesbian Social Services, 10*(3/4), 49–64.

Martin, A. D. (1982). Learning to hide: Socialization of the gay adolescent. *Adolescent Psychiatry, 10*, 52–64.

Martin, A. D., & Hetrick, E. S. (1988). The stigmatization of the gay and lesbian adolescent. *Journal of Homosexuality, 15*, 163–183.

Maynard, J. (2002). Answering the call. *In the Family, 7*, 22–24.

McAnarney, E. (1985). Social maturation: A challenge for handicapped and chronically ill adolescents. *Journal of Adolescent Health Care, 6*, 90–101.

Meehan, P., Lamb, J., Saltzman, I., & O'Carroll, P. (1992). Attempted suicide among young adults: Progress toward a meaningful estimate of prevalence. *American Journal of Psychiatry, 149*, 41–44.

Monteiro, K. P., & Fuqua, V. (1994). African American gay youth: One form of manhood. *High School Journal, 77*, 20–36.

Morris, R. E., Baker, C. J., & Huscroft, S. (1992). Incarcerated youth at risk for HIV infection. In R. J. DiClemente (Ed.), *Adolescents and AIDS: A generation in jeopardy* (pp. 52–70). Thousand Oaks, CA: Sage Publications.

Morrow, S. L. (1997). Career development of lesbian and gay youth: Effects of sexual orientation, coming out, and homophobia. *Journal of Gay & Lesbian Social Services, 7,* 1–15.

National Coalition for the Homeless. (1990). *Fighting to live: Homeless people with AIDS.* Washington, DC: Author.

Nichols, J., & Howard, J. (1998). Better dead than gay? *Youth Studies Austria, 17,* 28–33.

O'Brien, C., Travers, R., & Bell, L. (1993). *No safe bed: Lesbian, gay and bisexual youth in residential services.* Toronto: Central Toronto Youth Services.

Offer, D., Ostrov, E., & Howard, K. I. (1981). *The adolescence: A psychological self-portrait.* New York: Basic Books.

Olson, E. D., & King, C. A. (1995). Gay and lesbian self-identification: A response to Rotheram-Boras and Fernandez. *Suicide and Life-Threatening Behavior, 25,* 35–39.

Painter, K. (1998, August 15). "Conversion" of gays: Morality or bigotry? *USA TODAY,* p. 1D.

Patterson, C. J. (1994). Children of the lesbian baby boom: Behavioral adjustment, self-concepts, and sex role identity. In B. Greene & G. M. Herek (Eds.), *Psychological perspectives on lesbian and gay psychology: Theory, research, and clinical applications* (pp. 156–175). Newbury Park, CA: Sage Publications.

Pazos, S. (1999). Practice with female-to-male trangendered youth. *Journal of Gay & Lesbian Social Services, 10,* 65–82.

Pederson, W. B. (1994). HIV risk in gay and lesbian adolescents. *Journal of Gay & Lesbian Social Services, 1,* 131–147.

Pela, R. J. (1997). Boys in the dollhouse, girls with toy trucks. *The Advocate, 746,* 55–60.

Peters, A. J. (1997). Themes in group work with lesbian and gay adolescents. *Social Work with Groups, 20,* 51–69.

Peterson, J. W. (1989, April 11). In harm's way: Gay runaways are in more danger than ever, and gay adults won't help. *The Advocate,* pp. 8–10.

Proctor, C. D., & Groze, V. K. (1994). Risk factors for suicide among gay, lesbian, and bisexual youths. *Social Work, 39,* 504–513.

Radkowsky, M., & Siegel, L. J. (1997). The gay adolescent: Stressors, adaptations, and psychosocial interventions. *Clinical Psychology Review, 17,* 191–216.

Remafedi, G. (1987). Adolescent homosexuality: Psychosocial and medical implications. *Pediatrics*, *79*, 331–337.

Remafedi, G. (1988). Preventing the sexual transmission of AIDS during adolescence. *Journal of Adolescent Health Care*, *9*, 139–143.

Remafedi, G. (1990). Fundamental issues in the care of homosexual youth. *Medical Clinics of North America*, *74*, 1169–1179.

Remafedi, G. (1994). Cognitive and behavioral adaptations to HIV/AIDS among gay and bisexual adolescents. *Journal of Adolescent Health*, *15*, 142–148.

Remafedi, G., Farrow, J. A., & Deisher, R. W. (1991). Risk factors for attempted suicide in gay and bisexual youth. *Pediatrics*, *87*, 869–875.

Remafedi, G., French, S., Story, M., Resnick, M. D., & Blum, R. (1998). The relationship between suicide risk and sexual orientation: Results of a population-based study. *American Journal of Public Health*, *88*, 57–60.

Robertson, M. J. (1989). *Homeless youth in Hollywood: Patterns of alcohol use.* Berkeley, CA: Alcohol Research Group.

Robinson, K. E. (1991). Gay youth support groups: An opportunity for social work intervention. *Social Work*, *36*, 458–459.

Rosario, M., Hunter, J., & Gwadz, M. (1997). Explorations of substance abuse use among lesbian, gay, and bisexual youth: Prevalence and correlates. *Journal of Adolescent Research*, *12*, 454–476.

Rosario, M., Hunter, J., Maguen, S., Gwadz, M., & Smith, R. (2001). The coming-out process and its adaptational and health-related associations among gay, lesbian, and bisexual youths: Stipulation and sexploration of a model. *American Journal of Community Psychology*, *29*, 133–160.

Rosario, M., Rotherham-Borus, M. J., & Reid, H. (1992). *Personal resources, gay-related stress, and multiple problem behaviors among gay and bisexual male adolescents.* Unpublished manuscript, Columbia University, New York.

Rotheram-Borus, M. J., & Bradley, J. (1990). Evaluation of suicide risk. In M. J. Rotheram-Borus, J. Bradley, & N. Obolensky (Eds.), *Planning to live: Evaluating and treating suicidal teens in community settings* (pp. 109–136.) Tulsa: University of Oklahoma, National Resource Center for Youth Services.

Rotheram-Borus, M. J., & Fernandez, M. I. (1995). Sexual orientation and the developmental challenges experienced by gay and lesbian youths. *Suicide and Life Threatening Diseases*, *25*(Suppl.), 26–34.

Rotheram-Borus, M. J., Hunter, J., & Rosario, M. (1994). Suicidal behavior and gay-related stress among gay and bisexual male adolescents. *Journal of Adolescent Research*, *9*, 498–508.

Rotheram-Borus, M. J., & Koopman, C. (1991). Sexual risk behavior, AIDS knowledge, and beliefs about AIDS among predominantly minority gay and bisexual male adolescents. *AIDS Education Prevention*, *3*, 305–312.

Rotheram-Borus, M. J., Rosario, M., & Koopman, C. (1991). Minority youths at high risk: Gay males and runaways. In M. E. Colten & S. Gore (Eds.), *Adolescent stress: Causes and consequences* (pp. 181–200). New York: Aldine de Gruyter.

Rotheram-Borus, M. J., Rosario, M., Meyer-Balburg, H.F.L., Koopman, C., Dopkins, S. C., & Davies, M. (1992). *Sexual and substance use behaviors among homosexual and bisexual male adolescents in New York City*. Unpublished manuscript, New York State Psychiatric Center, HIV Center for Clinical and Behavioral Studies.

Rotheram-Borus, M. J., Rosario, M., Meyer-Balburg, H.F.L., Koopman, C., Dopkins, S. C., & Davies, M. (1994). Sexual and substance use acts of gay and bisexual male adolescents in New York City. *Journal of Sex Research*, *33*, 47–57.

Ryan, C., & Futterman, D. (1997). *Gay and lesbian youth: Care and counseling*. Philadelphia: Handley & Belfus.

Safren, S. A. (1998). Suicidality in gay, lesbian, and bisexual youth. *Behavior Therapist*, *21*, 147–152.

Safren, S. A., & Heinberg, R. G. (1998). Depression, hopelessness, suicidality and related factors in sexual minority and heterosexual adolescents. *Journal of Consulting & Clinical Psychology*, *67*, 859–866.

Sanford, N. D. (1989). Providing sensitive health care to gay and lesbian youth. *Nurse Practitioner*, *14*, 30–47.

Savin-Williams, R. (1994). Verbal and physical abuse as stressors in the lives of lesbian, gay male, and bisexual youths: Associations with school problems, running away, substance abuse, prostitution, and suicide. *Journal of Consulting and Clinical Psychology*, *62*, 260–269.

Savin-Williams, R. (1995a). An exploratory study of pubertal maturation timing and self-esteem among gay and bisexual male youths. *Developmental Psychology*, *31*, 56–64.

Savin-Williams, R. C. (1995b). Lesbian, gay male, and bisexual adolescents. In A. R. D'Augelli & C. J. Patterson (Eds.), *Lesbian, gay, and bisexual identities over the lifespan* (pp. 165–189). New York: Oxford University Press.

Savin-Williams, R. C. (1998). *". . . and then I became gay": Young men's stories*. New York: Routledge.

Savin-Williams, R. C. (2001). Suicide attempts among sexual-minority youths: Population and measurement issues. *Journal of Consulting and Clinical Psychology, 69,* 983–991.

Savin-Williams, R., & Cohen, K. M. (1996). Psychosocial outcomes of verbal and physical abuse among lesbian, gay, and bisexual youths. In R. C. Savin-Williams & K. M. Cohen (Eds.), *The lives of lesbians, gays, and bisexuals: Children to adults* (pp. 181–200). Fort Worth, TX: Harcourt Brace.

Schneider, M. (1989). Sappho was a right-on adolescent: Growing up lesbian. *Journal of Homosexuality, 17,* 111–130.

Seattle Commission on Children and Youth. (1988). *Report on gay and lesbian youth in Seattle.* Seattle, WA: City of Seattle, Department of Human Services.

Shaffer, D. (1993). Suicide risk factors and the public health [Editorial]. *American Journal of Public Health, 83,* 171–172.

Shaffer, D., Fisher, P., Hicks, R. H., Parides, M., & Gould, M. (1995). Sexual orientation in adolescents who commit suicide. *Suicide and Life-Threatening Behavior, 25,* 64–71.

Shaffer, D., Garland, A., Gould, M., Fisher, P., & Trautman, P. (1988). Preventing teenage suicide: A critical review. *Journal of the American Academy of Child Psychiatry, 27,* 675–687.

Shifrin, F., & Solis, M. (1992). Chemical dependency in gay and lesbian youth. *Journal of Chemical Dependency Treatment, 5,* 67–76.

Stall, R., Barrett, D., & Bye, L. (1992). A comparison of younger and older gay men's HIV risk-taking behaviors: The communications technologies 1989 cross-sectional survey. *Journal of Acquired Immune Deficiency Syndromes, 5,* 682–687.

Strommen, E. F. (1990). Hidden branches and growing pains: Homosexuality and the family tree. *Marriage & Family Review, 14,* 9–34.

Sullivan, T. R., & Schneider, M. (1987). Development and identity issues in adolescent homosexuality. *Child and Adolescent Social Work, 4,* 13–23.

Turner, J. S., & Helms, D. B. (1991). *Lifespan development* (4th ed.). Fort Worth, TX: Holt, Rinehart & Winston.

Uribe, V., & Harbeck, K. (1991). Addressing the needs of lesbian, gay, and bisexual youth: The origins of PROJECT 10 and school-based intervention. *Journal of Homosexuality, 22,* 9–28.

U.S. Department of Health and Human Services. (1989). Report of the Secretary's Task Force on Youth Suicide (Vol. 3): *Prevention and interventions in youth suicide* (DHHS publication ADM 89–1622.). Rockville, MD: Author.

U.S. General Accounting Office. (1989). *Homelessness: Homeless and runaway youth receiving services at federally funded shelters.* Washington, DC: Author.

Valleroy, L., Secura, G., MacKellar, D., & Behel, S. (2001, February). *High HIV and risk behavior prevalence among 23- to 29-year-old men who have had sex with men in six U.S. cities.* Paper presented at the 8th Conference on Retroviruses and Opportunistic Infections, Foundation for Retrovirology and Human Health, Chicago.

Waldo, C. R., Hesson-McInnis, M. S., & D'Augelli, A. R. (1998). Antecedents and consequences of victimization of lesbian, gay, and bisexual young people: A structural model comparing rural university and urban samples. *American Journal of Community Psychology, 26,* 307–334.

Whitlock, K. (1989). *Bridges of respect: Creating support for lesbian and gay youth* (2nd ed.). Philadelphia: American Friends Service Committee.

Yates, G., MacKenzie, R., Pennbridge, J., & Swofford, A. (1991). A risk profile comparison of homeless youth involved in prostitution and homeless youth not involved. *Journal of Adolescent Health, 12,* 545–548.

Zenilman, J. (1988). Sexually transmitted diseases in homosexual adolescents. *Journal of Adolescent Health Care, 9,* 129–138.

Zibalese-Crawford, M. (1997). A creative approach to HIV/AIDS programs for adolescents. *Social Work in Health Care, 25,* 73–88.

CHAPTER 14
MIDLIFE AND AGING

What are issues for midlife gay and lesbian persons in education, work, and income?

What are family issues for midlife and older gay and lesbian persons?

What are positive experiences at midlife for gay and lesbian persons?

What particular worries face gay and lesbian persons at midlife?

What issues do midlife lesbians and gay persons bring to practitioners?

What issues do older gay and lesbian persons bring to practitioners?

What are some of the obstacles that older gay persons

face when trying to link with other gay persons?

How can practitioners be involved with community services for older lesbian
and gay persons?

WHEN DOES MIDLIFE OR OLDER AGE HAPPEN?

The age boundaries for middle adulthood are approximately between 40 and 64 years, with most researchers in adult studies using age 65 as the entry point into older age. The boundaries of these life periods, however, are not clearly definable by age (Bumpass & Aquilino, 1995), stages (Clausen, 1986), or tasks (Rothblum, Mintz, Cowan, & Haller, 1995). Additional factors that make the boundaries ambiguous are the ever-expanding life expectancy rates and the expanding number of persons working beyond age 65 (Herdt, Beeler, & Rawls, 1997).

Gay and lesbian persons who view themselves as "older" grew up from the 1920s through the 1950s or before the "gay liberation" movement of the late 1960s and the 1970s (Herdt et al., 1997). Persons living during this pre-Stonewall era (prior to the revolt against a police raid at the Stonewall Inn in 1969) experienced no concepts such as "gay pride" (Christian & Keefe, 1997) and "out" was not "in" (Wahler & Gabbay, 1997). Anyone identified as "homosexual" was called "sick by doctors, immoral by clergy, unfit by the military, and a menace by the police" (Kochman, 1997, p. 2). Invisibility, fear, and loneliness dominated the lives of these persons. Coming out and reaching self-acceptance and self-esteem were long and arduous processes for them (Fassinger, 1997). They also invested much effort in keeping their sexual identity hidden (Friend, 1987, 1990; Jones, Nystrom, Fredriksen, Clunis, & Freeman, 1999).

The current midlife cohort of gay and lesbian persons also reached adulthood without visible role models or other cultural resources to support the development of their identities. The issues around sexual identity did not reach resolution for many persons in this cohort until well into their 20s or even 30s (Cohler & Galatzer-Levy, 2000; Cohler, Hostetler, & Boxer,

1998). Yet, this cohort charted a new path as the first generation of this population to reach midlife since the 1969 Stonewall rebellion and the evolving modern gay liberation movement (Kimmel & Sang, 1995).

PRIMARY LIFE ARENAS

The primary life arenas for midlife and older lesbian and gay persons include education, work, income, family, and community. The literature in these areas, however, does not always cover both groups.

Education and Work

The levels of education and income of gay persons are generally high in comparison to the general population of men (Adams & Kimmel, 1991; Quam & Whitford, 1992). Yet, some midlife and older gay persons may not pursue higher level positions in their work because of actual, or fear of, discrimination and the consequent efforts to hide their sexual orientation (Kimmel & Sang, 1995). In preliminary results from a Chicago study of lesbian and gay adult development and aging, many older gay persons reported that they worked in low-profile positions—for example, librarians or engineers—whereas others worked in gay-identified jobs-for example, interior design (Cohler et al., 1998; Herdt et al., 1997; Hostetler & Cohler, 1997).

Many midlife lesbians have extensive educations. Among a national sample of midlife lesbians studied by Bradford and Ryan (1991), 24 percent graduated from college or completed some graduate work; 48 percent completed a graduate or professional degree. Lesbian baby boomers also benefited from job and career opportunities advanced by the feminist movement (Rothblum et al., 1995). Compared with employed lesbians women in the general population, midlife lesbians are four times as likely to work in professional or technical fields (Bradford & Ryan, 1991). Over three-fourths of the midlife lesbians studied by Sang (1990, 1991) were professionals. Half of them were in nontraditional careers or jobs such as university deans, financial analysts, or truck drivers although their earned income does not reflect their academic and employment accomplishments. Over half (55 percent) of Sang's respondents were at least five times as likely as other women their age to experience distressing financial difficulties.

Family

Midlife and older gay and lesbian persons have families of origin and families of friends, partners, and children. In contrast with younger generations today who may have children through means such as donor sperm insemination, midlife and older persons who have children most often had them in heterosexual marriages.

Parents. When their gay or lesbian children are at midlife, parents may decrease attempts to change them. Realizing that their sexual orientation is not just a phase, the parents may finally accept it. If the adult child has a long-time partner, the parent's familiarity with this partner may make the relationship more acceptable to them. The parents may also be happy that their child is not alone (Rothblum et al., 1995; Weinstock, 2000). Some families, however, continue to dictate rules to their adult children such as not disclosing their sexual orientation to certain family members (Brown, 1995), and some midlife children remain severed from their families of origin (Weinstock, 2000).

An added family role for many midlife women is that of caregiver to elderly parents. Though the general caregiving literature is extensive, only rare mention is made of midlife lesbians as caregivers. After marital partners, daughters are usually the "selected" caregivers (Brody, 1990). Midlife lesbians are likely, therefore, to sometimes perform this role, as are gay persons (Kimmel & Sang, 1995). In a rare survey of 1,466 gay and lesbian persons with adult care responsibilities, Fredriksen (1999) reported that about 40 percent were between ages 30 and 39, and slightly more than one-quarter (26 percent) were between ages 40 and 49.

Friends. Usually, friends are the major source of social support for lesbian and gay persons over the life course (for example, Bradford & Ryan, 1991; Sang, 1991; Weinstock, 2000). Several studies reported that both midlife and older lesbian and gay persons have close friends, mostly of their same sexual orientation (for example, Bradford & Ryan, 1991; Grossman, D'Augelli, & Hershberger, 2000; Jones et al., 1999). Especially if they were not open with their families of origin, midlife lesbians are closer to and more comfortable with their lesbian friends (Bradford & Ryan, 1991), and they receive more support (81 percent) from friends, ex-lovers, and lovers (Fertitta, 1984). A closeted lesbian may have only ex-lovers for friends because they are the only ones who know of her sexual identity (Rothblum et al., 1995).

Older lesbian and gay persons studied by Herdt and colleagues (1997) were closer to their friends than their families of origin. Their friendship networks provided significantly more support than did their families of origin (Dorfman et al., 1995). Eighty-nine percent of another sample of older lesbian and gay respondents indicated that if they had a serious difficulty they could turn to at least three friends for advice and emotional support; 60 percent had six or more such friends (Beeler, Rawls, Herdt, & Cohler, 1999). Friendship networks provide other positive outcomes besides support, such as increased life satisfaction for older lesbian and gay persons (Adelman, 1991; Lee, 1987), psychological well-being for older gay persons (Friend, 1980), and higher self-esteem and adaptation to aging for older lesbians (Raphael & Robinson, 1984).

Partners. Midlife lesbian couples range from those who have a long history together to those who have just met and fallen in love (Mitchell, 2000). Midlife lesbians may be more definite than younger lesbians about what they are looking for in a partner. They also may be less willing to spend time in casual interactions and may go out with another woman only if the development of a serious relationship seems likely. Fewer partners may be available because lesbians who are single in the 40 to 65 age group are rare. When midlife lesbians find another single midlife lesbian, they may move at a faster pace toward involvement (Rose & Zand, 2000).

Much of the limited data on midlife and older gay or lesbian primary linkups focused on demographics. From earlier data that combined samples of older lesbian and gay persons, about 70 percent of older gay persons and 50 percent of older lesbians had no primary same sex–gender link (for example, Almvig, 1982; Kehoe, 1986). A more recent sample showed that 48 percent of older lesbian and gay persons lived alone, 38 percent were with a partner, and 5 percent had a nonromantic roommate (Beeler et al., 1999). Over half (56 percent) of the

Herdt and colleagues (1997) sample of older lesbian and gay persons were in a link with a lover or partner, but a greater number of lesbians (79 percent) were partnered than gay persons (46 percent). Nearly half of the respondents in a sample of midlife and older gay persons studied by Brown, Sarosy, Cook, and Quarto (1997) were involved in committed relationships.

In studies on midlife and older lesbians, the proportion with lovers or partners ranged from 18 percent to more than 74 percent (Almvig, 1982; Bradford & Ryan, 1991; Raphael & Robinson, 1984; Schreurs & Buunk, 1996). Midlife lesbians not in long-term partnerships generally reported wanting to be in one (Rose, 1996; Rothblum et al., 1995). The data on the involvement of midlife and older gay persons in partner relationships were also variable in the findings, ranging from 24 percent to 43 percent (Berger, 1996; Quam & Whitford, 1992). The partners of 5 percent of the older men studied by Quam and Whitford were deceased. Older gay persons studied by Christian and Keefe (1997) were reluctant to recommit to a primary link after losing a partner to death or a breakup.

Several researchers (Berger, 1980, 1996; Lee, 1987) found that older gay persons in long-term partnerships, whether with same–sex gender or cross sex–gender partners, were more likely to be satisfied with their lives than those who lived an unattached single life. Other studies found that, among older gay persons, having a partner was associated with higher levels of psychosocial adaptation and self-esteem (Brown et al., 1997), better physical health, and less loneliness (Grossman et al., 2000). The older men studied by Brown and colleagues in committed relationships were uniformly positive about their relationships because partners provided much of the support and satisfaction in their lives. Relationships among older lesbians studied by Kehoe (1989) were more caring, gentle, emotionally close, and sexually satisfying than their heterosexual relationships had been. Older lesbians studied by Raphael and Robinson (1984) preferred other older women for their intimate partners. The older the participants in lesbian couples studied by Schreurs and Buunk (1996), the more satisfied they were.

Children. Many midlife women have children, including one-third in the Bradford and Ryan (1991) sample. Compared to heterosexual mothers, however, Rothblum and colleagues (1995) reported that for many lesbian mothers, children came later in life. This includes many lesbian baby boomers who did not desire motherhood earlier in their lives, changed their minds later, and began motherhood around age 40. Nine midlife mothers (mostly nonbiological mothers, ages 45 to 62) who were parenting young children in the San Francisco Bay area reported that their experiences with mothering in midlife were overwhelmingly positive. They felt that they had reached new levels of maturity, patience, and self-confidence that helped with parenting (Donaldson, 2000).

Midlife lesbians who are raising teenagers experience challenges as do all parents with children at this life stage, but they also may fear that their children will become hostile and rejecting because of their mothers' sexual orientation. As discussed in Chapter 7, adolescents typically adopt hostile peer attitudes toward same sex–gender sexual orientation (Kirkpatrick, 1989b). If mothers are just coming out as lesbians in midlife, their children may react negatively to the sudden divergence from the norm in sexual orientation (Sang, 1992). They may fear embarrassment and ridicule or being stigmatized and repudiated by their peers and therefore will undergo an adjustment process regarding their mothers' revelations (Rothschild, 1991).

Sexuality

Sex is important to midlife gay and lesbian persons, and most of them want a sexual life (Bradford & Ryan, 1991; Brown et al., 1997; Rothblum et al., 1995). Not having a sex life is usually not a voluntary state (Kehoe, 1986, 1989). Most of Deevey's (1990) sample of older lesbians reported they were still sexually active, and Loulan (1987) found that lesbians over age 60 experienced sex more often (two to three times a month) than any other age group. Older gay persons with the lowest frequency of sexual encounters are often unsatisfied with their sex lives (Brown et al., 1997). The current sex lives for the majority of older gay persons, however, are satisfactory especially in the qualitative aspects. In their sample of older gay persons, Pope and Schulz (1990) found that gay persons experienced no change in sexual enjoyment with age (69 percent); some even reported greater sexual enjoyment (13 percent).

In one of the rare studies of 56 midlife bisexual persons, Weinberg, Williams, and Pryor (2001) found that in midlife, sexual involvements decreased and a move toward sexual activity with one sex–gender only increased for half of the group. In part, the decrease in sexual involvements was attributed to menopause, aging, a perceived decrease in sexual attractiveness, and distractions of other responsibilities. Limiting sexual activity to one sex–gender was often related to the desire for monogamy.

Community

Only about a third of midlife lesbians (34 percent) studied by Woodman (1987) affiliated with the gay and lesbian community. Often these women experienced the dilemma of fearing the disclosure of their sexual orientation but not wanting to be isolated from others who might be potential friends. In contrast, almost all the 68 midlife lesbians studied by Fertitta (1984) involved themselves in the lesbian community, an involvement that was significant to them for self-acceptance and a positive lesbian identity. A majority of the midlife lesbians (52 percent) in the Bradford and Ryan (1991) study attended events for lesbians at least once or twice a month. The most frequent activities were supportive, social, or political. Those who participated in lesbian and gay rights organizations (37 percent) were more likely to be open about their sexual orientation.

Many older lesbians in couples socialized only in their own homes. Yet, some lesbians after retirement might experience greater freedom to participate in the lesbian community when job loss is no longer a threat (Kirkpatrick, 1989a, 1989b). Some older lesbians, however, might not venture into lesbian communities if they thought they were not welcomed by younger, more political and radical women (Barrett, 1989). In a sample of older gay and lesbian persons studied by Beeler and colleagues (1999), over half (59 percent) were "moderately" or "exceedingly" involved with the gay and lesbian community. Compared to the men, however, the women were less involved. Only 19 percent were "exceedingly" involved; almost half (48 percent) were not "very" involved. Adelman (1991) found that adjustment to later life and high life satisfaction for older lesbians and gay persons were associated with low involvement with other lesbian and gay persons. But other studies report positive results from participation in the lesbian and gay communities. Persons well-integrated into the lesbian and gay community were less fearful of aging, more self-accepting, less depressed (Berger, 1996); higher in self-esteem and self-worth; higher in psychological well-being (Weinberg &

Williams, 1974); and happier (Lee, 1987). Participation in social and religious activities in the gay community was associated with an increase in the quality of life for older gay persons. These positive factors were especially prominent among men 50 to 59 years of age (Whitford, 1997).

POSITIVE LIFE EXPERIENCES

Midlife LGB persons experience positive changes and endeavors during this life period. The literature on older lesbian and gay persons also indicates that the majority of them seem to adjust well and experience satisfaction with their lives.

Positive Changes and Sources of Meaning for Midlife Lesbian and Gay Persons

For the particular group of midlife lesbians studied so far (primarily White, well-educated, professional, and middle to upper middle class), changes at midlife were mostly positive. They experience greater self-acceptance, perspective, and wisdom (Fertitta, 1984); confidence and optimism about the future and their growth and development as persons (Sang, 1991); self-understanding, fulfillment, liking of themselves, enjoyment of themselves and others, self-direction, and better balance of commitments. Many felt that midlife was the best time of their lives (Dorell, 1991). Most midlife bisexual persons (women and men) studied by Weinberg and colleagues (2001) were more certain and positive about their bisexual identity.

Generative Endeavors

Erikson (1980) identified the major issue of midlife as "generativity" (contributing to future generations) versus stagnation. Children are a common generative source for lesbian and gay persons. They may have their own children, may serve as foster or adoptive parents (Cohler et al., 1998), or may reach out to help other relatives such as nieces, nephews, godchildren, or children of other lesbian and gay persons (Humphreys & Quam, 1998). Many gay persons reach out to future generations through mentoring, teaching, social work, and activism (Isay, 1996). Contributions to future generations of lesbian and gay persons can also come through participation in the struggle for the civil rights of all LGBT persons (Humphreys & Quam, 1998). The AIDS epidemic provides numerous opportunities for generative endeavors. Some midlife men were leaders in the creation of services for gay persons with HIV/AIDS (Kimmel & Sang, 1995). Aside from providing services for persons with HIV/AIDS and caring for these persons, generativity also includes efforts to curtail the epidemic for the next generation. Lesbians have adopted their own mission in breast cancer prevention groups and concern for the health of the next generation of women (Cohler et al., 1998). Many lesbians also participate in caregiving for gay persons with AIDS and fund raising for research and services (Brown, Sarosy, Cook, & Quatro, 1997).

Adjustments and Life Satisfaction for Older Lesbian and Gay Persons

Older lesbian and gay persons have many obstacles to overcome in their lives. Besides the stigma of their sexual orientation, they are also stigmatized because of their stage of life. This creates particularly negative stereotypes, for example, being sexually frustrated, lacking support of family and friends, and being lonely, unhappy, and depressed (Berger, 1980, 1996; Deevey, 1990; Friend, 1980, 1990). Older ethnic and racial gay and lesbian persons also contend with racism. Older African American gay persons studied by Adams and Kimmel (1997) were more aware of racism than age discrimination or antigay discrimination. Another layer of bias and discrimination in the lives of older lesbians is sexism. More negative views are directed at older women than older men (for example, Schoonmaker, 1993). Gay persons, on the other hand, may contend with "accelerated or premature" aging, or losing physical attractiveness (Sarosy, 1997), especially in the gay community (Kertzner & Sved, 1996).

Given the situations recounted above, what is life like for older LGB persons? Much of the research on these persons has centered on countering the negative stereotypes about their lives and is now largely outdated, having been published several decades ago. Fortunately reports from several new investigations are available (Beeler et al., 1999), and they largely confirm the earlier results. Though variation exists among older lesbian and gay persons as it does among heterosexual persons (Reid, 1995), studies show that most of the respondents do not match the depressed, lonely, and isolated stereotypes attributed to them (for example, Brown et al., 1997; Dawson, 1982; Dorfman et al., 1995). They seem psychologically well-adjusted, happy, generally satisfied with their lives, and are adapting well to getting older (for example, Adelman, 1988; Friend, 1991; Jones et al., 1999). Most lesbian and gay persons recognize the positive aspects of their identities and feel satisfied about themselves (Lee, 1987; Quam & Whitford, 1992).

CONTRIBUTIONS TO ADJUSTMENT AND SATISFACTION

Some research findings exist on factors that may influence the adjustment and satisfaction of older lesbian and gay persons. These factors fall into two categories: sources of strength and sources of well-being.

Strengths include mastering independence and stigma, developing crisis competence, and developing sex–gender role flexibility. Both older gay and lesbian persons can fend for themselves (Friend, 1991; Quam & Whitford, 1992). They probably worked all their adult lives and planned to take care of themselves physically and financially when they became older (Quam & Whitford, 1992). They also learned how to negotiate systems needed for services (for example, Adelman, 1991; Fassinger, 1996). In addition, high levels of independence from families resulted in forming "families of friends" for support groups (Brown et al., 1997).

For the gay persons studied by Brown and colleagues (1997), the mastery of stigma developed slowly throughout their lives. Strong barriers existed to breaking through fear and hidden identities (Fassinger, 1997). Many researchers proposed, though, that successful resolution of the crises of coming out and disclosure prepares one to cope with later life crises (for example, Quam & Whitford, 1992; Sharp, 1997). Yet, if the coming–out and disclosure processes can lead to personal growth and development, they can also overwhelm persons and their coping resources (Reid, 1995).

Another researcher, Lee (1987), found in a study of older gay persons that the happiest participants reported the fewest number of crises, whether associated with sexual orientation or not. They also reported that self-acceptance developed more easily for them than other participants. However, some of the exceedingly satisfied men experienced long periods of identity crisis, while some who did not go through a crisis of this kind were unhappy.

Cohort effects may also impact crisis competence. The current midlife cohort may demonstrate more crisis competence in later life because they have already dealt more directly with heterosexism at work and in the larger public arena. Or sexual orientation may be less significant for them and for younger cohorts of lesbian and gay persons when they reach later life (Cohler & Galatzer-Levy, 2000).

The strength of sex–gender role flexibility may develop because as they age lesbian and gay persons potentially attain more freedom to behave in nontraditional ways; they do not play out traditional sex–gender roles (Fassinger, 1997). In old age, then, they can take care of themselves better because they can perform tasks associated with both males and females, such as financial management and cooking (Friend, 1991). Lesbians also feel strengthened to cope with later life because they broke out of the social prescriptions for women to be passive, dependent, and powerless (Fassinger, 1997; Sharp, 1997).

SOURCES OF WELL-BEING

The major factors that gay persons identify as benefiting them in old age include a strong support system, good physical health, adequate financial resources, openness to growth and change, and interests and activities that they feel passionate about (Brown et al. 1997). No doubt, older lesbians would include similar items on such a list. Another factor, addressed in some detail here, includes three variations of well-being identified by Friend (1990, 1991): *affirmative* (resists stereotypes), *conforming* (internalizes stereotypes), and *passing* (accommodates to stereotypes).

A number of studies found that *affirmative* older lesbian and gay persons attained high levels of psychological adjustment. These persons constructed a positive identity by rejecting the negative views of the larger culture. They accepted and valued themselves and saw advantages in their sexual orientation (Friend, 1991). Most of these respondents also reported that they were close to their families and in frequent communication with them. They were also more likely to be open with and accepted by their families and to encourage accepting family members to challenge heterosexism through participation in groups such as the Parents, Families, and Friends of Lesbians and Gays (Friend, 1990).

The two other outcomes observed by Friend (1990, 1991) were less optimal. In the conforming groups, lesbian and gay persons capitulated to negative beliefs and attitudes and incorporated these beliefs into their views of themselves. Older lesbian and gay persons who were conforming matched the popular stereotypes of these persons as alienated, lonely, and depressed and still living with self-loathing, shame, and guilt. They hid all or parts of themselves from families and friends, creating a wall of separation and distance. They did not challenge their negative beliefs about themselves largely because of their separation from affirmative lesbian and gay persons. They continued to be distanced from other lesbian and gay persons and were unlikely to develop social or emotional support systems. In a report on older gay African American men, Icard (1996) observed that those who viewed their sexual attractions as a disease or sin did not associate with either black or White gay persons.

The *passing* option comprises the middle range of the three outcomes that Friend (1990, 1991) observed among older lesbian and gay persons. Though members of this group were not much different from those in the conforming group, they did not totally accept society's negative views, marginally accepted their sexual orientation, and were a little less isolated. They could not fully accept their sexual orientation because they largely capitulated to the heterosexist ideology. Probably because they thought heterosexuality was the superior sexual orientation, they were often heterosexually married and closeted. Many persons in this group kept their distance from identifiable lesbian or gay persons, although some interacted with them and sometimes participated in a long-term primary relationship with someone of the same sex–gender. Even if they entered a same sex–gender relationship, they still passed as heterosexual. The emotional costs of this incongruent life, however, were high.

WORRIES IN MIDLIFE AND OLDER LIFE

Beyond midlife, the concerns of growing older are no different from those of older heterosexual men and women with the distinct exception of contending with heterosexism (Almvig, 1982; Quam & Whitford, 1992). Older gay persons reported that the most difficult aspects of their lives were physical deterioration, worsening health, and the deaths of friends, family, and loved ones (Quarto, 1996). Almost three-quarters of the sample of gay persons studied by Brown and colleagues (1997) feared dying in a nursing home without family or friends. In a survey by Herdt and colleagues (1997), lesbians over age 50 seemed more positive than older gay persons about their lives and about themselves although nearly half experienced concerns about their physical health and appearance. Gay persons seemed to feel more positive when they were younger than age 50 but grew more anxious as they grew older, and by age 50 they felt more negative about their bodies and futures.

Other concerns for both older lesbian and gay persons included maintenance of autonomy, reduced social and employment roles, difficulties protecting themselves, difficulties managing finances, and age discrimination (Fassinger, 1997; Quam, 1993; Reid, 1995). Seventy-one self-identified LGB persons ages 50 to 80 in San Diego County, CA, were surveyed by Jacobs, Rasmussen, and Hohman (1999). Their concerns included income (24 percent), loneliness (17 percent), health care (14 percent), crime (10 percent), use of free time (8 percent), age discrimination in the larger community (4 percent), transportation (2 percent), and housing (2 percent). The most common concerns about aging for older lesbians surveyed by Jones and colleagues (1999) included housing, financial security, illness, effect of losing the support of partners and friends through death, and how to ensure that they and their partners would continue to have control over their own lives. They were hopeful that their support networks would be available to help them maintain control of their lives when they got older. Most of those with partners made provisions to protect the right of inheritance for their partners. Many expressed an interest in living among older lesbian and gay persons in communities where they could live together and support each other. Other studies found that 50 percent to 88 percent of gay and lesbian persons were interested in gay and lesbian retirement communities (Lucco, 1987; Quam & Whitford, 1992).

Another way to contemplate the issues discussed here is to ask older lesbian and gay persons what they want instead of what they worry about. In the Beeler and colleagues (1999) sample of older gay and lesbian persons living in Chicago, future goals included striving for financial security (31 percent), maintaining health and well-being (30 percent), having positive social relations (21 percent), achieving success in career and work (19 percent), and attaining a comfortable retirement (19 percent). Most importantly, 73 percent said they wanted expanded opportunities to socialize with other older gay and lesbian persons. Most (89 percent: 98 percent of women, 85 percent of men) said that Chicago should have a gay and lesbian community center but when asked whether they would use such a center, only 25 percent said yes. About two-thirds (62 percent) said their use would depend on the nature and focus of such a center.

Health Issues

Physical health was not a worry for most of the midlife lesbians surveyed by Bradford and Ryan (1991). Four out of five respondents perceived their health as excellent or good. Yet, maintaining good health was a new concern for some midlife lesbians (35 percent) studied by Sang (1993). For both older lesbian and gay persons declining health was a serious concern (Brown et al., 1997; Quam & Whitford, 1992). About two-thirds of the men studied by Beeler and colleagues (1999) reported concerns about their physical health and independence compared to 23 percent of the women. The same concerns were experienced by almost half (47 percent) of the men over age 51 compared to 29 percent of the women (Cohler et al., 1998; Herdt et al., 1997; Hostetler & Cohler, 1997). Although women were not as concerned about their health—because they are more likely to reach older age than men—they are more vulnerable later to the chronic and often disabling illnesses of old age such as arthritis and diabetes (Fassinger, 1997).

HIV/AIDS

The general health picture is totally different for both midlife and older gay persons than for lesbians because of HIV/AIDS. This epidemic is now in its third decade, leaving the gay community "saturated with the consciousness and experiences of mortality" (Hopcke, 1992, p. 106). It hit the current cohort of midlife men the hardest by shortening the expected life course for many of them (Cohler et al., 1998). Most gay and bisexual men in midlife have friends and partners infected with HIV or AIDS who may be dying or have died. They probably know twice as many who are living with the infection (Hopcke, 1992; Quarto, 1996). These men may also be living with this illness and impending death (Kimmel & Sang, 1995).

Although older lesbian and gay persons came of age long before the HIV/AIDS epidemic began (Herdt et al., 1997), this epidemic affects the health picture for gay and bisexual men over age 50 (Catania et al., 1989; Kooperman, 1994). Seven percent of a sample of older gay persons studied by Beeler and colleagues (1999) was HIV positive, and 15 percent currently had HIV-positive partners. AIDS affected the lives of many more in this sample (70 percent of men and 46 percent of women) usually because of lovers, friends, and family members claimed by this disease.

Older persons with HIV experience special difficulties such as faster progression of the disease. In addition, older gay persons who are not out about their sexual orientation might delay being tested for HIV or upon learning of the diagnosis keep it a secret from family and friends (Kooperman, 1994). Older gay persons with an HIV-positive diagnosis and a low sense of self-worth could feel even greater shame about their sexual orientation. Some men in their 60s and 70s might believe that HIV/AIDS confirms the worthlessness they always thought was true about themselves (Kochman, 1993).

A greater number of persons with HIV/AIDS are now living longer. Linsk (1997) studied older men plus one woman over age 50 with HIV and discovered that several of these persons received a diagnosis of HIV many years ago.

OTHER STRUGGLES OF AGING

Although the majority of older gay and lesbians persons seem well-adjusted and happy, some struggle more than others with heterosexism and stigma, lack of acceptance of aging, despair about their lives, and low income. The most worrisome issue for many older lesbian and gay persons is loneliness. Lesbians over age 60 studied by Kehoe (1989) reported that besides economic security their most serious concern was loneliness. Samples of older gay persons reported feeling more isolated from other gay persons as they grew older (Berger, 1996) and they worried about being without friends and membership in a couple (Whitford, 1997).

One of the loneliest times for an older gay or lesbian person can occur when a partner dies (for example, Kochman, 1997; Saunders, 1990). Without accepting and supportive family-of-origin members, no one else may be available who knows what is happening to the surviving person. Even other lesbian and gay persons may not be aware of the situation if the couple was isolated from other gay and lesbian persons (Brown et al., 1997). The remaining partner in a lesbian relationship, for example, may never have applied the word lesbian to the link and may feel it necessary to hide grieving over the loss of the partner (Fullmer, 1995). Mourning in seclusion, without support from others, can make one vulnerable to despair (Humphreys & Quam, 1998).

Although this is not always easy to do, it is crucial that older lesbian and gay persons rebuild their support systems when members are lost. Older lesbian and gay persons studied by Grossman and colleagues (2000) who were most satisfied with their social support networks felt less lonely. Those living with partners were also less lonely. The availability of social support in later life will depend partly on factors such as partners, children, and other relatives. Several studies found that lesbians who came out later in life, compared to those who did so earlier in life, tended to maintain closer and supportive ties to relatives (Cohler & Galatzer-Levy, 2000; Kehoe, 1989). Both older lesbian and gay persons who have children are more likely to experience more social support than those who are childless (Herdt et al., 1997). If one has no partner, children, or contacts with relatives, it appears that the best next investment is close friends and others who know about one's sexual orientation (Grossman et al., 2000). Friendships can provide many resources for support (Friend, 1980; Kehoe, 1989), although the resources may not be equivalent depending on whether one's friends are new or long term (Matthews, 1986).

PRACTICE WITH MIDLIFE AND OLDER LESBIAN AND GAY PERSONS

Because we live in a society that is ageist, as lesbian and gay persons get older they may need assistance in overcoming negative attitudes about aging. This requires accomplishing several tasks, such as seeking out positive role models for successful aging, developing new age-suitable standards of attractiveness, visualizing a positive future as mature adults, and working on life planning and goal setting. Diverse models of older gay and lesbian persons can counter stereotypical and stigmatized images and provide alternative ways to approach older age (Kooden, 1997). The most useful models are older gay and lesbian persons who are active, productive, self-motivated, and sexual (Friend, 1990). Affirmative books with accurate information countering myths and misconceptions of older lesbian and gay persons can also help (Friend, 1987). Several possibilities include *Gay and Gray* by Berger (1996) and *Rubyfruit Jungle* by Brown (1973). Interactions with lesbian and gay persons of different ages can also provide varied role models as well as social stimulation (Friend, 1987). For gay persons who are troubled by no longer feeling that they are physically attractive, Linde (1994) suggested that they redefine their own self-worth as well as learn new ways to associate with other men without trying to emulate a youthful version of sexual attractiveness.

Several other issues that midlife and older lesbian and gay persons may bring to practice are discussed here. Many of the practice concerns of older lesbian and gay persons focus on the development of and access to various social services. This practice focus was addressed in Chapter 12 as a community practice endeavor.

Midlife Lesbian and Gay Persons

Many midlife lesbians may not perceive a need for professional assistance because they are happy during this stage of life. This is not the whole story, however, as some of these women experience worries and anxieties, especially about finances (Bradford & Ryan, 1991). For these clients, referrals to persons who specialize in financial planning can be useful as is retirement planning for the many midlife lesbians who are self-supporting (Sang, 1992).

The midlife lesbians surveyed by Bradford and Ryan (1991) sought mental health services mostly for emotional distress and difficulties with lovers. These concerns topped the list of the reasons these women gave for seeking a practitioner: feeling sad or depressed (62 percent), difficulties with lovers (62 percent), difficulties with family members (39 percent), feeling anxious or afraid (36 percent), personal growth (32 percent), difficulties with sexual orientation (27 percent), loneliness (24 percent), alcohol and drug difficulties (20 percent), work difficulties (20 percent), difficulties with friends (10 percent), and difficulties with racism (4 percent). Long-term use of mental health services was significantly associated with the distress associated with disclosing one's sexual orientation. Except for issues around sexual orientation and disclosure, many of the concerns listed here can be addressed by standard interventions, including cognitive restructuring, behavioral techniques, self-nurturing, and social skills training.

Another issue that may bring some midlife women to seek a practitioner is the experience of new feelings about another woman. These women may need assistance in conceptualizing coming out as a life transition; clarification of the challenges ahead may facilitate a more positive transition. Lesbians in prior marriages may hold a variety of negative images of lesbians. It is important, therefore, to provide them with accurate and affirming views. The primary means for this is positive contact with other lesbians in addition to affirmative books, support groups, and cognitive restructuring (Bridges & Croteau, 1994).

No comparable surveys have focused on midlife men and the concerns they may bring to a practitioner though men who did not come out as gay until midlife may seek counseling. Before coming out, they may have experienced a wrenching struggle, accompanied by guilt, secrecy, and traumatic crisis in the family or heterosexual marriage (Kimmel & Sang, 1995). When gay persons have been in long-term marriages and have had little or no experience with the gay community, they often struggle with tasks usually associated with adolescence instead of with midlife. They are suddenly in an unfamiliar world and experience considerable uncertainty. They not only have to redefine themselves but navigate the new environment (Herdt et al., 1997).

Some gay persons also feel that heterosexual marriage did not prepare them for being single and dating in this new world. They expressed a sense of "being different" from other gay persons because of their many years in heterosexual marriages. They wondered whether gay persons not formerly married could understand their feelings about the importance of their children to them, how time-consuming children can be, and the difficulties of divorce, coming out in later life, and disclosure to their children. These struggles left them feeling as if they were living in two worlds. Some of these gay persons may want to learn dating skills applicable to the gay community and want resources such as support groups for persons in similar situations (Herdt et al., 1997). The experiences of formerly married lesbians are probably similiar, including lesbians who lived as single mothers or reared children from a prior marriage within a lesbian relationship (Laird, 1996).

It is not unusual for persons at midlife to reassess their life decisions and to desire more purpose and meaning in their lives and a more authentic sense of self (Hopcke, 1992). The use of groups for midlife gay persons (also applicable to lesbians) was recommended by Frost (1997) to assist in creating more meaning in their lives, learning to love themselves and others, and contemplating issues of generativity or ways to give back to the gay and lesbian community or to society at large.

Planning Ahead for Midlife Lesbian and Gay Persons

It is imperative that coupled or single lesbian and gay persons plan ahead for their later years. Planning for older age includes disability and health insurance and knowledge of the health care and legal systems before a crisis occurs. A will and a power of attorney are significant legal instruments if a partner becomes severely ill or dies (Dunker, 1987; Martin & Lyon, 1992). Midlife and older lesbian and gay persons must ensure that these agreements and others such as living wills, funeral arrangements, and distribution of personal and joint property are honored (Friend, 1990; Reid, 1995). To protect as much personal, medical, and property rights as possible, planning should begin in midlife. Human services practitioners need to know the legal resources that can assist in such planning (Humphreys & Quam, 1998).

Social Services for Older Lesbian and Gay Persons

A community assessment of the needs of older lesbian and gay persons was discussed in Chapter 12. Social services organizations for older lesbian and gay persons are growing in the United States and Canada to meet their needs. Several organizations in large urban areas provide comprehensive social and support services. The most comprehensive program is Senior Action in a Gay Environment (SAGE) in New York (Friend, 1987; Grenwald, 1984). Founded in 1977, SAGE offers a variety of support and counseling services, education, outreach, and case management. It also uses the assistance of older lesbian and gay volunteers to plan and conduct the programs. Examples of other programs include the Society for Senior Gay and Lesbian Citizens/PROJECT RAINBOW in Los Angeles (Galassi, 1991); Gay and Lesbian Outreach to Elders (GLOE) in San Francisco (Reid, 1995); and Gay and Lesbian Elders Active in Minnesota (GLEAM) in Minneapolis. Prime Timers, a self-help group that originated in Boston, now exists in other parts of the United States (McDougall, 1993). Gays and Lesbians Older and Wiser (GLOW) is a support group that operates out of a university-based geriatric clinic in Ann Arbor, Michigan (Slusher, Mayer, & Dunkle, 1996).

Older LGB persons prefer to use social and support services provided in LGB programs, but such organizations do not always exist where they live. Social work administrators can develop programs in mainstream agencies once they learn what is needed for specialized, functional, and accessible social services for this population. SAGE invests considerable efforts in educating professional communities and the general public about the needs of older lesbian and gay persons in a wide variety of settings and through a diverse array of media. This organization advocates for more sensitive services delivery, support, and advocacy. In-service training programs at local agencies sensitize the staff to the issues and needs of older LGB persons. Information is disseminated at conferences, and a speaker's bureau provides leaders for panels and group discussions. Educational materials are published in newsletters and magazines and broadcast on television and radio (Jacobs et al., 1999).

In working with older lesbian and gay persons, it is particularly important for human services professionals to move beyond the training they might have received in individual, intrapsychic approaches to the use of advocacy and consultative interventions. The community organizing approach discussed in Chapter 12 offers more promise of meeting the needs of this population than the direct provision of specific services. For example, the preference of older lesbians for existing friendships and social networks in meeting their needs means that a group specialist might be most effective as a consultant or supervisor in setting up self-help groups in a community. This would replace or expand one's usual role as a direct provider of group services. Advocacy for other social services is also important for these older clients (Fassinger, 1997) once this population has identified what services they need. Many older lesbian and gay person will also be resources for some of the needed services (see Chapter 12).

A set of practice principles with older lesbian and gay persons developed by Humphreys and Quam (1998) addresses attitudes, knowledge, and skills. These principles, which could also apply to midlife and younger persons, include:

- *Respect the client's right to privacy and confidentiality.* Many older lesbian and gay persons do not want their sexual orientation known.
- *Recognize diversity among older LGB persons.* Different persons are at different levels of comfort with their sexual orientation and in how open or closeted they are. Some are out to everyone whereas others might never have acknowledged to anyone that they are gay, lesbian, or bisexual. Some might have a history of acceptance from family and friends where-

as others might have experienced humiliating discrimination and rejection. The age at which they discovered they were gay, lesbian, or bisexual could have been at 20 or 50. Important differences also emerge depending on the era in which they were born and when they acknowledged a lesbian gay, or bisexual orientation. For example, Jacobson (1995) pointed out that both middle age and older gay and lesbian persons might use different terminology in referring to themselves and to their sexual orientation than younger gay and lesbian persons do. Humphreys and Quam (1998) emphasized that it is important to inquire about and use terms that are most comfortable for the client. Some lesbians who are older or unaffiliated with the modern women's movement continue to refer to themselves as "gay" instead of "lesbian." In addition, although in a sexual history it might appear as if a client is bisexual, the client, if an older person, might not use this term.

- *Recognize that not all the difficulties being experienced by a person are associated with being old or gay or lesbian.* It is easy to fall into an ageist trap of thinking that because someone is old, they are tired or frail. Similarly, a heterosexist bias might lead the practitioner to see clients as frightened or depressed when clients can feel depressed about many things other than age or sexual orientation.

- *Treat identified family as family.* As discussed in various places in this book, gay and lesbian persons create their own families. Older gay and lesbian persons fear that in times of critical decisions about their health, medical professionals will not acknowledge members of their family of choice as the ones the client wants involved in the decisions.

- *Plan activities and discussions that are neutral with respect to sexual orientation.* In one senior center, a discussion group that offered a Valentine's Day discussion about "husbands and wives" changed the topic to "those I have loved." Another senior center started having round dances and ethnic dancing that did not involve male–female partners.

- *Create an atmosphere among staff that is open to discussion about differences and an environment that does not tolerate discrimination based on sexual orientation or sex–gender expression.* Though many agencies do good work with staff training and developing sensitivity to diversity, including sexual orientation and sex–gender expression, personnel changes over time. New questions also occur particularly with new clients and circumstances that might challenge the norms of an agency. The environment needs to be one in which staff members can safely express their lack of knowledge about these challenges or how to handle them.

In a study done in San Diego, California, study, Jacobs and colleagues (1999) found that older lesbian and gay participants used social and support groups within the lesbian and gay community, but they also used general community health services. They rated lesbian and gay services in San Diego as more adequate in meeting needs in times of emotional crises than nonlesbian and nongay services. The future utilization of social services among the respondents was also addressed: about one-third (32 percent) said they would participate once a week in programs for older lesbian and gay persons; 20 percent every other week; and 25 percent once a month. Some (9 percent) would participate more than once a week. Nearly half (49 percent) would never participate in lesbian and gay programs within nongay and nonlesbian organizations. Both women and men indicated that they would be interested in participating in social groups within the lesbian and gay community segregated by sex–gender. About one-third (31 percent) would never participate in mixed sex–gender social programs; 41 percent would participate but only once a month. When asked what types of programs or social services they would like to see available, the respondents requested social groups and support groups more than any other services. About one-third also said they would use phone contact services, bereavement groups, and transportation services. Women (53 percent) were significantly more interested in bereavement groups than men (24 percent). Other types of services that older lesbian and gay persons would use if available include peer counseling, employment, dating, and help with finding affordable housing.

Group Services for Older Lesbian and Gay Persons

One of the key needs that older lesbian and gay persons want fulfilled is social support and expanded opportunities to meet others. Various group services can meet the needs for support and social/recreational involvements as well as provide counseling, education, and advocacy. Specific benefits of groups, identified by Fassinger (1997), include (a) *affiliation* (for example, countering isolation); (b) *affirmation* (for example, understanding one's feelings for a lost partner); (c) *universality* (for example, normalizing one's experiences); (d) *ventilation/catharsis* (for example, talking about and expressing feelings about issues in one's life); (e) *integration* (for example, integrating one's sexual orientation into one's overall identity); (f) *altruism and meaningful roles* (for example, mentoring, sharing knowledge and skills); (g) *socializing techniques and interpersonal learning* (for example, using others as guides for transitions, benefiting from hearing about their experiences); and (h) *information, resources, and problem solving* (for example, learning about community resources and how to access them). Frost (1997) also recommended a group setting for gay persons to help combat isolation resulting from losses, to examine the myths and stereotypes about aging, and to develop deeper nonsexual relationships with other gay persons.

SUMMARY

- Research indicates that generally midlife gay and lesbian persons are well-educated, many having college or professional degrees. They work across a variety of settings. Although gay persons are at least as well educated as their heterosexual counterparts, they may not have experienced the same level of career success because of heterosexism in the workplace or because of their own choices about how to balance career and personal life. As for all women, income levels for lesbians are lower than their training and education would imply.
- Many midlife lesbian and gay persons experience positive relationships with their families of origin. Parents have usually reconciled their differences with their children by the time they reach midlife. At this time in life, adult children are often assuming caregiving responsibilities for aging parents and this no doubt includes lesbian and gay adult children.
- Often, gay and lesbian persons have formed families of "choice," a supportive collection of friends and, sometimes, family members who provide nurturance and companionship. These networks are valuable sources of strength to midlife and older gay and lesbian persons. In addition, most of these persons want relationships with partners, and many want or had children.
- Despite its stress, midlife offers gay and lesbian persons much satisfaction. Many persons in midlife undertake generative tasks such as volunteer work that give them a sense of con-

tributing to something larger than themselves. Many gay persons have participated in the development of AIDS outreach programs, and many lesbians have worked to eliminate breast cancer and AIDS for future generations. Other strengths emerge in midlife and beyond to give gay and lesbian persons a "mastery of independence" that helps them adjust to aging and prepare for it financially and socially. Also, many gay and lesbian persons have overcome their fears of stigma and have learned how to cope with the crises of living in a heterosexist society. In short, they have achieved a positive sense of self that brings life satisfaction and well-being. Older lesbian and gay persons are not different from heterosexual persons in psychological adjustment, morale, or rates of depression.

- Although most lesbian and gay persons have achieved contentment in life, many report worrying about security and aging. Some fear that they will lose physical attractiveness, they will be alone in old age, they will have insufficient financial resources, and they will be in poor health. In addition to living with heterosexism, they are facing ageism and the discrimination that comes with it in work and social situations. Women, particularly, face health difficulties associated with aging, as well as financial difficulties. Gay persons face the specter of AIDS in their own lives and in the lives of their friends.

- In midlife, lesbians seek help for many of the same issues that heterosexual women do, but women who are coming out in midlife confront unique issues. Self-identifying as lesbian can be a difficult transition requiring education and support (in groups as well as individually). Women in couples for the first time with other women are learning new ways of relating physically and emotionally with their partners, and they are experiencing these new feelings in the midst of the busiest time of life. Gay persons coming out in midlife typically have a history of marriage and lifelong efforts to deny their gay identity. When these men do come out, they have little experience with the gay community and may go through developmental phases more similar to adolescence than to midlife.

- Some men may focus on the loss of physical attractiveness for aging gay persons; these men may perceive that they are no longer able to attract younger men or even men of their own age. These feelings can bring on depression and anxiety that need to be addressed by practitioners.

- Most older lesbian and gay persons seem well-adjusted and happy, but some struggle more than others with heterosexism and stigma, lack of acceptance of aging, despair, and low income. Especially painful for these persons is loneliness.

- When gay and lesbian programs are unavailable (as is often the case), other agencies must take responsibility for outreach to aging gay and lesbian persons. This outreach will include educating the general public about the needs of these clients and advocating for the funding of social and support services. This will involve extensive staff training in certain realities of practice with gay and lesbian persons. The importance of community organizing on behalf of these persons and of group services must also be emphasized.

CHAPTER 14
REFERENCES

Adams, C. L., & Kimmel, D. C. (1991, November). *Older African-American gay men*. Paper presented at the annual meeting of the Gerontological Society of America, San Francisco.

Adams, C. L., & Kimmel, D. C. (1997). Exploring the lives of older African American gay men. In B. Greene (Ed.), *Ethnic and cultural diversity among lesbians and gay men* (pp. 132–151). Thousand Oaks, CA: Sage Publications.

Adelman, M. (1988). Quieting our fears: Lesbians and aging. *Outlook: National Lesbian and Gay Quarterly, 1*, 78–81.

Adelman, M. (1991). Stigma, gay lifestyles, and adjustment to aging: A study of later-life gay men and lesbians. In J. A. Lee (Ed.), *Gay midlife and maturity* (pp. 1–32). New York: Haworth Press.

Almvig, C. (1982). *The invisible minority: Aging and lesbians*. Syracuse, NY: Syracuse University, Utica College.

Barrett, M. B. (1989). *Invisible lives: The truth about millions of women loving women*. New York: Morrow.

Beeler, J. A., Rawls, T. W., Herdt, G. H., & Cohler, B. J. (1999). Needs of older lesbians and gay men in Chicago. *Journal of Gay and Lesbian Social Services, 9*, 31.

Berger, R. M. (1980). Psychological adaptation of the older homosexual male. *Journal of Homosexuality, 5*, 161–175.

Berger, R. M. (1996). *Gay and gray: The older homosexual man* (2nd ed.). Binghamtom, NY: Haworth Press.

Bradford, J., & Ryan, C. (1991). Who we are: Health concerns of middle-aged lesbians. In B. J. Warshow & A. J. Smith (Eds.), *Lesbians at midlife: The creative transition* (pp.147–163). San Francisco: Spinsters.

Bridges, K. L., & Croteau, J. M. (1994). Once-married lesbians: Facilitating changing life patterns. *Journal of Counseling & Development, 73*, 134–140.

Brody, E. M. (1990). *Women in the middle: Their parent care years*. New York: Springer.

Brown, L. B., Sarosy, S. G., Cook, T. C., & Quarto, J. G. (1997). *Gay men and aging.* New York: Garland.

Brown, L. S. (1995). Are we family? Lesbians and families of origin. In K. Jay (Ed.), *Dyke life: From growing up to growing old, a celebration of the lesbian experience* (pp. 19–35). New York: Basic Books.

Brown, R. (1973). *Rubyfruit jungle.* New York: Daughters.

Bumpass, L. L., & Aquilino, W. S. (1995). *A social map of midlife: Family and work over the middle life course.* Vero Beach, FL: MacArthur Foundation Research Network on Successful Midlife Development.

Catania, J., Turner, H., Kegeles, S., Stall, R., Pollack, L., & Coates, T. (1989). Older Americans and AIDS: Transmission risks and primary prevention research needs. *Gerontologist, 29,* 373–381.

Christian, D. V., & Keefe, D. A. (1997). Maturing gay men: A framework for social service: Assessment and intervention. *Journal of Gay and Lesbian Social Services, 6,* 47–78.

Clausen, J. A. (1986). *The life course: A sociological perspective.* Englewood Cliffs, NJ: Prentice Hall.

Cohler, B. J., & Galatzer-Levy, R. M. (2000). *The course of gay and lesbian lives: Social and psychoanalytic perspectives.* Chicago: University of Chicago Press.

Cohler, B. J., Hostetler, A. J., & Boxer, A. M. (1998). Generativity, social context, and lived experience: Narratives of gay men in middle adulthood. In D. P. McAdams & E. de St. Aubin (Eds.), *Generativity and adult development* (pp. 265–309). Washington, DC: American Psychological Association.

Dawson, K. (1982, November). Serving the older gay community. *Siecus Report, 17,* 5–6.

Deevey, S. (1990). Older lesbian women: An invisible minority. *Journal of Gerontological Nursing, 16,* 35–37, 39.

Donaldson, C. (2000). Midlife lesbian parenting. *Journal of Gay & Lesbian Social Services, 11,* 119–138.

Dorell, B. (1991). Being there: A support network of lesbian women. *Journal of Homosexuality, 20,* 89–98.

Dorfman, R., Walters, K., Burke, P., Hardin, L., Karanik, T., Raphael, J., & Silverstein, E. (1995). Old, sad and alone: The myth of the aging homosexual. *Journal of Gerontological Social Work, 24,* 29–44.

Dunker, B. (1987). Aging lesbians: Observations and speculations. In Boston Lesbian Psychologies Collective (Eds.), *Lesbian psychologies: Explorations and challenges* (pp. 72–82). Urbana: University of Illinois Press.

Erikson, E. H. (1980). *Identity and the life cycle.* New York: W. W. Norton.

Fassinger, R. E. (1996). Notes from the margins: Integrating lesbian experience into the vocational psychology of women. *Journal of Vocational Behavior, 48,* 160–175.

Fassinger, R. E. (1997). Issues in group work with older lesbians. *Group, 21,* 191–210.

Fertitta, S. (1984). *Never married women in the middle years: A comparison of lesbians and heterosexuals.* Unpublished doctoral dissertation, Wright University, Los Angeles.

Fredriksen, K. I. (1999). Family caregiving responsibilities among lesbians and gay men. *Social Work, 44,* 142–155.

Friend, R. A. (1980). GAYging: Adjustment and older gay males. *Alternative Lifestyles, 3,* 231–248.

Friend, R. A. (1987). The individual and social psychology of aging: Clinical implications for lesbians and gay men. *Journal of Homosexuality, 14,* 307–331.

Friend, R. A. (1990). Older lesbian and gay people: Responding to homophobia. *Marriage and Family Review, 14,* 241–263.

Friend, R. A. (1991). Older lesbian and gay people: A theory of successful aging. *Journal of Homosexuality, 20,* 99–118.

Frost, J. C. (1997). Group psychotherapy with the aging gay male: Treatment of choice. *Group, 21,* 267–285.

Fullmer, E. M. (1995). Challenging biases against families of older gays and lesbians. In G. C. Smith, S. S. Tobin, E. A. Robertson, T. Chabo, & P. W. Power (Eds.), *Strengthening aging families: Diversity in practice and policy* (pp. 99–119). Thousand Oaks, CA: Sage Publications.

Galassi, F. S. (1991). A life-review workshop for gay and lesbian elders. *Journal of Gerontological Social Work, 16,* 75–68.

Grenwald, M. (1984). The SAGE model for serving older lesbians and gay men. *Journal of Social Work and Human Sexuality, 2,* 53–61.

Grossman, A. H., D'Augelli, A. R., & Hershberger, S. L. (2000). Social support networks of lesbian, gay, and bisexual adults 60 years of age and older. *Journal of Gerontology: Psychological Sciences, 55B,* 171–179.

Herdt, G. H., Beeler, J., & Rawls, T. W. (1997). Life course diversity among older lesbians and gay men: A study in Chicago. *Journal of Gay, Lesbian, and Bisexual Identity*, *2*, 231–246.

Hopcke, R. H. (1992). Midlife, gay men, and the AIDS epidemic. *Quadrant*, *25*, 101–109.

Hostetler, A. J., & Cohler, B. J. (1997). Partnership, singlehood, and the lesbian and gay life course: A research agenda. *Journal of Gay, Lesbian, and Bisexual Identity*, *2*, 199–230.

Humphreys, N. A., & Quam, J. K. (1998). Middle-aged and old gay, lesbian, and bisexual adults. In G. A. Appleby & J. W. Anastas (Eds.), *Not just a passing phase: Social work with gay, lesbian, and bisexual people* (pp. 245–267). New York: Columbia University Press.

Icard, L. D. (1996). Assessing the psychosocial well-being of African American gays: A multi dimensional perspective. *Journal of Gay & Lesbian Social Services*, *5*, 25–49.

Isay, R. A. (1996). *Becoming gay: The journey of self-acceptance*. New York: Pantheon Books.

Jacobs, R. J., Rasmussen, L. A., & Hohman, M. M. (1999). The social support needs of older lesbians, gay men, and bisexuals. *Journal of Gay and Lesbian Social Services*, *9*, 1–30.

Jacobson, S. (1995). Methodological issues in research on older lesbians. *Journal of Gay and Lesbian Social Services*, *3*, 43–56.

Jones, T. C., Nystrom, N. M., Fredriksen, K. I., Clunis, D. M., & Freeman, P. (1999, March). *Looking back . . . looking forward: Addressing the lives of lesbians 55 and older.* Paper presented at the annual program meeting, Council on Social Work Education, San Francisco.

Kehoe, M. (1986). Lesbians over 65: A triple invisible minority. *Journal of Homosexuality*, *12*, 139–152.

Kehoe, M. (1989). *Lesbians over 60 speak for themselves*. New York: Harrington Park.

Kertzner, R. M., & Sved, M. (1996). Mildife gay men and lesbians: Adult development and mental health. In R. Cabaj & T. S. Stein (Eds.), *Textbook of homosexuality and mental health* (pp. 289–304). Washington, DC: American Psychiatric Press.

Kimmel, D. C., & Sang, B. E. (1995). Lesbians and gay men in midlife. In A. R. D'Augelli & C. J. Patterson (Eds.), *Lesbian, gay, and bisexual identities over the lifespan: Psychological perspectives* (pp.190–214). New York: Oxford University Press.

Kirkpatrick, M. (1989a). Lesbians: A different middle-age? In J. Oldham & R. Liebert (Eds.), *New psychoanalytic perspectives: The middle years* (pp. 135–148). New Haven, CT: Yale University Press.

Kirkpatrick, M. (1989b). Middle age and the lesbian experience. *Women's Studies Quarterly*, *1/2*, 87–96.

Kochman, A. (Speaker). (1993). *AIDS and the elderly* (Cassette Recording No. ASA3-691). San Francisco: American Society on Aging.

Kochman, A. (1997). Gay and lesbian elderly: Historical overview and implications for social work practice. *Journal of Gay & Lesbian Services*, *6*, 1–10.

Kooden, H. (1997). Successful aging in the middle-aged gay man: A contribution to developmental theory. *Journal of Gay & Lesbian Social Services*, *6*, 21–43.

Kooperman, L. (1994). A survey of gay and bisexual men age 50 and older: AIDS related knowledge, attitude, belief, and behavior. *AIDS Patient Care*, *8*, 114–117.

Laird, J. (1996). Family-centered practice with lesbian and gay families. *Families in Society: Journal of Contemporary Human Services*, *77*, 559–572.

Lee, J. A. (1987). What can homosexual aging studies contribute to theories of aging? *Journal of Homosexuality*, *13*, 43–71.

Linde, R. (1994). Impact of AIDS on adult gay male development: Implications for psychotherapy. In S. A. Cadwell, R. A. Burnham, & M. Forstein (Eds.), *Therapists on the front-line: Psychotherapy with gay men in the age of AIDS* (pp. 25–31). Washington, DC: American Psychiatric Press.

Linsk, N. L. (1997). Experience of older gay and bisexual men living with HIV/AIDS. *Journal of Gay, Lesbian, and Bisexual Identity*, *2*, 285–308.

Loulan, J. (1987). *Lesbian passion: Loving ourselves and each other*. San Francisco: Spinsters/Aunt Lute.

Lucco, A. J. (1987). Planned retirement housing preferences of older homosexuals. *Journal of Homosexuality*, *14*, 35–56.

Martin, D., & Lyon, P. (1992). The older lesbian. In B. Berzon & R. Leighton (Eds.), *Positively gay* (pp. 111–120). Berkeley, CA: Celestial Arts.

Matthews, S. (1986). Friendships in old age: Biography and circumstance. In V. Marshall (Ed.), *Later life: The social psychology of aging* (pp. 233–270). Beverly Hills, CA: Sage Publications.

McDougall, G. J. (1993). Therapeutic issues with gay and lesbian elders. *Clinical Gerontologist*, *14*, 45–57.

Mitchell, V. (2000). The bloom is on the rose: The impact of midlife on the lesbian couple. *Journal of Gay & Lesbian Social Services*, *11*, 33–48.

Pope, M., & Schulz, R. (1990). Sexual attitudes and behavior in midlife and aging homosexual males. *Journal of Homosexuality*, *20*, 169–177.

Quam, J. K. (1993). Gay and lesbian aging. *Siecus Report*, *21*, 10–12.

Quam, J. K., & Whitford, G. S. (1992). Adaptation and age-related expectations of older gay and lesbian adults. *Gerontologist*, *32*, 367–374.

Raphael, S., & Robinson, M. (1984). The older lesbian: Love relationships and friendship patterns. In J. T. Darty & S. Potter (Eds.), *Women-identified women* (pp. 67–82). Palo Alto, CA: Mayfield.

Reid, J. D. (1995). Development in late life: Older lesbian and gay lives. In A. R. D'Augelli & C. J. Patterson (Eds.), *Lesbian, gay, and bisexual identities the over the lifespan: Psychological perspectives* (pp. 215–240). New York: Oxford University Press.

Rose, S. (1996). Lesbian and gay love scripts. In E. D. Rothblum & L. A. Bond (Eds.), *Preventing heterosexism and homophobia* (pp. 151–173). Thousand Oaks, CA: Sage Publications.

Rose, S., & Zand, D. (2000). Lesbian dating and courtship from young adulthood to midlife. *Journal of Gay & Lesbian Social Services*, *11*, 77–104.

Rothblum, E. D., Mintz, B., Cowan, D. B., & Haller, C. (1995). Lesbian baby boomers at midlife. In K. Jay (Ed.), *Dyke life: From growing up to growing old, a celebration of the lesbian experience* (pp. 61–76). New York: Basic Books.

Rothschild, M. (1991). Life as improvisation. In B. Sang, J. Warshow, & A. Smith (Eds.), *Lesbians at midlife: The creative transition* (pp. 91–98). San Francisco: Spinsters.

Sang, B. (1990). Reflections of midlife lesbians on their adolescence. *Journal of Women and Aging*, *2*, 111–117.

Sang, B. (1991). Moving toward balance and integration. In B. Sang, J. Warshow, & A. Smith (Eds.), *Lesbians at midlife: The creative transition* (pp. 206–214). San Francisco: Spinsters.

Sang, B. (1992). Counseling and psychotherapy with midlife and older lesbians. In S. Dworkin & F. Gutiérrez (Eds.), *Counseling gay men and lesbians: Journey to the end of the rainbow* (pp. 35–48). Alexandria, VA: American Association for Counseling and Development.

Sang, B. (1993). Some existential issues of midlife lesbians. In L. D. Garnets & D. C. Kimmel (Eds.), *Psychological perspectives on lesbian and gay male experiences* (pp. 500–516). New York: Columbia University Press.

Sarosy, S. G., Jr. (1997). *Pink and gray: An exploratory study on gay men and aging.* Unpublished master's thesis, Department of Social Work, California State University, Long Beach.

Saunders, J. M. (1990). Gay and lesbian widowhood. In R. J. Kuys (Ed.), *Keys to caring: Assisting your gay and lesbian clients* (pp. 224–243). Boston: Alyson Press.

Schoonmaker, C. V. (1993). Aging lesbians: Bearing the burden of triple shame. In N. D. Davis, E. Cole, & E. D. Rothblum (Eds.), *Faces of aging* (pp. 21–31). New York: Harrington Park.

Schreurs, K.M.G., & Buunk, B. P. (1996). Closeness, autonomy, equity, and relationship satisfaction in lesbian couples. *Psychology of Women Quarterly, 20,* 577–592.

Sharp, C. E. (1997). Lesbianism and later life in an Australian sample: How does development of one affect anticipation of the other? *Journal of Gay, Lesbian, and Bisexual Identity, 2,* 247–263.

Slusher, M. P., Mayer, C. J., & Dunkle, R. E. (1996). Gays and lesbians older and wiser (GLOW): A support group for older people. *Gerontologist, 36,* 118–123.

Wahler, J., & Gabbay, S. G. (1997). Gay male aging: A review of the literature. *Journal of Gay & Lesbian Social Services, 6,* 1–20.

Weinberg, M. S., & Williams, C. J. (1974). *Male homosexuals: Their problems and adaptations.* New York: Oxford University Press.

Weinberg, M. S., Williams, C. J., & Pryor, D. W. (2001). Bisexuals at midlife: Commitment, salience, and identity. *Journal of Contemporary Ethnography, 30,* 180–208.

Weinstock, J. S. (2000). Lesbian friendships at midlife: Patterns and possibilities for the 21st century. *Journal of Gay & Lesbian Social Services, 11,* 1–32.

Whitford, G. S. (1997). Realities and hopes for older gay males. *Journal of Gay & Lesbian Social Services, 6,* 79–95.

Woodman, N. J. (1987, September). *Lesbian women in their midyears: Issues and implications for practice.* Paper presented at the Health/Mental Health Conference of the National Association of Social Workers, New Orleans.

EPILOGUE: RESEARCH

Although alluded to elsewhere in the book, various issues about the research on LGBT persons are addressed here. This book is "research based," but research is not equal. Rarely is any of the research cited in this book based on random samples or many other requirements necessary for solid research projects. One of the reasons for this state of the research is that carrying out research projects in LGBT communities is formidable work. It involves social, political, and methodological issues that affect both the conduct of research and its conclusions. Heterosexist assumptions that heterosexual sexual orientation is the only acceptable form of affectional and sexual expression result in missing or distorted data about LGBT persons, their communities, and their cultures. Researchers may also purposively ignore LGBT persons or devalue and stigmatize them (Herek, Kimmel, Amaro, & Melton, 1991). They are ignored, for example, by talking about generic women and men, which equals heterosexual women and men. This is an error of commission. Errors of omission also occur such as failing to act on or disregarding the silence about LGBT persons in most research projects (Braun, 2000). Even when researchers sincerely want to "study" LGBT populations in nonbiased ways, numerous challenges emerge including sampling and generalizability, measurement and instrumentation, and methodologies.

The most basic challenge of sampling involves attaining a group of persons who represent the populations of interest in order to generalize the findings beyond the study sample. Yet, these groups differ across many factors and most studies cannot account for all the variations (T. S. Stein, 1997). Operational definitions for the study respondents also vary widely and hold limited capability to explain the variations among LGBT persons (T. S. Stein, 1997). The most common means of assessing sexual orientation for research projects is to ask respondents to choose a categorical label to apply to themselves. Being gay, bisexual, or lesbian, however, are not homogenous experiences (see Chapter 3), and what these labels mean to persons who use them may vary from one person to the next (Gonsiorek, Sell, & Weinrich, 1995). Following a constructionist perspective, Russell and Bohan (1999) suggested that researchers listen to individuals' experiences rather than look at only those aspects that fit into identity categories. Perhaps respondents can give their own definitions of their sexual identities. Also, some persons may be more willing to describe their experiences in an open-ended format instead of one in which they are asked to categorize themselves. Understandings of constructionist portrayals of sexual identity may best be explored through qualitative analyses. Whatever the "measurements" of sexual orientation used, E. Stein (1999) recommended that research studies should explicitly define and justify them.

The fluidity of sexual identity and sexual behavior during adolescence also creates obstacles in ascertaining accurately which respondents are lesbian, gay, or bisexual (Shaffer, 1993). No one knows how to explain changes in sexual identity or whether a certain sexual identity claimed by a youth is still in flux. Data collected by Rosario et al. (1996) showed that at least half of the youth identifying as lesbian or gay had contemplated a bisexual identity formerly, and vice versa.

Usually, populations of LGBT persons are concentrated in urban rather than rural settings (Laumann, Gagnon, Michael, & Michaels, 1994). Depending on the derivation of samples, therefore, these persons can be either underrepresented or overrepresented (T. S. Stein, 1997). True random samples of LGBT populations are not possible as these persons are still partly hidden. This commonly results in researchers using purposive or convenience samples including techniques such as the snowball method or finding respondents through gay and lesbian friends, organizations, magazines, or conferences. These techniques can yield large samples, but they limit generalizability of study findings. The samples generally do not include diversity by race, ethnicity, class, education, disability, or age, or any persons who do not, for example, attend gay and lesbian organizations or conferences. Additional difficulties exist in representing racial and ethnic LGBT persons including test instruments that were standardized on White populations and research results that are not tabulated for each ethnic and racial sexually subordinated group represented (Croom, 2000).

A multisite (urban, suburban, and rural), population-based, longitudinal study of the experiences of LGBT persons would be ideal, with matched controls of heterosexual peers. But, no reliable and valid methodology, sampling strategy, and instrumentation are available for doing this (Olson & King, 1995).

Given that rigorous research on LGBT populations will not be easy and that it is expensive and time-consuming, E. Stein (1999) recommended the following suggestions for designing better research:

- Take all possible steps to avoid sampling biases. Select respondents using sophisticated statistical sampling methods such as used by Laumann and colleagues (1994). If not possible, at the least recruit respondents in a way to encourage "closeted" lesbian and gay persons to participate, recognizing that it will be difficult to find an adequate number of respondents willing to provide the data needed without introducing sampling bias.
- Involve respondents from various cultures, especially those whose sexual orientations are conceptualized differently than in the mainstream culture.
- Be careful in assigning respondents to a sexual orientation.
- Be careful not to seek a causal link where the data do not support it.

Good research is essential to understanding the diversities among LGBT (and intersex) persons across the life course. Delivery of effective, affirmative services evolves from this knowledge.

EPILOGUE
REFERENCES

Braun, V. (2000). Heterosexism in focus group research: Collusion and challenges. *Feminism & Psychology, 10,* 133–140.

Croom, G. L. (2000). Lesbian, gay, and bisexual people of color: A challenge to representative sampling in empirical research. In B. Greene & G. L. Croom (Eds.), *Education, research, and practice in lesbian, gay, bisexual, and transgendered psychology: A resource manual* (Vol. 5, pp. 263–281). Thousand Oaks, CA: Sage Publications.

Gonsiorek, J. C., Sell, R. L., & Weinrich, J. D. (1995). Definition and measurement of sexual orientation. *Suicide and Life-Threatening Behavior, 25,* 40–51.

Herek, G. M., Kimmel, D. C., Amaro, H., & Melton, G. B. (1991). Avoiding heterosexist bias in psychological research. *American Psychologist, 46,* 957–963.

Laumann, E. D., Gagnon, J. H., Michael, R. T., & Michaels, S. (1994). *The social organization of sexuality: Sexual practices in the United States.* Chicago: University of Chicago Press.

Olson, E. D., & King, C. A. (1995). Gay and lesbian self-identification: A response to Rotheram-Boras and Fernandez. *Suicide & Life-Threatening Behavior, 25,* 35–39.

Rosario, M., Meyer-Bahlburg, H.F.L., Hunter, J., Exner, T. M., Gwadz, M., & Keller, A. M. (1996). The psychosexual development of urban lesbian, gay, and bisexual youths. *Journal of Sex Research, 35,* 113–126.

Russell, G. M., & Bohan, J. S. (1999). Implications for clinical work. In J. S. Bohan & G. M. Russell (Eds.), *Conversations about psychology and sexual orientation* (pp. 31–56). New York: New York University Press.

Shaffer, D. (1993). Suicide risk factors and the public health [Editorial]. *American Journal of Public Health, 83,* 171–172.

Stein, E. (1999). *The mismeasure of desire: The science, theory, and ethics of sexual orientation.* New York: Oxford University Press.

Stein, T. S. (1997). Deconstructing sexual orientation: Understanding the phenomena of sexual orientation. *Journal of Homosexuality, 34,* 81–86.

APPENDIX
GENERAL PRACTICE APPLICATIONS

How is the PIE classification system applicable to LGBT clients?

What are examples of intervention goals for LGBT clients?

What are the four broad classes of "therapy" approaches that can be used with LGBT clients and what are the benefits and detractions for each of these approaches?

What are the differences between the essentialist and constructionist perspectives on practice?

ASSESSMENT, INTERVENTION GOALS, AND INTERVENTION: APPROACHES FOR LGBT CLIENTS

Presented here are the person-in-environment classification system (PIE) that is useful in the assessment of LGBT clients, a categorization of possible intervention goals, and an analysis of a selection of intervention approaches. The PIE system is presented first because it offers an extensive assessment procedure (only briefly presented here) that is a guide to practice goals and interventions.

Person-in-Environment Classification System

LGBT clients face difficulties from multiple sources. Human services practitioners, then, must view them from a broad perspective. Karls and Wandrei (1994b) developed the PIE system as a tool for collecting and categorizing a broad array of information about a client and then determining targets for intervention.

Four factors can be addressed in a PIE assessment leading to a descriptive classification of the client according to each factor. The practitioner identifies "problems" across the four factors: "problem" types, severity of the disruptions caused by the "problems," duration of the "problems," and the client's capacity for dealing with each "problem" (Karls & Wandrei, 1994a). The four factors identified by Karls and Wandrei (1994a, 1994b) are

Factor I: social functioning
Factor II: environmental
Factor III: mental health
Factor IV: physical health.

The social functioning factor considers a person's functioning in social roles. Roles are grouped into four categories: (1) family, (2) other interpersonal, (3) occupational, and (4) special life situations. Each of these categories has subcategories. The family category, for example, contains the subcategories of parent, child, spouse, sibling, other family roles, and significant other.

The environmental factor focuses on aspects that are external to the client that may impact social functioning arenas. This factor draws on the ecosystems model and its emphasis on the interaction of the client and the environment. Six environmental arenas are examined: (1) economic–basic needs systems; (2) education–training systems; (3) judicial–legal systems; (4) health, safety, and social services systems; (5) voluntary association systems; and (6) affection support systems. Each of these categories also contains subcategories of specific problems. A client may experience difficulties, for example, in the economic needs system because of employment difficulties, with the specific subcategory of unemployment. An additional dimension of the environmental factor is discrimination experienced by the client. The practitioner classifies discrimination in any of 12 categories, such as age, sex–gender, race and ethnicity, and sexual orientation.

The mental health factor provides a way for the practitioner to integrate the client's mental health problems, if present, into the overall picture of the client. Axes I and II of the *Diagnostic and Statistical Manual of Mental Disorders* (American Psychiatric Association, 1994) are used as guides. The physical health factor includes current physical health conditions that may be pertinent to understanding the client's situation.

The case study below illustrates the application of the PIE system to coming-out and disclosure experiences.

CASE STUDY: SUE

Sue, a 40-year-old woman, sought a social worker to assist her in determining her sexual identity. She experienced intimate relations with both men and women. Previously married, Sue had two daughters. Sue's husband was granted custody of the children because he asserted that Sue "liked women." The judge ruled that Sue would be a detrimental influence on her daughters and granted her visitation only on alternating weekends.

Currently, Sue was experiencing an involvement with a woman but could not seem to commit herself solely to a primary relationship with a woman. She remained in relationships with women only a short time, and then followed with relationships with men. Sue admitted, however, that she did not feel the strength of attraction for men that she felt for women. What she most wanted to discover was what she called her true sexual identity: What is she? Heterosexual, lesbian, or bisexual? If lesbian or bisexual, should she disclose this to her children and parents?

The practitioner completed a PIE assessment on Sue. Factor I and Factor II seemed the most pertinent areas of concern. Factor I issues focused on Sue's roles as parent, former marital partner, worker, and adult child. Did aspects of these roles block her clarity about her sexual identity? Sue filled out several scales, including the Klein scale (discussed in Chapter 3), and came to her own conclusion that because most of her sexual fantasies involved women, she was probably a lesbian. Although the practitioner wanted to present both the essentialist and the social–constructionist views of sexual orientation to Sue, it was important to accept Sue's assessment of her situation (see Introduction, Chapter 4, and later discussion in this appendix). The practitioner did explain to Sue, however, that sexual identity can be fluid and that she may rethink her conclusion later. The reason was not to de-emphasize the personal importance of this client's coming-out experience but to increase her understanding of its tie to social contexts. For now, Sue seemed comfortable in declaring a lesbian identity. Her main concern then became disclosures. This concern involves the Factor II category of discrimination as an obstacle to disclosures.

The practitioner provided education about other person's experiences with the disclosure process as well as ways to cope with disclosure outcomes such as possible disrupted relationships (Hollander & Haber, 1992). A pro and con list to address disclosure helped Sue make thoughtful decisions. She felt concerned about what to tell her daughters, as they experienced confusion about the separation from their mother. The practitioner told Sue about the research on the influence of age differences in children's responses to parent's disclosures. Sue determined that her daughters were old enough to discuss her sexual identification with them but young enough (not yet adolescents) so that hostile responses were unlikely. She also wanted to make disclosures to other family members, including her parents. The practitioner involved Sue in several role-playing activities to help her feel confident about what to say and to decrease her anxiety about the disclosures. The practitioner recommended to Sue that family disclosures be made separately so as to pace her adjustments to the responses (see Chapter 10). Sue decided to delay additional family disclosures for now although she plans disclosures to her parents in the near future.

An additional pertinent Factor II category system for Sue is employment. Several women whom Sue had lesbian relationships with were unhappy about exclusion from social activities with her work colleagues. Sue did not want to be known in her workplace as a lesbian. The practitioner discussed the pros and cons of disclosures in the workplace with Sue and the need to determine whether her workplace had a nondiscrimination policy. Sue decided against disclosure at work until she could better assess her situation there.

Sue felt isolated from lesbians other than the ones she met at a local bar. Hollander (1989) advised that assistance in developing new support will help reduce the stress associated with coming out and disclosure. The practitioner referred Sue to a support group and provided a list of other resources for meeting lesbians. The practitioner emphasized the importance of support groups (especially friends) in the lives of LGBT persons. In a follow-up session several months later, Sue reported that she was much happier because she could be open with her children and had met several lesbians who also had children in various custody arrangements. They were becoming a support network for each other. Sue was also exploring friendships with several other lesbians she met in her support group.

Another Take on Intervention Goals

D'Augelli (1996) developed a comprehensive plan for operationalizing intervention goals for LGBT persons, drawing from Rappaport (1977) and Thomas (1984). Although D'Augelli applied this plan to LGB youth, it is adapted here for persons across the life course. It can also be used at the different system levels of practice (individuals, small groups, organizations, and institutions), in specialized programs, and in general human services programs. The goals can also provide options to look at following a PIE assessment. The goals and accompanying examples of system targets and interventions include:

- *"Remediation" or remedying sources of difficulty for clients.* System targets and examples of interventions include the individual (affirmative practice, cognitive–behavioral work for depression, role playing for disclosing, solution-focused work for coping strategies); small groups (groups on coping with parental rejection, communication training for couples, anger management for perpetrators of intimate violence); organizations (alternative protective programs for high-risk youth, alternative programs for alcohol or drug misuse, alternative programs for LGBT public school students); institutional and community (community coalitions for services development and staff training such as in social services agencies, public schools).

- *"Enhancement" or raising functioning above an already satisfactory level.* System targets and examples of interventions include the individual (self-acceptance enhancement and social skills training); small groups (dating-skills training, parent training); organizations (Project 10 programs in public schools); and institutional and community (alternative schools, events in which heterosexual community members can learn about LGBT persons).

- *"Competence" or developing strengths to handle both existing and future difficulties in selected areas.* System targets and examples of interventions include the individual (assertiveness training); small groups (problem-solving skills for relationship building); organizations (methods for reporting discrimination in organizations); and institutional and community (community safe-sex promotion).

- *"Education" or providing information to facilitate both knowledge and skills.* System targets and examples of interventions include the individual (reading materials, videos, learning models for a variety of topics such as coming out); small groups (information on child development and parental management of children); organizations (information on antidiscrimination and violence policies); and institutional and community (information on local and national sources of assistance and on building community programs).

- *"Prevention" or addressing potential difficulties before they arise or become sufficiently problematic to require remediation.* System targets and examples of interventions include the individual (maintaining physical and mental health); small groups (developing successful relationships, developing and maintaining clear boundaries); organizations (procedures for maintaining an affirmative workplace); and institutional and community (safe-sex campaigns for LGB persons, campaigns against hate crimes).

- *"Advocacy" or defending and taking actions on behalf of LGBT persons such as protecting their rights and pursuing their interests.* System targets and examples of interventions include the individual (advocacy for custody rights by offering testimony on the research on gay and lesbian families in court hearings); small groups (advocacy for inclusion of materials on same sex–gender issues in classes and same sex–gender support groups in public schools); organizations (advocacy for explicit equal protection clauses in educational settings); and institutional and community (advocacy for protective legislation and funds for services).

- *"Resource provision" or providing basic resources such as food, clothing, shelter, money, or medicine.* System targets and examples of interventions include the individual (telephone helplines and Internet materials); small groups (mentor and buddy systems); organizations (funding for youth outreach programs in human services settings, safe houses, and medical clinics); and institutional and community (advocacy for education and protective legislation and funds for services).

- *"Legal controls" or providing legal information and legal advocacy*. System targets and examples of interventions include the individual (legal rights for LGBT persons); small groups (seminar on legal issues focused on couples); organizations (assurance of confidentiality in youth practices); and institutional and community (protective legislation and penalties for violence and discrimination against LGBT persons).

Assessment of Therapy Approaches

The PIE program does not dictate any particular theory of human behavior or intervention nor does D'Augelli's (1996) classification system recommend any particular interventions. Many issues that LGBT clients bring into practice situations are no different from what heterosexual clients bring. So, all the possible interventions and approaches available to practitioners are acceptable for LGBT clients as long as they do not pathologize a same sex–gender or bisexual sexual orientation, or sex–gender expression (Hunter & Mallon, 2000; Stein, 1988), or are not sexist, ageist, or racist. The personal characteristics of the practitioner, especially nonheterosexist attitudes and the capacity to establish an empathic relationship with clients, may be far more important than any particular theoretical school or model of practice (for example, Freidlander, Wildman, Heatherington, & Skowron, 1994; Lambert & Bergin, 1994).

Fassinger (2000) reviewed four broad classes of practice approaches (humanistic, cognitive–behavioral, psychodynamic, and systems–cultural), including a focus on their usefulness and the objections to their use for same sex–gender and bisexual clients. They also appear useful for transgender clients. A brief summary of this analysis follows.

Humanistic approaches include person centered (Rogers, 1961), gestalt (Perls, 1973), existential (Yalom, 1981), and transactional analysis (Berne, 1964). Humanistic approaches are the foundation of all work with LGBT clients because of the ameliorative effects of a supportive, respectful relationship with the practitioner. The practitioner is empathetic and accepting. This helps to counterbalance heterosexism and internalized oppression. Humanistic approaches share core assumptions of self-determination and a positive growth orientation (Fassinger, 2000).

Humanistic approaches are especially useful for clients experiencing life transitions or developmental crises. Clients can explore their needs, values, feelings, and goals. The goals can include self-acceptance, pride, more openness and honesty, and coherence in self-image. Clients are helped to remove roadblocks to growth and freedom and take responsibility for their choices (Fassinger, 2000).

Some of the techniques of gestalt approaches, such as dialogues between polarities and empty-chair strategies, can help elucidate internal conflicts about one's sexual identity. Role playing can be useful in practicing disclosures (see the discussion on this strategy in the case study above and in Chapter 10). Gestalt empty-chair techniques can help bring into awareness all sides of the ambivalence and confusion about same sex–gender sexual orientation, as well as help clients vicariously talk to family, friends, coworkers, and others about their same sex–gender sexual orientation. Transactional analysis techniques can be useful in learning maturity in interpersonal interactions such as whether one acts as a child, parent, or adult. The adult-to-adult model promotes mature intimate relationships (Fassinger, 2000).

Among the objections to the humanistic approaches are a lack of formal assessment procedures, little challenge and confrontation, a passive practitioner that may not provide information desired by clients, and polarities in the gestalt approach that may reinforce dichotomous thinking and lead to identity foreclosure or premature self-labeling. Some of these shortcomings can be addressed with the more directive cognitive–behavioral approaches (Fassinger, 2000).

Cognitive–behavioral approaches include rational–emotive (Ellis, 1989); other cognitive approaches (Beck, 1976); behavioral, cognitive–behavioral, and social learning approaches (Bandura, 1982; Wolpe, 1990); reality (Glasser, 1980); Adlerian (Mosak, 1989); and multimodal (Lazarus, 1989). These approaches emphasize that we learn cognitive and behavioral responses within person-in-environment interactions, and that difficulties result from faulty learning (Fassinger, 2000).

Cognitive–behavioral approaches involve a thorough assessment, clear goals, experimentation, evaluation, and establishment of new goals. The client is an active learner and participant in a collaborative process. These approaches can be useful with LGBT clients who internalized myths and misinformation by helping them to overcome negative thinking and develop a positive sense of self. The practitioner challenges problematic patterns of thinking and behavior while the clients take an active role in reading and seeking resources either independently or as assigned through homework. Relaxation techniques and stress inoculation are helpful in preparing for disclosures (Fassinger, 2000).

Objections to cognitive–behavioral approaches include a lack of attention to feelings that may inhibit progress. The challenging of one's thinking and behaving may also feel overwhelming if one is already feeling under attack by a heterosexist society. The practitioner may seem insensitive and critical. Some practitioners may impose their belief systems on clients with no attention to the clients' cultural beliefs and values. These approaches also ignore clients' past experiences in their families and other arenas (Fassinger, 2000).

Psychodynamic approaches include psychoanalysis and psychoanalytic approaches (Freud, 1949; Jung, 1961), ego psychology (Erikson, 1963), object relations theory (Mahler, 1968), self-psychology (Kohut, 1984), and attachment theory (Bowlby, 1969). These approaches are more personality theories than practice frameworks, so implications for practice are more difficult to draw. They share an emphasis on intrapsychic processes and influences on the present self from early experiences with caregivers and other significant adults. These are intellectual approaches and require motivation of the client for deep self-understanding based on exploring and analyzing family background. The practitioner brings unconscious motivations into consciousness, analyzes dreams and fantasies, and uses this material to help clients understand their current behavioral difficulties. The practitioner is an interpreter and explainer and more detached than practitioners using other approaches. Generally, these approaches require long-term work with clients.

These approaches can be useful for persons seeking insights such as resistance to coming out. Objections to these approaches include paternalistic aspects and emphasis on psychopathology and intrapsychic processes to the exclusion of contextual and environmental issues. The long-term nature of many of these approaches is also unrealistic for most persons (Fassinger, 2000).

In a qualitative study of the approaches psychodynamic and psychoanalytic psychotherapists in Britain used with lesbian and gay clients, Phillips, Bartlett, and King (2001) found that the practitioners regarded the lives of these clients as difficult and leading to loneliness and social exclusion. The researchers concluded that because of their essentially negative views these practitioners would not likely be of help to lesbian and gay clients.

Systems–cultural approaches include traditional models of family approaches (Ackerman, 1966), more recently developed feminist therapy (Brown, 1994), and multicultural practice (Sue, Ivey, & Pederson, 1996). All these approaches share an emphasis on context in determining behavior; persons influence others as well as are influenced by others in their various systems such as couples, families, cultural groups, or larger institutions. Also emphasized are concepts of homeostasis, resistance to change, and quickly filled system voids. Because of the resistance to change, practitioners are more active and proactive as teachers, coaches, models, and consultants. They actively challenge the clients' assumptions about the existing systems and their location in them. Often practitioners are advocates for clients in confronting systems. Family sculptures, genograms, skills training, political analysis, social or political action, drama, movement, and art are techniques that fit with these systems–cultural approaches (Fassinger, 2000).

These approaches can be useful in couples, families, and other groups. Family systems and couples interventions are useful for working with an array of relationship issues. As noted earlier, the feminist approach is important in minimizing power differences and creating a supportive atmosphere. Multicultural counseling emphasizes political analysis and action, personal empowerment, and cultural awareness and sensitivity. These approaches are important with culturally diverse clients (Fassinger, 1991). Objections to these approaches include the excessive focus on the family that may obscure what clients want to address. Some clients may think it is rude to talk about their families. Political analysis of sexism, racism, and heterosexism can also be premature (Fassinger, 2000).

Two additional practice perspectives discussed by Russell and Bohan (1999) are essentialist and social constructivist. The essentialist perspective proposes that persons have no control over their sexual identity; they do not choose it. Sexual identity is a core, fixed part of themselves. The practitioner's task when following the essentialist perspective is to guide their clients in the discovery of their true sexual selves.

Although the essentialist perspective is suitable for many LGB persons, coming to terms with sexual identity is not so straightforward as many clients are not comfortable with their attractions to the same sex–gender, at least initially. And, how can practitioners assume that clients are right about what they say they discover? In addition to these cautions, objections to this approach include giving clients the view that their sexual identity is beyond their control and not examining the meanings clients give to sexual expressions in their lives (Haldeman, 1999).

The social–constructionist perspective proposes that understandings, including those of sexual identity, result from social constructions. Sexual identity is not a quality of individuals but instead is a social construct. Sexual expressions are also more complex and fluid than the essentialist perspective presents them to be. For example, what about a heterosexually married person who is also gay or lesbian identified who seeks a practitioner to resolve the conflict? This person needs exploration not uncritical encouragement to "come out" and be one's true self. Whereas the essentialist practitioner asks, "Who are you?" the constructionist practitioner asks "Whom do you want to be?" (Bohan & Russell, 1999).

The social–constructionist perspective has some similarities with the existential and feminist approaches, including an emphasis on a dialogic relationship between the client and practitioner. The practitioner is not an expert except in asking questions or prompting explorations toward new understandings of oneself, others, and contexts. The practitioner and client discuss how the client's understanding of sexuality and sexual identity developed over time and the influence of different relationships and contexts. No one lives outside social contexts, and these contexts influence what clients bring to a practitioner. The practitioner especially challenges clients who want to put themselves in a category by asking them to be open to self-examination and self-questioning. Clients are asked to move beyond all categories of sexual identity so that they can create their own meaning about their sexual identity as influenced by cultural, social, familial, and other contexts. They move to trusting themselves, their perceptions, and their choices (Bohan & Russell, 1999).

Objections to the constructionist approach include the necessity of clients being able to tolerate ambiguity and draw on internal and external resources to get through the self-examination process. Not every client has these abilities or is open to this type of work. The practitioner may offer the opportunity to explore assumptions that underlie a client's essentialist assumptions, but doing so is always up to the client (Bohan & Russell, 1999).

No single approach is suitable for all client issues and difficulties, and every approach falls short in some ways. Outcome research does not support the efficacy of one approach over another for work with LGBT clients nor have any specific unique interventions for LGBT persons and families been identified in the literature (Fassinger, 2000; Scrivner, 1997). Although the role of one's sexual orientation or sex–gender expression in one's life may need to be considered for some issues, most of the issues of concern to LGBT persons are the same as those for heterosexual persons and have little or nothing to do with sexual orientation or sex–gender expression. For example, to say that one drinks too much because one is gay or is depressed because one is lesbian represents an erroneous process of thought. It is also important to keep in mind that there are in-group differences so that the reasons for depression in one gay person, for example, may not be the same reasons for depression in another gay person. When the issues that LGBT persons are contending with do link to sexual orientation or sex–gender expression, the issues are societal in terms of the hostility, discrimination, and violence that can result from being LGB or T (Davidson, 2001).

When flexible and open-minded practitioners working with LGBT clients use approaches that best fit a given client system, they have to integrate theories and techniques (Fassinger, 2000). Interventions with these clients cannot be only psychological but must also be sociological and political. Relief from heterosexism, for example, will only come through social change. Since this has yet to happen, the task of practitioners is in part to compensate for the absence of support for these clients through operating at the highest levels of affirmative practice. They also must often act as advocates for these clients in various systems such as legal, education, medical, and political (Martin, 1998).

SUMMARY

• The PIE classification system is applicable because of its use of multiple system levels for assessment. There are also multiple intervention goals that can come out of this assessment ranging from remediation to advocacy, resource provision, and legal controls.

• Four broad classes of "therapy" that can be used with LGBT clients include humanistic, cognitive–behavioral, psychodynamic, and systems–cultural. Although these therapies are all beneficial, they also all have limitations.

• When practitioners follow the essentialist perspective in practice, they help clients to discover their "real selves." If approached from the social–constructionist perspective, however, they help clients examine and question categories and move beyond them so that they can determine their own meaning about their sexual identities as influenced by various contexts.

• No one approach is suitable for all clients. Practitioners have to explore approaches that best fit any particular client and some integration of various approaches will likely be part of the best fit.

APPENDIX
REFERENCES

Ackerman, N. (1966). *Treating the troubled family*. New York: Basic Books.

American Psychiatric Association. (1994). *Diagnostic and statistical manual of mental disorders* (4th ed.). Washington, DC: Author.

Bandura, A. (1982). Self-efficacy mechanisms in human agency. *American Psychologist, 37,* 122–147.

Beck, A. T. (1976). *Cognitive therapy and emotional disorders*. New York: International Universities Press.

Berne, E. (1964). *Games people play*. New York: Grove Press.

Bohan, J. S., & Russell, G. M. (1999). Conceptual frameworks. In J. S. Bohan & G. M. Russell (Eds.), *Conversations about psychology and sexual orientation* (pp. 11–30). New York: New York University Press.

Bowlby, J. (1969). *Attachment and loss* (Vol. 1). New York: Basic Books.

Brown, L. S. (1994). *Subversive dialogues: Theory in feminist therapy*. New York: Basic Books.

D'Augelli, A. R. (1996). Enhancing the development of lesbian, gay, and bisexual youths. In E. D. Rothblum & L. A. Bond (Eds.), *Preventing heterosexism and homophobia* (pp. 124–150). Thousand Oaks, CA: Sage Publications.

Davidson, G. C. (2001). Conceptual and ethical issues in therapy for the psychological problems of gay men, lesbians, and bisexuals. *Session: Psychotherapy in Practice, 57,* 695–704.

Ellis, A. (1989). Rational–emotive therapy. In R. J. Corsini & D. Wedding (Eds.), *Current pscyotherapies* (4th ed., pp. 197–240). Itasca, IL: F. E. Peacock.

Erikson, E. H. (1963). *Childhood and society* (2nd. ed.). New York: W. W. Norton.

Fassinger, R. E. (1991). The hidden minority: Issues and challenges in working with lesbians and gay men. *Counseling Psychologist, 19,* 157–176.

Fassinger, R. E. (2000). Applying counseling theories to lesbian, gay, and bisexual clients: *Pitfalls and possibilities*. In R. M. Perez, K. A. DeBord, & K. J. Bieschke (Eds.), *Handbook of counseling and psychotherapy with lesbian, gay, and bisexual clients.* Washington, DC: American Psychological Association.

Freidlander, M. L., Wildman, J., Heatherington, L., & Skowron, E. A. (1994). What we do and don't know about the process of family therapy. *Journal of Family Psychology, 8*, 390–416.

Freud, S. (1949). *An outline of psychoanalysis.* New York: W. W. Norton.

Glasser, N. (1980). *What are you doing? How people are helped by reality therapy.* New York: Harper & Row.

Haldeman, D. C. (1999). Therapeutic responses to sexual orientation. In B. Greene & G. L. Croom (Eds.), *Psychological perspectives on lesbian and gay lives* (Vol. 5, pp. 244–262). Thousand Oaks, CA: Sage Publications.

Hollander, J. (1989). Restructuring lesbian social networks: Evaluation of an intervention. *Journal of Gay and Lesbian Psychotherapy, 1*, 63–72.

Hollander, J., & Haber, L. (1992). Ecological transition: Using Bronfenbrenner's model to study sexual identity change. *Health Care for Women International, 13*, 121–129.

Hunter, J., & Mallon, G. P. (2000). Lesbian, gay, and bisexual adolescent development: Dancing with your feet tied together. In B. Greene & G. L. Croom (Eds.), *Psychological perspectives on lesbian and gay lives* (Vol. 5, pp. 226–243). Thousand Oaks, CA: Sage Publications.

Jung, C. G. (1961). *Memories, dreams, reflections.* New York: Vintage Books.

Karls, J. M., & Wandrei, K. E. (1994a). *Person-in-environment system.* Washington, DC: NASW Press.

Karls, J. M., & Wandrei, K. E. (1994b). *PIE manual: Person-in-environment system.* Washington, DC: NASW Press.

Kohut, H. (1984). *How does psychoanalysis cure?* Chicago: University of Chicago Press.

Lambert, M. J., & Bergin, A. E. (1994). The effectiveness of psychotherapy. In S. L. Garfield & A. E. Bergin (Eds.), *Handbook of psychotherapy and behavior change* (4th ed., pp. 143–189). New York: John Wiley & Sons.

Lazarus, A. A. (1989). *The practice of multimodal therapy.* Baltimore: Johns Hopkins University Press.

Mahler, M. S. (1968). *On human symbiosis or the vicissitudes of individuation.* New York: International Universities Press.

Martin, A. (1998). Clinical issues in psychotherapy with lesbian-, gay-, and bisexual-parented families. In C. J. Patterson & A. R. D'Augelli (Eds.), *Lesbian, gay, and bisexual identities in families: Psychological perspectives* (pp. 270–291). London: Oxford University Press.

Mosak, H. H. (1989). Adlerin psychotherapy. In R. J. Corsini & D. Wedding (Eds.), *Current psychotherapies* (4th ed., pp. 65–118). Itasca, IL: F. E. Peacock.

Perls, F. (1973). *The Gestalt approach and eye witness to therapy.* New York: Bantam Books.

Phillips, P., Bartlett, A., & King, M. (2001). Psychotherapists' approaches to gay and lesbian patients/clients: A qualitative study. *British Journal of Medical Psychology, 74,* 73–84.

Rappaport, J. (1977). *Community psychology.* New York: Holt, Rinehart & Winston.

Rogers, C. R. (1961). *On becoming a person.* Boston: Houghton Mifflin.

Russell, G. M., & Bohan, J. S. (1999). Implications for clinical work. In J. S. Bohan & G. M. Russell (Eds.), *Conversations about psychology and sexual orientation* (pp. 31–56). New York: New York University Press.

Scrivner, R. (1997). Ethical and legal issues in lesbian, gay, and bisexual family therapy. In D. T. Marsh & R. D. Magee (Eds.), *Ethical and legal issues in professional practice with families* (pp. 140–160). New York: John Wiley & Sons.

Stein, T. S. (1988). Theoretical considerations in psychotherapy with gay men and lesbians *Journal of Homosexuality, 15,* 75–95.

Sue, D. W., Ivey, A., & Pederson, P. (1996). *A theory of multicultural counseling and therapy.* Pacific Grove, CA: Brooks/Cole.

Thomas, E. M. (1984). *Designing interventions for the helping professions.* Beverly Hills, CA: Sage Publications.

Wolpe, J. (1990). *The practice of behavior therapy* (4th ed.). Elmsford, NY: Pergamon Press.

Yalom, L. D. (1981). *Existential psychotherapy.* New York: Basic Books.

INDEX

Affirmative Practice: Understanding and Working with Lesbian, Gay, Bisexual, and Transgender Persons

disclosure and, 147–148, 152–154, 272

dual-career issues for, 148

duration of, 147

effects of HIV/AIDS on, 277–278, 282

employment benefits for, 46

family-of-origin issues for, 148

fusion-interventions for, 274–276

impact of external obstacles on, 152–153

internalized oppression as issue for, 272

interracial issues for, 148–149

intimacy and closeness of, 146–147, 274

issues facing, 271–274

legal protections for, 279–280

marriage and, 44–45

midlife and older, 351–352

models for same sex–gender, 142–143

safe-sex issues facing, 277

satisfaction of, 145, 147

severing of, 153–154

sex–gender role issues for, 149–150, 272–274

sexuality issues facing, 276–277

social support for, 279

stage models for, 278–279

Courage group, 203

Cracker Barrel restaurants, 46, 47

Crimes. *See* Hate crimes; Violence

Cross-dressers

explanation of, 75

marriage with transgender, 124

needs of, 249

Cultural heterosexism, 39

D

Dating process, 142

Daughters of Bilitis, 20

Defense of Marriage Act of 1996, 45

Democratic heterosexuality, 220

Department of Defense, 46

Depression, 336

Developmental tasks, 321

Diagnostic and Statistical Manual of Mental Disorders (American Psychiatric Association), 1, 380

Diagnostic and Statistical Manual of Mental Disorders (DSM-III) (American Psychiatric Association), 197, 201

Diagnostic and Statistical Manual of Mental Disorders (DSM-IV) (American Psychiatric Association), 197

Dickinson, Emily, 39

Dignity (support group), 246

Disabilities, 102

Disclosure. *See also* Coming out
  case study of, 381
  to children, 124, 178–180
  during coming-out process, 93, 95, 99, 126
  in couple relationships, 147–148, 152–154, 272
  decision making regarding, 126
  delay of, 323
  explanation of, 7
  to families, 115–117, 252–254, 310
  to friends, 124–125, 310
  HIV/AIDS and, 251
  during identity acceptance stage, 247
  to marital partners, 123–124
  in marriages with transgender partner, 124
  motivations for, 114
  overview of, 113–114
  parents' progression over time with, 121–122
  preparation for, 251–252
  in racial and ethnic families, 117–120, 122, 257–258
  range of, 114
  to siblings, 122–123
  violence following, 117, 255
  in workplace, 125–126

Discrimination
  employment, 43, 45–47, 259, 298
  racial and ethnic, 148–149
  sexual orientation, 43
  Walt Disney Company, 47, 299

Divorce, 123

Donor sperm insemination, 170, 171, 174, 175

Drag kings, 79

Drag queens, 79

Dual-branch model
  explanation of, 93–94
  interventions for, 247
  phases in, 94–95

Dual-career issues, 148

E

couple relationships and, 148, 152
disclosure to, 115–120, 252–254, 310
interventions for distressed, 254–255
Latinos and, 24, 257
providing information to, 256
racial and ethnic, 23
support groups for, 256–257
Family and Medical Leave Act of 1993, 46
Fathers. *See* Gay fathers; Parents
Federal legislation, 47, 298
Female impersonators, 79
Feminist approach, 201
Feminist movement, 22–23
For Lesbian Parents (Johnson & O'Connor), 283
Foster care, 170–171, 173, 174
Fourteenth Amendment, Equal Protection Clause, 43–44
Freud, Sigmund, 195
Friends. *See also* Relationships
disclosure to, 124–125, 310
of midlife and older lesbians and gays, 351
Fusion interventions, 274–275

G

Gay, Lesbian, and Straight Teachers Network, 303
Gay American Indians, 26
Gay and Gray (Berger), 360
Gay and Lesbian Education Commission (Los Angeles), 302
Gay and Lesbian Elders Active in Minnesota (GLEAM), 362
Gay and Lesbian Outreach to Elders (GLOE), 362
Gay families
children in, 170, 180–183
community support for, 180, 284
demographics of, 169–170
legal issues facing, 284–285
practitioners working with, 282–283
school issues and, 283–284
Gay fathers
children of, 182–183
disclosure to children and others and, 178–180
explanation of, 176–177
parenting models and, 177
Gay Liberation Movement, 21, 23, 196
Gays. *See also* LGBT persons

I

Identity acceptance stage
    explanation of, 93
    interventions for, 247
Identity comparison stage
    explanation of, 92
    interventions for, 247
Identity confusion stage
    explanation of, 92
    interventions for, 246
Identity pride stage
    explanation of, 93
    interventions for, 247
Identity synthesis stage
    explanation of, 93
    interventions for, 247
Identity tolerance stage
    explanation of, 93
    interventions for, 247
Immigrants, 101–102
Immigration Act of 1917, 101
Inheritance law, 284
Insurance benefits, 285
Integrative heterosexuality model, 227
Integrity (support group), 246
Intellectual competency, 225
Internalized oppression, 272, 275
Internet, 142
Intersex persons
    advocacy groups for, 28
    explanation of, 5
    surgery and, 76, 198
Intersex Society of North America (ISNA), 198
Intimacy
    in couple relationships, 146–147, 274
    link between sex and, 248
Iowa State University, 300
Isolation
    in bisexuals, 26
    in youth, 335

J

Jealousy, 281
Jones, L. E., 2

Person-in-environment classification system (PIE)

Q

Queer, as term, 6

Queer Nation, 26, 48

Queer politics, 48

The Queer Parent's Primer (Brill), 283

Questions

    asked by parents, 255–256

    open-ended and neutral, 226

R

Racial and ethnic groups. *See also specific groups*

    coming out and, 96–97

    conflicting loyalties and, 24

    counterdevelopments in communities and, 25–26

    cross-cultural and mixed-race couples and, 148–149

    disclosure in, 117–120, 122, 257–258

    overview of, 23

    sexual identity and, 73, 114, 328

    terms used by, 5–6

    variations in primary allegiances and, 24–25

Radical transgender, 79

Reality testing, 250

Relationships. *See also* Couples; Friends; Parenting issues

    balancing attachment and automony in, 150

    breakup of, 154, 280

    chosen families and, 141–142

    commitment in, 144–145, 151–152

    conflict resolution in, 145–146

    couples scripts and, 142–143

    duration of, 147

    external obstacles on, 152–153

    family-of-origin issues in, 148

    finding dates and partners, 142

    identity management and disclosure issues in, 147–148

    interracial, 148–149

    intimacy and closeness in, 146–147

    of midlife and older lesbians and gays, 350–352

    satisfaction in, 145, 147

    severing of, 153–154

    sex–gender role issues in, 149–150

    transgender, 144

    work issues and, 148

Religiosity

MORE RESOURCES FROM NASW PRESS!

Affirmative Practice: Understanding and Working with Lesbian, Gay, Bisexual, and Transgender Persons, *by Ski Hunter and Jane Hickerson. Affirmative Practice* is a groundbreaking new book that contributes to the intellectual and emotional capacity of social workers and social work students who work with or will work with lesbian, gay, bisexual, and transgender clients. Specific topics include the development of communities among LGBT persons, social and legal issues and advances, coming out and disclosure, and more.

ISBN: 0-87101-325-0. June 2003. Item #3250. $44.99.

Foundations of Social Work Practice: A Graduate Text, 3rd Edition, *Mark A. Mattaini, Christine T. Lowery, and Carol H. Meyer, Editors.* In the context of a professional evolution in which potent forces are driving advances in social work knowledge and practice, the third edition of the best-selling textbook *Foundations of Social Work Practice* builds on and, in some cases, wrestles with these developments. Individual chapters may be used in any order consistent with an instructor's syllabus. Group and skills-building class exercises are useful teaching tools for different modalities and learning styles.

ISBN: 0-87101-349-5. July 2002. Item #3495. $49.99.

Women at Midlife: Life Experiences and Implications for the Helping Professions, *by Ski Hunter, Sandra S. Sundel, and Martin Sundel.* The number of women at midlife served by the helping professions is substantial. *Women at Midlife* fills a gap in the organized research knowledge on this population and examines a wide variety of the issues and concerns that women encounter during this life period, including family contexts and relationships, physical health, menopause and sexuality, emotional concerns, personality and identity, and life satisfaction.

ISBN: 0-87101-351-7. October 2002. Item #3517. $44.99.

Clinical Practice with Individuals, *by Mark A. Mattaini.* Practitioners and educators alike will find this guidebook invaluable. Mattaini provides practice guidelines that are firmly rooted in contemporary state-of-the-art knowledge and are both accessible and immediately applicable to practice. Using more than 30 figures to illustrate practice, an interview guide for assessment, and sample exercises, the book presents an ecobehavioral approach that can be very effective in short-term treatment.

ISBN: 0-87101-270-7. 1996. Item #2707. $28.95.

Clinical Intervention with Families, *by Mark A. Mattaini.* (Companion Volume to *Clinical Practice with Individuals.*) Written for social workers in family practice as well as for instructors and advanced-level students, this book is a state-of-the-art and state-of-the-science treatment guide of family practice. An essential volume for those seeking to understand the extrinsic family factors affecting the theory and practice of family social work.

ISBN: 0-87101-308-8. 1999. Item #3088. $39.99.

(Order form and information on reverse side)

ORDER FORM

Qty.	Title	Item #	Price	Total
__	Affirmative Practice	3250	$44.99	_____
__	Foundations of Social Work Practice	3495	$49.99	_____
__	Women at Midlife	3517	$44.99	_____
__	Clinical Practice with Individuals	2707	$28.95	_____
__	Clinical Intervention with Families	3088	$39.99	_____

Subtotal	_____
Postage and Handling	_____
DC residents add 6% sales tax	_____
MD residents add 5% sales tax	_____
Total	_____

POSTAGE AND HANDLING
Minimum postage and handling fee is $4.95. Orders that do not include appropriate postage and handling will be returned.

DOMESTIC: Please add 12% to orders under $100 for postage and handling. For orders over $100 add 7% of order.

CANADA: Please add 17% postage and handling.

OTHER INTERNATIONAL: Please add 22% postage and handling.

❏ **Check** or **money order** (payable to NASW Press) for $ _____.

❏ **Credit card**
 ❏ NASW Visa* I ❏ Visa I ❏ NASW MasterCard* I ❏ MasterCard I ❏ Amex

_____   _____
Credit Card Number   Expiration Date

Signature _____

Use of these cards generates funds in support of the social work profession.

Name _____

Address _____

City _____ State/Province _____

Country _____ Zip _____

Phone _____ E-mail _____

NASW Member # (if applicable) _____

(Please make checks payable to NASW Press. Prices are subject to change.)

NASW PRESS
P. O. Box 431
Annapolis JCT, MD 20701
USA

Credit card orders call
1-800-227-3590
(In the Metro Wash., DC, area, call 301-317-8688)
Or fax your order to 301-206-7989
Or order online at http://www.naswpress.org

Visit our Web site at http://www.naswpress.org.   CPAP03